The History of Sexuality in Europe

The History of Sexuality in Europe: A sourcebook and reader is a dynamic introduction to the latest debates in the history of sexuality in Europe. It begins with an introduction, "The magnetic poetry kit of sex," that surveys the field of sexuality and introduces the new concept of sexual grammar. The *Reader* focuses on the modern age, but has three chapters on the ancient and medieval worlds to demonstrate their very different cultures of sexuality.

Each section of the *Reader* pairs the latest chapters and articles by experts with primary sources, addressing questions such as:

- Why did ancient Greek philosophers and medieval Islamic poets celebrate men's desire for each other?
- Was Jesus a queer eunuch?
- Were Victorians sexually repressed?
- How did nonwestern cultures change some Europeans' ideas about sex?
- Does regulating prostitution protect or punish women who sell sex?
- How did sexologists learn from feminists, and men and women who desired those of the same sex?
- Were 1960s feminists pro- or anti-sex?

An essential collection for all students of the history of sexuality.

Anna Clark is a Professor of History at the University of Minnesota. Her publications include *Women's Silence, Men's Violence: Sexual assault in England, 1770–1845* (1987), *The Struggle for the Breeches: Gender and the making of the British working class* (1995), *Scandal: The sexual politics of the British constitution* (2003) and *Desire* (Routledge, 2008).

Routledge Readers in History

The Decolonization Reader
Edited by James Le Sueur

The Enlightenment: A sourcebook and
reader
Edited by Olga Gomez, Francesca
Greensides and Paul Hyland

The European Women's History
Reader
Edited by Christine Collette and
Fiona Montgomery

The Fascism Reader
Edited by Aristotle A. Kallis

The Feminist History Reader
Edited by Sue Morgan

The Global History Reader
Edited by Bruce Mazlish and
Akira Iriye

The History and Narrative Reader
Edited by Geoffrey Roberts

The History on Film Reader
Edited by Marnie Hughes-Warrington

The Irish Women's History Reader
Edited by Alan Hayes and
Diane Urquhart

The Modern Historiography Reader
Edited by Adam Budd

The Nature of History Reader
Edited by Keith Jenkins and
Alun Munslow

The New Imperial Histories Reader
Edited by Stephen Howe

The Oral History Reader
Edited by Robert Perks and
Alistair Thomson

The Postmodern History Reader
Edited by Keith Jenkins

The Postmodernism Reader:
Foundational texts
Edited by Michael Drolet

Renaissance Thought: A reader
Edited by Robert Black

The Slavery Reader
Edited by Gad Heuman and
James Walvin

The Terrorism Reader
Edited by David J. Whittaker

The Victorian Studies Reader
Edited by Kelly Boyd and
Rohan McWilliam

The Witchcraft Reader
Edited by Darren Oldridge

The World War Two Reader
Edited by Gordon Martel

The History of Sexuality in Europe

A sourcebook and reader

Edited by

Anna Clark

Routledge
Taylor & Francis Group

LONDON AND NEW YORK

First published 2011
by Routledge
2 Park Square, Milton Park, Abingdon, Oxon OX14 4RN

Simultaneously published in the USA and Canada
by Routledge
270 Madison Ave, New York, NY 10016

Routledge is an imprint of the Taylor & Francis Group, an informa business

Typeset in Perpetua and Bell Gothic by
Florence Production Ltd, Stoodleigh, Devon
Printed and bound in Great Britain by
TJ International Ltd, Padstow

British Library Cataloguing in Publication Data
A catalogue record for this book is available from the British Library

Library of Congress Cataloging-in-Publication Data
The history of sexuality in Europe : a sourcebook and reader / edited by
Anna Clark.
        p. cm. — (Routledge readers in history)
    1. Sex—Europe—History.   2. Sex customs—Europe—History.
  3. Sex—Social aspects—Europe.   4. Europe—Social life and customs.
I. Clark, Anna.
HQ18.E8H57 2010
306.7094—dc22   2010022078

ISBN13: 978–0–415–78139–8 (hbk)
ISBN13: 978–0–415–78140–4 (pbk)

Contents

Acknowledgments   ix

Anna Clark
INTRODUCTION: THE MAGNETIC POETRY KIT OF SEX   1

PART 1
**Did the ancient Greeks accept love, desire, and
relationships between men?**   13
INTRODUCTION

1   Giulia Sissa
    SEX AND SENSUALITY IN THE ANCIENT WORLD (2008)   16

2   Aeschines
    AGAINST TIMARCHUS (346 BCE, 1919 EDITION)   29

PART 2
Was Jesus a queer eunuch?   37
INTRODUCTION

3   Halvor Moxnes
    PUTTING JESUS IN HIS PLACE: A RADICAL VISION OF
    HOUSEHOLD AND KINGDOM (2003)   40

4   JESUS ON SEXUALITY   56

PART 3
Did the medieval and early modern Islamic world accept men who had sex with male youths?   59
INTRODUCTION

5   Khaled El-Rouayheb
BEFORE HOMOSEXUALITY IN THE ARAB-ISLAMIC WORLD,
1500–1800 (2005)   61

6   Abū Muḥammad ʿAlī ibn Ḥazm al-Andalusī
A BOOK CONTAINING THE *RISĀLA* KNOWN AS THE DOVE'S
NECK-RING ABOUT LOVE AND LOVERS (1022, 1931 EDITION)   82

PART 4
Are sexual morality and sexual prohibitions universal, or should they vary by culture?   95
INTRODUCTION

7   Claudia Moscovici
AN ETHICS OF CULTURAL EXCHANGE: DIDEROT'S
SUPPLÉMENT AU VOYAGE *DE BOUGAINVILLE* (2001)   98

8   Denis Diderot
SUPPLEMENT TO BOUGAINVILLE'S *VOYAGE*
(1796, 1993 EDITION)   107

PART 5
Were Victorians sexually repressed?   115
INTRODUCTION

9   Hera Cook
THE LONG SEXUAL REVOLUTION: ENGLISH WOMEN, SEX,
AND CONTRACEPTION 1800–1975 (2004)   118

10 ARISTOTLE'S COMPLEAT MASTERPIECE: DISPLAYING THE
SECRETS OF NATURE IN THE GENERATION OF MAN (1755)   130

11 HANDBOOK OF DR. KAHN'S MUSEUM (1863)   135

PART 6
Did female marriages undermine conventional marriage in the Victorian era?   141
INTRODUCTION

12 Sharon Marcus
BETWEEN WOMEN: FRIENDSHIP, DESIRE, AND MARRIAGE
IN VICTORIAN ENGLAND (2007)   144

13 Anne Lister
    I KNOW MY OWN HEART (1988 EDITION)   156

PART 7
How were definitions of prostitution influenced by race,
and were experts able to control prostitution?   **161**
INTRODUCTION

14 Philippa Levine
    PROSTITUTION, RACE AND POLITICS: VENEREAL DISEASE AND
    THE BRITISH EMPIRE (2003)   164

15 Joseph Edmondson
    AN ENQUIRY INTO THE CAUSES OF THE GREAT SANITARY
    FAILURE OF THE STATE REGULATION OF SOCIAL VICE (1897)   176

PART 8
Did sexologists impose definitions of homosexuality on
men and women who desired those of the same sex?   **183**
INTRODUCTION

16 Harry Oosterhuis
    STEPCHILDREN OF NATURE: KRAFFT-EBING, PSYCHIATRY,
    AND THE MAKING OF SEXUAL IDENTITY (2000)   186

17 Richard Krafft-Ebing
    PSYCHOPATHIA SEXUALIS (1886, 1926 EDITION)   198

PART 9
The problem of heterosexuality. Could men and women
find happiness together?   **209**
INTRODUCTION

18 Edward Ross Dickinson
    'A DARK, IMPENETRABLE WALL OF COMPLETE INCOMPREHENSION':
    THE IMPOSSIBILITY OF HETEROSEXUAL LOVE IN IMPERIAL
    GERMANY (2007)   211

19 Grete Meisel-Hess
    THE SEXUAL CRISIS: A CRITIQUE OF OUR SEX LIFE (1917)   223

PART 10
Was banning clitoridectomy humanitarian or imperialist?   **233**
INTRODUCTION

20 Bodil Folke Frederiksen
    JOMO KENYATTA, MARIE BONAPARTE AND BRONISLAW MALINOWSKI
    ON CLITORIDECTOMY AND FEMALE SEXUALITY (2008)   236

21   Jomo Kenyatta
     FACING MOUNT KENYA (1953, 1978 EDITION)   252

22   SPEECHES BY THE DUCHESS OF ATHOLL AND
     ELEANOR RATHBONE (1929)   260

PART 11
Was abortion reform motivated by eugenics, leftwing
politics, or Nazi power?   **267**
INTRODUCTION

23   Cornelie Usborne
     CULTURES OF ABORTION IN WEIMAR GERMANY (2007)   269

24   Dr. J. Leunbach
     ABORTION AND STERILIZATION IN DENMARK (1930)   288

PART 12
Did 1960s feminists hate sex?   **295**
INTRODUCTION

25   Lynn Walter
     THE REDSTOCKING MOVEMENT: SEX, LOVE, AND POLITICS
     IN 1968 (2004)   297

26   Mette Ejlersen
     I ACCUSE! (1969)   317

PART 13
Should prostitution be legalized or punished?   **325**
INTRODUCTION

27   Yvonne Svanström
     THROUGH THE PRISM OF PROSTITUTION: CONCEPTIONS OF
     WOMEN AND SEXUALITY IN SWEDEN AT TWO FINS-DE-SIÈCLE
     (2005)   327

28   Elizabeth Bernstein
     TEMPORARILY YOURS: INTIMACY, AUTHENTICITY, AND THE
     COMMERCE OF SEX (2007)   337

     Index   353

Acknowledgments

The publishers would like to thank the following for permission to reprint their material:

Yale University Press for permission to reprint extracts from Giulia Sissa, *Sex and Sensuality in the Ancient World* (New Haven: Yale University Press, 2008), pp. 50–65. Reprinted with kind permission of the author.

Westminster John Knox Press for permission to reprint extracts from Halvor Moxnes, *Putting Jesus in His Place: A Radical Vision of Household and Kingdom* (Louisville: John Knox Publisher, 2003), pp. 72–84, 88–90. Reproduced from *Putting Jesus in His Place*. © 2003 Halvor Moxnes. Used by permission of Westminster John Knox Press and the author. www.wjkbooks.com.

University of Chicago Press for permission to reprint extracts from Khaled El-Rouayheb, *Before Homosexuality in the Arab-Islamic World, 1500–1800* (Chicago: University of Chicago Press, 2005), pp. 13–34. Reprinted with kind permission of the author.

Abu Muḥammad ʿAlī ibn Ḥazm al-Andalusī, *A Book Containing the* Risāla *Known as the Dove's Neck-Ring about Love and Lovers,* trans. A. R. Nykl (Paris: Librarie Orientaliste Paul Geuthner, 1931), pp. 6–7, 56–59, 62–63, 176–180, 186–188, 199–201.

Clio for permission to reprint extracts from Claudia Moscovici, "An Ethics of Cultural Exchange: Diderot's 'Supplément au Voyage de Bougainville'," *Clio* 30, no. 3 (2001): 1–3, 6–12, 13, 16.

P. N. Furbank for permission to reprint extracts from his translation of Diderot's "Supplement to the Voyage of Bougainville," in P. N. Furbank, ed. and trans., *This Is Not a Story and Other Stories* (Oxford: Oxford University Press, 1993). Reprinted with permission of the editor, P. N. Furbank.

Oxford University Press for permission to reprint extracts from Hera Cook, *The Long Sexual Revolution: English Women, Sex, and Contraception 1800–1975* (Oxford: Oxford University Press, 2004), pp. 90–106. Reprinted with kind permission of the author.

Sharon Marcus, *Between Women* © 2007 by Princeton University Press. Reprinted by permission of Princeton University Press. pp. 193–204. Also reprinted with kind permission of the author.

Helena Whitbread and the Caroline Davidson Literary Agency for permission to reprint excerpts from Helena Whitbread, ed., *I Know My Own Heart: The Diaries of Anne Lister, 1791–1840* (London: Virago, 1988) [31 Aug. 1818. p. 57; 18 Nov. 1819. pp. 104–105; 4 April 1820. pp. 119–120; 13 June 1820. p. 154; 27 June 1821. p. 189; 20 Aug. 1823, p. 281; 17 Sept. 1832. p. 297; 2 March 1824 p. 328.

Taylor & Francis Group/Routledge Publishing Inc. and the author for kind permission to reprint extracts from Philippa Levine, "The Sexual Census and the Racialization of Colonial Women," in *Prostitution, Race and Politics: Venereal Disease and the British Empire* (London: Routledge, 2003), pp. 199–202, 207–213. www.routledge.com.

Joseph Edmondson, *An Enquiry into the Causes of the Great Sanitary Failure of the State Regulation of Social Vice* (London, 1897), pp. 1–9.

University of Chicago Press for permission to reprint extracts from Harry Oosterhuis, *Stepchildren of Nature: Krafft-Ebing, Psychiatry, and the Making of Sexual Identity* (Chicago: University of Chicago Press, 2000), pp. 195–208. Reprinted with permission of the author.

Richard Krafft-Ebing, *Psychopathia Sexualis*, trans. J. R. Rebman (New York: Medical Art Agency, 1926), pp. 282–297, 404–408.

Cambridge University Press for permission to reprint Edward Ross Dickinson, "'A Dark, Impenetrable Wall of Complete Incomprehension': The Impossibility of Heterosexual Love in Imperial Germany," *Central European History* 40, no. 3 (2007): 467–472, 480, 482–485, 491–493, 494, 496–497. © 2007 Conference Group for Central European History of the American Historical Association, published by Cambridge University Press, reproduced with permission. Reprinted with the kind permission of the author.

Grete Meisel-Hess, *The Sexual Crisis: A Critique of Our Sex Life*, trans. Eden Paul and Cedar Paul (New York: The Critic and Guide Company, 1917), pp. 17–19, 22–26, 83–86, 324–328.

Oxford Journals and Oxford University Press for permission to reprint extracts from Bodil Folke Frederiksen, "Jomo Kenyatta, Marie Bonaparte and Bronislaw Malinowski on Clitoridectomy and Female Sexuality," *History Workshop Journal* 65, no. 1, (2008): 23–40, 42. Copyright © 2008 by the Oxford University Press.

From *Facing Mount Kenya* by Jomo Kenyatta, published by Secker and Warburg. Reprinted by permission of the Random House Group.

HMSO and the Office of Public Sector Information for permission to reprint extracts from parliamentary material: Duchess of Atholl and Eleanor Rathbone's speech. Hansard Parliamentary Debates, 5th series, vol. 233, Dec. 11, 1929, cols. 599–608. 4 pages. 2220 words. Parliamentary licence number P2010000148.

Berghahn Books and the author for permission to reprint extracts from Cornelie Usborne, *Cultures of Abortion in Weimar Germany* (London: Berghahn Books, 2007), pp. 202–203, 213.

Dr. J. Leunbach, "Abortion and Sterilization in Denmark," in Norman Haire, ed., *Sexual Reform Congress. World League for Sexual Reform Proceedings of the Third Congress, 1929* (London: Kegan Paul, 1930), pp. 133–138, 139–142.

Lynn Walter, "The Redstocking Movement: Sex, Love, and Politics in 1968," August 15, 2004. Also published in Danish as "Rødstrømpebevægelsen: sex, kærlighed og politik i 1968," in Morten Bendix Andersen and Niklas Olsen, eds., *1968, Dengang og Nu*, Copenhagen: Museum Tusculanums Forlag, Københavns Universitet, 2004, pp. 259–282. Reprinted with kind permission of the author. www.uwgb.edu/walterl/denmark/The%20Redstocking%20Movement.htm abridged.5687.

Mette Ejlersen, *I Accuse!*, trans. Marianne Kold Madsen (London: Tandem, 1969), pp. 84–100.

Taylor & Francis for permission to reprint extracts from Yvonne Svanström, "Through the Prism of Prostitution: Conceptions of Women and Sexuality in Sweden at Two Fins-de-Siècle," *Nora, Nordic Journal of Women's Studies* 13 (2005): 48–58. Reprinted by permission of the publisher (Taylor & Francis Ltd, www.tandf.co.uk/journals).

University of Chicago Press for permission to reprint extracts from Elizabeth Bernstein, *Temporarily Yours: Intimacy, Authenticity, and the Commerce of Sex* (Chicago: University of Chicago Press, 2007), pp. 145–156, 163–166. Reprinted with kind permission of the author.

Disclaimer

Acknowledgements

I would like to thank Laura Doan, Paul Deslandes, Susie Steinbach and Marjorie Levine-Clark for advice on the selections, and for comments on the introduction, Kevin Murphy and Regina Kunzel. The staff at Routledge were very helpful – thanks to Eve Setch and Vicky Peters for commissioning the Reader and working with me on it, and Emily Kindleysides, Frances Brown, and Anna Callander for their meticulous work on permissions, copy-editing and production. My gratitude to the University of Minnesota and the Samuel Russell Chair for helping to fund my work on this Reader, and Anne Carter for her moral support, as always.

Introduction

The magnetic poetry kit of sex

ANNA CLARK

REMEMBER THOSE MAGNETIC poetry kits from the 1990s? You bought a little box of words, which you could scramble and then mix and match to try to create sentences and verses on your refrigerator. You were limited by the words available to you in the box, and you needed a subject and verb, at least, for your phrase to make sense, even if it was poetic and ridiculous. But you could come up with surprising combinations, which made the best poetry. Today, anyone from cat lovers to sex lovers can find a magnetic poetry kit with a vocabulary for them.

To apply this idea to sex, each culture has its own sexual vocabulary, which shapes the way we can think about sex. We can start with the words for the genitals. On one level, we might think that sexual bodies are fairly straightforward, so to speak. Penis in vagina leads to ejaculation, and perhaps to pregnancy. But bodies themselves are more complicated – it is not just a matter of putting Tab A in Slot B. Procreation and pleasure are two different goals.

Furthermore, people need to have the words for their body parts to use and understand them. For instance, for women, anatomically speaking, the orgasm comes from the nerves of the clitoris, not the vagina. However, the word for the clitoris was not always known, which may have made it more difficult, although of course not impossible, for women to have orgasms. As seen in Part 5 of this Reader, the eighteenth-century popular sex manual *Aristotle's Masterpiece* clearly explained the role of the clitoris in women's sexual pleasure, but this was because it was thought women needed to have orgasms to conceive. However, in Part 12, we will also read an excerpt by Mette Ejlersen, a Danish journalist, who pointed out that pornography and sex manuals in the 1960s ignored or downplayed the role of the clitoris in women's sexual pleasure, leaving women frustrated.

Yet the sexual poetry kit also contains creative possibilities. Just as we can mix and match words in the magnetic poetry kit, the genitals can be mixed and matched.

The penis and vagina is not the only possibility – hands and mouths can stimulate as well. Men can pleasure men, and women women. Some sexual vocabularies acknowledge these possibilities, but others do not. For instance, the ancient Romans had an extremely elaborate sexual vocabulary with different words for the act of giving and receiving oral sex with a man, and even different words for the motions made by a woman or man being penetrated.[1] However, for medieval Europeans, sodomy became the crime "not to be named among Christians."

The Latin sexual vocabulary had its own rules of grammar, changing the form of the word according to who performed the action. However, it was a matter not just of word endings, but of the deeper structures of power – expressed in oppositions – that made a sentence intelligible. Today, modern American culture tends to think in terms of what is normal and abnormal, natural and unnatural. Until recently this mapped on to heterosexual and homosexual. If a man has sex with another man, he is considered to be gay. But the ancient Romans had a completely different understanding of sexuality. Although they could conceive of a wide variety of sexual possibilities, their sexual attitudes were not fluid. Rather, they were structured by a rigid dichotomy between dominance and submission. Citizen men were supposed to be dominant over others, such as slaves and women. If a man submitted sexually to another man, he was considered to be feminine, and inferior. But if a man took the dominant role sexually with another man or male youth and kept in control, he was considered masculine. He was not supposed to have sex with a male citizen or his son, or with another man's wife, because that would violate property relations.[2] As this example indicates, the dichotomy between masculine and feminine (not necessarily between male and female bodies, but those socially constructed as masculine and feminine) is probably the most important way our understanding of sexuality has been structured, but different societies have very different ways of depicting masculinity, femininity, and sexuality.

Every culture has rules about who can use what words when, to harness the power of sexual words, and different understandings of public and private. In ancient Rome, the crudest sexual words would be scrawled on the walls of Pompeii, but elite poets such as Martial sometimes used them in otherwise elegant verse. But in nineteenth-century Europe, the time of the supposedly prudish Victorians, sex was not supposed to be discussed openly in print or in public, especially by ladies. At the same time, some authorities have always been able to write about sex legitimately – such as religious and medical authorities, with their power over bodies and souls. In the Victorian era, as philosopher Michel Foucault points out, doctors wrote more and more heavy tomes about how to manage sex and reproduction, and, more daringly, about "deviant" sexual desires. Their words shaped our modern understanding of sex.

Foucault insisted that Victorian sexuality was not repressed and driven underground, but instead, that there was an explosion of discourses about sex.[3] Hera Cook, as we shall see in an excerpt in Part 5, criticizes Foucault's argument, declaring that the Victorians did indeed try to limit people's knowledge about sex. She notes that those discourses about sex which were available were very negative about sex.[4] For instance, in the same part we shall read a guide from the Victorian museum of Dr. Kahn which contained repulsive models of sexual organs as diseased and deformed, intended to deter people from masturbation and venereal disease.

Nonetheless, both Foucault and Cook agree that sexuality is not an inborn drive which people just express naturally. Rather, even our most intimate sexual feelings are shaped by social messages, and more importantly, sexual language has immense social power. Foucault's counter-intuitive proclamation about Victorian repression was part of a larger argument about the connections between sexual words, power, and knowledge. Foucault defined sexuality as a "great surface network in which the stimulation of bodies, the intensification of pleasures, the incitement to discourse, the formation of special knowledges, the strengthening of controls and resistances, are linked to one another."

This Reader will use a simpler definition of sexuality: the *Oxford English Dictionary* defines sexuality in biological terms, as "Sexual nature, instinct, or feelings"; or as "the possession or expression of sexual identity" – the latter therefore being only one possible meaning of sexuality. Here, then, sexuality means not just identity, but bodies, desires, acts, identities, or relationships having to do with sex and eroticism.

Nonetheless, Foucault's definition has led to great insights into the connection between sexuality, knowledge, and power. To put his definition in simpler terms, Foucault argued that discourses about sex stimulate bodies, but they also control and regulate people's behavior. Discourses such as legal codes or psychiatric writings convey power in institutions such as asylums and prisons and exert power over people in that context. For instance, psychiatrists developed the discourse of sexology, which in some versions defined homosexuality as a form of mental degeneration, and they used this discourse in mental asylums to treat men who had sex with men.

Foucault argued that these discourses controlled and shaped our understanding of the self. For instance, in the eighteenth century, he argued, French philosophers invented the notion that sexuality – sexual identity – was the truth about the self, our innermost secret. In the late nineteenth century, sexology, a discipline that grew out of medicine and psychiatry, expanded on this idea to argue that sexuality defined our personalities – that homosexuals, for instance, were a certain type of person. We think we are very original, that our sexuality is part of our true inner nature, but in fact we are just participating in the discourse that sexuality is the truth of the self.

Contemporary theorists often refer to the idea of "heteronormativity," that society forces people to conform to the norm of marriage and family, and only heterosexuals are seen as normal.[5] But as Karma Lochrie and other thinkers such as Foucault point out, the notion of the "norm" as the average, regular, and natural was invented in the nineteenth century by such disciplines as sexology, biology, and statistics.[6] Scientists tried to discern what was average and most commonly occurring, as well as the ideal. Darwinism impelled them to reject religious notions of sexual morality to discern what would be ideal for reproduction and the survival of the fittest. Of course, Victorian values shaped what was seen as normal – for instance, male sexual aggression and female sexual passivity. Scientists began to define those who did not fit this paradigm as unfit and abnormal, as unnatural. Behaviors such as sex between men came to be seen as diseased rather than sinful or criminal. Furthermore, scientists feared that human beings were degenerating, rather than progressing, on the evolutionary path.[7]

Eugenics, the pseudo-science of human breeding, held that judgments about the propriety of sexual conduct should be based on what would produce the healthiest offspring. Eugenicists declared that people should be licensed to marry, and that only certain types of people should reproduce. They feared that unfit working-class people were having too many children, while well-educated middle-class women were refusing to have large families.[8] In this context, homosexuality could be seen as degenerative since it was not reproductive. Eugenics also contributed to the racial thinking so characteristic of nineteenth-century European imperialism, since fitness was defined in terms of race, and most eugenicists wanted sex to be strictly controlled in the colonies lest mixed-race children be produced.[9]

As Edward Ross Dickinson points out in Part 9 of this Reader, eugenics was not just an institutional discourse about managing populations; it influenced more popular debate about conflict between men and women over marriage, a sense that sexual antagonism and competing needs poisoned the love between men and women. Yet eugenics also appealed to those on the left who wanted to manage and transform society. Some, such as Grete Meisel-Hess, an Austrian feminist whose work is also excerpted in Part 9, argued that sex would only produce healthy children if it were freely chosen and passionate and pleasurable, and if women could use birth control and even abortion to give birth to only healthy, fit, and chosen children. Some leftwing eugenicists believed that interracial marriages would produce more vital children by hybridizing desirable traits.[10]

Institutional discourses also exerted power by naming and categorizing as deviant people such as men who had sex with men and women who sold sex. For instance, several European countries forced women who sold sex to register as prostitutes with the police, to undergo medical exams and treatment for venereal disease, and often to work in official brothels.[11] The British government came late to this project, but in the 1860s it passed the Contagious Diseases Acts, which mandated that women who sold sex in garrison towns and ports had to register as prostitutes, submit to painful examinations for venereal disease, and undergo useless treatments in lock hospitals, as we shall see in Part 7.[12]

The category of the homosexual also emerged in nineteenth-century sexology. Previously, argued Foucault, authorities regarded men who had sex with men as committing a sin or serious criminal act, but they thought that the devil might ensnare any man into such behavior – authorities did not see these men, claimed Foucault, as having a specific personality type. But in the late nineteenth century, sexologists began to diagnose the "homosexual" as a type of personality. In Part 7 we will read an excerpt from *Psychopathia Sexualis*, by German sexologist Richard Krafft-Ebing, in which he diagnoses homosexuals as suffering from inherited, congenital degeneracy and mental illness. This discourse was so powerful that it shaped law and psychiatric practice, as men who had sex with men underwent painful therapies in order to try to overcome what was perceived as an illness. They looked back into their family histories for signs of degeneration, as we can see in the excerpt, examining their personalities for signs of "inversion" – the notion that they had traits of the opposite sex in their personalities.

Foucault also argued, however, that homosexuals and others could engage in a reverse discourse, using the terms of the discourse of sexology against itself, to create and defend a positive identity for themselves. They reversed the negative connotations of homosexuality and instead proclaimed, as gay rights activists still do today, that homosexuality is inborn. They influenced some sexologists like Havelock Ellis, who suggested that homosexuality was not degenerate but rather just a harmless difference, like left-handedness, and might even be associated with special talents.[13] However, these activists were still trapped in the assumptions of sexology's vocabulary to explain themselves. Recently, as we shall see, historians have argued that institutional discourses were not just imposed on the subjects they defined; rather, these subjects participated in and helped originate these discourses. As Harry Oosterhuis has found, excerpted in Part 7, Krafft-Ebing actually borrowed some of the concepts and words about homosexuality from gay rights activist Karl Ulrichs. Furthermore, as he corresponded more and more with homosexual men and women, he became more sympathetic to their cause, and eventually spoke out against the persecution of homosexuals.

European cultures believed that their own versions of heteronormativity were superior to those of the cultures they conquered, such as Aztecs or Indians, and tried to impose their own standards of sexual morality upon them. For instance, the British were shocked at the practice of clitoridectomy among the Kikuyu people in their Kenya colony in the 1920s and 1930s, so missionaries urged the government to forbid it. In response, African nationalists such as Jomo Kenyatta appropriated the discourse of anthropology to proclaim that clitoridectomy was an important rite of passage which ensured that young women belonged to their community, as we shall see in an excerpt from his book *Facing Mount Kenya* in Part 10. The issue became a rallying cry in the nationalist struggle against British rule.

However, some Europeans learned from these cultural encounters that their own society's morality was not fixed by nature, but varied geographically. In Part 10, we shall also learn that Princess Marie Bonaparte, a Freudian analyst, wanted to meet Kenyatta and find out more about clitoridectomy, because she thought African women might be able to have vaginal orgasms rather than the clitoral orgasms Freud condemned as immature. Earlier, as we see in Part 4, Enlightenment philosopher Denis Diderot had celebrated the people of Tahiti for having a natural sexual morality based on fertility, rather than fear and guilt.

Some scholars and activists have taken Foucault's work even further into what has been called "queer studies." Queer studies critics point out that while cultural discourses such as sexology seem to uphold the value of heteronormativity, at the same time they are wrought with internal contradictions that undermine heteronormativity. Queer studies is based on the premise that sexual (or any) identities are never stable – whether heterosexual or homosexual. Queer desires are those which come from an odd angle, which subvert conventional sexualities. As Judith Butler points out, queer theory also undermines the stability of gender.[14] For instance, Krafft-Ebing defined true homosexuals as those who were born with an inverted nature, sometimes the wrong sex in the wrong body, whose desires focused on the same sex and shaped their whole personalities. At the same time he wrote that many men might be susceptible to desire for other men in certain situations, such as at a boarding school or in prison, or in old age. The new category of the homosexual coexisted with the recognition that such categories were not so stable after all.

Queer theorists insist at the same time that homosexual identity is never stable either. They have taken up Foucault's insistence on the specificity of the modern discourse of homosexuality to declare that before the modern era the notion of homosexuality did not exist. They criticize earlier historians for trying to go back and discover gay men and lesbians who have been "hidden from history," for those categories simply did not exist in the past. For instance, in ancient Rome, as we have learned, men who took the dominant role in sex with other men were not considered to have any kind of sexual identity or a certain kind of personality. Indeed, they would not be condemned or even mildly criticized, unless they indulged too much in sex with male prostitutes or raped a citizen's son – just as they would be criticized for spending too much time with female prostitutes or seducing another man's wife. Indeed, some queer critics assume that the premodern period was a time of greater sexual fluidity, when men would occasionally have sex with men, or women with women, without being labeled and stigmatized.

Contemporary critics sometimes broaden this out to an assumption that premodern societies had more fluid attitudes about sexuality and gender more generally. However, it is important to recognize that premodern societies actually labeled, categorized, and regulated men who had sex with men, and women who were prostitutes, albeit in much different ways than today. For instance, in Elizabeth Bernstein's otherwise excellent book on modern prostitution, she asserts that "the forms of sexual commerce that prevailed prior to this period were self-organized, occasional exchanges in which women traded sexual favors during limited periods of hardship," in contrast to the modern period where prostitutes were labeled, stigmatized, and forced into brothels.[15] In fact, although such casual sexual commerce has always existed and continues to flourish, in the middle ages authorities constantly attempted to label women who sold sex as prostitutes, and forced them to wear stigmatizing clothing and work in municipal brothels.[16]

In instances too many to list, modern historians and literary critics often assert that, "before" the nineteenth century, men could have sex with male youths and nothing was thought of it. The actual picture was more complex. Even in ancient Rome, the word *cinaedus* was a term for a recognizable type of man – an effeminate man, who might earn his living as a dancer or as a male prostitute. But he was not the same as the modern homosexual – the *cinaedus* was also reviled for seducing other men's wives.[17] In fifteenth-century Florence, it was very common for men to have sex with male youths, but the city established an Office of the Night to prosecute them. Punishments were generally very mild. But theologians characterized the sodomite as a particular type of sinner whose sins were quite egregious. In times of social crisis, men accused of sodomy were burnt at the stake in waves of persecution.[18] Of course, these social identities based on notions of internal evil desires and external sinful acts were very different from our modern understanding of sexuality as a psychological truth about the self.[19] This Reader includes three parts on the premodern period in order to make the point that each era has its own sexual vocabulary that controls sexual understanding and regulates behavior; it is a mistake to regard the premodern era as more fluid.

Furthermore, the notion of heteronormativity does not really apply to premodern societies.[20] This is not to say that sexuality was more fluid; rather, marriage was the ideal of relations between men and women, and other sexual relations between men and women were considered disturbing to the social order. In ancient Greek, Roman, and Islamic societies, marriage and family, on the one hand, and romantic love and erotic desire, on the other, were not necessarily considered to be the same thing, since marriages were founded for the purposes of property relations. Husbands and wives often loved each other, but poetry and philosophy represented romantic desire as something which occurred outside of marriage.

To get back to our magnetic poetry kit, desire plays an interesting role in putting together sentences about sex. Modern people tend to assume that desire is transitive, that it must have an object – the sentence would read "he desires her." However, desire can be an intransitive verb, as well as a noun. In ancient Greece, desire seems to have been thought of as a free-flowing emotion that seized the lover and could be attached to a young man or a young woman. Poetry and romance celebrated erotic desire as the motive force of the universe, leading to creativity and fertility. But any erotic desires could be excessive and dangerous, because they led to a loss of control.

In Part 1, we will learn the story of Timarchus, a young man in classical Athens who squandered his fortune on female prostitutes, drinking, and gambling, and then submitted himself to the sexual demands of other men for money. His political enemy Aeschines accused him of prostituting himself, and demanded that Timarchus be stripped of his political privileges as a citizen of Athens. But Aeschines did not object to the fact that Timarchus went to female prostitutes, or that he loved men – rather, Timarchus did not control his desires and became weak, effeminate, and corrupt.

The medieval Islamic world provides an interesting counterpoint to this debate, as we shall see in Part 3. Poets and writers celebrated the beauty of slave girls or male youths in the same romantic, yearning language we find in Ibn Ḥazm's *The Dove's Neck-Ring*. At the same time, the Qu'ran and other religious authorities strictly condemned sodomy and adultery. We shall see how the writer Ibn Ḥazm tried to reconcile the two important strands in his culture.[21] One way was to celebrate secret, hidden, unfulfilled desires, and condemn only their fulfillment and publicity. Historians of the premodern Islamic world accept Foucault's claim that the notion of homosexuality as a category did not apply to their societies. However, the formulation that only acts were judged, not identities, does not hold up either, for as historian Khaled El-Rouayheb points out, early Islamic societies did label men who committed certain acts with each other, although these labels did not correspond to our modern notion of the homosexual.[22]

Christianity had rather different notions of desire: carnal or erotic desire was sinful, but the desire for God was spiritual. Early Christianity, furthermore, was not what could be called heteronormative. In Part 2, Halvor Moxnes provocatively suggests that Jesus opened up a queer space in Palestinian society, because he called on believers to reject their families to follow him, and even to become eunuchs "for the kingdom of heaven." The desire for romance, marriage, and family distracted from the love of God. Of course, as Christianity became established as an institution, it upheld marriage and the family. But as Karma Lochrie explains, the early Church regarded all sexual desire, whether same sex or opposite sex, as a distraction from the contemplation of God. They thought that sexual desire was the result of original sin, the fall from grace in the Garden of Eden, even if it was an unfortunate necessity for procreation.[23] The Church tried to regulate strictly when and where even married people could have sex – not on fast days, not at night, not naked, and without excessive desire. Anything else was seen as sinful and unnatural by the Church.[24] Of course, for most people, this was not average or everyday behavior; as moderns would term it, the norm. Rather, the Church was not concerned with the norm in terms of how people actually behaved, but held up the ideal as a pure, unattainable, sinless state.

Some sexual desires which do not live up to society's ideals may be indulged in without threatening social structures, or without incurring permanent labeling into a stigmatized identity. I term these "twilight moments."[25] They were behaviors hidden from the light of day, dimly perceived as in the hushed light of dusk, veiled but not totally concealed. For instance, the love of a poet for a male youth was supposed to be hidden and secret. As we shall see from Ibn Ḥazm, it was considered shameful when it became open. Although the ancient Greeks celebrated the erotic love of adult men for male youths in philosophy, poetry, and vase painting, male youths were not supposed to yield themselves sexually. They may have submitted to penetration between the thighs; and/or the sex may have been a twilight moment, a temporary phase in the youth's life, and never openly acknowledged.

Similarly, women expressed very strong romantic feelings for each other in Victorian Britain, writing in letters that they wanted to kiss and hug each other all night, even kicking their husbands out of bed to enjoy each other's company. The Victorians did not regard these emotions as sexual, and thought of these friendships as touching if not sentimental. In Part 6, literary critic Sharon Marcus even claims that female friendships strengthened rather than undermined Victorian marriage. If these relationships were erotic, they may have been twilight moments, unacknowledged perhaps even by the female lovers, and unrecognizable to society.

The rules of sexual grammar help determine what is intelligible or not. In some ways, women could get away with intense female friendships in nineteenth-century Britain because some sexual combinations, such as women with women, simply were not intelligible. In the eighteenth century, louche poets and sophisticated intellectuals occasionally used the word "tribade" or "sapphist," but other educated men thought it was impossible for two women to be sexual with each other. For instance, when two school teachers were accused of having a sexual affair in a boarding school, the judge proclaimed that the notion of English women having sex with each other was as extraordinary and unlikely as witchcraft and sorcery.[26] As we shall see in Part 6, Anne Lister, an early nineteenth-century gentlewoman, thought of herself as a singular person because she desired only women, but she did not have the word "lesbian" to describe an identity. In order to explain her feelings to herself, she searched in the classics for precedents, finding the words for clitoris and tribade.[27] Other women, as critic Martha Vicinus has shown, might borrow the vocabulary of romantic desire, calling each other husband, or the language of family, describing each other as mother and child.[28]

Even when the rules of sexual grammar were clear, people could evade the labels imposed on them, carrying out their desires and sexual acts as twilight moments. For instance, the British government found it very difficult to enforce its Contagious Diseases Acts because many women who sold sex refused to label themselves as prostitutes. Men who had sex with other men often did not define themselves as homosexual, even when that identity emerged and became more positive. In the nineteenth century, many working-class women had sex before marriage, but they did not regard themselves as fallen women. As Cornelie Usborne writes in Part 11, women in Weimar Germany sometimes went to quack doctors for a solution to blocked menstruation. Of course, the doctors were really performing abortions. Women also whispered the names of abortionists as they stood gossiping on their front stoops. But abortion was not something that was supposed to be admitted in public. Then the sex reform movement, inspired by socialists and feminists, proclaimed that too many women were dying of illegal abortions and excessive childbirth; they demanded access to birth control and a loosening of the restrictions on abortions. As we shall see in the speech by Dr. J. Leunbach in Part 11, they attacked the hypocrisy of regular doctors and government officials who tacitly allowed upper-class women to have abortions while forbidding them for working-class women.

To get beyond the impasses of Foucauldian thought and queer theory, but also build on their insights, we might return to the magnetic poetry kit with which this introduction started. The notion of a sexual vocabulary and sexual grammar can augment Foucault's focus on discourses, and provide a more flexible, open understanding of the power of language. Discourses shape people's thoughts and exert power, but people also have the ability to use the magnetic poetry kit of sex available in their cultures to create new sentences, to protest the power of institutional discourses, and to create new ways of articulating desire.

Feminists challenged the fundamental structure of sexual discourses, based on masculinity and femininity and the double standard. For instance, Josephine Butler, a respectable Victorian lady, organized other women to protest against the Contagious Diseases Act, which they believed meant that the state sanctioned prostitution. Of course, Butler's own words were still structured by Victorian assumptions that sex was polluting, but she declared that women should not be forced to serve the sexual needs of men. By the end of the nineteenth century, some feminists went even further, to attack the very assumptions of marriage. Why should women subordinate themselves to men in marriage? Grete Meisel-Hess asked, as we shall see in Part 9. Perhaps women should be able to rear children independently of men. By the 1960s, Danish feminists challenged the notion that women's goal in life was to be beautiful, sexy, and attractive to men. But Mette Ejlersen pointed out that women were not having satisfactory orgasms.

But the feminist movement has always been deeply divided over the question of whether the priority should be fighting the dangers of sexual exploitation or insisting on the need for sexual pleasure. For instance, Josephine Butler and her allies focused on sexual purity. But Grete Meisel-Hess, who we read here, insisted that women have the right to sexual pleasure. In the 1960s, as we have mentioned, Mette Ejlersen insisted on women's right to sexual pleasure by informing them about the clitoris. But other feminists, such as the Danish Redstockings, claimed that sex appeal was a way of keeping women down. Some feminists revived Butler's attack on prostitution as the sexual exploitation of women by men. By the 1990s, Swedish feminists successfully obtained the prosecution of men for soliciting prostitution. Other feminists oppose this, calling for the legalization of prostitution. But overall, feminists have tried to restructure the sexual grammar which had governed our understanding of sexuality — sex should be judged not on whether a woman was pure or impure, but on whether she consented to sex and enjoyed it.

This Reader is organized chronologically, to give a sense of change over time, but it could also be used thematically. For instance, Parts 1, 3, and 8 discuss male homosexuality. Heterosexuality and fertility are touched on in Parts 4, 5, 9, and 10. Prostitution is the focus of Parts 7 and 13. Parts 5, 6, 9, and 12 consider female sexuality.

This Reader focuses on European sexuality, because there are plenty of excellent works available on American sexuality. The roots of many American sexual attitudes, especially those to do with Christianity, can be found in European culture. At the same time, European cultures are very different among themselves. For the modern period, this Reader includes material from French, British, German, Danish, and Swedish sources. Many ideas about sex flowed between countries, but at the same time nations experienced different chronologies in terms of sexual attitudes.[29] The British government engaged in much more censorship than the German government was able to do, and in the early twentieth century a modern sex reform culture and homosexual and lesbian culture flourished in Berlin and other cities. However, the Nazi government then tried to control sex for the purposes of the state. Scandinavia has been notorious for sexual freedom since the 1960s, but as we shall see this freedom emerged from intense conflict between the government, conservatives, and socialists and feminists. Today, the Danes regard the Swedes as much too willing to engage in government regulation of sex.

Instead of addressing global sexualities, this Reader also includes several parts on imperialism. In fact, there is no such thing as nonwestern sexuality; rather, there are hundreds of varied cultures, too many to discuss in one book. However, by covering imperialism, we gain a sense of the relativity of sexual power and sexual vocabularies.

This volume is structured as a series of debates. Readers can examine an article or part written by a modern historian or critic, and then analyze a primary source document, written during the past, to see whether the historian's argument holds up, or they can examine debates between two critics.

By thinking of sexual words in terms of a magnetic poetry kit, we can acknowledge that the sexual vocabulary available in a culture limits how people can think about sex, especially when it is formulated in discourses linked to institutional power, such as medicine and psychiatry. Yet people can still mix and match the words, and create new sentences, and new ways of thinking about sex.

Notes

1   J. N. Adams, *The Latin Sexual Vocabulary* (Baltimore: Johns Hopkins University Press, 1982), 126.
2   Craig A. Williams, *Roman Homosexuality: Ideologies of Masculinity in Classical Antiquity* (New York: Oxford University Press, 1999), 270–286.
3   Michel Foucault, *The History of Sexuality: An Introduction,* trans. Robert Hurley (New York: Vintage Books, 1990).
4   Hera Cook, *The Long Sexual Revolution: English Women, Sex, and Contraception 1800–1975* (Oxford: Oxford University Press, 2004).
5   Michael Warner, *The Trouble with Normal* (New York: Free Press, 1999).
6   Karma Lochrie, *Heterosyncrasies: Female Sexuality When Normal Wasn't* (Minneapolis: University of Minnesota Press, 2005), 6.
7   Daniel Pick, *Faces of Degeneration: A European Disorder, c. 1848–1914* (Cambridge: Cambridge University Press, 1989).
8   Mark B. Adams, *The Wellborn Science: Eugenics in Germany, France, Brazil, and Russia* (New York: Oxford University Press, 1990); Edward Ross Dickinson, "Biopolitics, Fascism, Democracy: Some Reflections on Our Discourse about 'Modernity'," *Central European History*

37, no. 1 (2004): 1–48; Paul Weindling, *Health, Race and German Politics between National Unification and Nazism, 1870–1945* (Cambridge: Cambridge University Press, 1989); Amir Weiner, "Nature, Nurture, and Memory in a Socialist Utopia: Delineating the Soviet Socio-Ethnic Body in the Age of Socialism," *American Historical Review* 104, no. 4 (1999): 1114–1155.

9   Dan Stone, "Race in British Eugenics," *European History Quarterly* 31, no. 3 (2001): 397–425, at 419.

10   Ellen Key, *Love and Marriage*, trans. Arthur G. Chater (New York: Putnam's, 1911), 166; George Robb, "The Way of All Flesh: Degeneration, Eugenics, and the Gospel of Free Love," *Journal of the History of Sexuality* 6, no. 4 (1996): 589–603, at 593.

11   Alain Corbin, *Women for Hire: Prostitution and Sexuality in France after 1850* (Cambridge, MA: Harvard University Press, 1990); Barbara Alpern Engel, "St. Petersburg Prostitutes in the Late Nineteenth Century: A Personal and Social Profile," *Russian Review* 48, no. 1 (1989): 21–44; Mary Gibson, *Prostitution and the State in Italy*, 2nd edn (Columbus: Ohio State University Press, 1999); Sophie de Schaepdrijver, "Regulated Prostitution in Brussels, 1844–1877: A Policy and Its Implementation," *Historical Social Research* [West Germany] 37 (1986): 89–108; Jolanta Sikorska-Kulesza, trans. Agnieszka Kreczmar, "Prostitution in Congress Poland," *Acta Poloniae Historica* [Poland] 83 (2001): 123–133; Carine Steverlynck, "La Traite des blanches et la prostitution enfantine en Belgique," *Paedagogica Historica* [Belgium] 29, no. 3 (1993): 77–98.

12   Judith Walkowitz, *Prostitution and Victorian Society: Women, Class and the State* (Cambridge: Cambridge University Press, 1980).

13   Havelock Ellis, *Studies in the Psychology of Sex*, vol. 2: *Sexual Inversion* (New York: Random House, 1936), 22–65

14   Judith Butler, *Undoing Gender* (New York: Routledge, 2004), 183.

15   Elizabeth Bernstein, *Temporarily Yours: Intimacy, Authenticity, and the Commerce of Sex* (Chicago: University of Chicago Press, 2007), 24.

16   Alice Dreger also writes that "Historical records in the West suggest that until well into the twentieth century intersex people tended simply to blend in with the general population . . . if genital ambiguity had been considered terribly disturbing throughout western history, there would likely exist significantly more records of legal, religious, and medical examples." But then she goes on to demonstrate that medical and religious authorities did insist that those people known as hermaphrodites choose a gender. Alice D. Dreger and April Herndon, "Progress and Politics in the Intersex Rights Movement: Feminist Theory in Action," *GLQ: A Journal of Lesbian & Gay Studies* 15, no. 2 (2009): 204.

17   John R. Clarke, "Representations of the Cinaedus in Roman Art: Evidence of 'Gay' Subculture?," *Journal of Homosexuality* 49, no. 3/4 (2005): 271–298; Williams, *Roman Homosexuality*, 193.

18   Mark D. Jordan, *The Invention of Sodomy in Christian Theology* (Chicago: University of Chicago Press, 1997), 45; Michael Rocke, *Forbidden Friendships: Homosexuality and Male Culture in Renaissance Florence* (New York and Oxford: Oxford University Press, 1996).

19   Ruth Mazo Karras, "Prostitution and the Question of Sexual Identity in Medieval Europe," *Journal of Women's History* 11, no. 2 (1999): 139–171.

20   Lochrie, *Heterosyncrasies*, 10.

21   Abu Muḥammad ʿAlī ibn Ḥazm al-Andalusī, *A Book Containing the* Risāla *Known as the Dove's Neck-Ring about Love and Lovers*, trans. A. R. Nykl (Paris: Librarie Orientaliste Paul Geuthner, 1931), 6–9, 51–59.

22   Kathryn Babayan, "'In Spirit We Ate Each Other's Sorrow': Female Companionship in Seventeenth-Century Safavi Iran," in *Islamicate Sexualities*, ed. Kathryn Babayan and Afsaneh Najmabadi (Cambridge, MA: Harvard Center for Middle Eastern Studies, 2008), 251; Khaled El-Rouayheb, *Before Homosexuality in the Arab-Islamic World, 1500–1800* Chicago: University of Chicago Press, 2005), 20; Joseph A. Massad, *Desiring Arabs* (Chicago: University

of Chicago Press, 2007); Afsaneh Najmabadi, "Types, Acts, or What? Regulation of Sexuality in Nineteenth-Century Iran," in *Islamicate Sexualities*, ed. Babayan and Najmabadi, 215–296.

23   Gary Anderson, "Celibacy or Consummation in the Garden? Reflections on Early Jewish and Christian Interpretations of the Garden of Eden," *Harvard Theological Review* 82, no. 2 (1989): 121–148.

24   Lochrie, *Heterosyncrasies*, 84.

25   Anna Clark, "Twilight Moments," *Journal of the History of Sexuality* 14, no. 1/2 (2005): 139–160.

26   Jonathan Katz, *Miss Marianne Woods and Miss Jane Pirie against Dame Helen Cumming Gordon* (New York: Arno Press, 1975), 13.

27   Anna Clark, "Anne Lister's Construction of Lesbian Identity," *Journal of the History of Sexuality* 7, no. 1 (1996): 23–50.

28   Martha Vicinus, *Intimate Friends: Women Who Loved Women, 1778–1928* (Chicago: University of Chicago Press, 2004).

29   Dagmar Herzog, "Syncopated Sex: Transforming European Sexual Cultures," *American Historical Review* 114, no. 5 (2009): 1287–1308.

PART 1

Did the ancient Greeks accept love, desire, and relationships between men?

Introduction

WE IMAGINE THE ANCIENT GREEKS as the esteemed thinkers, memorialized in pure white marble sculptures, who inspired the founding fathers of the United States with their ideals of democracy. Indeed, Athens was a city state, where all citizens discussed, debated, and decided on politics. Yet these citizens were male slave holders, and not as high minded as we imagine. The marble statues would have been painted in bright colors, and Greek men feasted at banquets, drinking wine and enjoying the dancing girls – *hetairai*, female entertainers who sold sex – and beautiful boys. Their wives were secluded in the women's quarters, in part because Greek men believed that female sexual desire could be uncontrolled and dangerous. But a man could have sex with a slave girl, a boy or a foreign man.[1]

Did this mean that the ancient Greeks tolerated homosexuality? The Greeks did not have a concept of the homosexual or the heterosexual. However, historians debate whether the Greeks accepted or tolerated love or sex between males. Kenneth Dover argued that the Greeks thought of sex in terms of domination and submission – they judged each other on whether a man was dominant and penetrated his sexual partner, or whether he submitted to penetration. If a man penetrated his slave or a foreigner, he was still dominant. Foucault took up Dover's ideas, but the word toleration was much too simple for him. Instead, he argued, the Greeks were concerned with the control of desire. Desire was natural, since we need appetites to live. But a man who was a slave to his desires was like a slave in general – and the passive partner by definition could not control his desire for this shameful act.[2] Worst of all was the *kinaidos* (*cinaedus*): the *kinaidos* was chiefly defined as an effeminate man, but some sources portray him as taking the passive role in sex with other men, and also pursuing pleasure with women.[3]

For ancient Greece, of course, it is difficult to find evidence to resolve these debates. Vase paintings often depict adult men having sex with — usually inserting their penises between the thighs of — male youths. Male prostitutes were a regular part of city life. On a more elevated scale, some philosophers celebrated intense, romantic love between an older man and a younger man, and debated what it meant for a younger man to "yield." However, citizen youths were not supposed to submit themselves sexually, especially for money. But there were no laws condemning sex between males in itself, unless a man violated or seduced a citizen boy.[4]

One of the most important sources for this issue is the trial of Timarchus, a male citizen accused of prostituting himself to other men. This would seem to undermine the notion that ancient Greeks accepted or tolerated sex between men. Timarchus faced the penalty of *atimia*, or deprivation of his right to participate in politics and public life. But his accuser, Aeschines, acknowledged that Athens taxed male prostitutes rather than condemning them, and that society admired some men who loved other men, and even admitted that he himself still felt desire for beautiful boys. How can these two things be reconciled? Some historians, such as John Winkler and David Halperin, argue that Athenians did not reject sex between men, but only men who took the passive role.[5] Furthermore, the case was really about politics; as Winkler asserts, if Timarchus had not wanted to play a role in politics, he could have indulged in his pleasures unpunished. James Davidson, however, argues that the problem was that Timarchus engaged too much in pleasure — he was self-indulgent, and Athens' enemies could easily buy him off by paying for his pleasures. Like Halperin, Giulia Sissa asserts that the problem was that Timarchus was becoming too much like a woman, uncontrolled and submissive. She argues that the problem was not pleasure, but desires which could not be controlled. Furthermore, she points out that desire between men was associated with the aristocracy; plebeian men may have resented them because they could not afford the sexual pleasure of prostitutes.

Aeschines was the author of the speech accusing Timarchus of being a prostitute. In analyzing this speech, historians have asked what seems to have motivated Timarchus, in Aeschines' view: was Timarchus exclusively interested in sex between men? Was he portrayed as masculine or feminine? Were Timarchus' lovers scorned, even though they took the masculine role? How could Aeschines defend some kinds of love between men and condemn Timarchus? For instance, Athenians often lauded Harmodius and Aristogeiton. The tyrant Hipparchus wanted to enjoy the sexual favors of the beautiful youth Harmodius. But Harmodius was the beloved of Aristogeiton, so he spurned Hipparchus, who took his revenge by insulting Harmondius' sister. In revenge, the two lovers plotted to kill Hipparchus and thus overthrew tyranny and freed Athens. Aeschines also refers to Achilles, the hero of Homer's *Iliad*, who was heartbroken when his companion Patroclus was killed by the Trojans. Why should Timarchus' sexual conduct matter to Athenian politics? Timarchus and the famous Demosthenes, after all, were political enemies of Aeschines. In the end, Aeschines triumphed, and Timarchus lost his political rights.[6]

Notes

1   For a useful overview, see Marilyn B. Skinner, *Sexuality in Greek and Roman Culture* (Malden, MA: Blackwell, 2005).

2   Michel Foucault, *The Uses of Pleasure*, trans. Robert Hurley (New York: Vintage, 1990), 68.

3   For different approaches, see James N. Davidson, *The Greeks and Greek Love* (London: Weidenfeld and Nicolson, 2008), 60–64; Skinner, *Sexuality in Greek and Roman Culture*, 56.

4   David Cohen, *Law, Sexuality and Society* (Cambridge: Cambridge University Press, 1994), 176.

5   David M. Halperin, "The Democratic Body: Prostitution and Citizenship in Classical Athens," *differences: a Journal of Feminist Cultural Studies* 2, no. 1 (1990): 1–27; John J. Winkler, "Laying Down the Law: The Oversight of Men's Sexual Behavior in Ancient Athens," in *Before Sexuality: The Construction of Erotic Experience in the Ancient Greek World*, ed. David M. Halperin, John J. Winkler, and Froma I. Zeitlin (Princeton: Princeton University Press, 1990), 171–210.

6   Chris Carey, *Aeschines* (Austin: University of Texas Press, 2000).

Chapter 1

Giulia Sissa

SEX AND SENSUALITY IN THE ANCIENT WORLD (2008)

Pleasure (*Hēdŏnḗ*)

G REEK PLEASURE IS SWEETNESS. It is sweetness to the palate: wine and delicious foods. It is the melodious voice of the Muses and the charming song of the poet. Greek pleasure is oblivion. A pleasurable mood is defined by the ability to forget the torment, the worries and the anxieties we have already encountered as some of the meanings of *kêdos* and *kḗdĕa lugrắ*. The dulcet voice, *glukĕrḗ*, of the Muses makes us forget the *kḗdĕa* (*Theogony*, 97–104). As the daughters of memory, the Muses came into the world with an 'uncaring spirit' (61) and the mission to make people forget their ills and to alleviate anxiety (55). Art is calming and narcotic. It acts like wine or the drug nepenthe, the analgesic and tranquilliser that Helen poured into her guests' cups on a memorable evening. We are at her home in Sparta, the war with Troy is over, and the beautiful woman is reconciled with her husband. Suddenly a shy young man arrives wanting to hear news of the heroes of that war, particularly Ulysses. During the meal, the remembrance of the battles, carnage and death creates a grim atmosphere. Everyone is intent on remembering and renewing the pain of mourning. Helen wishes to distract them from those distressing reflections. She therefore mixes this Egyptian drug into the watered-down wine in a large bowl, and the drug has the power to anesthetise the memory, extinguish grief and placate anger (*The Odyssey*, iv, 220–30). The same is true of all causes of pleasure.

Pleasure is respite, the extinction of pain and an end to unease. Eros is associated with *húpnos* (sleep), as we have seen in Hera's seduction of Zeus. Desire, which we normally see as arousal, was primarily perceived in these texts as paralysis and petrification. Knees that go weak are knees that cannot run or leap forward. The act itself and the sensuousness it produces are a kind of powerlessness and withdrawal from life, similar to exhaustion.

The symposium was the most fulfilling hedonistic ritual for the ancients; it was the setting in which all the ingredients of pleasure came together. When Plato wants to show what citizens would do in a city governed not by concern for the common good but by the principle of pleasure, he produces the following scene: those who should be dealing with the management of the city would indulge in a life of continuous feasting, those who should be working to produce goods would put on extravagant clothes, cover themselves with jewels and relax in an unending symposium, making the occasional useful gesture if they find it amusing (*Republic*, iv, 420e–421c). The coming together of food, wine, music and eroticism in an event that inevitably costs a great deal of money was a celebration of the triumph of the feral soul and of the disintegrative power of pleasure (*hēdŏnē*). And pleasure had to be excluded from the ideal city precisely because it resulted in anxieties being forgotten.

Unsurprisingly, therefore, the ancients associated relaxation, eroticism and conviviality with one posture of the body and one piece of furniture. In Greece and Rome, they slept, made love and dined while reclining on comfortable couches. The frescoes in the House of the Chaste Lovers in Pompeii show how a triclinium would have been set out. It is a room containing three beds placed in a horseshoe shape around low tables, on which there are plates and goblets – a dining room. A man and a woman lie in sensuous proximity and amorous languor on each of the beds. Greek vases – the very things which were used at table and were often decorated with scenes pertinent to the table and its universe – depicted relaxation and abandon on couches (*klînaĭ*) in dining rooms between men and boys, or between men and *hĕtaîraĭ*, sensuous female companions.

Mollitia and *malakía*, which designated yielding, laziness and laxity, were traits of character that were associated with physical characteristics and positions. Resting and lying down – the acts of making oneself soft and releasing the tension in one's body – require something comfortable as support. The convivial *klînē*, with its wide mattress, provided this for men and youths who met in a house for a banquet or a symposium: a place prepared for pleasure in all its forms. Wine, conversation, music, food and erotic titillation: all this was enjoyed with elegant abandon. 'Come and lie on the couch,' the youthful Anticleon invites his father Procleon who, because of his coarseness, is in need of re-education, 'and I'll teach you how to behave at a symposium' (Aristophanes, *Wasps*, 1208–15). Participants at these events had to lie down with grace, by stretching out their knees and languidly slipping down like a gymnast. The Aristotelian author of the *Problems* wrote that you can lie on the left side with pleasure (*hēdĕos*), whereas on your right side you fall asleep. You stay awake while resting on your left elbow because, with the active right hand free, you can make all the gestures you want (vi, 5 and 7). You digest better with your body bent, as a result of the warmth the position allows you to conserve (vi, 3). We can see this in the symposium scenes painted on the pottery used at the symposia themselves: reclining men, with one leg stretched out and the other slightly bent, and with one arm holding up the body and the other free, so that the hand can raise a goblet or caress a drinking partner.

Respectable women did not get involved in such worldly pleasures: to recline beside a table meant also going to bed in euphoric and animated company, which was created in order to abolish distances and expose scantily dressed bodies (the clothing was not stitched) to contact with all the others. For this reason it was generally believed that a woman who frequented banquets was a *hĕtaîra*, a prostitute or mistress (Pseudo-Demosthenes, *Against Neaira*). No husband who cared about his honour would have exposed his wife to such promiscuity. Banquet scenes on vases do indeed show women at symposia, but only in the most unrestrained erotic situations.

Pleasure was hypnotic, and pleasure was lethargy. Plato revived this ancient perception of pleasure, but added an idea of his own: it is impossible to partake of *hēdŏnē* in small doses that are compatible with an industrious and balanced life, because desire is insatiable. Once you give in to desire, you sink into a different kind of existence. The power of sensuousness does not therefore depend on its intensity, but rather on that continuous movement of want, refilling and want again, which ends up absorbing all the time of those who live like plovers, grazing cattle or jars with a leaky bottom. The symposium of those who abandoned themselves to the game was full-time indolence.

The problem of pleasure, let me insist, is not its excessiveness – its excessive intensity, duration or beauty. Indeed, pleasure paradoxically becomes illusory and unreachable in its purity because of the desire that pursues it asymptotically. With its despotic and inordinate demands, appetite prevails and renders satisfaction impossible. The excess, therefore, is to be found in desire and not in pleasure (*Laws*, 783a–b). This is why Platonic ethics cannot be reduced to a simple call for moderation, as though it were a matter of curbing an overindulgence; it actually proposes ascetic abstinence. The guardians in the ideal city have to renounce property and a private life in which they would be able to express their taste for luxury. They have to eat communal meals precisely in order to avoid the exquisite ambivalences of symposia. They have to form sexual partnerships that are unrelated to their erotic inclinations. The city has to be happy, but its happiness is not the one its citizens aspire to, which is individual pleasure. In other words, they have to prefer something else. The black horse has to be tamed.

Thus, regarding erotic pleasure, sexual acts themselves are not the substance of ethics, because what matters is, rather, the risks inherent in *la dolce vita*. Sexual acts were perceived as the effects and expression of a certain kind of persistent inclination – what I call sensuality. Although each one can be isolated and described, they all depend on a yearning for a state of completeness that can never be achieved.

Democratic life

Platonic thought was a corrective, polemical and paedagogic response to a particular vision of human existence. Callicles, a character in the *Gorgias*, speaks for those who believe that happiness is made up of powerful passions, which come together in a continuous enjoyment of life. Unless you want to live like a corpse or a stone, the movement of appetite must never be halted. Life is desire and the satisfaction of desire. As we have already seen, Socrates responds to this Heraclitean manifesto with one of his usual dramatic reversals of ideas. Who is really living like a dead person? Aren't the dead – the souls of the Danaids in the underworld – those who pass their time vainly filling leaking jars? Is not this continuous filling the opposite of what we really want to obtain, which is plenitude? The soul of a pleasure-seeker is like a holed jar – it is like a plover. Callicles obstinately refuses to agree. But then happiness would be like being hungry and eating, being thirsty and drinking and feeling the itch and scratching oneself all the time. This argument has no effect, and Callicles continues in his beliefs. At this stage, Socrates uses a less paradoxical example: the *cinaedus*, a type who was well known to everyone. He asks whether such a person could be considered the model for a happy life. Callicles finally surrenders. The public image of such a contemptible and ignominious person removes all doubts. No one would dare to support such an idea, even in jest.

The *cinaedus* represented an extreme, and typified covetousness in all its forms, but particularly shameless sexual frenzies. He was the human equivalent of the plover – an inexhaustible body, always hungry for pleasure. He had a male body that resembled a woman's. We encounter this in a speech Aeschines delivered in 346 BC: *Against Timarchus*.

Those who had committed one or several of the following crimes were banned from speaking in the assembly by Athenian law: abandonment of one's shield on the battlefield, that is, desertion; mistreatment of, or failure to maintain, one's parents; dissipation or waste of inherited wealth; and prostitution. A citizen who dared to stand up and give a speech to the people after having committed one of these acts was liable to face legal action. If the accusation was confirmed by the courts, the guilty party could lose his civil rights, including the right to be elected or chosen by lots for political and religious offices, and even the simple right to take part in the assembly of the people. He could be punished by *atīmía* (19–32).

The law on *atīmía* followed a logic which provides us with a crucial element for understanding what the Greeks, or at least the Athenians, thought of individual and private life. It affords us a glimpse into a question which is increasingly relevant for contemporary societies: the importance of sex for the integrity and credibility of political actors. When ancient and modern democracies are compared, it can be argued that the law and Aeschines' comments demonstrate the existence, already in the ancient world, of a distinction: between the private sphere and the public and political one. The absence of legal norms affecting private life demonstrates the Athenians' great concern with negative freedom or freedom from oppressive rules. Prostitution is not prohibited: the only violation of the law occurs when someone who has committed this act appears in the assembly. The law did not interfere with those who minded their own business in the privacy of their own home (Wallace, 1996: 127–215).

Following this argument, the city's restraint in not interfering in such activities as management of the home or the use to which one puts one's own body confirms Pericles' proud boast in his famous *Funeral Oration* (Thucydides, ii, 37). Under Athenian democracy, citizens did not look on each other with mutual suspicion when it came to everyday behaviour, lifestyles and forms of pleasure. People did not get emotionally involved or become irritated with their neighbours simply because the latter were living in a particular manner, just as they pleased. The Athenians did not ill-treat others even with attitudes which, stopping short of actual injury, could hurt or make life unpleasant. In other words, the Athenian was discrete and had an open mind, free from envy. This meant that all those habits and manners that we associate with the personal and domestic sphere – how we dress, how we eat, how, when and where we make love, and how we bring up our children – were left to individual choice and preferences: everyone was free to behave as they thought best. This assertion can be found in a whole series of texts on the nature of democracy. Democracy was by definition a regime, the only regime, in which everyone lived as he pleased (Lysias, xxvi, 5; Isocrates, vii, 20; Plato, *Republic*, viii, 557a–b; Aristotle, *Politics*, $1317^a40–^b14$).

When comparing the freedoms of the ancients and the freedoms of the moderns, however, we need to be aware of a much more radical distinction. In democratic Athens, nobody claimed that the city should allow complete sexual freedom to all consenting adults. One could not find in the Athenian constitution a fundamental right to privacy

(Rahe, 1992: 196). One of the proofs of this theory is precisely the speech *Against Timarchus*. Hence the comments of such philosophers as Plato, Aristotle and Isocrates concerning the licence that democracy allowed to proliferate in the private sphere, must be considered polemical exaggerations by critics of the *dễmos* and its *laissez-faire* (ibid., 189–90). Athens was an 'illiberal democracy', a pre-modern state that knew nothing of the principle that a state must allow its subjects to behave freely, pursue their own happiness and live in safety.

Without any doubt, the ancients were aware of a symbolic and real separation between *tà ídia* and *tà dēmósia*: distinct spaces, specific activities, and different levels of intrusion by the law. This distinction is, however, compatible with a constant and fundamental relevance of the private in relation to the public and political. As Paul Rahe asserts, the right to privacy – that is, the right to respect, principally consisting of non-interference in people's preferences and habits, which are considered irrelevant outside the home – could not become a value in a society which linked so closely together what a man did in his bedroom and what he said before the people. This connection goes to the heart of the law on *atīmía*: a way of life – one involving waste of one's own money, selling off family property cheap, failing in gratitude to one's relations and, above all, using oneself and one's body for mercenary reasons in an erotic lifestyle – engenders a discrimination in public life. To be more precise, it creates an absolute and drastic exclusion: the law deprived those citizens who dared to do these things not only of their right to election to particular positions, but also of their right to the most fundamental activity in a system of direct democracy: the freedom to speak in the assembly.

The private therefore had a very heavy impact on political activity. In his rhetorical use of the law, Aeschines reminded his fellow citizens of their familiarity with what it was that linked those two worlds: prejudice and reputation, the instruments of shame. Let us see how the use of one's body relates to political ability.

The management of one's own house is relevant to the holding of high office and to the expression of one's opinion on communal decisions. Aeschines asserted that this was because the private and the public are similar or *paraplễsioi* (*Against Timarchus*, 153). It is possible to infer or predict (*manteũŏmaï*) how a person will act in political life from the way they have acted in their own home (127). How has this man treated his relations, his inheritance and, most importantly, himself – his *sỗma*? That is the way in which he will treat the city. The past gives a foretaste of the future, and the manner in which he looked after himself will be reflected in the way he looks after the common good (153). An elementary semiotics makes it possible for anyone to assess the qualities of a politician in advance.

There is an ethical aspect to this view of sexuality as something politically significant. To judge a man in his capacity as a citizen meant examining his life in its most intimate moments, as though political competence were a component of the person taken as a whole. At stake is a man's integrity in the literal sense of his wholeness, and this presupposes that the individual has a coherent, homogeneous and unchanging identity. The actions a person carries out at different times and in different places are supposed to follow a repetitive pattern: they are always the same because the person is the same. Desire for pleasure is the thing that unifies all of Timarchus' actions. And reputation is the thing that gives the impression of continuity. Aeschines warded off possible difficulties: no one was supposed to ask him to refer to particular deeds as everyone knew what Timarchus' behaviour was like (*Against Timarchus*, 89–122). His listeners had acknowledged the kind of things he got up to, by laughing at him in a recent assembly (*Against Timarchus*, 79 and 85).

This focus on the entire person, from head to toe and from the beginning to the present, was unsurprising, because democracy – whose spirit the orator attributed to his public – rejects in principle any criterion based on social status (27). Pericles proclaimed in his defence of the aristocratic Athenian democracy that obscurity or origins lacking in prestige or renown do not interfere with the opportunity to acquire reputation and glory through personal merit (Thucydides, ii, 37). Aeschines took up the same theme to introduce his political attack on Timarchus and his defence of the democratic values shared by his listeners. He asserted that the Athenians did not ask that those who took part in politics be descendants of generals or noble ancestors; they simply asked that they should live a decent life. Instead of aristocratic virtues, which were the product of education in childhood and of a particular social environment, democracy demanded personal guarantees from individuals. Their deeds, habits, manners and life histories became the exclusive source on which the people based their evaluations. Public trust therefore depended on private matters.

This is why, for all the claims concerning the fundamental freedom of behaviour inherent in the power of the dêmos, it proves to be mercilessly intrusive towards this very behaviour. Morality, habits and customs were the sole material by which the politically active democratic individual could be judged. There had to be complete transparency. Reputation and gossip were its instruments. Through Rumor, who, as Aeschines reminded his listeners, is a goddess (*Against Timarchus*, 127–31), the community came to know how each person lived. There was nowhere to hide. *Tà ídia*, one's private affairs, ended up being exposed to the eyes and ears of everyone. The rumours that circulated about an individual – the people he mingled with, the places of ill repute where he went at night to have his fun, and the things that happened to him when he got drunk – provided the information needed to assess the dignity of that individual in relation to the workings of democracy, once the right person had been able to collect it and present it to the public in the proper place, which was a court of law. What kind of man would live like that? How could he make himself useful to the city, if he behaved in such a destructive and dishonourable manner towards himself, his people and his things?

The Athenian democracy was prying and puritanical in the name of the rejection of class distinction, as Thucydides admitted when he examined the popular resentment against another famous pleasure-lover, Alcibiades. The same exemplary fellow citizens whom Pericles idealised for their lack of envy and for their capacity not to interfere in other people's affairs displayed extremely intense feelings when it came to this young dandy, with his hair after the Spartan fashion, his horses and his life wasted amongst *hĕtaîrai*, young men and banquets. While admitting his great skills as a general, people were offended by his extravagance, intemperance and luxury to the point where they entrusted the state to others and hence, concludes the historian, brought about its ruin (Thucydides, vi, 15, 4). What is evident here is a criticism of the regime's stupidity, as it sacrificed the best interests of the state to vulgar emotions – resentment, indignation and envy – which might have had nothing to do with a policy based on more politically appropriate emotions, or rational choices. Was this a manifestation of human nature in historical events? It was certainly the emergence of a contradiction inherent in ancient democracy.

If what counts for political participation is the individual, irrespective of his origins, then it must be his life that counts, hence his acts and their methods, because this is what the essential person comes down to. But this means that an individual is not free to live exactly as he pleases. He is going to be judged in accordance with a shared sense of proper behaviour, and this traditional and collective perception will prevail over an assessment of his intelligence and competence. It was democracy's boast that it attributed value to a man on the basis of his merits, in contrast with the aristocratic perception of excellence as the product of a certain genealogy and a given *paĭdeĭa*, which can only be obtained if one has the good fortune to be born into a noble family. The democratic man was a competent adult, born on Attic soil, who was responsible for his own qualities and was only accidentally someone's son. He was not born well, but he lived well. However, his value depended on the values of those who had the power to acknowledge it, that is, of the *dêmos* in the sense of the 'people'. It was the people who sat in judgement of individual decency in the *dŏkĭmăsĭaĭ* (the examinations of candidates or retiring magistrates) and in trials like the one against Timarchus. The individual thus had to conform to communal standards of morality and passions. Above all, he had to know how to show contrition.

In an ancient Mediterranean city, which was a relatively small community where everyone more or less knew everyone else, shame and fear of other people's opinion – *aischŭnē* or *aidŏs* – act as the most important factors in social cohesion and moral control (Cohen, 1987). Shame means experiencing displeasure over what others might find deplorable in our behaviour. It means that our happiness becomes dependent on other people's opinion, and especially on received beliefs. This is not an entirely passive apprehension, because we are only sensitive to the opinions of people we respect and with whom we share precisely these same opinions. We relate to others in a reciprocal manner through the use of restraint and embarrassment, but only in so far as they represent the values we believe in (Aristotle, *Rhetoric*, 2, 6; Williams, 1992). Someone who knows no shame also fears no one. If we cannot blush, then we do not belong to a community.

Democracy can only accentuate the role of the public dominion. Shame becomes a fundamental passion, because of the importance of the way the *dêmos* judges individual and politically acceptable behaviour. And sex becomes a political matter. Indeed, shame concerns sexual behaviour more than any other aspect of life. The sexual organs were called *aidŏĭa*, or (in Latin) *pudenda*, [in French] *parties honteuses* ('shameful things'). Dishonourable behaviour (*aischrǎ*) included unions with inappropriate persons at inappropriate times and in inappropriate places, because such transgressions resulted from incontinence (*akŏlăsía*) (Aristotle, *Rhetoric*, 2, 6, 4). Timarchus' entire life was ignominious (*aischrŏs*): as his behaviour was as shameful as he was shameless, he had lost all fear of other people's disapproval and was no longer able to blush (*Against Timarchus*, 28 and 38).

Shameless living

In 346, Timarchus was a prominent politician. He and Demosthenes accused Aeschines of having betrayed the city's interests during the famous embassy to King Philip II of Macedonia. He thus exposed himself to the public gaze, and Aeschines wanted to get his revenge and destroy an undesirable opponent. His personal attack was cynical and purely concerned with the end result. It was, however, an opportunity provided by the law on *atīmía*, which made it possible to eliminate a political adversary with arguments of a personal nature. This was the punishment that Aeschines wanted the judges to inflict on Timarchus: he wanted him to be condemned to disappear from the political arena because he had continued to speak in front of the people after having wasted a considerable paternal inheritance, after having ill-treated an ageing and infirm uncle and, above all, after having shamelessly sold his body and having been unrestrainedly maintained by other men. Timarchus was culpable of every single one of the ignominious acts detailed in the law.

We are interested here in an extreme interpretation of the law, and the relentless ferocity with which an orator managed to provoke his listeners, the *ándrĕs Athēnaõi*, into feeling repugnance at the simple rehearsal of something they were already well aware of, as everyone was talking about it. Democratic rhetoric, by echoing gossip, manipulated that quintessentially social emotion we call shame, in order to destroy a man completely There is, however, a special fierceness in the arguments about sex. Aeschines examined Timarchus' sex life in its most intimate details – using prurient insinuation and euphemistic reticence – and exploited those details as his main argument. They were supposed to be infinitely more important than Timarchus' squandered inheritance and his poor neglected uncle when it came to excluding him from public life.

Since his early youth, Timarchus had indulged in ceaseless erotic pursuits with *hĕtaîrai*, youths and mature men, one after another. This craving of his was the cause of his dissipated fortune, of the ease with which he could be corrupted and of his habit of selling off his assets cheap. But, the culmination of this insatiability included behaviour without which Timarchus could not have been arraigned (rather than simply gossiped about): that behaviour was prostitution. The fact that he had sold his body – in other words, himself – to other men was the central point to Aeschines' rhetoric.

Now this is the really interesting problem in our argument: what was so despicable about Timarchus' love life? What persuaded the Athenians to deprive him of his honour (*tĩmẽ*)? Was it the fact that he allowed himself to be penetrated sexually and that he subjected himself to a humiliating power that debased him and his identity as a citizen (Dover, 1978; Halperin, 1990; Foucault, 1984a; 1984b)? Was it his general dissipation, which included his passions for fish, gambling, courtesans, female flautists, extravagant dinners, and so on (*Against Timarchus*, 42)? If this was the case, then Timarchus was simply a bottomless pit and a slave to his insatiable desires, which needed to be paid for by someone else (*Against Timarchus*, 75–6; Davidson, 1997).

When we consider the violence and vehemence of Aeschines' speech, which commented on the law using general assertions on sexual morality, we have to ask ourselves whether it was the venality or the actual sexual behaviour that made prostitution incompatible with political activity. Now male prostitution was not only a form of immoderate hedonism, like the mania for flautists and mullet: it was a sexual transaction. This was the point that rhetoric managed to magnify and dramatise. The only important relationships were those between Timarchus and his various male partners, because these were the only ones that involved money, gifts and maintenance in exchange for sexual favours, and these were the ones that were presented as truly scandalous. The other things fleshed out the depiction of his lifestyle, but this was the decisive factor as far as his public disgrace was concerned.

The law referred to selling oneself, not to having sex with another man. It is also true, however, that we do not know of a law inflicting *atĩmía* upon men kept by women. And it is also true that Aeschines spoke of other things and extended his attack far beyond the financial aspects of Timarchus' sex life. The speech ends by vilifying the kind of relationship this man created with other men. Timarchus, Aeschines insists, has made his body impure and therefore unacceptable within the confines of the political space (*Against Timarchus*, 188 and 195). He has used his male body in unspeakable positions, as though it were a woman's body (185). He has cultivated an unnatural sexuality, *parà phŭsin (ibid.)*.

All this went beyond the simple act of prostitution and threw a disturbing light on the intolerance that the orator wished to arouse in his public. Precisely because he was so keen to demolish the reputation of Timarchus, we have to assume that he was using plausible arguments and could count on the sympathy of those who were listening and preparing to make their decision. By using words that stigmatised unnatural, effeminate and impure eroticism, Aeschines was touching on what must have been a sensitive matter for the Athenians.

We do not know exactly what these unmentionable acts were, but the allusion to femininity and nature suggests they concerned anal eroticism. In fact it was considered against nature (*parà phūsin*) for male bodies to behave like female ones and to wish to be passive (*ĕpithūmeîn páscheîn*). In the section on sexuality in the Aristotelian *Problems*, we find a detailed explanation of the changes that desire undergoes in certain people (iv, 26). In naturally effeminate men (*phūseî thēlūdríai*), the tubes that carry semen to the penis and to the testicles are obstructed either because of a congenital malformation or because these men are eunuchs or impotent. The fluid therefore flows towards the posterior (*hĕdra*), where it accumulates and creates a store of material which is sensitive to erotic stimulation. In contact with a depiction, perception or thought, that is the area that experiences the desire to be rubbed. The pleasure of the sexual act is also experienced there because that is where a secretion of semen occurs, as is demonstrated by the fact that during the sexual act the anus contracts and the surrounding tissues are consumed.

This is analogous to what occurs in active males – those who act (*drân*) in the sexual encounter – because it involves a redirected ejaculation. Effeminate men always remain men, and they can have short erections (otherwise they would become women). Their partial mutilation makes them only similar to women: like women, they are insatiable (*áplēstoi*) because the seminal liquid does not come out with sufficient force to empty the anal area completely. They therefore remain permanently in a state of erotic sensitivity and potential arousal: their erogenous zone always retains a little stagnant material, ready to respond to stimulation. This is why their sensuality is pure lasciviousness (*lagneía*). Anyone who desires to be the passive partner, either all the time or on alternate occasions, has a physiology which can never free itself from desire: it is like having a constant itch, in the manner of the Platonic hedonist. For Aristotle, the itch is the exact model for erotic pleasure: it is an enjoyment that culminates in the expulsion of a fluid full of hot air, which was trapped in the body against nature. The expulsion of semen is the ejection of a humour of this kind in accordance with nature (*Problems*, iv, 15).

Men who desire the passive role are insatiable because their bodies never dry out. Their bodies never manage to expel the humour completely for an anatomical reason: the anus does not have the necessary force to eject it all. It is not designed for this purpose. The natural function of the penis is to fill itself with hot air and liquid in quantities sufficient to eject the semen that has accumulated in the testicles (*Problems*, iv, 21). In a very hot and humid body such as that of hirsute, lame, melancholic or young men, the abundant outflow of semen is accompanied by a great capacity for replenishment and by an intense sexuality, which inevitably involves a series of erections (*Problems*, iv, 30 and 31; v, 31). The anus, on the other hand, is inadequate, just like the female sex organs. Its weakness is effeminacy. Its lasciviousness has a timing which is quite unlike that of the penis: this is the consequence of the residues that constantly impregnate its tissues.

This physiology applied to both Plato's *cinaedus* and Timarchus. The *cinaedus* is the paradigm for insatiable desire (*áplēstos*), because he passes his life 'scratching himself', maddened by a chronic sexual itch. He is like the plover, the leaky jar, the grazing cattle. Timarchus had extravagantly indulged in all manner of pleasures, but the pleasure of pleasures remained the sexual voracity of his youth, which drove him to let himself be maintained by several men, in spite of being rich (*Against Timarchus*, 95). The young Timarchus was not driven to humiliate himself by need; he was not forced into an involuntary slavery. He chose that life (160) because he liked it and desired it (95; 191). He gave it up only when his faded beauty ceased to be profitable. Then he sold his properties and continued to live as he had done. It was the hedonistic gratuitousness of his lascivious nature that strengthened his enemy's hand.

The application of Aristotelian physiology to Timarchus poses a problem. Are we attributing a theory of sex founded on nature to the Greeks, or at least to the people to whom our belligerent orator addressed his arguments?

Like Plato, Aristotle perceived sexual pleasure as the drive for procreation (*Problems*, iv, 15; *History of Animals* 8, 1). And procreation is the work of the *phúsis*. Sexual dimorphism exists in order to allow the transmission of life, while the intestine has a different and specific purpose. The use of the anus for erotic purposes does not fulfil the natural duty to procreate, but if this act is possible as a sexual act – if anal penetration is pleasurable and can be desired – then there must be an explanation. How can sexual pleasure shift to that area? The answer is: through the redirection of the flow of semen, which is a material that acts specifically upon the erotic *diánoiă*. This shift therefore results from processes that occur within the body, and these can be either congenital or the product of habit. We have a dilemma: anal eroticism is in the body, but it is still unnatural. Let us examine this point more closely.

Those who are exposed to sexual relations in adolescence conserve a memory of those acts and of their associated pleasure. By acquiring a habit, they come to desire passivity as though it were natural. In many cases, habit becomes nature. If the person is also lascivious, weak and humid, then this process occurs all the more quickly (*Problems*, iv, 26). This artificial nature, which could be defined as the product of inurement, is indeed a modification of the body: the pleasure of those who acquire the desire to be penetrated occurs because they enjoy and secrete semen in a particular place (*ibid.*, 879b34–5). The acquired nature becomes a memory which is both psychological and corporeal. However, this is not enough to make it natural in the sense of conforming to the ends of *phúsis*. It is the *body* in which the semen is not directed towards the penis that is defined as 'not in accordance with nature' (*mè katà phúsin*, 879b6).

Let us cast Aeschines' speech against the background of this Aristotelian theory. His insinuations portrayed Timarchus as the perfect example of a man who had given himself over entirely to effeminate and unnatural pleasure, both because of his lasciviousness (his repugnant nature) and because of his assiduously cultivated habit, which in turn had resulted from his uncontrollable desire (*Against Timarchus*, 95). Like Plato's *cinaedus*, he had a desire for passivity, which explains why he voluntarily engaged in prostitution.

Érōs kalós

We have therefore come to the very core of the most widely known question concerning ancient sexuality. What was the attitude of the Greeks towards sex between men and youths? It is an attitude, I will argue, that depends on the social environment, and changes radically between the rarefied world of the enlightened aristocracy and that of the ordinary Athenians, engaged in the performance of democracy.

This question is usually posed by taking Plato as the starting point. But, with Plato, the setting is that of the palaestra and the symposium. In the gymnasium, naked young men ran, threw javelins and wrestled. They sweated, covered themselves in oil and sand, and then dried themselves by running a strigil over their thighs and biceps. They would sit on the ground and leave traces of their genitals in the dust. Older men would look on, admire and comment upon them. They would meet and socialise. And then a youth comes in: he is of such beauty that everyone, older men and peers alike, are unsettled and turn to look at him (Plato, *Charmides*, 154b–d). In the symposium, grown men and youths reclined on beds in pairs, in studied proximity; they chatted, drank and listened to music. The only women present were flautists and the *hĕtaîrai*. There was warmth and euphoria. It was then they asked themselves about the nature of *eros*. And it was then, in the company of nobles and philosophers, that they eulogised Love as though it had nothing to do with women and the dilemmas of passion and chastity, and as if pleasure and devotion were a matter exclusively for and between men.

Timarchus' trial projects us into an entirely different world. Here we meet the people and find ourselves in the midst of the *dễmos*. Pleasure is something else. There are no women, but the men are family men, mostly landowners, who had time to engage in political activities while their slaves worked their fields. Here the ancient and still current argument of 'nature', contamination and disgust could be used with impunity. Aeschines became the mouthpiece for frightening intimidation, secure in the knowledge that he was stroking the beast in the direction of its fur: his public was going to follow him. It was the same public that laughed at Aristophanes' crude obscenities: the playwright, too, liked to direct his sarcasm against love between men. In this context, Timarchus, who ultimately wasn't that different from Alcibiades, had reason to be afraid.

However, the public was mixed, and you never knew who might have wormed their way into the crowd. Aeschines cunningly reckoned that he had to take at least one precaution. He asked the people to imagine what would happen if a general, one of those pompous and pedantic characters who frequented gymnasia and symposia, were to come to the court. Such a man would most probably see the thing in a completely different fashion, and appreciate and cultivate male love in its refined form as in its noble and literary history. There had been mythical couples, like Patroclos and Achilles, and historical ones, like Harmodius and Aristogiton, the tyrannicides. The general might have referred to that authoritative and aristocratic image of heroic excellence associated with erotic friendship between men. He would have demanded his right to teach his fellow Athenians that this type of *eros* is good. In the name of this tradition, he might have wanted to defend Timarchus and his various partners.

Thus there was another sort of listener. The general represented a potential public, whose presence could not be excluded in the anonymity of the audience. In response to this objection, which came not so much from a particular person as from the circles that frequented gymnasia and symposia where love was considered in exclusively male terms, Aeschines admitted that such noble forms of love exist. But, of course, Timarchus' ignominious sexuality had nothing to do with them, as they were ultimately dissociated from sex. That *eros* was good because it was chaste, just and legitimate (*Against Timarchus*, 136–7; 139–40). The wise moderation (*sōphrŏsŭnē*) that typified it was the exact opposite of the overindulgence in pleasure.

During his rhetorical peregrinations, Aeschines addressed two very different audiences. First there was the Athenian multitude, which was ready to snigger at his portrayals of Timarchus wandering outside the city walls at night (80–4), inclined to blush at the spectacle of his all too public exposure in that memorable assembly, and sensitive to the disgust (*bdĕlŭría*) which his actions and the marks it left on his body provoked (189). It was all right to speak of unmentionable acts against nature and of defilement in front of such people, because they were already disposed to receive these kinds of argument favourably. The other possible presence, as I have said, was that of people who thought differently because they lived differently. The general and people like him would have been well disposed towards Timarchus and willing to defend him against Aeschines, by associating him with famous historical and mythical male couples. As they would have been disinclined to accept the orator's premises and conclusions, he challenged them by dwelling at great length on the two types of *eros*, the chaste one and the ignominious one. Aeschines, in sum, attempted to head off the arguments by insisting that love can only be virtuous if it is Platonic.

By distinguishing between the two types of listener to whom he had to address his oratory – the aristocracy and the commoners to whom Aristophanes appealed – Aeschines has provided us with two very distinct sets of beliefs on sexual morality in Greek society. A Greek who stood up in defence of a man with an intensely erotic past, a pleasure-seeking individual who loved grown men as well as youths, and accepted gifts and money would have approved of anything, including venality, and regarded these activities as insignificant detail. This was the viewpoint expressed by the famous general, in whose eyes Achilles, Patroclos, Harmodius, Aristogiton and Timarchus shared the same kind of sex life. Any form of sensuality between males was welcome, whether it was active or passive, mercenary or not. On the other hand, a Greek who fiercely criticised Timarchus for his prostitution, ridiculed his nightly escapades and showed contempt for his unnatural effeminacy was attempting to stir up revulsion against that kind of sex, both in itself and in all its various aspects. Such a Greek would end up feeling nauseated in the presence of Timarchus, not just because he had sold himself but also because he engaged in that kind of eroticism.

According to this logic, those who prized love between males perceived it as an affair between partners both of whom were worthy of respect, and those who scorned it reduced it to nothing more than an inherently imbalanced and ruinous relationship: destructive for the youth, who would lose his good reputation forever (160), and ignominious for the grown man, who would be the cause of such dishonour. The general spoke clearly: the magnificent fame of couples – Patroclos and Achilles, or Aristogiton and Harmodius – had to be defended against Aeschines' vulgar attack on Timarchus. It would indeed have been unjust to harm the handsome young man for the beauty which exposed him to the desires of others (132–6). It was not a crime to be attractive, because comeliness is involuntary and irresistible: it was well known that you could run into that terrifying animal, the beautiful young man, in the world of the palaestra and symposium, and the only solution was to flee abroad for a year (Xenophon, *Memorabilia*, i, 3, 13). Aeschines, who had to answer for his own loves, replied in the affirmative: there can be a wonderful *erǎsthaĭ*, the state of being loved which becomes noble passivity (*Against Timarchus*, 137). But allowing oneself to be loved for one's beauty falls into the same category as loving with elegance: it is a just, lawful and chaste love.

In other words those who speak in favour of *eros*, whether or not they perceive it as sensual, praise the whole relationship. Those like Aristophanes or Aeschines in his speech to the *ándrěs Athēnaîoi*, who wish to make it hateful, start by distinguishing between the active role (*práttein*) and the passive role (*páschein*), and then go on to discredit both. Both members of the couples which were formed – first Misgolas and Timarchus, then Timarchus and Hegesander – came out pretty poorly, according to the portrayal Aeschines gave of them. By accepting money and gifts and allowing himself to be maintained, Timarchus placed himself in the position of a wife or, in other words, he renounced his virility and revealed his effeminate *phŭsis*. By engaging him for money, Misgolas behaved in a shameful manner (41). The enjoyment of a body which has been hired is the act of an arrogant man (*hubristés*) who lacks education *(apaídeūtos)* (137). In their case, neither avoids criticism.

References

David Cohen, 'Law, Society and Homosexuality in Classical Athens,' *Past and Present* 117 (1987): 3–21.

James Davidson, *Courtesans and Fishcakes: The Consuming Passions of Classical Athens*. London: HarperCollins, 1997.

Kenneth Dover, *Greek Homosexuality*. Cambridge, MA: Harvard University Press, 1978.

Michel Foucault, *L'Usage des plaisirs* [*The Use of Pleasure*]. Paris: Gallimard, 1984a.

Michel Foucault, *Le Souci de soi* [*The Care of the Self*]. Paris: Gallimard, 1984b.

David Halperin, *One Hundred Years of Greek Homosexuality and Other Essays on Greek Love*. London and New York: Routledge, 1990.

Paul Rahe, *Republics Ancient and Modern: Classical Republicanism and the American Revolution*. Chapel Hill: University of North Carolina Press, 1992.

Robert W. Wallace, 'Law, freedom, and the concept of citizens' rights in democratic Athens,' in Josiah Ober and Charles W. Hedrick, eds., *Demokratia: A Conversation on Democracies, Ancient and Modern*. Princeton: Princeton University Press, 1996.

Bernard Williams, *Shame and Necessity*. Berkeley: University of California Press, 1992.

Chapter 2

Aeschines

AGAINST TIMARCHUS
(346 BCE, 1919 edition)

Law

If any Athenian shall have prostituted his person, he shall not be permitted to become one of the nine archons, nor to discharge the office of priest, nor to act as an advocate for the state, nor shall he hold any office whatsoever, at home or abroad, whether filled by lot or by election; he shall not be sent as a herald; he shall not take part in debate, nor be present at public sacrifices; when the citizens are wearing garlands, he shall wear none; and he shall not enter within the limits of the place that has been purified for the assembling of the people. If any man who has been convicted of prostitution act contrary to these prohibitions, he shall be put to death.

[40] **FIRST OF ALL**, as soon as he was past boyhood he settled down in the Peiraeus at the establishment of Euthydicus the physician, pretending to be a student of medicine, but in fact deliberately offering himself for sale, as the event proved. The names of the merchants or other foreigners, or of our own citizens, who enjoyed the person of Timarchus in those days I will pass over willingly, that no one may say that I am over particular to state every petty detail. But in whose houses he has lived to the shame of his own body and of the city, earning wages by precisely that thing which the law forbids, under penalty of losing the privilege of public speech, of this I will speak.

[41] Fellow citizens, there is one Misgolas, son of Naucrates, of the deme Collytus, a man otherwise honorable, and beyond reproach save in this, that he is bent on that sort of thing like one possessed, and is accustomed always to have about him singers or cithara-players. I say this, not from any liking for indecent talk, but that you may know what sort of man Misgolas is. Now this Misgolas, perceiving Timarchus' motive in staying at the house of the physician, paid him a sum of money in advance and caused him to change his lodgings, and got him into his own home; for Timarchus was well developed, young,

and lewd, just the person for the thing that Misgolas wanted to do, and Timarchus wanted to have done.

[42] Timarchus did not hesitate, but submitted to it all, though he had income to satisfy all reasonable desires. For his father had left him a very large property, which he has squandered, as I will show in the course of my speech. But he behaved as he did because he was a slave to the most shameful lusts, to gluttony and extravagance at table, to flute-girls and harlots, to dice, and to all those other things no one of which ought to have the mastery over a man who is well-born and free. And this wretch was not ashamed to abandon his father's house and live with Misgolas, a man who was not a friend of his father's, nor a person of his own age, but a stranger, and older than himself, a man who knew no restraint in such matters, while Timarchus himself was in the bloom of youth.

[52] But if, saying nothing about these bestial fellows, Cedonides, Autocleides, and Thersandrus, and simply telling the names of those in whose houses he has been an inmate, I refresh your memories and show that he is guilty of selling his person not only in Misgolas' house, but in the house of another man also, and again of another, and that from this last he went to still another, surely you will no longer look upon him as one who has merely been a kept man, but – by Dionysus, I don't know how I can keep glossing the thing over all day long – as a common prostitute. For the man who follows these practices recklessly and with many men and for pay seems to me to be chargeable with precisely this.

[53] Well, when now Misgolas found him too expensive and dismissed him, next Anticles, son of Callias, the deme Euonymon, took him up. Anticles, however, is absent in Samos as a member of the new colony, so I will pass on to the next incident. For after this man Timarchus had left Anticles and Misgolas, he did not repent or reform his way of life, but spent his days in the gambling-place, where the gaming-table is set, and cock-fighting and dice-throwing are the regular occupations. I imagine some of you have seen the place; at any rate you have heard of it.

[54] Among the men who spend their time there is one Pittalacus, a slave-fellow who is the property of the city. He had plenty of money, and seeing Timarchus spending his time thus he took him and kept him in his own house. This foul wretch here was not disturbed by the fact that he was going to defile himself with a public slave, but thought of one thing only, of getting him to be paymaster for his own disgusting lusts; to the question of virtue or of shame he never gave a thought.

[73] Only one alternative then remains: that the man who submitted to the act shall acknowledge it. But he is on trial on precisely this charge, that after such conduct as this, he breaks the laws by speaking before the assembly. Shall we, then, drop the whole affair, and make no further inquiry? By Poseidon, a fine home this city will be for us, if when we ourselves know that a thing has been done in fact, we are to ignore it unless some man come forward here and testify to the act in words as explicit as they must be shameless.

[74] But pray consider the case with the help of illustrations; and naturally the illustrations will have to be like the pursuits of Timarchus. You see the men over yonder who sit in the bawdy-houses, men who confessedly pursue the profession. Yet these persons, brought to such straits as that, do nevertheless make some attempt to cover their shame: they shut their doors. Now if, as you are passing along the street, any one should ask you, "Pray, what is the fellow doing at this moment?" you would instantly name the act, though you do not see it done, and do not know who it was that entered the house; knowing the profession of the man, you know his act also.

[75] In the same way, therefore, you ought to judge the case of Timarchus, and not to ask whether anyone saw, but whether he has done the deed. For by heaven, Timarchus, what shall a man say? What would you say yourself about another man on trial on this charge? What shall we say when a young man leaves his father's house and spends his nights in other people's houses, a conspicuously handsome young man? When he enjoys costly suppers without paying for them, and keeps the most expensive flutegirls and harlots? When he gambles and pays nothing himself but another man always pays for him?

[76] Does it take a wizard to explain all that? Is it not perfectly plain that the man who makes such demands must himself necessarily be furnishing in return certain pleasures to the men who are spending their money on him? I say "furnishing pleasures," because, by the Olympian Zeus, I don't know how I can use more euphemistic language than that in referring to your contemptible conduct.

[94] And yet a certain speech-writer who is concocting his defense says that I contradict myself; since it seems to him impossible, he says, for the same man to have been a prostitute and to have consumed his patrimony. For, he says, to have sinned against one's own body is the act of a boy, but to have consumed one's patrimony is that of a man. And furthermore he says that those who defile themselves exact pay for it. He therefore goes up and down the marketplace expressing his wonder and amazement that one and the same man should have prostituted himself and also have consumed his patrimony.

[95] Now if anyone does not understand the facts of the case, I will try to explain them more clearly. Hegesandrus, who kept Timarchus, had married an heiress. So long as her inheritance held out, and the money that Hegesandrus had brought back with him from his voyage with Timomachus, they lived in all luxury and lewdness. But when these resources had been wasted and gambled away and eaten up, and this defendant had lost his youthful charm, and, as you would expect, no one would any longer give him anything, while his lewd and depraved nature constantly craved the same indulgences, and with excessive incontinence kept making demand after demand upon him,

[96] Then, at last, incessantly drawn back to his old habits, he resorted to the devouring of his patrimony. And not only did he eat it up, but, if one may so say, he also drank it up! He sold one piece of property after another, not for what it was worth — he couldn't wait for a higher offer nor even for the bare value, but let it go for what it would fetch on the instant, so urgently did he hasten to gratify his lusts.

[110] In the same year in which Timarchus was a member of the senate, Hegesandrus, the brother of Crobylus, was a treasurer of the funds of the goddess, and together, in right friendly comradeship, they were in the act of stealing a thousand drachmas which belonged to the city. But a reputable man, Pamphilus of the deme Acherdous, who had had some trouble with the defendant and was angry with him, found out what was going on, and at a meeting of the assembly arose and said, "Fellow citizens, a man and a woman are conspiring to steal one thousand drachmas of yours."

[111] Then you in astonishment cried, "How 'a man and a woman,' what are you talking about?" After a little he went on: "Don't you understand," said he, "what I mean? The man is our friend Hegesandrus there, a man now, though he too used to be a woman, Laodamas's woman; as for the woman, she is Timarchus yonder. How the money is being stolen I will tell you." He then proceeded to give a full account of the matter, and in a way that showed that there was no guesswork about it. After he had given you this information, "What is it, fellow citizens," said he, "that I advise? If the senate sustains the charge against this man and expels him, and then hands him over to the courts, give the

senate the usual testimonial; but if they fail to punish him, refuse to give it, and lay up this thing against them for that day."

[119] The eminent orator Demosthenes says that you must either wipe out your laws, or else no attention must be paid to my words. For he is amazed, he says, if you do not all remember that every single year the senate farms out the tax on prostitutes, and that the men who buy this tax do not guess, but know precisely, who they are that follow this profession. When, therefore, I have dared to bring impeachment against Timarchus for having prostituted himself, in order that I may deprive him of the right to address the people in assembly, Demosthenes says that the very act complained of calls, not for an accuser's arraignment, but for the testimony of the tax-gatherer who collected this tax from Timarchus.

[131] In the case of Demosthenes, too, it was common report, and not his nurse, that gave him his nickname; and well did common report name him Batalus, for his effeminacy and lewdness! For, Demosthenes, if anyone should strip off those exquisite, pretty mantles of yours, and the soft, pretty shirts that you wear while you are writing your speeches against your friends, and should pass them around among the jurors, I think, unless they were informed beforehand, they would be quite at a loss to say whether they had in their hands the clothing of a man or of a woman!

[132] But in the course of the defense one of the generals will, as I am told, mount the platform, with head held high and a self-conscious air, as one who should say, Behold the graduate of the wrestling schools, and the student of philosophy! And he will undertake to throw ridicule upon the whole idea of the prosecution, asserting that this is no legal process that I have devised, but the first step in a dangerous decline in the culture of our youth. He will cite first those benefactors of yours, Harmodius and Aristogeiton, describing their fidelity to one another, and telling how in their case this relationship proved the salvation of the state.

[133] Indeed, they say he will not even spare the poems of Homer or the names of the heroes, but will celebrate the friendship between Patroclus and Achilles, which, we are told, had its source in passion. And he will pronounce an encomium on beauty now, as though it were not recognised long since as a blessing, if haply it be united with morality. For he says that if certain men by slandering this beauty of body shall cause beauty to be a misfortune to those who possess it, then in your public verdict you will contradict your personal prayers.

[134] For you seem to him, he says, in danger of being strangely inconsistent; for when you are about to beget children, you pray one and all that your sons still unborn may be fair and beautiful in person, and worthy of the city; and yet when you have sons already born, of whom the city may well be proud, if by their surpassing beauty and youthful charm they infatuate one person or another, and become the subject of strife because of the passion they inspire, these sons, as it seems, you propose to deprive of civic rights – because Aeschines tells you to do it.

[135] And just here I understand he is going to carry the war into my territory, and ask me if I am not ashamed on my own part, after having made a nuisance of myself in the gymnasia and having been many times a lover, now to be bringing the practice into reproach and danger. And finally – so I am told – in an attempt to raise a laugh and start silly talk among you, he says he is going to exhibit all the erotic poems I have ever addressed to one person or another, and he promises to call witnesses to certain quarrels and pommellings in which I have been involved in consequence of this habit.

[136] Now as for me, I neither find fault with love that is honorable, nor do I say that those who surpass in beauty are prostitutes. I do not deny that I myself have been a lover and am a lover to this day, nor do I deny that the jealousies and quarrels that commonly arise from the practice have happened in my case. As to the poems which they say I have composed, some I acknowledge, but as to others I deny that they are of the character that these people will impute to them, for they will tamper with them.

[137] The distinction which I draw is this: to be in love with those who are beautiful and chaste is the experience of a kind-hearted and generous soul; but to hire for money and to indulge in licentiousness is the act of a man who is wanton and ill-bred. And whereas it is an honor to be the object of a pure love, I declare that he who has played the prostitute by inducement of wages is disgraced. How wide indeed is the distinction between these two acts and how great the difference, I will try to show you in what I shall next say.

[138] Your fathers, when they were laying down laws to regulate the habits of men and those acts that inevitably flow from human nature, forbade slaves to do those things which they thought ought to be done by free men. "A slave," says the law, "shall not take exercise or anoint himself in the wrestling-schools." It did not go on to add, "But the free man shall anoint himself and take exercise;" for when, seeing the good that comes from gymnastics, the lawgivers forbade slaves to take part, they thought that in prohibiting them they were by the same words inviting the free.

[139] Again, the same lawgiver said, "A slave shall not be the lover of a free boy nor follow after him, or else he shall receive fifty blows of the public lash." But the free man was not forbidden to love a boy, and associate with him, and follow after him, nor did the lawgiver think that harm came to the boy thereby, but rather that such a thing was a testimony to his chastity. But, I think, so long as the boy is not his own master and is as yet unable to discern who is a genuine friend, and who is not, the law teaches the lover self-control, and makes him defer the words of friendship till the other is older and has reached years of discretion; but to follow after the boy and to watch over him the lawgiver regarded as the best possible safeguard and protection for chastity.

[140] And so it was that those benefactors of the state, Harmodius and Aristogeiton, men pre-eminent for their virtues, were so nurtured by that chaste and lawful love – or call it by some other name than love if you like – and so disciplined, that when we hear men praising what they did, we feel that words are inadequate to the eulogy of their deeds.

[141] But since you make mention of Achilles and Patroclus, and of Homer and the other poets – as though the jury were men innocent of education, while you are people of a superior sort, who feel yourselves quite beyond common folks in learning – that you may know that we too have before now heard and learned a little something, we shall say a word about this also. For since they undertake to cite wise men, and to take refuge in sentiments expressed in poetic measures, look, fellow citizens, into the works of those who are confessedly good and helpful poets, and see how far apart they considered chaste men, who love their like, and men who are wanton and overcome by forbidden lusts.

[142] I will speak first of Homer, whom we rank among the oldest and wisest of the poets. Although he speaks in many places of Patroclus and Achilles, he hides their love and avoids giving a name to their friendship, thinking that the exceeding greatness of their affection is manifest to such of his hearers as are educated men.

[143] For Achilles says somewhere in the course of his lament for the death of Patroclus, as recalling one of the greatest of sorrows, that unwillingly he has broken the promise he had given to Menoetius, the father of Patroclus; for he had promised to bring his son back safe to Opus, if he would send him along with him to Troy, and entrust him to his care. It is evident from this that it was because of love that he undertook to take care of him.

[144] But the verses, which I am about to recite, are these: "Ah me, I rashly spoke vain words that day When in his halls I cheered Menoetius. I told the hero I would surely bring His famous son to Opus back again, When he had ravaged Ilium, and won His share of spoil. But Zeus does not fulfil To men their every hope. For fate decrees That both of us make red one spot of earth."

[145] And indeed not only here do we see his deep distress, but he mourned so sorely for him, that although his mother Thetis cautioned him and told him that if he would refrain from following up his enemies and leave the death of Patroclus unavenged, he should return to his home and die an old man in his own land, whereas if he should take vengeance, he should soon end his life, he chose fidelity to the dead rather than safety. And with such nobility of soul did he hasten to take vengeance on the man who slew his friend, that when all tried to comfort him and urged him to bathe and take food, he swore that he would do none of these things until he had brought the head of Hector to the grave of Patroclus.

[146] And when he was sleeping by the funeral pyre, as the poet says, the ghost of Patroclus stood before him, and stirred such memories and laid upon Achilles such injunctions, that one may well weep, and envy the virtue and the friendship of these men. He prophesies that Achilles too is not far from the end of life, and enjoins upon him, if it be in any wise possible, to make provision that even as they had grown up and lived together, even so when they are dead their bones may be in the same coffer.

[147] Weeping, and recalling the pursuits which they had followed together in life, he says, "Never again shall we sit together alone as in the old days, apart from our other friends, and take high counsel," feeling, I believe, that this fidelity and affection were what they would long for most. But that you may hear the sentiments of the poet in verse also, the clerk shall read to you the verses on this theme which Homer composed.

[148] Read first the verses about the vengeance on Hector. "But since, dear comrade, after thee I go Beneath the earth, I will not bury thee Till here I bring thee Hector's head and arms, The spoils of that proud prince who took thy life."

[149] Now read what Patroclus says in the dream about their common burial and about the intercourse that they once had with one another. "For we no longer as in life shall sit Apart in sweet communion. Nay, the doom Appointed me at birth has yawned for me. And fate has destined thee, Achilles, peer Of gods, to die beneath the wall of Troy's Proud lords, fighting for fair-haired Helen's sake. More will I say to thee, pray heed it well: Let not my bones be laid apart from thine, Achilles, but that thou and I may be In common earth, I beg that I may share That golden coffer which thy mother brought To be thine own, even as we in youth Grew up together in thy home. My sire Menoetius brought me, a little lad, from home, From Opus, to your house, for sad bloodshed, That day, when, all unwitting, in childish wrath About the dice, I killed Amphidamas' son. The knightly Peleus took me to his home And kindly reared me, naming me thy squire. So let one common coffer hide our bones."

[150] Now to show that it was possible for him to have been saved had he refrained from avenging the death of Patroclus, read what Thetis says. "Ah me, my son, swift fate indeed will fall On thee, if thou dost speak such words. For know, Swift after Hector's death fate brings thine own. To her divine Achilles, swift of foot, In turn made answer. Straightway let me die, For when my friend was slain, my dearest friend, It was not granted me to succor him."

[185] Such, then, was the judgment of your fathers concerning things shameful and things honorable; and shall their sons let Timarchus go free, a man chargeable with the most shameful practices, a creature with the body of a man defiled with the sins of a woman? In that case, who of you will punish a woman if he finds her in wrong doing? Or what man will not be regarded as lacking intelligence who is angry with her who errs by an impulse of nature, while he treats as adviser the man who in despite of nature has sinned against his own body?

[191] No, the impetuous lusts of the body and insatiate desire – these it is that fill the robbers' bands, that send men on board the pirates' boats; these are, for each man, his Fury, urging him to slay his fellow citizens, to serve the tyrant, to help put down the democracy. For such men reck not of disgrace, nor yet of punishment to come, but are beguiled by the pleasures they expect if they succeed. Therefore, fellow citizens, remove from among us such natures, for so shall you turn the aspirations of the young toward virtue.

PART 2

Was Jesus a queer eunuch?

Introduction

SURPRISINGLY, EARLY CHRISTIANITY CHALLENGED the family values of the Graeco-Roman and Jewish worlds. All these cultures celebrated marriage and sexual pleasure to ensure the reproduction of humans and therefore societies in an era when crops often failed and military conflict could destroy vulnerable groups. To be a full man in Jewish culture, for instance, one had to marry. To be sure, at the time of Jesus, some radical Jewish groups, such as the Essenes, valued celibacy for a spiritual elite.[1] But in the gospels, Jesus is portrayed as telling his followers to leave their families and come with him; he even admonishes them to hate their mothers and fathers. His followers wandered around Palestine, begging for food and penniless. No doubt his enemies made fun of them as single men without the status of husband and father. In response, the gospel records Jesus as provocatively suggesting that some of his followers might make themselves "eunuchs for the kingdom of heaven."

What did this mean? As Halvor Moxnes points out, in Roman-occupied Palestine, eunuchs would have been visible as prestigious servants in Roman courts, and as the *galli*, a cult of mother-goddess worshipers who castrated themselves and traveled around the countryside in feminine attire. While they were seen as having magical powers, they were also hated and feared.

Moxnes provocatively argues that Jesus created a "queer space" outside of the family. What does "queer" mean in this context? Is Moxnes arguing that Jesus was gay? As we have seen, in the ancient world there was no concept of heterosexuality or homosexuality as we think of it. Today, activists have also criticized the notion that human beings have fixed, inborn sexual identities. Reclaiming the insult "queer," they use the term to depict those desires which do not fit into rigid, conventional categories – queerness is also a way of thinking of society that is critical, coming from an oblique angle.

There are few relevant verses that reveal Jesus' attitude toward sexuality. Jesus said nothing at all about sex between men or abortion, but he denounced divorce. So Jesus valued marriage, even though he admonished his followers to leave their families. How could these two views be reconciled? As Moxnes later argues, it was hoped that the followers would found new families, and find a new, loving type of family in Christianity.

In subsequent decades, the followers of Jesus believed that he would return imminently, so the task of marrying and procreating was less urgent. They wanted to focus on a spiritual relationship with God; the apostle Paul argued that marriage was only second best to chastity.

Foucault argued that, by celebrating celibacy, Christians were just following trends in the Judaeo-Graeco-Roman world.[2] Some Stoic philosophers, for instance, advocated celibacy, or, if that was not possible, only having sex to procreate. However, in another work, Moxnes shows that Christians differed from Roman philosophers in important ways. Paul warns men that if they had sex with prostitutes, they not only lacked sexual self-control, they unified their bodies with prostitutes, whereas their bodies ought to be unified with Christ. Whereas Roman culture denigrated men if they lost self-control or submitted passively in sex, Paul denigrates men who are dominant in sex as well as men who are passive. Early Christians challenged the conventional equation of sexuality with dominance.[3]

By remaining celibate, monks could concentrate on love of God, rather than of women or family. But the Church fathers worried that some monks might take the verse too seriously and castrate themselves – indeed, it is rumored that Origen castrated himself as a young man to make it easier to control his desires; to him, virginity represented the purity of the soul.[4] Historian Matthew Kuefler suggests that self-castration "may have expressed a belief in the ultimate human restoration to original existence as angels, a return from multiplicity in male and female unity to androgyny." Horrified at such ideas, the Church fathers interpreted Jesus' statement about eunuchs to mean that he was a virgin. They denigrated Roman eunuchs such as the *galli* as effeminate, degenerate, and pagan. Kuefler argues that when the apostle Paul denounced men "who do shameless things with men" he was actually attacking the *galli* for prostituting themselves in temples. Self-castration threatened the perpetuation and growth of Christianity through the formation of families. So the Church fathers urged monks to control sexual desire with the unruly will.[5] Monks, therefore, could prove their manliness, since this task required incredible strength.[6] However, it took centuries to firmly establish the principle that priests should be celibate.[7]

Notes

1   Peter Brown, *The Body and Society: Men, Women, and Sexual Renunciation in Early Christianity* (New York: Columbia University Press, 1988), 38.
2   Michel Foucault, *The Care of the Self*, trans. Robert Hurley, 3 vols., vol. 3, *The History of Sexuality* (New York: Vintage Books, 1988), 52.
3   Halvor Moxnes, "Asceticism and Christian Identity in Antiquity: A Dialogue with Foucault and Paul," *Journal for the Study of the New Testament* 26, no. 1 (2003): 22.
4   Brown, *The Body and Society*, 170.

5   Matthew Kuefler, *The Manly Eunuch: Masculinity, Gender Ambiguity, and Christian Ideology in Late Antiquity* (Chicago: University of Chicago Press, 2001), 256–263.

6   Daniel F. Caner, "The Practice and Prohibition of Self-Castration in Early Christianity," *Vigiliae Christianae* 51, no. 4 (1997): 396–415.

7   R. I. Moore, "Property, Marriage, and the Eleventh-Century Revolution: A Context for Early Medieval Communism," in Michael Frassetto, ed., *Medieval Purity and Piety* (New York: Garland, 1998), 179–208.

Chapter 3

Halvor Moxnes

PUTTING JESUS IN HIS PLACE
A radical vision of household and kingdom (2003)

Leaving male space: eunuchs in the Jesus movement

YOUNG MEN WHO LEFT THEIR HOUSEHOLDS and followed Jesus became displaced persons. By putting themselves "out of place" they represented a provocation to the very order of the community. One of the most provoking ways that men might be put out of place was by being—or standing accused of being—a eunuch. It is probably such an accusation that caused the eunuch saying in Matt. 19:12, one of the strangest words attributed to Jesus: "For there are eunuchs who have been so from birth, and there are eunuchs who have been made eunuchs by men, and there are eunuchs who have made themselves eunuchs for the sake of the kingdom of heaven. He who is able to receive this, let him receive it." Although there are strong arguments for regarding this as a saying of Jesus, it is little used in descriptions of the historical Jesus. This may be because the image of *eunuch* threatens common presuppositions about Jesus as a male figure.

In this chapter we shall use the eunuch saying for entry into a discussion of what it meant to Jesus and his followers to leave their place as males in a household.[1] Within a house and household, everybody had "their place," both in terms of material practice, what kind of work they did, and in terms of social and ideological place. Men had their specific place as fathers, sons, brothers, and husbands. Their position was privileged compared to that of mothers, daughters, sisters, and wives. To leave this male place in the household meant to abdicate from an important part of their identity as men.[2] Outside of this location their identity was threatened and open to question. It is this questioning of masculine identity that will provide the starting point for our investigation.

[. . .]

Withdrawal from one's (male) place is part of a larger discussion of *asceticism*.[3] Often asceticism is spoken of in terms of what specific practices or things are given up, but a more fruitful approach places these specific practices within the larger context of the purpose of asceticism.[4] One such suggestive attempt at a definition says that "Asceticism may be defined as performances within a dominant social environment intended to inaugurate a *new* subjectivity, *different* social relations, and an *alternative* symbolic universe."[5] The emphasis on "new," "different," and "alternative" places asceticism at odds with "the dominant social environment." According to this definition, asceticism is a set of performances that will create something other than that which exists within the dominant culture. That is, asceticism is a critical activity. It is an attempt from a nondominant, even marginal position, to create something that transcends or even transgresses the existing order.[6] In the sayings of Jesus it is the patriarchal household that is the "dominant social environment." We may therefore characterize it as "male space." By that I mean not only the practical and social structure of the house and the household activities, place in practical terms, but also the ideological and mental structures and the place of men, women, and children within that space. Therefore, I will look at the asceticism of Jesus, his call to leave male space, as a challenge to the standards of masculinity in antiquity.

In antiquity asceticism was viewed in terms of self-control and -mastery, and it was regarded as a masculine characteristic. Eunuchs, on the other hand, were regarded as "half-men." These views on masculinity and asceticism were shared by early Christian writers, some of whom, all men, commented on Matt. 19:12. They strongly defended the ascetic renunciation of sexuality as a male virtue, and therefore distanced Jesus from any association with castrated eunuchs. Against this background, I will return to the saying in its historical context and examine the saying in the context of a break with the masculine, patriarchal patterns of society at the time.

But first we shall see how modern interpreters of the passage in Matt. 19 have defended the masculinity of Jesus against the accusation that he was a eunuch. It appears that they find it threatening to imagine that the masculinity of Jesus may be questioned. It may be permissible to view Jesus as an ascetic, but not to question his masculinity. Here I think that we are dealing with strong cultural patterns and presuppositions among (mostly) male scholars.

Unsettling a male space: modern interpretations of Matt. 19:12

The history of interpretation shows that Matt 19:12 has caused problems to interpreters throughout the centuries.[7] Even today, modern interpreters are in a quandary how to explain it. I am interested to find out why this saying has been as problematic as it obviously has been, and I suggest that it has to do with the interpreters' presuppositions about masculinity, both that of Jesus and his followers and that of their interpreters. The eunuch is a highly problematic and ambiguous figure who, because he is a male figure, threatens the very idea of masculinity. To imagine Jesus or his disciples as eunuchs, as men who were physically unfit for marriage, unable to perform sexually, is perhaps an unsettling picture. But this strange and uncomfortable picture of the eunuch is a useful place to start. By so effectively denying masculine sexuality, it suddenly makes us think about the sexuality and masculinity of Jesus. To start "off center," with the image of the emasculated man, may help us to see more clearly what male images we hold of Jesus, what presuppositions about masculinity we bring with us when we try to construct our picture of "Jesus the man."[8] In texts from antiquity we find that the figure of the eunuch often was the "other" that triggered reflection on male identity.[9] In this effect the eunuch shared similarities with women as the "other" over against which masculinity was defined. We will start with modern interpreters and then move back to early Christian expositions of this saying.

Most often the eunuch saying in Matt. 19:12 has been regarded as a conclusion to the conflict dialogue between Jesus and the Pharisees about divorce. In Matt. 19:3–11 Jesus sharpens the command against divorce, and especially against remarriage after divorce. The following verse has often been interpreted in light of this discussion, as an exhortation to a divorced husband to live in chastity or celibacy. The most common understanding of "eunuchs for the sake of the kingdom of heaven" has therefore been that it meant "chaste" or "celibate," and that it had nothing to do with castration.

However, many commentators have realized that Matt. 19:12 does not fit well together with 19:3–9, and have suggested that it was Matthew's redaction that combined the two sayings.[10] Thus, it is very likely that Matt. 19:12 was originally an independent saying, and there are good reasons to think that in some form it goes back to Jesus.[11] Although it is attested only in Matt. 19:12 in the New Testament, the suggestion that it is an ancient saying is supported by a version of the saying in Justin I *Apol.* 15:4 that most likely is independent of Matthew.[12] If the addressee for the saying is no longer a divorced husband who is encouraged to live a celibate life, we may have to consider other possibilities for the implications of the word "eunuch."

If it was an independent saying, it probably goes back to a polemical exchange with Jesus' opponents.[13] The opponents may have used the word "eunuch" to denigrate or slander Jesus and his disciples, in effect to remove them from their position as "real" men. In response, Jesus picked up the word, and accepted it: yes, in a certain sense they were eunuchs, unable to live a married life. The saying lists three different types of eunuchs. The first two were commonly known in antiquity, also from Jewish sources (*Jebamot* 8.4): one by nature, that is, from birth, the other through human intervention, by castration. To these two Jesus added a third, referring to his disciples. They were eunuchs of a very special type, not by nature, not "man-made" by forced castration, but "for the sake of the kingdom of heaven." In the first two instances the term "eunuch" was commonly used not of someone who was celibate or who abstained from marriage, but of someone who was physically (made) *unfit* for marriage and incapable of performing sexually. The central question is therefore whether the last group was parallel to the others in this respect, or whether "eunuch" was here used in another, figurative meaning.

Many scholars have accepted this proposal of a polemical exchange as the context of the saying, but when it comes to further interpretation, they still do not seem to grasp the challenge that the use of this word eunuch posed.[14] In his otherwise very perceptive discussion of the asceticism of Jesus, Dale C. Allison provides an illuminating example. He twice mentions that this saying in Matt. 19:12 may be pejorative or due to slander,[15] but finds that it could still be a word by Jesus since it corresponds to his habit of taking up slander and using it for his own purpose. But this seems to be forgotten when Allison offers his own interpretation of the saying. He says that

> [Jesus'] urgent eschatological mission was sufficiently important and consuming
> as to disallow family entanglements. This is, after all, and as argued above,
> the plain meaning of Mt 19:12. The eunuchs that Jesus defended were those
> who, as heralds of the coming kingdom, had as little time for marriage as for

business. To leave all for the sake of the grand cause was to leave behind the world and its attendant affairs once and for all. If the discipline of the Spartans was to prepare for war, and if the exercises of the Greek athlete were to prepare him for the athletic contest, the asceticism of the pre-Easter Jesus movement was similarly a strategy to meet a specific goal. The missionary endeavor to restore Israel in the face of judgment demanded complete dedication. In other words, the proclamation of the coming kingdom required sacrificing a normal course of life.[16]

It is noteworthy that Allison here so easily enters into a language of asceticism that is full of stereotypical masculine categories. Within one sentence it has acquired "discipline," "prepare for war," "exercise," "athlete," and "contest." The Spartan warrior and the Greek athlete are the ideal figures, the "grand cause" of exploration or conquest is the metaphor. In this interpretation, the insight that "eunuch" was a word of slander has gotten lost. There is no trace left of the specific meaning of being a eunuch in the saying in Matt. 19:12. Allison continues an interpretation of the saying as an exercise in the manly business of self-mastery over the body and mastery over the world, and the result is a disciplined virility. But the image of a eunuch in fact represented the very opposite of the masculine discipline of the Spartans or of the Greek athlete. His was a body that had been emasculated, and therefore did not conform to the ideal standards of the male body that Allison invokes. Thus, in the context of various images of "eunuch," the associations that the word evoked could hardly have been that of warrior or athlete.

I use this quotation not so much to single out Allison's interpretation in particular for criticism, but to illustrate how it belongs to a tradition of male interpretation that has had great trouble in interpreting this verse. This is not so much due to individual short-comings but because of a cultural pattern that views the world from a masculine perspective. For male authors, asceticism is so obviously a masculine place, a war field or a sport arena, and this perception filters the information that can get through.[17] Therefore we may ask: What position did the eunuchs represent within the field of male asceticism that made them so unsettling? Let us first look at how masculinity and asceticism were combined and how asceticism was regarded as a male ideal.

Asceticism as male space

The masculine ideals of the warrior and athlete invoked by Allison have a long tradition and actually go all the way back to antiquity.[18] This idea implied not only mastery over others, but also mastery over self, self-control. The dominant meaning could change over time and in various situations. On an individual basis, there were different aspects to the mastery or control that a male could exercise. One was the mastery over others in the household, performed by the male head of the house, reflected for instance in the household codes in early Christian letters.[19] Another was the mastery over self in terms of control of one's body. In the ancient world there were two areas that were of primary concern regarding self-control: sexuality and food.

This masculine ideal was shared by many cultures within the Greco-Roman world; there were many similarities between ancient Greek, Roman, and Jewish ideals.[20] Therefore, we shall use passages from the Jewish authors Philo and Josephus about ascetic movements as examples of this ideal of male self-mastery. These passages are particularly useful since they have often been adduced as parallels to leaving home in the Jesus movement. But the explicitly masculine character of this ideal of renunciation has not been discussed, and as a result it has been taken for granted that Jesus' asceticism built on the same ideals.[21]

Continence or renunciation of sexuality was based on the ideal of self-mastery or self-control. In Jewish sources, as well as in Greek and Roman ones, this ideal was gendered as male.[22] In contrast, a lack of self-mastery was gendered as female. Self-mastery was part of a set of masculine virtues, like courage, whereas weaknesses like softness and servility were associated with women. Among Jewish writers in the first century C.E., Philo emphasizes that through ascetic regimens men can transcend their corporeal and feminine aspects, and he portrays his male heroes as possessing the self-mastery that was required. Women, on the other hand, lacked this self-control, and are identified with negative and unmanly characteristics.[23]

Philo's description of the Therapeutae in *De Vita Contemplativa* is a good example of this masculine self-control. His picture of the Therapeutae is most likely not a historical description, maybe not even meant to be,[24] but it tells much about the gendered value system that Philo shared with many of his elite contemporaries. The Therapeutae followed an ascetic lifestyle in a male community, with the goal to do philosophical contemplation. There were also women in the community, but they are described as having renounced their femaleness by becoming "virgins." They had sacrificed that which made them women, bodily pleasures and desire for children, and behaved like men in their yearning for wisdom (Philo *Contempl.* 68–69). Thus, masculine and feminine do not correspond directly to (biological) man and woman; there is a possibility also for women to "become male," but then they must leave behind "the ways of women."

This criticism, or rather disdain, of women becomes even more outspoken in Philo's description of the Essenes (*Hypoth.* 11:1–18). He sets up a contrast between marriage, which due to the character of the wife is described in negative terms, and communal life (*koinōnia*), which is characterized by the ideal of self-control (*enkrateia*). Philo's view reflects the position of popular Greek moral philosophers. He portrays a wife as selfish, jealous, casting shame, foreign to communal life. In contrast, communal life is identified by male characteristics—it is not jealous, it has a sovereign mind, and it is not slave, but free.

Josephus's picture of the Essenes, as a male community, follows the same lines (*B.J.* 2.119–61; *Ant.* 18.18–22). Their special virtue, he says, is control of their passions. He says that they do not oppose marriage on principle, but then goes on to a very hard criticism of women: "They wish to protect themselves against women's wantonness, being persuaded that none of the sex keeps her plighted troth to one man" (*B.J.* 2.120–21). Philo and Josephus are male voices, addressing other men. Their heroes are all men, or women who have become like men. The dangers are represented as women. In these pictures of the Therapeutae and the Essenes, the ultimate male mastery over self was represented as ascetic community life, free from everything that was identified with women. In Josephus and Philo the ascetic body is determined as male; asceticism is a male space. Women have to become male in order to enter that space. This shows, though, flexibility—that it was possible for some women to "become male."

This was a discourse in which the masculine ideal (be it in men or women) was contrasted with the feminine counterimage. The language of asceticism could be inscribed in the culturally formed language of male–female contrasts, with binary opposites. Philo and Josephus were thoroughly familiar with the Greco-Roman cultural ideals, and they displayed in their writings a typical combination of masculine self-control and sexual abstinence. Asceticism and masculinity as ideals were combined, so one might say that asceticism was entering more deeply into a male space, not leaving it. This was the reason that the combination of asceticism and an emasculated man, a eunuch, who had left male space, was so controversial.

Eunuchs in borderland

It was this ambiguity, that the eunuch represented renunciation but also had renounced masculinity, that made it so difficult to find a defined place for the eunuchs. In attempts to characterize them, we find that eunuchs did not have their own "essence," but only a position in relation to others. They could be described in relation to men as "half-men" (*semiviri*), and in slander they would be compared to women as "soft" and "feminine."[25] Although they were men, they were prime examples that "man" was not a category that all who were born male automatically belonged to but was something that had to be earned and defended. To be a man was an honorable position, but it could always be put into question, and a man must always be prepared to fight for it. In antiquity, as well as in many modern cultures, this male honor was associated above all with a sexual role as the one who initiated and dominated a sexual and social relationship.[26] In all these areas the eunuch was at a disadvantage and could not compete.

Eunuchs are known from antiquity in the East as well as in the Greco-Roman world.[27] The best-known examples from the Middle Ages were the court eunuchs in Byzantium,[28] and at Muslim courts. In modern times, the imperial court in China and shrines in Mecca and Medina had well-known groups of eunuchs.[29] The following description refers primarily to eunuchs and attitudes toward eunuchs in antiquity.

First, to be a eunuch due to involuntary castration was an indication of an inferior or disadvantaged social position. After loss in war, members of the losing army or tribe might suffer castration as an act of ultimate shame and emasculation. Prisoners of war might also be castrated and sold off as slaves. Thus slave trade was the most common source for castrated slaves in the Western parts of the Roman Empire. Consequently, slaves were (mostly) at the bottom of society, and at the will of their master, to fulfill both his needs for work and his sexual desires. Some young men were castrated with the specific purpose of being sold as slaves for sex.

Their social situation as castrated males made eunuchs useful in several specific areas. In the Persian and other Eastern empires, eunuchs were important and powerful officials for the king. This was also true in the late Roman and Byzantine empires. Likewise, eunuchs could hold important positions in private households, for instance, as guardians of women or teachers for sons. Their social position resulting from their sexual status might give some explanation for this. Since they were cut off from having a family of their own, they were outside the power of family structures, and therefore could more easily serve as confidants for rulers or masters and mediate between them and the outside world. Eunuchs were part of a complex social structure, in which their ambiguous social and sexual status made them useful. An Arabic collection of verses, anecdotes, and proverbs from the fourteenth century, on the ideal home, places eunuchs in a significant and highly charged part of a wealthy house: in the vestibule (*dihliz*), the hallway between the door and the actual dwelling.[30] The vestibule served as the corridor between the public and the private. The eunuchs were guardians of the vestibule, and decided who was allowed to enter further into the house and who was denied entry. The eunuchs acted as representatives of the master of the household in the area that protected the inner, sacred space of the house. But their in-between position, socially and sexually, made the eunuchs vulnerable and exposed to criticism and slander.[31]

The various groups of eunuchs were either eunuchs by birth, or castrated, mostly against their will. They correspond therefore to the first two categories listed in the saying in Matt. 19:12: "eunuchs who have been so from birth," and "eunuchs who have been made eunuchs by men." But there was one more group, those who had chosen to become eunuchs—in the words of Matt. 19:12, those "who have made themselves eunuchs" for a higher purpose. This group was, in antiquity, mostly associated with cults that originated in Asia Minor, especially the fertility cults of Cybele (and Attis) from Phrygia[32] and of Dea Syria from Syria.[33] This institution of self-castrated men was called galli.[34] They had special functions at festivals, in particular at processions, but they were not priests. There was likely a link between the main myth of the Cybele and Attis cult, in which Attis castrates himself (or is castrated by Cybele), and the act of self-castration by male devotees during the main spring festival. Castration may therefore originally have been associated with a fertility rite, and its ascetic connection may be a later development.[35]

These galli do not seem to have had a fixed organization, but were wandering groups, with song and music. They carried with them a picture of the goddess, gave oracles, and begged. For local participants in the cults of Dea Syria and Cybele, visits by these groups of galli must have served as contact with the goddess. Groups of galli were more common in the Orient than in Rome and the Western parts of the Roman Empire. But the galli of the Cybele cult, originating in Phrygia, must have contributed to the spreading of the cult also in Greece, Rome, and the Western part of the Mediterranean.[36] One reason for the fascination the galli evoked was their chastity, which was especially important in relation to fertility rituals.

In contrast to popular opinion, the literary elite was more skeptical. We have most of our knowledge of the cults, the festivals, and also the institution of the galli from detailed descriptions in Lucian of Samosata, Apuleius, and other satiric writers.[37] Lucian and Apuleius turn a very critical eye towards the galli. Their narratives are satirical and critical, and thus their information about the cults is onesided. Lucian (*Syr.d.* 20ff.) tells the myth of Combabus, which is related to the practice of castration. He says that after they were castrated, the men became "as women" (*thēlynontai*), no longer dressing as men, but wearing women's clothes and doing women's work. Apuleius (*Metam.* 7.24–31) tells how a band of galli traveled through villages and lured people to give them gifts, how they performed acts of flagellation and self-mutilation almost as theater. He describes them as *semiviri* and *effeminati* (7.28), and tells how they, although they posed as chaste priests, were caught in the act of seducing a young man.

Such descriptions provide a stock list of accusations against the galli.[38] In addition to accusations of greediness, which puts their begging in a bad light, the main attack was directed at the effect of castration on their masculine role. There is a whole series of invectives that shows how difficult it was to define somebody who had gone beyond the secure male boundaries. They are neither men nor women, they are "half-men" or effeminate. The accusations of sexual misconduct revolve around a lack of masculinity as well as a lack of chastity. When the Cybele-Attis cult was officially established in Rome, excessive elements and the institution of galli were curtailed, for instance, by laws against castration. But the galli remained an ambiguous sign of the Oriental cults, partly admired, partly despised.[39]

Eunuchs occupied an ambiguous place in various respects: They did not fit into the common ways of making boundaries and drawing borders. They could not be placed securely either as male or as female. Likewise, the galli threatened the distinction between sacred and profane. And, maybe most provoking, the eunuchs could not be placed within the area of chastity. They also appeared to belong in the location of desire. Thus, the challenge of eunuchs was that they could not be securely placed, they were in a position of "betwixt and between," in a permanent liminal position.

The masculine ascetic in early Christian writers

Early Christian writers, who belonged to the educated class of men, shared masculine ideals and the critical attitude to eunuchs common among the Roman elite.[40] With regard to the galli of the Cybele and other cults, these Christian writers showed their abhorrence toward the excesses of Oriental cults.[41] These cults were part of the religious and cultural context when Christian writers discussed what place eunuchs might have within Christian asceticism. But eunuchs not only represented the pagan "other," religious competitors from whom the Christians could distance themselves. Extreme asceticism in the form of castration was also practiced among Christians themselves.[42] It must have been a problem in many communities, since the Council of Nicaea in 325, in its first canon, condemned self-castration and decided that self-castrated eunuchs could not serve as priests.[43]

The interpretation of the eunuch saying in Matt. 19:12 is part of a controversy among early Christians over how radical sexual asceticism should be. There are relatively few direct references to Matt. 19:12 in gospel commentaries and homilies of the early church.[44] One reason may have been the fear that it could support radical asceticism. In the second century, Justin tells about persons who took the saying about making themselves eunuchs for the sake of the kingdom in a literal sense (1 *Apol.* 29). The eunuch saying from Matt. 19:12 is mentioned in a context that deals with *sōphrosyne*, moderation or self-control. This makes it likely that Justin understands Jesus' eunuch saying in the sense of chastity,[45] that is, in a figurative sense, and not about castration.

This hypothesis is supported by the following story about a young man who wanted to become a eunuch (1 *Apol.* 29). Set in Alexandria, this story gives interesting insight into the situation after the decrees against castration by several Roman emperors, starting with Domitian.[46] A young man in the Christian community contacted doctors to have them make him a eunuch. But they said that they were forbidden to do that, unless he received permission from the prefect, Felix. The prefect, however, refused to give his permission. Justin tells how the young man then decided nevertheless to remain celibate, supported by his own conscience and that of his fellow believers. Here the contours of an interpretation of the eunuch saying become visible. If castration was not possible, it was still possible to remain single, and that decision could be supported by one's conscience. Thus, one's decision to remain single and true to one's conscience was more important than physical castration.[47] With this story, Justin has laid out much of the pattern that later interpretations of Matt. 19:12 would follow in their arguments for a figurative understanding of the eunuch.

Early Christian writers were concerned to interpret Matt. 19:12 in such a way that it supported a commitment to chastity, but prevented this commitment from going too far. So how do they argue that "[making] themselves eunuchs for the . . . kingdom" shall be read not literally, but figuratively?[48] There are some instances in which the writer shows horror over the "murder" involved in castration. But in most cases the arguments seem to be driven by a logic where two possible causes for an act are positioned as binary opposites. Clemens of Alexandria (*Paed.* 3.4.26) says that a true eunuch is one who is not married, not because he does not have the (generative) power (*mē dynamenos*), but because he does not want to (*mē bouloumenos*). Clemens thus sets up a contrast between somebody who is a eunuch, either by nature or by castration, and a man who makes a deliberate decision not to marry. And it is obviously the latter who is the morally superior.

This figurative understanding of "eunuchs for the kingdom" is found also in Origen. In his commentary on Matt. 19:12, Origen (*Comm. Matt.* 15.1) is concerned with consistency in interpretation. Therefore he protests against what he sees as an inconsistent interpretation, which takes the two first classes of eunuchs in a literal sense, and the last one in a figurative sense. On the basis of 2 Cor. 3:6 (letter versus spirit), Origen holds that either one must understand all three of them in a literal way, or all of them in a figurative way. He argues for a figurative interpretation of all three groups of eunuchs.[49] Origen, notwithstanding the reports that he had castrated himself as a youth,[50] associates himself with those who were opposed to a form of extreme asceticism that practiced castration. Origen recognizes that those who were castrated may have undergone this operation out of fear of God, but he considered it to be a misguided fear, and too much love for renunciation. And his main argument against taking the third group (eunuchs for the sake of the kingdom) in a literal sense is that eunuchs would attract slander, even shame, both from outsiders and from people within the Christian church. Christian eunuchs were probably part of his social environment, but they were not highly regarded by the mainline groups that Origen now represented, and were exposed to slander and shame. One wonders how it could be possible for Origen to write this if he actually had castrated himself. But if he in fact had done it,[51] it might explain why he was relatively mild in his criticism of castration and why he was concerned with the shame and slander that eunuchs experienced. He distanced himself from the eunuchs, but nevertheless showed a certain sympathy. Eunuchs were not made into something totally "other."

Origen's figurative interpretation of the third group, those who were eunuchs "because of the kingdom," is filled with masculine metaphors (*Comm. Matt.* 15.4). His starting point is that castration is performed by the word of God, which is "sharper than any two-edged sword" (Heb. 4:12). The ideal eunuch is a man who takes this word, which the apostle also calls "the sword of the Spirit" (Eph. 6:17), so that he may cut out the passions of his soul, without touching the body. Since passions are gendered female,[52] by cutting out the passions the masculine sword (word) of God turns the ascetic man into "a real man," since his physical body is not touched. Thus, the eunuchs are "dephysicalized,"[53] and as a result the ascetic male can preserve and heighten his masculinity. Origen's figurative interpretation was clothed in war and warrior categories, those most masculine of male images.

For Jerome also it was important to make a moral distinction between eunuchs who had been castrated and true Christian ascetics. In his commentary on Matt. 19:12 he argues that the first two groups of eunuchs (by birth and made by men) are inferior to the last group, those who are eunuchs because of Christ. His argument is similar to that of Clemens of Alexandria, that the first two groups are eunuchs from necessity and not from (free) will.[54] This binary opposite between necessity or lack of power on the one hand, and will on the other, is a contrast between the negative and the positive with regard to moral value. Commonly, also, the contrast between feminine and masculine is associated with such binary opposites. In this set of comparisons, the eunuchs come down on the feminine and morally negative side. Whether the terminology used is "nature," "necessity," or "lack of power," all these terms refer to the physical fact of being a eunuch. They made him unfit for the physical aspects of marriage, sexual intercourse, and procreation, but did not require an act of will or a moral decision. Thus, being a eunuch in the physical sense was devalued; it came down on the "left" and feminine side of the comparison, and therefore it was also lower in the hierarchy of values.[55]

Jerome makes this absolutely clear when he goes on to contrast the two groups, the involuntary and the voluntary eunuchs. To leave no doubt, he identifies the voluntary eunuchs as truly masculine, saying that "although they could have been men, they made themselves eunuchs for Christ."[56] In the allegoric interpretation of "eunuchs by men," Jerome follows Origen, and attributes such castrations to the influence of philosophers, the cult of idols, or to heresy. In the description of what the cults do to their adherents, he employs stock accusations against the gallis of the Cybele or other Oriental cults: "They are softened into feminines [emolliuntur in feminas]." Only those who have (figuratively) castrated themselves for Christ will obtain the kingdom of heaven. Jerome exhorts his readers in an exposition of Matt. 19:12d: "He who is able to receive this, let him receive it." It is necessary that he consider his powers (vires). And it is as if the voice of the Lord exhorted and encouraged his soldiers to receive the reward for their chastity: "He who can fight, fight! Conquer and triumph!"

This whole discourse on the ideal spiritual eunuch versus the two other types in the flesh is expressed as a contest over masculinity. It is obvious that the very question of entering into a position of nonprocreation brought the fear of losing male power and virility. So therefore it was imperative for Jerome to say that "to castrate oneself [spiritually] for Christ" was nothing of the sort. Those who did it might have been (real) men, and in a way they continued to be just that, because to be a virgin required strength. It was like being a soldier, to go into battle, to win a prize. Spiritual eunuchs had nothing in common with the (real) eunuchs of Oriental cults, who were written off as feminine, or with more radical Christian ascetics, who were written off as just "simulating chastity." Jerome wanted to show the superiority of the spiritual eunuchs over the bodily ones. His real fear seems to be the loss of virility and masculine status that being a eunuch represented. This is why he argues so vehemently that voluntary chastity is a truly masculine endeavor that wins the prize, the kingdom of heaven. And he uses the most masculine of all images: these men are soldiers of the Lord, with the Lord himself as commander in chief. Thus, the military metaphor is appropriated for these men who had actually rejected the world with its military power.[57]

When we look at this early history of the interpretation of Matt. 19:12, "real" eunuchs have all but disappeared from Jesus' saying about those who are eunuchs for the sake of the kingdom of heaven. They have been subsumed under the category of continence or celibacy. And the reason for a spiritual interpretation of this third group of eunuchs is not just the extreme demand that castration represented. It has also to do with the figure of the eunuch and the representations of that figure. The eunuch was an intensely problematic and ambiguous figure. The problem was that the eunuch represented both the goal, asceticism, and something extremely problematic—a lack of virility and of masculinity. And for these male writers (in antiquity and today) masculinity was more difficult to give up than married life or sexuality. The challenge was how to combine asceticism with masculinity, to turn the body into an ascetic male by spiritual means, without touching the body with the knife. In this male space the eunuchs did not fit. Implied in the figure of the eunuch was the shame of losing masculinity.

The traditional interpretation of Matt. 19:12 attempted and succeeded in domesticating the eunuch saying, and brought it back home into a male space. It made the spiritualized eunuch into a male ideal and stripped the saying of its "queer" qualities. Characteristics of the eunuch that seemed to contradict the male ideals were removed and attributed to the "others," one's opponents—the heretics or those who belonged to other cults. In this way that which was offensive about the saying, that it identified Jesus and his followers with eunuchs, was interpreted away. Consequently, the renunciation practiced by Jesus and his followers was interpreted in light of an utterly masculine asceticism, far removed from real eunuchs. That appears to be a successful strategy, which still works today.

[. . .]

Eunuch is a term used of a man, but of a man who lacks many of the characteristics of a "real man." Therefore eunuchs were unfit for marriage. This affected a broad spectrum of the role of a man. Jesus' saying should be read in the context of masculinity as it was constructed through role models, demands, and expectations for men in Jewish society. One aspect was, of course, sexuality. Another was power, and a third was place, to be integrated as husband and father in a household. All these aspects of male identification were challenged by the figure of the eunuch.

With the figure of the eunuch Jesus held on to a metaphor that violated masculine identity. It was a metaphor that moved those men that experienced castration, either literally or figuratively (e.g., by slander), out from a secure male place into an uncertain zone of ambiguity and suspicion. It would be tempting to say that Jesus by the phrase "because of the kingdom" made an allusion to the king's eunuchs, that is, the court eunuchs,[58] and transferred that title to the kingdom of heaven. But the association with the kingdom would not take away the ambiguity of the phrase.[59] Most shocking to Jesus' Jewish environment was probably the way in which he associated the shameful identity and life of eunuchs with the kingdom of heaven, even saying that it was "for the sake of" the kingdom, that the kingdom actually motivated it.[60] By picking up the slander, Jesus both rejected it and confirmed it. It must have worked as a defiant defense for a strange group of single men who associated with women and even with children. Consequently, the combination of eunuchs and kingdom is not a positive ideal, as it is when "eunuch" is read as "celibate," alongside Matt. 19:1–9. Rather, it is a controversial saying by Jesus, and to be placed together with other statements about the excluded groups that are to be included in the kingdom. The saying in Matt. 19:12 is similar to sayings of Jesus where he picks up on or responds to criticism and slander; for instance, when he associates sinners and tax collectors with the kingdom (Matt. 21:31; Luke 15:1–2).[61]

This leaves Matt. 19:12, I think, with a message that is not fully explored. I think it is highly significant that the saying, just because it was and continues to be so countercultural, probably goes back to Jesus in some form. Because he does not simply refute the term "eunuch," but takes it up and plays around with it, so to speak, Jesus creates an ambiguity over the male identity of himself and his followers. If the origin of the saying was slander from Jesus' opponents, its point was to dislocate Jesus and his followers from their identity as "real" men, to move them out of that space and into an "outside" position. And Jesus does not question this position; he takes up and identifies with the word "eunuch," and now puts it into the new context of the approaching kingdom.

The eunuch saying of Jesus questioned the masculine identity that was taken for granted for Jewish men in the first century. And the difficulties of interpretation show that it also challenges modern presuppositions about masculinity and the male identity of Jesus. Jesus has been seen through the lenses of modern masculinity, which have provided the categories within which to understand him. Since the masculinity of Jesus has been taken for granted, it has been impossible even to contemplate that Jesus might be a eunuch in a physical sense, that is, castrated. The intellectual energy of both ancient and modern interpreters has been spent on rejecting that possibility in order to defend the masculinity of Jesus. As a result, the possibility that Jesus embraced the term "eunuch" as a designation for himself and his followers, and the meaning this term entailed (with or without castration), has not been explored.

Eunuchs were men who were permanently out of place, in a liminal position where there was no possibility of integration into the order of masculinity. The institution of eunuchs is not well known in the modern Western world, and that may be one of the reasons that it is difficult to find suitable models of interpretation and understanding. I suggest that the modern term that can best provide a lens for viewing the material and a category for interpretation is that of "queer." This is in contrast to suggestions that Jesus could be understood by means of categories like feminine or gay. These would be categories that once more attempted to view Jesus in terms of a fixed identity, as feminine in contrast to masculine, or gay in contrast to heterosexual. "Queer," on the other hand, does not indicate another category. Rather, it signals a protest against fixed categories.[62] As a protest or opposition to fixed categories of identity, it points out that all categories are historically and socially constructed, and that human experiences are forced into these categories. The use of the term "eunuch" in antiquity illustrates this point. It defied categorization. It did not fit into the categories of either male or female. In modern terminology, it is sometimes spoken of as "third gender."[63] The term queer is often used in questions of gender and identity, but it can be used in much broader terms than sexuality. It concerns power, social roles, place in hierarchies, in short, all aspects of identity. I suggest, therefore, that "queer" is the most useful term to apply when we try to make sense of Jesus' eunuch saying from a modern perspective.

The closest parallel to the function of this saying I can imagine is the way in which oppressed or marginal groups take up pejorative names used by the dominant culture and adopt them and use them about themselves, as a way to turn the labeling and oppression around. Marginalized groups thereby turn the terms into something else. Terminology that has been used to keep groups and individuals in "their place" suddenly becomes something else, more dangerous and undefined. Blacks and gays are two communities where this has been used as a counterstrategy against the abuse of power in labeling. Maybe those who identify themselves as "queer" in protest against fixed male or female identities provide the closest parallel to Jesus' use of "eunuch" today.

We started by stating that the eunuch saying has been little used in historical studies of Jesus. The reason may be that it was regarded as so strange, almost weird, that it could not easily be integrated into a plausible picture of Jesus. I suggest, however, that the saying about those who made themselves eunuchs for the sake of the kingdom fits very well with other sayings of Jesus about *who* belongs in the kingdom.

Notes

1   See the previous chapter. In sayings where the gender of the persons called to follow Jesus
    could be identified, they appear to be young men.
2   M. Kuefler, *The Manly Eunuch: Masculinity, Gender Ambiguity, and Christian Ideology in Late
    Antiquity* (Chicago: University of Chicago Press, 2001), 274.
3   For this discussion, see V. Wimbush and R. Valantasis, eds., *Asceticism* (New York: Oxford
    University Press, 1995); L. E. Vaage and V. Wimbush, eds., *Asceticism and the New Testament*
    (New York: Routledge, 1999). Especially for the use of Scripture in asceticism, see now
    the magisterial study by Elizabeth A. Clark, *Reading Renunciation: Asceticism and Scripture in
    Early Christianity* (Princeton, N.J.: Princeton University Press, 1999).
4   Richard Valantasis, "Constructions of Power in Asceticism," *JAAR* 63 (1995): 775–821;
    idem, "A Theory of the Social Function of Asceticism," in *Asceticism* (ed. V. Wimbush and
    R. Valantasis; New York: Oxford University Press, 1995), 544–52.
5   Valantasis, "Power in Asceticism," 797, my italics.
6   This definition corresponds to the theoretical perspectives in Edelman and Harvey and
    Lefevbre (chap. 1) about the possibility of creating a new embodiment of the subject, and
    of new ways to structure the world.
7   For a general overview of the history of interpretation, see Ulrich Luz, *Das Evangelium nach
    Matthäus*, vol. 3 (1997), 104–6; for patristic exegesis, see Walter Bauer, "Matt 19,12 und
    die alten Christen," in *Aufsätze und kleine Schriften* (ed. G. Strecker; Tübingen:. Mohr, 1967;
    publ. orig. 1914), 253–62; Clark, *Reading Renunciation: Asceticism and Scripture*, 90–92.
8   For illuminating examples, see David J. A. Clines, "*Ecce Vir*, or, Gendering the Son of Man,"
    in *Biblical Studies/Cultural Studies* (JSOT Sup 266; ed. J. Cheryl Exum and S. D. Moore;
    Sheffield: Sheffield University Press, 1998), 352–75; David Morgan, "The Masculinity of
    Jesus in Popular Religious Art," in *Men's Bodies, Men's Gods* (ed. Björn Krondorfer; New
    York: New York University Press, 1996), 251–66; Stephen D. Moore, "Ugly Thoughts:
    On the Face and Physique of the Historical Jesus," in *Biblical Studies/Cultural Studies*, 376–99.
9   For an excellent and illuminating discussion, see M. Kuefler, *Manly Eunuch*.
10 J. Blinzler, "*Eisin eunouchoi*," *ZNW* 48 (1957): 254–70; Luz, *Matthäus* 3:107; K.
    Niederwimmer, *Askese und Mysterium* (FRLANT 113; Göttingen: Vandenhoeck & Ruprecht,
    1975), 55.
11 This is the evaluation by Meier (*Marginal Jew*, 1:344–45) which, applying by the criteria of
    embarrassment, discontinuity with early Christianity and coherence with Jesus' other
    teachings, may be typical; see also Dale C. Allison, *Jesus of Nazareth: Millenarian Prophet*
    (Minneapolis: Fortress, 1998), 183–84; Luz, *Matthäus*, 3:109; Heinrich Baltensweiler, *Die
    Ehe im Neuen Testament* (ATANT 52; Zürich: Zwingli Verlag, 1967), 103.
12 It has a different wording; the list starts with those who have been made eunuchs by men;
    see Josef Blinzler, "Justinus *Apol.* I 15,4 und Matthäus 19:11–12," in *Mélanges Bibliques: En
    homage au R.P. Beda Rigaux* (ed. A. Descamps and A. de Halleux; Gembloux: Duculot,
    1970), 45–55.
13 Blinzler, "*Eisin eunouchoi*," 268–70; Luz, *Matthäus*, 3:110–11; Francis Moloney, "Matthew
    19:3–12 and Celibacy: A Redactional and Form Critical Study," *JSNT* 2 (1979): 42–60;
    Allison, *Jesus of Nazareth*, 183.
14 Arthur J. Dewey ("The Unkindest Cut of All? Matt 19:11–12," *Forum* 8:1–2 [1992]: 113–22)
    is an exception in that he notices the ambiguities of the term "eunuch" and the challenges
    it poses for understandings of masculinity.
15 Allison, *Jesus of Nazareth*, 183–84.
16 Ibid., 202.
17 In a discussion of how fieldwork among anthropologists is also constructed by "heroic
    masculinism," Matthew Sparke asks: "What is the spatiality not represented yet implied
    (unseen) by the masculinist fielding of the field?" in "Displacing the Field in Fieldwork:
    Masculinity, Metaphor and Space," in *Bodyspace: Destabilizing Geographies of Gender and Sexuality*
    (ed. N. Duncan; London: Routledge, 1996), 220.

18   I use the category "antiquity" to include both Greco-Roman and Jewish cultures in the period under discussion, the centuries around the time of Jesus.

19   Eph. 5:22–6:9; Col. 3:18–4:1; 1 Pet. 2:13–3:7.

20   Studies of families as well as of masculinities have shown that there are many similarities that cut across ethnic and cultural boundaries, and that many of the differences are found within the various cultures, rather than between them. We should also notice that "male" means the free male, as a member of the society under discussion; slaves and "others" are not included. See S. J. D. Cohen, ed., *The Jewish Family in Antiquity* (Atlanta: Scholars Press, 1993); Stephen D. Moore and Janice C. Anderson, "Taking It Like a Man: Masculinities in 4 Maccabees," *JBL* 117 (1998): 249–73; Halvor Moxnes, "Conventional Values in the Hellenistic World: Masculinity," in *Conventional Values in the Hellenistic World* (ed. P. Bilde et al.; Aarhus: Aarhus University Press, 1997), 263–84; Michael L. Satlow, "'Try to Be a Man': The Rabbinic Construction of Masculinity," *HTR* 89 (1996): 19–40; Steve Young, "Being a Man: The Pursuit of Manliness in the Shepherd of Hermas," *JECS* 2 (1994): 237–55.

21   E.g., Stephen Barton, *Discipleship and Family Ties*. Barton finds parallel to passages about leaving family in Mark and Matthew in Jewish sources: "There is no lack of material from the biblical and Jewish sources which provides further evidence for what we found in the analysis of Philo, Josephus and the Qumran documents: that, fundamentally speaking, allegiance to God and devotion to the will of God transcends family ties and legitimates their subordination" (55–56). Barton does not seem to notice the misogynistic tendencies in this material.

22   Satlow, "Masculinity," 21–26.

23   Richard A. Baer, *Philo's Use of the Categories Male and Female* (ALGHJ 3; Leiden: Brill, 1970), 38–4.

24   T. Engberg-Pedersen, "Philo's *De Vita Contemplativa* as a Philosopher's Dream," *JSJ* 30 (1999): 40–64.

25   Apuleius, *Golden Ass* VII.28.

26   Gilmore, "Introduction: The Shame of Dishonour."

27   Peter Guyot, *Eunuchen als Sklaven und Freigelassene in der griechisch-römische Antike* (Stuttgarter Beiträge zur Geschichte und Politik 14; Stuttgart: Klett-Cotta, 1980); Johannes Schneider, "Eunochos, eunochizo," TDNT 2: 765–68; Piotr O. Scholz, *Der ermannte Eros* (Düsseldorf: Artemis & Winkler, 1997).

28   Kathryn M. Ringrose, "Living in the Shadows: Eunuchs and Gender in Byzantium," in *Third Sex, Third Gender* (ed. G. Herdt; New York: Zone, 1994), 85–109; Shaun F. Tougher, "Byzantine Eunuchs: An Overview, with Special Reference to Their Creation and Origin," in *Women, Men and Eunuchs: Gender in Byzantium* (ed. L. James; London: Routledge, 1997), 168–84.

29   Scholz, *Eros*, 116–62; Shaun Marmon, *Eunuchs and Sacred Boundaries in Islamic Society* (Oxford: Oxford University Press, 1995).

30   *The Book of the Risings of the Full Moon of the Dwellings of Joy*, by Ala al-Din al Ghuzuli, discussed in Marmon, *Eunuchs and Sacred Boundaries*, 3–15.

31   Jaqueline Long, *Claudian's In Eutropium: Or, How, When and Why to Slander a Eunuch* (Chapel Hill: University of North Carolina Press, 1996).

32   Garth Thomas, "Magna Mater and Attis," *ANRW* II. 17.3 (1984): 1500–1535.

33   Monika Hörig, "Dea Syria – Atargatis," *ANRW* II.17.3 (1984): 1537–81.

34   G. Sanders, "Gallos," *RAC* 8: 984–1034.

35   Ibid., 990.

36   Ibid., 996.

37   Louis Richard, "Juvenal et les galles de Cybèle," *Revue de l'Histoire des Religions* 169 (1966): 51–67.

38   G. Sanders, "Gallos," 1024.

39   G. Sanders, "Kybele und Attis," in *Die Orientalischen Religionen im Römerreich* (ed. M. J. Vermaseren; Leiden: Brill, 1981), 283–84.

40   Kuefler, *Manly Eunuch*, passim.
41   G. Sanders, "Kybele and Attis," 268.
42   G. Sanders, "Gallos," 1026–27.
43   "If any one in sickness has been subjected by physicians to a surgical operation, or if he has been castrated by barbarians, let him remain among the clergy; but if any one in sound health has castrated himself, it behoves that such an one, if (already) enrolled among the clergy, should cease (from his ministry), and that from henceforth no such person should be promoted. But as it is evident that this is said of those who wilfully do the thing and presume to castrate themselves, so if any has been made eunuchs by barbarians, or by their masters, and should otherwise be found worthy, such men the Canon admits to the clergy," *The Seven Ecumenical Councils*, Nicene and Post-Nicene Fathers Ser. 2, 14 (ed. H. R. Percival; Edinburgh: T. & T. Clark, 1991), 8. See also *Apost. Const.* 21–22 (ibid., 595): "21. An eunuch, if he has been made so by the violence of men, or (if his *virilia* have been amputated) in times of persecution, or if he has been born so, if in other respects he is worthy, may be made a bishop. 22. He who has mutilated himself cannot become a clergyman, for he is a self-murderer, and an enemy to the workmanship of God."
44   Bauer, "Matt 19:12"; Clark, *Reading Renunciation*, 90–92.
45   L. W. Barnard (Justin Martyr, *The First and Second Apologies* [Introd. by L. W. Barnard; New York: Paulist Press, 1997], 32) translates *sōphrosyne* with "chastity." For the tendency among early Christian Latin fathers to translate *sōphrosyne* with terms for chastity, see Clark, *Reading Renunciation*, 103–5.
46   Guyot, *Eunuchen*, 45–51.
47   Justin contrasts this young man as an example of the heroic virtue of chastity with Antinous, Hadrian's young Greek favorite. The latter had drowned (himself?) in the Nile some years earlier, and was now venerated as a god, although "they knew both who he was and what was his origin." This was a not-so-veiled criticism of Antinous, whom Justin with Christian eyes would regard as both sexually licentious and effeminate.
48   For the term "figurative reading," which encompasses both allegorical and typological reading, see Clark, *Reading Renunciation*, 76–78.
49   Origen, *Comm. Matt.* 15.1; Clark, *Reading Renunciation*, 91–92.
50   Eusebius, *Hist. Eccl.* 6.8, 1.2.
51   Brown (*The Body and Society: Men, Women and Sexual Renunciation in Early Christianity* [New York: Columbia University Press, 1988], 168) thinks that the sources are reliable.
52   Clark, *Reading Renunciation*, 173.
53   The phrase is from Clark, *Reading Renunciation*, 91.
54   Jerome, "necessitas non voluntas est," *Commentaire sur S. Matthieu*, vol. 2 (introd. E. Bonnard; SC 259; Paris: Éditions du Cerf, 1979), 72. Similarly, in his letter to Eustochium, *Epist.* 22.19, Jerome makes a contrast between *necessitas* and *voluntas*: "Some people may be eunuchs from necessity; I am one of free will." In *Hom. Matt.* 62.2 to Matt. 19:12, John Chrysostom makes a similar distinction between *nature* and *choice*. He offers many arguments against an understanding of "made themselves eunuchs" as castration: it would be murder, it would give reason to slander God's creation, it would give the Manichaeans an argument, and it would be as unlawful as similar acts among the Greeks (probably the galli). But his strongest argument is the contrast between human choice and freedom on the one hand and nature on the other, or between mind and nature.
55   For Jerome's hierarchy of ascetic over nonascetic, and of various levels of asceticism, see Clark, *Reading Renunciation*, 167–69.
56   "Cum possint esse viri, propter Christum eunuchi fiunt."
57   Kuefler, *Manly Eunuch*, 275–78.
58   According to Josephus (*A.J.* 16. 230; *B.J.* 1.488), Herod the Great had eunuchs at his court; Guyot, *Eunuchen*, 100, 231–34.
59   It is not certain that all references to eunuchs at the courts of Babylon or Jerusalem are to castrated men, but sufficiently many are for the ambiguity to remain. Many court eunuchs

experienced slander and plotting where accusations of feminine traits were common; see Long, *Claudian's In Eutropium*; Ringrose, "Byzantium"; Tougher, "Byzantine Eunuchs."

60   Sand, *Reich Gottes*, 56–57.

61   Davies and Allison, *Matthew* 3, 25 n. 131.

62   William B. Turner, *A Genealogy of Queer Theory* (Philadelphia: Temple University Press, 2000), 1–35.

63   Herdt, *Third Sex, Third Gender*.

Chapter 4

JESUS ON SEXUALITY

Matthew 5:31–32 It hath been said, Whosoever shall put away his wife, let him give her a writing of divorcement: But I say unto you, That whosoever shall put away his wife, saving for the cause of fornication, causeth her to commit adultery: and whosoever shall marry her that is divorced committeth adultery.

(KJV)

Matthew 5:27–28 Ye have heard that it was said by them of old time, Thou shalt not commit adultery: But I say unto you, That whosoever looketh on a woman to lust after her hath committed adultery with her already in his heart.

John 8:1–11 (New International Version) But Jesus went to the Mount of Olives. At dawn he appeared again in the temple courts, where all the people gathered around him, and he sat down to teach them. The teachers of the law and the Pharisees brought in a woman caught in adultery. They made her stand before the group and said to Jesus, 'Teacher, this woman was caught in the act of adultery. In the Law Moses commanded us to stone such women. Now what do you say?' They were using this question as a trap, in order to have a basis for accusing him. But Jesus bent down and started to write on the ground with his finger. When they kept on questioning him, he straightened up and said to them, 'If any one of you is without sin, let him be the first to throw a stone at her.' Again he stooped down and wrote on the ground. At this, those who heard began to go away one at a time, the older ones first, until only Jesus was left, with the woman still standing there. Jesus straightened up and asked her, 'Woman, where are they? Has no one condemned you?'

'No one, sir,' she said.

'Then neither do I condemn you,' Jesus declared. 'Go now and leave your life of sin.'

Mark 7:17–23 When He had entered a house away from the crowd, His disciples asked Him concerning the parable. So He said to them, 'Are you thus without understanding also? Do you not perceive that whatever enters a man from outside cannot defile him, because it does not enter his heart but his stomach, and is eliminated, thus purifying all foods?' And He said, 'What comes out of a man, that defiles a man. For from within, out of the heart of men, proceed evil thoughts, adulteries, fornications, murders, thefts, covetousness, wickedness, deceit, lewdness, an evil eye, blasphemy, pride, foolishness. All these evil things come from within and defile a man.'

Did the medieval and early modern Islamic world accept men who had sex with male youths?

Introduction

D ID ISLAMIC SOCIETY follow the model of what we think of as premodern sexuality as espoused by Foucault, with no concept of sexual identity, and therefore no distinction between heterosexual and homosexual? Scholar Khaled El-Rouayheb and others have argued that in fact the Qur'an and Islamic legal codes harshly condemned anal intercourse between men as *liwat*. In the wider culture, men who had sex with male youths could be condemned as engaging in a vice, like drinking or gambling, but adult men who desired to be penetrated were scorned as effeminate and ruled by their vices. Yet in another strand of Islamic culture, active sodomy was identified with aggressive masculinity, a way of humiliating one's opponents. In Sufism (a mystical practice of Islam), poetry celebrated the love of adult men for boys as an erotic metaphor for a love of God. And between the eighth and ninth centuries, poems and other literature praising beautiful youths became an established part of the Arabic literary canon.

One early example is *The Dove's Neck-Ring*, written around AD 1022 in Spain, and excerpted here. Much of early medieval Spain – known as al-Andalus – was dominated by Muslim rulers who had invaded from North Africa. Islamic Spain was a distinctive culture, but Khaled El-Rouayheb notes that his findings about the later Ottoman and Arab world from 1500 to 1800 also apply to the wider Arabic world in the earlier period as well.

The author of *The Dove's Neck-Ring*, Ibn Hazm, was born in AD 994. A sickly boy, he was raised in the women's quarters of the noble court, where the ladies educated him in the Qur'an, poetry, and writing. Later he became a vizier, or minister at a royal court, but he really wished to devote himself to poetry, theology, law, medicine, and Greek lore. He praised the love of both slave girls and male youths, but he also condemned sexual sin. How can we reconcile such contradictions? The answer lies in Ibn Hazm's focus on love. Love itself was not seen as sinful, no matter what the object, because it was an overwhelming force over which its victim had no control. But this elevated, intense passion was not seen as something that usually led to marriage. Respectable young women were kept secluded from men who might try to seduce them. This is why slaves and male youths became the objects of desire.

Yet even these loves still had to be concealed. Muslim literature admired the person who suffered from an impossible love as a martyr; the poetry is replete with images of secret loves flickering in the "concealment of night."[1] In the excerpt about "Divulging (the secret)," does Ibn Hazm treat the man who revealed his love for a slave girl differently than the man who revealed his love for the son of a silversmith? In the excerpt about "Submissiveness," did the submissive love of Muqaddam Ibn-ul-Asfar for a page, or the love of Saʿīd b. Mundir b. Saʿīd for a slave girl, turn out well?

In his conclusion, Ibn Hazm condemns adultery as sinful, but he rebukes men who commit sodomy even more harshly. Yet Ibn Hazm believes that any man could be attracted to a beautiful youth. Virtue lay in controling oneself and not giving in to these desires. Ibn Hazm recounts the terrible consequences when elite men openly indulge their passions for young men. But in telling these tales, what did Ibn Hazm find most shameful? Loving a Christian youth? Exposing a harem to immorality to gain the favors of a youth? Submissiveness? Ibn Hazm is mostly concerned with the male perspective. Although he writes of many women respectfully, in a passage not reprinted here he doubts that women would ever be able to overcome passion, since they were too irrational and sexual.

Although neither Ibn Hazm nor Khaled El-Rouayheb discusses the topic, the theme of women loving women does appear in medieval Arabic literature, such as *The Thousand and One Nights*, and in Iran, from the seventeenth century onwards, there was a tradition of close female friendships.[2]

By the late nineteenth century, Arab and Persian nationalists began denouncing the tradition of desire of women for each other or of men for male youths as decadent, for they wanted to reform their own societies in order to make them free from the West. The long tradition of homoerotic poetry was censored and criticized.[3] The paradox had disappeared.

Notes

1   Ruqayya Yasmine Khan, "On the Significance of Secrecy in the Medieval Arabic Romances," *Journal of Arabic Literature* 31, no. 3 (2000): 243–247.

2   Shahar Amer, "Cross-Dressing and Female Same-Sex Marriage in Medieval French and Arabic Literatures," in *Islamicate Sexualities*, ed. Kathryn Babayan and Afsaneh Najmabadi (Cambridge, MA: Harvard Center for Middle Eastern Studies, 2008), 92; Kathryn Babayan, "'In Spirit We Ate Each Other's Sorrow': Female Companionship in Seventeenth-Century Safavi Iran," in *Islamicate Sexualities*, ed. Kathryn Babayan and Afsaneh Najmabadi (Cambridge, MA: Harvard Center for Middle Eastern Studies, 2008), 239–274.

3   Joseph A. Massad, *Desiring Arabs* (Chicago: University of Chicago Press, 2007), 143. Janet Afary, *Sexual Politics in Modern Iran* (Cambridge: Cambridge University Press, 2009), 140.

Chapter 5

Khaled El-Rouayheb

BEFORE HOMOSEXUALITY IN THE ARAB-ISLAMIC WORLD, 1500–1800 (2005)

Pederasts and pathics: sex as polarization

TOWARD THE END OF THE YEAR 1701, a Druze chieftain (Emir) from the Wādī al-Taym area in Syria came to Damascus to be officially invested as head military official (*Yāyābāshī*) of his home region by the governor of the city. According to a contemporary chronicler, the Emir was a notorious womanizer, who "in Damascus was determined to conduct himself with his characteristic lewdness." Once, while at the house of a local woman, he was surprised by around twenty Turcoman soldiers, who gang-raped him and robbed him of his clothes, leaving him barefoot and clad only in his inner garments. "He who encroaches upon the womenfolk (*ḥarīm*) of the Muslims deserves more than this," they reportedly said before letting him go. "News of the incident," the chronicler added, "reached the women and children [of the city], and songs about him [i.e., the Emir] were composed and performed by singers . . . He then departed to the land of the Druzes, his home, and it was said that the woman remained untainted [i.e., she was not dishonored before the arrival of the soldiers], and thus God forsook the damned Emir at the hands of the Turcomans."[1] The quoted remarks make it clear in what terms the chronicler, and the Muslim population of Damascus in general, viewed the reported action of the soldiers. An outsider, and a non-Muslim at that, by his attempt to seduce or rape a local woman, had threatened the honor of the community at large. The threat was not only averted, but the potential dishonorer was himself dishonored by being buggered, and the Turcoman troops came in this particular case to be seen as instruments of poetic justice. Underlying the interpretation, of course, is a tacit identification of sexual penetration, both the one averted and the one committed by the soldiers, with dishonor. This assumption is one that will be all too familiar to anyone acquainted with the more bawdy or ribald aspects of present-day Arab (and Mediterranean) culture, as manifested for example in jokes and insults: to penetrate phallically is to dominate, subjugate, and

ultimately to humiliate. According to the oneiromantic handbook of the Damascene scholar
'Abd al-Ghanī al-Nābulusī (d. 1731), to dream that one is sexually penetrating a rival or
enemy forebodes that one will get the better of him in real life, whereas being penetrated
by him is ominous, signifying the reverse.[2] A strikingly uncompromising expression of
this way of conceiving phallic penetration is contained in the following defamatory poem
in which Ibrāhīm al-Ghazālī (d. 1678), deputy judge at one of the courts of Damascus,
lampooned a contemporary:

> By God ask, on my behalf, the gross character: "Of what do you disapprove
>   in so-and-so?" and you will be amazed.
> You will not find the reason to be other than that I did not fuck him since he
>   has long disgusted me.
> And had I inflicted upon him my penis and given it to him, he would not
>   have reckoned I had any faults.
> But I now cauterize his ulcerous arse with the fire of my penis, and ascend
>   the ranks [of virtue] in his eyes.
> I impose on my self what is contrary to its preference; before me many did
>   what I am now doing . . .
> O penis! Arise! Put on your armor, and enter his interior like a raider, and
>   give us his guts as spoils.
> Make him wide as you hump and shake within him, and if you cannot,
>   delegate in your place a piece of wood.[3]

As described in this context, the act of penetration can hardly be called "sexual," as
it is dissociated, not only from love and intimacy, but also from desire and pleasure. It
is explicitly stated that the penetrator has to overcome his feeling of disgust and impose
on his self "what is contrary to its preference," whereas the fact that the penetrated is
said to derive pleasure from the act simply adds to the insult. "You who closes his thighs
around the manhood from pleasure! You pasture-ground of penises!" a seventeenth-century
Egyptian scholar wrote to an adversary.[4] As has been noted by the psychiatrist T. Vanggaard,
it seems to be a misconception to assume that men are only able to sustain an erection
and have intercourse if they are attracted sexually (in any ordinary sense of the word) to
the person in question. In some cases, the erection may be sustained by feelings of
aggressive hostility.[5] The possibility of what Vanggaard calls "phallic aggression" seems to
have been conceived in the premodern Arab East. The Iraqi scholar Maḥmūd al-Alūsī (d.
1854), for example, stated that some people in his time used sodomy as a way of getting
revenge in vendettas (akhdhan li-al-tha'r).[6] In addition, some of the traditions which were
invoked by Muslim religious scholars to explain the rise of sodomy among "the people of
Lot" (Qawm Lūṭ) stated that they started to sodomize strangers as a way of driving them
off their land, "without having any sexual desire to do that (min ghayr shahwah bihim ilā
dhālik)."[7]

Instead of references to desire and pleasure, the quoted verses of Ibrāhīm al-Ghazālī
contain a remarkable profusion of metaphors derived from the language of violence and
war: infliction, fire, armor, raid, spoils. Conversely, literary descriptions of battles in
classical Arabic often conjure up, perhaps unconsciously, the imagery of sexual intercourse:
the defeated soldiers "turn tail" (wallaw al-adbār); the swords of the victorious ravage the
turned tails (fataka or 'amila fī adbārihim) of their enemies; the sword of the powerful

military commander was said to "make courageous men into women" (*yu'annithu al-buhm al-dhukūr*) or to "make male enemies menstruate" (*ja'ala al-dhukūr min al-a'ādī ḥuyyaḍan*).[8] The word *futūḥ* can be used equally of military conquest and of sexual penetration or deflowering. If the act of penetration can be seen as a uniting of two persons or as "making love," it can also be perceived as a deeply "polarizing" experience, which distinguishes the dominant from the dominated, the dishonorer from the dishonored, and the victorious from the defeated.[9] Some recent writers seem to want to juxtapose the two views, and attribute the former to the modern West and the latter to the Mediterranean–Middle Eastern area.[10] Yet the idea of sex as *jimā'* (i.e., bringing together, combining) was not foreign to the premodern Middle East, nor is the idea of "screwing" in the sense of defeating or insulting in any way absent in the contemporary West. Having said this, it is still undeniable that the aggressive, masculine-centered view featured much more prominently in the public (male-dominated) discourse of the early Ottoman Arab East than the affectionate-androgynous view. In the ongoing rivalries for posts, money, status, and influence in the exclusively male public sphere, allusions to phallic penetration were always near at hand. When the poet Māmāyah al-Rūmī (d. 1579) was appointed as interpreter at one of the courts of Damascus at the expense of the previous holder of the position, a Turk by the name of Amrallah, he composed the following lines in celebration:

> Thanks to God, I achieved my desired aim, and the opponent was
>   discharged.
> And I received what I had hoped for, and God's will (*amr Allah*) was done
>   (*maf'ūlan*).[11]

Since *maf'ūl bihi* is the term usually used to denote the passive sexual partner, the allusion is very clear in Arabic: Amrallah has been "screwed" by his successful rival for the post.

The modern concept of "homosexuality" elides a distinction that, in the Middle East, was (and still is) fraught with symbolic significance: that between the penetrator and the penetrated. Not surprisingly, in ordinary language there was no corresponding concept that would apply to both those who preferred the active-insertive role and those who preferred the passive-receptive role in a homosexual act. The term *lūṭī* was typically used of the former, while *mukhannath* or *ma'būn* or (more colloquially) *'ilq* was reserved for the latter. It is worth dwelling on this point, since there is a persistent tendency among some modern scholars to overlook this distinction and render the indigenous term *lūṭī* as "homosexual."[12] In Islamic law, the *lūṭī* is a man who commits *liwāṭ* (i.e., anal intercourse with another man), regardless of whether he commits it as an active or passive partner.[13] However, in ordinary, nontechnical language (as manifested in, for example, bawdy-satirical anecdotes) the term *lūṭī* almost always meant "pederast." One short anecdote illustrates the fact that a stereotypical *lūṭī* was thought to be interested in active-insertive anal intercourse with boys: "of another person it was related that he was a *lā'iṭ* [variant of *lūṭī*], and so his wife told him: I have what boys have (*'indī mā 'ind al-ghilmān*). He replied: Yes, but it has an unpleasant neighbor [i.e., the vagina]."[14] A tradition related by the Shī'ī scholar Muḥammad al-Ḥurr al-'Āmilī (d. 1693) also confirms that *liwāṭ* was normally understood to be equivalent to sodomizing boys: a heretic (*zindīq*) asked 'Alī ibn Abī Ṭālib (the Prophet Muḥammad's son-in-law) for the reason behind the religious prohibition of *liwāṭ*. 'Alī supposedly answered: "If carnal penetration of a boy (*ityān al-ghulām*) were permitted, men would dispense with women, and this would lead to the disruption of procreation."[15] In the Egyptian version of the popular, orally transmitted epic *Sīrat Baybars*, the term *lūṭī* is used of adult males who make sexual advances to beardless youths, and the term is used interchangeably with the colloquial term *bita 'al-Ḥighār*, which roughly translates as "he who is for youngsters."[16] According to an anonymous and tongue-in-cheek couplet cited in both a late seventeenth-century Egyptian and a late eighteenth-century Damascene text:

> The lover of beardless boys is known among people as a *lūṭī*, and the lover
>   of young women is called a fornicator [*zānī*]
> So, out of chastity, I turned to those with beards, and thus I am neither a *lūṭī*
>   nor a *zānī*.[17]

The Egyptian scholar and poet Aḥmad al-Khafājī (d. 1659) complained in verse of the age in which he was living, claiming that it was similar to "the people of Lot" in giving preference to young upstarts at the expense of the older and venerable.[18] In a love poem, the Iraqi scholar 'Abd al-Bāqī al-'Umarī (d. 1697/8) said of the eulogized female that, "if the people of Lot had seen her beauty, they would never have turned to a boy."[19]

The image of "the people of Lot" in the Islamic tradition was, to be sure, not entirely uniform. In commenting on the just-quoted verse of 'Abd al-Bāqī al-'Umarī, the Iraqi scholar Muḥammad Amīn al-'Umarī (d. 1788) reminded readers that the people of Lot not only sodomized boys but also adult male strangers.[20] This was the standard dual image of the "people of Lot" in the Qur'anic commentaries of the time: on the one hand they were portrayed as pederasts and, on the other, as an aggressive people who anally raped trespassers.[21] In both cases, however, they were assumed to be the "active" or "insertive" party, and this assumption tended to reflect back on the juridical literature itself. The Palestinian religious scholar Muḥammad al-Saffārīnī (d. 1774), for example, defined *liwāṭ* or "the act of the people of Lot" (*'amal qawm Lūṭ*) as "carnal penetration of males in the anus (*ityān al-dhukūr fī al-dubur*)."[22] Though Saffārīnī was committed to the idea that the man who willingly assumes the passive-receptive role in anal intercourse has committed sodomy and may be prosecuted accordingly, it still seemed natural for him to define sodomy in a way which suggests that it is only the active-insertive party who commits it. Similarly, the Egyptian jurist Ibrāhīm al-Bājūrī (d. 1860) stated that *liwāṭ* was "the act committed by the people of Lot (*fi'l qawm Lūṭ*), for they were the first to sodomize men (*fa-innahum awwal man atā al-rijāl fī adbārihim*)." He went on to claim that the habit disappeared after the destruction of Sodom, and was only resurrected after the Islamic conquest of the Middle East. Many soldiers were away from their women, and availed themselves of native, subservient males instead, and so they "did it to them and treated them as women" (*fa'alū bihim wa ajrawhum majrā al-nisā'*).[23] Bājūrī's remarks are not particularly valuable as a historical observation, but again reveal that even jurists were prone to make the tacit assumption that *liwāṭ* ("the act of the people of Lot") was active rather than passive sodomy, and that the paradigmatic *lūṭī* was therefore the active-insertive partner. The assumption was articulated clearly in nonjuridical discourse, such as the following defamatory poem by the Aleppine poet Ḥusayn al-Jazarī (d. ca. 1624):

> Does the offspring of al-Naḥḥās Fathallah seek satisfaction for his scratchy
>   arse?
> Trust my maternal cousin in *liwāṭ* and trust his extended, erect prick.

Take it and forgo my penis, for I see no one suitable for that effeminate man
(*mukhannath*) except that *lūṭī*.[24]

The confusion resulting from the assumption that *lūṭī* translates as "homosexual" may
be seen, for example, in a modern discussion of the collection of erotic anecdotes entitled
Nuzhat al-albāb fīmā lā yūjad fī kitāb by the Egyptian scholar Aḥmad al-Tīfāshī (d. 1253).
Having apparently been misled by a French translation, Robert Irwin asserts, in his
absorbing and rewarding book *The Arabian Nights: A Companion*, that the sixth chapter of
Tīfāshī's work deals with homosexuals, and goes on to give the "characteristic features"
attributed to them:

> The homosexual should have a pleasant lodging, well-furnished with books
> and wine, and made pleasanter yet by the presence of doves and singing birds.
> A homosexual can be recognized by the way he stares directly at one, this
> direct gaze often being followed by a wink. The typical homosexual has thin
> legs with hairy ankles and tends to wear robes which reach right down to the
> ground. When he walks, his hands and his legs sway.[25]

Chapters 6–8 of al-Tīfāshī's book are in fact devoted to *al-lāṭā* (plural *of lūṭī*) and *al-murd
al-muʾājirīn*. Even a cursory reading of the Arabic text (to which Irwin did not have access)
reveals that the former term refers to adult men who desire to sodomize boys—that is,
to "pederasts" rather than "homosexuals"—while the term *murd muʾājirīn* refers to beardless
boy prostitutes who render sexual services to *al-lāṭā* . The quoted account of "characteristic
features" runs these two categories together: it is the pederast who should have pleasant
lodgings, books and wine, but it is the boy prostitute who may be recognized by his gaze,
his legs, and the way he walks.[26] What is even more damaging to the assumption that the
term *lūṭī* is synonymous with "homosexual" is the fact that a later chapter of Tīfāshī's
work (chapter 12) deals with *al-khināth*—that is, effeminate adult men who desire to be
sodomized by (preferably very masculine) men. This category is clearly treated by the
author as distinct from the previously mentioned *lāṭā* and *muʾājirīn* (the latter are beardless
boys and their motives are depicted as pecuniary). It should be clear by now that the
modern term "homosexual" hopelessly muddles certain native distinctions, and that insisting
on using it in translation or paraphrase leads to serious misunderstanding.[27] It is also clear
that Tīfāshī's work cannot be invoked, as Irwin does, in support of the idea that some
medieval Arabs thought of homosexuality as a "single condition" shared by those who
prefer the active role and those who prefer the passive, nor of the idea that this single
condition was considered by some to be "a form of illness." There does not seem to be
any support at all for the idea that pederasts were thought to suffer from an illness. One
may admittedly encounter a few passages in which *liwāṭ* was called a *dāʾ*, and the latter
term may in appropriate contexts mean "disease." However, the term *dāʾ* was frequently
used in a loose sense to cover any habit or character trait that was held to be reprehensible.
The very passages or works that use the term *dāʾ* of *liwāṭ* also use it, for example, of
stinginess (*bukhl*) or ignorance of religious stipulations (*jahl*).[28] There were no medical
discussions of *liwāṭ* or any other indication that a tendency to commit *liwāṭ* was held to
be a disease in the strict sense, with a physiological basis, physical symptoms, and natural
remedies.[29] The *lūṭī* was instead widely represented as a morally dissolute person, a
libertine (*fāsiq*), and this latter word was sometimes used as its synonym. Being a pederast

was often spoken of in the same breath as being a drinker of wine: "he is suspected of drinking wine and being inclined to beardless boys"; "[he] loves boys and drink"; "he became famous for drinking wine and loving boys"; "both of them are unscrupulous wine-drinkers and rakes, well known for their carousing, and famous among rich and poor for kissing fair boys and fair girls."[30] As in the case of drinking alcohol, the antidote to pederasty was repentance. A story in a collection of humorous anecdotes, perhaps dating from the seventeenth century, started thus: "It was related that one of the *lūṭīs* repented (*tāba*) from sodomy (*liwāṭ*)."[31] In the romance of Baybars, men who make sexual advances to the young hero and his groom 'Uthmān are regularly beaten up until they say: "I repent at your hands, and swear by your head and eyes that I will no longer meet youngsters and commit *liwāṭ*," or, "My master! I repent and recant for what I did, and regret and repent at your hands from this time on, and if I should revert to anything of the kind then kill me."[32] The following couplet by the poet Māmāyah al-Rūmī also illustrates the tendency to assimilate pederasty to sins such as (heterosexual) fornication and drinking alcohol:

> My career in pursuit of fancy is ruined, so have mercy on me, O Bestower
> and Benefactor!
> I've lost this world and the next, on fornication, booze, and beardless boys
> in my time.[33]

It was the *ma'būn* or *mukhannath* who was viewed as a pathological case. The Arabic medical tradition, following the Greek, tended to regard the male who desires to be anally penetrated as being afflicted with a disease—*ubnah*—at least from the time of Abū Bakr al-Rāzī (d. ca. 925), and this continued to be the verdict of the medical treatises of the early Ottoman period.[34] *Ubnah* was classified as a disease with prescribed remedies in the medical works of 'Abd al-Wahhāb al-Sha'rānī (d. 1565), Dāwūd al-Anṭākī (d. 1599), and Aḥmad al-Qalyūbī (d. 1658).[35] Of the three, only Anṭākī discussed the etiology of the disease. He considered it to be caused by the presence of a boric substance (*māddah būrāqiyyah*) in the veins of the rectum, which burns and tickles the anus until it becomes like an itching wound, inducing the person with the disease to seek to have his anus penetrated. Though usually inherited (*mawrūth*), the disease could also be caused by being subjected to penetration, since the anal itch could be the effect of especially pungent semen. The person with *ubnah* was most often effeminate, and typically suffered from flabbiness, cough, a dull, languid look, dried lips, a fleshy face, and a large posterior. As a remedy, Anṭākī mentioned liquid potions of lapis lazuli, agaric, aloe, mastic, or clove with yogurt, all of which supposedly counteract pungent humors. He also suggested the efficacy of rubbing the anus with ash obtained by burning hair from the right thigh of a hyena.[36]

Even outside a strictly medical context, the desire of the passive sodomite was perceived as anomalous and as requiring a special explanation, for example in terms of a worm-infected anus.[37] Of course, the fact that passive sodomy was widely regarded as disease-induced did not imply that it ceased to be judged as morally and religiously reprehensible. However, it was not simply a sin that in principle anyone could commit—like, say, drinking alcohol or stealing. *Ubnah* was something a *ma'būn* had or suffered from, whereas *liwāṭ was* simply something a *lūṭī* did. The difference is strikingly illustrated in jurists' discussion of insults that qualify as formal accusations of illicit sexual intercourse. Calling a man a *lūṭī* always qualified as such an accusation, but in the case of calling someone a *ma'būn* opinions were less uniform. The Egyptian jurist Manṣūr al-Buhūtī (d. 1641), for example, asserted that the latter insult did not qualify as an accusation of illicit sexual intercourse, since it referred to a condition of the insulted person and did not explicitly claim that he acted in accordance with it (*al-ubnah al-mushār ilayhā lā tu'tī annahu yaf'al bi-muqtaḍāhā*).[38]

The concept of *liwāṭ* was thus to a large extent "behavioristic," whereas *ubnah* was more likely to be seen as an inner condition that gave rise to, and hence explained, peculiar behavior. *Ubnah* was a pathological or abnormal state which, permanently or recurrently, overwhelmed the person afflicted: "I would see him drink alcohol until he was intoxicated . . . and his *ubnah* would be aroused and he would remain restless until he would be done in his anus"; "I heard of a person of honorable status who was afflicted with the disease of *ubnah*, so, fearing that this would be divulged . . . he had a piece of wood in the shape of a penis made, and when the disease would be roused he would seclude himself . . . and lock the doors from fear of being discovered and treat himself with the wood . . . [afterwards] he would implore of God . . . that this disease would cease."[39] At least during the phase in which his disease is active, the *ma'būn* was seen as being thoroughly saturated with his deviant sexual preference, and he was typically portrayed in the works of bawdy comedy (*mujūn*) as insatiable and indiscriminately promiscuous (except perhaps for his preference for virile and well-endowed men).[40] Such a stock association is reiterated in a defamatory poem composed by the Damascene poet 'Abd al-Ḥayy al-Khāl (d. 1715) of a contemporary whom he accused of being a passive sodomite (*'ilq*):

> You of wide and generous posterior—and how many marks have we
>   left on it!
> You who, if a penis appears in the Hijaz and the land of Rāmah,
> Cries and wails, saying, "I am tired of my residence [in Damascus]."
> Or if he smells a penis in al-Yamāmah says: "By God, to al-Yamāmah!"
> He prefers to everlasting bliss with wine [in paradise],
> A penis as the neck of a camel and as long as the legs of an ostrich.
> If the pricks that he has used to quench his cravings were put end to end,
> And he mounted them, he would reach the sky, and truly exceed the
>   stars in stature.[41]

A common insult (attested for sixteenth- and seventeenth-century Damascus, seventeenth-century Cairo, and seventeenth- and eighteenth-century Mosul) which denigrated the passive male sodomite, and associated him with a ravenous sexual appetite, is the term *wasī'*, or "wide[-arsed]."[42]

The mentioned differences in the stereotypes of the *lūṭī* and the *ma'būn* seem to be related to the fact that only the latter was perceived as being at odds with the ideal of masculinity. Effeminacy was not a part of the image of the *lūṭī*. Soldiers, for instance, had a reputation for being active sodomites.[43] The *Sakbāns*, mercenary soldiers who roamed the Syrian countryside in the early seventeenth century, were according to a contemporary source notorious pederasts and took many boys captive when they looted the suburbs of Damascus in 1606, as did the Egyptian troops of Muḥammad Bey Abū al-Dhahab after their sacking of Jaffa in 1775.[44] The Ottoman historian and belletrist Muṣṭafā 'Alī (d. 1600), who visited Egypt in 1599, held that a large proportion of the cavalrymen (*jundīs*) there were pederasts.[45] According to the above-mentioned poet Māmāyah al-Rūmī:

> The art of *liwāṭ* is the way of masculinity (*fuḥūliyyah*), and might ('izz), so
>   leave to Majnūn Laylah, and with Kuthayyir 'Azz[ah],
> And go up to every handsome beardless boy, strip him, and, even if he cries,
>   present him with your prick and fuck him by force.[46]

Liwāṭ was simply one of the temptations to which a man was exposed. On the other hand, a preference for the passive-receptive, role in sexual intercourse was seen as the very antithesis of masculinity. A common synonym for *ma'būn* was *mukhannath*, an effeminate man. The two terms were, to be sure, not perfect synonyms. A person suffering from *ubnah* could hide this fact and thus not behave in a way likely to be considered effeminate by his peers. It was also recognized that it was possible to be outwardly effeminate without being a passive sodomite. However, it seems misguided to expect a strictly literal use of what were, after all, very derogatory epithets. That the two terms were usually used interchangeably is clear from the bawdy-erotic literature, and is also confirmed by jurists of the period who discussed insults that qualify as formal accusations of illicit sexual intercourse. The Egyptian scholar Aḥmad al-Dardīr (d. 1786), for example, asserted that someone who calls a man a *mukhannath* has made such an accusation, and is thus bound to substantiate his claim or face punishment for slander. This is so, wrote Dardīr, even if the person swears that he only intended the strict lexical meaning of the term, because according to the prevalent norm ('urf), the term *mukhannath* was used of the passive sodomite.[47] The Damascene jurist 'Alā' al-Dīn Muḥammad al-Ḥaṣkafī (d. 1677) also explicated the term *mukhannath* as "he who is penetrated like a woman" (*man yu'tā ka-al-mar'ah*).[48]

The passive male sodomite was seen as being in possession of a female sex drive, but without any of the constraints imposed on women in a patriarchal, gender-segregated society, and his image in bawdy-humorous works is similar to the image of promiscuous women (*al-qiḥāb*).[49] The parallel is also revealed at the level of insults: a woman could be called "wide" (*wasī'ah*) and the passive sodomite a "slut" (*qaḥbah*); or at the level of folk-etiology: the sex drive of the nymphomaniac could also be explained by a worm-induced itch.[50] The existence of the *ma'būn* or *mukhannath* challenged what was, in the premodern Middle East, one of the most sharp and consequential of boundaries: the distinction between genders. Lying outside the bounds of normality, *ubnah* was seen as a force that was powerful and uncontrollable (capable of overturning the familiar order of things) but also comparatively rare. When jurists of the Ḥanafi school sought to defend their ruling that sodomy was not a subvariety of fornication (*zinā*)—and was therefore not subject to the same punishment—one of the arguments to which they resorted was that the incitement to fornication typically came from both parties, whereas the incitement to sodomy came from one party only.[51]

The conceptual distinction between the active and passive sodomite, and the association of the latter—but not the former—with the transgression of gender roles, is hardly distinctive of the early Ottoman Arab East. The same could more or less be said of contemporary Arab, southern European, or Latin American culture, or, for that matter, the culture of classical Greece and Rome, Viking-age Scandinavia, or pre-Meiji Japan. One is clearly dealing with a conceptualization that is very widespread, both geographically and historically. Transgressions of culturally sanctioned gender roles tend to provoke particularly strong feelings of unease and condemnation, and this is especially so in the case of men who, in strongly patriarchal societies like those mentioned above, adopt behavior seen as proper only to women.[52] The contempt and ridicule aroused by the *ma'būn* thus tended to be greater than the disapproval allotted to the *lūṭī*. It was generally understood that one would rather be known as an active than a passive sodomite, as is clear from the following anecdote:

> It was related that a certain man entered his home with a beardless boy . . . when the beardless boy came [back] out he claimed that he had been the active party, so this was related to him [the man], so he said: "Trustworthiness is debased and sodomy is [therefore] forbidden except in the presence of two witnesses."[53]

It should be pointed out that it would be rash to assert on the basis of this passage, or the story of the rape of the Druze chieftain, or the defamatory poem of Ibrāhīm al-Ghazālī, that the active, "male" role in homosexual intercourse was regarded as being entirely free of opprobrium. Such an assertion has nevertheless been made, and an analogy is often drawn to what has been called the "double-standard" of traditional Mediterranean societies: outside of marriage (and historically also slavery) sexual relations are dishonoring for the female (the penetrated) but not for the male (the penetrator). As is to be expected, moral valuations are somewhat more complex than such a neat contrast suggests. First, the very distinction between male/penetrator and female/penetrated is much less relevant in one—hardly unimportant—context, namely the religious-juridical. It is in such contexts than one may encounter the otherwise atypical use of the word *lūṭī* to designate the passive as well as the active sodomite.[54] Second, there is abundant evidence that to say or insinuate of a man that he was a fornicator or an active sodomite was perceived and intended as a derogatory remark. For example, in a defamatory poem, the Damascene scholar Badr al-Dīn al-Ghazzī (d. 1577) said of his rival Muḥammad al-Ījī (d. 1577):

> and how many times has he not crept up on a beardless boy at night, and caused an opening in the upper part of the porch [*riwāq*—an allusion to the boy's rear].[55]

That this was not only the attitude of puritanical scholars is clear from the way the biographer Ḥasan al-Būrīnī (d. 1615) relates the following incident in his entry on the Damascene scholar Ismā'īl al-Nābulusī (d. 1585):

> He was falsely suspected of [an affair with] a boy . . . and the religious scholars (*'ulamā'*) supported him in this ugly affair but he encountered during that time extreme coldness from both elite and commoners, and this was because the boy went up to the hall of the governor . . . with blood flowing down his legs, claiming that this was due to his being penetrated.[56]

The different popular reactions to the reported act of Ismā'īl al-Nābulusī in the late sixteenth century, and to the reported act of the Turcoman soldiers in the early eighteenth, is a testimony, not to changed sensibilities in the intervening period, but to the fundamentally context-dependent nature of the perception and evaluation of homosexual intercourse. In the first case, it is the alleged penetrator, a distinguished notable and scholar, who is highlighted and bears the brunt of public disapproval, whereas the identity and moral character of the penetrated boy is left out of consideration as being of secondary interest. In the second case, the reverse is true: the Emir occupies center stage, while the soldiers remain more or less anonymous. The social status of the people involved was thus one factor determining the interpretation and judgment of a particular case. In the oneiromantic handbook of ʿAbd al-Ghanī al-Nābulusī, dreaming that one is being anally penetrated by a social equal or inferior (a rival, a younger brother, a slave) usually has an inauspicious portent, while being penetrated by a social superior (the Sultan or one's father) is a good omen.[57] It is as if the aggressive, polarizing significance of phallic penetration, and therefore the humiliation of being the passive partner, is toned down in a situation in which the penetrated is already clearly a social inferior, whereas it is emphasized when the status of the partners is roughly equal, or when the penetrated is socially superior to the penetrator. An illustration of this point is contained in the following anecdote in an anonymous collection of humorous stories that seems to date from the seventeenth century: Satan assumes the form of a beautiful boy to lead a repentant sodomite astray. After he has succeeded, he reassumes his original form—that of an ugly, one-eyed old man—and reveals his true identity, whereupon the initially disappointed sodomite says: "Look at my prick up your hole."[58] What was merely sodomy with some boy became an act of "screwing"—and thus a cause of pride—when the passive partner turned out to be none other than Satan himself.

Where the attitude toward the passive partner tended to be unequivocally negative, the evaluation of the active partner was more ambivalent. From the perspective of the ideal of masculinity, the penetrator emerges from the sexual encounter with his honor unimpaired, if not enhanced. From the perspective of the ideal of conformity with the religious-moral norms of society, the penetrator is dishonored. It would be misleading to try to establish a correspondence between these two points of view and specific social groups. The religious scholars could, as we have seen, make unabashed use of the language of aggressive masculinity, while religious considerations were hardly irrelevant to the moral evaluations of the man on the street. Which perspective was adopted had more to do with the particularities of each concrete case than with the social background of the evaluator. Moral judgments are not, as is often supposed, a matter of the automatic application of clear and consensual principles. Rather, they typically involve selective and sometimes contestable use of the stock of generally accepted and usually loosely integrated maxims by individuals and social groups according to a myriad of contextual factors that cannot be exhaustively enumerated.[59] Within one culture (and subculture), the same act may be appraised differently according to the interest of the observer, the way in which the act becomes public knowledge, whether it is carried out discreetly or flauntingly, whether the perpetrator is male or female, young or old, a friend or a rival, a prominent religious scholar or a common soldier, and so on. In the words of the anthropologist J. Pitt-Rivers:

> A system of values is never a homogeneous code of abstract principles obeyed by all the participants in a given culture and able to be extracted from an informant with the aid of a set of hypothetical questions, but a collection of concepts which are related to one another and applied differentially by the different status groups defined by age, sex, class, occupation, etc. in the different social . . . contexts in which they find their meaning.[60]

Transgenerational homosexuality

The significance attributed to biological gender seems to vary both geographically and historically. Whereas some cultures are relatively androgynous, other cultures have strongly developed gender roles, sometimes to the point of "gender polarity"—that is, valuing, on the whole, opposing character traits in the two sexes, such as timidity in women and assertiveness in men. The early Ottoman Arab East evidently belonged to the latter category, with its separate and clearly demarcated male and female spheres, which legitimately overlapped only in certain well-defined contexts. Merely by virtue of his biological sex, a man was expected to participate in a world from which women were in principle excluded. This was the public world in which men competed and cooperated in the pursuit of money, status, and power. Succeeding in this world was to succeed as a male, to live up to the demands of masculinity, and was thus on the symbolic level linked to virility. Defeat, on the other hand, was symbolically equivalent to calling into question male gender identity, to emasculation.[61] Hence, the pervasiveness of sexual allusions to express nonsexual rivalries between men. The victor (e.g., the above-mentioned poet Māmāyah) figuratively "screws" the defeated (e.g., Māmāyah's rival Amrallah), depriving him of his gender and transforming him into a woman. Male honor was symbolically associated with the biological expressions of masculinity, shame with their diminishment or loss. According to the oneiromantic handbook of 'Abd al-Ghanī al-Nābulusī, an increase in the size of the penis or testicles in a dream forebodes an increase in the dreamer's reputation, honor, and money. A decrease indicates the reverse: impoverishment and humiliation.[62]

In the "homosocial" world of the early Ottoman Arab East, sexual symbolism was thus never far from the surface. Yet actual sexual intercourse between adult men was clearly perceived as an anomaly, linked either to violence (rape) or disease (ubnah). Homosexual relations in the early Ottoman Arab East were almost always conceived as involving an adult man (who stereotypically would be the "male" partner) and an adolescent boy (the "female"). The latter—referred to in the texts as amrad (beardless boy); ghulām or ṣabī (boy); or: fatā, shābb, or ḥadath (male youth)—though biologically male, was not completely a "man" in the social and cultural sense; and his intermediate status was symbolized by the lack of the most visible of male sex characteristics: a beard. The cultural importance of beards and/or moustaches in the early Ottoman Arab East is attested by both the European travel literature and the indigenous literature. The beard or moustache was a symbol of male honor, something one swore by or insulted. Slaves were expected not to wear a beard, and in early Ottoman Egypt at least, the phrase "he let his beard grow" (arkhā liḥyatahu) was a standard way of designating a master's emancipation of his slave.[63] The appearance of a beard on the cheeks of a youth was frequently celebrated in verse, and was often used in the biographical literature as an age marker, the third stage, after tamyīz (i.e., the age of discernment—traditionally set at around seven) and bulūgh (puberty). The association of the beard or moustache with male virility is a circum-Mediterranean trait, and is clearly brought out in the dream analysis of 'Abd al-Ghanī al-Nābulusī:

> The beard in a dream means for the man wealth and honor, so if he sees it
> grow in length to an agreeable, handsome, not immoderate extent, he will

encounter honor, prestige, beauty, money, power, and comfort . . . He who sees it [the beard] sparse to an ugly extent, his prestige and standing among people will diminish.

By comparison:

The penis of a man is his reputation and honor among people, and an increase in its size indicates an increase in these . . . and he who sees that his penis is transformed into a vagina, his fortitude and strength will become impotence, weakness, feebleness, and submissiveness.

The symbolic equivalence of beard and penis is underlined in the following:

It is said that if a woman dreams that she has a penis or beard or wears the clothes of men, she will become impudent toward her husband.[64]

Corollary to the tacit association of coarse facial hair with masculinity was the relative feminization of the teenage boy whose beard was as yet absent or soft and incomplete. This feminization must have been enhanced by the fact that, in the urban centers at least, women's faces were normally veiled in public.

The feminization of male youths is apparent in pederastic courtship, which tended to follow the typical heterosexual pattern in societies in which premarital contact between unrelated men and women is not hindered by gender segregation and arranged marriages. The part of the pursuer was assumed by the man; that of the pursued by the boy. The latter would walk a tightrope between being considered haughty and arrogant (a frequent complaint in the love poetry of the period) and being "easy" or "cheap." It was apparently the latter sort of boys that the Damascene poet Abū al-Fatḥ al-Mālikī (d. 1567/8) frequented, to the detriment of his reputation.[65] Similarly, the Egyptian poet Ismāʿīl al-Khashshāb (d. 1815), who himself fell in love with a young scribe during the brief Napoleonic rule of Egypt, warned a friend who had become infatuated with a boy not to fall for a worn hackney (mubtadhal).[66] A boy's reputation for being "easy" would be an embarrassing liability in his older days, upon which opponents and detractors could pounce. In a defamatory poem, the Damascene Amīn al-Dīn Muḥammad al-Ṣāliḥī al-Hilālī (d. 1596) said of a rival:

. . . and who was in his youth a female camel, led to the worst of men and ridden.[67]

Though it was clearly held disreputable for the boy to display too much enthusiasm for his role as a coveted object, there are indications that many boys made the most of the interest shown in them by adult men. While they submitted to the sexual desires of men only at a peril to their reputation, they could hold a lover (or several lovers) suspended in hope, conceding a rendezvous or a kiss now and then, and playing admirers off against each other. Some boys clearly lorded it over their lovers, refusing to speak to them unless they composed a love poem, or asking them to prove their love by slitting a wrist or jumping into a moat.[68] A man could be taunted by other men if the boy he pursued ended up bestowing his favors upon another. The Yemeni poet Sha'bān al-Rūmī (d. 1736) was, for example, teased by an acquaintance when a handsome shopkeeper he loved moved store and started showing favor to another man called al-Iṣfahānī:

> O Sha'bān, we have noticed the dark-lashed, tender-handed [fellow] leave your quarter so as not to see you, and treat his eyes with Iṣfahānī [kohl] (al-Iṣfahānī).[69]

The family of the boy was expected to shield him from the sexual interests of older men, and were liable to be dishonored if they failed to do so. This is underlined in the following anonymous couplet purporting to address a handsome boy:

> Your beauty has deprived the gazelle of his attributes, and all beauty has
> gathered in you.
> You have his neck, eyes, and shyness, but as to the [cuckold's] horns, they
> are your father's.[70]

The Meccan jurist Ibn Ḥajar al-Haytamī (d. 1566) asserted that fornication was not only a transgression of the law of God but could also be seen as a crime against other persons, since it reflected dishonorably on the relatives of the passive-receptive party—the woman or the sodomized (al-malūṭ bihi).[71] The Egyptian scholar Ibn al-Wakīl al-Mallawī (d. ca. 1719) related with unconcealed sympathy a number of pederastic love stories that unfolded in Egypt in his own time. A recurrent feature of these stories is the intervention of fathers to prevent the adult lovers from frequenting their sons.[72] A mother in sixteenth-century Aleppo ended her son's apprenticeship with a tailor when she learned that the master had developed a liking for him, and one of the students of the Aleppine scholar Raḍī al-Dīn ibn al-Ḥanbalī (d. 1563) was evicted from the doorsteps of his beloved's home by the boy's father.[73] Other parents seem to have been willing to look the other way, especially if the suitor came from a socioeconomic class far above their own. The attention of a rich notable would often translate itself into concrete material benefits for both the boy and his parents. The Damascene judge Aḥmad al-Shuwaykī (d. 1598) was, according to a colleague, in the habit of paying regular subsidies to the youths he courted, as well as conferring certain "worldly benefits" upon their parents.[74]

The outlined pattern of pederastic courtship could suggest that boys functioned as ersatz women, and thus at first sight lend support to the oft-heard idea that (supposedly) widespread "homosexuality" in the Arab world is caused by the segregation of women. Men did not, however, simply turn to boys because of the unavailability of women. There are indeed a few remarks in the biographical literature that linked a person's interest in boys with his unmarried status. For example, the aforementioned biographer Ḥasan al-Būrīnī said of the Damascene poet Aḥmad al-'Ināyātī (d. 1606) that "he did not marry throughout his long life, and did not incline toward a female beloved (khalīlah) who would fortify him (tuḥṣinahu) against having a male beloved (khalīl)."[75] Būrīnī's use of the term tuḥṣinahu reflects the assumption that marriage could provide protection (iḥṣān—a widely used synonym for marriage) against the temptation to have paramours (male or female). However, it is far from clear that Būrīnī believed that 'Ināyātī was unable to marry, and thus turned to boys only as an alternative sexual outlet. It is more likely that 'Ināyātī's unmarried status was voluntary, and that Būrīnī believed that he might have gotten involved in fewer love affairs with boys had he married. The case of Māmāyah al-Rūmī lends support to the idea that sexual interest in boys was not necessarily the effect of the segregation—and hence "unavailability"—of women, but could just as well be the result of a considered decision to remain unmarried. In a long poem in his *Dīwān*, he described how he had been hounded into divorcing his wife by his mother-in-law and her family. He concluded the poem by expressing his resolve to avoid women and to resort to beardless boys when lust got the better of him.[76] In any case, even if it was widely believed that most unmarried men would be interested in boys (either because they constituted an alternative sexual outlet for unmarried men, or because men who chose to remain unmarried were not sufficiently interested in women), this does not show that it was also believed that most of those who were interested in boys were unmarried. Many of those who courted boys were married, and this was not depicted by the sources as in any way remarkable or strange. At most, the husband's pederastic escapades were said to have led to domestic discord because of resentment and jealousy on the part of the wife.[77] What little evidence we have of marital norms in the premodern Middle East suggests that marriage was nearly universal and was, moreover, usually entered into at a relatively early age, often at the onset of puberty.[78] The Egyptian scholar and historian 'Abd al-Raḥmān al-Jabartī (d. 1825/6), for example, was married at the age of fourteen, while his grandfather died at the age of sixteen, one month after his wife had given birth.[79] To be sure, not all scholars married that early, and some remained unmarried all their lives, but this was unusual enough to be considered noteworthy in the biographical notices dedicated to them. It is possible that early marriage was the prerogative of the wealthier segment of the population, but the abundant evidence we have concerning pederasty in the premodern Arab East relates primarily to this social class, so that the purported explanation of widespread "homosexuality" in terms of the unavailability of women still fails to gain any credence. It is also worth mentioning that there is evidence for the availability of female prostitutes in the major Arab cities during the centuries under consideration.[80] It is thus far from clear that there were no heterosexual outlets even for the minority of adult men who were unmarried. There may indeed be some connection between gender segregation and widespread pederasty in the premodern Middle East. However, crude notions of blocked heterosexual libido being diverted toward boys fail to do justice to the complexity of the connection. Gender segregation in public, and arranged marriages, did not prevent women from being sexually available to adult men, but they may have severely restricted the possibilities for heterosexual courtship. One could suppose that courting fulfils certain emotional (rather than sexual) needs on the part of the courter, such as the thrill of fancying someone who is not straightforwardly available for sexual intercourse (in contrast to wives and prostitutes), the challenge of trying to win the favor of that someone, and the satisfaction of succeeding. In the premodern Middle East such needs could most easily be met by courting boys, not women.[81] An explanation along these lines was offered by the French traveler Volney, who visited Egypt in the 1780s. Speaking of the Mamluk elite of that country, he wrote: "They are, above all, addicted to that abominable wickedness which was at all times the vice of the Greeks . . . It is difficult to account for this taste, when we consider that they all have women, unless we suppose they seek in one sex that poignancy of refusal which they do not permit the other."[82]

It is not a straightforward affair to determine the age during which a male youth was considered to be sexually attractive to adult men. The relevant terms, such as *amrad* or *ghulām*, tend to be impressionistic and somewhat loosely employed in the sources. For example, the term *amrad* (beardless boy) could be used to refer to prepubescent, completely smooth-cheeked boys, as opposed to adolescent, downy-cheeked youths, but it could also refer to all youths who did not yet have a fully developed beard, and hence to youths who were as old as twenty or twenty-one. According to a saying attributed to the first Umayyad Caliph Mu'āwiyah (d. 680) and quoted in an eighteenth-century dictionary:

> I was beardless for twenty years, fully bearded for twenty years, I plucked gray hairs from it for twenty years, and dyed it for twenty years.[83]

If the upper age limit was physical maturity at around twenty, the lower age limit for the sexual interest of the pederasts seems to have been the recognized transition from childhood to youth, at the age of seven or eight. The weight of the available evidence tends to support the conclusion that the pederasts' lust tended to be directed at boys whose age fell within this interval, and that the boy's attractiveness was usually supposed to peak around halfway through, at fourteen or fifteen. The Egyptian Yūsuf al-Shirbīnī, writing in the late seventeenth century, opined that a boy's attractiveness peaks at fifteen, declines after the age of eighteen, and disappears fully at twenty, by which time he will be fully hirsute: "So infatuation and passionate love is properly directed only at those of lithesome figure and sweet smile from those who are in their tens (*awlād al-'ashr*)."[84] Similarly, an anonymous poem cited by the Damascene chronicler Ibn Kannān al-Ṣāliḥī (d. 1740) on the natural ages of man associated the "son of ten" (*ibn al-'ashr*—presumably in the sense of "in his tens" rather than "exactly ten years old") with incomparable beauty, the "son of twenty" with the heedless pursuit of pleasure, the "son of thirty" with the apogee of strength, etc.[85] In love poetry and rhymed prose, the age of the beloved was often said to be fourteen, probably a standard rhetorical device engendered by the conventional comparison of the face of the beloved with the moon, which reaches its apogee around the fourteenth of each month of the Muslim lunar calendar.[86] However, there is independent evidence from European travel accounts that catamites were "likely of twelve, or fourteene years old, some of them not above nine, or ten."[87] Much depended, however, on the eye of the beholder as well as the individual rate of maturation. As will be seen in the next chapter, the comparison of the respective charms of beardless and downy-cheeked youths was a conventional topic in the belles-lettres of the period. Many poets expressed the opinion that a boy ceased to be attractive already at the appearance of beard-down (*'idhār*) on his cheeks, which would imply a somewhat lower upper age limit. The Damascene scholar and biographer Muḥammad Khalīl al-Murādī (d. 1791) seems to have had enough beard-down by the age of fourteen to merit a poem celebrating the occasion. A grandson of 'Abd al-Ghanī al-Nābulusī was seventeen, and a son of the Iraqi scholar Maḥmūd al-Alūsī eighteen, when they elicited similar poems.[88] The prominent Syrian mystic Muḥammad ibn 'Irāq (d. 1526) veiled his son 'Alī between the age of eight and sixteen, "to keep people from being enchanted by him," suggesting that by the latter age his features were deemed by the father to be developed enough to make him unattractive to other men.[89] On the other hand, the chronicler Ibn Ayyūb al-Anṣārī recorded the death of a seventeen-year-old Damascene youth who left behind a host of lamenting male admirers.[90] The Iraqi poet Qāsim al-Rāmī (d. 1772/3) traced in verse the development of a boy from the age of ten, when he "became settled in the sanctuary of beauty," to the age of sixteen, when he (disreputably) started to pluck the hairs from his cheeks.[91] Plucking beard-down from the face seems to have signaled, in a too direct and indiscreet manner, that the boy actually enjoyed being coveted by men, and was in no hurry to become a bearded adult. To that extent, it was associated with the behavior of boy prostitutes or effeminate males. The above-mentioned Yūsuf al-Shirbīnī thus stated that the term *natīf* (literally "plucked") was used of the beardless boy who, "if his beard starts to grow, and he enjoys being effeminate (*al-khināth*) or—God forbid—he has *ubnah*, will constantly shave his beard and beautify himself for the libertine (*fāsiq*) . . . for souls incline toward the beardless boy as long as his cheeks are clear."[92]

Interestingly, an adolescent youth was himself expected to be sexually attracted to women and it seems to have been a common ploy of those desirous of a youth to adopt a woman as bait.[93] It is also possible that adolescent youths themselves regularly courted younger, prepubescent boys. "Serial" relationships (*al-'ishq al-musalsal*), in which the beloved of one man is himself the lover of a woman or boy, are not unknown to the Arabic lore on profane love.[94] According to a couplet by the Damascene Ibrāhīm al-Su'ālātī (d. 1684):

> The beloved has fallen in love with a gazelle like himself, and is afflicted by
> 　　amorous rapture.
> He was a beloved and is now a lover, and thus love has passed its judgment
> 　　[both] for and against him.[95]

The "male" sexual potential of an adolescent youth was not confined to intercourse with women or younger boys. Behind closed doors, one could not tell for certain whether the man or the boy had been the active partner, and the uncertainty could be exploited in the bawdy and defamatory literature, as shown by the previously mentioned anecdote involving a man and a boy each insisting that they had been the active partner. An anonymous line of poetry spelled out this latent uncertainty:

> He who is civil in *liwāṭ* is not assumed to involve a third party, and if he is
> 　　alone with his boy, only God knows who does the fucking.[96]

Such poems and anecdotes are clearly "parasitical" in the sense that they consciously break with the dominant, stereotypical representation of pederastic relationships. Yet they do suggest that these dominant depictions were not always adequate to the actual behavior of individuals, and that there was some awareness of this at the time. Not only does there exist the odd indication that boys could sometimes assume the "active" role, but there are also indications that some men had sex with other adult men. Thus the effeminate adult men portrayed in the bawdy literature do not seem to have had particular difficulties in finding other adult men willing to have sex with them. It is also likely that some pederastic relationships continued long after the "passive" partner could reasonably be passed off as a "boy." Yūsuf al-Shirbīnī claimed that this was precisely what some heretical Egyptian dervishes tended to do, and saw therein a confirmation of their rustic, unrefined character.[97] It is doubtful whether such men were thought to actually prefer adult men to boys or women. It seems more likely that the assumption was that they were helping themselves to whatever orifice happened to be at hand. The assumption that rough and masculine men will behave in this manner is one that is still very much alive, as evinced by the stereotype that contemporary Latin American or Arab men, though they may actually prefer to have sex with women, will readily resort to effeminate men or Western homosexual tourists as the second-best thing.[98] The tendency to bugger men of all ages was also denounced by the above-mentioned Iraqi scholar Muḥammad Amīn al-'Umarī as "an abomination (faḥishah) which is not perpetrated except by someone with a coarse character and a malicious soul."[99]

The social context of pederasty

The homosexuality represented in the texts of the early Ottoman period was, on the whole, of the pederastic, "transgenerational" or "age-structured" type well known from classical Greece and Rome. It is not that this was the only type that was thought to exist; nor was it the only type that was acceptable—it was not acceptable to many—but it was the type that was conceived as being usual. Even those religious scholars who inveighed the most strongly against sodomy and its antecedents warned against gazing at *boys*, against being alone with a *boy* in a private place, against composing love poetry of *boys*, and so on. That an adult man who was not a *ma'būn* or *mukhannath* should actually prefer fully developed adult men to teenage boys is an idea that seems not to have been seriously entertained.

Rather than desiring and having intercourse with each other, pederasts competed and sometimes fought amongst themselves for boys. The Damascene poet Darwīsh al-Ṭālawī (d. 1606) alluded in verse to one such conflict between a chief judge of Damascus and a footman (çuhadār), and was himself deprived of a young, handsome slave whom he loved by the Druze Emir of Mt. Lebanon, Fakhr al-Dīn al-Ma'nī (d. 1635), while passing through the city of Sidon.[100] The above-mentioned Muṣṭafā 'Alī, in his description of Egypt in 1599, noted that the cavalrymen there often quarreled amongst themselves, usually about boys or horses—this in contrast to soldiers in the Turkish regions of the Empire, among whom he claimed "nobody covets another person's possessions or horse or boy."[101]

In the modern West, sexual relations between men tend to be perceived as essentially relations between two persons of the same gender who, because of a psychological orientation or the unavailability of members of the opposite sex, have intercourse with one another. Such liaisons are therefore thought to be especially common in all-male environments: the military, boarding schools, saunas, monasteries, prisons, etc. In the early Ottoman Arab East, liwāṭ was usually thought to involve a man and a boy, and it thus tended to be associated, at least in the popular imagination, with social contexts in which the mixing of generations was especially marked. This is not to say that liwāṭ was, or was believed to be, confined to such contexts. The generations were not segregated in the way the genders were, and the opportunities for pederastic courtship were correspondingly diffuse. However, it seems clear that certain social environments were thought to be especially suspect (or promising) precisely to the extent that, in them, the mixing of men and boys was particularly intense, or could occur hidden from the public eye. This applies first and foremost to the following realms: education; mystic orders; slavery and servitude; coffeehouses and public baths.

Notes

1   Ibn Kannān, *al-Ḥawādith al-yawmiyyah*, 51–52.
2   Nābulusī, *Taʾṭīr al-anām*, 2:210 (*liwāṭ*) and 2:294 (*nikāḥ*); see also Munāwī, *al-Fuyūḍāt al-ilāhiyyah*, fol. 70b–71a.
3   Muḥibbī, *Nafḥat al-rayḥānah*, 1:395–96; Muḥibbī, *Khulāṣat al-athar*, 1:47.
4   Muḥibbī, *Nafḥat al-rayḥānah*, 4:607–8.
5   Vanggaard, *Phallos*, ch. 6.
6   al-Alūsī, *Rūḥ al-maʾānī*, 8:152.
7   al-Baḥrānī, *al-Burhān*, 2:348, 4:233.
8   For example, al-Manīnī, *al-Fatḥ al-wahbī*, 1:323, 325; al-Isḥāqī, *Akhbār al-uwal*, 125; the two quotations are from poems cited in al-Manīnī, *al-Fatḥ al-wahbī*, 1:156, and in al-ʾĀmilī, Bahāʾ al-Dīn, *al-Kashkūl*, 1:319.
9   I have adopted the term "polarizing" from Halperin's discussion of the classical Greek attitude toward sexual intercourse (Halperin, *One Hundred Years of Homosexuality*, 30).
10   This seems to me to be the tendency of many of the contributions to Schmitt and Sofer, eds., *Sexuality and Eroticism among Males in Muslim Societies*. For another criticism of the simplistic juxtaposition of "Western" and "Arab" attitudes, see Massad, "Re-Orienting Desire," 363.
11   Ibn Ayyūb, *al-Rawḍ al-ʾāṭir*, 84; Māmāyah al-Rūmī, *Rawḍat al-mushtāq*, fol. 191a. For another example of sexual imagery being used in a case of rivalry for position, see Ṭalawī, *Sāniḥāt dumā al-qaṣr*, 1:217–19.
12   For recent examples, see Abu Khalil, "A Note on the Study of Homosexuality in the Arab/Islamic Civilization"; Hopwood, *Sexual Encounters in the Middle East*, 176.
13   The strict juridical concept of *liwāṭ* will be discussed in chapter 3.
14   Jazāʾirī, *Zahr al-rabīʾ*, 31.
15   al-Ḥurr al-ʾĀmilī, *Wasāʾil al-shīʾah*, 14:248ff. (tradition 12). The term *ityān*, which I have rendered as "carnal penetration of," clearly connotes assuming the active-insertive role in sexual intercourse, and passive forms of the word are regularly used to denote the assumption of the passive-receptive role.
16   See *Dīwān khidmat al-usṭā ʿUthmān*. On *lūṭīs* who are attracted to boys: 12, 26–27; on *bitāʾ al-ṣighār*: 7, 37.
17   Shirbīnī, *Hazz al-quḥūf*, 94.; Murādī, *Silk al-durar*, 2:206.
18   Khafājī, *Rayḥānat al-alibbā*, 1:431–32.
19   al-ʾUmarī, ʿUthmān, *al-Rawḍ al-naḍir*, 1:62.
20   al-ʾUmarī, Muḥammad Amīn, *Manhal al-awliyāʾ*, 1:228.
21   The image of the people of Sodom in the Qurʾanic commentaries will be discussed in chapter 3.
22   Saffārīnī, *Qarʾ al-siyāṭ*, fol. 10b. Again, the term *ityān* clearly indicates assuming the insertive role.
23   Bājūrī, *Ḥāshiyah*, 2:240.
24   Jazarī, *Dīwān*, fol. 72a.
25   Irwin, *The Arabian Nights: A Companion*, 169.
26   Compare Tīfāshī, *Nuzhat al-albāb*, 141 (on the helpful tools of the pederast) with 144–45 (on the visible characteristics of boy prostitutes). Incidentally, Irwin's references to hairy ankles, thin legs, and long robes are also inaccurate. Tīfāshī wrote that the boy prostitutes usually remove the hair from their legs and wear short robes that reveal their ankles. It is only those who do not shave their legs, or who have thin legs, who try to conceal this by wearing long robes.
27   E. Rowson makes a similar point in "The Categorization of Gender and Sexual Irregularity in Medieval Arabic Vice Lists," as does T. Bauer, in *Liebe und Liebesdichtung*, 166.
28   For example, *liwāṭ* is called *al-dāʾ al-ladhī lā dawāʾ lahu* in a tradition cited in Baḥrānī, *al-Burhān*, 2:348; but the very same tradition goes on to state: *fa-ayy dāʾ adwaʾ* [variant: *aʾdā*]

min al-bukhl? Muḥammad al-Saffārīnī calls *liwāṭ* a *dā'* in his short tract *Qarʾ al-siyāṭ* (fol. 10b), which relies heavily on *al-Dāʾ wa al-dawāʾ* by Ibn Qayyim al-Jawziyyah (d. 1350). However, the latter work clearly uses the term *dāʾ* in a broad, nonmedical sense, calling *jahl* the fundamental *dāʾ*, and repentance (*al-tawbah*) the most important antidote.

29   Medieval Latin translations of Avicenna's *Canon* (book 3, chapter 20) refer to *alu-buati* (or *aluminati* or *alguagi*). Joan Cadden takes these to be Latinizations of the Arabic *al-liwāṭ* ("Western Medicine and Natural Philosophy," 64). They are in fact Latinizations of the Arabic *al-ubnah*. See Ibn Sīnā, *al-Qānūn fī al-ṭibb*, 3:228–29. See also the discussion of this passage in Nathan, "Medieval Arabic Medical Views on Male Homosexuality." Nathan, however, insists on using the unhelpful term "homosexual" to translate the Arabic term *maʾbūn*, even though, as he himself admits, the latter term only applied to the passive partner.

30   Ibn Ayyūb, *al-Rawḍ al-ʾāṭir*, 23; Ibn Kannān, *al-Ḥawādith al-yawmiyyah*, 38; al-Makkī al-Mūsawī, *Nuzhat al-jalīs*, 1:242; Tietze, *Mustafa ʿAli's Description of Egypt*, 60.

31   *Nuzhat al-udabāʾ*, MS I, 95a; MS II, 208a. This work is sometimes attributed to a certain ʿUmar al-Halabī, who seems to have flourished in the seventeenth century. See Brockelmann, *Geschichte der arabischen Literatur*, Supplement, 2:414; and Arberry, *A Second Supplementary Hand-List*, no. 128.

32   *Dīwān khidmat al-usṭā ʿUthmān*, 13, 31.

33   Māmāyah al-Rūmī, *Rawḍat al-mushtāq*, fol. 192b–193a.

34   On Rāzī's diagnosis of *ubnah*, see Rosenthal, "Ar-Razi on the Hidden Illness." The Arabic text is reproduced in al-Tīfāshī, *Nuzhat al-albāb*, 302–8.

35   Anṭākī, *al-Nuzhah al-mubhijah*, 2:216; Shaʿrānī, *Mukhtaṣar*, 55; Qalyūbī, *al-Tadhkirah*, 58. See also Jazāʾirī, *Zahr al-rabīʿ*, 511; Isḥāqī, *Akhbār al-uwal*, 48; Shaʿrānī, *Laṭāʾif al-minan*, 2:211.

36   This last remedy is also mentioned in the discussions of Shaʿrānī, Qalyūbī, and Jazāʾirī. The idea goes back at least to Pliny the Elder (d. 79), see Williams, *Roman Homosexuality*, 180–81. A variant also appears in the medieval Western medical tradition. Albertus Magnus (d. 1280) suggested burnt and ground fur from the neck of *alzabo* (Arabic *al-ḍab'*) as an effective cure for "sodomy." As pointed out by J. Boswell, Albertus's source was probably a Latin translation or adaptation of an earlier Arabic medical or zoological work (*Christianity, Social Tolerance, and Homosexuality*, 316–17). Apparently, the Arabic *ubnah*, which refers to a condition of the passive partner, became role-unspecified *sodomia* in Latin.

37   Isḥāqī, *Akhbār al-uwal*, 47; Ibn Nujaym, *al-Baḥr al-rāʾiq*, 5:50; Ibn ʿĀbidīn, *Radd al-muḥtār*, 3:201–2.

38   Buhūtī, *Sharḥ muntahā al-irādāt*, 3:358; a similar ruling is given in Ibn Ḥajar, *al-Fatāwā al-kubrā al-fiqhiyyah*, 4: 201.

39   Ibn Ayyūb, *al-Rawḍ al-ʾaṭir*, 101; al-Isḥāqī, *Akhbār al-uwal*, 47.

40   *Nuzhat al-udabāʾ*, MS I, fol. 93b–97a; MS II, fol. 208a–209a (ch. II: *fī al-mustaṭrab min aḥādīth al-maʿābīn wa al-mukhannathīn*); Tīfāshī, *Nuzhat al-albāb*, 249–308 (ch. 12: *fī al-khināth wa al-mukhannathīn*); Isḥāqī, *Akhbār al-uwal*, 44–48.

41   al-Khāl, *Dīwān*, fol. 35b. The term *ʿilq* is a colloquial term with the same meaning as *mukhannath* or *maʾbūn*. This is explicitly stated in Darbīr, *al-Sharḥ al-jalī*, 230. See also Hinds and Badawi, *A Dictionary of Egyptian Arabic*, 593, and *Dīwān khidmat al-usṭā ʿUthmān*, 37: "No one washes his arse except the *ʿilq* boy so that he will be loved by *bitāʾ al-Ḥighār*."

42   Ibn Ayyūb, *al-Rawḍ al-ʾāṭir*, 79–80; Khafājī, *Rayḥānat al-alibbā*, 2:125; Muḥibbī, *Khulāṣat al-athar*, 1:47; al-ʾUmarī, *ʿUthmān, al-Rawḍ al-naḍir*, 68. The same insult (*euruprôktos*) was used in classical Greece, see Dover, *Greek Homosexuality*, 140; Thornton, *Eros*, 110.

43   Winter, *Egyptian Society under Ottoman Rule*, 9–10 (citing the chronicle of Ibn Iyyās), 230 (citing the chronicle of Aḥmad Çelebī).

44   Būrīnī, *Tarājim al-aʿyān*, 2:280; Jabartī, *ʿAjāʾib al-āthār*, 1:413.

45   Tietze, *Mustafa ʿAli's Description of Egypt*, 51–54.

46 Ibn Ayyūb, *al-Rawḍ al-ʾāṭir*, 87–88; Māmāyah al-Rūmī, *Rawḍat al-mushtāq*, fol. 219b. Majnūn and Laylah and Kuthayyir and ʿAzzah are legendary (male/female) love couples from the early Islamic period.

47 Dardīr, *al-Sharḥ al-kabīr*, 4:339.

48 Ḥaṣkafī, *al-Durr al-muntaqā*, 1:609–10.

49 See the anecdotes in Isḥāqī, *Akhbār al-uwal*, 113–16; and Tīfāshī, *Nuzhat al-albāb*, 99–126.

50 Bullough, *Sexual Variance in Society and History*, 232; Irwin, *The Arabian Nights*, 175. Both works cite *The Arabian Nights*.

51 Shaykhzāde, *Majmaʾ al-anhur*, 1:595–96; Ibn Nujaym, *al-Baḥr al-rāʾiq*, 5:17–18.

52 Gilmore, "Introduction: The Shame of Dishonour," 9.

53 ʿĀmilī, Bahāʾ al-Dīn, *al-Kashkūl*, 1:361; Jazāʾirī, *Zahr al-rabīʾ*, 45.

54 For example, Buhūtī, *Sharḥ muntahā al-irādāt*, 3:345: "*wa lūṭī fāʾil wa mafʿūl bihi . . .*"

55 Būrīnī, *Tarājim al-aʿyān*, 1:252.

56 Būrīnī, *Tarājim al-aʿyān*, 2:73–74. For another independent allusion to this incident, see Ibn Ayyūb, *al-Rawḍ al-ʾāṭir*, 30.

57 Nābulusī, *Taʿṭīr al-anām*, 2:210 (*liwāṭ*), 236–38 (*mujāmaʿah*), 294 (*nikāḥ*). Compare the strikingly similar interpretations of Artemidorus (2nd century AD), analyzed in Foucault, *The History of Sexuality*, 3:4–36, and Winkler, *The Constraints of Desire*, 17–44. On this theme, see also Oberhelman, "Hierarchies of Gender, Ideology, and Power in Medieval Greek and Arabic Dream Literature."

58 *Nuzhat al-udabāʾ*, MS I, fol. 95a; MS II, fol. 208a–b.

59 This is one of the main points in Bourdieu, *The Logic of Practice*; see especially "The Social Uses of Kinship," 162–99.

60 Pitt-Rivers, *The Fate of Shechem*, 16.

61 Gilmore, "Introduction: The Shame of Dishonour," 10–11 (speaking of contemporary Mediterranean culture in general).

62 Nābulusī, *Taʿṭīr al-anām*, 1:223–27 (*dhakar insān*), 19 (*unthayān*), 192 (*khaṣī*). See also Munāwī, *al-Fuyūḍāt al-ilāhiyyah*, fol. 68b–69a. For a similar observation concerning the contemporary Mediterranean area, see Pitt-Rivers, *The Fate of Shechem*, 22.

63 For example, Jabartī, *ʿAjāʾib al-āthār*, 1:100, 111; see also Lane, *An Account of the Manners and Customs of the Modern Egyptians*, 37, 561 (n. 4); and Volney, *Travels through Syria and Egypt*, 1:118.

64 Nābulusī, *Taʿṭīr al-anām*, 2:206–8 (*liḥya*), 1:223–27 (*dhakar insān*). See also Munāwī, *al-Fuyūḍāt al-ilāhiyyah*, fol. 66b (*al-ṭūl fī al-liḥyah*) and fol. 68 (*kibr al-dhakar wa ṭūluhu*). On the symbolic importance of the beard or moustache in the Mediterranean area, see Gilmore, *Manhood in the Making*, 31, 47 (Italy and Greece); and Bourdieu, *The Logic of Practice*, 211 (the Kabyle of Algeria).

65 Ibn al-Ḥanbalī, *Durr al-ḥabab*, 2:145; Ghazzī, *al-Kawākib al-sāʾirah*, 3:23.

66 Jabartī, *ʿAjāʾib al-āthār*, 2:217. For al-Khashshāb's love of the scribe, see ibid, 4:238–41.

67 Muḥibbī, *Khulāṣat al-athar*, 4:35–36; Muḥibbī, *Nafḥat al-rayḥānah*, 1:380.

68 The theme will be dealt with at greater length in the following chapter.

69 Shawkānī, *al-Badr al-ṭāliʿ*, 1:281–82 (the editor's footnote, quoting an unpublished biographical dictionary of eighteenth-century Yemeni poets).

70 Darbīr, *al-Sharḥ al-jalī*, 220.

71 Ibn Ḥajar al-Haytamī, *al-Fatāwā al-kubrā al-fiqhiyyah*, 4:359.

72 Ibn al-Wakīl al-Mallawī, *Bughyat al-musāmir*, fol. 131b–133a.

73 Ibn al-Ḥanbalī, *Durr al-ḥabab*, 1:688–89, 2:159.

74 Ibn Ayyūib al-Anṣārī, *al-Rawḍ al-ʾāṭir*, 23.

75 Būrīnī, *Tarājim al-aʿyān*, 1:108. For another example, see Ghazzī, *Lutf al-samar*, 2:581–82.

76 Māmāyah, al-Rūmī, *Rawḍat al-mushtāq*, fol. 331b–334a.

77 ʿUrḍī, *Maʿādin al-dhahab*, 244–45; Ibn al-Ḥanbalī, *Durr al-ḥabab*, 1:687–93; al-Budayrī al-Ḥallāq, *Ḥawādith Dimashq al-yawmiyyah*, 185.

78 Lane, *An Account of the Manners and Customs of the Modern Egyptians*, 159–60; Russell, *The Natural History of Aleppo*, 1:281–82; Volney, *Travels through Syria and Egypt*, 2:485–86; Marcus, *The Middle-East on the Eve of Modernity*, 196.

79 Jabartī, *'Ajā'ib al-āthār*, 1:67, 361.

80 Pitts, *A Faithful Account*, 98–100; Burckhardt, *Travels in Arabia*, 1:364; Jabartī, *'Aja'ib al-āthār*, 1:144, 3:219; al-Budayarī al-Ḥallāq, *Ḥawādith Dimashq al-yawmiyyah*, 39, 57, 92, 112, 134; al-Suwaydī 'Abdallah, *al-Nafḥah al-miskiyyah*, fol. 95a.

81 For related remarks on courtship of boys in ancient Greece, see Cohen, *Law, Sexuality, and Society*, 185–87.

82 Volney, *Travels through Syria and Egypt*, 1:185.

83 Zabīdī, *Tāj al-'arūs*, 9:166 (m-r-d).

84 Shirbīnī, *Hazz al-quḥūf*, 94. This is strikingly similar to the pre-Meiji Japanese views analyzed in Pflugfelder, *Cartographies of Desire*, 31.

85 Ibn Kannān, *al-Ḥawādith al-yawmiyyah*, 417.

86 Būrīnī, *Tarājim al-a'yān*, 2:241; Muḥibbī, *Nafḥat al-rayḥānah*, 1:412; Khafājī, *Rayḥānat al-alibbā*, 1:247. An eighteenth-century Turkish work of bawdy comedy also states that for pederasts the ideal age of boys is fourteen (see Schmidt, "Sünbülzāde," 24).

87 Blount, *A Voyage into the Levant*, 14.

88 Murādī, *Silk al-durar*, 1:247; Ghazzī, *al-Wird al-unsī*, fol. 110b–111a; al-Alūsī, Maḥmūd Shukrī, *al-Misk al-adhfar*, 98–99. In these cases, the last hemistich of the poems contains the date of composition in letter-code. Together with the date of birth, they allow the calculation of the age of the youth at the time.

89 Ibn al-Ḥanbalī, *Durr al-ḥabab*, 1:1109. Ibn al-Ḥanbalī knew the son in question personally.

90 Ibn Ayyūb, *Nuzhat al-khāṭir*, 2:204.

91 al-'Umarī, 'Uthmān, *al-Rawḍ al-naḍir*, 2:270–73.

92 Shirbīnī, *Hazz al-quḥūf*, 233.

93 Tīfāshī, *Nuzhat al-albāb*, 198; for a concrete example, see Ibn Kannān, *al-Ḥawādith al-yawmiyyah*, 180.

94 Antākī, *Tazyīn al-aswāq*, 2:84; the above-mentioned poem of Qāsim al-Rāmī also stated that the handsome boy himself fell in love, when he was fourteen.

95 Muḥibbī, *Nafḥat al-rayḥānah*, 1:301.

96 al-'Āmilī, Bahā' al-Dīn, *al-Kashkūl*, 1:361; Jazā'irī, *Zahr al-rabī'*, 287.

97 Shirbīnī, *Hazz al-quḥūf*, 94.

98 This is a recurrent theme in Schmitt and Sofer, eds., *Sexuality and Eroticism among Males in Muslim Societies*. For a criticism of the "blind phallus" stereotype that infects some of the contributions to that work, see Murray, *Homosexualities*, 266–72.

99 al-'Umarī, Muḥammad Amīn, *Manhal al-awliyā'*, 1:228.

100 Būrīnī, *Tarājim al-a'yān*, 1:87; Khafājī, *Rayḥānat al-alibbā*, 1:62. For another example, see Ibn Kannān, *al-Ḥawādith al-yawmiyyah*, 38.

101 Tietze, *Mustafa 'Ali's Description of Egypt*, 54.

Chapter 6

Abū Muḥammad ʿAlī ibn Ḥazm al-Andalusī

A BOOK CONTAINING THE *RISĀLA* KNOWN AS THE DOVE'S NECK-RING ABOUT LOVE AND LOVERS
(1022, 1931 edition)

THERE IS A GOOD DEAL OF DISPUTE among people about the *nature of love*, and there is much lengthy discussion. What I believe myself is that it is a *reunion of parts of the souls, separated in this creation (world), within their original higher element*, not according to what Muḥammad b. Dāwūd, may God have mercy on him, said, basing himself upon (the views of) some philosophers that: "Spirits are divided spheres" but along the line of the resemblance of their (motive) forces in the (*firm*) *abode of their higher world* and their mutual approximation to the form of their make-up. We well know that the secret of commingling and estrangement in creation (things created) is nothing but attraction or repulsion; and so one kind zealously yearns for one of its kind, and like dwells with its like, and the resemblance of forms has a psychological action and an evident influence: the mutual repulsion of opposites and mutual accord of likes, and yearning between things mutually similar, all this is found among us (in this world). How much more is it true of the *soul* whose world is a pure, ethereal world and its essence is the essence of a straight, well-balanced lance; it is basically shaped to take on mutual agreement, and inclination, and sympathy, and aversion, and passionate desire and avoidance: all this is known in our day in (the various) circumstances as man fluctuates between them and dwells in them; and God, Most High and Exalted, says: "He it is who created you *from one soul*, and made therefrom its mate to dwell therewith," and as the cause of (this) dwelling He made the fact that she is made of him. If the cause of love were the beauty of bodily form it would be necessary (to find) that something more defective in form would not find approval—but we find many people who prefer something worse (inferior), and though they know something better than that, yet they find for their heart no swerving from it—and were it on account of mutual agreement of character then man would not fall in love with someone who does not help him or does not agree with him. We know, then, that it is something within the soul *itself*: and maybe love is caused by certain causes and such a love passes away when its cause passes away; so that if someone loves you on account of something he will turn away from you when that something passes away. And on that subject I say:

> (*Ṭawīl*)
> My affection for you is permanent in accordance with its *being*:
> It attains its utmost limit, and (then) does not decrease in any way, nor
>   increase;
> There is no cause for it except *will*,
> And there is no other cause but this that anyone could know;
> Whenever we find a thing to be its own cause
> Such an existence does not pass away in all eternity:
> And if we do find in something to have its cause in something different
>   from it,
> The coming to naught of that thing will be caused by our being bereft of
>   that to which it owed its existence!

And what corroborates this saying is our knowing that there are *various kinds of love*. The noblest of these is the love of those who mutually love each other in God, Most High and Exalted, either for the sake of zeal in work, or harmony in the basic laws of a sect or creed, or for the sake of the nobility of knowledge which is granted to man. Then comes love of blood relatives, and love of intimate friendship, and sharing of things desired, and love of companionship and knowledge, and love because of a virtue attributed by man to his neighbor, and love on account of coveting the beloved's high rank, and love of those who love each other because the secrecy with which they clandestinely meet obliges them to cover it up, and love in order to obtain pleasure and satisfy (the object of) one's desires, and passionate love, the cause of which is nothing else but what we mentioned about the reunion of souls. And all these kinds cease upon the cessation of their causes, and grow in intensity if the causes grow intense, or grow less intense if the causes are diminishing; they are strengthened by their proximity, grow weaker when distant from them, except the *true, passionate love, emanating from the soul*; this is a love which never passes away except through death. Thus you will find a man who thinks he has (willingly) forgotten (his ardent desire), and has already reached the extreme old age, who, if you mention it to him, will remember it, and rejoice, and be rejuvenated, and his emotion comes back and his yearning desire becomes excited; and in the (other) kinds (of love) mentioned nothing happens like mental preoccupation, pain, constant obsession, change of innate character, mutation of firmly impressed nature, emaciation, and sighing, and other indications of deep sorrow as happens in passionate love.

Thus it is proved true that love is a spiritual approval and a mutual commingling of souls. Someone may say: "If this were so, then love between the two would be equal on either side, since the two parts would be joined in equal partnership in the reunion and their share in it would be equal." The answer to this is for us to say: "By my life, this is a true objection, but the soul of him who does not love the one who loves him is surrounded on all sides by some mysterious accidents; and by a veil of earthly nature which envelops it, so that it does not feel (come in sensory contact) with the part which was joined to it before its present dwelling; but if it were freed, the two would have an equal share in the reunion and in love. And the soul of the one (of the two) who loves is free, knows of the place where it was its companion in proximity, is asking for it, endeavoring to reach it, searching for it, ardently desirous of meeting it, gravitating toward it when it can—like magnet and iron. The force of the essence of the magnet which is bound up with the force of the essence of iron does not reach out, as a result of its make-up nor its purity towards iron, although it is of its kind and element, but rather the power of iron, on account of its strength, inclines toward its kind and is attracted to it: since motion always comes from the stronger: and the force of iron when left to itself is not prevented by an obstacle to desire what resembles it, and to giving itself up to it, hurrying toward it according to nature and necessity, not because of (free) choice and firm purpose. But while you take iron in your hand it will not be attracted, since there has not also come from it an overpowering force which would be more powerful than the strength of him who has picked it up. When the particles of iron are numerous they only act upon one another and check their kind from the desire to follow a small part of their forces far removed from it. But when the volume of the magnet is large and its force matches all the force of the volume of iron, the latter will come back to its usual nature (behavior). Similarly, fire in a flint; the latter does not overcome the force of fire by simple joining and approximation of its particles wherever they might be, except after rubbing and approaching the two pieces (of stone) by mutual pressure and friction; otherwise, fire will remain hidden in its inside, and will not start or become visible. And an argument in favor of this is also the fact that you will not find two persons who love each other except if there is between them an accord and agreement of natural qualities. This is absolutely necessary, even if it be in a small measure. And whenever the resemblance is greater the similarity (of species) increases and love becomes firmer. And if you look around you will see this plainly yourself, and this saying of the Prophet of God corroborates it: "Spirits are troops gathered: those who mutually recognize each other will unite (join in a friendly manner), and those who mutually disavow each other will disagree (take opposite stand)." And there also is a saying of a traditionist about one of the just: "Spirits of the believers mutually recognize each other." And it was this that saddened Hippocrates when an unintelligent man was described to him as loving him, and he was told about it, and said: "He surely would not love me, unless I resembled him in some of his characteristics." And Plato records that some king put him in jail unjustly, and he went on bringing proofs in favor of himself until he clearly showed his innocence, and the king knew that he was dealing unjustly with him. His wazīr, who had been delegated to bring Plato's message to the king, said to him: "O king, now it has become clear to you that he is innocent, so what have you against him?" And the king said: "By my life, I have nothing against him, except that I find him loathsome to me; I do not know what it is." And this was repeated (by the wazīr) to Plato. He said: "So I argued that I must search in my soul and character for something in which I could meet his soul and character (on a common ground) wherein they would resemble each other. And I looked into his character and found him to be a lover of justice and abhorrer of injustice—and I discerned the same nature within myself. And in the very moment I stirred up this accordance and met his soul upon the ground of this innate nature which was in my soul he ordered that I be freed." And the king said to his wazīr: "All (the aversion) I had felt against him was dissolved in my soul."

As regards the cause because of which love ever occurs in most cases, it is an outwardly beautiful form; because the soul is beautiful and passionately desires anything beautiful, and inclines toward perfect images: and if it sees such an image it fixes itself upon it; and if it discerns, after that, something of its nature in it, draws close to it, and true love comes to pass: and if it does not discern behind it something of its kind, its affection does not go beyond the *form*. Thus it is with *passion*. Truly, images are a wonderful vehicle of bringing about a union between parts of the souls distant from each other.

[. . .]

Love, my dear friend, is an incurable disease and in it there is remedy against it, according to the manner of dealing with it; it is a delightful condition and a disease yearned for: he who is free from the disease does not like to stay immune, he who suffers from it does not find pleasure in being cured of it; it makes appear beautiful to a man what he has been abstaining from because of shame, and makes appear easy to him what was difficult for him, to the extent of changing inborn characteristics and innate natural traits: and all this will be analyzed in detail in its chapter, if it please God.

    Story. I used to know a young man among some of my acquaintances, who plunged into the bog of love and was hurled into its snares, and his mad love affected his health, and a grave illness enervated him, and his soul did not seek relief in praying to God, Most High and Exalted, revealing to Him what was the matter, and his tongue did not unburden itself of it; and his only prayer was for union, and for becoming the possessor of the person whom he loved to his great woe and long pain. What do you think of a sick person who does not wish to be rid of his illness? One day I sat with him, and saw how downcast and ill he was, and how he let his head hang down; all this afflicted me, and I said to him among other things: "May God cheer you up" and I saw indications of disgust on his face! And about people like that I say in a long poem:

> (*Basīṭ*)
> I take delight in my woes on your account, my hope,
> And will not depart from you during all my days!
> If I were told: "You will obtain relief by forgetting loving him,"
> My answer would be nothing but Lām Alif (= No)!

Story. And these symptoms are just the opposite of what I was told by Abū Bakr Muḥammad b. Qāsim b. Muḥammad al-Qurašī, known as Aš-Šilšī, one of the sons of Imām Hišām b. ʿAbd-ur-Raḥmān b. Muʿāwiya, about himself; namely, that he had never loved anyone at all and had never experienced any grief on account of a friend who left for a far-away place, and never went beyond the limit of friendship and companionship to the limit of sexual love and passionate love since he was born.

Divulging (the secret)

And in love there happens the divulging (of it); and this is one of the blamable accidents which occur in it. It has its causes.

One of them is that the perpetrator of it wishes to adorn himself with the fashion of lovers and be counted one of them. This is an insufferable rascality, and a detestable brazen-facedness, and a spurious longing after love.

Another cause of disclosing love may perchance be the overpowering force of love, and predomination of (the desire for) publicity over modesty; and in such an event man is incapable of restraint or measure (just proportion). This is one of the extreme limits of passionate love and its most powerful domination over reason: it goes to the extent of representing the beautiful in the shape of the ugly and the ugly in the form of the beautiful, and then good is seen as evil and evil is seen as good. And in the case of how many a one who well guarded his veil, and who let down the curtain, and let down the cover, did love lift his veil, and made lawful his things forbidden, and made him *nonchalant* in his not-permitted things, so that it became common knowledge after careful guarding and a proverb (talk of the town) after quietness; and shameful acts became his most favorite in what, had it been presented to him prior to that time, shivering fever would have seized him at (mere) mentioning it; and he would have prayed for a long time taking refuge in God from it. Thus what was very arduous became level, and what was difficult became easy, and what was hard became smooth. And I remember having known a youth of the finest people, and from among my friends of the highest rank, who was struck with love for a slave-girl kept in a palace, and became crazy about her, and his love for her deprived him of many of his ennobling qualities, and signs of his love became apparent to anyone who could see: until she herself reprimanded him for what could be seen in him of the things to which love was leading him.

Story. I was told by Mūsā b. 'Āsim b. 'Amru: he said: "I was in the presence of Abū-l-Fatḥ, my father, may God have mercy upon him; he ordered me to write a letter. As I was writing it my eye caught the sight of a slave-girl with whom I was passionately infatuated, and I lost all self-control, threw the letter from my hand, and hastened toward her. My father was astonished and thought it was some fit I was having. Then my reason made me come to again and I wiped my face off, and I came back apologizing that I had been overcome by nose-bleeding."

And know that this is a cause which leads to the estrangement of the beloved, a bad way to do things, and a weak policy. And there is no other thing which would cause him who adopts it as his method and way—in case he who seeks something goes beyond it, or is not skillful in following it—to reverse (the aim) of his work for him; and his exertion (will turn) into fatigue, and his toil into dust, and his investigation will be superfluous; and whenever his deviation from the right way, and his excessive keeping away from it and hastening outside of the (right) road, is growing, it increases the distance between him and the reaching of his goal: and on this subject I have a poem from which I quote:

> (*Ṭawīl*)
> Do not treat jestingly a difficult matter,
> Nor put too much effort in the easy thing you desire:
> But meet the vicissitudes of Time when they reach you,
> And there is plenty of them coming on!
> For their varying kinds depend on your clever work:
> Let the easy suffice to you instead of something else, and what goes by
>   let it go by!
> Have you not seen that when a lamp is first lighted and kindled,

How blowing on it puts out its blaze?
But once its burning and flame is fully ablaze
Your blowing makes it keener and lengthens its extension?

Story. And I know among the people of Córdoba one who is the son of a scribe and in a high service (government job), whose name is Aḥmad b. Fatḥ. I knew him to be very circumspect among the seekers of knowledge and pursuers of good education; he surpassed his friends in being reserved, and excelled them in quietness. He frequented only noble circles and showed himself only in decent society; his behavior was praiseworthy, his conduct was pleasing and manifested his soul; and he was acting in accordance with it. Then God's decrees separated my house from his, and the first news I received unexpectedly after my arrival in Xātiba was that he had despoiled himself of his virtue by reason of his love for a youth, son of a silversmith, named Ibrāhīm b. Aḥmad, whom I know: I do not believe his qualities to be worthy of love of a person of good family, pre-eminence, vast riches, and opulence in wealth. And it was confirmed to me that he disclosed his head and showed his face, and threw off his halter, and uncovered his countenance, and tucked up the garment on his forearms and directed himself toward (vicious) passion, and became the subject of storytellers' talk, and a *protégé* among tellers of news, and stories about him were making rounds in the country, and rumors about him spread in the land traveling in company with wonderment: and he obtained nothing from it, except the uncovering of the veil, and the divulging of the secret, and ugly talk, and repulsive gossip, and running away of his beloved from him completely, and being entirely prevented from seeing him; and he had no need of all this, and had a most complete freedom, and a secluded place where he could be at his ease. And had his secret remained hidden, and the troubles of his soul under cover, he would have continued to keep the clothing of safety, and he would not have worn out the (woolen) cloak of caution, but he may have found in the meeting of the person by the love for whom he was smitten, and in his conversation and companionship a kind of hope and sufficient contentment; but (as it was) there was no excuse for him: and the argument against him is incontrovertible; unless he was confused in his understanding or struck with (disease) in his reason, because of the great (misfortune) which crushed him. That alone might call for a real excuse; but in case there was the slightest vestige (of reason) left to him he was wrong in undertaking to do what he knew his beloved disliked or was harmed by. This is not a quality of people in love; and this will be explained in the chapter dealing with submissiveness, if it please God, Most High.

There is a third aspect to the causes of disclosing (love) and this is considered by reasonable people as a contemptible one and a base action, namely, when the lover experiences betrayal, *ennui* or dislike from his beloved and finds no way of getting even with him except in something that would do him harm and the most advantageous for him in his purpose is the disclosing and making public (the secret); this is the greatest shame and the most despicable disgrace, and the strongest proof of the absence of reason and the presence of poor wit. And it may be that the disclosing comes from the talk that spreads about, and rumors that become circulated; and this coincides with the little care that the lover attaches to it, and his approval of seeing his secret made public; either for the sake of admiration, or for the purpose of making known something he is hoping for; and I have seen this done by some of my friends from among the sons of chiefs. Also I read in some of the stories of Bedouins that their women were not contented and did not believe their lovers to be passionately in love with them, until their love was widely spoken of and disclosed, and their name made public, and advertised, and praised above all others. I do not know what the meaning of this is, even if their chastity is praised: and what chastity can there be in a woman whose acme of happiness and joy is to be renowned in this respect?

[. . .]

> (*Kāmil*)
> Submission in love is not odious,
> For in love the proud one humbles himself:
> Do not be surprised at my docility in my condition,
> For before me Al-Mustanṣir has suffered the same lot!
> The beloved is not to be considered your equal (in strength),
> So that your patience, if you bear it patiently, would be vile:
> An apple fell and its falling caused pain:
> Would cutting it be on your part a triumph worth mentioning?

Story. I was told by Abū Dulaf, the paper dealer, as from Maslama b. Aḥmad, the philosopher known as Al-Maǧrīṭī, that he said, in the mosque, which is east of the cemetery of Qurais in Córdoba, opposite the house of the wazīr Abū ʿOmar Aḥmad b. Muḥammad b. Ǧadīr, may God have mercy upon him: In this mosque was the permanent staying place of Muqaddam Ibn-ul-Aṣfar, in the days of his youth, on account of his passion for ʿAǧīb, a page of the wazīr Abū ʿOmar mentioned before. He was giving up the prayer in the Masrūr mosque in which was his abode, and he would come day and night to this mosque on account of ʿAǧīb. More than once the guard came upon him at night when he was leaving after the last evening prayer, and he was sitting and looking at ʿAǧīb: until (once) the young man became angry and annoyed, and went to him, and struck him, and slapped him on both his cheeks and eyes: and he was overjoyed by it, saying: "This, by God, is my highest bliss and now I am happy!" And he walked along with him after that for quite a while. Said Abū Dulaf: "Maslama told us this story more than once in ʿAǧīb's presence, when he saw the might of Muqaddam Ibn-ul-Aṣfar, and the display of his power and prosperity. The situation of Muqaddam Ibn-ul-Aṣfar became very powerful. He became a very intimate friend of Al-Muẓaffar b. Abī ʿĀmir, and became closely attached to the latter's mother and relatives; it was through him that mosques and drinking fountains were built, and not a few beneficial works were undertaken; besides his engaging in whatever men of power undertake in matters meant for the welfare of the people and other purposes."

Story. The most abominable of (cases of submissiveness) is this: Saʿīd b. Mundir b. Saʿīd, the prayer leader in the Great Mosque of Córdoba in the days of the reign of Al-Ḥakam Al-Mustanṣir billāhi, may God have mercy upon him, had a young slave-girl whom he loved very much: and he proposed to her that he would free her and marry her. And she said to him making fun of him—for he had a mighty beard: "I find your great beard detestable, and if you had it cut off, that would be what I should like." So he put scissors to work on it until it became dainty. Then the two called a number of witnesses and he made them to be witness of her being set free: then he asked her in marriage for himself, and she did not accept him. And among those present was his brother Ḥakam b. Mundir and he said to those present: "I propose to her that I ask her to be my wife." And he did so, and she consented, and he married her in that very assembly. And he (Saʿīd) consented to this crushing shame, despite his piety, and devotion, and religious zeal. I knew this Saʿīd: he was killed by the Berbers on the day when they entered Córdoba by force and sacked it.

Ugliness of illicit practices

Said the author, may God have mercy upon him: Many people obey their souls and disobey their reason(s), and follow their passions and abandon their religion; and keep aloof from what God, Most High, encourages (people to do) and what he put into sound minds in the way of moderation, and forsaking sinful acts, and fighting passion successfully. They oppose God, their Lord, and please Iblīs in what he likes in the way of ruinous passions, and *practice (illicit sexual) aberrations in their love.* We know indeed that God, Most High and Exalted, combined in man two opposite natures: one of them advises nothing but VIRTUE, and incites to nothing but GOODNESS, and nothing is conceived by it except whatever is AGREEABLE: and this is REASON and its guide is JUSTICE: and the other, its *opposite*, advises nothing but passions and leads only to perdition: this is the SOUL and its guide is PASSION, and God, Most High, says: "Verily, the soul is very urgent to evil"; and He used the word "heart" as a metonymy for "reason", and therefore said: "Verily, in that is a reminder to whomsoever has a heart, or gives ear, and is a witness thereto," and the Most High has said: "He has made faith beloved by you, and has made it seemly in your hearts, and he addressed those endowed with minds."

And these two natures are the two poles in man, and they are two forces among the forces of the body which is the operator of them both, and two reflectors among the reflectors which throw the beams of these two marvelous, lofty, and sublime essences; and each body has its share of the two, in proportion to its responsiveness to them, according to the disposition of the One, Eternal, whose names are Holy, when He created it and shaped it: they forever are in opposition to each other, and continually litigate with each other. And if Reason conquers the Soul, man abstains and overpowers the fits (of inward corruption) which have suddenly attacked him, and is enlightened by God's light, and follows Justice; and if Soul conquers Reason, man's perspicacity is blinded, and he cannot make a proper distinction between the Beautiful and the Ugly; and he increasingly becomes enveloped in (this blindness), rolls into the abyss of perdition and the chasm of ruin, and by reason of these (two situations) things commanded and forbidden are appraised, and the fulfillment (of the law) is (made) obligatory, and the reward or punishment is (judged as) correct, and the reward (of Paradise) is merited. And the spirit unites itself with these two natures, and connects them between them, and is the vehicle of their confluence. And indeed the stopping at the limit (boundary line) of obedience (= observance of law, avoidance of sin) is *non-existent except after long and continual (ascetic) practice*, and *right knowledge*, and *perspicacity of understanding*, together with keeping away from exposing one's self to temptations, and being intimate with people in general, and sitting in houses and dwellings; so that a warranted safety could take place; or that a man be sexually defective so he has no need of women; or has no (bodily) organ which would help him (to have intercourse with) them since a long time.

He who has been preserved from the evil of his "waggler," and his "din-ner," and his "wiggler," has been preserved against the evils of the world in their entirety: the "waggler" is the tongue, the "din-ner" is the belly, and the "wiggler" are the private parts. And I was informed by Abū Ḥafs, the secretary, one of the sons of Rauḥ b. Zinbāʿ al-Ġaḏāmī, that he had heard a famous story teller, who had himself called (an expert) in *fiqh*, that he was asked about this story, and he said: "A *qabqaba* is a melon!"

And we were told by Aḥmad b. Muḥammad b. Aḥmad, and were told by Wahb b. Masarra and Muḥammad b. Abī Dalīm, from Muḥammad b. Waddāḥ, from Yaḥyā b. Yaḥyā, from Malik b. Anas, from Zaid b. Aslam, from ʿAṭā b. Yasār, that the Prophet of God said in a long *ḥadīt*: "Whom God has preserved from the evil of the two will enter the Paradise." And he was asked about it, and said: "Namely, of what in between his two lips and his two legs."

And verily I hear many people who say: "Integrity in the subduing of passions is (to be found) in men, not in women, and I greatly wonder at this talk. I have said and I shall not deviate from it: Men and women in the matter of *inclination* toward these two things are equal. There is no man who, if a pretty woman proposes love to him, and prolongs her attitude, and if there is no obstacle, but will fall into the Šaiṭān's net, and will be overcome by the passion for sinful acts, and excited by covetousness, and carried away by desire; and there is no woman who, when invited by a man in a similar circumstance, but she would deliver herself to him, by God's decree and absolute rule, from which there is no swerving at all.

And I was informed by a very trustworthy friend of mine, one of those accomplished in *fiqh* (jurisprudence), and dogmatic theology, and knowledge, and firmness in his religion, that he fell in love with a slave-girl who was very intelligent, educated, and of superlative beauty, he said: "I proposed (love) to her and she ran away, then I proposed (love) to her again and she refused, and the affair continued thus a long time and my love for her increased, and she was of the type that will not listen at all to (pleadings); until my excessive love for her and the blindness of my youth brought me to the making of a vow that when I would obtain from her the gratification of my wish I would repent with a true repentance." He said: "And not many days and nights passed when she surrendered after all this stubbornness and running away." And I said to him: "Well, Abū N., have you been faithful to your vow?" And he said: "Yes, indeed, by Allāh!" And I laughed and was reminded by that action of what is being constantly and frequently dished up to our hearing about the custom according to which in the land of the Berbers, which is neighboring with our Andalus, the adulterer repents, provided that he has accomplished his business with whomever he wishes to repent of, and he is not hindered in this; and they reprove anyone who would address a hint to him in a word, and they say to him: "Can a Muslim man be deprived of repenting?" And he said: "I remember that she wept and said: By God, now you have brought me to a situation which I never could imagine (as possible), and I did not think I would yield in this to anyone."

And I do not consider it inconceivable that there does exist righteousness in men and women, and I take refuge in God, lest I should have different belief! But I have seen people making an error in the meaning of this word, namely, *righteousness*, a far-reaching error indeed. The correct and true explanation of it is that a righteous woman is the one who, if she is kept straight becomes stronger in virtue, and if her means by which evil may come indirectly are cut off, she allows herself to be held fast; and the bad woman is the one who, if she is kept straight does not become stronger in virtue, and if a hindrance intervenes between her and between causes which facilitate depravity, she will seek means to reach them by various tricks. And the righteous man is he who does not mix with depraved people, and does not expose himself to sights which would bring forth passions nor does he lift his eyes to marvelously composed images; and the bad man is he who seeks the company of vicious people, and unfolds his sight to beautifully made faces, and applies himself to seeing evil sights, and loves solitary places which lead to ruin. Righteous men and women are like fire covered by ashes which does not burn those who approach it, unless it be stirred up; and iniquitous (men and women) are like a kindled fire which burns everything. And as regards a neglected woman and a man who exposes himself, both are led to ruin and perish. For this reason it was forbidden to a Muslim to take delight in hearing the melodious voice of a *strange woman*, because the first look would be made at you and the second against you; and the Prophet said: "Whosoever contemplates with attention a woman while fasting so that he sees the fleshy curves of her anatomy, has broken his fast;" and indeed, what has been said by way of interdiction concerning love in the text of the Revelation is quite sufficient. And in the modes of usage of this word, namely *hawā*, a word which conveys (many) shades of meanings, and their derivation among the Arabs, (there is a great variety): and this is a proof of the inclination of the souls and their *penchant* toward such situations; and truly he who abstains from them is in conflict with his soul and is combatting it.

[. . .]

And Abū-l-Ḥusein Aḥmad b. Yaḥyā b. Isḥāq Ar-Ruweidī mentions in the book *Rhetoric and Correct Speech* that Ibrāhīm b. Sayyār an-Naẓẓām, chief of the Muʿtazilites, despite his high rank in dogmatic theology and his power and mastery in perfect knowledge, was carried away by what God has forbidden, by reason of a Christian youth for whom he conceived a passion to such an extent that he wrote for him a book about the greater excellence of Trinity against Unity—we implore your help, oh Lord, in your protection against the Šaiṭān's intrigues, and the happening of your abandonment! At times the evil grows greater, and the passion rages, and the ugly seems unimportant, and religion grows weaker, until man, in order to arrive at his wish, consents to side with ugly deeds and shameful acts: such (misfortune) befell, for example, ʿObeid-ullāh b. Yaḥyā al-Azdī, known as Ibn Al-Ġazīrī, who consented to the abandonment of his household, and profanation of his wives (harem), and exposing of his household (to evil), because of a desire in obtaining his wishes from a youth with whom he was infatuated—let us take refuge in God from aberration, and let us ask for His protection, and for the improvement of our reputation and the amelioration of our good name!—until the poor man became a public talk, with which all places of gathering were filled, and about whom poems were being composed. And this is what the Arabs call *dayyūt* (sexual complaisance), which is derived from *tadyīt* (humiliation, submission) which means "being soft"; and there is no "being soft" greater than in the case of one who permits himself to be thus far "obliging" in this matter. In the same way one says "an indifferent" camel, namely abased (brow-beaten); and by my life, jealousy is found in the natural disposition of animals: and with us how much more so, since our law has confirmed it! There is no greater misfortune than this—*dayyūt*! And I knew the aforementioned man as discreet, until Šaiṭān possessed him with lust—let us take refuge in God from abandonment! And on the subject ʿĪsā b. Muḥammad b. Muḥammal al-Ḥaulānī says:

> (*Kāmil*)
> You who make the pudenda of your own (lawful) women
> As a net to hunt young fawns;

I see the net tearing completely, and then
Your gain will be only the shame of a mishap!

And I also say:

(*Tawīl*)
Abū Merwān permitted his free women (to be used),
In order to attain what he desired from one young fawn;
And I blamed him for his complaisance in his ugly deed,
But he recited to me in a manner of a hard-boiled sharper:
"I had obtained the object of my desire, only
My wives were jealous of me because I alone had obtained it!"

[. . .]

We were told by Al-Hāmdani, from Abū Isḥaq, from Muḥammad b. Yusuf, from Muḥammad b. Ismāiʿīl, from ʿAbd-ul-ʿAziz b. ʿAbdullah, who said: We were told by Suleiman, from Ṭaur b. Yazid, from Abū-l-Geiṭ, from Abū Hureira, from the Prophet, that he said: "Avoid seven capital sins." They said: "What are they, Prophet of God?" He said: "*Association of other deities with God, sorcery, killing of a person which God had forbidden, except by right, usury, consuming the property of an orphan, turning one's back on the day of battle, and casting of imputations of adultery on chaste women who are negligent, yet believing.*"

Verily, in adultery there is a profanation of women, and corruption of progeny, and separation between husband and wife—a fact which God has considered grave and what cannot be regarded lightly by any man endowed with reason and by him who has the least moral character: and were not this element in man so important, and because it is not safeguarded from being overcome—God would not have lightened the punishment of the unmarried ones, and made it heavier on the married ones. Thus it is with us (Muslims) now, and in all the ancient laws revealed by God, Most High and Exalted, as a permanent verdict, which was not abrogated and will not be caused to cease (repealed): blessed be the one who observes His servants, who is not prevented from—by anything, however mighty it may be, in His creation; nor does anything in His universes, however great it may be, lessen His power of His observing the least little thing in them: for He is as the Mighty and Exalted One said: "the living, the self-subsistent, slumber takes Him not, nor sleep." And He said: "He knows what goes into the earth, and what comes forth therefrom, and what comes down from the sky, and what ascends thereto." "He knows things hidden, not the weight of an atom escapes from Him in earth or in heaven."

Verily, the greatest sin that a servant may commit is the disclosure of the protection of God, Most High and Exalted, about His servants; and there is recorded about the sentence of Abū Bakr, the Truthful, may God be pleased with him, that he struck a man who had pressed himself against a youth until he had the orgasm, a blow which caused his death; and about the admiration of Malik, may God have mercy upon him, at the religious zeal of the Emīr who struck a young man who gave a man a chance to kiss him so long until the man's semen was ejected: he beat him until he died; (enough) to make people forget the assaults of the motives in this matter and its causes. And the increase of *Iǧtihād*, though we do not hold that opinion, is commended by many learned men whose view is followed by the learned among the people: and as regards the one we follow, it is the one we were told by Al-Hamdānī, from Al-Balkhī, from Al-Firibrī, from Al-Bukhārī, who said: "We were told by Yaḥyā b. Suleimān, we were told by Ibn Wahb, who said: I was told by ʿAmru that Bukeir had told him from Suleimān b. Yasār, from ʿAbd-ur-Raḥmān b. Ǧābir; from his father, from Abū Burda Al-Anṣārī, who said: "I heard the Prophet of God say: "There shall be no scourging above ten stripes, except in a punishment among the punishments of God, the Mighty and Exalted." And this is the belief of Abū Ǧaʿfar Muḥammad b. ʿAlī An-Nasāʾī Aš-Šafiʿī, may God have mercy upon him.

And as regards the act of Lot's people it is hideous and despicable. Said God, Most High: "Do ye approach an abomination which no one in all the world ever anticipated you in?" And God threw upon those who practiced it stones of marked clay, and Malik, may God have mercy upon him, holds that the active and passive doer of it should be stoned, be they married or not married. And some of the partisans of Malik argue in proof of it that God, Most High and Exalted, says about the hitting of the doers of this by stones "and these are not so far from the unjust!"; hence it is necessary, according to this, that if anyone acted wrongly now, practicing what they did, stones are near him. And to defend a dissenting opinion in this matter does not belong here.

Abū Isḥāq Ibrāhīm b. As-Sirrī mentioned that Abū Bakr, may God be pleased with him, burned by fire because of it, and Abū ʿObeida Maʿmar b. Al-Mutannā mentioned the name of the one burned, and said: "It was Šuǧāʿ b. Warqa Al-Asadī, whom Abū Bakr, the Truthful, had burned by fire, because he offered his hindquarters as a woman offers (her forequarters.) And an intelligent man has indeed ample ways of behavior apart from immoralities, because God did not forbid anything but He put in its place for His servants things permitted which are better than the forbidden and nobler; there is no God but He!"

Are sexual morality and sexual prohibitions universal, or should they vary by culture?

Introduction

ENLIGHTENMENT PHILOSOPHERS OFTEN FANTASIZED about non-European societies in what they saw as a state of nature in order to challenge the values of their own societies. Reading accounts of explorers, they found that other cultures had very different notions of sexual morality. Some started to wonder if Christian moral codes were not endowed by nature, but culturally constructed and perhaps relative. Of course, Europeans also drew on these observations to argue for their own moral superiority. Even those who criticized imperialism might still think of the cultures they encountered as "primitive" and "savage." Enlightenment thinkers challenged the notion that traditional European society, along with its admiration of royalty and its Christian obsession with purity, was based on the law of nature, and imagined a different, more free and egalitarian law of nature. But they still saw the law of nature as universal.

In 1768, the explorer Louis Antoine de Bougainville published an account of his voyage to the South Seas. Bougainville depicted Tahiti as a romantic paradise filled with beautiful women. As the Europeans arrived, he claimed, the natives offered up a lavish feast. The European men were pleased when they were also offered young women to have sex with, but shocked when they were expected to perform the act in public, on a flower-strewn floor, accompanied by musicians. Some anthropologists hypothesize that this may have been a religious ritual to propitiate the god Oro, carried out by the sect of the Ariori. The Ariori were an aristocratic elite, who behaved unlike everyday Tahitians. The Ariori could have sex with many partners until marriage, but once married, they had to have abortions or kill their offspring if they wanted to keep their ritual power.[1] Other anthropologists surmise that the Tahitians may have been trying to propitiate the Europeans with food and females, fearing that they would attack them with guns as the English had done the year before.[2]

Bougainville's work inspired the philosopher Denis Diderot to present his ideas about the cultural relativity of morality in his *Supplement to the Voyage of Bougainville*. Diderot was a philosopher whose main accomplishment was to edit the famous *Encylopédie*, which contained material ranging from articles on printing and engineering to studies of sexual pleasure. Because his work challenged conventional authority, it was often censored. Indeed, Diderot circulated the *Supplement* in manuscript by 1772, but only published it in 1798.

Diderot often wrote in the form of a dialogue, so that he could present several provocative points of view. The entire *Supplement to the Voyage of Bougainville* contains several dialogues, between Bougainville and a Tahitian leader, a chaplain and a Tahitian man named Orou, and between readers A and B. Diderot begins the work by presenting a dialogue in which A and B question Bougainville's motives and debate whether "savages" were like children, or more moral than Europeans. Next Diderot presents a speech by an old man who denounces the Europeans for bringing terrible things to this once idyllic island. While the Tahitians shared women harmoniously, once they gave their women to the Europeans jealousy and bloodshed erupted. European guilt now tainted their natural enjoyment of love. (In fact, Europeans brought venereal disease to the islands.) However, is the critic Moscovici correct to suggest that the Tahitian leader who denounced the explorers may have been prejudiced against the Europeans?

In the excerpt presented here, the European chaplain is staying with the family of Orou, a Tahitian. Orou offers his daughter to the chaplain for the night, but he refuses indignantly. Surprised, Orou asks him why, and the two men compare Tahitian and Catholic morality. On what grounds do the Tahitians permit or forbid sexual behavior? What was more important – sexual purity or fertility? In a later part of the supplement not excerpted here, the Tahitians report that older women who are sterile wear a black veil to indicate they are not supposed to have sex. They also reveal that the real reason they gave their daughters to Europeans was to improve their blood stock. But the chaplain also learns, to his horror, that Tahitians allow incest.

In the conclusion, Diderot argues that the Tahitians are closest to the law of nature. He asks why nature's gift of sexual attraction has become the source of evil, and answers, "it is because of the tyranny of Man, who has turned possession of women into a property right." But is Moscovici right to suggest that the Tahitians regarded women as property as well? Did Diderot want any kind of sexual control, or did he think people should just follow the law of nature? What was the law of nature?

Notes

1   Martha Warren Beckwith, "Review: Die Geheime Gesellschaft der Arioi," *American Anthropologist* 35, no. 2 (1933): 379–380; D. G. Charlton, *New Images of the Natural in France* (Cambridge: Cambridge University Press, 1984), 127; Pamela Cheek, *Sexual Antipodes: Enlightenment Globalization and the Placing of Sex* (Stanford: Stanford University Press, 2003), 160; Michel Hénaff, "Supplement to Diderot's Dream," in *The Libertine Reader*, ed. Michel Feher (New York: Zone Books, 1997), 52–60.
2   Andy Martin, "The Enlightenment in Paradise: Bougainville, Tahiti, and the Duty of Desire," *Eighteenth-Century Studies* 41, no. 2 (2008): 203–216.

Chapter 7

Claudia Moscovici

AN ETHICS OF CULTURAL EXCHANGE
Diderot's *Supplément au* Voyage *de Bougainville* (2001)

ARE THERE ANY UNIVERSAL or singular, eternal, and static-moral standards that all human societies and groups should adopt regardless of cultural differences? In other words, is universalist ethics a desirable or even possible moral option in a multi-cultural world? Contemporary critics of universalism argue that such ethics turn out to be a form of cultural chauvinism, a way of imposing culturally specific standards upon societies where they would not be useful or appropriate. Even the most seemingly universalist rules – such as the injunctions not to harm or steal from other people – are always created by particular cultures or groups to serve their interests. Such injunctions, the argument goes, involve culturally specific and recent rather than atemporal and cross-cultural principles.[1] They depend upon the notion of the sanctity of the individual, human life, and property which, at least in Europe, emerged during the eighteenth century with the decline of aristocratic regimes and the rise of an increasingly powerful middle class.

If we accept the proposition that universalism is, indeed, always a form of ethnocentrism which is blind to its own biases, then are we led to the conclusion that cultural relativism is the only plausible ethical theory modern societies can adopt? Should cultural differences preclude all cultures or groups from judging one another? Without universal values, however, the very notion of ethics, or of morally desirable codes of conduct, risks meaninglessness. This kind of reasoning oscillates between the poles of universalism and relativism, without settling on either. If neither universalism nor relativism can adequately solve ethical problems, however, then what kind of ethical theory can? Is a path between universalism and relativism possible? What form would it take? I believe that Diderot's *Supplément au Voyage de Bougainville* (1770)[2] represents one of the most significant attempts in eighteenth-century French fiction to come to terms with ethical differences among and within cultures.

Diderot's *Supplément* is a fictitious supplement to a French explorer's account of his visit to Tahiti. It consists of a series of conversations, anecdotes, and speeches between the French explorers and the Tahitian people. The text contrasts not just two cultures – the French and the Tahitian – but also, and more importantly, two attitudes toward cultural exchange: an ethnocentric one that regards itself as universal and a more tolerant one that accepts some degree of cultural relativism. The only way to claim the universality of one's own values, Diderot suggests paradoxically, is by respecting cultural differences, or the relative. Only this dual perspective affords a balance between relativism and universalism that ultimately critiques and rejects both extremes. To arrive at a moral equilibrium, the *Supplément* observes a doubled dialectical process. On the one hand, the narrative rejects (or negates) complete cultural relativism because it still upholds the superiority of one's own cultural ethics over those of others. On the other hand, the text also rejects (or negates) absolutist – and ultimately ethnocentric – universalism because it endorses respecting the mores of a host society. Let us follow the dialectical narrative process that leads to what might be called an "ethic of cultural exchange": one, that is, that negates both relativism and universalism.

The *Supplément* begins by emphasizing cultural differences. Its series of monologues and dialogues contrast the happy and natural life of the Tahitians, and particularly their freer codes of sexual behavior, with the restrictive sexual mores of French society. Consequently, ethical distinctions are translated into sexual differences. Gender-based behavior functions as a litmus test as to whether a society observes or violates the universal laws of nature. Diderot establishes a complex correlation between the laws of nature and the universalist ethics that should govern human behavior.[3] The emerging French Enlightenment discourse of natural laws and rights proposed by the *philosophes* such as Rousseau, Montesquieu, and Diderot himself, a discourse which supposedly represents universal human values, is projected onto Tahitian society. This projection is openly acknowledged by the text.

Diderot indicates that readers will not have direct access to the words of the Tahitian people. The words of Orou, for example, the main Tahitian character, are subject to several translations by Spanish and then French explorers. As two of the French characters observe, Orou's ethical critiques and visions, are "modelé(s) à l'européenne" (177). Like Montesquieu in the *Lettres persanes* (1721), Diderot fictionalizes other cultures in order to problematize the aspects of French aristocratic society that he considers dated and wants to change. It is therefore not surprising that Orou provides a typical Enlightenment critique of traditional Western values. Does this mean Diderot's travel narrative has absolutely nothing to teach us about respect for other cultures? No, it does not. The *Supplément*, along with other travel narratives such as the *Lettres persanes* and *Lettres d'une Péruvienne* (1752), continue to interest contemporary scholars because they raise a question that is becoming increasingly pertinent today: how can one respect and fairly represent other cultures without pretending to abandon one's own cultural perspectives and values?'[4] This question, more so than the critique of aristocratic French culture, is the main ethical problem explored by the *Supplément*.[5]

The *Supplément* takes the form of several nested dialogues. The dialogic form, as Dena Goodman observes, not only allows for the expression of vastly different points of view, but also quite explicitly opens up the text to interpretation by readers. "Unlike drama," writes Goodman, "the dialogue's nonmimetic character calls for critical thought and distance on the part of readers. This distance, when looked at from another angle, defines the reader's position as firmly rooted in the real world, where political action can be taken."[6] This essay will explain how the nested dialogues of the *Supplément* help create such a critical and potentially political readership by encouraging readers to perceive the limitations of a hierarchical (or single dialectical) model of culture, while also making them aware of the advantages of a more open (or double dialectical) model of cultural exchange.[7]

[. . .]

The *Supplément* begins as a dialogue between two typical French Enlightenment men, called simply "A" and "B." . . . The discussion between the two Frenchmen reviews culturally entrenched assumptions about the nature of exploratory voyages: the belief that they constituted useful sources of knowledge about human evolution and geographical change; that the explorer, if well-educated, was an objective (i.e., truthful and impartial) source of knowledge; and that Western cultures had attained the pinnacle of human civilization. As is generally the case in exotic narratives,[8] the two Frenchmen describe "savage life" with ambivalence rather than unqualified praise. "Savage life" lies far behind the stage of development and complexity of "civilized life." Character "B" uses the same analogy as La Mettrie – the man-machine – to contrast the simplicity of "primitive" societies with the complexity of "advanced" societies, "[that] are such complicated machines." From the analogy between man and machine, the text goes on to describe the relation between Europeans and natives in terms of two different – and distant – stages of human development: "The Tahitian touches upon the origin of the world and the European upon its old age."

   Character "B" offers the qualification that this description of non-Western and Western man as part of the same evolutionary development can only be analogical since "the interval which separates him from us is greater than the distance between a new-born infant and an old man." Using the language of natural history, character "B" compares non-European people to children and observes their practices in order to comprehend the more baffling behavior of "civilized man." The relationship between the Western observers and the non-Western observed is obviously hierarchical and non-reciprocal, the product of a single dialectical understanding of cultural difference. For while Bougainville is assumed to have the expertise and authority to observe Tahitian behavior, the Tahitian subject supposedly does not understand and instinctively rejects, out of a desire for liberty, the constraints of civilization. The preliminary dialogue between the two Frenchmen obviously outlines a diffusionist model of culture, whereby Western subjects justify colonial expansion in terms of sharing their higher knowledge with less advanced societies. As we will see, Diderot implies that diffusionism could not prove more mistaken, since the most astute cultural wisdom provided in this narrative is offered not by a European, but by Orou, a Tahitian.

[. . .]

Having depicted the false universalism proposed by the two Frenchmen in their monological conversation, Diderot goes on to sketch two clashing ethnocentric perspectives, epitomized by Bougainville and the Tahitian chief. These two monologues also conform to a single dialectical logic. Some critics interpret the chief's attitude as a mark of ethical complexity and even as a call for respect among cultures. Most notably, Goodman maintains in *Criticism in Action* that the Tahitian chief's ethics are complex and call for respect among different cultures. She argues, "the [chief's] reasoning here takes the following form:

(a) You are neither greater nor lesser and are therefore a man. (b) How can you then assert yourself above those to whom you are equal? (c) If all are men and thus equal, then your right to declare Tahiti as your property implies the Tahitian's right to claim France as his property. (d) You see the absurdity and the injustice of the latter and from there can see that the former must be equally absurd and equally injust" (187). By performing a dialectical reading, however, I would like to show that the chief neither assumes nor proclaims the equality of all men. Instead, he adopts a single dialectical stance, which establishes the superiority of Tahitian society by negating the value of European culture.

The Tahitian leader narrates a "before" and "after" story that sets up a series of juxtapositions between Tahitian and French cultures. Before the advent of the French army and their general Bougainville, the chief claims, the Tahitians lived a natural, virtuous, and innocent life. They were at peace with themselves and their environment. This idyllic existence was destroyed by the advent of the Europeans. To the chief, the Europeans represent evil itself. They have traveled to Tahiti only to pillage the country and to dominate its people. When the Tahitians bemoan Bougainville's departure, the chief chastises them: "Cry misfortunate Tahitians! cry; but about the arrival, not the departure, of these mean and ambitious men: one day you will know them better" (147).

It is not that the chief is wrong. With historical hindsight, we know that the Europeans did indeed colonize other cultures. Although correct, however, the Tahitian chief allows for no complexity in his vision of the two societies, which he describes in binary terms as the good Tahitian versus the bad European civilizations. Even before the Europeans manifested their imperialist intentions, the chief does not know or want to know anything about the Europeans. Readers are told that "Upon the arrival of the Europeans, he cast a glance full of disdain upon them, without showing either surprise, fear, or curiosity. They approached him; he turned his back on them and retired into his cabin" (147). His hatred of Europeans comes not so much from foresight, as from prejudice.

The chief's assumptions about European societies, appropriately expressed in a monologue to his people, exactly parallel those of the two anonymous Frenchmen and of Bougainville himself. Both reflect single dialectical understandings of culture. For these men, the world is divided into two asymmetrical parts: from the Frenchmen's perspective, civilized Europe versus uncivilized non-Europe; from the chief's perspective, pure Tahiti versus corrupt non-Tahiti. Each side establishes the superiority of its own culture by defining the other culture only negatively, as that which their own culture is not. Consequently, as previously noted, the Europeans praise the rationality, civilization, and morality of Western civilization by depicting non-Western societies as irrational, uncivilized, and immoral. The Tahitian chief follows the same dialectical process to declare cultural superiority. He establishes the innocence, happiness, and morality of his own culture by describing Europeans as their opposites, meaning as non-innocent, unhappy, and immoral. Starting with such ethnocentric premises, it follows that nothing could be more dangerous for either society than cultural mixture. Cultural exchange, be it economic, social, or sexual, would displace the (single) dialectical structure of us versus non-us and its accompanying hierarchies. Western cultural influence, the chief argues, risks destroying the peace and corrupting the innocence of the Tahitian people: "We are innocent, we are happy; and you can't but destroy our happiness. We follow the pure instinct of nature . . . Here everything is ours; and you have imparted to us I don't know what kind of distinction between yours and mine. We share our wives and daughters; you enjoyed this privilege with us; you came to stir in them unknown desires" (148).

The binary opposition between Europeans and Tahitians would be incomprehensible without having a common standard of comparison, what can be called, borrowing Marxist terminology, a "general equivalent." By offering a common measure, the general equivalent enables us to assign comparative value to dissimilar entities. In this text, the standard that transcends and measures all cultural differences, I wish to argue, is provided by what might be called "fraternal patriarchy." That is to say, both the French and the Tahitian cultures define ethics in terms of how women are exchanged among men for the purposes of sexual and cultural reproduction.

By way of contrast to Anderson's claim in *Diderot's Dream* that Diderot proposes a gender-neutral analysis of the economy of value, I would like to show that such an economy is directly linked to sexual valorization and power. According to Anderson, reproduction rather than gender, is what matters most in Tahitian society: those who can reproduce are valued because they can contribute to the society; those who cannot reproduce are less valued. This interpretation, however, does not explain the androcentrism of the narrative, whereby women are depicted as "owned," shared, and exchanged among men.

In Tahiti, as in Europe, women are assumed to be the property of men. As Orou explains to his guest, Tahitian men "share [their] wives and daughters." Relying upon this common cultural foundation, the chief uses fraternal patriarchy to distinguish between the two societies. If women are assumed to be the property and sexual right of all men in a society, as is supposedly the case in Tahiti, then that society is natural and innocent. By way of contrast, if women are regarded as the property of one man, as in European monogamy, then that society is unnatural and immoral. Clearly, insofar as the *Supplément* describes Tahiti in order to critique France, it critiques neither a biological definition of sexual difference nor the social inequality between men and women. Instead, Diderot's narrative objects to the particular manner in which the Western patriarchal economy is organized by means of the exchange of women.

If we pursue the logic of both Bougainville's and the chief's monologues, we would be led to the conclusion that the Tahitians attain a better form of culture because they base their values upon natural sexual difference. Unlike the French, the Tahitians make no mistake about gender. For example, in a brief but significant scene of the *Supplément*, Diderot describes the rape of a female European servant, who was disguised as a man, by a group of Tahitian men. Although the servant's "true" sexual identity had gone unnoticed by the European officers, the more "natural" Tahitians "guess[ed] his gender from the first glance" (152–53). Corrupted by centuries of dissimulation and artifice, the text implies, Europeans can no longer recognize sexual difference. By way of contrast, truly natural people will immediately perceive sexual identity in the visible, biological signs of the body. Literary critics generally stop here, regarding the *Supplément* as representing Tahitian culture in order to critique Western culture. For example, as Carol Blum argues in *Diderot: The Virtue of a Philosopher*,

> For Diderot, the central virtue of Tahitian culture was not that it liberated
> from law, that primitive anarchy would be preferable to civilized order, but
> that the islanders' laws, customs and religion were based upon nature and in
> harmony with her designs. Unlike the European who was constantly torn
> between the demands of contradictory authorities, the Tahitian was permitted
> to experience himself as a whole. The voice of nature and the voice of society
> were in unison and the word they spoke was: procreate."[9]

Such interpretations of the *Supplément*, however, focus upon the monologic narratives and thus read the entire text according to the logic of the single dialectic. They argue that the *Supplément* contrasts the natural and artificial foundations of society, regarding the Tahitian culture as based on nature and the French culture as its dialectical contrary – specifically, as based on lack of natural principles and therefore as arbitrary and conventional.

Diderot's text, however, is not that one-sided. At the same time that the author uses gender differences to critique the ethical norms of French culture, he also uses cultural similarities to critique Tahitian culture. As we have observed, the chief resembles Bougainville in that he shares a desire to control and manipulate the Tahitian people. By the end of the narrative, most Tahitians reject Bougainville and follow their native leader. In so doing, the text implies, they uncritically exchange one form of ethnocentrism for another.

After showing us how not to engage in cultural exchange through a series of single dialectical or monological narratives, Diderot stages a third conversation, between the Tahitian patriarch Orou and the French chaplain, that presents a better model of intercultural communication which pursues the logic of the double dialectic. By all appearances, this conversation resembles the exchanges between Bougainville and the Tahitian chief. As before, fraternal patriarchy provides an appropriate standard by which to measure both cultures because it is the blindspot, or unquestioned foundation, of both societies. Unlike all the other cultural values debated in this narrative, patriarchy is assumed to be universal not only in validity but also in fact.

I will illustrate, however, that while Diderot begins his text with monological narratives that, following a single dialectical process, present Tahitian culture as the positive term in order to critique French civilization as its negation, he also stages a dialogical narrative that quite literally doubles the single dialectic. In making the transition from the single (or monologic) to the double dialectical (or dialogic) narratives, the *Supplément* turns around and represents French "culture" as the positive term in order to critique Tahitian "nature."

The very circumstances of this third conversation create the possibility for dialogue. Although Orou and the chaplain are still character types, they are dissimilar. In fact, each can be regarded as a spokesman for his society. Furthermore, because the chaplain is a guest in Orou's home, both have the incentive to be polite and open-minded. The crux of the debate between Orou and the chaplain concerns the issue of which culture implements the best sexual mores. The chaplain claims that his culture, which is based largely on sexual prohibitions – against incest, and extramarital or premarital sex – is superior because it conforms to both human and divine law. Orou pretends not to understand how a divinity could be so removed from human nature as to dictate rules that "prevent one from tasting that innocent pleasure that nature, that sovereign mistress, invites us all to enjoy; to give life to a being that resembles us" (153). Reproduction, he maintains, yields not only personal satisfaction but also general utility, since it produces more able bodies for the clan and country. Orou posits that a code of ethics is universal only if it conforms to the following principles: "Do you wish to know what is good and bad everywhere and for all time? Look upon the nature of actions and things; upon your relations to your peers; upon the effect of your behavior upon your personal utility and the general good" (158). Aspiring to the general good and personal utility dictates precisely the ethics observed by the Tahitian people: sharing all women among men; subsuming sexuality to reproduction; and thus imposing absolutely no restrictions upon sexual behavior other than the ones imposed by reproduction itself.

Upon first glance, the most plausible interpretation of the text is the one offered by Lester G. Crocker, who argues that the *Supplément* confers more value upon the Tahitian, or "natural" view of sexuality over the French, or "cultural" suppression of it. Crocker maintains that "Sexual restrictions foment disorder, since they are ineffective and only promote rebellion by an impulse overwhelming in its power."[10] This reading, however, also presumes a single dialectical textual logic, in which Tahitian nature and European culture are viewed as opposites, where one must overrule the other. By way of contrast to such interpretations, I will argue that the dialogue between the monk and Orou more plausibly reveals a double dialectical logic in which two cultures negotiate their understandings of nature in a process of mutual social critique.

In Tahiti, Orou explains, there is no incest taboo; no rule against premarital or extramarital sex; no shame attached to single motherhood. On the contrary, a nubile female is considered more desirable if she already has a few children – a sign of her fertility – some of whom are the result of sexual relations with her own father – a sign of her desirability. Single motherhood is thus not only a right, but also a point of pride. "The birth of a child," Orou elaborates, "is a happy domestic and public occasion: it is a growth of fortune for the household, and of strength for the nation" (161). Despite the wide divergence in European and Tahitian attitudes toward single mothers, however, the chaplain is able to understand, if not altogether accept, Orou's argument because they adopt similar androcentric language. To them, a welcome child is a male child. As Orou continues to explain, children, "represent more arms and hands in Tahiti; we see in him a farmer, a fisherman, a hunter, a soldier, a husband, a father" (161). Furthermore, as Wilda Anderson observes, in both cultures children are viewed as patrilineal property, particularly in Tahitian society, where "Children thus are treasured not as persons, but as the source of material riches."[11]

[. . .]

What this system of values and hierarchies based upon fecundity implies is that no civilization is natural. Tahiti cannot be plausibly viewed, after all, as the dialectical opposite of France. Orou explains as much when he observes that the Tahitians have sexual prohibitions that are, like the injunctions themselves, related to reproduction. Women or men who are not at the peak of their fertility – either because of age or impotence – cannot engage in sexual relations. The only vice consists of "the sign of sterility, an innate evil, or the result of advanced age. The woman who takes off her veil and mingles with men, is a libertine, the man who takes off such a veil and approaches a sterile woman is a libertine" (169). For the Tahitians, sexuality needs to be tied to reproduction in order to remain natural and hence ethical. Such ethics are an ethics of utility, since the production of children is equivalent to the production of wealth. As Anderson notes, "From the drive to amass wealth, Orou derives a coherent notion of utility, and from utility, a lucid morality. From this same concept of morality, he then derives social rank and status: they are an index of fecundity."[12] The ethic of useful fecundity in turn depends upon the education of women, meaning the regulation of their reproduction. Gender-based education thus forms "the main object of private education and the most important principle of public mœurs" in Tahiti. (163)

Given these cultural values, it makes sense that Orou and his family feel offended when the chaplain refuses to engage in sexual relations with his wife and nubile daughters, all of whom are close to the peak of their fertility. Confronted with a systematic explanation of Tahitian mores, the chaplain responds defensively. He declares that his religion and state forbid him to engage in sexual relations with Orou's daughters and wife. His answer, repeated without further explanation like a refrain, provides a caricature rather than a fair description of contemporary French values. His defensive reaction fails to address the obvious problems with Orou's arguments, problems that the text nonetheless underscores. For although Orou wants to convince his interlocutor that the Tahitians live in a non-hierarchical, non-normative, and free society, it is rather clear that this society is neither non-hierarchical nor free, but rather impelled by an ethic of fecundity that establishes hierarchies based on age and fecundity.[13]

More important than the chaplain's defense of his own culture, however, is his attitude toward another. Eventually the chaplain gives in to Orou's wishes and, out of respect for Tahitian values, engages in sexual relations with Orou's youngest daughter without ceasing to believe, however, in the validity of his own ethics. The only real dialogue of the *Supplément* thus describes Tahitian and European cultures in terms of a double dialectical process or reciprocal critique that negates the possibility of any utopian society. As Anderson argues,

> The poignant picture of the Tahitian "natural culture," of villagers destroyed by Bougainville's sailors' syphilis and their equivalent contamination by European mores and religion seems at first glance to be a classic Enlightenment – even Rousseauist – denunciation of the corrupting effect of increasing civilization. But against the backdrop of his materialism, Diderot's story takes on a different cast, a much more ambiguous one, and replaces the primitive innocence of Rousseau's noble savages with the shifting and disabused morality of Rameau's nephew. Diderot's salon philosophers, by abandoning utopian visions, whether negative or positive, accede (seemingly paradoxically) to a position superceding the fatalistic determinism associated with materialism.[14]

Only if we perceive the double dialectical narrative logic of the *Supplément* are we in the position to grasp the complexity of Diderot's non-utopic ethical vision. More specifically, a dialectical reading illustrates that the text plausibly combines the cultural bias inherent in universalism with the open-minded respect implied by relativism.

In his depiction of several voyages from Europe to Tahiti, Diderot is able to offer both positive and negative models of cultural exchange. The successful traveler, the author suggests, is one who reconciles what he may consider to be the universalist values of his own culture with the relative values of another. Characters such as the Tahitian leader and Bougainville are never able to see beyond the supposed universalism of their own culture. Both assume that only their values are correct. Paradoxically, this cultural chauvinism has the textual effect of relativizing the universal, since it represents universalist ethics as a form of blind ethnocentrism. By way of contrast, Orou and the chaplain are open-minded enough to engage in mutually beneficial dialogues about the validity of their values.

In the conclusion, one of the Frenchmen urges readers to have a modest attitude toward their own ethics and a tolerant one toward those of others: "Let's imitate the good monk: monk in France, savage in Tahiti" (186). The Frenchman thus suggests that only individuals who can question the ethical norms of not only different cultures but also of their own gain a truly ethical consciousness that benefits from cultural exchange. The *Supplément* transforms the general Enlightenment question "should we civilize man?" into an open-ended discussion about what constitutes civilization and which forms are best suited for different peoples. While not completely resolving the impasse between relativist and universalist ethics, the text offers a good start by presenting generations of critical readers with a model of dialogue that functions as the basis of a double dialectical, and thus more reciprocal and non-hierarchical, understanding of cultural difference.[15]

Notes

1   See, for example, the arguments presented by Edward Said in *Orientalism: Western Representations of the Orient* (London: Routledge and Kegan Paul, 1978).

2   Denis Diderot, *Supplément au Voyage de Bougainville* (1770; rpt. Paris: Garnier-Flammarion, 1972). The translations from French are my own.

3   For more information concerning the complex interrelations Diderot establishes between sexuality and ethics, see Wilda Anderson, *Diderot's Dream* (Baltimore: Johns Hopkins UP, 1990).

4   As Pierre Saint-Amand aptly poses this question in *The Laws of Hostility: Politics, Violence, and the Enlightenment* (Minneapolis: U of Minnesota P, 1996): "It is not difficult to understand how the incommunicability of cultures subsequently becomes the main subject of Diderot's book. Indeed, the Supplement is a theorization of passage from one place to another and of the possibilities of all forms of exchange . . . Are we condemned to the impossibility of exchange, to the untranslatability of mores and languages? . . . Do we have eyes only to see no further than ourselves, bounded as we are by our cultural narcissism?" (123).

5   James Creech, for example, regards the insoluble ethical tension of the *Supplément* as an epistemological contradiction in modes of representation: "The conclusion I have been implying up to now is this: representation . . . brings with it a problem of similarity and difference. This problem fuels epistemological systems. It is what those systems are trying to accommodate, but the effort itself is incommodious." *Diderot: Thresholds of Representation* (Columbus: Ohio State UP, 1986), 19.

6   Dena Goodman, *Criticism in Action: Enlightenment Experiments in Political Writing* (Ithaca: Cornell UP, 1989), 142.

7   Cf. Wilda Anderson, *Diderot's Dream*, 129.

8   As Tsvetan Todorov indicates in *On Human Diversity: Nationalism, Racism, and Exoticism in French Thought* (Cambridge: Harvard UP 1993), because the exotic is often equated with one's own cultural ideals, it cannot be attributed to a well-known culture, since familiarity with the shortcomings of that society might tarnish the gloss of the ideal. Exoticist discourse thus depends upon a dissatisfaction with one's own culture combined with a vague and distant knowledge of another culture upon which one projects one's own cultural fantasies.

9   Carol Blum, *Diderot: The Virtue of a Philosopher* (New York: Viking, 1974), 121.

10   Lester G. Crocker, *Diderot's Chaotic Order* (Princeton: Princeton UP, 1974), 80.

11   *Diderot's Dream*, 135.

12   *Diderot's Dream*, 138.

13   As Anderson perceptively observes, "The Tahitians view their society as being in equilibrium with nature – or better, they feel that they have realized an ideal, the creation of a fixed social structure that accommodates the changeability of the natural world. Notice that their culture does have a directional development of a sort. It must have been more egalitarian years before; it becomes relentlessly more hierarchized as the years go by, according to the principle of a single parameter meritocracy. The Tahitians, however, do not perceive this vector" (*Diderot's Dream*, 141).

14   *Diderot's Dream*, 127–28.

15   As Goodman observes in *Criticism in Action*, "In this rhetoric can be seen a new form of politics, a politics not based on the authority of the absolute but one whose means – and perhaps even whose end – is reasoned discourse and whose authority is common sense . . . . And the agents of this reform, the critical politicians, are the critical readers themselves, the enlightened public that had been created by fifty years of philosophic and critical activity" (226).

Chapter 8

Denis Diderot

SUPPLEMENT TO BOUGAINVILLE'S
VOYAGE
(1796, 1993 edition)

The Chaplain's conversation with Orou

IN THE SHARING-OUT of Bougainville's crew, the Chaplain fell to Orou. They were about the same age, thirty-five or thirty-six. Orou at this time had a wife and three daughters, called Asto, Palli, and Thia. They undressed the Chaplain, washed his face, hands, and feet, and served him a wholesome and frugal meal. As he was about to go to bed, Orou, who had gone off with his family, reappeared and presented his wife and his three naked children, saying: "You have had supper, you are young, you are in good health; if you sleep alone, you will sleep badly, a man needs a companion at his side at night. Here is my wife, here are my daughters: choose the one who suits you, but if you wish to oblige me, you will give the preference to the youngest of my daughters, who has not yet had any children."

The mother added: "Alas, it is not for me to complain. Poor Thia! It is not her fault."

The Chaplain replied that his religion, his calling, and sheer decency and good morals forbade him to accept these offers.

Orou replied: "I do not know what this thing is that you call 'religion,' but I cannot believe it is good, since it prevents you from enjoying an innocent pleasure, one to which nature, our sovereign mistress, invites us all; since it prevents you from giving existence to a fellow mortal, from doing a service asked of you by a father, a mother, and their children, from repaying a host who has given you a warm welcome, and from enriching a nation by endowing it with another citizen. I do not know what kind of thing a 'calling' is, but your first duty is to be a man and to show gratitude. I, Orou, your host and your friend, do not ask you to carry my customs back to your own country; but I beg you to fall in with them here. Are the customs of Tahiti better or worse than yours? There is an easy answer to that: does the country where you were born have more men than it can feed? In that case your customs are neither worse nor better than ours. Could it feed more than it has? Then our customs are better than yours. As to the matter of decency that you mentioned, I understand, I see I was wrong and I beg your pardon. I do not wish you to injure your health; if you are tired, then you must sleep. Only I hope you will not always sadden us in this way. See the look of concern on those faces: they are afraid you have seen some defect in them which makes you despise them. But even were it so, would it not be pleasure enough for you to honor one of my daughters among her companions and sisters and so perform a good deed? Be generous!"

THE CHAPLAIN It's not that. They are all equally beautiful. But think of my religion! Think of my calling!

OROU They belong to me, and I am offering them to you. They belong to themselves, and they give themselves to you. However pure a conscience the thing named *religion* and the thing named a *calling* demand, you can accept them without scruple. It is no abuse of authority on my part; I assure you I know and I respect the rights of individuals.

Here the honest Chaplain has to admit, Providence had never exposed him to such a pressing temptation. He was young; he was in a fever; he tore his gaze away from the amiable suppliants, he let it be drawn back to them; he lifted his eyes and his hands to heaven. Thia, the youngest, clasped his knees and said: "Stranger, do not distress my father, do not distress my mother, do not distress me! Do me honor in the hut and among my own people; raise me to the rank of my sisters, who make fun of me. Asto, the eldest, already has three children; Palli, the second, has two; and Thia has none! Stranger, worthy stranger, do not rebuff me! Make me a mother. Give me a child whom, one day, I can walk with hand in hand; a child all may see at my bosom in nine months' time; an object of pride and a part of my dowry when I pass from my father's hut to another's. I shall perhaps be more lucky with you than with our young Tahitians. If you grant me this favor, I shall never forget you; I shall bless you all my life; I shall write your name on my arm and on your son's; we will always repeat your name with joy, and when you quit these shores, my wishes will pursue you across the seas till you are safely home."

The ingenuous Chaplain says that she clasped his hands and gave him such touching and expressive looks; that she wept; that her father, her mother, and her sisters left the scene; that, left alone with her and still repeating "My religion! My calling!" he woke next morning to find himself beside this young woman, who was covering him with caresses and invited her father, her mother, and her sisters, when they came to the bedside, to add their thanks to hers.

Asto and Palli went away and returned with meats of the country and fruit and wine. They embraced their sister and wished her happiness. The party all breakfasted together, after which Orou, being left alone with the Chaplain, said to him: "I can see that you have made my daughter happy, and I thank you. But could you explain to me that word *religion*, which you have so often pronounced and with such sadness?"

The Chaplain, after a moment's meditation, replied: "Who made your hut and the utensils in it?"

OROU I did.

THE CHAPLAIN Well, we believe that this world and all it contains is the work of a workman.

OROU Does he have feet, hands, and a head?

THE CHAPLAIN No.

OROU Where does he live?

THE CHAPLAIN Everywhere.

OROU Even here!

THE CHAPLAIN Even here.

OROU We have never seen him.

THE CHAPLAIN One cannot see him.

OROU He does not seem much of a father. But I suppose he must be rather old. He must be at least as old as his creation.

THE CHAPLAIN He does not age. He spoke to our ancestors; he gave them laws; he told them how he wished to be honored; he commanded them to perform certain actions, as being good, and forbade them to commit others, as being bad.

OROU I see; and one of the actions he forbade was to sleep with a woman or a girl? If so, why did he create two sexes?

THE CHAPLAIN So that they might unite; but on certain specified conditions and after certain preliminary ceremonies, after which a man belongs to a woman and belongs only to her, and a woman belongs to a man and only to him.

OROU For their whole life?

THE CHAPLAIN For their whole life.

OROU So that if a wife happens to sleep with another man, or a husband to sleep with another woman . . . but that will not happen, since, he being there, and such a thing being displeasing to him, he can prevent it.

THE CHAPLAIN No, he lets them do as they will, and if they do it they sin against the law of God (for that is the name we give to the great workman) and against the law of the country, and they commit a crime.

OROU I would hate to offend you. But if you would allow me, I could give you my own opinion.

THE CHAPLAIN Do so.

OROU I find those strange commands you mention opposed to nature and contrary to reason; they seem to me designed to multiply crimes and produce continual annoyance for the old workman—the one who made everything without the aid of a head or hands or tools, who is everywhere and is not to be seen anywhere, who exists today, exists tomorrow, and is never a day older, who commands and is not obeyed, who could prevent things and does not. I find them contrary to nature because they imply that a feeling, thinking, and free being can be the property of another being of the same kind. What could be the grounds for such a right? Do you not see that in your country you have made a confusion between things which have neither feeling, nor thought, nor desire, nor will and can be given or taken, kept or exchanged, without suffering or complaint, and things which *cannot* be exchanged or owned, things which have liberty and will and desire, can give or withhold themselves for a moment or forever, things which complain and suffer and can never be made items of commerce without forgetting their character or doing violence to their nature. I find these commands contrary to the general law of beings. Does anything, really, seem more senseless than a commandment which makes a sin of the changeableness which is in all of us and dictates a constancy which is not to be found in any of us, which violates the nature and the liberty of man and woman by chaining them to each other forever? Could anything seem more mad than a fidelity which confines the most capricious of enjoyments to a single individual? Than a vow of immutability by two creatures of flesh and blood, in the sight of a heaven never two instants the same, beneath caverns which menace ruin, under a rock crumbling into dust, at the foot of a tottering tree and standing upon shifting stone? Believe me, you have brought mankind to a plight worse than the animals. I know nothing of your great workman, but I am glad he did not speak to our fathers, and I hope he will not speak to our children, for he might by chance tell them the same stupidities, and they might perhaps be stupid enough to believe them. Yesterday at supper you talked to us about magistrates and priests. I do not know what sort of thing they are, these *magistrates* and *priests* whose authority regulates your conduct, but tell me, are they the masters of good and evil? Can they make just things unjust and unjust things just? Have they the power to attach goodness to harmful actions and evil to innocent and useful ones? You can hardly believe so, for, on that basis, there would be neither true nor false, neither good nor bad, neither beautiful nor ugly— or at least only what it pleases your great workman, your magistrates, and your priests to pronounce as such, and from moment to moment you would have to change your ideas and your conduct. One day, by one or other of your three masters, you would be given the command *kill*, and you would be obliged, in conscience, to kill; another day, *steal*, and you would be expected to steal; or, *do not eat that fruit*, and you would not dare to eat it; or *I forbid you that vegetable, or that animal*, and you would take care not to touch it. There is no sort of goodness that might not be forbidden you, or wickedness you might not be ordered to do. And where will you be if, your three masters being apt to disagree, one of them decides to permit, one to command, and one to forbid you to do the same thing, as I imagine often happens? Then, to please the priest you will have to quarrel with the magistrate, to satisfy the magistrate you will have to displease the great workman, and to keep on good terms with the great workman you will have to renounce nature. And do you know what the result will be? It means you will despise all three, and you will be neither a man, nor a citizen, nor pious; you will be nothing at all; you will be on bad terms with every kind of authority, on bad terms with yourself, malevolent, tormented by your own heart's feelings, and unhappy, as I saw you last night, when I offered you my daughter and you cried: "Think of my religion, think of my calling!" Do you want to know what is good and what is evil at all times and in all places? Then fix your eye on the nature of things, on your relationship with your fellow-men, on the influence of your conduct on your private benefit and on the public good. You are mad if you think there is anything in the universe, high or low, which can add to or take away from the laws of nature. Her eternal will is that the good shall be preferred to the bad and the general good to the particular. Command the opposite as much as you wish, you will not be obeyed. You will multiply evildoers and the unhappy by fear, by punishment, and by remorse; you will deprave consciences; you will corrupt minds; people will no longer know what they are supposed to do or avoid doing. Troubled when they are innocent, at peace with themselves in crime, they will have lost sight of their Pole star, their right road.

Tell me honestly: despite the express commands of your three legislators, does not a young man ever sleep with a young woman?

THE CHAPLAIN It would be a lie if I said so.

OROU Does a woman who has sworn to belong to none but her husband never give herself to another man?

THE CHAPLAIN Nothing is more common.

OROU Either your legislators penalize it severely, or they do not. If they do, they are savage brutes doing violence to nature; if they do not, they are idiots who have exposed their authority to scorn by a useless prohibition.

THE CHAPLAIN The guilty parties, if they escape legal penalty, are punished by public censure.

OROU That is to say: justice only comes into its own where common sense fails, and the law has to be helped out by the madness of public opinion.

THE CHAPLAIN A girl who is disgraced cannot find a husband.

OROU Disgraced? Why?

THE CHAPLAIN An unfaithful wife is more or less generally despised.

OROU Despised? Why?

THE CHAPLAIN The young man is called a cowardly seducer.

OROU Cowardly! A seducer! Why?

THE CHAPLAIN The father, the mother, and the child herself are all grief-stricken. An unfaithful husband is a libertine; a husband who has been betrayed shares in his wife's shame.

OROU What a monstrous tissue of absurdities you are describing. And you have not told me all: for as soon as one is allowed to apply the ideas of justice and property as one chooses, allowed to give or deny qualities to things arbitrarily, allowed to attribute good and evil and their opposites to actions according to one's fancy, one will begin blaming others, accusing others, suspecting and tyrannizing over others, becoming envious and jealous, deceitful and hurtful, secretive and false; one will spy and lay traps and quarrel and lie. Daughters will deceive their parents, husbands their wives and wives their husbands. Girls—yes, it will come to that—will suffocate their young; suspicious fathers will despise and neglect theirs; and mothers will abandon them to the mercy of fate, and crime and debauchery will flourish in a hundred forms. I know all this, as if I had lived among you. It is so, because it must be so; and society, which your leader so praises for its beautiful "order," will be no more than a collection, either of hypocrites, who secretly trample on the law, or unfortunates, the willing instruments of their own suffering, or imbeciles, in whom prejudice has quite stifled the voice of nature, or mere monsters and freaks in whom nature renounces her rights.

THE CHAPLAIN It is not an unfair picture. But in your country, do you not marry?

OROU Yes, we marry.

THE CHAPLAIN What is marriage, with you?

OROU Consent to live in the same hut and sleep in the same bed, so long as we are happy in doing so.

THE CHAPLAIN And when you are not?

OROU We separate.

THE CHAPLAIN What becomes of your children?

OROU O stranger! Your last question finally shows me the depths of your country's misery. Know, my friend, that here the birth of a child is always an occasion for happiness and its death a subject for regret and tears. A child is a precious good, because it must become a man, and we cherish it with a quite different care than we give to our animals and our plants. A newborn infant causes both private and public joy: it is an increase of wealth for the hut and of strength for the nation; it means more arms and hands in Tahiti; we see in the child a future farmworker, fisherman, hunter, soldier, husband, and father. On returning from her husband's hut to her parents', a wife will bring back with her the children she took there as a dowry. The ones born during their life together are shared out; and we try to keep a balance, giving each partner the same number of girls and boys.

THE CHAPLAIN But children have to be looked after for many years before they become useful.

OROU We assign a sixth part of the country's wealth to their support and to the needs of the old. This grant follows them wherever they go. Thus, you see, the bigger a Tahitian family is, the richer it becomes.

THE CHAPLAIN A sixth part!

OROU It's a sure way of encouraging population and respect for old age and proper care of children.

THE CHAPLAIN Do your husbands and wives sometimes reunite?

OROU Very often. However, the shortest length for a marriage is from one moon to another.

THE CHAPLAIN Unless the wife is pregnant; and then they must live together for at least nine months?

OROU No, not so. Paternity, like the child-grant, follows the child everywhere.

THE CHAPLAIN You mentioned children brought by a wife as a dowry?

OROU Exactly. Take the case of my eldest daughter. She has three children; they can walk; they are healthy; they promise to be strong. When the fancy takes her to marry again, she will take them with her. They are hers. Her husband will receive them with joy, and she will please him all the more if she is pregnant with a fourth.

THE CHAPLAIN By him?

OROU By him, or by some other man. The more children our daughters have, the more they are sought after; the more vigorous and good-looking our sons are, the richer they will be. Also, to the same degree that we carefully protect the one from approaches by men and the other from dealings with women before the age of fecundity, when the boys reach puberty and the girls are marriageable we are urgent with them to reproduce. You cannot imagine what a service you will have done my daughter Thia if you have given her a child. Her mother will not have to say to her at each new moon, "Thia, what can you be thinking of? You are not pregnant. You are nineteen years old; you ought to have had two children already, and you have none. Who is going to take care of you? If you waste the years of your youth like this, what will you do in your old age? Thia, you must have some defect which puts men off. Take yourself in hand my child. At your age, I had been a mother three times."

THE CHAPLAIN What precautions do you take to protect your adolescent girls and boys?

OROU That's the leading part of home education and the most important point in public morality. Our boys, up to the age of twenty-two, that is to say two or three years after puberty, wear a long tunic and a little chain round their loins. Our daughters, before marriageable age, would not dare go out without a white veil. To take off one's chain, to raise one's veil, is a crime that only rarely they commit, because from early on we teach them its dangerous consequences. But at the moment when the young male reaches his full strength, when the symptoms of his virility are continuous and the frequency of his emissions and the quality of the seminal fluid give us confidence; at the moment when a young girl begins to droop and languish and is of an age to conceive desires, to provoke them, and to satisfy them effectively; at this moment, a father will remove his son's chain and cut the nail of his right-hand middle finger, and a mother will lift her daughter's veil. The one is allowed to solicit women and be solicited by them, and the other to walk in public with her face uncovered and her bosom bare and accept or refuse a man's caresses.

We merely indicate to them in advance which girls the boys, and which boys the girls, would do best to prefer. The emancipation of a girl or a boy is a great celebration. If it is a girl, the young men gather outside her hut the night before and all night the air resounds with song and the sound of instruments. On the day itself, her father and mother lead her to an enclosure where there is dancing and jumping, wrestling and running. They display the man naked before her, so she can see him from all sides and in every posture. Or if it is a young man's day, it is for the girls to do the honors and display the young woman naked to him, without reserve or secrecy. The ceremony is finally completed on a bed of leaves, as you saw when you came among us. At the fall of night the girl may return to her parents' hut or may go to that of her chosen man, where she will stay as long as she feels inclined.

THE CHAPLAIN So that celebration may be, or may not be, a wedding day?

OROU Exactly . . .

PART 5

Were Victorians sexually repressed?

Introduction

MICHEL FOUCAULT INFLUENTIALLY ARGUED against the stereotype that the Victorians were sexually repressed, asserting that in fact there was an explosion of discourses about sex during this period by experts such as psychiatrists, sexologists, and doctors. To be sure, Foucault also acknowledged that during the Victorian era it may have been more difficult for ordinary people to talk about sex, but in arguing for an explosion of discourses, he downplayed the fact that, in Victorian Britain at least, sexual language was heavily censored.

Foucault also argued against the repressive hypothesis because it assumed that sexual desire is a fixed, natural, biological force, that must be allowed an outlet, or it would fester and explode, much like a pressure cooker or hydraulic system. Instead, he asserted that sexuality was socially constructed through discourses. Even discourses which prohibited sexual acts or desires could be titillating and incite the very acts they tried to forbid, he contended. But at the end of his book, he optimistically suggested that "bodies and pleasures" may be a way of resisting this deployment of power.[1]

Hera Cook challenges Foucault's assumption that Victorian repression was a myth, and asserts that it did in fact have an impact on people's experiences. At the same time, she is also building on Foucault's insistence that sexuality is socially constructed. While discourses scold their readers to avoid sexual practices, by describing them in great detail, they may in fact be titillating. But when people know little about sexual anatomy, and silence reigns about sexuality, sexual desires may not be incited very much at all, or, at the very least, people will be inhibited from acting on what desires they have. Furthermore, physical dangers, such as venereal disease and pregnancy, imposed limits on female sexuality. Cook surmises that in the absence of reliable birth control techniques, couples often relied on abstinence to control their fertility. What sources does she use? Are birth rates or first-person accounts reliable indicators of sexual behavior?

It is not just a matter of exploring the body and its pleasures, for according to Foucault's own logic, sexual techniques usually must be learned. Cook and other historians argue that the availability of information about sex changed over time. The eighteenth century was much more open about sex, but in the early nineteenth century this information became more restricted, and the British government cracked down on it harshly, especially after the Obscene Publications Act of 1857.

Two sources are provided to contrast sexual information in the eighteenth and nineteenth centuries. First is *Aristotle's Masterpiece*, a popular pamphlet that circulated widely, mostly in the eighteenth century, with a few nineteenth-century editions. This manual of fertility had nothing to do with Aristotle, although some of its anatomical assumptions derived from the Greek writer Galen.[2] *Aristotle's Masterpiece* focused its message on fertility: sexual pleasure, including the female orgasm, was necessary to conceive. The pamphlet provided detailed knowledge about anatomy, including the fact that the clitoris was the seat of women's sexual pleasure. (By the mid-nineteenth century, medical experts proved that women did not need to have orgasms to conceive.) How did the pamphlet portray men and women as different?[3] Could the information about conception be used to avoid conception?

From the eighteenth century, pamphlets warning against venereal disease also provided information on sexual anatomy. The *Catalogue of Dr. Kahn's Celebrated Anatomical Museum* described the detailed wax models of human anatomy, including the genitals, available in this popular London museum. Historian Michael Mason asserts that this demonstrates the widespread availability of sexual knowledge, and indeed when the museum opened in 1851 men and women visited it and the esteemed medical journal *The Lancet* praised it.[4] What kind of sexual information would they learn from this pamphlet and the museum? Would it stimulate or inhibit their desires? How was race depicted? Kahn lost his reputation when it was revealed he provided men anxious about venereal disease with ineffective quack treatments, and then blackmailed them.[5] After years of attack by anti-vice organizations, the museum was forced to close under anti-obscenity laws in 1873.[6] The social purity movement that helped force its closure warned against masturbation in less explicit terms, but it spoke more and more about sex.[7]

Notes

1   Michel Foucault, *The History of Sexuality: An Introduction*, trans. Robert Hurley (New York: Vintage Books, 1990), 157.
2   Mary Fissell, "Hairy Women and Naked Truths: Gender and the Politics of Knowledge in *Aristotle's Masterpiece*," *William and Mary Quarterly* 60, no. 1 (2003): 43–74.
3   Roy Porter and Leslie Hall, *The Facts of Life: The Creation of Sexual Knowledges in Britain, 1650–1950* (New Haven: Yale University Press, 1995), 39.
4   Michael Mason, *The Making of Victorian Sexuality* (Oxford: Oxford University Press, 1994), 190–203.
5   Letter to editor from W. B. Kesteven, *Associated Medical Journal* 1, no. 49 (1853): 1094.

6   A. W. Bates, "Dr Kahn's Museum: Obscene Anatomy in Victorian London," *Journal of the Royal Society of Medicine* 99 (2006): 618–624.

7   Alan Hunt, "The Great Masturbation Panic and the Discourses of Moral Regulation in Late Nineteenth-Century and Early Twentieth-Century Britain," *Journal of the History of Sexuality* 8, no. 4 (1998): 575–585; Frank Mort, *Dangerous Sexualities: Medico-Moral Politics in England since 1830* (London: Routledge and Kegan Paul, 1987), 105. For social purity more generally see Lucy Bland, *Banishing the Beast: English Feminism and Sexual Morality 1885–1914* (London: Penguin, 1995).

Chapter 9

Hera Cook

THE LONG SEXUAL REVOLUTION
English women, sex, and contraception
1800–1975 (2004)

'ONE MAN IS AS GOOD AS ANOTHER IN THAT RESPECT': WOMEN AND SEXUAL ABSTINENCE

IN THIS CHAPTER THE SIGNS of women's increasing confidence and assertiveness in the late nineteenth century and the growing female consciousness of the, impact of sexuality upon women are briefly charted. The evidence for a shift toward female rejection of sexual pleasure during the nineteenth century is considered and it is argued that this took place. Women's belated, even churlish, acceptance of birth control in the twentieth century is then described. This produces an account of changing sexuality in, the nineteenth century which is incompatible with the account by Michel Foucault that has dominated the history of Victorian sexuality over the last three decades. Foucault rejected the 'repressive hypothesis', that is the claim that sex had been increasingly repressed since the seventeenth century, and put a counter-argument that the Victorian period incited sexuality, producing a multiplicity of sexual discourses and the privileging of sexuality as the core of identity. Little attention has been paid to the limits Foucault placed upon his subject matter:

> It is quite possible that there was an expurgation—and a very vigorous one— of the authorised vocabulary . . . Without question, new rules of propriety screened out some words: there was a policing of statements. A control over annunciations as well: where and when it was not possible to talk about things became much more strictly defined; in which circumstances, among which speakers and within which social relationships . . . This almost certainly constituted a whole restrictive economy . . . At the level of discourses and their domains, however . . . practically the opposite phenomenon occurred . . . an institutional incitement to speak about [sex] and to do so more and more.[1]

So Foucault was not making an argument about everyday speech. This was increasingly subject to a 'restrictive economy' in which talk of sex was repressed. His rejection of the 'repressive hypotheses' referred to a phenomenon that was occurring primarily, perhaps only, at the level of discourses produced by institutions and disciplines. English women were far less willing to speak of sex than English men; indeed they were heavily stigmatized for doing so, they also had a lesser degree of involvement with institutions and disciplines until the late nineteenth century, and thus they contributed little to such discourses. A focus on women's engagement with discourses on sexuality, and on what is known of women's experience of physical sexual activity, foregrounds the restrictive economy.

Foucault saw the subject's construction of self as resulting from the internalizing of the disciplinary gaze and the acceptance of the demands of society as her or his own needs. The lived experience of the body was, thus, the historical outcome of power/knowledge formations: the product of discourses. The residual category of a natural, untrammelled transhistorical body and its pleasures was posited by him as the site of resistance to power. But the sexual body of which Foucault speaks is a male body. It is evident that in the period studied coitus was assumed to be the aim of sexual desire and means to sexual pleasure by the vast majority of people. Conception and pregnancy take place within the female body. The risk/consequence of pregnancy exists prior to discursive power/knowledge formations, institutions, or the state. The female body cannot be only a source of resistance, it must also be a source of restrictions and regulation in the lives of women. Conception and pregnancy impose physical constraints upon the woman, as does use of contraception. She can resist these by rejecting the pregnancy or the child but there is no natural, untrammelled female sexual body to act as the site of resistance to power. Female sexual pleasure could not act as resistance to internalized discipline, rather, one way or another, discipline was necessary in order that pleasure could be experienced. To put this into Foucauldian terms, in relation to sexuality, the female body was not an active, unrestrained body that had to be rendered docile by the internalizing of controls which had previously been imposed externally. To remain active women had first to resist their own bodies. This theoretical basis for the emergence of resistance to sexuality from within female discourse suggests a radically different account of sexuality in this period, one in which sexual repression does not come only from external forces imposing a social order, but also wells up from within and below.

The double standard

Mid-century middle-class England saw the apogee of the double standard of sexual morality; male sexual access to women was a necessity but any slip from sexual purity on a woman's part cut her off from respectable society. Josephine Butler (1826–1906), who later became the leader of the campaign against the regulation of prostitution, lived in Oxford in the 1850s. She described hearing strong rumours that a don had seduced a 'very young girl', who then bore his child. But, she explained, when she expressed the hope that the don would be brought to a 'sense of his crime' to a man whom she believed to carry moral authority in the university, he advised her that a 'pure woman . . . should be absolutely ignorant of a certain class of evils in the world'. For women 'silence was thought to be the greatest duty of all on such subjects', she wrote.[2] Around the same time Barbara Leigh Smith (1827–1891, later Bodichon) was writing a pamphlet summarizing the laws of

England as they concerned women. She was advised to omit any mention of prostitution as 'no more than is absolutely necessary should be said upon subjects, which are considered as forbidden to women'.[3] These statements were quite clear. The subject of male sexuality was *forbidden* to women. It was women's *duty* as women to be silent. The dominant sexual culture in mid-Victorian Britain was shaped by the acceptance of purchased sexual relief for men and respectable women were forbidden to discuss it. This is the foundation of Victorian sexual hypocrisy, and it is intimately tied into the emergence of feminism because that silence was imposed upon women for the benefit of men. This mid-century double standard was a radically different position from the stance taken by moral reformers in the early nineteenth century, and still adhered to by Dissenters and evangelical Anglicans as they had demanded that men also be moral.

In his recent history of Victorian sexuality, Michael Mason argues that too much has been made of sexual hypocrisy. He tells us that 'as a matter of plain fact, sexual hypocrisy in the lives of notable Victorians is rare . . . it is interesting that when sexual secrets have been disclosed they have often been revelations of non-performance, as . . . it may be in the extra-marital life of Dickens.'[4] The sexual secret was the existence of Charles Dickens's (1812–70) extramarital life, not his sexual performance. The hypocrisy lay in the immurement of Ellen Ternan (1839–1914), Dickens's mistress, in a suburban villa to serve his sexual and emotional needs, while he continued to benefit economically from his professions of belief in Victorian family values. Dickens's sexual performance once he got to the villa is of almost no significance whatsoever in relation to hypocrisy. Such a life could be imposed upon a woman like Ternan because her family's financial resources were so slender that she had little choice but to seize the opportunity Dickens offered and no means of supporting herself if she tired of her isolation.[5] As Butler wrote, it angered her that such men were able to 'go about smiling at dinner parties' while the women they privately consorted with were '*branded* openly'.[6]

It was in this social context that concern about sexuality began to be voiced publicly by middle-class and upper-middle-class women. The topic of male conjugal rights formed the starting point for a new public discussion by women of female sexuality. Leigh Smith was discouraged from speaking of prostitution but in the finished pamphlet on English law, she wrote that 'A woman's body belongs to her husband; she is in his custody; and he can enforce his right by a writ of *habeus corpus*.'[7] Historian James Hammerton has used evidence from cases heard under the new Divorce Act in 1857 and the Matrimonial Causes Act of 1875, which permitted the granting of separation orders in the magistrates' courts. In court, husbands and wives revealed that both parties accepted normative social attitudes and beliefs, such as a wife's duty of submission to her husband and an acceptance of male conjugal rights. The household was both a set of relationships and a physical terrain in which wives had a rightful place. A husband's acceptance of these boundaries gave his wife a degree of customary authority and control. But the cases reveal the vulnerability of wives where husbands were unwilling to abandon expectations of literal and unquestioning obedience and service.[8] Hammerton argues that the publicity divorce cases gave to women's resistance to male domination, including insistence on their conjugal rights, contributed to the development of feminism.

Nationally the issue that had most salience among women was probably venereal disease. The Contagious Diseases Acts provided for the compulsory medical examination for venereal disease of prostitutes working in specified military districts, and were passed in 1864, 1866, and 1869.[9] Initially these Acts provoked little public attention. However the campaign for the repeal of the Acts continued for seventeen years, and during this period the medical understanding of syphilis and gonorrhoea grew substantially. Both the support for the Acts and the campaign against them can be thought of as publicity that raised people's awareness of the dangers of venereal diseases and of the high rates of infection. Treatments for venereal diseases remained highly unpleasant, and were of uncertain efficacy until the early twentieth century when the drug Salvarsan was introduced. Syphilis had a low mortality rate but as late as 1924 the disease killed 60,335, a year when only 50,389 died of cancer and 41,103 of tuberculosis.[10] The open insistence by male supporters of the Contagious Diseases Acts on men's need for sexual relief in spite of the risks to wives and children alienated many women. Elaine Showalter has pointed out that men saw women working as prostitutes as the source of contamination, while women believed the source of the disease to be men.[11] The churches and the social purity movement exploited fears about venereal disease to reinforce the existing negative Christian association between sexuality and sin. Thus the emerging discourse on sexuality was powerfully negative and gender specific. Much effort had also been put into raising standards of personal hygiene over the course of the nineteenth century, increasing perceptions of the genitals as dirty and potentially disgusting.[12] In this context of sin, dirt, and disease, a growing distrust and perception of physical sexual activity as repugnant was unsurprising.

In the last quarter of the nineteenth century, working-class women's literacy was rising fast and the education of middle-class women was starting to be taken seriously.[13] Female education has been consistently associated with increased female autonomy. In 1995, demographer Shireen Jejeebhoy reviewed contemporary research on female education and reproduction since the 1960s. She found that educating women has been found to have a substantial downward impact on their fertility in a wide range of developing countries. Her complex analysis has much to offer beyond this point. Education works indirectly, enhancing women's knowledge, decision-making power, and confidence in interacting with the outside world. Their emotional closeness to their husband and children, and their economic and social self-reliance, are also increased. The impact of education differed according to the degree of gender stratification, that is, equality or lack of it, in a given society. In very unequal circumstances, relatively high levels of education may be necessary to make a difference to levels of fertility. In settings that are more egalitarian, less education is required.[14] There was considerable regional variation in gender and sexual cultures in England. Thus the increase in education is likely to have enabled women to act upon their desire for fertility control and protection from venereal diseases more effectively but the impact would have varied in different communities.[15]

During the last quarter of the century, employment opportunities for lower-middle-class women began to widen and middle- and upper-class women were being elected to positions at the municipal level and on boards. There was increasing agitation in support of legislative changes, such as the Married Woman's Property Acts, that would ensure women were less vulnerable to unreasonable husbands.[16] In 1867, the London-based National Society for Women's Suffrage was organized. Similar groups sprang up in Manchester, Edinburgh, Bristol, and Birmingham, creating a loose federation of suffrage societies. By the end of the century, the struggle for women's suffrage was becoming a mass movement with support from women in all regions and classes.[17] The emergence of the movement and rising literacy suggest that women were growing in confidence and assertiveness.

Women and sexuality

There is limited evidence about women's physical sexual experience in the nineteenth century but what is available is consistent with the trajectory suggested by fertility rates. It is probable that a substantial alteration in women's experience of genital sexuality, and in their attitudes, was taking place in the second half of the nineteenth century. Early to mid-century accounts suggest that many women had passionate physical sexual desires and felt able to express these. Middle-class Effie Gray's (b. 1817) marriage in 1848 to the art critic John Ruskin (1819–1900) was, notoriously, annulled after six years because of his refusal to consummate it. It appears that Effie fully undressed on the first night of her marriage, that Ruskin held her in his arms, and that she allowed him to look at her body, probably including her genitals, in the light. Her letter to her parents entreating their help suggests that she questioned him at length about his reasons. Such readiness to speak of sexuality and her anger about his disgust at 'her person' suggests a confidence about her own sexuality, which is reinforced by the erotic success of her second marriage.[18] Erotic confidence comes through clearly in the letters, and/or descriptions, of Sarah Austin (1793–1867), Sarah Walker (b. approx. 1800), Fanny Kingsley (1814–91), and other women in the first half of the nineteenth century.[19] Even with no experience of physical sexuality other than that with her prudish and self-absorbed husband John Austin, Sarah Austin was aware of her body's potential for pleasure and deeply desired further sexual experience.

Effie's initial acceptance of Ruskin's behaviour suggests she was speaking the truth when she wrote that, before marriage, 'I had never been told the duties of married persons to each other and knew little or nothing about their relations in the closest union on earth.'[20] Fanny Kingsley had been similarly ignorant of what sexual intercourse entailed before her marriage but this did not prevent her from enjoying physical sexual desire.[21] By the last quarter of the century such ignorance of physical sexuality and reproductive processes was said to be frequently devastating for young women, and a rising chorus of blame was directed toward mothers of all classes who, it was claimed, had failed to teach their daughters about sexuality.[22] It seems probable that mothers' responsibility for educating daughters about physical sexual acts was a new requirement. Previously girls of all classes had probably obtained this information gradually in the course of observation, premarital sexual exploration as described in the previous chapter, and conversations with other women such as married cousins and elder sisters.[23] By the late nineteenth century, these avenues of information were increasingly strictly proscribed for young women in all classes and increasing numbers of young men.

The possibility for adolescent observation of adult sexual affection and reproductive processes diminished during this period as adults restricted their own behaviour. Historian M. J. Peterson has described the mid-century marriage of Lydia North (1815–95) and James Paget. This upper-middle-class couple appear to have had a mutually pleasurable physical relationship, but James wrote to Lydia that the 'extreme and ardour of affection when openly exhibited is as displeasing to me as, when privately shown, it is delightful'.[24] This retreat from easy acceptance of open physical affection as well as of physical sexuality appears to have taken place in many early and mid-Victorian households, and minimal physical demonstrativeness appears to have become increasingly usual in middle-class families.[25] When parents reject the open expression of sexual affection then children lose the opportunity to learn how this is expressed. There is a notion that women who live in a society that condemns female sexual passion are nonetheless able to express their sexuality fully in private, but this is difficult to accept when careful attention is paid to generational change.[26] Rather, it appears that the impact of changes in behaviour and attitudes related to sexual expression on succeeding generations grew over these decades.

Ruskin's behaviour calls for comment. Mary Lutyens argued convincingly that the reason for the non-consummation and breakdown of the marriage was due to Ruskin's horror of babies and his dishonesty in concealing his determination to avoid them from Effie before the marriage.[27] This horror would easily produce the disgust he evinced toward female genitals (not merely pubic hair) in a period when coitus could not proceed without risk of conception. He also felt intense anxiety about his masturbation. Ruskin was the only child of upwardly mobile, rigid, and disciplined parents. He belonged to one of the occupational categories, authors, editors, journalists, that Joseph Banks identified as pioneers of the small family in the 1850s, as did Thomas Carlyle and John Stuart Mill, also known to have had low levels of physical sexual interest.[28] But Banks's range of categories suggests that varied strategies were being employed to lower family size. For example, officers of the navy and marines and army officers were certainly not embracing new sexual inhibitions.[29] Venereal diseases in the army and navy reached record heights in the third quarter of the century. There was no norm of male sexuality in nineteenth-century England just as there was no norm of family size; rather, several male sexual cultures existed, shaped by factors such as religion, income, region, degree of urbanization, and homosocial environment as well as personal temperament and ambition.[30]

Newly married women's increasing lack of sexual knowledge and experience when compared to that of their husbands arises as a problem in the last third of the century. Daniel Minertzhagen (1842–1910) had extensive sexual experience while Georgina Potter (1850–1914) had none when the couple married in 1873. Their son wrote that 'Mother in her puritan chastity could not respond to father's exuberance.'[31] Daniel lacked the sensitivity and interest necessary for the creation of a mutual sexual relationship. As the marriage continued he spent as much time as possible away from home and did nothing to support Georgina during her frequent pregnancies. Edwin Lutyens (1869–1944) came to his marriage in 1897 'pure' although he was without the strong religious convictions that had previously been associated with such attitudes. Unlike John Austin (1790–1859) nearly a century earlier, he was also socially adept and skilled at pleasing others, yet Emily, his wife, later told her daughter that her honeymoon was 'a nightmare of physical pain and mental disappointment'. It appears Edwin lacked previous sexual experience, and had intercourse rapidly without any sensitivity to Emily's feelings, making the experience 'increasingly disagreeable to her', and one she came to find 'disgusting'[32]. Emily was probably hampered in any effort to alter his behaviour because both she and Edwin would have found it unacceptable for her to make sexual demands. In the absence of premarital sexual petting she would, in any event, have had little opportunity to learn how her needs might be met physically or emotionally. It is evident that other women did learn to enjoy coitus after marriage, but for many 'a sense of sin or degradation . . . accompan[ied] the sexual act' and where this was so the woman's participation might be limited. Rosie Williams, who was physically repelled by a prospective second husband was told by her elder sister that 'One man is as good as another in that respect'.[33]

During the nineteenth century upper-middle-class sexual culture shifted substantially. In the early decades women and men were often aware of the possibility of physical passion and subdued their sexual desires with difficulty. By the middle decades of the century, there was a thriving culture of sexual commerce available, which many middle-class men took advantage of, but respectable women were expected to control their sexual feelings.[34] By the later decades of the nineteenth century, there appears to have been considerable female and some male ignorance of physical sexual activity along with diminishing mutual sexual pleasure. Middle- and upper-working-class 'new women' were struggling with new ideas about sexuality from the 1890s, but few appear to have had much actual sexual experience.[35] Those women who did tentatively express positive support for female sexual expression in public insisted this was only possible in the context of continence and self-control.[36] The costs of defying sexual conventions were often high for those bohemians and radical socialists who attempted to live differently.[37]

Among the working classes illegitimacy and premarital conception rates reveal that premarital sexual intercourse between couples who had agreed to marry continued to be usual well into the nineteenth century.[38] From the 1840s, illegitimacy fell steadily, hitting a low point in 1901 when the ratio of illegitimate births to all live births reached 38.9 (Fig. 1). The twentieth-century trends make it evident that this reflects changing levels of sexual activity outside marriage. The ratio rose from 1900 in spite of improving contraception, and actually doubled between 1955 and 1980, during which period contraception became widely available to single women for the first time.[39] There are two sharp peaks, of 62.6 in 1918 and 93.3 in 1945, which clearly occur as a result of the First and Second World Wars. Male access to condoms increased during the wars but this seems to have had little impact.[40] During the war men were less likely to be present when women discovered their pregnancies and failure to marry is revealed by the relationship between the rise in the number of illegitimate births during the Second World War and the fall in pre-nuptial pregnancies.[41] If we put the two world wars to one side, then from 1875 until the 1950s the ratio stays below 50 (Table 1). From the inter-war period, some illegitimate pregnancies would have been prevented by use of contraception. However, the high numbers of pre-nuptial pregnancies reveal that the unmarried had difficulty obtaining such information and therefore the trends continue to reflect sexual mores. This period of sexual restraint is both consistent with and reinforces the other evidence about sexual behaviour.

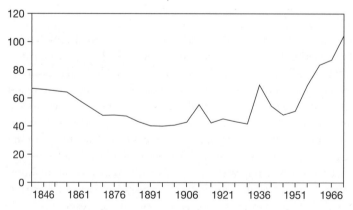

Figure 1 Illegitimate live births per 1,000 total live births

Source: *Birth Statistics: Historical Series of Statistics from Registrations of Births in England and Wales, 1837–1983* OPCS Series FM1 no. 13. T. 1.1, 19.

Table 1 Illegitimate live births per 1,000 total live births

Period	Ratio
1846–50	67.1
1851–5	65.9
1856–60	64.9
1861–5	63.6
1866–70	58.4
1871–5	52.1
1876–80	47.5
1881–5	48.0
1886–1890	46.3
1891–5	42.4
1896–1900	41.0
1901–5	39.5
1906–10	40.2
1911–15	43.1
1916–20	53.9
1921–5	42.7
1926–30	44.6
1931–5	43.5
1936–40	42.0
1941–5	68.7
1946–50	54.9
1951–5	47.5
1956–60	50.1
1961–5	69.0
1966–70	82.9
1971–5	86.8
1976–80	104.6

Source: *Birth Statistics: Historical Series of Statistics from Registrations of Births in England and Wales, 1837–1983*, OPCS Series FM1 no. 13 (1983).

There is little direct evidence of working-class women's physical sexual experiences but it is probable that many engaged in genital sexual petting with more than one partner before settling down. William Hazlitt's (1778–1830) bitter tirade, against Sarah Walker (b. *c.*1800), the daughter of an artisan and a lodging house keeper, provides a unique account of a young woman experimenting with physical sexual pleasure. Walker enjoyed sexual activity, choosing from among the limited pool of male lodgers in her mother's house those to whom she was attracted. Hazlitt writes of her 'sitting in my lap, twining herself around me, [letting me enjoy her through her petticoats] looking as if she would faint with tenderness and modesty, admitting all sorts of indecent liberties'. She sat in his lap 'rubbing against' him, 'hard at it' for an hour at a time. Marriage with Hazlitt did not interest her; 'Why could we not go on as we were', she told him, 'and never mind about the word, *forever?*' He associates female physical desire with whoring, as is usual in nineteenth-century sources, but Sarah refused to be bought. Though he bribed her mother by paying the huge sum of £100 in advance for his lodgings, she returned his books and would not marry him.[42]

A minimum of around two-thirds of working-class women were engaged in small businesses or other paid employment.[43] There was less emphasis on self-control and discipline among the upper working classes and lower middle classes and many of these women had greater economic autonomy than did upper-middle-class women. Their sexual mores appear to have been relatively fluid. Where backgrounds are given for the small number of women who made successful careers associated with non-marital sexual activity, including prostitution, artist's models, mistresses, and actresses, they frequently came from the upper working classes.[44] Research by Ginger Frost into breach of promise cases between 1870 and 1900 reveals that most of the plaintiffs were respectable small businesswomen and either upper working class or lower middle class. Sexual intercourse was reported to have taken place in 25 per cent of the cases, including some women who had been cohabiting for long periods. Some men were willing to make false promises of marriage as 'all men do', but it is perhaps more important that if circumstances changed even men who had sincerely intended to marry felt able to change their minds.[45] The cases reveal that these women often desired sexual activity but they were anxious and aware of their vulnerability once intercourse had taken place. In these cases, the consequences of the breakdown of community control over young men described in the previous chapter can be observed. The falling illegitimacy rates are evidence of women's increasing sexual caution and diminishing opportunity for relaxed premarital sexual activity with a variety of partners, which would in turn have contributed to diminishing physical sexual pleasure.

Nonetheless, working-class women still had more opportunity to experience physical sexual activity before they began having children than did middle-class women. But given their poor nutritional status and living conditions it is probable that once they had children the impact of high fertility on working-class women's sexuality was even greater.[46] Two mid-twentieth-century studies of English women living in poverty with limited access to contraception found that their pleasure in sexual intercourse rapidly diminished with successive pregnancies.[47] In some regions working-class couples had already begun to lower their fertility by ceasing childbearing earlier in women's lives. This is achieved by couples having sexual intercourse less often later in marriage (or other long-term relationship).[48] This behaviour may not be parity specific, that is, dependent on the number of children already born (desired family size), as demographers have argued, but rather dependent on a woman's health and levels of fatigue, her willingness to continue sexual relations, and the degree of control she could exercise over her partner. From the 1870s, the slowing down of a half-century of rapid urbanization led to the establishment of more settled urban working-class communities enabling women (and parents) to establish networks of support and surveillance.[49] Respectability was increasingly central to working-class women's identity. Openly expressed enthusiasm for sexual pleasure, especially if it resulted in several affairs or was expressed by single women, became deviant and stigmatized behaviour. As with all such behaviour this does not mean that it did not take place but that the incidence was diminished because it was shameful and had to be hidden. Sexually active young women, such as Sarah Walker, still existed but the majority of women around them rejected such behaviour.

Nineteenth-century scholars now support a revisionist view of female sexuality, rejecting the construction of Victorian women as excessively prudish or anxious regarding sexuality. However, the evidence suggests that the error lay in placing the peak of these attitudes in the early or mid-nineteenth century and the presentation of them as monolithic and uncontested. By the late nineteenth and early twentieth centuries there is a wealth of evidence regarding a wide range of women, which reveals that the trajectory from the mid- to late nineteenth century was in the direction of increasing anxiety and diminishing sexual pleasure. This includes evidence relating to birth control use and sexuality, as well as autobiographies, and the testimony collected by oral historians.[50] Caveats include the probability that those women who did enjoy sexual intercourse were not willing to admit to such pleasure when interviewed by comparative strangers, but nonetheless, the responses obtained have been remarkably consistent; with only occasional hints of pleasure. The other potential source of bias toward a more negative view of female sexuality is quite simply the limited volume of sources available for the earlier period, including the over-representation of Nonconformists, who had stricter sexual mores than was then usual. However, the trends suggested by these sources are supported by the birth rates.

Notes

1   M. Foucault, *The History of Sexuality* (*La Volonté de Savoir*) (1978; 1984), 17–8 n. 1.
2   J. Butler, *Recollections of George Butler* (1892), 96.
3   The advice came from Matthew Davenport Hill, who was a Liberal MP and reformer of the criminal law. He found the project amusing. Barbara was herself illegitimate and the double standard had shaped her life. P. Hirsch, *Barbara Leigh Smith Bodichon* (2001), 89–90.
4   M. Mason, *The Making of Victorian Sexuality* (1995), 43. It is unclear how Mason defines sexual hypocrisy. The OED 2nd edn. definition of hypocrisy can be summarized as the 'assuming of a false appearance of virtue or goodness, with dissimulation of real character or inclinations'. Examples that meet this definition abound. The Victorians certainly used the word in a sexual context: 'Behold one of our [brothel] patrons . . . apparently participating in the delights of a chaste wife . . . He "does the agreeable" to admiration. The arch hypocrite!' J. Talbot, *The Miseries of Prostitution* (1844), 37.
5   For Nell Ternan's relationship with Dickens, see C. Tomalin, *The Invisible Woman* (1990).
6   Letter to Fanny Smyttan, 27 Feb. 1867, cited in J. Jordan, *Josephine Butler* (2001), 81.
7   Hirsch, *Bodichon*, 90.
8   A. J. Hammerton, *Cruelty and Companionship* (1992), 6–7, 112–13, 132.
9   See J. Walkowitz, *Prostitution and Victorian Society: Women, Class and the State* (1980).
10 E. T. Burke, 'The Toll of Secret Disease', *Nineteenth Century* (1927), cited in R. Davenport-Hines, *Sex, Death and Punishment* (1991), 246.
11 E. Showalter, *Sexual Anarchy: Gender and Culture at the Fin de Siècle* (1991), 193–8. See also L. Bland, *Banishing the Beast: English Feminism and Sexual Morality, 1885–1914* (1995), ch. 1.
12 There is little existing historiography. S. Sheard, 'Profit is a Dirty Word: The Development of Public Baths and Wash-Houses in Britain, 1847–1915', *Social History of Medicine*, 13/1 (2000). A. Wear, 'The History of Personal Hygiene', in R. Porter and W. F. Bynum (eds.), *Companion Encyclopedia of the History of Medicine* (1993). Cleanliness is mentioned regularly in 19th-century sources, see e.g. G. Gissing, *New Grub Street* (1891; 1968), 278–9. F. Place, *The Autobiography of Francis Place* (*1771–1854*), ed. M. Thale (1972), 108, 225. H. Wilson, *Harriette Wilson's Memoirs*, ed. L. Blanch (1825; 1957), 112–13, 131.
13 D. Vincent, *The Rise of Mass Literacy: Reading and Writing in Modern Europe* (2000), 60–1.
14 S. Jejeebhoy, *Women's Education, Autonomy, and Reproductive Behaviour: Experience from Developing Countries* (1995), 37, 178.
15 Regional cultures, e.g. Ellen Ross, *Love and Toil: Motherhood in Outcast London, 1870–1918* (1993), 59–65. B. Reay, 'Sexuality in Nineteenth-Century England: The Social Context of

Illegitimacy in Rural Kent', *Rural History*, 1/2 (1990). D. Gittins, 'Marital Status, Work and Kinship, 1850–1930', in J. Lewis (ed.), *Labour and Love: Women's Experience of Home and Family 1850–1940* (1986).

16   See M. L. Shanley, *Feminism, Marriage and the Law in Victorian England, 1850–1895* (1989).

17   L. Leneman, 'A Truly National Movement: The View from Outside London', in M. Joannou and J. Purvis (eds.), *The Women's Suffrage Movement: New Feminist Perspectives* (2000). Jill Liddington and Jill Norris, *One Hand Tied Behind Us: The Rise of the Women's Suffrage Movement* (1978; 1994). An indication of the magnitude of movement by the early 20th century is given by the large-scale marches and the ability to sustain nationwide campaigns such as the arson attacks, see A. Rosen, *Rise up Women! The Militant Campaign of the Women's Social and Political Union 1903–1914* (1974). C. Jorgensen-Earp, *'The Transfiguring Sword': The Just War of the Women's Social and Political Union* (1997).

18   M. Lutyens, *The Ruskins and the Grays* (1972), 108–9, 184–5, 234, 284.

19   L. and J. Hamburger, *Contemplating Adultery* (1992), 117–18; see also 119, 127. S. Chitty, *The Beast and the Monk* (1974). H. M. Sikes (ed.), *The Letters of William Hazlitt* (1978). See also J. Tosh, *A Man's Place: Masculinity and the Middle Class Home in Victorian England* (1999), 58–9.

20   M. Lutyens, *Millais and the Ruskins* (1967), 155.

21   Chitty, *Beast*, 74.

22   Mothers, e.g. M. Llewellyn Davies, *Maternity: Letters from Working Women Collected by the Women's Co-operative Guild* (1915; 1978), 44, 48, 50, 58, 64. Bland, *Banishing*, 139–43. P. Keating, *The Haunted Study: A Social History of the English Novel, 1875–1914* (1989), 188–9. Gittins, *Fair Sex*, 79–90. Ross, *Love*, 107. M. Stephens, *Women and Marriage: A Handbook* (1910; 1918), 40–1. L. Tait, *Diseases of Women and Abdominal Surgery*, vol. i (1889), 51–5.

23   For sexual learning, see Chs. 7, 8.

24   M. J. Peterson, 'No Angels in the House: The Victorian Myth and the Paget Women', *American Historical Review*, 89 (1984), 701.

25   For comment on the emotional tone of the late 19th century, see P. T. Cominos, 'Late-Victorian Respectability and the Social System', *International Review of Social History*, 8/1–2 (1963). B. Caine, *Destined to be Wives: The Sisters of Beatrice Webb* (1985), 93, 127–8. R. Keynes, *Annie's Box: Charles Darwin, his Daughter and Human Evolution* (2001; 2002), 83, 216–17. G. Raverat, *Period Piece: A Cambridge Childhood* (1952), 110, 113. Davenport-Hines, *Sex*, 70–2, 124. His perceptive comments on male homosexuality and the denial of emotion in that context after 1885 are also relevant, e.g. Brian Masters, *The Life of E. F. Benson* (1991; 1993), 209, 245–6.

26   See Ch. 7.

27   Lutyens, *Ruskins*, 108–9.

28   Also see D. Hudson, *Munby Man of Two Worlds: The Life and Diaries of Arthur J. Munby, 1828–1910* (1972); for Thomas Carlyle, John Stuart Mill see P. Rose, *Parallel Lives* (1983; 1994), 64, 125–6.

29   The other occupations were painters, sculptors, artists; civil, mining engineers; accountants, physicians, and solicitors; ministers of other than the Established Church. J. A. Banks, *Victorian Values: Secularism and the Size of Families* (1981), 40.

30   M. Anderson, 'The Emergence of the Modern Life Cycle in Britain', *Social History*, 10 (1985), 80.

31   Caine, *Destined*, 95–6, *passim*.

32   M. Lutyens, *Edwin Lutyens* (1980), 56, 76.

33   Caine, *Destined*, 103.

34   See Ch. 3.

35   T. Thompson (ed.), *Dear Girl: The Diaries and Letters of Two Working Women 1897–1917* (1987), 80, 138–9, 154, 195.

36   F. Mort, *Dangerous Sexualities: Medico-Moral Politics in England since 1830* (1987), 111–16. Bland, *Banishing*, ch. 7.

37   e.g. Eleanor Marx's suicide on 31 Mar. 1898 followed repeated betrayals by her lover
      Edward Aveling. R. Brandon, *The New Women and the Old Men* (1990), 139–59. Ida Nettleship
      (1877–1907), who in 1901 married the painter Augustus John (1878–1961), invited his
      (first) mistress Dorelia McNeill (b. 1881) to share their home. Ida rapidly had four sons
      and was unable to continue with her own painting. In spite of her fondness for Dorelia she
      became deeply depressed. Dorelia's qualities enabled her to prosper. She had no personal
      ambitions other than to be an artist's muse, she did not demand fidelity from her lovers or
      herself, and she had little concern about personal comforts; e.g. giving birth to her first
      child alone in an isolated caravan did not disturb her. M. Holroyd, *Augustus John* (1974),
      191–200, 244, 251.

38   Garret et al., *Changing Family Size*, 281.

39   The connection between illegitimacy and sexual mores was rejected by E. Shorter, J. Knodel,
      and E. van de Walle, 'The Decline of Non-Marital Fertility in Europe', *Population Studies*,
      25 (1971), 376. For a more recent discussion, see R. Adair, *Courtship, Illegitimacy and
      Marriage in Early Modern England* (1996).

40   C. Chinn, *They Worked All their Lives: Women of the Urban Poor in England, 1880–1939* (1988),
      143. J. Peel, 'The Manufacture and Retailing of Contraceptives in England', *Population Studies*,
      17 (1963), n. 60, 162.

41   *Birth Statistics: Historical Series of Statistics from Registrations of Births in England and Wales,
      1837–1983*, OPCS Series FM1 no. 13 (1983), tables 1.1, 5.5.

42   The square brackets are missing words added by the editor of the letters. Sikes (ed.), *Letters*,
      63–72, 81–2, 263–4, 300–1.

43   M. Anderson, 'The Social Position of Spinsters in Mid-Victorian Britain', *Journal of Family
      History* (Winter 1984), table 2, 380, source 1851 census.

44   e.g. F. Barret-Ducrocq, *Love in the Time of Victoria* (1992), 51–5, 72–3. H. E. Blyth, *Skittles:
      The Last Victorian Courtesan: The Life and Times of Catherine Walters* (1970). T. C. Davis, *Actresses
      as Working Women: Their Social Identity in Victorian Culture* (1991), 72–3. B. Hemyng,
      'Prostitution', in H. Mayhew (ed.), *London Labour and the London Poor* (1862), 216–17, 243,
      255; 147. Hudson, *Munby*, 40–1. Wilson, *Memoirs*. This continued to be true into the 20th
      century; e.g. Dorelia McNeill's father was a mercantile clerk. Holroyd, *John*.

45   G. Frost, *Promises Broken: Courtship, Class, and Gender in Victorian England* (1995), 11, 104–5,
      114.

46   For childbearing, see Llewellyn Davies, *Maternity*.

47   M. Kerr, *The People of Ship Street* (1958), quoted in J. Klein, *Samples of English Culture*,
      vol. i (1965), 72. P. Shapiro, 'The Unplanned Children', *New Society* (1962).

48   B. Reay, 'Before the Transition: Fertility in English Villages, 1800–1880', *Continuity and
      Change*, 9 (1994), 103, 108, 110.

49   G. Stedman Jones, *Languages of Class: Studies in English Working Class History, 1832–1982*
      (1983), 27. M. Tebbutt, *Women's Talk? A Social History of Gossip in Working-Class Neighbourhoods,
      1880–1960* (1995), 77–9. J. R. Walkowitz, 'Male Vice and Female Virtue', in A. Snitow,
      C. Stansell, and S. Thompson (eds.), *Powers of Desire: The Politics of Sexuality* (1983), 46.

50   Chinn, *They Worked*, 142–3. K. Fisher, ' "She was Quite Satisfied with the Arrangements
      I Made": Gender and Birth Control in Britain 1920–1950', *Past and Present* 169 (2001), 177.
      N. Higgins, 'Marriage in mid 20th Century North England' (D.Phil. thesis, 2003), 175–88.
      E. Roberts, *A Woman's Place: An Oral History of Working-Class Women, 1890–1940* (1984).
      Ross, *Love*, 162. W. Seccombe, 'Starting to Stop: Working-Class Fertility Decline in Britain',
      Past and Present, 126 (1990), 175–7. P. Townsend, *The Family Life of Old People: An Inquiry
      in East London* (1957), 75. M. Woodside, 'Orgasm Capacity Among 200 English Working-
      Class Wives', in A. Ellis and A. P. Pillay (eds.), *Sex, Society and the Individual* (1953), 105.
      More obliquely, P. Thompson, *The Edwardians: The Remaking of British Society* (1975; 1977),
      75–80. Mixed experiences, see S. Rowbotham and J. McCrindle, *Dutiful Daughters: Women
      Talk about their Lives* (1977), 36–41.

Chapter 10

Aristotle's Compleat Masterpiece

DISPLAYING THE SECRETS OF NATURE IN THE GENERATION OF MAN (1755)

Thus Nature nothing does in vain produce,
But fits each part for what's its proper use;
And though of different sexes formed we be,
Yet betwixt these there is that unity,
That we in nothing can a greater find,
Unless the soul that's to the body joined:
And sure in this Dame Nature's in the right,
The strictest union yields the most delight.

Ch. II. Of the Restriction laid upon Men in the Use of Carnal Copulation, by the Institution of Marriage; with the Advantage that it brings to Mankind, and the proper Time for it.

'THO THE GREAT ARCHITECT OF THE WORLD has been pleased to frame us of different Sexes, and for the Propagation and Continuation of Mankind has indulged us the mutual Embraces of each other, the Desire whereof, by a powerful and secret Instinct, is become natural to us; yet he would leave them to the Law of the Creator, who has ordained, That every Man shall have his own Wife: And though since Man, by sinning against his Creator, hath fallen from his primitive Purity, and has multiplied Wives and Concubines, by which the first institution is violated, and the grossest Affront to the Divine Lawgiver; for the Holy Jesus has told us, That in the Beginning it was so; the Marriage of one Man to one Woman. So that as these conjugal Delights cannot be enjoyed but in a married State, so neither in that State can they lawfully be participated of with more than one Wife. And it is the breaking of this Order, that has filled the World with Confusion and Debauchery, has brought Diseases on the Body, Consumption on

Estates, and eternal Ruin to the Soul, if not repented of. Let all those therefore of either Sex, that have a Desire to enjoy the Delights of mutual Embraces, take care that they do it in a married State with their own Wives or Husbands, or it will become a curse to them instead of a Blessing.

[. . .]

Having taken a survey of the Parts of Generation, both in Men and Women, it is requisite that, according to my intended Method, I should shew the Use and Action of these parts in the Work of Generation, which will excellently inform us that Nature has made nothing in vain.

The external Parts in Women's Privities; or that which is most obvious to the Eye at first View, commonly called the Pudendum, as which being seen by a Man causes Shame and Blushing in the Cheeks of the Fair Sex, are designed by Nature to cover the great orifice, as that Orifice is to receive the Penis or Yard in the Act of Coition, and also give passage to the Urine, and at the Time of Birth of the Child. The use of the wings and knobs like myrtle berries, shutting the orifice and neck of the bladder, and by the swelling up, cause titulation and delight in those parts, and also to obstruct the involuntary passage of the urine.

The Use and Action of the Clitoris in Women, is like that of the Penis or Yard in Men, that is Erection; its extreme End being like that of the Glans in the Man, the Seat of the greatest Pleasure in the Act of Copulation, so is this of the Clitoris in Women, and therefore called the Sweetness of Love and the Fury of Venery.

The Action and Use of the Neck of the Womb is the same with that of the Penis, that is Erection, which is occasioned sundry Ways. For, First, in Copulation it is erected, and made strait for the Passage of the Penis to the Womb. Secondly, whilst the Passage is replete with Spirits and vital Blood, it becomes more strait for the embracing the Penis. And for the Necessity of Erection, there is a two-fold Reason: One is, that if the Neck of the Womb was not erected, the Yard could have no convenient Passage to the Womb. The other, is, that it hinders any Hurt or Damage that might ensue, through the violent Concussion of the Yard, during the Time of Copulation.

PART II DISPLAYING THE SECRETS OF NATURE IN THE PRODUCTION OF MAN

Ch. I. What Conception is; what is pre-requisite thereto; how a Woman may know whether she has conceived; and whether a boy or a girl. etc.

The first part of this Book does most properly contain the Foundation and Ground-Work of the Secrets of Nature in the Generation of Man; the Instruments of Generation in both Sexes having been described, and the Use of those Instruments, and the Aptness of them to the Uses for which Nature intended them, I have also shewed what must by done by both Sexes, in order to their having a lawful Use of each other: And then having shewn when they are fit to enter into a married State, and are capable of performing the Work of Generation; I have treated of Virginity, and shewn what it is, and wherein it consists, as also how it may be known and the Several Ways of it being lost: But still all these are but the Proemiums of Generation-Work, or the Begetting or Procreation of Children. We must therefore in this Second Part proceed on, and shew what conception is; the signs and tokens thereof; and what are the pre-requisites thereunto; for when once a woman has conceived, the work of generation is begun, and time with nature's help, will perfect the work: And what at first is but Conception, will issue in a perfect birth.

Now in Conception, that which is first to be regarded, and without which it cannot be, is the Seed of the Man, that being the active Principle, or efficient Cause of the Foetus, the Matter of which is arterial Blood and animal Spirits, which are elaborated into Seed in the Testicles, and from thence by proper Vessels conveyed into the Yard, and in the Act of Copulation, it is injected or emitted into the Womb. The next Thing is the passive Principle of the Foetus (for there must be both in order to conception) and this is an ovum or egg, impregnated by the man's seed; on being conveyed to it the womb closes up, that no air may enter therein, but the impregnated ovum may swell into a foetus. This is that which is truly and properly conception, and the pre-requisites thereunto I shall make the subject of the next section.

SEC. II. Of the pre-requisites of Conception.

I HAVE shown in the former section that there are two things to be regarded chiefly in conception, to wit, the active and passive principles. This in part shows that difference of sexes is a prerequisite to conception. So nature has ordained, there must be a proper vehicle for the active principle to be injected thereinto, and there must also be a passive principle to be impregnated thereby; so the woman has no active principle to impregnate, and therefore, without different sexes, there can be no conception.

But this is not all; for it is not enough that there be different sexes, but these different sexes must unite, and there must be coition, in order to conception; and it is coition, or the mutual embraces of both sexes, which nature has made so desirable to each other; which, when authorised in the way heaven has ordained, there is no need of ravishing; for the fair bride will quickly meet her bridegroom with equal vigour. But since in that there may be over-doing, and such errors committed by their giving way to the impetuosity of their desires, as may be prejudicial to conception, it will not be amiss to give some directions to make this operation the more effectual.

SEC. III. A Word of Advice to both Sexes; of Directions respecting the Act of Coition or Carnal Copulation.

THOUGH there are some that desire not to have children, and yet are very fond of nocturnal embraces, to whom these directions will be no way acceptable, because it may probably produce those effects which they had rather be without; yet I doubt not but the generality of both sexes, when in a married state, have such a desire to produce the fair image of themselves, that nothing can be more welcome to them than those directions that may make their mutual embraces most effectual to that end; and therefore let none think it strange that we pretend to give directions for the promoting that which nature itself teacheth all to perform; since 'tis no solecism for art to be a handmaid to nature, and to assist her in her noblest operations. Neither is it the bare performing of that act which we here direct to, but the performing of it so as to make conducive unto the work of generation. And since this act is the foundation of generation, and without which it cannot be, some care ought to be taken, and, consequently, some advice given, how to perform it well; and therein I am sure the proverb is on our side, which tells us, *That what is once well done is twice done.* But yet what we shall advance on this nice subject shall be offered with that caution, as not to give offence to the chastest ear, nor put the fair sex to the trouble of blushing. What I shall offer will consist of two parts; First, something previous to it; and secondly, something consequential to it.

For the first, When married persons design to follow the propensions of nature for the production of the fair image of themselves, let everything that looks like care and business be banished from their thoughts, for all such things are enemies to Venus; and let their animal and vital spirits be powerfully exhilarated by some brisk and generous restoratives; and let them, to invigorate their fancies, survey the lovely beauties of each other, and bear the bright ideas of them in their minds; and if it happens, that instead of beauty there is anything that looks like imperfection or deformity (for nature is not alike bountiful to all), let them be covered over with a veil of darkness and oblivion. And since the utmost intention of desire is required in this act, it may not be amiss for the bridegroom, for the more eager heightening of his joy, to delineate the scene of their approaching happiness to his fair languishing bride, in some such amorous rapture as this:

> Now, my fair bride, now I will storm the mint
> Of love and joy and rifle all that is in't.
> Now my infranchis'd hand on ev'ry side,
> Shall o'er thy naked polish'd ivory glide.
> Freely shall now my longing eyes behold,
> Thy bared snow, and thy undrained gold:
> Nor curtain now, tho' of transparent lawn
> Shall be before thy virgin treasure drawn.
> I will enjoy thee now, my fairest; come,
> And, fly with me to love's elysium;
> My rudder with thy bold hand, like a try'd
> And skilful pilot, thou shalt steer, and guide
> My bark in love's dark channel, where it shall
> Dance, as the bounding waves do rise and fall.
> Whilst my tall pinnace in the Cyprian streight,
> Rides safe at anchor, and unlades the freight.

Having by these and other amorous acts (which love can better dictate than my pen) wound up your fancies to the highest ardour and desires.

> Perform those rites nature and love requires,
> Till you have quench'd each other's am'rous fires.

And now for the second thing proposed: When the act of coition is over, and the Bridegroom has done that Nature has prompted him to, he ought to take heed of withdrawing too suddenly out of the field of battle, lest he should, by so doing, make way for cold to strike into the Womb, which might be of dangerous consequence. But when he has given time for the matrix to close up, he may withdraw, and leave the bride to her repose, which ought to be with all the calmness possible, betaking herself to rest on the right side, and not removing without great occasion, till she has taken her first sleep. She ought also to have a care of sneezing, and, if possible, to avoid both that and Coughing, or anything that agitates or causes a motion of the body. Neither should they too often reiterate those amorous engagements till the conception is confirmed. And even then the Bridegroom should remember that 'tis a Market that lasts all the year, and be careful that he does not not spend his stock too lavishly. Nor will his Wife like him at all the worse for it; for generally Women rather chuse to have a Thing done well than have it often. And in this case, to do it well, and often too is inconsistent. But so much shall suffice for this.

AFTER the means made use of in order to conception, according to the directions given before, there is reason to expect that conception should follow; but because the success of all our actions depends upon the Divine Blessing, and that Things do not always succeed according to our desires, therefore conception does not always follow upon coition. For which Reason it is, that many women, especially those newly married, who know not whether they have conceived or not, after coition; which if they were assured of, they might and would avoid several inconveniences which they now run upon thro' Ignorance thereof. For, when after conception a woman finds an alteration in herself, and yet not knows from whence it arises, she is apt to run to the doctor, and inquires of him what is the matter, who not knowing that she is with child, gives her perhaps a strong cathartical potion, which certainly destroys the conception. There are others who, out of foolish bashful coyness, though they know that they have conceived, yet will not confess it, that they may be instructed how to order themselves accordingly. Those that are coy may learn in time to be wise; and for the sake of those that are ignorant, I shall set down the signs of conception, that women may know thereby whether they have conceived or not.

If a woman hath conceived, the vein under the eye will be swelled, i.e., under the lower eyelid; the vein in the eyes appearing clearly, and the eyes somewhat discoloured; if the woman hath not her terms upon her, nor hath watched the night before, there is a certain sign of her having conceived; and this appears most plainly just upon the conception, and holds for the first two months after.

Again, stop the urine of the woman close in a glass three days, and then strain it through a fine linen cloth rag; if you find small living creatures in it, she most assuredly conceived with child: for the urine, which was before part of her own substance, will be generative as well as its mistress.

Also, a coldness and chillness of the outward parts after copulation shows a woman to have conceived, the heat being retired to make the conception; and then the veins of the breasts are more clearly seen than they were before. The tops of the nipples look redder than formerly; the body is weakened and the face discoloured; the belly waxeth very fat, because the womb closes itself together to nourish and cherish the seed. If she drinks cold water a coldness is felt in the breast; she has also loss of appetite, sour belchings, and exceeding weakness of the stomach; the breasts begin to swell and wax hard, not without pain or soreness; wringing or griping pains like the cramp happen in the belly above the navel; also divers appetites and longings are engendered. The veins of the eyes are also clearly seen, and the eyes seem something discoloured, as a looking-glass will show.

Chapter 11

HANDBOOK OF DR. KAHN'S MUSEUM (1863)

CATALOGUE OF DR KAHN'S CELEBRATED ANATOMICAL MUSEUM

Open, daily and evening

DR. KAHN EXECUTES ORDERS for every description, of Anatomical Wax Models, at a short notice, and on reasonable terms.

253   The female sexual organs laid open; *a*, the greater labia or lips, *b*, the inner labia or nymphæ, *c*, the clitoris, *d*, the vagina, *e*, the urethra, *f*, the womb, *g*, the mouth of the womb, *h*, the left ovary, *i*, the right ovary laid open, *jj*, the fallopian tubes, *kk*, the fringed or fimbriated extremities of the fallopian tubes.

254   Spermatic animalculæ 500 times magnified.

255   do. do. 1000 do.

256   Immature female ovum or egg, 300 times magnified.

257   Mature female ovum, 300 times magnified.

258   Impregnated female ovum, 300 times magnified. By the three foregoing figures it will be seen that the female egg in an immature condition is composed of a congeries of cells, with a larger one in the centre, which, as the egg advances towards maturity, rises to its surface, forming the germinal spot. On this becoming impregnated by the attachment of the spermatozoon, a small white stripe is found on the germinal spot, and this shape is termed the *nota primitica*.

259   An ovary, showing the Graafian vesicles.

260   The fallopian tube laid open, showing a fecundated ovum.

261   Section of the womb and ovary, showing the mode in which the egg is seized by the fringed extremity of the fallopian tube: *a*, the womb, *b*, passage for the ovum, *c*, mucous secretion in the womb, or deciduary membrane, *d*, fringed ends of the fallopian tube, *e*, ovary laid open, *f*, enlargement of the Graafian vesicle, containing the ovum.

262   Ovary of a girl, who had apparently never copulated, but in whom, after death, a yellow spot, formed by the departure of the ovum, and called the corpus luteum, was

found in the ovary. This accords with Dr. Bischoff's theory, who says, that ova sometimes detach themselves during menstruation, or as the result of onanism.

263   An ovary taken from an old woman, who it was supposed had never copulated, yet in the ovary several old corpora lutea are discoverable.

264   Ovary of a woman who died seven months after conception, showing a recent corpus luteum.

265   Ovary of a woman who died 4 weeks after confinement, showing the corpus luteum.

266   Representation of the mode in which the Graafian vesicle bursts on the impregnation of the ovum. The fringed end of the fallopian tube is seizing the ovary, and the egg, passing into it, is carried along the tube into the womb to be developed, pushing back the deciduary membrane as it enters: a, ovary laid open, b, the Graafian vesicle burst, c, fallopian tube laid open, d, the ovum detached from the ovary, and arriving in the womb, e, deciduary membrane, f, inner deciduary membrane.

267   The womb of a girl who died suffocated, and who had, shortly before her death, an ovum detached from the ovary, which was found in the fallopian tube; in the womb itself may be observed the mucous secretion called the deciduary membrane.

268   Womb, laid open, unimpregnated; therefore the mucous secretion is not found

ROOM FOR MEDICAL GENTLEMEN.

OBSTETRICAL PREPARATIONS.

625   A child born in proper time, attached to the placenta by the umbilical cord.

626   Full-length figure representing the natural position of the child at time of birth; the hand is shown holding an instrument, raising the umbilical cord or navel string.

627   Transverse position of the child.—In this case the child must be turned in the accouchement; for this purpose, the accoucheur's hand is introduced to effect the turning by means of the feet.

628   Foot presentation.—Here the child makes its exit from the womb by the feet, instead of the head; a running knot is attached to the left hand of the fœtus, for the purpose of assisting delivery.

629   A preparation representing the left hand introduced, in order to disengage the placenta.

630   Face presentation.—Here, instead of the face being turned to one side, it is presenting; and in order to prevent the rupture of the perineum, the hand is placed beneath, for its support.

631   Breech presentation.—In this abnormal accouchement the child comes out the breech first; the infant's legs are bent upon the chest; the delivery is obtained by means of a blunt hook, and the child is usually much injured by this kind of operation.

632   Forceps delivery.—In many accouchements the instrument called forceps is used to disengage the head of the child. This operation, however, is not so dangerous as would appear by this model.

633   An operation termed craniotomy.—In this preparation is shown how the operator uses an instrument called a perforator, in order to pierce the child's cranium to procure delivery; of course this is only done when he is convinced of the infant's death, or that the accouchement cannot be performed in any other way.

634   Division of the ligament uniting the bones of the pelvis, which was unsuccessfully attempted, in order to obviate the necessity of the Cæsarian operation.

The six following figures are introduced for the purpose of showing the extraordinary influences exercised by climate over the female sexual organs.

641   The internal sexual parts of the European female in a state of virginity—*a*, the external labia, or lips, *b*, internal labia, and at their point of junction, is a little conical gland, called *c*, clitoris, *d*, the entrance to the bladder, *e*, the entrance to the vagina, which in virginity is partially closed by a membrane, called *f*, hymen, or virginal membrane; whose absence, however, is not by any means a proof of unchastity, as it is sometimes deficient from infancy, and at other time, is so slight, as to be ruptured by ordinary exertion.

642   The external female sexual organs, in a state of virginity.

643   Sexual parts of a Lapland woman, showing the hymen.

644   Sexual parts of a Hottentot woman, showing an enormous enlargement of the inner labia through which a ring has been passed for the purpose of preserving chastity.

645   A Hottentot woman with pendulous clitoris, or natural apron.

646   A Hottentot woman, with an enormous clitoris. It is said that women of that race purposely elongate the clitoris themselves, and mutually satisfy their sexual propensities.

647   By this is represented an elongated clitoris, seen in a girl, still living in Munich, and who since the age of eight years has practised onanism (or self abuse) to such an extent that the clitoris has become enlarged.

648   Enormous enlargement of the prepuce of the clitoris in an English female, also arising from onanism.

649   Elephantiasis of the female sexual parts.—In this figure is also seen the result of onanism.

650   Elongation of the testicle caused by onanism.

651   Head and face of a man who fell a victim to the demoralising and destructive habit of onanism.

652   Spinal cord diseased by the effects of onanism, taken from a boy 12 years of age, who died in the hospital in Vienna.

653   Sexual parts of an individual, who is still living in Paris; the scrotum is split, the penis like the clitoris of a woman, joined to the scrotum without being pierced; the evacuation of the urine is by an opening resembling a vagina, which is seen beneath the sexual parts.

654   Sexual parts of an individual named Gottlich, born near Dresden, in Saxony; his scrotum consists of two equal parts; instead of the penis there is a species of clitoris, beneath which is found an opening two inches deep, by which the urine is evacuated.

655   Sexual parts of an individual named Sandl, who is still living in Brunswick, his penis is very short, and not pierced; the urine is evacuated by an opening in the scrotum, which is split.

656   Prolapsus Uteri.—This malady occurs to women who have had many children, and those of a weak constitution, who are obliged to stand long in an upright position.

657   Representation, of Dr. Bourgerie's bandage, prolapsus uteri.

658   Figure of a man who had his penis torn off by a horse, rendering the constant wearing of a small silver tube necessary for the passage of the urine.

659   Section of the male sexual parts, showing—*a*, the gland, *b*, corpus cavernosum, *c*, urethra, *d*, bladder, *e*, prostate gland, *f*, seminal vesicles, *g*, spermatic ejaculatory duct, *h*, the part of the urethra generally first attacked by gonorrhœa.
660   Enlargement of the prostate gland.

VENEREAL DISEASES.

The venereal disease made its first appearance in central Europe in the year 1492, and is supposed to have been brought from Italy. It is of two kinds, the one being called gonorrhœa, and the other syphilis. Gonorrhœa, although originally a local disease, may give rise to most serious results; while syphilis, or the constitutional disease, will inevitably, unless immediately arrested, produce the most terrific effects: on the health and personal appearance of its unfortunate victims. Syphilis generally presents itself after impure connection, but it has been known to be communicated by a single kiss.

The question will naturally arise, on viewing a collection of this description, as to what its effect may be upon the minds of the rising generation. The mode hitherto adopted in the education of youth, has been to keep them in perfect ignorance of the perils which await them during the critical passage from adolescence to manhood. The evil results of this system have been shown by the destruction of many a promising young man, who, had he the least idea of the probable consequences of an illicit indulgence of his passions, might have brought reason to his aid, and resisted those temptations to which he unfortunately became a prey. "Forewarned forearmed," is a good motto, and Dr. Kahn trusts that the horrible results of vicious indulgence as shown in the following collection, will contribute as much to the promotion of morality and chastity, if not more, than the most earnest parental admonition, or even the solemn warnings from the pulpit. The gradations of these diseases are here faithfully delineated, and it is necessary to add that they are all models of real cases, and are not in the slightest degree exaggerated.

VENEREAL DISEASE IN THE MALE.

666   Purulent discharge from the urethra, called gonorrhœa, with curvature of the penis known by the name of chordee.
667   Malignant gonorrhœa, with the foreskin contracted behind the gland; this is called paraphymosis.
668   Operation for phymosis. This disease is caused by a chancre behind the corona glandis.—The operator endeavours to force the foreskin over the gland.
669   Operation of the paraphymosis.—This is caused by a stricture of the foreskin; there the operator has recourse to the lancet, and makes an incision in the foreskin.
670   Ten syphilitic ulcers or chancres on the prepuce and glans.
671   Destruction of the foreskin, exposing the gland; the result of neglecting phymosis.
672   Cancer of the penis.—In this case the amputation of the entire penis was necessary. This operation was performed in 1827, at the Venereal Hospital in Paris by Dr. Devergère.
673   Inflammation of the scrotum, frequently the result of gonorrhœa, when too quickly stopped by maltreatment. Several abscesses are formed in the scrotum.
674   Gangrene and mortification of the scrotum, with partial destruction of the skin of the penis, which occurred during a course of mercury, administered to cure an inguinal bubo on the right side; seen, in 1826, by Doctors Duvivier and Devergère.

675   Gangrene of penis and urethra, caused by urinary abscess and stricture.

676   Schirrous enlargement of the testicle.

677   Hydrocele, or water in the testicle, with application of the trocar.

678   Vegetations on and round the glans penis.

679   Schirrons disease seen after an incision made in the prepuce, showing ulceration of the glans.

680   Amputation of the penis, caused by gangrene and mortification.

VENEREAL DISEASE IN THE FEMALE.

681   Gonorrhœa in the female.

682   Syphilis in the female, showing chancres in the vagina and at the mouth of the womb.

683   Two tumours in the inguinal region, of the size of an egg, called buboes.

684   Two syphilitic ulcers, at the anterior lip of the right of the pudendum, which is red, and much inflamed.

685   Vulva almost entirely destroyed by chancres.

686   Abscess of the outer lip on the left of the pudendum, as well as many chancres at the two exterior lips.

687   Pointed warts on the great lips.

688   Humid warts on the perineum.

689   A number of humid warts, covering all the exterior part of the pudendum.

690   Lenticular ulcers, with humid warts of the anus and its environs.

691   Venereal disease in the parts of an individual who lived near Munich, and who was regarded as a woman until he attained his 20th year. For two years he had cohabited as a female; but having caught the venereal disease in the month of January, 1850, he was brought to Munich, and at the hospital of that town was declared to be of the masculine gender.

PART 6

Did female marriages undermine conventional marriage in the Victorian era?

Introduction

I N THE FIRST DECADE of the twenty-first century, American society debated gay marriage; conservatives feared it would destroy marriage, and activists demanded the right to form a lifelong, publicly sanctioned, monogamous relationship. By examining alternatives to marriage, we can illuminate marriage itself.

During the Victorian era, marriage was regarded as the foundation of society. The Victorians celebrated it as a romantic relationship of close affection, but they also acknowledged that it was a property relationship. Middle-class women were not supposed to earn money during marriage, and if they did, their husbands legally controlled their earnings. It was difficult for middle-class women to support themselves without marrying if they did not have a private income, although more opportunities in teaching and clerical work opened up later in the century. Husbands were supposed to go out into the world of work, while wives stayed at home. Men and women supposedly had very different personalities and interests. Although husbands and wives were supposed to love each other, men's and women's intense emotions could be focused on friends of the same sex with whom they had more in common.

Historian Carroll Smith-Rosenberg established many years ago that nineteenth-century middle-class women wrote to each other in highly charged, romantic terms, dreaming of kissing and embracing each other all night, even evicting their husbands from their beds when a beloved friend came to visit. As Smith-Rosenberg pointed out, these relationships were not seen as sexual; she suggested that these women may have had erotic feelings but they did not act on them.[1] Some women even engaged in what were called Boston marriages, or female marriages, when two close friends lived together for years.

Literary critic Sharon Marcus suggests that female marriages were socially, although not legally acknowledged. Marcus goes even further – she argues that such women could be widely accepted and seen as having marriage-type relationships. In a section not excerpted here, she goes on to say that such women helped reform the marriage laws by giving wives more rights to their property. Therefore they strengthened Victorian marriages, by making them more about romantic love and emotional support than just a property transaction. Charlotte Cushman, the actress, is her example of a woman in a female marriage who was accepted. Was Charlotte Cushman a typical woman in respectable Victorian society?

The diaries of Anne Lister, a gentlewoman in early nineteenth-century Yorkshire, England, changed the way we understand these relationships. Anne Lister kept some of her diaries in a secret code that was only recently deciphered. Contrary to the hypotheses of Carroll Smith-Rosenberg and others, Anne Lister not only loved women, she had sex with them – which she called "grubbling" or a "kiss" and noted with an X in the margins of her diaries. Born in 1791, she fell in love with Marianna Lawton when she was twenty-one years old – she is the "M" of the diaries. Marianna did not have her own income, and at that point, neither did Anne. So they could not live together, like the famed Ladies of Llangollen – two Irish gentlewomen who eloped together to live in Wales. In 1815, with Anne's connivance, Marianna married the wealthy Charles Lawton – "C" in the diaries. It was not a particularly happy marriage, and Charles infected Marianna with venereal disease (which she passed on to Anne). Marianna continued her sexual relationship with Anne despite being married to Charles. Although deeply in love with Marianna, Anne had other lovers: one was Isabella Norcliffe ("Tibb"), who would have liked to live with Anne and be her companion.

While Anne Lister had an established role in York society owing to her social position and wealth (as the heiress of her aunt and uncle), some society folk shunned her because she was seen as too masculine, and a few worried that she flirted with young women. Anne Lister's diaries provide a good way to test Sharon Marcus's hypothesis, for we can examine how Charles Lawton and Anne's aunt and uncle (who provided a home for her) reacted to her relationship with Marianna.[2]

Anne Lister could not join a lesbian community or even a female network like that of Charlotte Cushman. Indeed, the notion of the "lesbian" as an identity or indeed sexual practice was very shadowy in Britain at this time. So did Anne conceive of a sexual identity? She copied a quote from the philosopher Jean-Jacques Rousseau, beginning "Je sens mon Cœur et je connais les hommes. Je ne suis fait comme aucun de ceux que j'ai vus; j'ose croire n'être fait comme aucun de ceux,"[3] which means "I know my own heart, and I know men. I am not made like those others I have seen; I believe that another being like me does not exist." She declared she loved only women, and did not want to marry. Did she think of her erotic emotions as natural or unnatural?

Notes

1   Carroll Smith-Rosenberg, *Disorderly Conduct* (New York: Oxford University Press, 1985), pp. 53–73.
2   For more on Anne Lister, see Anna Clark, "Anne Lister's Construction of Lesbian Identity," *Journal of the History of Sexuality* 7, no. 1 (1996): 23–50; Helena Whitbread, ed., *No Priest but Love: The Journals of Anne Lister from 1824–1826* (Otley, W. Yorks: Smith Settle, 1992); Jill Liddington, *Female Fortune: Land, Gender, and Authority: The Anne Lister Diaries and Other Writings, 1833–36* (London: Rivers Oram, 1998).
3   Jean-Jacques Rousseau, *The Confessions*, trans. J. M. Cohen (Harmondsworth: Penguin, 1953), p. 1.

Chapter 12

Sharon Marcus

BETWEEN WOMEN
Friendship, desire, and marriage in Victorian England (2007)

The Genealogy of Marriage

DOES MARRIAGE HAVE A HISTORY? And if so, is it only the history of alliances between men and women? Social historians have answered the first question with a resounding yes, and in the past several decades have traced marriage's evolving relationship to the state, civil society, and private life, to friends and kin, to consent, contract, and pleasure. But most have also taken for granted that until very recently, marriage has been defined as the union of male and female.[1] In 2004, when legalization of same-sex marriage in Massachusetts sparked awareness that many same-sex couples were eager to wed, those on all sides of the ensuing debate viewed gay marriage as a sudden development with relatively shallow historical roots. Opponents charged that same-sex marriage lacked a past and would be the end of history, calling it a threat to "the most fundamental institution of civilization."[2] Supporters saw it as a new phenomenon made possible only by the very recent intersection of a gay civil rights movement and the modernization of heterosexual marriage. As Stephanie Coontz put it in a defense of same-sex unions, "Gays and lesbians simply looked at the revolution heterosexuals had wrought and noticed that with its new norms, marriage could work for them, too."[3]

Changes in heterosexual marriage have made lesbian and gay unions possible, but the influence has not been unilateral. For over a century, same-sex unions have also affected innovations in heterosexual marriage. To be sure, until very recently legal marriage has only been available to opposite-sex couples, most people have long taken it for granted that marriage takes place between men and women, and for decades, lesbian and gay activists have focused more on criticizing marriage than on demanding the right to it (as many continue to do). But the meaning of marriage is not exhausted by its legal definition, and socially accepted forms of marriage that exist outside the law have long informed legal changes to the institution. Far from having to wait for heterosexuals to make marriage more flexible, same-sex couples helped create that flexibility by using marriage as a model for their relationships and by actively working to change the laws governing unions between men and women.

Same-sex unions have been part of the history of marriage since at least the nineteenth century. As we saw in chapter 1, the female relations of Victorian England included women who lived together, owned property together, made vows of fidelity to one another, and were described as spouses by themselves and by others in their social networks. Women in female marriages created relationships that, like legal marriage, did the work assigned to sexuality in the nineteenth century: the management of shared households, the transmission of property, the expression of emotional and religious affect, and the development and care of the self.[4] Through individual, customized legal agreements, women in female couples obtained some of the rights that the state automatically conferred on married couples. Their legal status as unmarried women allowed them to have a socially recognized spouse and to keep the economic autonomy that legally married wives relinquished under the doctrine of coverture. Women in female marriages were thus in the vanguard of the movement to modernize marriage, for their relationships anticipated the increasing equality of husbands and wives gradually written into law over the course of the nineteenth and twentieth centuries. More concretely, several women in female marriages played a small but pivotal role in advocating for civil divorce, the property and custody rights of wives, and expanded opportunities for unmarried women. Although female marriages were the exception, not the rule, women in them were able to play a significant role in the history of marriage because they belonged to social networks that included legislators, journalists, activists, and anthropologists. They were, to use Michael Lucey's terms, agents "who both *work within* and *do work on* . . . social forms."[5] The pressures exerted by forms of kinship outside the law but inside the social were a crucial factor in making marriage a plastic institution.

Just as the "homosexual" is a recent invention, so too is the opposition between marriage and homosexuality. Nor is the history of same-sex unions congruent with the emergence of lesbian and gay identity, for same-sex unions existed long before sexology invented the "invert." Only once medical writers and social thinkers in the 1880s began to equate inversion with the infantile, the primitive, and the undoing of a civilization premised on monogamous, heterosexual marriage did homosexuality come to seem antithetical to marriage. Since then, many have perpetuated the association between homosexuality and primitivism by warning that gay marriage will lead to an undifferentiated presocial state in which anything goes. As United States senator Rick Santorum notoriously put it in 2002, if the right to privacy were extended to gay sex, then "you have the right to bigamy, you have the right to polygamy, you have the right to incest, you have the right to adultery. You have the right to anything."[6] In that view, gay sex is so external to the social order that it has the power to reverse the course of civilization by catapulting culture into a state of nature.

In the service of a diametrically opposed political vision, Gayle Rubin made a similar argument in her pathbreaking 1995 essay, "The Traffic in Women," when she famously observed that a critique of anthropological and psychoanalytical theories of culture relegates homosexuality to a precultural realm: "[T]he incest taboo presupposes a prior, less articulate taboo on homosexuality. A prohibition against *some* heterosexual unions assumes a taboo against *non* heterosexual unions." Prefiguring a point that Judith Butler developed in *Gender Trouble* and subsequent writings, Rubin showed that anthropological theories of kinship that posit the incest taboo and male exchange of women as necessary for the emergence of culture also exclude homosexuality from civilization, and thus establish an implicit equivalence between them.[7] Psychoanalysis and structural anthropology, by emphasizing that the incest taboo and the taboo on homosexuality make social and psychic coherence possible, raise the specter that to legitimate homosexuality would dissolve the very structure of kinship.

Homosexuality does indeed haunt Claude Lévi-Strauss's *The Elementary Structures of Kinship* (1949), one of Rubin's key texts, but interestingly, Lévi-Strauss does not associate homosexuality with incest or with the precultural. One can see the case for Rubin's argument that Lévi-Strauss's concept of the incest taboo assumes a prior taboo on homosexuality, for Lévi-Strauss's theory is not overtly hospitable to the possibility of formalized same-sex relationships and there is little in it to salvage for progressive sexual politics today. "[T]he rules of kinship and marriage," Lévi-Strauss wrote, "are not made necessary by the social state. They are the social state itself."[8] The rule of marriage is the prohibition on incest, which regulates the relation between the sexes as a dictate that men must exchange women (23). It would thus follow that sexual relationships that do not involve male exchange of women could not be part of the social state. Lévi-Strauss accordingly dismissed theories of kinship that depended on what he called "feminism"— by which he meant any explanation that assigned agency and autonomy to women. In this sense, 1940s structuralist anthropology proved less willing to recognize the possibility of female autonomy than its Victorian avatars, with their accounts of early matriarchy and polyandry. Victorian anthropologists, however, also argued that primitive societies lacked incest taboos. By asserting that the incest taboo was universal, Lévi-Strauss conferred structure and sociality on primitive society—and simultaneously aligned "the social state" with marriage, defined as male authority over women, and with culture, posited as a set of rules that require men to exchange women.

Surprisingly, however, Lévi-Strauss was also willing to recognize the sociality of homosexuality. He noted that homosexuality and fraternal polyandry can both be "solutions" to the scarcity of wives (38).[9] Responding to Brenda Seligman's argument that blood-brotherhood "disputes that the woman is the sole or predominant instrument of alliance," Lévi-Strauss conceded, "It is far from our mind to claim that the exchange or gift of women is the only way to establish an alliance in primitive societies" (483). He even claimed that before Seligman did so, he himself had already shown that among some groups, the cross-cousin and potential brother-in-law "is the one with whom, as an adolescent, one indulges in homosexual activities" (484). That is, he glossed, brothers-in-law are the same "whether they play the role of the opposite sex in the erotic games of childhood, or whether their masculine alliance as adults is confirmed by each providing the other with what he does not have—a wife—through their simultaneous renunciation of what they both do have—a sister" (484).

Lévi-Strauss recognized homosexuality only to the extent that he could subsume it within heterosexuality, but in the process he characterized homosexuality as cultural, as a form of alliance within the social, not banished from it. The universality of the incest taboo means not that homosexuality is equally taboo, but rather that even homosexuality is ultimately governed by the prohibition on incest and the imperative to exogamy. Hence the assertion that homosexual relationships are governed by the same rule of exchange as heterosexual ones: "[M]arriage serves as model for that artificial and temporary 'conjugality' between young people of the same sex in some schools and on which Balzac makes the profound remark that it is never superimposed upon blood ties but replaces them" (480). An artificial, temporary, imitative conjugality—Lévi-Strauss barely conceded the existence of homosexuality as such. But precisely because he could barely see it as different from heterosexuality, he did not distinguish between heterosexuality and same-sex alliances, nor did he locate homosexuality in a primordial state of nature before incest was prohibited.

Female marriage in the nineteenth century

Members of respectable Victorian society were also able to perceive women as married to one another, and they rarely confounded female marriages between white, middle-class women with the polygamous or incestuous arrangements they attributed to the peoples they sought to subjugate, using Christian ideals of marriage to justify the imperial mission. The life of Charlotte Cushman (1816–1876), documented in letters and memoirs, shows that even a woman who did have an illicit affair with her daughter-in-law differentiated between that illicit, quasi-incestuous affair and a more marital relationship, conducted in full view of her friends and the public, with a woman she called her wife. Charlotte Cushman was one of the most acclaimed and financially successful American actresses of the nineteenth century, best known for playing Romeo in the 1840s. Born in the United States, she lived outside it for most of her life, first in England and then in Italy, but returned often to play sold-out national tours. As Lisa Merrill has shown in a brilliant biography, Cushman used the language of marriage to conceptualize many of her sexual relationships with women, which after her rise to stardom usually consisted of a primary relationship with a peer and a secondary, clandestine relationship with a much younger woman, often a fan.[10] Cushman described her primary relationships as marriages that created a spousal bond and kinship network. In 1844, she noted in her diary, "Slept with Rose," and the following day wrote "'R.' Saturday, July 6th 'married.'" (9). As in heterosexual marriage, sex made marriage and marriage created kinship: Cushman called Rose's father "Father," as though he were her father-in-law, or as though in marrying Rose she had become her sister (74).

Cushman was involved in two long-term relationships with women: one with Matilda Hays, an author, translator, and feminist activist, and another with the sculptor Emma Stebbins, whom she met in 1857. Stebbins is best known today for her sculpture *Angel of the Waters*, which stands in Central Park's Bethesda Terrace and features prominently in Tony Kushner's *Angels in America*. Until her death in 1876, Cushman cultivated a public persona as a respectable artist and lived openly with Emma Stebbins in an elegant apartment brimming with friends and pets. After Cushman's death, Emma Stebbins wrote a biography of her former spouse that, with the reticence and impersonality typical of the lifewriting discussed in chapter 1, made only one direct statement about their relationship: "It was in the winter of 1856–57 that the compiler of these memoirs first made Miss Cushman's acquaintance, and from that time the current of their two lives ran, with rare exceptions, side by side." But Stebbins attested to her marital connection with Cushman through the very act of writing the biography as a memoir, in her pointed exclusion of Cushman's other lovers from her account, in her detailed description of their shared apartment in Rome, and in a ten-page inventory of their pets, including dogs named Teddy and Bushie.[11]

One of the women's many pets became the subject of a eulogy by Isa Blagden, a writer who lived in Florence and was close to Stebbins and Cushman, for whom she composed "To Dear Old Bushie. From One Who Loved Her," cited in full in Stebbins's biography. It would be naive to think that the Victorians were so naive as to be unaware of the connotations of "Bushie" as a pet name, so to speak, for female genitalia. The use of pronouns rather than proper names in the subtitle "From One Who Loved Her" invites us to read the poem symbolically, as a lament for a beloved dog and as an anticipation of the death of a beloved woman. That conflation is facilitated by the poem's rhetorical decision to apostrophize the absent dog directly in the second person as an unnamed but personified interlocutor: "Much loving and much loved, dare I, / With my weak, faltering praise, / Record thy pure fidelity, / Thy patient, loving ways; / Thy wistful, eager, gasping sighs, / Our sullen sense to reach; / The solemn meaning of thine eyes, / More clear than uttered speech?" The rest of the poem argues that animals equal humans in love and fidelity, and concludes, "A life-long love lies in thy dust; / Can human grave hold more?"[12] In its emphasis on the true devotion of a passionate love that remains tacit, the poem signals Blagden's genuine affection for Bushie and her appreciation for the "life-long love" between the two women with whom the dog lived.[13]

Cushman herself described her relationship to Stebbins as a marriage when she warned her young lover Emma Crow that she was not a free woman; as she put it, "Do you not know that I am already married and wear the badge upon the third finger of my left hand?" (211). Cushman began a clandestine relationship with the much younger Crow in 1858, soon after she exchanged rings with Emma Stebbins and began living with her. Cushman met Crow while touring the United States; their affair lasted years, spanned continents, and is documented in Cushman's many letters to Crow, which Crow preserved and bequeathed to the Library of Congress, despite her lover's many anxious requests that she burn them. In that correspondence, Cushman frequently tried to naturalize her adulterous betrayal of Emma Stebbins by calling the younger Emma Crow her daughter, niece, and baby, as if to suggest that Crow was not Stebbins's rival but simply an addition to the family. "Never did a mother love her child so dearly. Never did Auntie think so sweetly so yearningly of her Niece. Never did Ladie love her lover so intensely," Cushman wrote.[14]

Cushman took the incestuous fantasy of sex as kinship to its literal limits when she encouraged Crow to marry Cushman's nephew and adopted son, Ned Cushman. Cushman's plan was to have Crow live near her as her daughter-in-law, a situation to which Cushman's wife, Emma Stebbins, could not object. Crow was so in love with Cushman that she agreed to the arrangement, and she and Cushman continued their affair well after Crow's marriage to Ned made Charlotte Cushman young Emma's mother-in-law and aunt to the children Emma had with Ned. After Crow married Ned Cushman, Charlotte continued to address Emma as her lover, but also as a "dear new daughter" who had, in taking the Cushman name, also become in some sense Cushman's wife. Cushman called Emma's marriage with Ned her own "ultimate entire union" with Emma, and her letters to a pregnant Emma convey a sense, as biographer Lisa Merrill puts it, "that she and her 'little lover' were having this baby together." With a grandiosity that came easily to a rich and famous actress, Cushman arrogated to herself the roles of husband, wife, father, mother, aunt, and lover, saluting Emma as "Dearest and Sweetest daughter[,] niece, friend and lover" and referring to herself in other letters as "Big Mamma."[15]

Cushman's matrilineal, incestuous, adulterous, polygamous, homosexual household seems to realize the conservative fantasy of the primitive family in which no distinctions are made, no restrictions imposed, and patriarchal monogamy does not contain the promiscuity that results when women reign unfettered. For that very reason, Cushman provides an excellent point of departure for interrogating the equation of homosexuality with primitive sexual anarchy. Her affair with Emma Crow does not in fact show that those who disregard the taboo on homosexuality will also flout the prohibitions on incest and polygamy. Instead it demonstrates that, like most Victorians, Cushman's desires were shaped by taboos that incited the very desires they prohibited. Vows of monogamy, even when not legally binding, made adultery all the more alluring, and as Foucault shows in the first volume of the *The History of Sexuality*, nothing in the Victorian family was more normative than its obsession with incest. In societies that make "the family . . . the most active site of sexuality . . . incest occupies a central place; it is constantly being solicited and refused; it is an object of obsession and attraction, a dreadful secret and an indispensable pivot. It is manifested as a thing that is strictly forbidden . . . but it is also a thing that is continuously demanded in order for the family to be a hotbed of constant sexual incitement."[16] The mother-daughter axis was as subject to eroticization as any other aspect of family life, and incest fantasies, veiled and overt, were a prominent feature of Victorian culture (see chapters 3 and 4). Cushman's letters to Emma Crow blurred the lines between lover and family member in the same way as Dinah Mulock Craik's 1850 novel *Olive* did when describing a wife's love for her husband: "She loved him at once with the love of mother, sister, friend, and wife."[17] Pornographic novels obsessively depicted incest of every variety and in every possible gender configuration (see chapter 3), and Henry James easily translated his acquaintance with Charlotte Cushman's history into the heterosexual plot of *The Golden Bowl*, in which a father marries his daughter's husband's lover, also named Charlotte.[18]

The normative cast of even Cushman's most hidden desires helps to explain why she was not branded as deviant in her lifetime and why the relationships with women that she did make public were accepted by those surrounding her. Cushman was a recognized and often admired type: a nineteenth-century woman whose financial independence made it relatively easy for her to form a couple with another woman. Cushman enjoyed playing male roles on stage, and like many middle-class and aristocratic women in female marriages, she adopted masculine dress and nicknames.[19] But she lived openly with other women as a woman, and identified with both feminine and masculine roles. Cushman called Emma Stebbins her better half and described herself as married to her first lover, Rose, but she did not consistently or exclusively see herself as a husband. The language of marriage described the quality of her commitment to a sexual partner rather than a gendered division of roles. In this respect female marriage appears, on the basis of current historical evidence, to have been a primarily middle- and upper-class phenomenon. Working-class women who earned their own money also formed couples with other women, but it was more common for one member of the couple to live as a man. Such alliances were therefore not perceived as female marriages. Although in some technical sense they could be called marriages between women, in the eyes of the law, the couple's community, and even the couple themselves, they were marriages between a woman and a man. If caught or exposed as women, some female husbands were legally censured and mocked in ballads and broadsides for seizing male privileges, but others were not.[20] An 1869 article on "Modern Amazons," for example, wrote approvingly of two women who assumed the roles of "man and wife" and "lived together in good repute with their neighbours for eighteen years."[21]

Examples of two women using the language of marriage to describe their relationships in the relatively private context of journals and letters abound across the nineteenth century. Eleanor Butler referred to her beloved Sarah Ponsonby in her journals as "my better half."[22] Sculptor Harriet Hosmer, one of Cushman's friends in Rome, called the widowed Englishwoman Lady Louisa Ashburton "my sposa" and referred to herself as Ashburton's "hubbie," "wedded wife," and daughter. Writing to Ashburton of a marriage between monarchs, Hosmer added, "They will be as happy in their married life as we are in ours"; in another letter she promised "when you are here I shall be a model wife (or husband whichever you like)."[23] Early in the century, Anne Lister and Anne Walker decided to become "companions for life" in a relationship that would, according to both, "be as good as marriage." Lister sealed her union with Walker by giving her a ring and arranging to receive communion with her, along with a legal ceremony in which each woman willed the other her unentailed property.[24] An 1892 obituary of English-born Annie Hindle in the *Chicago Herald* reported that in 1886 the famous male impersonator was married to her "dresser and faithful companion" Annie Ryan, "a pretty little brunette of twenty-five" by "a minister of the gospel, Rev. E.H. Brooks," who "solemnly pronounced Annie Hindle the husband of Annie Ryan." Hindle married in male dress, using a male name, but the article noted that following the wedding she lived with Ryan while dressed as a woman: "The neighbors respected them . . . . That they could live together openly as man and wife, the husband always in female attire, and yet cause no scandal, is the best proof of the esteem in which those around them held them."[25]

The idea of female marriage was not simply a private metaphor used by women in same-sex relationships; it was also a term used by the legally married to describe relationships that were conducted openly and discussed neutrally in respectable society. Even among middle-class Victorians, marriages were not defined by law alone, and for couples with no legal status, social acceptance provided legitimation and established rules for beginning and ending relationships.[26] Charlotte Cushman assumed that many in her circle were aware of sexual romance between women, since she warned Emma Crow in an 1860 letter that "there are people in this world who could understand our love for each other, therefore it is necessary that we should keep our expression of it to ourselves."[27] The historical context leaves it surprisingly unclear whether Cushman demanded secrecy because Crow was a woman, or because Cushman was afraid of being exposed as adulterous. There are no similar records of Cushman attempting to conceal her relationships with Eliza Cook, Matilda Hays, or Emma Stebbins, which far from being open secrets were explicitly acknowledged by her social circle and in newspapers. Cushman and her lovers displayed their intimacy for all to see. In the 1840s Cook published a fervent poem, "To Charlotte Cushman," which described the two women as "captive in Affection's thrall," and when Hays published her translation of George Sand's *La Petite Fadette* in 1851, she dedicated it to Charlotte Cushman. On a tour of United States theaters in 1849, Cushman traveled with Hays, and a newspaper article praising Cushman as a "woman . . . worthy of homage and esteem" added, "Miss Cushman will be accompanied by her friend, novelist and translator, Matilda M. Hays."[28]

When grasping for a vocabulary to describe relationships between women, Victorians often, as we saw in chapter 1, resorted to a qualified, hyperbolic lexicon of friendship, but they also applied the concept of marriage to female couples. Elizabeth Barrett Browning wrote to her sister Arabel in 1852 about meeting Matilda Hays and Charlotte Cushman: "I understand that she & Miss Hayes [sic] have made vows of celibacy & of eternal attachment to each other—they live together, dress alike . . . it is a female marriage. I happened to say, 'Well, I never heard of such a thing before.' 'Haven't you?' said Mrs Corkrane [sic],

. . . 'oh, it is by no means uncommon.' They are on their way to Rome, so I dare say we shall see a good deal of them. Though an actress . . . Miss Cushman has an unimpeachable character."[29] Barrett Browning's informant was the wife of journalist John Frazer Corkran, a correspondent for the *Morning Chronicle*. Browning's reference to vows of celibacy suggests an equation of female marriage with sexual renunciation, but the conjunction of the women's celibacy with their "eternal attachment" to each other redefines celibacy as a mutual vow never to leave one another to marry men, one way of predicating Barrett Browning's next term, "a female marriage." The offhandedness of Barrett Browning's "I happened to say" sits uneasily with the emphatic nature of what she does say—"Well, I have never heard of such a thing"—but suggests her desire to demonstrate that she has already absorbed the lesson in urbanity imparted by her married interlocutor, who remarks, "[I]t is by no means uncommon." Browning's final comment on Cushman's reputation for respectability makes no connection, positive or negative, between her female marriage and her "unimpeachable character." Far from suggesting that she might want to avoid Cushman and Hays, Browning writes that she expects to see a good deal of them—and she did, often bringing along her husband and their young son.

To understand the social position of women in female marriages, it is helpful to distinguish between a subculture and a network. Charlotte Cushman did not belong to a subculture, a type of social group that tends to be organized around a limited number of shared traits and that coheres through its separation from the mainstream. She did, however, belong to a network, a form of social alliance whose strength derives from its relative openness and internal variety and from its links to other networks. Overlapping sets of acquaintances as well as shared identities define networks; the stronger the network, the greater the number and type of groups to which it is linked. Cushman's network thus included women in or interested in relationships with other women and had many links to people who were not in same-sex couples. Her circle overlapped considerably, for example, with the Browning circle, which consisted of highly respected artists who lived in Italy to get distance from their immediate families, access to a warmer climate, and exposure to Italy's historic culture. Charlotte Cushman's integration into multiple networks shows how easily same-sex relationships between women were assimilated to the model of marriage. Indeed, as Merrill notes, Cushman's relationships with Matilda Hays and Emma Stebbins helped incorporate the actress into many networks by giving her an aura of propriety and respectability (190).

Women in female marriages or interested in sexual liaisons with women banded together but also entered social circles organized around legally married couples. Robert and Elizabeth Barrett Browning spent time not only with Cushman and Hays but with several other women whose charged same-sex relationships included giddy flirtations, tempestuous infatuations, short-term love affairs, and long-term partnerships. The Brownings' letters recount numerous dinners, picnics, and excursions with Harriet Hosmer, Isa Blagden, Kate Field, and Frances Power Cobbe, as well as with Cushman and Stebbins. In some cases, the ties were deep: Blagden was one of Robert Browning's chief correspondents, Hosmer made a famous cast of the Brownings' hands, and after his wife's death, Robert gave Field a chain and locket Elizabeth had worn since childhood, adding to it some of his wife's hair.[30] Cushman, Hosmer, and Cobbe were on good social terms with married women such as Jane Carlyle, Mary Somerville, and Margaret Oliphant, and often socialized with their husbands as well. Harriet Hosmer adopted boyish dress and manners and flirted openly with women, but Victorian lifewriting attests that dozens of respectable Englishwomen traveling to Rome were eager to meet her. She knew the Gladstones, Sir William Boxall (director of the National Gallery and portraitist of leading figures of the day), and the Layards (Austen Layard was an archeologist, politician, and ambassador to Madrid in the 1870s; his wife was the daughter of Sir John and Lady Charlotte Guest). Her visitors in the late 1860s included a diplomat's wife, a philanthropic Christian woman, and Anne Thackeray, who traveled to Rome with Lady de Rothschild.[31]

In the 1860s and 1870s, a period when few knew of the sexological idea of inversion and many still associated sodomy with sexual acts absolutely opposed to nature and virtue, the female couple was accepted as a variation on legal marriage, not treated as a separate species. This suggests that Lillian Faderman and Carroll Smith-Rosenberg were absolutely right that Victorians considered love between women to be perfectly normal, whether that love involved intense, sensual friendships that existed alongside marriage to men (Smith-Rosenberg) or lifelong partnerships that replaced marriage to men (Faderman).[32] It also shows how they were wrong. Smith-Rosenberg erred in defining intimacy between women as a supplement to male-female marriage, for women in female marriages did not supplement marriage, they appropriated it. Faderman was wrong to argue that acceptance of female couples depended on the perceived asexuality of their relationships; the use of marriage as a term to describe female couples suggests that people believed sex was involved, for marriage, unlike friendship, was never an asexual term. For Victorians, marriage meant the union of sexual and spiritual impulses, the reconciliation of sexuality with propriety. Marriage was a socially acceptable exhibition of sexual intimacy because it was predicated on fidelity and thus advertised not only the sexuality of spouses but also their acceptance of restraints and limits. For this reason, female marriage was not associated with a savage state of sexual license but instead was readily integrated into even the most restrictive ideas of social order. As we will see, however, female marriage also differed from legal marriage between men and women in significant ways, and those differences made it a model for reformers seeking to modernize legal marriage.

Notes

1 For the social history of marriage in England, see Lawrence Stone, *The Family, Sex and Marriage in England 1500–1800* (New York: Harper Torchbooks, 1979), and John R. Gillis, *For Better, For Worse: British Marriages, 1600 to the Present* (New York: Oxford University Press, 1985). In *Same-Sex Unions in Pre-modern Europe* (New York: Vintage Books, 1994), John Boswell argued that medieval Christian churches conducted ceremonies to unite men in relationships that resembled marriage, but his claims did not impact subsequent scholarship on modern marriage.

2 President George W. Bush, February 2004 speech advocating a constitutional amendment to ban same-sex marriage, http://www.cnn.com/2004/ALLPOLITICS/02/24/elec04.prez.bush.transcript/index.html. In France, politicians made similar charges that same-sex unions would destroy the symbolic order of culture. On the French debates, see Didier Eribon, *Échapper à la psychanalyse* (Paris: Editions Léo Scheer, 2005); Michael Lucey, *The Misfit of the Family: Balzac and the Social Forms of Sexuality* (Durham, NC: Duke University Press, 2003), 15; and Judith Butler, *Undoing Gender* (New York: Routledge, 2004), 110–23.

3 Stephanie Coontz, "The Heterosexual Revolution," op-ed, *New York Times*, July 5, 2005, A17. George Chauncey similarly argues that developments in heterosexual culture preceded and enabled the lesbian and gay interest in marriage, and heterosexual "acceptance of sexual relations as a source of pleasure . . . made lesbians, bisexuals, and gay men bolder and more

confident"; *Why Marriage? The History Shaping Today's Debate over Gay Equality* (New York: Basic Books, 2004), 34.

4   Michael Lucey develops this definition of sexuality through a synthesis of Pierre Bourdieu and Michel Foucault in *The Misfit of the Family*; see 18, 28, 150.

5   Lucey, *The Misfit of the Family*, xxvii.

6   Hendrik Hertzberg, "Dog Bites Man," *New Yorker*, May 5, 2003, 33.

7   Gayle Rubin, "The Traffic in Women: Notes toward a Political Economy of Sex," in *Toward an Anthropology of Women*, ed. Rayna Reiter (New York: Monthly Review Press, 1975), 180. In *Gender Trouble: Feminism and the Subversion of Identity* (New York: Routledge, 1990), Judith Butler developed Rubin's argument into a groundbreaking critique of the "heterosexual matrix," which charges the incest prohibition with producing gender identity as heterosexuality. In *Antigone's Claim: Kinship Between Life and Death* (New York: Columbia University Press, 2000), Butler reconfigured that insight to argue that one must distinguish between prohibitions on incest and on homosexuality and decouple kinship from heterosexuality, 66.

8   Claude Lévi-Strauss, *The Elementary Structures of Kinship*, trans. James Harle Bell, John Richard von Sturmer, and Rodney Needham (1949; repr. Boston: Beacon Press, 1969), 490. All further references are to this edition and appear in the text.

9   The word in French is "homosexualité"; Claude Lévi-Strauss, *Les Structures élémentaires de la parenté* (1947; repr. Paris: Mouton, 1981), 44.

10   Lisa Merrill, *When Romeo Was a Woman: Charlotte Cushman and Her Circle of Female Spectators* (Ann Arbor: University of Michigan Press, 1999), 150. Further references are to this edition and appear in the text.

11   Emma Stebbins, ed., *Charlotte Cushman: Her Letters and Memories of Her Life* (Boston: Houghton, Osgood and Company; Cambridge: The Riverside Press, 1879), 100. For the description of their shared house, see 114–15; for a discussion of their servants, the other "members of this household," see 116–21; on pets, see 112–31. Merrill interprets Stebbins's elision of references to Cushman's former lovers as a suppression of overt references to lesbianism, 251, but it seems instead a subtle admission of a possessive relationship to her biographical subject.

12   Cited in Stebbins, *Charlotte Cushman*, 126–27.

13   The shared pet was a common trope of female marriages. Katherine Bradley and Edith Cooper, who lived together and wrote under the shared name Michael Field, were devoted to a trinity they formed with their dog Whym Chow, whom they saw as mediating their union; see Frederick S. Roden, *Same-Sex Desire in Victorian Religious Culture* (Houndmills: Palgrave Macmillan, 2002), 191–99. On the affinity between homoerotic love and the love of and for animals, see also Ruth Vanita, *Sappho and the Virgin Mary: Same-Sex Love and the English Literary Imagination* (New York: Columbia University Press, 1996), 215–41.

14   Cited in Julia Markus, *Across an Untried Sea: Discovering Lives Hidden in the Shadow of Convention and Time* (New York: Alfred A. Knopf, 2000), 175.

15   See Merrill, 221, 223, 217, 226, 231, 230.

16   Foucault, *The History of Sexuality. Volume 1: An Introduction*, trans. Robert Hurley (New York: Vintage Books, 1980), 109.

17   Dinah Mulock Craik, *Olive* (1850; repr., New York: Oxford University Press, 1999), 314.

18   Henry James discussed Cushman and Hosmer, whose Italian careers he deemed "likely to lead us into bypaths queer and crooked," in *William Wetmore Story and His Friends: From Friends, Diaries, and Recollections*, vol. 1 (1903; repr., New York: Da Capo Press, 1969), 258. In *Across an Untried Sea*, Markus notes the connection between James's acquaintance with Cushman's circle and the plot of *The Golden Bowl*, 72–73. Markus also notes that Emma Crow Cushman, both while married to Ned and after his death, continued to have female lovers, 231, 282.

19   As a specialist in trouser roles, Cushman was often perceived as masculine; her lover before Emma Stebbins, Matilda Hays, was often called Max or Mathew; Merrill, 160. Their friends

Harriet Hosmer, Frances Power Cobbe, and Rosa Bonheur were also often described as boyish or masculine. Merrill notes that reviewers often remarked on Cushman's virility as an actress but did not connect that characteristic to her sexuality, 125.

20   For overt hostility to passing women, see *Sinks of London Laid Open* (London: J. Duncombe, 1848), which described a woman who dressed as a man as a "singular being" and "creature" who "had a wife; and, as if that was not enough for any man, likewise had a mistress," 66, 67.

21   "Gleanings from Dark Annals: Modern Amazons," *Chambers's Journal of Popular Literature, Science and Arts* (May 30, 1863), 348–49. On women who dressed or lived as men in the nineteenth century, see Gretchen van Slyke, "Who Wears the Pants Here? The Policing of Women's Dress in Nineteenth-Century England, Germany and France," *Nineteenth-Century Contexts* 17.1 (1993), 17–33; Camilla Townsend, "'I Am the Woman for Spirit': A Working Woman's Gender Transgression in Victorian London," in *Sexualities in Victorian Britain*, eds. Andrew H. Miller and James Eli Adams (Bloomington: Indiana University Press, 1996), 214–33; Julie Wheelright, *Amazons and Military Maids: Women Who Dressed as Men in Pursuit of Life, Liberty and Happiness* (London: Pandora, 1989); and "Cross-dressing Women," in Alison Oram and Annmarie Turnbull, *The Lesbian History Sourcebook: Love and Sex Between Women in Britain from 1780 to 1970* (London: Routledge, 2001), 11–34.

22   Eleanor Butler cited in Rick Incorvati, "Introduction: Women's Friendships and Lesbian Sexuality," *Nineteenth-Century Contexts* 23.2 (2001), 176.

23   Dolly Sherwood, *Harriet Hosmer: American Sculptor 1830–1908* (Columbia: University of Missouri Press, 1991), 271; Markus, *Across an Untried Sea*, 247; and Martha Vicinus, *Intimate Friends: Women Who Loved Women, 1778–1928* (Chicago: University of Chicago Press, 2004), 51, 50.

24   Jill Liddington, *Female Fortune: Land, Gender and Authority. The Anne Lister Diaries and Other Writings* (London and New York: Rivers Oram Press, 1998), 62, 94.

25   *Chicago Herald*, December 27, 1892, cited in Erna Olafson Hellerstein, Leslie Parker Hume, and Karen M. Offen, eds., *Victorian Women: A Documentary Account of Women's Lives in Nineteenth-Century England, France, and the United States* (Stanford: Stanford University Press, 1981), 188–89.

26   In *Intimate Friends*, Vicinus wavers about the social status of relationships like Hosmer's with Ashburton; on the one hand, she writes that Victorians were "happy to let odd sexual relations flourish as long as no one spoke openly about them," 54, on the other that "Cushman and Hosmer . . . never pretended to be other than women who loved women, and they were accepted as such," 55.

27   Cited in Markus, *Across an Untried Sea*, 65.

28   Cook cited in Merrill, 138; 1849 article cited in Merrill, 163.

29   Cited in Robert Browning, *Dearest Isa: Robert Browning's Letters to Isabella Blagden*, ed. Edward C. McAleer (Austin: University of Texas Press, 1951), 27, n. 12; my attention was drawn to this quotation by its partial citation in Merrill, 160, and in Sherwood, 41. Browning misspelled her acquaintance's name, which was Corkran.

30   Lilian Whiting records Robert Browning's gift to Field in *The Brownings: Their Life and Art* (Boston: Little, Brown & Co., 1911), 153–54. On the Brownings's almost daily contact with Hosmer in 1857, see Cornelia Carr, ed., *Harriet Hosmer: Letters and Memories* (London: John Lane, 1913), 92.

31   See Carr, ed., *Harriet Hosmer: Letters and Memories*, 189; Martha Somerville, *Personal Recollections, from Early Life to Old Age, of Mary Somerville* (London: John Murray, 1873), 305, 359, who noted that Mr. Somerville also knew and liked Cobbe, 326. For instances of Englishwomen who mentioned meeting Hosmer (as well as William Story) while visiting Rome, see *Letters of Mary Mathison* (London: for private circulation only, 1875), 11; Georgiana Baroness Bloomfield, *Reminiscences of Court and Diplomatic Life*, vol. 2 (London: Kegan, Paul, Trench &Co., 1883), 301–2, 310; and Hester Ritchie, ed., *Letters of Anne Thackeray Ritchie* (London: John Murray, 1924), 137.

32   Carroll Smith-Rosenberg, "The Female World of Love and Ritual: Relations between Women in Nineteenth-Century America," in *Feminism and History*, ed. Joan Wallach Scott (Oxford: Oxford University Press, 1996), 366–97; Lillian Faderman, *Surpassing the Love of Men: Romantic Friendship and Love Between Women from the Renaissance to the Present* (New York: William Morrow, 1981).

Chapter 13

Anne Lister

I KNOW MY OWN HEART
(1988 edition)

Monday 31 August 1818 [Halifax]

LETTER FROM M– . . . Her letter breathes little of affection & indeed I do not estimate her feelings towards me very highly. She has not, she never had, the heart that Isabella has. I suppose she is more comfortable now than formerly with C–. She has her carriage & the luxuries of life & thinks proportionately less of me. Mrs Featherstone said, 'Give her these things & these are all she wants.' M–'s conduct to me has certainly been as strange a mixture of weakness, selfishness & worldly-mindedness. Consider her conduct on our first acquaintance; before her marriage; about her marriage; & ever since. An unfaithful friend to Isabella, a weak & wavering companion to me. On calm & mature reflection I neither much admire her nor much esteem her character. But she is specious, very specious, with much female vanity. I do not accuse her of premeditated deceit because perhaps she deceives herself as much as anyone else. She always seemed religious & talked piously. She believed herself, or seemed to believe herself, over head & ears in love, yet she sold her person to another for a carriage & a jointure, still keeping her intercourse with the one she loved & was seriously desirous of executing the prostituting of herself in disguise to any man who could make up the deficiencies & get her with child for the sake of fixing her importance by being the mother of an heir to Lawton. I know the scheme was originally my own proposing but she persisted in it till I utterly disclaimed it, shocked, as I said, at the serious idea of such a thing. Wherewith her morality? But I have acted very foolishly & wickedly. Oh that I may repent & turn me from my sin. Lord, forgive & help me.

Saturday 5 September 1819 [Halifax]

Not much conversation before getting into bed. C– made no objection to her coming to Manchester when he heard she was to meet me, tho' before he did not wish her to go farther than Wilmslow, he hurried them off before seven in the morning that she might have more time to be with me, & on this account, would give her till eight o'clock to be at home tomorrow . . . Asked her how often they were connected &, guessing, found it might be at the rate of about twenty times a year. Got into bed. She seemed to want a kiss. It was more than I did. The tears rushed to my eyes. I felt I know not what & she perceived that I was much agitated. She bade me not or she should begin too & I knew not how she should suffer. She guessed not what passed within me. They were not tears of adoration. I felt that she was another man's wife. I shuddered at the thought & at the conviction that no soffistry [sic] could gloss over the criminality of our connection. It seemed not that the like had occurred to her. (I said, just before we got up, 'Well, come, whatever C– has done to me, I am even with him. However, he little thinks what we have been about. What would he do if he knew?' 'Do? He would divorce me.' 'Yes,' said I, 'it would be a sad business for us both, but we are even with him, at any rate.' 'Indeed,' said M–, laughing, 'indeed we are.' Shewed no sign of scruples . . . What is M–'s match but legal prostitution? And, alas, what is her connection with me? Has she more passion than refinement? More plausibility than virtue? Give me a little romance. It is the greatest purifier of our affections & often an excellent guard against liberties.) From the kiss she gave me it seemed as if she loved me as fondly as ever. By & by, we seemed to drop asleep but, by & by, I perceived she would like another kiss & she whispered, 'Come again a bit, Freddy.' For a little while I pretended sleep. In fact, it was inconvenient. But soon, I got up a second time, again took off, went to her a second time &, in spite of all, she really gave me pleasure, & I told her no one had ever given me kisses like hers.

Tuesday 4 April 1820 [Halifax]

After coming up, M– was to look over some of our old letters. In getting them, happened to stumble on some memoranda I made in 1817 on her conduct, her selfishness in marrying, the waste & distraction of my love, etc. Began reading these & went on thoughtlessly till I heard a book fall from her hands &, turning round, saw her motionless & speechless, in tears. Tried very soothing & affectionate means. She had never before known how I loved her or half what her marriage had cost me. Had she known, she could not have done it & it was evident that repentance now pressed heavily. I endeavoured, & successfully, to prove it to have been done for the best. She said she had never deserved some of the remarks made, but it was quite natural in me to make them. She grieved over what I had suffered & would never doubt me again. I am indeed persuaded & satisfied of her love.

Wednesday 13 June 1821 [Halifax]

Finished my letter to M– . . . I have not exactly given her a promise in a set form of words but I have done nearly, in fact, the same thing, so that I cannot now retract with honour. Well, I am satisfied to have done. I love her & her heart is mine in return. Liberty & wavering made us both wretched & why throw away our happiness so foolishly? She is my wife in honour & in love & why not acknowledge her such openly & at once? I am satisfied to have her mind, & my own, at ease. The chain is golden & shared with M–. I love it better, than any liberty.

Thursday 27 June 1822 [Halifax]

Talking, after supper, to my uncle & aunt about M–. One thing led to another till I said plainly, in substance, that she would not have married if she or I had had good independent fortunes. That her having C– was as much my doing as hers & that I hoped she would one day be in the Blue Room, that is, live with me. I said we both of us knew we could not live on air. Besides, I did not like her being in Petergate [York] & had rather have her at Lawton than there. My uncle, as usual, said little or nothing but seemed well enough satisfied. My aunt talked, appearing not at all surprised, saying she always thought it a match of convenience.

Wednesday 20 August 1823 [Halifax]

Soon began on the erotics last night. Her warmth encouraging . . . Both awoke at five in the morning & talked till seven. Asked if this was not better than my sleeping in Micklegate [at the Duffins']. Yes, but it was prudence on her part. She had a feeling she could not describe. Would make any sacrifice rather than have our connection suspected. She seemed very affectionate & fond of me. Said I was her only comfort. She should be miserable without me . . . [I said] 'This is adultery to all intents & purposes.' 'No, no,' said she. 'Oh, yes, M–. No casuistry can disguise it.' 'Not this then, but the other.' 'Well,' said I, choosing to let the thing turn her own way. 'I always considered your marriage legal prostitution. We were both wrong. You to do it & I to consent to it. And, when I think of blaming others, I always remember nothing can at all excuse us but our prior connection.' I did not pursue the subject, nor did M– seem to think much of it. The fear of discovery is strong. It rather increases, I think, but her conscience seems seared so long as concealment is secure . . . Told her she need not fear my conduct letting out our secret. I could deceive anyone.

Wednesday 17 September 1823 [Scarborough]

Talked a little after we got into bed. Told M– I would not be with her again in strange places till I had an establishment of my own & that degree of importance which would carry me thro', for that she, & she owned it, had not consequence enough to, as it were, pass me off. If she were a Lady Mary it would be very different, but I knew her feelings & excused them. I felt for, & had a great deal of consideration for her, more than she was aware. I was going to offer never to be with her again till we could be together entirely, but I stopt short, tho' not before she guessed that I meant offering to be off altogether. This seemed to affect her. I said I had stopt short, doubting whether it would be right to make such an offer, for things had perhaps gone too far. It was necessary for people to meet sometimes & I had no right to propose what might weaken the tie between us. For the intellectuals might not be enough for me. She said I did not know her feeling; the objection, the horror she had to anything unnatural. I shewed her I understood her & then observed upon my conduct & feelings being surely natural to me inasmuch as they were not taught, not fictitious, but instinctive. Said from my heart, I could make any sacrifice for her, tho' she could not for me. I could have braved anything. Yes, I have often felt I could have rushed on ruin. She said it was lucky for us both her feelings were cooler. They tempered mine. I said this was not necessary. I had met with those who could feel in unison with me . . . My feelings now began to overpower me. I thought of the devotion with which I had loved her, & of all I had suffered. I contrasted these with all the little deceits she has put upon me & with those cooler feelings with which she thought it so lucky to have tempered mine. I thought of these things & my heart was almost agonized to bursting. The tears ran down my cheeks. I stifled my sobs but at last my agitation could not be concealed. M– bade me not try to hide it & it must have been about half past four before I could at all compose myself & drop to sleep quite exhausted. My head much swollen in the morning, yet I got up & cold water made me decent enough to appear at breakfast. M— cried a little last night & several times asked, 'Can I say nothing to console you?' 'No, my love,' said I, 'nothing human can just now or I am sure you could.' It was with great difficulty I could contain myself all the morning . . .

Tuesday 2 March 1824 [Halifax]

Walked with Mrs Priestley ½ way to Cliff-hill to meet Miss Walker with whom she was going in the carriage to make calls. They took me up & set me down at the top of our lane at 10¾. When walking with Mrs Priestley, said she would believe I should never marry if she knew me better. I had been pretty well tried. I might have had, & perhaps might still have, rank, fortune & talent, a title & several thousand a year with thorough worth & amiability added to great learning. In my own mind alluded to Sir George Stainton. But I refused from principle. There was one feeling – I meant love – properly so-called, that was out of my way, & I did not think it right to marry without. I should have a good fortune & had no occasion. Not that I could live without a companion. I did not mean to say that. She said I should be too fastidious. There would be none I should choose. 'No,' said I, 'I have chosen already.' Mrs Priestley looked. 'One can but be happy,' said I. 'It is a lady & my mind has been made up these fifteen years.' I ought to have said a dozen for, of course, I meant M—, but said I never mentioned this to anyone but my uncle & aunt. 'You will see, in time. I am sure you will like my choice.' Here Mrs Walker's carriage came up & stopt our conversation. I wonder what Mrs Priestley thought. She will not forget &, I think, was rather taken by surprise.

PART 7

How were definitions of prostitution influenced by race, and were experts able to control prostitution?

Introduction

BY THE NINETEENTH CENTURY, venereal disease had become a major social and medical problem. In response, evangelical social reformers had initiated studies of prostitutes in the earlier nineteenth century, as they sought to save them from the streets. They blamed English prostitutes for their lack of discipline and their love of fine dress. Later, doctors and social scientists in France and Britain combined this moralism with more detailed investigations, finding that low wages in women's work and the demand of men for sex pushed women into prostitution, which might be a temporary stage of their lives. The definition of prostitution turned out to be difficult. Was a woman a prostitute if she only occasionally sold sex? If she later married?

In an effort to control and define prostitution against this fluid sexual commerce, the authorities of some countries, such as France and Belgium, monitored and regulated prostitutes, requiring women who sold sex to register and subjecting them to police surveillance. The Belgians were particularly notorious for their official brothels.[1]

The British resisted such tactics for a long time, but the army was very concerned that one third of its soldiers were infected with venereal disease. So it instituted a series of contagious diseases laws. The first ordinance was actually passed for Hong Kong, then a British possession, in 1857, requiring brothel keepers to register their inmates and treat them for venereal disease. The Contagious Diseases Acts were expanded and extended to Britain's garrison and port towns in 1864, mandating women in port and garrison towns accused of being prostitutes to submit to forcible pelvic examinations, and if found to be infected with venereal disease, to be confined in a Lock hospital for treatment. Throughout the 1860s and 70s, these laws were implemented throughout the colonies. Unfortunately, the treatment, with mercury, was not effective, and the soldiers were not examined or treated.[2] Experts such as William Acton proclaimed that prostitutes were indecent by nature – they were not as sensitive as respectable ladies – therefore, they should be treated harshly in order to prevent venereal disease. The Contagious Diseases Acts seemed like the modern response to a medical problem.

A coalition of lady reformers, religious reformers, and working-class men protested vigorously against the acts. Josephine Butler, an academic's wife, ministered to prostitutes on the streets of Oxford. She hated the way the promulgators of the Contagious Diseases Acts assumed that the government basically needed to provide a supply of undiseased women to sexually service its soldiers. So she founded the Ladies' National Association to campaign against the acts, defying the disapproval of society which did not think ladies should know of such things, let alone protest them publicly – and also the violent hostility of pimps who did not want prostitutes rescued. The movement succeeded in getting the Contagious Diseases Acts suspended in Britain in 1883, and repealed in 1886.

Meanwhile the Contagious Diseases Acts had been extended into more and more colonies. Philippa Levine's book shows that in the colonial context women suspected of selling sex were studied and defined in terms of broader sexual and racial categories, not as individuals. How was the denigrated language used against them inflected by race, or class as well? Was this categorization and regulation effective? Later in the book, Levine reports that some dancing girls in India – who followed a historic traditional trade – complained that they were wrongly classified as prostitutes. Some registered women actually petitioned the authorities complaining they were not getting enough customers. What other power relations were prostitutes subjected to, outside of colonial regulations and discourses?

Pressure from missionaries, feminists, and Indian nationalists resulted in the repeal of the Acts in the colonies in 1887–8. However, in fact, the practice of registering prostitutes continued, as two American women discovered. Their findings fueled a parliamentary investigation, which found that despite Parliament's order that the Acts be repealed in the colonies, colonial officials continued to try to force women to undergo humiliating registration. Army officials wrote secret memoranda demanding that the officials ensure that the registered women were attractive, so the soldiers would patronize them. And the policy failed to control venereal disease.

The pamphlet excerpted here is by Joseph Edmondson, from Yorkshire, who campaigned with Josephine Butler against the continuation of registration in India and indeed in Europe as a whole. On what grounds does he criticize experts on prostitution? How does he describe the impact of registration and examination on a woman? How does he use racial language to describe prostitutes, and does this mean he was more sympathetic to them? Later in the pamphlet, he mocks those experts who believe that confining women in official brothels will prevent the spread of venereal disease. He warns that male customers will gain a false sense of security, and that the regulations will just encourage them to go to prostitutes more often, and thus, to spread venereal disease more quickly. At the end of the pamphlet, it becomes clear that Edmondson's goal was the religious reclamation of the prostitute, but he believed that forcible medical treatment would only harden women, not lead them to repentance. Religious concerns therefore continued to motivate debate on prostitution.

Notes

1   A.-J.-B. Parent-Duchatelet, *De la prostitution dans la ville de Paris*, vol. 2 (Paris: J.B. Ballière et fils, 1857); Sophie de Schaepdrijver, "Regulated Prostitution in Brussels, 1844–1877: A Policy and Its Implementation," *Historical Social Research [West Germany]*, 37 (1986): 89–109; Carine Steverlynck, "La traite des blanches et la prostitution enfantine en Belgique," *Paedagogica Historica [Belgium]* 29, no. 3 (1993): 779–820; Christelle Taraud, *La prostitution coloniale: Algérie, Tunisie, Maroc (1830–1962)* (Paris: Payot, 2003); Ambrose Tardieu, *Dictionnaire d'hygiène publique*, 4 vols., vol. 3 (Paris: J.B. Ballière, 1862).
2   Judith Walkowitz, *Prostitution in Victorian Society: Women, Class, and State* (Cambridge: Cambridge University Press, 1980).

Chapter 14

Philippa Levine

PROSTITUTION, RACE AND POLITICS
Venereal disease and the British Empire (2003)

The sexual census and the racialization of colonial women

> The passions of manhood and the penalties entailed upon their gratification are causes of more broken constitutions than all other indiscretions put together. *Lues* everywhere abounds and occupies a large figure in every sick report. This is the Scylla of European life in India; the Charybdis is left-handed alliances with native females; and the "*medio tutissimus ibis*" is either through the Straits of Continence or of Matrimony.
>
> John McCosh

THE AMBIVALENCE AND DIFFICULTIES that lawmakers as well as doctors experienced in actually defining prostitution did not stop them, and other figures of colonial authority, from nonetheless seeking to define those who worked in this simultaneously elusive and transparent trade. On the one hand, prostitution constantly eluded precise definition. On the other, those in the trade could be marked, enumerated, and elucidated. The sheer quantity of information about the rank, age, appearance, demeanor, medical condition, and behavior of women engaged in prostitution amounts, in effect, to a kind of sexual census akin to the growing blue-book sociology of the nineteenth century. These blue books were enormously influential; Philip Corrigan and Derek Sayer have dubbed them "the key instruments in the moral revolution of the nineteenth century."[1]

The new Victorian sociology—tracking not only the demographics of birth, life, and death but such things as economic growth, crop acreage, disease rates, and sanitary conditions—was by no means a practice confined to island Britain. The new emphasis on statistics and on expert witness, collated in a triumphant empiricism, helped guide government policy not only in Britain but throughout its colonies. By the late nineteenth century, the collection of census data was widespread, estimating population numbers and itemizing the characteristics and habits of a host of subject populations.[2]

Certainly, "instruments of control, surveillance and violence" predate the systematic employment of census-style empirical data as a weapon to control both colonial and metropolitan subjects.[3] Bernard Cohn has traced early attempts by the East India Company to gather demographic data as an aid to Indian revenue collection and more accurate mapmaking.[4] "The vast social world that was India had to be classified, categorized, and bounded before it could be ordered."[5] Gauri Viswanathan makes the point that "the state had a vital interest in the production of knowledge about those whom it ruled [and] . . . a role in actively processing and then selectively delivering that knowledge . . . in the guise of 'objective knowledge.'"[6] Veena Das similarly argues that this new social science was a necessary element "in the new complex of knowledge and power."[7] While India's size made the prospect perhaps a more daunting one, colonialists elsewhere in Asia and the Pacific were no less keen to know their adversities and advantages. The mapping of Australia's tropical north, Hong Kong's relation to Chinese trade, and the growth of informal British influence in Malaysia all relied on knowledge of local peoples and terrains, carefully garnered and usably classified.

The classification central to this storehouse of detail-as-knowledge was taken as a sign of progress and modernity, an index of British order, logic and efficiency.[8] This "English epistemological authority" relied on counting as its natural mode.[9] Census-style knowledge rested on two axes: the body as the site of counting (for while household and family remained troubled and shifting concepts, the body was indivisible); and the idea of differentiation, without which the vertical hierarchies of rule had meager purchase. It was a tactic that parlayed the notion of knowledge into a distinctive justification of imperial governance.

The census and other such mechanisms did not, of course, describe so much as they fashioned, producing the very categories by which "difference" could be hierarchically explained. The typologies that resulted, while represented as factual record-keeping, were in no sense anterior to the moment. There were no a priori and immovable definitions of race, civilization, or masculinity and femininity already available to the knowledge-makers, although in its certainty their work assumed that there was. The confusion and debate over what constituted prostitution, or who might be named as a prostitute, provides a good index of the slipperiness of these categories. Value and meaning were mutable, dependent in the colonial context on both local encounter and values imported from the metropolis. Census-making of this ilk tells us much about the anxieties and the concerns of ruling elites and their desire to impose order upon that which they considered dangerously disordered. In the mid-nineteenth century, sex, with its inevitable messiness, its apparent resistance to logic, and the seeming health consequences of its unbridled forms, was an obvious area in which such strategies of containment were regarded as purposeful.

Social commentators throughout the nineteenth century devoted pages to describing the physiology and the psychology of the prostitute, her family life and education, her marital state, the date of her "fall" from grace, her penchant for or abstinence from intoxicating substances, and her recourse to other forms of money earning. When physical anthropology became a serious discipline, the prostitute was a topic of study. Fiction and art were littered with representations of the fallen woman. Colonial officials tried hard to manage and understand both the sex trade and what they understood as native sexuality by detailing every observable particular of women they regarded as prostitutes. In effect, they were making a sexual census, using much the same techniques and ideas that informed the new science of the census and social description. They counted, enumerated, and categorized, producing estimates of how many women worked in prostitution, of how many willingly registered as such, of how many presented symptoms of disease. They logged appearance, race and nationality, and religion. They measured attractiveness and they classified brothels by hygiene, clientele, and fees. British officials elusively sought knowledge of indigenous sexual conditions, but in the process actively created indigenous sexual identities.

Edward Said has dubbed Orientalism as both an anatomical and an enumerative exercise.[10] The orientalizing knowledge that marked the particulars of the sexual census was both these things. It was anatomical not just in its literal counting of bodies but also in its commitment to the sexual body as a site of disorder, and enumerative in its attempt to manage and control that disorder—epitomized by the sex trade—through detailed empirical ordering. The understanding offered by this enumerative form of regulation was a crucial form of control. Moreover, the emphasis on the indigenous woman as a sexualized being underscored the sensuality said to define and to drive the east. The fallen woman was always and everywhere eagerly chronicled by the British, in the metropole as in the colonies, but while her domestic presence "proved" her anomalousness, her apparent ubiquity in the colonies defined both her and her homeland as depraved.[11]

Striking a dominant note was race which, while underlining distinction, rested on a notion of an indifferent and homogenous mass, a body of "natives" too large and too similar to one another to count, "the infinite substitutability of the native."[12] It was "groups, rather than individuals, who were said to possess distinctive psychologies and bodies."[13] Such homogenization was directly at work in the sexual census. Unlike the social commentaries of Nathaniel Caine, William Greg, Ralph Wardlaw, and a score of mostly male writers in the metropolis, this census tabulated collective and externally observable details rather than delving into the psychological.[14] It substituted the pathology of the mass for that of the individual. The common notion of the lushness and fecundity of the "orient" made this tendency to deindividualize easy.[15] The east was simply too much of everything: "too much colour, too many faces, too much hubbub."[16]

In Queensland, the focus was on both an indigenous Aboriginal population and on others whom white settlers regarded as foreign, the Chinese, Japanese, and Melanesian islanders engaged in agriculture, fishing, pearling, and trade in northern Australia. In India and in southeast Asia, both local and immigrant populations were scrutinized, labeled, and taxonomized. This less formal, but quite palpable, census-taking approach invited attention to, and indeed was dependent upon, a careful practice of differentiation. How else were the Hindu and the "Mussulman" to be distinguished from one another? the moral from the degenerate? the clean from the dirty? the foreign from the properly English?

This contradictory impetus combined a clear dismissal of colonial populations as multitudinous and unindividual, and yet insisted on minutely refining racial categories. Characteristically it showed a disregard for divisions other than those meaningful to colonial power. Thus while certain types of "blackness" needed delineating, colonial officials were seldom inclined to respect, for instance, locally important tribal distinctions. In nineteenth-century Canada, "the European category 'Chinese' collapsed whatever distinctions people of Chinese origin made among themselves, to the service of one distinction—that of differentiating 'them' from 'whites' and white domains."[17] It was much the same wherever immigrant populations settled. A twenty-two-year-old Australian woman, Annie Bowman, was described by Queensland's protector of Aboriginals as "an aboriginal half-caste girl with a Chinese father, the Chinese strain being very conspicuous."[18] Under scrutiny as a disease-carrying prostitute, and finally packed off to endure the rigors of Fraser's Island by the protector's dictate, Bowman's Aboriginal status was not qualified by tribe or region, despite the enormous differences among Queensland Aboriginals. Her blackness was made all the more threatening by her Chinese parentage, but her precise standing within Aboriginal society was irrelevant. The allegedly uncontrollable immorality that had brought her to the protector's attention in the first instance was seen by him as a product not of her *tribal* but of her *racial* status. The protector's description not only ignored the differences between Aboriginal groups (a sociology he did not even deem worth mentioning) but lumped together as racially alien the Aboriginal and the Chinese. In a recent essay, Ien Ang tells a story of her own hostile encounter with a white Australian a hundred years later in 1990s Australia, in which this very same gesture of a generalized racial exclusion takes center stage. It is Ang's contention that the ethnocentrism she encounters "is sourced precisely in the precariousness and fragility, the moot legitimacy and lack of historical density of white settler subjectivity."[19] Such instability as a necessary accompaniment to settler colonialism was equally visible in crown colonies, where a small European population constantly stressed its difference from and natural regnance over local peoples. In short, only those racial categories recognizable to the census-makers were legitimate; those that might resonate in subject populations could hardly serve the purposes of empire as conveniently and as neatly as European-inspired categories of racial difference and distinction.

Annie Bowman's fate—lonely confinement on a remote island reserved for the intractable—demonstrates vividly what Gayatri Spivak has called the "epistemic violence of colonialism" as it operated through the careful building of a body of data designed not only to manage disorder but to name it.[20] In like manner, the British census was "underpinned by hidden purposes and ideological preconceptions."[21] The attributions made by the racially cast sexual census in the colonies also served, as we have seen, to normalize and naturalize the idea of prostitution in colonial-racial settings. In this way, whiteness as a ruling norm could be distanced conceptually from unrespectable sexual practice, even while whites engaged in such activities.

Ann Stoler has persuasively argued that we need to place the management of sexuality at the core of our analysis of the operation of race and nationality in the colonial context.[22] The studied use of a census-style "Orientalist sociology," drawing on much the same methods and indeed stereotypes about the colonial body (and the colonial body politic) as did fact-grubbers intent upon demographic precision or the depth of the water table, was a crucial element in the invention of the exoticized sexualities that have been so constitutive in defining and labeling the colonized. Knowledge of sexual habits and preferences, of brothel management, and the like, was part of the way that colonialism set about constituting the need for particular forms of authority. The racially charged taxonomic care, the endless fine-tuning of the delineation of the prostitute—her race, class, caste, religion, and clientele—was drawn against the backdrop not only of legal imprecision with respect to the boundaries of her trade, but with the imprecision we have noted as to distinctions and divisions within the communities imagined, invented, and notated by census-minded colonists.

For all its dynamism and proclaimed modernity, then, the knowledge derived in this manner imposed upon colonized women a set of biological as well as cultural fixities, frozen in time. Charles Hirschman, and following him Benedict Anderson, have noted how census categories became more and more ordered over time by racial preoccupations and Sudipta Sen has noted "distinctively racial hierarchies fashioned out of the old great chain of being" in the eighteenth century, when data-gathering of this ilk was relatively new.[23] The minutiae by which prostitute women were taxonomized fixed them not only via racial characteristics but, fundamentally, by sex. As the previous chapter argued, whatever other definitions law and public opinion could *not* muster to define prostitution, it was always defined as female. While, as Hirschman has argued, "direct colonial rule brought European racial theory" to the colonies, "and constructed a social and economic order structured by 'race,'" women's lives were also ordered through a reading of fixed sexual characteristics.[24]

[. . .]

Race and hygiene

The racial-sexual hierarchy further figured native women as fixed in moral decadence. Reporting from the Malay Peninsula at the end of the nineteenth century, the resident general of Selangor district showed no hesitation in drawing direct links between race and hygiene. In his report on VD in Pahang, he excoriated the "incontinent Tamils" and the "dirty low class Chinese" for spreading syphilis, laid the origins of local gonorrhea on "Tamil women generally," and commented on the sanitary advantages enjoyed by "the cleaner and more sober Malay unfortunates and the more careful Japanese."[25] The low-caste Bombay prostitutes, thought police commissioner Edwardes, "live in great squalor" so "it is not surprising that venereal disease is extremely common and that the offering of four annas to Venus ends generally in a further expenditure of one or two rupees on quack remedies."[26]

The growing association between cleanliness and femininity fueled by Victorian readings of the domestic lent added meaning to the sanitary issues around prostitution and disease.[27] The sex trade mocked the idea of women as guardians of the sanitized and sanctified hearth. Their rejection of domesticated womanhood alongside their potential role in purveying disease brought together complex associations between race, sex, hygiene, and femininity. Hygiene became another means by which racial difference—and its effects upon sexual difference—was made visible. Dirty women were also racially marked women.

White Australians frequently alluded to Aboriginal filth, both in encampments and in terms of personal hygiene. It was a small step from this widely held opinion to the contention that "the Gins [common slang for Aboriginal women] are simply prostitutes. Wherever there is a camp there is prostitution and, more or less, venereal disease."[28] The sentiment was remarkably similar throughout the colonies. Charles Lucas at the Colonial Office claimed that 75 percent of the Chinese women living in Hong Kong were prostitutes.[29] Reports of Chinese brothels in both Hong Kong and the Straits Settlements dwelt on their filthiness, and proclaimed the civilizing success of the CD ordinances in cleaning them up. The association of dirt and disease, of disease and illicit sex, of dirt and immorality compounded the racialized reading of prostitution. A committee on VD reporting in the Straits in the 1920s claimed that, "European prostitutes set a high standard of cleanliness."[30]

Physical categories

Commentators frequently dwelt on the physical characteristics of prostitute women. Indian officials constantly complained that "registered women are as a rule old, ugly, dirty: therefore not acceptable to British soldiers; chiefly they receive the visits of native men."[31] Lock hospital reports frequently referred to them as "old hags," complaining that their presence actively encouraged soldiers to seek out more attractive but dangerously unregistered women. The Madras lock hospital report for 1879 declared that the "registered prostitutes are, as a rule, dirty, miserably clad, and physically repulsive."[32] W. Graves wrote angrily of the women he treated at the northern Indian hill station of Naini Tal. "The registered women are of the most loathsome, dirty, old and ugly description that one cannot be surprised at any intelligent European soldier seeking and soliciting a more desirable companion when obliged to do so."[33] Some went further: "steps ought to be taken to provide a younger and more attractive class of prostitutes for the use of British troops."[34] Yet the call to people the *lal* bazaars and the cantonments with attractive women was disingenuous. Though officials constantly distinguished the reality of the unlovely woman willing to register from the unregistered enchantress, in fact few officials ever claim to have found indigenous women who fit this latter description, for as Sander Gilman has pointed out, "the nineteenth century knew that blacks had no aesthetic sensibility."[35] The English aesthetic of this era united beauty with morality and thence with race.[36] Women might be alluring but they were not beautiful in a healthy way. They were dangerous by virtue of their race as much as by their profession.

Ugliness was only one of the negative visual attributes used to damn such women. They were represented as heavily made up, as hardened, as gaudily dressed. W. N. Willis, observing the "great gaudy centre of the Babylonian quarter" of Singapore, Malay Street, described the women as "[H]eavily painted and decked out with tinselled roses in their hair, low-necked blouses, silk stockings and worked slippers, their profession is unmistakable."[37] Such commentaries, focused as they were for the most part, on nonwhite and certainly on non-British prostitutes suggest a service, a standard of hygiene, and indeed, a rate of payment, lower than those of their European competitors. They suggest too, that in many respects these shameless hordes were less amenable to European control. Descriptions of the women, the brothels, and the red-light districts abound with disapproving descriptions of colorful chaotic loudness, of unembarrassed displays of flesh, of squalid cots open to the streets. This was the common language used throughout this period to depict the conditions, lives, and appearances of women engaged in prostitution. Their trade was a mirror of the bazaars of the East and the trading posts of Australia; their living conditions reflected those of the indigenous east in general—overcrowded, unhygienic, noisy, and immoral.

Of course, many of these same complaints about painted faces and uncontrolled loudness were the stuff of class tension in Britain as well. Working-class women, prostitutes, barmaids, and others outside the sphere of respectability attracted similar criticism in the metropole. The critique of proletarian aesthetics and morals was cast in a similar language of disgust, but in the colonial setting Britons could, at least theoretically, be elevated to a homogenous set of middle-class behaviors. This willing forgetfulness of the troublesome presence of the working classes suggests the contingency of political arithmetic and definition, the taxonomies, values, and emphases shifting according to the demands of the local context and of political necessity.

The visible and the invisible

Troubling as all of this was to colonial English sensibilities, it provided census-makers with a useful and immediate form of visual assessment. One of the most constant sources of frustration for officials, both in the era of formal regulation and after its abandonment, was the presence of women known variously as "clandestines," "amateurs," or "sly" prostitutes. Where registration was permitted, these were women who eluded the complex of rules by which the registered were bound. In places where, and times in which registration was forbidden, they were women who chose not to reveal a public association with commercial sex but to work outside the public or official gaze. Always vilified as a fertile source of disease and infection, such women defied the law as well as the census in their concern to remain anonymous and unlabelled.

> There are of prostitute women two distinct classes—the bona fide order, who live in a recognised quarter, and sit at their doors with painted faces, lanterns, and looking-glasses inviting all comers; and the secret set . . . who do not publicly confess prostitution, but are available when called upon.[38]

In this reading, and in marked contrast to prevailing domestic British sentiment, the author constructs what is, in effect, a class of authenticated prostitutes, discernible not only via their bending to the yoke of registration, but by appearance and domicile. *Real* prostitutes are identifiable; they dress and behave in certain ways. They are yielding both to a clientele and to the state's ordering of their trade.

Secrecy, avoidance of authentication, rejection of the rules connoted trouble, a trouble located in women engaging in an occupation to which they had, effectively, no right and thus rendering ineffectual a regulatory system crucially dependent for its running on prostitutes' acceptance of the definitions that bound them. George Newton, medical officer at the British-run Yokohama lock hospital in the Japanese treaty ports, complained bitterly about the "vagrant" unregistered women who were, unless checked, "noisy" and "clamorous."[39] Women who did not look the part, women who did not advertise in the accepted and open fashion, and women who concealed their activities from the state's eye were all renegades.

Disapprobation of the sly prostitute rested on her unwillingness to declare her profession publicly and yet the unregistered woman would have to let potential clients know of her willingness. In such circumstances, it would be hard for women to hide their intentions. At the same time, colonial attitudes to prostitution were premised on the notion that the occupation carried little shame in "depraved" societies. If this was so, then the clandestine woman's reluctance could only be seen as hostility to bureaucracy or doctors and not as an index of shame. It was a division that made the definitions that structured prostitution and regulation considerably less stable.

It was with some considerable ire that the deputy surgeon general in Burma explained how this "deception" derailed the sanitary system of the CD laws.

> . . . when the matter is looked into critically it will be seen that the source of all disease is *clandestine prostitution*, and that this exists to a great extent because the classes who seek the company of profligate females entertain a preference for those who do homage to virtue by dropping a veil over the

revolting character of their calling, a veil which is stript off the moment a woman is placed upon the register of a lock-hospital; for these reports teach also that when a woman's real life is exposed, and she is registered amongst those licensed to ply their calling without let or hindrance, she tries every device to withdraw from her new sisterhood . . . . *Clandestine* prostitution is a very widespread vice, and it may be classed amongst those most difficult to be suppressed or controlled by human laws which the Legislature is ever called upon to grapple with.[40]

Queensland, as a settler colony enjoying the privileges of responsible self-government, maintained a system of registration throughout this period. In general, the concern of residents and officials alike was to control and render invisible what was widely called the social evil. Neighborhood petitions complained about brothels creating upset and noise, and public servants echoed that concern, investing more in the idea of the ordered street than in the woman evading registration. In fact, even in Brisbane with a population of almost 400,000 in 1891, the numbers of registered women clearly did not reflect the extent of the sex trade. In 1868, the first year of the colony's CD act, 77 women were registered with the Brisbane police; a decade later, in 1877, the number had only risen to 115.[41] Yet these unrealistically small numbers did not raise the kind of concern they did elsewhere in the colonies. As in the cities of India, Australian women moved their residence and their business beyond the geographical limits of the act. Though occasional police reports from Brisbane allude to this, overall the idea of the clandestine, and of her potential to wreak medical and other havoc, was less shocking to Queensland sensibilities. As William Parry-Okeden, Brisbane's commissioner of police remarked in 1899, "Given that the 'Social evil' exists and . . . must be tolerated . . . it is very desirable that, in the public interest, the doings of the persons concerned in carrying on this loathsome trade, should be kept from being openly, flagrantly offensive and demoralizing."[42]

The situation in Queensland resembled domestic British policy more than direct colonial rule. Australian laws around sexual commerce were in general more coercive and far-reaching than their British counterparts, but they rested, as had the British CD Acts, on police initiative in finding and registering women who engaged in prostitution. Where nonwhite subject populations formed the bulk of those ruled, the law relied instead on self-declaration and self-registration.[43] Since prostitution was allegedly less morally repugnant to "orientalized" peoples, the clandestine thus became a symbol of defiance of the law and of the sanitary order, for her nonregistration was not attributed to shame.[44] In white settler arenas, by contrast, she was, while still perhaps medically dangerous, fittingly invisible. To be clandestine in white Australia was to be respectful of the moral law; when the Geraldton police chief reported the presence of six suspected Japanese prostitutes in his jurisdiction in 1894, he stressed that "[T]hey are never seen on the streets and there have not been any complaints of misconduct made against them."[45] These were not troublesome women.

But in India, the same invisibility constituted gross misconduct. One of the most common complaints of frustrated medical officers in India was of women, not prostitute-identified, *lurking* and *prowling* around soldiers' quarters. The language is clear in conveying the furtive subterfuge of the women's intent. "We are aware of the mischief wrought by the coolie and other women whose occupations bring them into the vicinity of the barracks."[46] Under cover of an alternative motive or occupation, such women could practice prostitution while not acknowledging it as a profession. The moral bankruptcy implied here extended beyond simply the perfidy of these always-available women, who were generally understood as seeking supplemental income.[47] Their casual morals extended further into a commentary on the colonized population; officials who complained about secret prostitution frequently described other ruses involving Indian male complicity. Local men, they charged, would pretend to be a woman's husband so that she could claim outward respectability and avoid the register.[48] Worse still, husbands might permit or even encourage their wives to seek out well-paying British customers.[49] India, then, was where the individual had urgently to be classified either as a clandestine or as a real prostitute, for healthy governance relied on policing this division.

Beyond India, too, the visible signification by which the unclean or the common woman might be known and classified was important. Queensland's white settlers might have breathed a sigh of relief that their well-mannered Japanese sex workers were not encouraging public brawls and upsets, but even where prostitution was successfully relegated behind closed doors, it was important that women in the trade were still in some way visibly marked, and thus authenticated. Clearly a painted face or a scanty outfit worked to disclose the signs of immorality but so too could a measuring and enumerating of distance from the popular conception of femininity. The stereotype of the hardened harlot, isolated from a softer, untainted femininity, found its way into this census-style knowledge of the sex trade. The protector of Chinese at the Straits thought that a "Cantonese girl of 20 years of age is often a hardened prostitute," a contrast with the soft innocent twenty-year old of Europe implied in his description.[50] Of course, the implied contrast necessitated forgetting the plethora of British literature that saw the young white prostitute in Britain as beyond help. Magdalen asylums, after all, premised their work on the divide between the truly penitent and the hardened unreachable. The rhetoric at work here normalized western women as always potentially virtuous, and colonized women as their moral opposite, alien and extraneous to proper womanhood. This was a racial geography mapping the vigilantly policed bounds of colonial sexual commerce, naming and bounding women marginalized not merely by their livelihood but by their relative and carefully gradated distance from the centrally definitional and definitionally respectable English woman. This geography of racial borders was mapped through a complex taxonomy of race and ethnic distinction, what Chandra Mohanty has called a "yardstick by which to encode and represent cultural others."[51]

In the brothel-based commerce characteristic of Hong Kong and the Straits Settlements, this racialized distance was measured both through the signification of the visible and via the organization of the brothel. After the compulsory genital examination was abolished, officials in these two dominantly Chinese colonies, where brothel registration remained a legal requirement, worried about the impact not of clandestine women, but of "sly brothels." The sly brothel was, of course, one that evaded government surveillance, and it was variously represented as a busy site of infection, a place of extreme brutality employing underage workers and overworking its employees, and barely selective about its clientele.[52]

These enumerations and definitions reinforced the tendency of regulationist policies to legitimize and authenticate certain forms and features of prostitution. Brothel regulation in effect legalized indoor prostitution. The prosecution of unregistered women and of sly brothels protected pliant traders from punitive sanctions. But since the law could not offer a fully encompassing definition of prostitution, it was this ersatz sexual census that did the work of defining who would be protected, making possible police and judicial action. As Corrigan and Sayer have so cogently argued: "The centralization of knowledge requires *facts*—and the legitimation of some facts, and the methods used to collect them, against the facts—to justify features and forms of policy" [emphasis in original].[53] The fact, of course, was knowledge made visible and material.

Notes

1   Philip Corrigan and Derek Sayer, *The Great Arch: English State Formation as Cultural Revolution* (Oxford: Basil Blackwell, 1985), 124.

2   Arjun Appadurai, "Number in the Colonial Imagination," in *Orientalism and the Postcolonial Predicament: Perspectives on South Asia*, ed. Carol Breckenridge and Peter van der Veer (Philadelphia, PA: University of Pennsylvania Press, 1993), 314–39; Bernard S. Cohn, "The Census, Social Structure and Objectification in South Asia," in *An Anthropologist Among the Historians and other Essays* (Delhi: Oxford University Press, 1987), 224–54, and introduction to *Colonialism and its Forms of Knowledge: The British in India* (Princeton, NJ: Princeton University Press, 1996); Charles Hirschman, "The Meaning and Measurement of Ethnicity in Malaysia: An Analysis of Census Classifications," *Journal of Asian Studies* 46, no. 3 (1987): 555–82 and "The Making of Race in Colonial Malaya: Political Economy and Racial Ideology," *Sociological Forum* 1, no. 2 (1986): 330–61. See too Ruth Lindeborg on the classifications proposed by missionary Joseph Salter: "The 'Asiatic' and the Boundaries of Victorian Englishness," *Victorian Studies* 37, no. 3 (1994): 395.

3   Sudipta Sen, "Colonial Frontiers of the Georgian State: East India Company's Rule in India," *Journal of Historical Sociology* 7, no. 4 (1994): 376; Lata Mani, *Contentious Traditions: The Debate on Sati in Colonial India* (Berkeley: University of California Press, 1998), 12.

4   Cohn, "The Census, Social Structure and Objectification," 231–2.

5   Cohn, *Colonialism and Its Forms of Knowledge*, 21–2.

6   Gauri Viswanathan, *Masks of Conquest: Literary Study and British Rule in India* (New York: Columbia University Press, 1989), 29.

7   Veena Das, "Gender Studies, Cross-Cultural Comparison, and the Colonial Organization of Knowledge," *Berkshire Review* 21 (1986): 59.

8   Chandra Talpade Mohanty, "Feminist Encounters: Locating the Politics of Experience," *Copyright* 1 (1987): 30.

9   David Ludden, "Orientalist Empiricism: Transformations of Colonial Knowledge," in *Orientalism and the Post Colonial Predicament*, 253.

10   Edward W. Said, *Orientalism* (London: Routledge and Kegan Paul, 1978), 72.

11   Joseph Alter points to similar anxieties around male sexuality in "Celibacy, Sexuality, and the Transformation of Gender into Nationalism in North India," *Journal of Asian Studies* 53, no. 1 (1994): 56.

12   Vinay Lal, "The Incident of the 'Crawling Lane': Women in the Punjab Disturbances of 1919," *Genders* 16 (1993): 46. And see Cheryl McEwan, "Encounters with West African Women: Textual Representations of Difference by White Women Abroad," in *Writing Women and Space: Colonial and Postcolonial Geographies*, ed. Alison Blunt and Gillian Roe (New York: The Guilford Press, 1994), 74.

13   Megan Vaughan, *Curing Their Ills: Colonial Power and African Illness* (Stanford, CA: Stanford University Press, 1991), 11.

14   Nathaniel Caine, *Prostitution: Its Aids and Accessories* (Liverpool: Egerton Smith, 1858); William Greg, "Prostitution," *Westminster Review* 53 (1850): 448–506; Ralph Wardlaw, *Lectures on Female Prostitution: Its Nature, Extent, Effects, Guilt, Causes, and Remedy* (Glasgow: James Maclehose, 1842). Women began writing about prostitution at a slightly later date: Elizabeth Blackwell, *Rescue Work in Relation to Prostitution and Disease* (London, T. Danes, 1881);

A. Maude Royden, ed., *Downward Paths: An Inquiry into the Causes which Contribute to the Making of the Prostitute* (London: G. Bell and Sons, 1916); and Helen M. Wilson, *On Some Causes of Prostitution, with Special Reference to Economic Conditions* (London: AMSH, 1916).

15 Robert J. C. Young, *Colonial Desire: Hybridity in Theory, Culture and Race* (London and New York: Routledge, 1995), 98.

16 Henry Champly, *The Road to Shanghai: White Slave Traffic in Asia* (London: John Long, 1934), 73.

17 Kay J. Anderson, *Vancouver's Chinatown: Racial Discourse in Canada, 1875–1980* (Montreal and Kingston: McGill-Queen's University Press, 1991), 168.

18 Harold Meston to Under Secretary, Home Office, 24 September 1902, Colonial Secretary's Office, QSA, COL/143.

19 Ien Ang, "I'm a Feminist But . . . 'Other' Women and Postnational Feminism," in *Transitions: New Australian Feminisms*, ed. Barbara Caine and Rosemary Pringle (St. Leonards, NSW: Allen and Unwin, 1995), 70.

20 Gayatri C. Spivak, "The Rani of Sirmur," in *Europe and Its Others*, vol. 1, ed. F. Barker, P. Hulme, M. Iverson, and D. Lozley (Colchester: University of Essex, 1985), 131.

21 José Harris, "Political Thought and the Welfare State 1870–1940: An Intellectual Framework for British Social Policy," *Past and Present* 135 (1992): 119.

22 Ann Laura Stoler, "'Mixed-bloods' and the Cultural Politics of European Identity in Colonial Southeast Asia," in *The Decolonization of Imagination: Culture, Knowledge and Power*, ed. Jan Nederveen Pieterse and Bhikhu Parekh (London: Zed Books, 1995), 128–29.

23 Hirschman, "The Meaning and Measurement of Ethnicity," and "The Making of Race"; Anderson, *Imagined Communities*, 164; Gyan Prakash, "Writing Post-Orientalist Histories of the Third World: Perspectives from Indian Historiography," *Comparative Studies in Society and History* 32, no. 2 (1990): 387; Sen, "Colonial Frontiers," 378.

24 Hirschman, "The Making of Race," 330.

25 F. Swettenham, Resident General, Selangor to High Commissioner, Federated Malay States, 31 July 1899, PRO, CO 273/251 (23660).

26 S. M. Edwardes, *The Bombay City Police: A Historical Sketch 1672–1916* (London, Bombay, Calcutta and Madras: Humphrey Milford/Oxford University Press, 1923), 94.

27 John and Jean Comaroff, "Home-Made Hegemony: Modernity, Domesticity, and Colonialism in South Africa," in *African Encounters with Domesticity*, ed. Karen Tranberg Hansen (Brunswick, NJ: Rutgers University Press, 1992), esp. 280; Anne McClintock, *Imperial Leather: Race, Gender, and Sexuality in the Colonial Context* (New York: Routledge, 1995), 207–8. See too Timothy Burke, *Lifebuoy Men, Lux Women: Commodification, Consumption, and Cleanliness in Modern Zimbabwe* (Durham, NC: Duke University Press, 1996).

28 Sergeant F. J. O'Connor, Boulia Sub District to Inspector of Police, 20 December 1898, QSA, COL/144 (12886).

29 C. P. Lucas to F. Meade, 6 May 1879, PRO, CO 129/184 (6690).

30 *Report of Venereal Diseases Committee*, 17 December 1923, PRO, CO275/109, C286.

31 *Seventh Annual Report on the Working of the Lock Hospitals in the Northwest Provinces and Oudh for the Year 1880* (Allahbad, n.p., 1881), 10, OIOC, V/24/2290.

32 *Annual Report on the Military Lock Hospitals of the Madras Presidency for the year 1879* (Madras: Government Press, 1880), 9, OIOC, V/24/2287.

33 Annual Report of Lock Hospital, Naini Tal, 1874, OIOC, P/525.

34 *Report on Voluntary Venereal Hospitals in the Punjab for the Year 1887* (Lahore: Civil and Military Gazette Press, 1888), 3, OIOC, L/MIL/7/13906.

35 Sander L. Gilman, *Inscribing the Other* (Lincoln: University of Nebraska Press, 1991), 20.

36 Inderpal Grewal, *Home and Harem: Nation, Gender, Empire, and the Cultures of Travel* (Durham, NC: Duke University Press, 1996), 47.

37 W. N. Willis, *Western Men with Eastern Morals* (London: Stanley Paul, 1913), 14.

38 Report on Lock Hospitals in British Burma for the Year 1873, Bassein Report, 13, OIOC, V/24/2296.

PROSTITUTION, RACE AND POLITICS

39   *Annual Medical Report of the Yokohama Lock Hospital for 1869* (Yokohama: Japan Gazette Office, 1870), 5, PRO, ADM125/16 (804).

40   J. McNeale Donnelly, Deputy Surgeon General, H.M. Forces, Burma Division to Inspector General of Jails, 18 February 1887, Lock Hospital Reports, Burma 1886–88, OIOC, L/MIL/7/13910.

41   Inspector of Contagious Diseases, Return of Examinations made under CDA, General Correspondence of Colonial Secretary, 1878, QSA CL A/268 (4353).

42   Memorandum of W. E. Parry-Okeden, n.d. 1899, QSA, HOM A/24 (10551).

43   Philippa Levine, "Venereal Disease, Prostitution, and the Politics of Empire: The Case of British India," *Journal of the History of Sexuality* 4, no. 4 (1994): 585–6.

44   Satadru Sen makes a similar point in arguing that the state consciously chose controlled and regulated prostitution over clandestine at the Indian convict settlement at Port Blair: "Rationing Sex: Female Convicts in the Andamans," *South Asia* 30 (1998): 29–59.

45   D. Seymour, Police Commissioner, Geraldton, to Colonial Secretary, 18 December 1894, QSA, COL/A788 (14408).

46   Military Despatch no. 73 of 1879, Lord Elgin et al. to Secretary of State for India, Lord Hamilton, 18 May 1897, OIOC, L/MIL/3/152.

47   See, for example, Lock Hospital reports, Madras 1887–89, OIOC, L/MIL/7/13904; W. H. Tarleton, Commissioner of Police, Rangoon to Chief Secretary to Government of Burma, 1 July 1914, OIOC, L/P& J/6/1448 (2987).

48   See for example *Fourth Annual Report on the Working of the Lock Hospitals in the Northwest Provinces and Oudh for the Year 1877* (Allahabad, n.p., 1878), 68, report for Naini Tal, OIOC, V/24/2290.

49   C. O. Mayne, Commander, Fourth Division to C. A. Elliott, Officiating Secretary to Government of the Northwest Provinces, 20 August 1870, NAI, Home Department, Public Consultations, A, Proceedings no. 188, 1870.

50   Sir Arthur Young to Walter Long, Colonial Office, 13 June 1917, PRO, CO 273/457 (41155).

51   Chandra Talpade Mohanty, "Under Western Eyes: Feminist Scholarship and Colonial Discourses," in *Third World Women and the Politics of Feminism*, 55; Ruth Frankenberg, *White Women, Race Matters: The Social Construction of Whiteness* (Minneapolis: University of Minnesota Press, 1993), 191–4; Trinh T. Minh-ha, "Difference: A Special Third World Women Issue," *Discourse* 8 (1986–7): 11–38.

52   Sir William Robinson to Joseph Chamberlain, 30 June 1897, PRO, CO 129/276 (17234); Reports of Colonial Surgeons, 1870s and 1880s, CO 129/203 (20349); G. W. Johnson to Mr. Bramston, Colonial Office internal memorandum, 21 May 1887, CO 273/144 (8507); various memoranda, 1893, CO 273/187 (8818).

53   Corrigan and Sayer, *The Great Arch*, 124.

Chapter 15

Joseph Edmondson

AN ENQUIRY INTO THE CAUSES OF THE GREAT SANITARY FAILURE OF THE STATE REGULATION OF SOCIAL VICE (1897)

The case briefly stated

THE CONSPICUOUS FAILURE of the Sanitary Regulation of Prostitution in India, as set forth by copious quotations from official and other trustworthy documents in a recent pamphlet,[1] strikingly corresponds with experience elsewhere. A body of writers on the Continent of Europe, so fully acquainted with the system down to its minutest details that they may well be termed Experts, and whose writings may be taken as "Text-Books" of the Art of Regulation, abundantly illustrate the fact of such failure as *essentially general*, and not merely *local*. Some of these writers belong to the medical profession and occupy important positions in the working of the system, while others are administrators who do not pretend to any medical skill, but who have a thorough and practical grasp of its operations and results. One of the latter, M. Lecour (for about fifteen years the chief of the *Police des Mœsurs*, who carry out the system in Paris), summing up in 1870 the final results of eighty years' experience in that city, wrote "The Administration has redoubled its activity . . . . and it has finally succeeded in maintaining the registered public women in a satisfactory sanitary condition."[2] And yet "Prostitution is increasing and becoming more dangerous to the public health."[3] The writings of the other Experts, though not so outspoken, are uniformly incompatible with anything but a precisely similar state of things in the cities of which they individually speak, viz., *increased and increasing danger*, side by side with *increased stringency and more perfect arrangements*.

It is the object of this paper to trace out the causes of this bewildering experience.

Not a medical question

The further our enquiry proceeds the more will it become evident that this is in no true sense a medical question, and that, so far from involving any technicalities as to the diagnosis or treatment of disease, its problems are administrative, and belong not to the domain of medicine but to the realm of morals. It is easy for The Profession to indicate the nature of the sanitary risks attaching to debauchery, and to formulate certain desiderata which from a merely medical point of view might be expected to eliminate or lessen those risks. But having done this they have only touched the fringe of the subject. The attempt to secure those desiderata, arousing, as it does, some of the most powerful of human motives to oppose it,—motives which operate not only to neutralise the attempt, but at the same time to intensify the risk—introduces considerations which The Profession discard as foreign to their aims and researches. Hence a medical education and training confer no special advantage in, or qualification for pronouncing a judgment upon the system.

As a matter of fact, although the system holds its ground mainly through the expressed opinions of the medical profession, very few of them know anything of its practical working or of the writings of the Experts. Their judgment is usually formed on the theory "that the retention of a certain number of diseased women in hospital must, *pro tanto*, reduce the number of men affected, and so have a certain salutary influence."[4] This seems so like an axiom, that few, either in the profession or out of it, see wherein its fallacy lies. Even the Experts, though conscious of failure, are blind to the flaw in their logic, and tenaciously cling to a system founded on this (to their minds) unassailable basis. Thus we find this description as applicable to their state of mind as to that of the Indian Medical Staff, to whom it more especially referred,—"Even after years of unsuccessful result it was still hoped that with increased care and greater stringency the desired end might yet be attained. But there can be no doubt that the outcome was a failure."[5] MORAL FORCES, which the administrator finds it necessary and yet impossible to trample under foot, combined with IMMORAL FORCES set in motion by the system itself and which he is powerless to withstand or turn aside, come in unbidden and make the system self-defeating at every stage.

Only half the area covered

Although both sexes are equally subject to, and equally liable to propagate the diseases at whose extinction the Regulationist aims, the system is applied to women alone. Aware of this inconsistency in their proceedings, the Experts here and there make feeble proposals with regard to men, but without any expectation of really carrying them out. Thus their operations embrace only one half the area of sanitary risk, and the hope of "stamping out" venereal contagion, so glibly advanced by superficial advocates of the system, is rendered hopeless at the very outset, and is at one stroke reduced to the more moderate dimensions of "promoting the public health." At the same time, the past experience already mentioned, of increased and increasing risk concurrent with increased stringency, negatives all probability that greater success would follow the inclusion of both sexes.

A sanitary cordon

The first step of the regulationist administrator consists in enrolling the women upon whom it is his aim to operate, with a view to establish a sanitary *cordon* within which men may safely practise debauchery. This enrolment or registration is merely the legal prelude to the compulsory medical examination of these women for the purpose of separating the healthy from the diseased, and detaining the latter until they are regarded as in a condition to resume their "trade" (so called by the Experts) without the risk of infecting their customers.

In this initial step the administrator finds (usually to his surprise) that he can only secure a mere fraction of the class, the whole of whom must be brought within the *cordon*, if he is even approximately to succeed. For, if the *cordon* be not all-inclusive as far as the women are concerned, men (being in no way under control) will gratify their passions sometimes *without* and at others *within* it. Hence there is an absolute certainty that contagion will be continually carried over the barrier, and the expected freedom from risk within it cannot be attained.

In Paris the efforts to make the *cordon* all-inclusive have been prodigious, and yet, according to M. Lecour[6] eighty years' experience had not devised means by which more than one-eighth of the estimated number of prostitute women could be brought within the "riskless" enclosure. This difficulty and the means, if any, by which it may be overcome, form the great theme of all the Experts. Though differing somewhat in their estimate of its precise extent, the Continental Experts are absolutely unanimous as to their ridiculously small success in this, the merely preparatory step towards the attainment of their object. Dr. Mauriac writes so recently as 1896, although "the medical inspection of licensed brothels and of regulated prostitution . . . . is conducted by a numerous, well-trained and experienced staff, how many cases both in Paris and the provinces escape their vigilance! Its efficacy . . . . only covers a relatively small number of cases, and this number decreases more and more."[7]

The experts demolish a fiction

Inexperts describe the system as a humanitarian agency, but the Experts (when writing for the professional, as distinguished from the public eye) plainly declare it to be the very reverse, and this fact is the key to the difficulty at present under review. Even a woman of loose morals is conscious that to be officially registered as a "common prostitute" is a further and great step in her downward course. But, degrading as *that* is, it is incomparably less debasing than the consequent "obligation" to submit to periodical medical examinations whose nature forbids their description here. The fulfilment of this obligation is enforced by severe penalties.

It is a common fiction of Inexperts that these women are too degraded to object to these examinations. Whence, then, all the difficulty in bringing them under its operation? It is said that they "don't care." The Experts know better, and they equally know "the reason why." One of them (M. Lenaers) speaking from his own experience as chief administrator of the system at Brussels, reported to the City Council that the inscription on the rolls of prostitution is an exceedingly grave and delicate matter when we consider the position in which it places the woman who is the object of it, for while this inscription is a purely administrative act the object of which is to compel the habitual prostitute to submit to the examination, none the less does it inflict (*inflige*) on the woman a patent of infamy and degradation, and exercise a disastrous and fatal influence on her future "life."[8] The Head of the Police in Berlin, in an Administrative Report for the decade 1881–90, acknowledges that the registration of prostitutes, with its consequences, horribly aggravates their abject condition.

Dr. Hippolyte Mireur (himself an Examining Surgeon at Marseilles) describes the "obligation" to submit to the examination in language which, if used by an *opponent* instead of a strenuous and skilled *advocate* of the system, would be denounced as sensational and exaggerated. He writes of it as "an obligation prodigiously degrading"; as "debasing and terrible";[9] and he characterises "the system" which enforces it, "which regularises and legitimates the sorrowful industry of the prostitute," as, "in fact, the sinister stroke by which the woman is cut off from society, after which she ceases to belong to herself and becomes the chattel (*chose*) of the Administration."[10]

Dr. Mauriac, who, though not an "Expert," has an intimate knowledge of the system, wrote in 1896:—"This terrible registration is one of the most abominable kinds of slavery inflicted on a free being."[11]

Small hope of success

Having such knowledge of the true character and effect of the examination, the Experts have no difficulty in understanding why the vast majority of even degraded women, so far from not caring about, abhor, and use all their ingenuity to escape it. They are, however, staggered at the number of these women who succeed in baffling all efforts to bring them within the sanitary *cordon*, and they recognise this "clandestine" or "illicit" prostitution as fatal to all efforts to make debauchery healthy. We shall see further on into how small a compass it reduces the hope of realising the limited expectation of promoting the "public health."

Even the heathen cannot be coerced

It might have been expected that in heathen lands, where a lower estimate of the dignity of womankind prevails, and where their normal condition is often little better than slavery, this difficulty would have disappeared. But it is not so. In India, precisely the same feature crops up; as is abundantly testified by the unimpeachable authorities quoted in the before-mentioned "History of a Sanitary Failure," to which the reader is referred. In Hong Kong, too, it was authoritatively stated, while the system was in force, "That the number of women caught under the sanitary regulations, has always been, as compared with those left unregulated, insignificant."[12] The same authority also pointed out that the objection of the Chinese prostitutes to submit to the examination was so intense that it could be inflicted only on *the lowest class*, found solely in brothels for Europeans. It was impossible to enforce it in those for Chinese and other Orientals, in which it had to be completely abandoned.

An unforeseen result

Now let it be assumed for a moment that *within* the *cordon* the system is more or less successful. It has an effect *outside* wholly unexpected, and in the opposite direction. The hatred of the "debasing" inspection and the fear of coming within the grasp of the officers who enforce it, prevents, to a very serious extent, the unregistered women from availing themselves of the means of healing provided by free hospitals or private practitioners, so that outside the *cordon* disease is more rife and the risk of contagion is, as a direct consequence of the so-called "protective" measures, greater than it otherwise would be. The Experts are continually pointing to this larger amount of disease, and the continual increase in the number of unregistered (and therefore unexamined) women, as the most formidable obstacle against which they have to contend. Even an Inexpert can see that a small increase in this outside risk, extending as it does over so large an area, may easily neutralise the effect of the comparative safety which we have momentarily assumed to exist within the *cordon*. Hence it becomes perfectly clear that, even from this cause alone, the attainment of the Expert's desideratum—the maintenance of "the registered public women in a satisfactory sanitary condition"—is no guarantee against prostitution "becoming more dangerous to the public health." This will be still more evident as we proceed.

The men's refinement of corruption

The study of this revolting subject is full of surprises. The large and increasing number of "clandestine" prostitutes is evidence of a much larger number of "clandestine" customers. "Clandestine sexual intercourse is to-day most in fashion. Nothing will be able to stop it. It has become and will always remain the most prolific source of venereal contagion."[13]

Why do not the men avail themselves of the sanitary *cordon* with its proffered benefits? It is because there is a certain refinement of corruption brought about by the regulation system itself. It flourishes equally in Europe, in India, in Hong Kong, and wherever else the system operates. Many men, seeing the way in which others rush in to take advantage of the regulations, seek for something less "common" outside the *cordon*, and, having found it, they try to keep it select, and to prevent its becoming known to the sanitary officers. They therefore aid the women in their evasion, and between the two the administrators are outwitted and checkmated at every turn. How delusive, then, is the hazy expectation of the Experts that, somehow or other, they will one day overcome the fatal defect, notwithstanding a century's experience to the contrary. Well may the British Army Sanitary Commission remark, that "to keep down clandestine prostitution 'would require a degree of zeal and hourly watchfulness which is never likely to be carried out.'"[14]

Notes

1   "The History of a Sanitary Failure. Extracts (mainly from official sources) shewing the results of 90 years' experiments in the Hygienic Regulation of Prostitution in India." Compiled by Henry J. Wilson, M.P.
2   Lecour, "La Prostitution à Paris et à Londres," Paris, 1870, p. 255.

3   *Ibid.*, p. 254.
4   "Memorandum by the [British] Army Sanitary Commission on the Statistics of Venereal Disease among British and Native Troops in India for the year 1892," in Parliamentary Paper No. 318 for 1895.
5   *Ibid.*
6   Lecour, "La Prostitution à Paris et à Londres." Compare the figures (30,000) on p. 120 with those (3,731) on p. 127.
7   "Traitement de la Syphilis," par Charles Mauriac, Médecin de l'Hôpital Ricord (Hôpital du Midi). Paris, 1896, p. 62.
8   "Report on, and Project for Regulating Prostitution in Brussels," presented to the College of the Burgomasters and Aldermen by M. Lenaers, Commissary of Police, 6th August, 1877.
9   Mireur, "La Syphilis et la Prostitution," p. 249.
10   *Ibid*, p. 248–9.
11   Dr. Mauriac, "Traitement de la Syphilis." Paris, 1896, p. 797.
12   "Report of Commissioners appointed to Inquire into the Working of 'the Contagious Diseases Ordinance, 1867'." Parliamentary Paper 118 of 1880, p. 63.
13   "Traitement de la Syphilis," par Charles Mauriac, Médecin de l'Hôpital Ricord (Hôpital du Midi). Paris, 1896, p. 62.
14   Report on Sanitary Measures in India, 1875–76, p. 26. Quoted in "The History of a Sanitary Failure."

Did sexologists impose definitions of homosexuality on men and women who desired those of the same sex?

Introduction

BY THE SECOND HALF of the nineteenth century, a new psychological science emerged, called sexology. Historians have debated whether sexologists were liberating Victorian society by speaking about sex, or if they were exercising a power discourse in Foucauldian terms. Sexologists asserted that sexuality was important – it was a powerful, human instinct necessary for reproduction, but it also inspired creativity, art, and music. Sexologists also expanded knowledge about sexual physiology. However, they also imposed diagnoses on men who had sex with other men, as well as other people with unusual sexual tastes – for instance, inventing the categories of sadism and masochism. The sexologists had the power to put their discourses into practice by having their patients confined to asylums, and when negative their accounts of homosexuals as degenerate justified persecution and hostility.[1]

Richard Krafft-Ebing, a German trained in medicine and psychiatry, was probably the most influential sexologist. He was very concerned with the development of what he called the sexual instinct, both physiologically, as the body evolved from embryo to adult, and psychologically, as the child developed into the adult. Like many at the time, he was worried that this development could go wrong, leading to degeneration. In mental asylums, he treated many men and women who desired their own sex, and diagnosed them as having a perversion. Perversion was not just a matter of performing "deviant" sexual acts, such as boys who had sex with each other in boarding school. Rather, homosexuality was a perversion which became part of the whole personality, and derived from physiological and psychological degeneration.

Not surprisingly, Krafft-Ebing portrayed homosexuals in negative terms: for instance, he asserted that "feminine timidity, frivolity, obstinacy and weakness of character rule among such individuals." As for women, he warned that "uranism may be suspected in females wearing their hair short , or who dress in the fashion of men, or pursue the sports and pastimes of their male acquaintances."[2]

The word "uranism" came from Karl Heinrichs Ulrich, a German lawyer who campaigned for the rights of men who desired men, and lost his job as a result. In his private life, he became acquainted with the urban subcultures of men who liked to take on feminine personas and even stage secret balls. Ulrichs hypothesized that they had a female soul in a male body and called them "urnings." Ulrichs derived the term "uranism" from Pausanius' speech in Plato's *Symposium*, in which he celebrated love and desire between men as heaven-sent. Uranists could refer to both men and women who desired the same sex.[3] Krafft-Ebing also borrowed the term "homosexual" from Karl Maria Kertbeny, another activist for homosexual rights.

Ulrichs was a patient of Krafft-Ebing, but at first the sexologist publicly criticized Ulrichs' celebration of homosexuality, arguing that it was pathological. However, over the course of decades, Krafft-Ebing corresponded with many self-defined homosexuals and others with same sex desires who read his book, *Psychopathia Sexualis*, and were inspired by it. Was this an example of what Foucault termed a "reverse discourse" – homosexuals or others defined as deviant using sexologists' own terms to create a more positive identity for themselves?

Oosterhuis goes further than Foucault and indeed challenges him. He argues that Krafft-Ebing actually derived many of his theories from his correspondences with homosexual men and women. They had created their own notion of what it meant to be homosexual, often inspired by Ulrichs' idea of a female soul in a male body. We can ascertain if the subjects of the case studies excerpted here agreed with Krafft-Ebing's ideas. Furthermore, the case of Miss L can also demonstrate why the female friendships discussed in the last section came under greater suspicion by the end of the century.[4]

Krafft-Ebing began to turn away from his insistence that homosexuality was unnatural and pathological in the 1890s. In some ways this was because scientists had shown that the human embryo was originally sexually undifferentiated, so perhaps bisexuality was natural. But Krafft-Ebing also changed his ideas because he met so many homosexual men and women who lived happy, healthy lives in loving relationships. By the twelfth edition he argued that "this abnormality must not be looked on as a pathological condition or as a crime." Instead, it was the outcome of sexual desires, which were important to all love, morality, ambition, and creativity. Such relations "may proceed with the same harmony and satisfying influence as in the normally disposed." Arguing that it was unfair to punish men for an inborn trait they could not resist, he also called for the repeal of the statute known as paragraph 175, which criminalized anal sex between men. The sexologist had changed his mind.[5]

Notes

1   Lucy Bland and Laura Doan, eds., *Sexology in Culture: Labelling Bodies and Desires* (Chicago: University of Chicago Press, 1998). For other sexologists, see Havelock Ellis, "Sexual Inversion," in *Studies in the Psychology of Sex* (New York: Random House, 1936); August Forel, *The Sexual Question,* trans. C. F. Marshall (New York: Rebman Company, 1908); E. Heinrich Kisch, *The Sexual Life of Woman in Its Physiological, Pathological and Hygienic Aspects,* trans. M. Eden Paul (New York: Rebman Company, 1910); Dr. L. Loewenfeld, *On Conjugal Happiness: Experiences and Reflections of a Medical Man,* trans. Ronald E. S. Krohn, 3rd edn (London: John Bale, Sons, and Danielsson Ltd, 1913); Paolo Mantegazza, *The Physiology of Love* (New York: Cleveland Publishing Co., 1894); Albert Moll, *Libido Sexualis,* trans. David Berger (New York: American Ethnological Press, 1933); Dr. Anton Nystrom, *The Natural Laws of Sexual Life: Medical-Sociological Researches,* trans. Carl Sandzen, 3rd Swedish edn (St. Louis: C. V. Mosby Company, 1913); Chris Waters, "Havelock Ellis, Sigmund Freud, and the State: Discourses of Homosexual Identity in Interwar Britain," in *Sexology in Culture,* ed. Bland and Doan. For French sexology, which was somewhat different than the Anglo-German-Scandinavian model, see Vernon Rosario, *The Erotic Imagination: French Histories of Perversity* (New York: Oxford University Press, 1997); L. Thoinot, *Medicolegal Aspects of Moral Offenses,* trans. Arthur W. Weysse (Philadelphia: F. A. Davis Company, 1913).
2   Richard Krafft-Ebing, *Psychopathia Sexualis,* 12th edn (New York: Putnam's, 1965), 321, 334.
3   Hubert Kennedy, *Ulrichs: The Life and Works of Karl Heinrich Ulrichs: Pioneer of the Modern Gay Movement* (Boston: Alyson Publications, Inc., 1988).
4   Harry Oosterhuis, *Stepchildren of Nature: Krafft-Ebing, Psychiatry, and the Making of Sexual Identity* (Chicago: University of Chicago Press, 2000), 370.
5   Krafft-Ebing, *Psychopathia Sexualis.*

Chapter 16

Harry Oosterhuis

STEPCHILDREN OF NATURE
Krafft-Ebing, psychiatry, and the making
of sexual identity (2000)

For science and humanity

BY PUBLISHING HIS PATIENTS' LETTERS and autobiographies and
by quoting their statements verbatim, Krafft-Ebing enabled voices to be heard that
were usually silenced. His case histories revealed to individuals with "odd feelings" that
they were not unique in their experience. In doing justice to the subjective experience
of patients in his writings, Krafft-Ebing represented a small minority within the medical
world of his day. According to Müller (1991) and Hansen (1992), physicians were rather
quick to generalize from a small number of cases and theorize without retelling individual
life histories. As a last resort, physicians might even tamper with individual cases so as to
construct a uniform set of evidence that perfectly fitted the established medical categories
(cf. Klabundt 1994, 126). However, my investigation of Krafft-Ebing's case histories offers
no support for such attitudes or practices. His unpublished case histories are in no way
different from the published ones. In his writings, individual meanings did not automatically
follow medical theories. Instead, contemporary readers could find subjective experience,
dialogue, multivocality, divergent meanings, and contradictory sets of values in *Psychopathia
Sexualis.*

Those readers who recognized themselves in Krafft-Ebing's cases were left enough
room to interpret their sexual feelings and experiences in their own way. The psychiatrist
quoted the words of perverts not solely as evidence in support of his medical diagnosis;
and, conversely, if their words challenged psychiatric doctrine, they were not censored.
Some of the autobiographers took the opportunity to vent their criticism of current social
norms. A twenty-year-old man was of the opinion that society did not have the right to
ban homosexual contact:

> Together with the majority of urnings, I claim that our sexual anomaly does
> not affect our mental condition or only slightly at best. Our desire may be

abnormal, but it is as intense as the normal urge and not unnatural. Therefore, legislators do not have the right to deny to us cooperative boys and men, just as they have no right to deprive paralytics of their crutches.

(*Ps* 1890, 161)

A thirty-six-year-old man who had lived a homosexual life in Paris, London, Rio de Janeiro, and in the United States stated that legal reforms were not enough to improve the social position of urnings:

> I myself don't foster any hope to witness a change for the better. That will be something of the future. Even if we will be treated by the courts in a more lenient way, there is still a question to be answered . . . . [W]ho will remove the prejudice against us, which from time immemorial has pervaded society? As long as that continues to exist, our moral suffering will not come to an end.
>
> (1890e, 55)

Even more militant was a medical student, aged twenty-three, who made it clear that he did not want a cure for his homosexual leanings. In his autobiography he stated:

> I intentionally and consciously curse contemporary moral standards, which force sexually abnormal people to offend against arbitrary laws. I think that sexual contact between two people of the same sex is at their individual discretion, without legislators having any right to interfere . . . . I only yearn for a time, when I can pursue my desires more easily and with less danger of being discovered, and thus enjoy a delight that will not harm anyone.
>
> (1890e, 63, 66; cf. *Ps* 1999, 571, 574)

Another urning wrote to Krafft-Ebing that his self-respect had been restored after he had read Plato's *Symposium* and a work by Gustav Jäger, but that his self-acceptance went hand in hand with a loathing of a social order that prevented him from organizing his life as he wished.[1] "From that moment, however, . . . a certain pent-up anger and an intense hate of modern social relationships took hold of me" (*Ps* 1887, 88). A technical engineer, too, was often, as he wrote,

> seized with bitterness and a deep hatred for the modern ideas that treat us poor urnings with such terrible harshness. For what is our fate? In most cases we are not understood, and we are derided and despised. Even when all goes well, and we are understood, we are still pitied like invalids or the insane— and pity has always been sickening to me.
>
> (1891h, 128; *Ps* 1999, 582)

The autobiography of a physician, which covered more than thirteen pages in small print and was published in several editions of *Psychopathia Sexualis*, was also remarkable, because of its criticism of the medical profession. By recounting his life's story in a novelistic style, this man explained that he had changed into a woman. In a letter accompanying his autobiography, he advocated that women should be allowed to study medicine because they had a more intuitive understanding of the body than men:

Finally, I wanted to present you with the results of my recollection and reflection to prove that one who thinks and feels like a woman can still be a doctor. I consider it a great injustice to bar women from medicine. A woman discovers the traces of many ailments through her intuition, while a man gropes in the dark, despite all his diagnostic skills, especially as far as women's and children's diseases are concerned. If I could have my way, every physician would have to live the life of a woman for three months. He then would have a better understanding and more consideration in matters affecting the half of mankind from which he himself is born. He then would respect woman's spiritual greatness, and at the same time also the harshness of their fate.

(1890e, 79; cf. *Ps* 1999, 268)

Other correspondents criticized their fellow sufferers because they did not demonstrate any critical awareness of their condition. Thus a Hungarian civil servant asserted that most urnings were generally kind-hearted but also superficial and addicted to backbiting (1890e, 45). A technical engineer reported that among the fifty-five urnings he knew, he had found the same character traits and habits:

Almost all of them are more or less idealists: they smoke little or not at all; they are bigoted, vain, desirous of admiration, and superstitious; and, unfortunately, I must confess that they embody more of the defects and reverse sides of both sexes than the good qualities.

(1891h, 130; cf. *Ps* 1999, 584)

The impact of Krafft-Ebing's medical work was multifaceted: it not only served as a guide for professionals and experts, but also as a forum for the individuals concerned. The book opened up a space in which they could begin to speak for themselves and look for models with which to identify. Despite the medical bias, many case histories served as go-betweens, linking individual introspection—the self-conscious and frequently painful recognition that one was a deviant kind of person—and social identification, the comforting sense of belonging to a community of like-minded individuals. Because Krafft-Ebing distinguished himself as an expert who took a stand against traditional moral-religious and legal denunciations of sexual deviance, individuals approached him to find understanding, acceptance, and support, as one letter of a Belgian urning clearly illustrates:

You will be able to empathize with what it means to lock forever within myself that which touches me deepest by far, and to not be able to confide in anybody, while I myself have often been the confidant in matters of great joy and grave suffering. You are the first to whom I open my heart. Use this letter in any way you please; maybe one day it will help lighten the fate of future men to whom nature will give the same feelings.

(*Ps* 1888, 87)

Another urning, who regretted that he had not read *Psychopathia Sexualis* earlier in his life because this would have prevented a lot of misery, confided to its author: "Nobody knows my true nature—only you, a stranger, you alone know me now, indeed better than father and mother, friend, wife, and lover. It is a real comfort to me to reveal, this one time, the heavy secret of my own nature" *(Ps* 1889, 138). Krafft-Ebing's humanitarian rhetoric did not ring hollow and had some real effect. In fact, many clients did not need medical treatment, because pouring out one's heart to someone was already something of a cure in itself: "Tout comprendre c'est tout guérir [To understand all is to cure all]," a thirty-five-year-old masochist wrote (1891h, 19; *Ps* 1999, 133). The psychiatrist's dealing with these men might be characterized as a form of "proto-psychotherapy." Several case histories create the impression that he showed an active interest in them, while simultaneously speaking reassuringly to them, thus making them feel at ease. A homosexual waiter, aged forty-two, was "pleased to obtain at last a professional explanation of the abnormal state that he had always considered a disease" *(Ps* 1887, 92; *Ps* 1999, 318). Being given a chance to tell their story in a leisurely, unhurried way and to explain themselves to the psychiatrist was frequently the first step toward self-acceptance. Writing their life history, giving coherence and intelligibility to their torn self, could result in a "catharsis" of comprehension: "I am very ashamed of myself because again I write down my confession, and yet it gives me great satisfaction to throw light on my condition," wrote the Dutch glove fetishist who had informed the psychiatrist earlier about his case.[2] Many suggested that his work had brought them relief: "I am very unhappy with my condition and have often considered suicide, but I was somewhat reassured after reading the *Psychopathia Sexualis*," a thirty-eight-year-old urning told Krafft-Ebing.[3] Another one wrote:

> Your work "Psychopathia Sexualis" gave me much comfort. It contains passages that I might have written myself; they seem to be unconsciously taken from my own life. My heart has been considerably lightened since I learned from your book of your benevolent interest in our disreputable class. It was the first time that I met someone who showed me that we are not entirely as bad as we are usually portrayed . . . . Anyway, I feel a great burden has been lifted from me.
>
> (1890e, 55)

To most private patients and correspondents, Krafft-Ebing was not simply a doctor treating diseases, but someone who answered their need to have themselves explained to themselves, an emotional confidant, and even an ally.[4] His German colleague Albert Moll, who corresponded with him on a regular basis, remembers in his autobiography that Krafft-Ebing was rather exceptional because his concern for his patients often went beyond mere professional commitment: he even answered letters of anonymous correspondents who were too ashamed to give their name (Moll 1936, 145). Displaying a humanitarian commitment to patients, Krafft-Ebing gained a reputation for trust and tolerance. For many he must have embodied the ideal of science as a means to improve their lot. "Your work 'Psychopathia sexualis' came to my attention a short time ago," a businessman informed Krafft-Ebing.

> I saw in the book that you were working and studying without prejudice in the interest of science and humanity. If I cannot tell you much that is new, I will still speak of a few things that I trust you will receive as one more brick for the construction of your work: in your hands, I am confident, this will aid in improving our social condition.
>
> (*Ps* 1890, 161; cf. *Ps* 1999, 566)

"This is my general confession. I never would have suspected that I would ever speak out to a man who is not one of us," another urning confided to the psychiatrist.

> Yet I have now opened my heart. Reading your work has warmed my heart; after all, contempt hurts, especially when one deserves only pity instead. Because of this low sexual drive, we are punished anyway . . . . I wish that public opinion on us unfortunate people would be alleviated . . . . A drowning person grasps at a straw. I hope to find something to hold on to, which protects me from sinking into the depths of misery and contempt.
>
> (1890e, 43)

Some of Krafft-Ebing's homosexual correspondents in particular believed that he was in a position to influence public opinion and to evoke more understanding for urnings in society. They appealed to him, not only to relieve their personal sufferings, but also with a call to mitigate the social ostracism of urnings in general. "Please, help to alleviate the painful pressure that burdens so many unfortunate men and carries them to despair," one addressed himself to Krafft-Ebing (*Ps* 1888, 93). What was especially depressing about his contrary sexual feeling, another autobiographer explained, was the fear that it might be revealed in public. He concluded his life history with an unequivocal appeal to science to enlighten the public: "Whoever will start to commit himself to the matter without prejudice, also before the general public? Science should discard its reservation and teach people about its insights" (1885a, 42). A thirty-three-year-old businessman declared that he was not the only one who was plagued with feelings of guilt and who had regularly considered committing suicide:

> Thousands are in this terrible situation. Should not every effort be made to liberate these thousands from the depressed feeling of having to hide a secret, which, if revealed, puts them below the criminal. This secret freezes any intellectual and spiritual impulse and causes great talents to be numbed, if it does not lead to insanity and suicide. If it is in your power to protect these unfortunates from public opinion, then please do so: you will save many noble people from ruin, men of genius among them.
>
> (*Ps* 1890, 115)

Far from resembling "a cluttered Victorian mansion," as Krafft-Ebing's mind was once characterized, within the limits of the moral climate of his time, he managed to be open-minded and pragmatic (Robinson 1976, 26). As a promoter of psychiatry at the university, he was guided by the positivist model of natural science, but at the same time his treatment of patients was rooted in a humanitarian tradition of asylum psychiatry and an anthropological approach in clinical psychiatry. He impressed upon his students that kindness and trust were often more helpful to patients than medication.[5] In his private practice, categories were not simply abstractions; "problems" were embodied in persons who often more or less stood on an equal footing with him. The letters of his upper- and middle-class patients suggest that he had a good relationship with many of them. With most of his private patients and informants, he shared a common bourgeois background, an attachment to individual achievement and independence, and a propensity toward a regular, well-ordered lifestyle. More than half of his patients and correspondents were members of the bourgeoisie or aristocracy, and the majority among them were private patients. Besides rich landowners, scholars, writers, artists, medical students, physicians, and engineers, there were also many common civil servants, businessmen, and employees. Apart from the unusual sexual life of some of them, most wanted to be respectable citizens. "After reading your work I hope that, if I fulfill my duties as a physician, citizen, father, and husband, I may still count myself among human beings who do not merely deserve to be despised," wrote one of Krafft-Ebing's correspondents (1890e, 79; *Ps* 1999, 268). A medical student who addressed himself to Krafft-Ebing because of his fetishism hoped "to become a useful employee, serving my country and science, in whatever position."[6] "I have a responsible occupation, and I think I can give the assurance," wrote a homosexual, "that my abnormal inclination has never, not even by a hair's breadth, caused me to deviate from the duty imposed on me" (1891h, 125; *Ps* 1999, 578–79). A high-level German civil servant who had sent Krafft-Ebing an extensive argument against the criminalization of homosexuality even reproached him for not being respectable enough, because *Psychopathia Sexualis*, which might have contributed significantly to the improvement of the social position of urnings, contained so many "obscene details" (1892i, 43).

To many of Krafft-Ebing's patients and correspondents, however, bourgeois respectability with all its sexual and moral constraints also posed a problem, which in part explains why some preferably looked for their sexual contacts among the lower classes in particular. As a possible escape from the restraints of bourgeois respectability, the looseness of lower-class sexuality, though generally considered dangerous, still seemed enticing, especially for homosexuals and masochists. In fact, many middle- and upper-class urnings indicated that they preferred sex with lower-class men; some of them stated that they were not sexually aroused by men of their own class or that they were even impotent with them. One of them explained that his attraction to men of his own social standing was merely platonic and that his sexual desire focused on lower-class "masculine characters":

> coarse, powerful men . . . who are mentally and socially beneath me. The reason for this strange phenomenon may be that my pronounced feeling of shame and innate apprehensiveness, when combined with my cautious disposition, produces an inhibitory effect with men of my own social position, so that with them I can only rarely and with difficulty induce sexual excitement in myself.
>
> (1891h, 129; *Ps* 1999, 583)

Apparently, some social distance made it easier for these men to discard any psychological inhibitions they might have—in this respect their attitude did not differ from heterosexual men having sex with lower-class prostitutes.

For homosexual men there was another reason to prefer lower-class sexual partners. Many refrained from having sex with other urnings because they were after "real men." According to Dr. G, two urnings were easily put off by each other, just as "two whores" would be, simply for reasons of competition (1882, 215). Rough lower-class men who did not consider themselves urnings but still engaged in same-sex contacts were viewed as hypermasculine; soldiers were especially sought after as well. "Generally, I seek my lovers among cavalrymen and sailors, and, eventually, among workmen, especially butchers and smiths," an estate agent wrote, adding that he especially favored "robust forms, with healthy facial complexions" (1891h, 100; *Ps* 1999, 603). "I loathe sexual contact with urnings," another correspondent reported. "I prefer lower-class men, servants, stable hands, soldiers, for example, if they are powerfully built."[7]

A special fascination for crossing boundaries of class manifested itself in some of the case histories of masochists. Being dominated by someone of an inferior social position seemed extra humiliating. Thus a high-ranking civil servant of thirty-two, homosexual as well as masochistic, was fascinated by "sturdy, dirty working-class figures" (1894e, 351). An aristocratic military officer, aged twenty-eight, was aroused by lower-class men in shining boots who incited

> sensually colored ideas, such as being his servant's servant and pulling off his boots; the idea of being stepped on by him or shining his boots was extremely pleasing . . . . It was only servants' boots that aroused him; the same kind of boots on persons of a similar social position did not affect him.
>
> (*Ps* 1888, 120; cf. *Ps* 1999, 296–97)

Another aristocrat believed that his masochism was inborn, "for already when he was still a boy he had longed to wear ragged clothes and to get in touch with proletarians." Krafft-Ebing reported that this aristocrat's sexual urge was very strong and that he was solely attracted to "sailors, coachmen, servants, journeymen with big, callous worker's hands."

> In order to experience such pleasure, it was necessary that he approached such men by changing his clothes, visiting cheap joints, etc. In his erotic dreams, which are all about masochist desires and sexual rape, only coarse masculine figures from the dregs of the nation play a role.
>
> (1899d, 151–52)

It is hard to think of a sharper contrast between this degraded milieu and the bourgeois and aristocratic worlds of many of Krafft-Ebing's private patients and correspondents as evoked in their stories and writings. Sent in by educated and often cosmopolitan men, several of these letters and personal narratives were filled with literary references, sophisticated self-analyses, and philosophical and medical speculations. Science was valued in particular. A thirty-four-year-old businessman declared:

> Convinced that the enigma of our existence can be solved, or, at least, illuminated only by the unprejudiced thought of scientific men, my only aim in portraying my life is, as far as is possible, to throw some light on this cruel error of nature, and to be useful to my companions in misfortune among generations to come, for as long as men are born, there will be urnings. It is a fact that they have existed in every age. With the progress of science in our age, one will view me and those like me not as objects of hatred, but as objects of pity, who deserve the warm compassion rather than the scorn of their more fortunate fellow men.
>
> (*Ps* 1888, 87–88; cf. *Ps* 1999, 586)

Remarkably, perhaps, religious references are found only sporadically in the case histories and personal narratives.[8] With reference to Darwin, some pointed out that their religious conviction was undermined by modern scientific insights. It seems that many of them were quite active in tracing scientific and literary writings that could throw light on their condition, and frequently they knew Krafft-Ebing's publications or other popular and scientific works on sexuality. "Even though I have not consorted with other urnings, I am, nevertheless, fully informed about my condition," wrote a homosexual businessman, "for I have succeeded in consulting almost all the literature on the subject" (Ps 1890, 161; cf. Ps 1999, 566). Others referred to classical culture to justify their homosexuality. Although he was ashamed of himself, a twenty-six-year-old patient had accepted his leanings. As Krafft-Ebing noted: "If he thinks of the magnificent classical masterworks of art, then he cannot imagine that it would be wrong to love a living embodiment of them" (1894e, 357). Above all it was the shared access to art and literature, or, in short, *Bildung*, the broad neo-humanistic and cultural education that defined the habitus of the upper echelons of the central European bourgeoisie, and that provided the intellectual basis for Krafft-Ebing, his private patients, and his correspondents to communicate with one another as equals. The aim of *Bildung* as a cultural ideal was not only intellectual education, but also the development of character: the self and its formation were cultivated as objects of observation and concern—as objects of self-reflection.

Next to class and education, gender is a crucial variable in Krafft-Ebing's casuistry. In the nineteenth century, women were generally considered to be more susceptible to mental disorders than men, and they often outnumbered men in asylums; but as far as sexual perversions were concerned, men were overrepresented (cf. Showalter 1987). Most of Krafft-Ebing's patients and correspondents discussed here, 322 out of 440, were male. Moreover, in more than half of the 118 case histories involving women, the issue was not so much sexual perversion per se, but mental disorders related to menstruation. Among the sadists, fetishists, exhibitionists, pedophiles, and zoo-erastes or zoophiles in Krafft-Ebing's casuistry, no women at all were represented. And they constituted only a minority among the masochists and homosexuals: out of 50 masochists 3 were female, and out of 168 homosexuals only 25.

This underrepresentation of women was no coincidence, since medical definitions of sexuality in general and perversion in particular were gender-specific and closely connected to norms about normal sexual behavior of men and women. Men were supposed to be active and aggressive, women passive and docile. It was assumed, for example, that mainly men were exhibitionists. Women were hardly considered as perverts if they showed their bodies to men, because they were supposed to be sexually passive and make themselves accessible to the male gaze. Conversely, if a woman observed the naked body of a man, she was not so much seen as a voyeur as he was considered to be an exhibitionist. Exhibitionism by a man was seen as a perversion inasmuch as the man was making himself into a passive object for the female gaze (McLaren 1997, 205).

The reason for the rarity of masochism among women is, paradoxically, that subjection and dependence were considered by Krafft-Ebing and other physicians as part of women's normal condition. In addition to the three female patients discussed under the category of masochism, another three women were diagnosed by Krafft-Ebing with so-called sexual bondage, a one-sided, extreme emotional dependency of women on their sexual partner. Sexual bondage, though considered an abnormality, was not a perversion because it did not interfere with normal intercourse. Mainly in men, who were supposed to be sexually dominant, was subjection considered a perversion. Moreover, since masochistic men, by adopting the passive female role, did not follow the supposedly normal biological order, this behavior was related to inversion. Like male exhibitionists, masochists undermined active heterosexual masculinity.

All sadists observed by Krafft-Ebing were men. Sadism was indeed defined as a problem of men: as he pointed out, sexual aggressiveness was part of the normal masculine psyche, but it sometimes transgressed the limits of the normal. As such it was an "anachronism" in modern civilization:

> From cultural history and anthropology we know that there were times and that there are still tribes in which cruel violence, plundering, and even the knocking out of women by blows with a club took and take the place of courtship. Nowadays, among civilized people, we still see such anachronisms in the form of rape.
>
> (1890e, 1)

The medical definition of this perversion reflected changing norms about masculinity and it also was differentiated according to class. Before Krafft-Ebing gave it a psychiatric label, the term *sadism* was first used by literary critics who in the 1850s commented on the decadent themes found in the writings of Gustave Flaubert (1821–1880) and Charles Baudelaire (1821–1867), and it began to be widely employed in the 1880s when the Marquis de Sade's work was rediscovered. The literary notion of sadism referred to a cultivated libertinism and decadence, and it included an elitist disdain for conventional bourgeois society. However, the men whom psychiatrists first labeled as sadists were for the most part lower-class sexual delinquents. Their crude and violent sexual behavior was considered compulsive, and it clearly transgressed the boundaries of normal masculine sexual aggressiveness. New notions of civilized and restrained masculinity placed restrictions on male aggression (McLaren 1997, 169–70, 205). Bourgeois masculinity was not only defined by aggressiveness but also by self-control, reason, and willpower, qualities that lower-class compulsive sadists failed to possess. Yet, some bourgeois men who were diagnosed with "ideal" sadism by Krafft-Ebing seemed quite capable of controlling their violent urges: these men were cruel only in their own imagination.

All fetishists who appear in Krafft-Ebing's work were men. Although he listed fetishistic tendencies in women regarding abstract qualities in men involving traits and talents like courage, chivalry, self-confidence, and other nonphysical aspects, he stated that cases of perverse fetishism in women were unknown to him. Typically, fetishists, obsessed with female body parts or female clothes and ornaments, were presented as actively desiring subjects while women played the role of passive object (Matlock 1993). Women, however, were seen as actors in another context: especially in France in the 1880s and 1890s, psychiatrists were confronted with middle- and upper-class women shoplifting in department stores, not out of poverty, but because they were obsessed by the objects of female fashion and supposedly suffered from excessive vanity. Psychiatrists diagnosed these women as kleptomaniacs, and they might well have been considered as the female equivalents of male fetishists (O'Brien 1983). Kleptomania was viewed as a typical female mental disorder. Like other derangements in women, psychiatrists often connected it to the female reproductive system, and they also noticed that women derived sexual pleasure from shoplifting. However, kleptomania was not seen as a sexual perversion. In *Psychopathia Sexualis* there is no reference to it, though Krafft-Ebing must have been familiar with the many case histories of kleptomania published by French psychiatrists. He probably saw no immediate ground to link this disorder to fetishism as French psychiatrists did, but, from the prevailing psychiatric perspective of his day, he might have done so with good reason (Rosario 1997, 113–14, 123–26).

In contrast to male homosexuality, female homosexuality largely remained a muted discourse in Krafft-Ebing's work, and his discussion of it was contradictory. On the one hand, he emphasized that lesbianism was comparable to male homosexuality and seemed as common as contrary sexual feeling in men:

> Careful observation of the ladies of large cities soon reveals that uranism is by no means a rarity. Females who wear their hair short, who dress in the fashion of men, who pursue the sports and pastimes of their male acquaintants, as well as opera singers and actresses who appear on the stage in male attire by preference may be suspected of it.
>
> (*Ps* 1903, 282; cf. *Ps* 1999, 328)

At the same time, however, he suggested that uranism was not as frequent among women as among men. Moreover, he contended that in the majority of cases, homosexuality in women was cultivated rather than inborn. Women were not only underrepresented in the casuistry, but they hardly spoke for themselves as well. In various case histories involving private female patients, who more often than men were sent by their partner or by relatives, Krafft-Ebing hinted at the fact that it was harder to elicit statements on their sexuality than from the men who consulted him (*Ps* 1887, 95; 1888e, 7). He seemed to have suspected that this might have been related to his own gender. "Details on the vita sexualis of women," he wrote as an aside in *Psychopathia Sexualis*, "will come to our knowledge only when medical women enter into the study of this subject" (*Ps* 1903, 21; cf. *Ps* 1999, 22). He also suggested that, in comparison to men, women experienced their homosexuality as less of a problem. After all, female homosexuality was not punishable in Germany while it was hardly persecuted in Austria. Moreover, lesbian women were supposed to have fewer problems with heterosexual intercourse than urnings, which is why many were married and invisible to the outside world.

To Krafft-Ebing, especially the appearance of women—more often than that of men who were more eager to tell their life stories—suggested their homosexuality, and in his therapeutical interactions with them, it was thus a factor in his trying to raise this issue. The few case histories on women also reveal that they, if already displaying a self-conscious attitude, were taken less seriously than men. It seems understandable, therefore, that his female patients could identify themselves much less with the medical-psychiatric discourse on sexuality of those days. Moreover, around 1900 a distinct sense of lesbian identity was still hardly developed in central European societies. For women, there were no public meeting places or an established sexual underground, while most also lacked economic independence and freedom of movement. In Germany and Austria, a self-defined lesbian identity and subculture did not emerge until the 1920s (Hacker and Lang 1986, 13–17; Hacker 1987; cf. Vicinus 1989).

This is not to deny, however, that some women may well have recognized themselves in Krafft-Ebing's case histories and that his work may have reinforced their sense of identity, even though there are only slight and indirect indications for this. The novel *Sind es Frauen? Roman über das dritte Geschlecht* (1901), by Aimée Duc, the penname of the Austrian author Minna Wettstein-Adelt, is one of the first literary works picturing the life and viewpoints of self-confident lesbian women, among them Minotschka Fernandoff, the leading character, and her lover Berta Cohn. While some of the women are out for an evening in Geneva, they are joined at their table by two men, who, referring to Lombroso, argue that emancipation and intellectual pursuits cause nervous disorders and hysteria in women. Biting back, Minotschka mentions Krafft-Ebing. Upon hearing the psychiatrist's name, one of the men intervenes:

> "Apropos: Krafft-Ebing! Is he not the one who stands up for perverse people?" Proudly he looked around the table. "Indeed," Minotschka said, "he is the same, the author of 'Psychopathia sexualis,' the book onto which many outsiders and uninitiated readers throw themselves eagerly and lustfully!"

Embarrassed, the men quickly leave the table:

> "We have chased them away!" cheered Berta Cohn. "What a pity," replied Minotschka, "I would have liked to teach them a little more! I wanted to tell them that we also belong to these 'Krafft-Ebing people'! I think that they would have fainted!"

(Duc 1976, 53–54)

Notes

1   Krafft-Ebing's correspondent probably referred to the second edition of *Entdeckung der Seele* (1880), in which the zoologist and anthropologist Jäger, influenced by Karl Maria Kertbeny, differentiated different types of homosexuals. Some of them, Jäger argued, were not effeminate but masculine, even hypervirile.
2   Letter of X (undated [1901/1902]), Nachlass Krafft-Ebing.
3   Case history of K (October 20–29, 1892), Nachlass Krafft-Ebing.
4   Not only perverts consulted Krafft-Ebing to find an emotional confidant. A married Russian woman, for example, who was hospitalized in Krafft-Ebing's sanatorium confessed that her mental distress was caused by the fact that she did not love her husband and that she had a lover, but that her husband did not agree to a divorce because he feared a scandal. "I write to you because . . . I know for sure that you keep this between us . . . . I am infinitely grateful to you for your help, but, unfortunately, not everybody can be helped in this world" (Letter IB to Krafft-Ebing [January 24, 1901], Nachlass Krafft-Ebing).
5   Dornblüth 1902; *Neues Wiener Journal* (undated [1902]), Nachlass Krafft-Ebing.
6   Letter of K (June 2, 1898), Nachlass Krafft-Ebing.
7   Case history of K (October 20–29, 1892), Nachlass Krafft-Ebing.
8   Krafft-Ebing's own remarks on Christianity tended to be ambivalent. On the one hand, he praised this religious tradition for its contribution to the control of sexual urges and the institutionalization of marriage in which, as a rule, husband and wife were equal partners. On the other hand, notably in *Psychopathia Sexualis*, he pointed to the darker sides of religious ecstasy, which, he believed, quickly degenerated into mysticism and zealotry. Sexuality and religion were both marked by transcendence of the self by means of love, surrender, and self-renunciation. The boundaries between various forms of Christian devotion and aspects of madness or sexual perversion, sadomasochism in particular, were fluid (1897e, 141). Although religiously inspired flagellants strove to move beyond the body by whipping themselves, the opposite was often the result, according to Krafft-Ebing (Ps 1903, 30; cf. 1879–80, 68). He also criticized celibacy: priests missed out on what he called "the ennobling influence exercised by love and marital life upon the character" (Ps 1903, 14; cf. Ps 1999, 16).

References

Archive

Nachlass Richard von Krafft-Ebing, Krafft-Ebing Family Archive, Graz: The Wellcome Institute for the History of Medicine, London.

Works by Richard Krafft-Ebing

1882. "Zur contraren Sexualempfindung." *Allgemeine Zeitschrift fur Psychiatrie* 38 (1882): 211–27.

1883e. "Ueber pollutionsartige Vorgange beim Weibe." *Wiener medizinische Press* 14 (1883): 107.

1885a. "Die contrare Sexualempfindung vor dem Forum. *Jahrbucher fur Psychiatrie und forensische Psychologie* 6 (1885): 34–47.

(*Ps* 1887). *Psychopathia Sexualis.* 2nd ed., 1887.

(*Ps* 1888). *Psychopathia Sexualis.* 3rd ed. Stuttgart: Ferdinand Enke, 1888.

(*Ps* 1889). *Psychopathia Sexualis.* 4th ed. Stuttgart: Ferdinand Enke, 1889.

(*Ps* 1890). *Psychopathia Sexualis.* 5th ed. Stuttgart: Ferdinand Enke, 1890.

1890e. Richard Krafft-Ebing. *Neue Forschungen aug dem Gebiet der Psychopathia Sexualis.* Stuttgart: Ferdinand Enke, 1890.

1891h. *Neue Forschungen aug dem Gebiet der Psychopathia Sexualis.* 2nd ed. Stuttgart: Ferdinand Enke, 1891.

1892i. "Zur contraren Sexualempfindung. Autobiographie und strafrechtliche Betrachtungen von einem contrar Sexualen." *Weiner medizinische Blatter* 15 (1892): 7–9, 42–44.

1894e. "Zur Aetiologie der contraren Sexualempfindung." *Jahrbucher fur Psychiatrie und Neurologie* 12 (1894): 338–65.

1897e *Lehrbuch der Psychiatrie auf klinischer Grundlage fur fractische Artzte und Studirende.* 6th ed. Stuttgart: Ferdinand Enke, 1897.

1899d "Beitrage zur Kenntniss des Masochismus. In *Arbeiten aus dem Gesammtegebiet der Psychiatrie und Neuropathologie* vol. IV. Leipzig: Barth, 1899. 160–69.

(*Ps* 1903). *Psychopathia Sexualis.* Edited by H. Gugl and A. Stichl. 12th ed. Stuttgart: Ferdinand Enke, 1902.

(*Ps* 1999). *Psychopathia Sexualis.* Burbank: Bloat, 1999.

Other works

Duc, A. 1976. *Sind es Frauen?* Berlin: Amazonen Frauen Verlag.

Hacker, H. 1987. *Frauen und Freundinnen: Studien zur "weiblichen Homosexualitat" am Beispiel Osterreich 1870–1938.* Weinheim: Beltz Verlag.

Hacker, H. and M. Lang, 1986. "Jenseits der Geschlechter, zwischen ihnen Homosexualitaten im Wien der Jahrhunderwende." In *Das lila Wien um 1900. Zur Asthetik der Homosexualitaten.* Ed. by N. Bei et al., pp. 8–18. Vienna: Promedia.

McLaren, Angus. 1987. *The Trials of Masculinity.* Chicago: University of Chicago Press.

Moll, Albert. 1936. *Ein Leben als Arzt der Seele. Erinnerungen.* Dresden: Carl Reissner, 1936.

O'Brien, Patricia. 1983. "The Kleptomania Diagnosis: Bourgeois Women and Theft in late 19th Century France," *Journal of Social History*: 65–77.

Showalter, Elaine. 1980. *The Female Malady: Women, Madness and English Culture, 1830–1980.* New York: Pantheon Books.

Vicinus, Martha. 1989. "'They Wonder to Which Sex I Belong': The Historical Roots of the Modern Lesbian Identity." In *Homosexuality: Which Homosexuality?* By D. Altman et al., pp. 171–98. Amsterdam: Dekker/Schorer, GMP Publishers.

Chapter 17

Richard Krafft-Ebing

PSYCHOPATHIA SEXUALIS
(1886, 1922 edition)

Antipathic sexuality

AFTER THE ATTAINMENT of complete sexual development, among the most constant elements of self-consciousness in the individual are the knowledge of representing a definite sexual personality and the consciousness of desire, during the period of physiological activity of the reproductive organs (production of semen and ova), to perform sexual acts corresponding with that sexual personality,—acts which, consciously or unconsciously, have a procreative purpose.

The sexual instinct and desire, save for indistinct feelings and impulses, remain latent until the period of development of the sexual organs. The child is *generis neutrius*; and though, during this latent period,—when sexuality has not yet risen into clear consciousness, is but virtually present, and unconnected with powerful organic sensations, —abnormally early excitation of the genitals may occur, either spontaneously or as a result of external influence, and find satisfaction in masturbation; yet, notwithstanding this, the *psychical* relation to persons of the opposite sex is still absolutely wanting, and the sexual acts during this period exhibit more or less a reflex spinal character.

The existence of innocence, or of sexual neutrality, is the more remarkable, since very early in education, employment, dress, etc., the child undergoes a differentiation from children of the opposite sex. These impressions remain, however, devoid of psychical significance, because they apparently are stripped of sexual meaning; for the central organ (*cortex*) of sexual emotions and ideas is not yet capable of activity, owing to its undeveloped condition.

With the inception of anatomical and functional development of the generative organs, and the differentiation of form belonging to each sex, which goes hand in hand with it (in the boy as well as in the girl), rudiments of a mental feeling corresponding with the sex are developed; and in this, of course, education and external influences in general have a powerful effect upon the individual, who now begins to observe.

If the sexual development is normal and undisturbed, a definite character, corresponding with the sex, is developed. Certain well-defined inclinations and reactions in intercourse with persons of the opposite sex arise; and it is psychologically worthy of note with what relative rapidity each individual psychical type corresponding with the sex is evolved.

While modesty, for instance, during childhood, is essentially but an uncomprehended and incomprehensible exaction of education and imitation, expressed but imperfectly in the innocence and *naiveté* of the child; in the youth and maiden it becomes an imperative requirement of self-respect; and, if in any way it is offended, intense vaso-motor reaction (blushing) and psychical emotions are induced.

If the original constitution is favourable and normal, and factors injurious to the psycho-sexual development exercise no adverse influence, then a psycho-sexual personality is developed which is so unchangeable and corresponds so completely and harmoniously with the sex of the individual in question, that subsequent loss of the generative organs (as by castration), or the *climacterium* or senility, cannot essentially alter it.

This, however, must not be taken as a declaration that the castrated man or woman, the youth and the aged man, the maiden and the matron, the impotent and the potent man, do not differ essentially from each other in their psychical existence.

An interesting and important question for what follows is, whether the peripheral influences of the generative glands (testes and ovaries), or central cerebral conditions, are the determining factors in psycho-sexual development. The fact that congenital deficiency of the generative glands, or removal of them *before* puberty, have a great influence on physical and psycho-sexual development, so that the latter is stunted and assumes a type more closely resembling the opposite sex (eunuchs, certain viragoes, etc.), betokens their great importance in this respect.

That the physical processes taking place in the genital organs are only co-operative, and not the exclusive factors, in the process of development of the psycho-sexual character, is shown by the fact that, notwithstanding a normal anatomical and physiological state of these organs, a sexual instinct may be developed which is the exact opposite of that characteristic of the sex to which the individual belongs.

In this case, the cause is to be sought only in an anomaly of central conditions,—in an abnormal psycho-sexual constitution. This constitution, as far as its anatomical and functional foundation is concerned, is as yet unknown. Since, in nearly all such cases, the individual tainted with antipathic sexual instinct displays a neuropathic predisposition in several directions, and the latter may be brought into relation with hereditary degenerate conditions, this anomaly of psycho-sexual feeling may be called, clinically, a functional sign of degeneration. This inverted sexuality appears spontaneously, without external cause, with the development of sexual life, as an individual manifestation of an abnormal form of the *vita sexualis*, having the force of a *congenital* phenomenon; or it develops upon a sexuality the beginning of which was normal, as a result of very definite injurious influences, and thus appears as an *acquired* anomaly. Upon what conditions this enigmatical phenomenon of acquired homo-sexual instinct depends, remains still unexplained, and is a mere matter of hypothesis. Careful examination of the so-called acquired cases makes it probable that the predisposition—also present here—consists of a latent homo-sexuality, or, at any rate, bi-sexuality, which, for its manifestation, requires the influence of accidental exciting causes to rouse it from its dormant state.

In so-called antipathic sexual instinct there are degrees of the phenomenon which quite correspond with the degrees of predisposition of the individuals. Thus, in the milder cases, there is simple hermaphroditism; in more pronounced cases, only homo-sexual feeling and instinct, but limited to the *vita sexualis*; in still more complete cases, the whole psychical personality, and even the bodily sensations, are transformed so as to correspond with the sexual inversion; and, in the complete cases, the physical form is correspondingly altered.

The following division of the various phenomena of this psycho-sexual anomaly is made, therefore, in accordance with these clinical facts.

A. Homo-sexual feeling as an acquired manifestation in both sexes

The determining factor here is the demonstration of perverse feeling for the same sex; not the proof of sexual acts with the same sex. These two phenomena must not be confounded with each other; *perversity* must not be taken for *perversion*.

Perverse sexual acts, without being dependent upon perversion, often come under observation. This is especially true with reference to sexual acts between persons of the same sex, particularly in pederasty. Here *parœsthesia sexualis* is not necessarily at work; but hyperæsthesia, with physical or psychical impossibility for natural sexual satisfaction.

Thus we find homo-sexual intercourse in impotent masturbators or debauchees, or *faute de mieux* in sensual men and women under imprisonment, on ship-board, in garrisons, bagnios, boarding-schools, etc.

There is an immediate return to normal sexual intercourse as soon as the obstacles to it are removed. Very frequently the cause of such temporary aberration is *masturbation* and its results in youthful individuals.

Nothing is so prone to contaminate—under certain circumstances, even to exhaust—the source of all noble and ideal sentiments, which arise of themselves from a normally developing sexual instinct, as the practice of masturbation in early years. It despoils the unfolding bud of perfume and beauty, and leaves behind only the coarse, animal desire for sexual satisfaction. If an individual, thus depraved, reaches the age of maturity, there is wanting in him that aesthetic, ideal, pure and free impulse which draws the opposite sexes together. The glow of sensual sensibility wanes, and the inclination toward the opposite sex is weakened. This defect influences the morals, the character, fancy, feeling and instinct of the youthful masturbator, male or female, in an unfavourable manner, even causing, under certain circumstances, the desire for the opposite sex to sink to *nil*; so that masturbation is preferred to the natural mode of satisfaction.

Sometimes the development of the nobler sexual feelings toward the opposite sex suffers, on account of hypochrondriacal fear of infection in sexual intercourse; or on account of an actual infection; or as a result of a faulty education which points out such dangers and exaggerates them. Again (especially in females), fear of the result of coitus (pregnancy), or abhorrence of men, by reason of physical or moral defects, may direct into perverse channels an instinct that makes itself felt with abnormal intensity. On the other hand, premature and perverse sexual satisfaction injures not merely the mind, but also the body; inasmuch as it induces neuroses of the sexual apparatus (irritable weakness of the centres governing erection and ejaculation; defective pleasurable feeling in coitus, etc.), while, at the same time, it maintains imagination and *libido* in continuous excitement.

Almost every masturbator at last reaches a point where, frightened on learning the results of the vice, or on experiencing them (neurasthenia), or led by example or seduction to the opposite sex, he wishes to free himself of the vice and reinstate his *vita sexualis.*

The moral and mental conditions are here the most unfavourable possible. The pure glow of sexual feeling is destroyed; the fire of sexual instinct is wanting, and self-confidence is lost; for every masturbator is more or less timid and cowardly. If the youthful sinner at last comes to make an attempt at coitus, he is either disappointed because enjoyment is wanting, on account of defective sensual feeling, or he is lacking in the physical strength necessary to accomplish the act. This fiasco has a fatal effect, and leads to absolute psychical impotence. A bad conscience and the memory of past failures prevent success in any further attempts. The ever present *libido sexualis,* however, demands satisfaction, and this moral and mental perversion separates further and further from woman.

For various reasons, however, (neurasthenic complaints, hypochondriacal fear of results, etc.), the individual is also kept from masturbation. At times, under such circumstances, bestiality is resorted to. Intercourse with the same sex is then near at hand,—as the result of seduction or of the feelings of friendship which, on the level of pathological sexuality, easily associate themselves with sexual feelings.

Passive and mutual onanism now become the equivalent of the avoided act. If there is a seducer,—which, unfortunately often happens,—then the cultivated pederast is produced, i.e., a man who performs *quasi* acts of onanism with persons of his own sex, and, at the same time, feels and prefers himself in an active *role* corresponding with his real sex; who is mentally indifferent not only to persons of the opposite sex, but also to those of his own.

Sexual aberration reaches this degree in the *normally* constituted, *untainted,* mentally healthy individual. No case has yet been demonstrated in which perversity has been transformed into perversion—*i.e.,* into an inversion of the sexual instinct.[1]

With *tainted* individuals, the matter is quite different. The latent perverse sexuality is developed under the influence of neurasthenia induced by masturbation, abstinence, or otherwise.

Gradually, in contact with persons of the same sex, sexual excitation by them is induced. Related ideas are coloured with lustful feelings, and awaken corresponding desires. This decidedly degenerate reaction is the beginning of a process of physical and mental transformation, a description of which is attempted in what follows, and which is one of the most interesting psychological phenomena that have been observed. This metamorphosis presents different stages, or degrees.

1. Degree: simple reversal of sexual feeling

This degree is attained when a person exercises an aphrodisiac effect over another person of the same sex who reciprocates the sexual feeling. Character and instinct, however, still correspond with the sex of the individual presenting the reversal of sexual feeling. He feels himself in the active *role*; he recognizes his impulse toward his own sex as an aberration, and finally seeks aid.

With episodical improvement of the neurosis, at first even normal sexual feelings may reappear and assert themselves. The following case seems well suited to exemplify this stage of the psycho-sexual degeneration:—

Case 125. *Acquired Antipathic Sexual Instinct.* "I am an official, and, as far as I know, come from an untainted family. My father died of an acute disease; my mother, still living, is *very nervous. A sister has been very intensely religious for some years.*

"I myself am tall, and, in speech, gait and manner, give a perfectly masculine impression. Measles is the only disease I have had; but since my thirteenth year I have suffered with so-called nervous headaches.

"My sexual life began in my thirteenth year, when I became acquainted with a boy somewhat older than myself, *quocum alter alterius genitalia tangendo delectabar.* I had the first ejaculation in my fourteenth year. Seduced to onanism by two older school-mates, I practised it partly with others and partly alone; in the latter case, however, always with the thought of persons of the female sex. My *libido sexualis* was very great, as it is to-day. Later, I tried to win a pretty, stout servant-girl who had very large *mammae;* id solum assecutus sum, ut me præsente superiorem corporis sui partem enudaret mihique concederet os mammasque osculari, dum ipsa penem meum valde erectum in manum suam recepit eumque trivit.

"Quamquam violentissime coitum rogarem hoc solum concessit, ut genitalia ejus tangerem.

"After going to the university, I visited a brothel and succeeded without special effort.

"Then an event occurred which brought about a change in me. One evening I accompanied a friend home, and in a mild state of intoxication I grasped him *ad genitalia.* He made but slight opposition. I then went up to his room with him, and we practised mutual masturbation. From that time we indulged in it quite frequently; in fact, it came to *immissio penis in os*, with resultant ejaculations. But it is strange that I was not at all in love with this person, but passionately in love with another friend, near whom I never felt the slightest sexual excitement, and whom I never connected with sexual matters, even in thought. My visits to brothels, where I was gladly received, became more infrequent; in my friend I found a substitute, and did not desire sexual intercourse with women.

"We never practised pederasty. That word was not even known between us. From the beginning of this relation with my friend, I again masturbated more frequently, and naturally the thought of females receded more and more into the background, and I thought more and more about young, handsome, strong men with the largest possible genitals. I preferred young fellows, from sixteen to twenty-five years old, without beards, but they had to be handsome and clean. Young labourers dressed in trousers of Manchester cloth or English leather, particularly masons, especially excited me.

"Persons in my own position had hardly any effect on me; but, at the sight of one of those strapping fellows of the lower class, I experienced marked sexual excitement. It seems to me that the touch of such trousers, the opening of them and the grasping of the penis, as well as kissing the fellow, would be the greatest delight. My sensibility to female charms is somewhat dulled; yet in sexual intercourse with a woman, particularly when she has well-developed mammae, I am always potent without the help of imagination. I have never attempted to make use of a young labourer, or the like, for the satisfaction of my evil desires, and never shall; but I often feel a longing to do it. I often impress on myself the mental image of such a man, and then masturbate at home.

"I am absolutely devoid of taste for female work. I rather like to move in female society, but dancing is repugnant to me. I have a lively interest in the fine arts. That my sexual sense is partly reversed is, I believe, in part due to greater convenience, which keeps me from entering into a relation with a girl; as the latter is a matter of too much trouble. To be constantly visiting houses of prostitution is, for aesthetic reasons, repugnant to me; and thus I am always returning to solitary onanism, which is very difficult for me to avoid.

"Hundreds of times I have said to myself that, in order to have a normal sexual sense, it would be necessary for me, first of all, to overcome my irresistible passion for onanism,—a practice so repugnant to my aesthetic feeling. Again and again I have resolved with all my might to fight this passion; but I am still unsuccessful. When I felt the sexual impulse gaining strength, instead of seeking satisfaction in the natural manner, I preferred to masturbate, because I felt that I would thus have more enjoyment.

"And yet experience has taught me that I am always potent with girls, and that, too, without trouble and without the vision of masculine genitals. In one case, however, I did not attain ejaculation because the woman—it was in a brothel—was devoid of every charm. I cannot avoid the thought and severe self-accusation that, to a certain extent, my inverted sexuality is the result of excessive onanism; and this especially depresses me, because I am compelled to acknowledge that I scarcely feel strong enough to overcome this vice by the force of my own will.

"As a result of my relations for years with a fellow-student and pal, mentioned in this communication—which, however, began while we were at the university, and after we had been friends for seven years—the impulse to unnatural satisfaction of *libido* has grown much stronger. I trust you will permit the description of an incident which worried me for months:—

"In the summer of 1882, I made the acquaintance of a companion six years younger than myself, who, with several others, had been introduced to me and my acquaintances. I very soon felt a deep interest in this handsome man, who was unusually well-proportioned, slim, and full of health. After a few weeks of association, this liking ripened into friendship, and at last into passionate love, with feelings of the most intense jealousy. I very soon noticed that in this love sexual excitation was also very marked; and, notwithstanding my determination, aside from all others, to keep myself in check in relation to this man, whom I respected so highly for his superior character, one night, after free indulgence in beer, as we were enjoying a bottle of champagne in my room, and drinking to good, true and lasting friendship, I yielded to the irresistible impulse to embrace him, etc.

"When I saw him next day, I was so ashamed that I could not look him in the face. I felt the deepest regret for my action, and accused myself bitterly for having thus sullied this friendship, which was to be and remain so pure and precious. In order to prove to him that I had lost control of myself only momentarily, at the end of the semester I urged him to make an excursion with me; and after some reluctance, the reason of which was only too clear to me, he consented. Several nights we slept in the same room without any attempt on my part to repeat my action. I wished to talk with him about the event of that night, but I could not bring myself to it; even when, during the next semester, we were separated, I could not induce myself to write to him on the subject; and when I visited him in March at X., it was the same. And yet I felt a great desire to clear up this dark point by an open statement. In October of the same year I was again in X., and this time found courage to speak without reserve; indeed, I asked him why he had not resisted me. He answered that, in part, it was because he wished to please me, and, in part, owing to the fact that he was somewhat apathetic as a result of being a little intoxicated. I explained to him my condition, and also gave him "Psychopathia Sexualis" to read, expressing the hope that by the force of my own will I should become fully and lastingly master of my unnatural impulse. Since this confession, the relation between this friend and me has been the most delightful and happy possible; there are the most friendly feelings on both sides, which are sincere and true; and it is to be hoped that they will endure.

"If I should not improve my abnormal condition, I am determined to put myself under your treatment; the more because, after a careful study of your work, I cannot count myself as belonging to the category of so-called urnings; and also because I have the firm conviction, or hope, at least, that a strong will, assisted and combined with skilful treatment, could transform me into a man of normal feeling."

Case 126. Ilma S.,[2] aged twenty-nine; single, merchant's daughter; of a family having bad nervous taint. Father was a drinker and died by suicide, as also did the patient's brother and sister. A sister suffered with convulsive hysteria. Mother's father shot himself while insane. Mother was sickly, and paralysed after apoplexy. The patient never had any severe illness. She was bright, enthusiastic and dreamy. Menses at the age of eighteen without difficulty; but thereafter they were very irregular. At fourteen, chlorosis and catalepsy from fright. Later, *hysteria gravis* and an attack of hysterical insanity. At eighteen, relations with a young man which were not platonic. This man's love was passionately returned. From statements of the patient, it seemed that she was very sensual, and after separation from her lover practised masturbation. After this she led a romantic life. In order to earn a living, she put on male clothing, and became a tutor; but she gave up her place because her mistress, not knowing her sex, fell in love with her and courted her. Then she became a railway employee. In the company of her companions, in order to conceal her sex, she was compelled to visit brothels with them, and hear the most vulgar stories. This became so distasteful to her that she gave up her place, resumed the garments of a female, and again sought to earn her living. She was arrested for theft, and on account of severe hystero-epilepsy was sent to the hospital. There inclination and impulse toward the same sex were discovered. The patient became troublesome on account of passionate love for female nurses and patients.

Her sexual inversion was considered congenital. With regard to this, the patient made some interesting statements:—

"I am judged incorrectly, if it is thought that I feel myself a man toward the female sex. In my whole thought and feeling I am much more a woman. Did I not love my cousin as only a woman can love a man ?

"The change of my feelings originated in this, that, in Pesth, dressed as a man, I had an opportunity to observe my cousin. I saw that I was wholly deceived in him. That gave me terrible heart-pangs. I knew that I could never love another man; that I belonged to those who love but once. Of similar effect was the fact that, in the society of my companions at the railway, I was compelled to hear the most offensive language and visit the most disreputable houses. As a result of the insight into men's motives, gained in this way, I took an unconquerable dislike to them. However, since I am of a very passionate nature and need to have some loving person on whom to depend, and to whom I can wholly surrender myself, I felt myself more and more powerfully drawn toward intelligent women and girls who were in sympathy with me."

The antipathic sexual instinct of this patient, which was clearly acquired, expressed itself in a stormy and decidedly sensual way, and was further augmented by masturbation; because constant control in hospitals made sexual satisfaction with the same sex impossible. Character and occupation remained feminine. There were no manifestations of virginity. According to information lately received by the author, this patient, after two years of treatment in an asylum, was entirely freed from her neurosis and sexual inversion, and discharged cured.

[. . .]

Case 155. *Homosexuality*. Miss L., fifty-five years of age. No information about her father's family. The parents of her mother were described as irascible, capricious and nervous. One brother of her mother was an epileptic, another eccentric and mentally abnormal.

Mother was sexually hyperaesthetic, and for a long time a messalina. She was considered to be psychopathic and died at the age of sixty-nine of cerebral disease.

Miss L. developed normally, had only slight illnesses in childhood, and was mentally well endowed, but of a neuropathic constitution, emotional, and troubled with numerous fads.

At the age of thirteen, two years previous to her first menstruation, she fell in love with a girl-friend ("a dreamy feeling, quite pure of sensuality").

Her second love was for a girl older than herself who was a bride; this was accompanied by tantalising sensual desires, jealousy, and an "undefined consciousness of mystical impropriety". She was refused by this lady and now fell in love with a married woman, who was a mother and twenty years her senior. As she controlled her sensual emotions, this lady never even divined the true reason of this enthusiastic friendship which lasted for twelve years. Patient described this period as a veritable martyrdom.

Since she was twenty-five she had begun to masturbate. Patient seriously thought that, perhaps, by marriage she might save herself, but her conscience objected, for her children might inherit her weakness, or she might make a sincere husband unhappy.

At the age of twenty-seven she was approached with direct proposals by a girl who denounced abstinence as absurd, and plainly described the homosexual instinct which ruled her and was very impetuous in her demands. She suffered the caresses of the girl, but would not consent to sexual intercourse, as sensuality without love disgusted her.

Mentally and bodily dissatisfied the years fled by, leaving the consciousness of a spoiled life. Now and then she became enthusiastic about ladies of her acquaintance, but controlled herself. She also rid herself from masturbation.

When she was thirty-eight years of age she became acquainted with a girl nineteen years her junior, of exceptional beauty, who came from a demoralized family, and had been at an early age seduced by her cousins to mutual masturbation. It could not be ascertained whether this girl A. was a case of psychical hermaphrodism or of acquired sexual inversion. The former hypothesis seems the likelier of the two.

The following is taken from an autobiography of Miss L.:—

"Miss A., my pupil, began to show me her idolatrous love. She was sympathetic to the highest degree. Since I knew that she was entangled in a hopeless love affair with a dissolute fellow and continued intimate intercourse with demoralized female cousins,

I decided not to repulse her. Compassion and the conviction that she was surely drifting into moral decay determined me to suffer her advances.

"I did not consider her affection as dangerous, as I did not think it possible that (considering her love affair) in ONE soul *two* passions (one for a man and another for a woman) could exist simultaneously. Moreover, I was certain of my power of resistance. I kept, therefore, Miss A. about me, renewed my moral resolutions, and considered it to be my duty to use her love for me for ennobling her character. The folly of this I soon found out. One day whilst I lay asleep Miss A. took occasion to satisfy her lust on me. Although I woke up just in time, I did not have the moral strength to resist her. I was highly excited, intoxicated as it were—and she prevailed.

"What I suffered immediately after this occurrence beggars description. Worry over the broken resolutions, which to keep I had made such strenuous efforts, fear of detection and subsequent contempt, exuberant joy at last to be rid of the torturing watchings and longings of the single state, unspeakable sensual pleasure, wrath against the evil companion, mingled with feelings of the deepest tenderness towards her. Miss A. calmly smiled at my excitement, and with caresses soothed my anger.

"I accepted the situation. Our intimacy lasted for years. We practised mutual masturbation, but never to excess or in a cynical fashion.

"Little by little this sensual companionship ceased. Miss A.'s tenderness weakened; mine, however, remained as before, although I felt no longer the same sensual cravings. Miss A. thought of marriage, partly in order to find a home, but especially because her sensual desires had turned into the normal paths. She succeeded in finding a husband. I sincerely hope she will make him happy, but I doubt it. Thus I have the prospect before me to linger on the same joyless, peaceless life as it ever was in youthful days.

"It is with sadness that I remember the years of our loving union. It does not disturb my conscience to have had sexual intercourse with Miss A., for I succumbed to her seduction, having honestly endeavoured to save her from moral ruin and to bring her up an educated and moral being. In this I honestly think I have succeeded after all. Besides, I rest in the thought that the moral code is established only for normal humans, but is not binding for anomalies. Of course, the human being who is endowed by nature with sentiments of refinement, but whose constitution is abnormal and outside the conventionalities of society, can never be truly happy. But I experienced a sad tranquillity and felt happy when I thought Miss A. to be so too.

"This is the history of an unhappy woman who, by the fatal caprice of nature, is deprived of all joy of life and made a victim of sorrow."

The author of this woeful story was a lady of great refinement. But she had coarse features, a powerful but throughout feminine frame. She passed through the *climacterium* without trouble, and since then had been entirely free from sensual worry. Sexually she had never played a defined *role* towards the woman she loved; for men she never felt the slightest inclination.

Her statements about the family relations and the health of her paramour, Miss A., establish a heavy taint beyond doubt. The father died in an insane asylum, the mother was deranged during the period of her *climacterium*, neuroses were of frequent occurrence in the family, and Miss A. herself suffered at times heavily from hysteropathy, with hallucinations and delirium.

Notes

1   *Garnier* ("Anomalies Sexuelles," Paris, pp. 508, 509) reports two cases (cases 222 and 223) that are apparently opposed to this assumption, particularly the first, in which despair about the unfaithfulness of a lover led the individual to submit to the seductions of men. But the case itself clearly shows that this individual *never found pleasure in homo-sexual acts.* In case 223, the individual was effeminated *ab origine*, or was at least a psychical hermaphrodite.

Those who hold to the opinion that the origin of homosexual feelings and instinct is found to be exclusively in defective education and other psychological influences are entirely in error.

An untainted male may be raised ever so much like a female, and a female like a male, but they will not become homo-sexual. *The natural disposition is the determining condition; not education and other accidental circumstances, like seduction.* There can be no thought of antipathic sexual instinct save when the person of the same sex exerts a psycho-sexual influence over the individual, and thus brings about *libido* and orgasm,—*i.e.*, has a psychical attraction. Those cases are quite different in which, *faute de mieux*, with great sensuality and a defective esthetic sense, the body of a person of the same sex is used for an onanistic act (not for coitus in a psychical sense).

In his excellent monograph, *Moll* shows very clearly and convincingly the importance of original predisposition in contrast with exciting causes *(cf. op. cit.*, pp. 212–231). He knows "many cases where early sexual intercourse with men was not capable of inducing perversion." *Moll* significantly says, further: "I know of such an epidemic (of mutual onanism) in a Berlin school, where a person, who is now an actor, shamelessly introduced mutual onanism. Though I now know the names of very many urnings in Berlin, yet I could not ascertain, even with anything like probability, that among all the pupils of that school at that time there was one that had become an urning; but, on the other hand, I have quite certain knowledge that many of those pupils are now normal sexually in feeling and intercourse."

2   *Cf.* author's "Experimental Study in the Domain of Hypnotism," third edition, 1893.

PART 9

The problem of heterosexuality. Could men and women find happiness together?

Introduction

A T THE TURN OF THE CENTURY, many questioned the romantic ideal of marriage and feared that a sexual crisis caught men and women in its grip. Daring playwrights such as Ibsen and Strindberg limned tumultuous and agonizing conflicts between husbands and wives. Evolutionary thought rejected the notion of marriage as an elevated spiritual state and exposed it as a social arrangement meant to harness biological instincts.[1] Sexologists believed that male aggression was natural – the deflowering of wives on their wedding night and rape were just two points on a continuum of natural male sexuality. Robert Michel, otherwise quite a radical sexologist, baldly stated, "the use of physical force to overcome the object of erotic desire, the forcible attainment of sexual possession of the female, is one of the normal biological elements of the erotic function as such, as may be seen daily in animal life."[2]

The new pseudoscience of eugenics, or human breeding, argued that degeneration was a danger when unfit men and women married and procreated, producing offspring who would damage the "race" (which could mean white race or human race). On the other side, the feminist movement criticized the double standard which allowed men to go to prostitutes and punished women who had sexual affairs. Both the sexologists and some feminists saw men as motivated mainly by lust, and women by love and the need to reproduce. For sexologists, this was normal, and for feminists, it was a tragedy. As Edward Ross Dickinson writes, men and women seemed to be on two sides of a great chasm. Dickinson suggests that there was a way out. Some radicals, inspired by the homosexual rights movement, argued that men and women were not utterly different – people had different balances of masculinity and femininity in them. By the early twentieth century, Dickinson argues, some sexologists took up the ideas of feminists who argued for women's sexual pleasure and began to explore the ways in which mutual sexual pleasure might strengthen conventional marriages. Indeed, some socialists and feminists began to assert that greater sexual freedom would lead to more fit reproduction of children, because women were forced to marry wealthy men who might be stunted, diseased, and degenerate. By enjoying sexual pleasure, men and women could tap into the life forces of the universe.[3]

Our primary source reading is from Grete Meisel-Hess (1879–1922), a novelist, feminist and activist in late nineteenth- and early twentieth-century Vienna and Berlin.[4] She espoused the work of the League for the Protection of Motherhood and Sexual Reform, which opposed the double standard and supported greater access to birth control, in order to allow women to plan their childbearing intelligently, as well as enjoying fulfilling emotional and work lives.[5] The League was a small but significant wing of the women's movement. Most women in the German women's movement did not advocate sex reform, because they saw sexuality more as a source of danger rather than pleasure for women: they wanted to rescue prostitutes and protect mothers, but they espoused conventional bourgeois values of chastity and opposed eugenics.

Meisel-Hess is a good example of a different, more radical feminist perspective on eugenics. While she was influenced by the eugenics arguments of Ernest Haeckel, who also inspired the Nazis, she repudiated his racial theories, and indeed she declared that marriage across racial lines would have a positive eugenic effect. Like many at the time, Meisel-Hess thought that marriage was in crisis: marriages were too unhappy, there were not enough men to marry because of the expense of supporting a wife, and women were so financially dependent they could not choose whom to marry. What did she see as the solution, and did it uphold Dickinson's argument?

Notes

1   Max Nordau, *Degeneration*, 2nd edn (Lincoln: University of Nebraska Press, 1993); Daniel Pick, "The Degenerating Genius," *History Today* 42, no. 4 (1992): 17–23.

2   Robert Michels, *Sexual Ethics: A Study of Borderland Questions* (London: Walter Scott Publishing Co., 1914), 123.

3   Carolyn Burdett, "The Hidden Romance of Sexual Science: Eugenics, the Nation and the Making of Modern Feminism," in *Sexology in Culture*, ed. Lucy Bland and Laura Doan (London: Routledge, 1998), 44–59; Ellen Key, *Love and Marriage*, trans. Arthur G. Chater (New York: Putnam's, 1911); George Robb, "The Way of All Flesh: Degeneration, Eugenics, and the Gospel of Free Love," *Journal of the History of Sexuality* 6, no. 4 (1996): 589–603; Richard A. Soloway, "The 'Perfect Contraceptive:' Eugenics and Birth Control Research in Britain and America in the Interwar Years," *Journal of Contemporary History* 30, no. 4 (1995): 637–664.

4   Ellinor Melander, "Toward the Sexual and Economic Emancipation of Women: The Philosophy of Grete Meisel-Hess," *History of European Ideas* 14, no. 5 (1992): 695–713.

5   Ann Taylor Allen, "Feminism, Venereal Diseases, and the State in Germany, 1890–1918," *Journal of the History of Sexuality* 4, no. 3 (1993): 35; Ann Taylor Allen, *Feminism and Motherhood in Western Europe 1890–1970* (New York: Palgrave Macmillan, 2005), 117.

Chapter 18

Edward Ross Dickinson

'A DARK, IMPENETRABLE WALL OF COMPLETE INCOMPREHENSION'
The impossibility of heterosexual love in imperial Germany (2007)[1]

IN THE YEARS AROUND THE TURN of the twentieth century, the "war between the sexes" was a major topic of public discussion and concern in Germany—in the daily press, in academic sexology journals and organizations, among medical and psychiatric professionals, in the women's movements, among conservative Christians, in art and music. Jacques Le Rider has even referred to the "obsessive leitmotif of male-female confrontation" in central European culture in this period.[2] Much of what has been written about this topic in recent years posits a crisis of gender relations produced by the growth of the women's movement, and by the backlash against it.[3] The idea that the feminist challenge generated hostility between men and women in this period was one that was also common at the time, particularly among anti-feminists. As Hedwig Dohm put it in 1913, "In all anti-feminist speeches and writings, the hostility between men and women is tirelessly denounced as a characteristic of the times, and a product of the women's movement."[4]

There was, and is, no doubt a great deal of truth to this diagnosis. The women's movement and the backlash against it posed very unsettling questions for Germans at the time about the nature and potentials of relations between men and women. One striking feature of the period, however, is that major groups active in the discussion of relations between the sexes argued not so much that the women's movement was creating conflict between men and women, as that men and women were very different so that they *could not* live together happily or peacefully—feminism or no feminism. This was particularly true in the discussion surrounding male and female sexuality; but it applied by extension to the whole question of love between men and women. Clearly the women's movement and the general sense that gender relations were in crisis—or at least in flux—was an important source of this conviction. But the breadth and depth of the discussion of the incompatibility of men and women suggest that it cannot be explained *only* in these terms.

This essay examines the discussion of the "war" between the sexes from three perspectives. First, it examines the central terms of this discussion as it was conducted within two different social and organizational milieux—among male sexologists and within the mainstream women's movement. Surprisingly, these two groups were largely in agreement concerning *what* the problem was—though they disagreed as to *who* the problem was, or rather who had a problem. Second, it presents a speculative but, I hope, plausible explanation of the social and psychological origins of the idea that there was such a "war": that this idea was a symptom not of the crisis of the "bourgeois" or "Christian" or "traditional" family order (defined by monogamous single-earner procreative marriage), but rather of its growing success and power. And third, it examines the early stages of the development of the ideas that would eventually resolve that "war," at least in discursive terms. This resolution was initiated not primarily by conservative defenders of marriage and traditional family values, but rather by the champions of radical feminist sex reform and homosexual emancipation. It was in these circles that the idea that there was a physiological and sexual common ground between men and women was pioneered—in the teeth of resistance from those who regarded both sexual women and homosexual men as pathological deviants.

From complementary to conflicting natures

Among educated Germans in the nineteenth century the dominant understanding of relationships between men and women was focused on the idea that the sexes were compatible and complementary. In the Anglo-American literature, this understanding is often referred to as the "ideology of separate spheres." In it, men and women were understood to have mutually exclusive but complementary social functions: competitive struggle in the public sphere of work, politics, and social activism for men; nurture and cooperation in the private sphere of the family for women. Similarly, they had diametrically opposed but complementary "natures" to match these tasks—pragmatic, intellectual, and creative in men, and idealistic, emotional, and "conservative" in women. In the family, these functions and characteristics complemented each other, creating a synthesis more "whole" than either of its parts, in which each appreciated and relied on the strengths and compensated for the weaknesses of the other. Heterosexual love was necessary for the achievement of the spiritual, emotional, characterological, and social "wholeness" of the individual; and to be in a heterosexual couple was the precondition for happiness and well-being. As Christoph Sachsse put it in his classic account of 1986, the nineteenth-century ideal of the family was "utopian" in the sense that it posited the existence, or at least the possibility, of the family as "a place of harmony, of peaceful comfort and romantic love," a "community founded on mutual love, respect, and tolerance." This ideal was made possible by what Karin Hausen long ago called the "polarization of sexual characteristics," but also by what she referred to as the corresponding "emotionalization of the family."[5] That is, the family was held to be not only a necessary and stable social institution, but also the locus of any individual's most intense emotional attachments and satisfactions.

In fact, it was these emotional ties—and not the pragmatic financial considerations or the advantages of the division of reproductive labor—that were regarded as the legitimate foundation of the family. The family had to be founded on "love," an emotion that one man and one woman felt exclusively for one another. This concept of love was heavily freighted with religious associations: love was understood to be redemptive, both in that it raised each partner above selfishness and allowed them to care more for someone else than for themselves, and in that it harnessed otherwise anarchic and selfish sexuality to that redemptive function, both by spiritualizing and emotionalizing physical desire and by linking it to procreation and child-rearing.

Reiterations of these ideas were still commonplace at the beginning of the twentieth century. A good example of this ideology of true love is an article on the "new marriage" published in the sex-reform journal *Geschlecht und Gesellschaft* (*Sex and Society*) in 1905. The author asked what "true love" might be, and answered, "it is not 'two souls with one thought,' but rather one soul, which appears in two different concrete manifestations (*Daseinsformen*), in two different people."[6] The explicitly religious irrationalism of this vision, not of harmony but in fact literally of unity, is typical of the nimbus of sanctity that, for many middle-class Germans in the late nineteenth century, surrounded the ideas of love and marriage.

And yet, again, by the beginning of the twentieth century there was a growing chorus of skepticism about the reality of this highly idealistic understanding of relations between the sexes. Always the peculiar cultural property of the middle classes, increasingly this understanding of love appears to have been confined to a culturally isolated and apparently shrinking group of *Bildungsbürger* with more conservative cultural commitments. It was challenged from multiple points within the broad and expanding middle-class reformist culture of the period—among those seeking to reformulate social relations in response to the social, economic, and cultural transformations attendant upon industrialization, urbanization, and modernization more broadly.

The emerging discipline of sexology—a field of theory and study taking shape from the 1880s and particularly after 1900, largely dominated by medical men—was an important locus of this challenge to the idealistic concept of romantic heterosexual love. In the first part of this essay I want to focus (for reasons that will become clear further on) on the ideas of several men who joined the most important sex reform organization of the period, the League for the Protection of Motherhood (*Bund für Mutterschutz*, or BfM) at its foundation in 1905, and then left it shortly afterward after coming into conflict with the feminists who would come to dominate it.

It is useful to identify four propositions concerning the incompatibility of the sexes that were, in varying degrees, subscribed to by academic and medical sexologists, and by a surprising proportion of the broader educated public as well. In fact, for the most part these propositions were widely regarded as "common sense," as self-evident, at the latest by 1914.

First was the belief that men's and women's sexual pleasure was incompatible. The classic formulation of this view was published by Albert Moll, who held that men seek "*Detumeszenz*," or release, while women seek "*Kontrektation*," or touch.[7] Whereas men sought intercourse and orgasm, women's sexuality was more diffuse and more emotionally charged. As Heinrich Kisch put it in a massive study of *The Sexual Life of Women* (1904), women sought "contact with the other sex, in a physical and emotional sense (*Kontrektationstrieb*)," while men had "the need to see a change brought about in the genitals (*Detumeszenztrieb*). The former instinct drives the sexes to physical and emotional intimacy, the latter to more localized functions."[8] The conservative doctor Hugo Sellheim put the same argument in slightly less clinical terms in his 1909 study of "The Charms of Woman": The man's desire, he held, "soon takes on a particular form. He sets his eyes on the goal, has at it directly, and takes the obstacles by storm." Women, in contrast, had no "primary understanding" of "male charms," but rather only "adaptability"—the ability to accommodate men's desires for the sake of emotional closeness.[9] Such ideas were, again, "common knowledge" at the turn of the century—and not only in Germany, obviously.

Second, as a corollary, it was widely believed that the emotional economy of sex was quite different for women and men. Sexual love was believed to be an overwhelmingly important experience for women, but not for men. Max Marcuse, a founding member of the Bund who later left to edit the two leading sexological journals in Germany, summed up two or three decades of received wisdom when he argued in 1919 that for men love was "separate, or at least separable, from sex," whereas for women the two were inextricably related. Sex for men was "superficial and episodic," whereas for women, who were more emotionally involved, it was "lastingly and deeply influential."[10] Eduard Fuchs had made this point twelve years earlier in *Geschlecht und Gesellschaft*, claiming that for men "the erotic cannot be separated from feelings of love, so that love is to a certain extent localized," whereas in women "exactly the opposite is true"; love is "for women psychic in a way that it is only in very rare cases for men."[11] Again, Sellheim was more circumspect, asserting merely that whereas "if a woman loves, this love dominates all her thoughts and efforts (*Denken und Trachten*)," for the man "love fades into the background as soon as his thoughts are claimed by his profession."[12]

Third, many educated Germans held in fact that men and women had sex for quite different reasons. For men, sexual pleasure was the sole aim of sex; for women, in contrast, the primary purpose of sex was to make babies. Thus Alfred Hegar, professor of gynecology in Freiburg, wrote in 1894 that men had "a much more pronounced desire for intercourse," and that the "natural inclination of the woman to physical love is in general . . . not very great." Women did have, however, a "much greater desire for procreation."[13] Max Flesch, a Frankfurt venerologist and leading social policy expert (and early member of the Bund), argued that "the physiological fact" was "that the initially motivating factor in causing people to enter into a sexual relationship is for the man sexual intercourse, for the woman motherhood."[14] As *Geschlecht und Gesellschaft* put it in 1906, quoting from the Italian criminologist Cesare Lombroso, for women sexual "love is a subordinate function of motherhood."[15] Again, Max Marcuse summed up the wisdom of the prewar decades in 1919, remarking on the "separability of the sexual from the love-complex in men as compared to their unity in woman."[16]

An important corollary was the belief that men's sexual drive was stronger, more tempestuous, and less easily controlled than that of women. The locus classicus for such views was Richard von Krafft-Ebing's *Psychopathia Sexualis* of 1886, in which he asserted—in a much-quoted passage—that:

> without doubt the man has a livelier sexual need than the woman . . . His love is sensual, his choice is determined by physical attractions. Guided by a powerful natural drive, he is aggressive and stormy in his love-play. And yet the demands of nature do not occupy his entire mental universe. If his need is fulfilled, his love recedes temporarily in favor of other vital and social interests.
>
> Woman is quite different. If a woman is mentally normally developed and well-raised, then her sensual desire is scant. If that were not so, the whole world would be a brothel, and marriage and family unthinkable . . . But the

sexual makes itself more evident in the consciousness of woman. The need for love is greater than in man, it is constant, not episodic, but this love is more spiritual than sensual.[17]

In this passage, the connection between the qualitative difference and the difference in intensity is particularly clear.

[. . .]

Fourth and finally, it was widely agreed that men and women "naturally sought to structure sexual relations in quite different ways. Men were by nature polygynous, seeking to have sex with many women; women were by nature monogamous. At the fringes of respectable opinion, some racial theorists actually proposed creating a polygynous sexual order in central Europe in these years.

[. . .]

In much of sexological discourse in the early twentieth century, there is an oddly compulsive rejection of the idea of love—a tendency to ridicule the idea and to discover that something else, something that could be explained in much more clinical and objective terms, was behind it. Ehrenfels was particularly explicit, arguing that monogamous marriage was a "pointless utopia," that the feminist radicals who believed in the possibility of monogamous love between men and women were "up to their necks in the moonlight romanticism of anemic little girls," and that marriage is "in the final analysis sexual provision for two persons of opposite sex through mutual, exclusive, and contractual agreement to intercourse. Our morality . . . tries to cover up this core of the matter . . . ; instead of sexual provision we speak of a unity of souls, and contractual agreement to coitus . . . [is] more or less transparently veiled by the term 'community of bed and table.'"[18] Paul Kompert, writing in *Geschlecht und Gesellschaft* in 1908, adopted a similar posture, suggesting that "the man values the woman as a means to satisfying the sex drive," and that one could analyze his behavior with respect to women in the same way one would analyze his behavior in respect:

> to any other item of consumption. Though we try to hide this fact, and to surround it with an aura of secrecy and specialness, an analysis that dispenses with all extraneous non-essentials must reach this conclusion. Certainly considerations of an ethical nature play a role in determining the value of a woman for marriage. Certainly the man is also often interested in getting a good housekeeper, assistant, status symbol, and educator for his children. But if one leaves aside all these non-essentials, and regards the woman as an *instrumentum cupidinis*, then she is subject . . . to the same general economic laws as any other means of satisfying needs.[19]

Love, in short, was really just the need for a highly desirable item of consumption—sex. A related strategy was to suggest that sexual desire in turn was itself simply racial instinct. Love was not a feeling; it was the will of the "race" for procreation and evolutionary betterment. In fact evolutionary biology—the function of the sexual drive in motivating reproduction and competition—was absolutely ubiquitous in the sexological literature of the period. Virtually every academic tome on sexuality opened with the obligatory first chapter on the sex lives of amoebas, annelids, birds, and lower mammals; and references to evolution were usually sprinkled throughout such texts, as they were in the periodical literature. Thus, for example, in an article on "Marriage and Evolution," published in *Geschlecht und Gesellschaft* in 1906, Wilhelm Brönner argued that the high racial "quality" of a man or woman was "the secret magnetic force that drives two lovers together . . . Here the instinct for reproduction and the creation of an ever better product of pairing [*Paarungsproduktes*] is always subconsciously the main goal."[20] And Bloch, while waxing poetic about the transcending of mere animal instinct by individualizing, emotional love, in fact recurred again and again to the behavior of egg and sperm as "the fundamental cause of the deep differences in the nature of the sexes" and to the importance of sexuality to "the progress of development"—a clear reference to evolutionary, as well as cultural, change.[21]

[. . .]

The radical sex reformer Ellen Key, for example, also believed that romantic choices were determined by the secret will of the "race" or species to create advantageous reproductive pairings.[22] Whereas for Key, however, this was part of an attempt to create a new "religion of life" in which sexual, romantic love was the most sacred value and the most important experience in human life, the male sex reformers appear to have intended precisely the opposite. "Love" was for them inessential, unimportant, trivial, illusory, unserious, mere superstructure. It was a concern, in short, of women; men need not, should not, be troubled by it.

Women view men

In some rather surprising ways, the views of many female participants in the discussion of the "sexual problem" in this period were similar to those of male sexologists. Whereas men held women to be inscrutable, the general consensus among women in this period appears to have been that men were all too knowable. But these women, too, held that the central fact known about men was that they do not love.

This was a view quite common in the more radical branch of the women's movement. Thus, for example, Adele Schreiber, one of the founding members of the BfM, wrote in 1909 that "the unwillingness and incapacity for love of today's *men* is the tragedy of today's *women*."[23] Rosa Mayreder, similarly, wrote in 1912 that "we can take as a given the fact that, in the emotional life of the average man, sexuality is not constitutionally connected with the higher spiritual functions (*den höheren Seelentätigkeiten*)."[24] And Johanna Elberskirchen, a particularly vehement critic of men's behavior, put the same view in more poetic language in 1908:

> The male's capacity for love is essentially very poorly developed . . . and hardly appears at all outside the zone of sexual desire and lust . . . His sexual love and sexuality is essentially lustful and focused on mere intercourse, and is

basically satisfied, or exhausted, with the act of intercourse . . . The man, then, is basically incapable of loving woman . . . spiritually . . . , whereas the woman's soul joyously rushes out to meet the man she loves . . . Oh what a cruel delusion! . . . Her soul, drunk with love, thirsting for love, crashes against a dark, impenetrable wall of complete incomprehension.[25]

The so-called "moderate" feminists who formed the mainstream of the German women's movement, and who vehemently rejected most of the arguments of the feminist sex reformers in the BfM, actually had quite similar notions about men. Gertrud Bäumer, for example, a leading "moderate" and chairwoman of the National League of German Women's Associations (Bund Deutscher Frauenvereine, or BDF) after 1910, held that monogamy had its origins in "the biological connection between love and motherhood in women," believed that "inherent in the love of any normal woman is the desire for children," and concluded that "the mingling of soul and senses is different in the love life of women than in that of men." For women, she wrote in 1905, "the sexual question is really the tension between the demands of their feelings of love and the erotic life of men"—which was not spiritual, emotional, or procreative, but simply physical and hedonistic.[26] Helene Lange, the grand dame of the "moderate" faction, held that the Christian ideal of monogamy was actually "a victory of Woman over the polygamous instincts of men."[27] Marianne Weber believed that monogamous marriage had been invented in order to "soften brutal male power" through contractual ties and that "the great mass of men still regard women as a sex object."[28] And Katharina Scheven, a leader in the movement against regulated prostitution, suggested that one should not forget that "the sexual drive is, and should be, first and foremost a drive to procreate," and that greater sexual freedom would "release the polygamous drives and passions of men once again, and [thereby] destroy the cultural achievements of millennia."[29]

A 1905 article by one Freya von Dohme in *Geschlecht und Gesellschaft* drew the logical conclusion from such postulates, arguing that lesbians had "a much deeper, more spiritualized love" than the average heterosexual, "a necessary consequence" of the fact that in lesbian relationships two "womanly creatures" loved each other. "If the normal marriage does not demonstrate this depth of feeling . . . the fault is that the erotic feelings of men are so very different. Their whole 'I' demands . . . , with much more elemental force, union with the loved one. But when he has found deliverance from the tortures of his hot blood with the chosen [love] object, he is calmed" and once again distracted by quotidian detail—whereas women were dreamier, more languid, and emotionally more deeply affected by love-making.[30]

Within the women's movements, these ideas were, of course, given a very different valence than in the thinking of the male sexologists. Most observers in the women's movements argued not that men were *constitutionally* incapable of love, but rather that love was not part of the prevailing male culture. Because they were economically, socially, and legally privileged, and could essentially do with and to women as they would, men were pathologically "oversexed" and sexually undisciplined. Their predatory, irresponsible, and essentially abusive sexual culture reflected their power over and contempt for women, their brutal enforcement and enjoyment of their sexual privilege. Lida Gustava Heymann, for example, reported that it was only when she discovered Hamburg's brothels that she came to understand the origins of "the brutal contempt of men for the female sex."[31]

If that privilege was revoked, sexual life would become healthy and loving. As Helene Lange put it, there was a natural difference in the interests and perspective of men and women, but it was not absolute, it did not make the sexes different "races." Drawing on the dominant nineteenth-century conception of gender relations, she insisted that it was precisely this difference "that makes them (i.e., the sexes) so ideally suited to complement each other." She believed that the conflict between the sexes was essentially evidence of the "immaturity" of relations between the sexes in German society.[32]

And yet clearly this analysis of men echoed, rather precisely, the self-descriptions published by male sexologists—their assertions that men just want to have orgasms, not complicating emotional attachments; their assertions that sexuality and emotionality were separable for men but not for women; their assertion that women wanted tenderness, love, and children while men didn't have much time for feelings. Whatever might happen in the future, for the time being, in Lange's words, "the two sexes are driven apart like the different nations at the building of the tower of Babel—a process one can view, in microcosm . . . , after any dinner-party." [33]

For the male sexologists, then, the relationship between the sexes was about men's efforts to "conquer" and "take possession of" and use women; for many women, it was the story of women's efforts to conquer men's anarchic and animalistic sexual drives. For many in the women's movement the "crisis" of gender relations derived from the fact that men did not love; for many men, the "crisis" was that some women expected them to.

Sexuality, bisexuality, homosexuality, and the idea of "peace" between the sexes

Whatever the reasons, in any case, there appears to have been a widespread conviction in Germany around the turn of the century that men and women were sexually and emotionally incompatible. This belief would soon be called into question, however. As students of the history of sexology in Europe will know, by the late 1920s a very different understanding of the fundamentals of gender relations would prevail. In that new understanding, the notion of radical sexual difference survived—men were still believed to be more aggressive and less emotional than women. The problems this difference created, however, could be bridged by the adoption of appropriate sexual technique. If men were considerate in bed, sex could become a positive and fulfilling—rather than brutal and alienating—experience for women, too.[34] Being considerate included engaging in foreplay in order to compensate for women's "slower" sexual responses; but it also meant using condoms, since fear of unwanted pregnancy was believed to be a major reason for women's aversion to sex. The crucial assumptions in this model, of course, were that—contrary to received wisdom—women *did* want to have sex without getting pregnant, and that they *did* want to reach orgasm.

This model was not completely unfamiliar within mainstream sexual theory before the war. Some sexual theorists had long held that even normal women could become "fallen women"—that is, become sexually corrupted to the point of being just as sexually voracious and undiscriminating as men (or even more so).[35] And again, some sexologists argued well before World War I that women were fundamentally masochistic, and, in effect, liked being sexually assaulted. Finally, in the years around the turn of the century, as we have seen, some sex experts gave this idea a more optimistic twist, arguing that it was possible for husbands to "awaken" their wives sexually, creating a mutually satisfying sex life within marriage. This latter position was, however, clearly a minority one; most continued to believe that there was a natural sexual hostility between men and women.

There were two groups of sexual radicals who *did* vehemently question the prevailing model before 1914, however. One of these groups was made up of members of the radical women's movement, and particularly participants in the BfM. In the decade before World War I, a number of these women argued quite forcefully that there actually was no great difference either in the quality or in the degree of sexual desire in men and women. Women wanted sex, not babies; they wanted orgasm, not cuddling; and some even held that women, too, were "naturally" just as polygamous as men. By arguing that men and women actually had shared sexual goals, these critics built a bridge across the chasm of radical difference.

Johanna Elberskirchen is a striking example of this "pro-sex" feminist analysis. For despite her apparent despair over the animal nature of masculine love, she held in fact that the prevailing pattern of male sexuality was not natural but pathological, a product of specific social conditions, and specifically of male power. In an essay of 1903 on "Sexual Feeling in Woman and Man," she argued that the sex drive in men and women derived from precisely the same physiological source (the "reproductive glands"), that "the sexual drive of women and its satisfaction has nothing to do with so-called motherhood, with breeding," and that the simple fact that women continued to have sex outside marriage in a society in which single mothers and illegitimate children were doomed to poverty, misery, and often early death showed "how strong the sex drive is in women, that it is equal in strength and power to the sex drive of men—and how woman hungers, hungers." Elberskirchen asserted that in women, too:

> body and soul, the whole person is subject to a single powerful feeling and drive, a single desire floods nerves and blood, cries out through them and drives and thrusts woman with commanding force toward man . . . And it is this elemental sexual longing that befuddles the mind of woman, that drives her into the arms of the man, that makes her forget all the threatening dangers for the [unborn] child, that makes her forget all the shame that threatens her and the child, that makes her seek out sexual union—and not the longing for a child.[36]

Like other feminist sex reformers, however, she insisted that this sexual drive was not in itself evil or destructive; what explained the sexual and social misery of the day, instead, was the fact that men had used their social power to create the double standard of sexual morality. Allowing their own sexual drives free reign, they reduced women to a state of "sexual slavery" and established themselves as "for women, in the field of sexuality, the capitalist," the exploiter. These relations of power had come to be embedded in the sexual economy of each of the sexes: "the sexual needs of men have come to exceed the physiologically necessary [measure], sexual activity has become for men a primary purpose in life, a goal, in its own right." At the same time, the sex drive of *some* women—those who were not, as prostitutes, required to service this "pathological, hysterical . . . sexual need in men"—was suppressed. The apparent differential in the sex drives of men and women was not a natural fact, but a product of a distorted social relationship of the sexes and of "immoral laws of morality."[37]

[. . .]

The second group working to undermine the prevailing model of heterosexual gender relations were, perhaps counterintuitively, men in the homosexual rights movement. Whereas that prevailing model held that men and women were effectively sexual opposites, the argument of many of these men was that every individual is essentially bisexual and that any given individual's sexual identity and sexuality falls somewhere along a continuum from pure (or ideal-typical) male to pure female. Both maleness and femaleness were present in every individual; the varying proportions in any one person explained some of the great variety of sexual orientations and sexual preferences.

[. . .]

For all the clinical rhetoric, then, sexology had clearly adopted a central aim of the radical sex-reform movements of the pre-war years, and particularly of the BfM. Those movements had been committed to using modern means—science and social change, eugenic and evolutionary ideas, contraception, and the emancipation of women—to rescue romantic love from its modern crisis. Sexologists before the war had scoffed at such ideas. By the late 1920s, even the more conservative and patriarchalist men in the field of sexology had re-"discovered" love by way of sex. In 1900 there had been virtual consensus that men and women could scarcely live with each other; by 1930, there was virtual consensus that they could scarcely live without each other (or at least without each other's bodies).

  The "biologization" of romantic love between the 1890s and the 1920s, then, was not a straightforward process. It seems to have been characterized, rather, by some surprising and ironic twists and turns. The discourse of difference constructed in the early nineteenth century appears to have begun to self-destruct by the 1890s, as difference-and-compatibility became difference-and-hostility. That process seems to have been driven, however, as much by the success of the social model built around the idea of sexual difference as by its failure. Appropriately, therefore, the primary impetus for formulating a discursive response to that "crisis" appears to have come, not from sexual conservatives, but from radicals bent on sexual revolution rather than sexual restoration—a sexual revolution that would rescue love from the pathologies of patriarchy and capitalism. And yet, at least some of the influential formulations of that response in the 1920s were clearly committed to the sexual authority of men. And a final irony—one still further beyond the proper scope of this essay—is that so far from "saving" marriage, the emergence of the new ideal of sexual companionship coincided with the beginnings of the "divorce revolution" that would transform it in the second half of the century. The divorce rate in Germany doubled from the 1910s to the 1920s, and then rose another twenty-five percent by the early 1930s (which suggests that the jump in the early 1920s was not only a product of the stresses of the war, though that clearly played a role).[38] In the 1920s Germans were much less enamored of the idea of the incompatibility of the sexes, but they were also beginning to get divorced at what would become, historically, a furious rate. The discussion of the "war of the sexes" appears, then, to be a marvelous illustration of the way in which discourses and social practices can subvert themselves, and each other, in multiple, cross-cutting, and unpredictable ways.

Notes

1   Work on this article was made possible by grants from the Charles Phelps Taft Memorial Fund at the University of Cincinnati and from the German Academic Exchange Service.

2   Jacques Le Rider, *Modernity and Crises of Identity* (Cambridge: Polity, 1993), 119. On European art in this period, see Bram Dijkstra, *Idols of Perversity: Fantasies of Feminine Evil in Fin-de-Siècle Culture* (New York: Oxford, 1986); Lynda Nead, *Myths of Sexuality: Representations of Women in Victorian Britain* (Oxford: Blackwell, 1988); Barbara Eschenburg, "Der Kampf der Geschlechter," in *Der Kampf der Geschlechter. Der neue Mythos in der Kunst 1850–1930*, ed. Helmut Friedel (Cologne: DuMont, 1995); and, for a later period, Maria Tatar, *Lustmord: Sexual Murder in Weimar Germany* (Princeton: Princeton University Press, 1995).

3   See, for example, Ute Planert, *Antifeminismus im Kaiserreich. Diskurs, soziale Formation und politische Mentalität* (Göttingen: Vandenhoeck & Ruprecht, 1998); Christina Klausmann and Iris Schröder, "Geschlechterstreit um 1900," in *Feministische Studien* 18 (2000); Michael Salewski, "Frauenbilder—Männerängste. Zum Geschlechterdiskurs im Fin de Siècle," *Historische Mitteilungen* 13 (2000); Atina Grossmann, *Reforming Sex: The German Movement for Birth Control and Abortion Rights, 1920–1950* (New York: Oxford University Press, 1995).

4   Hedwig Dohm, "Der Hass der Geschlechter," in *Hedwig Dohm. Erinnerungen und weitere Schriften von und über Hedwig Dohm*, ed. Hedda Korsch (Zurich: Ala, 1980), 153.

5   Christoph Sachsse, *Mütterlichkeit als Beruf. Sozialarbeit, Sozialreform und Frauenbewegung, 1871–1929* (Frankfurt: Suhrkamp, 1986), 110, 111, 112; Karin Hausen, "Family and Role-Division: The Polarization of Sexual Stereotypes in the Nineteenth Century—An Aspect of the Dissociation of Work and Family Life," in *The German Family*, ed. Richard J. Evans (London: Taylor & Francis Books Ltd., 1981). On love, see Anne-Charlotte Trepp, "Emotion und bürgerliche Sinnstiftung oder die Metaphysik des Gefühls. Liebe am Beginn des bürgerlichen Zeitalters," in *Der bürgerliche Wertehimmel. Innenansichten des 19. Jahrhunderts*, ed. Manfred Hettling and Stefan-Ludwig Hoffmann (Göttingen: Vandenhoeck & Ruprecht, 1998).

6   Hans Adner, "Von der neuen Ehe," *Geschlecht und Gesellschaft* (hereafter *GG*) 1 (1905): 117.

7   Albert Moll, *Untersuchungen über die Libido sexualis* (Berlin: Fischer, 1898), 8–11.

8   Enoch Heinrich Kisch, *Das Geschlechtsleben des Weibes in physiologischer, pathologischer und hygienischer Beziehung* (Berlin: Urban & Schwarzenberg, 1904), 179. Kisch is summarizing Moll here.

9   Hugo Sellheim, *Die Reize der Frau und ihre Bedeutung für den Kulturforischritt* (Stuttgart: Enke, 1909), 9.

10   Max Marcuse, "Über die Problematik der Sexualpsychologie des Weibes und der vergleichenden Sexualpsychologie der Geschlechter," *Zeitschrift für Sexualwissenschaft* (hereafter *ZSW*) 6 (1919): 274.

11   Eduard Fuchs, "Die weibliche Sinnlichkeit," *GG* 2 (1907): 482–83.

12   Sellheim, *Reize*, 9.

13   Alfred Hegar, *Der Geschlechtstriebes. Eine Social-Medicinische Studie* (Stuttgart: Ferdinand Enke, 1894), 5, 7.

14   Johanna Elberskirchen, *Die Sexualempfindung bei Weib und Mann, betrachtet vom physiologisch-soziologischen Standpunkte* (Leipzig: Jacque Hegner, 1903), 4.

15   Cesare Lombroso, "Weibliche und männliche Liebe," *GG* 1 (1906): 327.

16   Marcuse, "Über die Problematik," 274.

17   Richard von Krafft-Ebing, *Psychopathia sexualis* (Munich: Matthes & Seitz, 1984), 12–13.

18   Ehrenfels, "Sexuales Ober- und Unterbewusstsein," *Politisch-Anthropologische Revue* 2 (1903/1904): 473; Ehrenfels, "Sexuale Reformvorschläge," *PAR* 4 (1905/1906): 442; Ehrenfels, "Die Ehe nach Mutterrecht," 633.

19   Paul Kompert, "Vorschläge zu einer Sexualökonomie," *GG* 4 (1909): 533.

20   Wilhelm Brönner, "Ehe und Entwicklungslehre," *GG* 1 (1905): 150–151.

21   Bloch, *Das Sexualleben*, 12–13.

22   See Ellen Key, *Über Liebe und Ehe* (Frankfurt: Fischer, 1911), 48.

23   Adele Schreiber, "Heiratsbeschränkungen," *Die Neue Generation* (hereafter *NG*) 5 (1909): 97.

24   Rosa Mayreder, "Zur Psychologie der freien Liebe," *NG* 8 (1912): 7.

25   Johanna Elberskirchen, quoted in "Rundschau," *SP* 4 (1908): 152, 153.

26   Gertrud Bäumer, "Die 'neue Ethik,'" *Die Frau* 12 (1905): 711–712.

27   Helene Lange, *Die Frauenbewegung in ihren modernen Problemen* (Leipzig: Quelle & Meyer, 1908), 60.

28   Marianne Weber, "Sexual-ethische Prinzipienfragen," in Gertrud Bäumer et al., *Frauenbewegung und Sexualethik. Beiträge zur modernen Ehekritik* (Heilbronn: Eugen Salzer, 1909), 29, 41.

29   Katharina Scheven, "Sexualethik und Kulturfortschritt," *Abolitionist* 12 (1913): 23, 26; Scheven, "Selbtsbeherrschung order freie Liebe?," *Abolitionist* 4 (1905): 96. It is worth noting that many conservative Christians had very similar views. Thus the Protestant sexual ethicist Gustav von Rohden held in 1911 that for men sex was "an episode," but for women it was "the meaning of life." The history of monogamous marriage was the history of the "assertion and recognition of woman's individuality," since men were "polygamous by instinct." Gustav von Rohden, *Ehe und freie Liebe. Ein Won zum Individualismus in der Frauenfrage* (Berlin: Martin Warneck, 1911), 39, 46, 43. Similarly, the Catholic moral philosopher Friedrich Wilhelm Foerster argued in 1907 that Christian, monogamous marriage was the necessary antidote to men's "vagabondish tendencies." Friedrich Wilhelm Foerster, *Sexualethik und Sexualpädagogik* (Kempten: Josef Kösel, 1907), 32.

30   Freya von Dohme, "Lesbische Liebe," *GG* 1 (1906): 68.

31   Lida Gustava Heymann, "Die rechtliche Grundlage und die moralischen Wirkungen der Prostitution," *Frauenbewegung* 9 (1903): 163.

32   Lange, "Intellektuelle Grenzlinien," 207, 211.

33   Ibid., 207.

34   See in particular Sheila Jeffries, *The Spinster and Her Enemies: Feminism and Sexuality, 1880–1930* (London: Pandora, 1985); Margaret Jackson, *The Real Facts of Life: Feminism and the Politics of Sexuality c. 1850–1940* (London: Taylor & Francis, 1994).

35   See, for example, Forel, *Die sexuelle Frage*, 97.

36   Elberskirchen, *Die Sexualempfindung*, 6, 7, 2829, 2526.

37   Ibid., 30, 31, 39, 47, 48, 38.

38   See Phillips, *Putting Asunder*, 518, 523.

Chapter 19

Grete Meisel-Hess

THE SEXUAL CRISIS
A critique of our sex life (1917)

CRITIQUE OF MARRIAGE IN ITS PRESENT FORM

Causes of the increase in the number of celibates. Perversion of courtship

TO EVERY EPOCH BELONGS its own established "order." If everyone had remained contented with this order, our development out of the protoplasmic slime of the sea-depths into the condition in which we now find ourselves would never have taken place. It is tantamount to an absolute negation of the idea of evolution to regard an established order as above criticism, as immaculately perfect. The sexual life of our civilization is grounded on marriage, and marriage is an order which has good reasons for its existence. Nevertheless, we have to ask ourselves what marriage costs us. Within the limits of this sexual order, mothers, delivered in secret, bleed to death for lack of aid; infants are drowned like superfluous kittens, or perish at the hands of the baby-farmer; women become prostitutes because no other livelihood is open to them: syphilitics, drunkards, consumptives, and persons suffering from mental disorder can marry without any obligation to disclose their infirmity to their partner in wedlock; undesired children are born for whom no sustenance can be found, sickly children, bred in corruption, unfitted from their very birth for the struggle for existence, who, when full grown, can only hinder and hamper the working of the social machinery, and who drag out their weary lives as a burden to themselves and to others; by this sexual order millions of healthy men and women are forbidden to reproduce their kind, whilst simultaneously, in mockery of the notion of racial selection, it is the most pushing and self-seeking, the least scrupulous and the least heroic of our race, those who by any rational standard are the most unworthy to perpetuate their type, that prove themselves the "fittest" to survive and propagate most rapidly and most abundantly; millions, too, are debarred, not merely from reproduction but further from any natural sexual life, this privation being in part dependent upon a total lack of opportunities for sexual gratification, and in part upon a restriction of such opportunities and upon the imposition of *artificial obstacles to sexual satisfaction*; to many millions of persons the only sexual life available is the life of prostitution: all these varied manifestations are the inseparable associates of our sexual order based on marriage, and so long as they persist we cannot fail to consider that this order urgently needs reform.

Surprise is often expressed at the fact that it is women, above all, who attack marriage as the only socially authorized variety of sexual relationships. We are told: "It is for women's sake that the institution of marriage exists; it has arisen for their protection, not for that of men." We are asked: "For what reason is it that among those who attack marriage, or object to the claim that marriage is the only permissible sexual relationship, women constitute the preponderant majority?" These questioners are apt to answer their own inquiry by telling us that the advocates of "Women's rights" attack marriage because "the grapes are sour!" Agreed. It is a deplorable truth that in the case of many women marriage is as completely unattainable as were the grapes to the fox in the fable. But it cannot be admitted that an institution which is inaccessible to millions of sound and healthy persons, well fitted for love and for parentage, can justly claim to be regarded as the only socially permissible form of sexual relationship.

[. . .]

Among all savage races the basis of sexual selection is constituted by the greater desirability of certain women. A Maori proverb runs: "However handsome a man may be, he is not the object of desire; however homely a woman may be, she will still be the object of desire." This is how it is among the Maori. But with us it is just the opposite. A woman may be beautiful and charming, and endowed with all possible gifts of mind and heart, and may yet find it difficult "to get a husband." On the other hand, the most pitiable creature among men can find hundreds of women willing to marry him, a fact proved by the career of those who make a regular profession of marrying women and deserting them. Where shall we find the woman, however good and attractive she may be, with whom hundreds of men would enter the bonds of marriage, and to whom they would all, one after another, make over their savings? "In unions between a member of a higher and a member of a lower race," writes Westermarck, "we almost invariably find that it is the man who belongs to the higher race." But within the limits of our own white race the very reverse of this prevails; and in a union between higher and lower types the woman commonly belongs to the higher, the man to the lower, type. We often encounter couples in which the husband is conspicuously degenerate, while the wife is beautiful and well developed. Very significant in this connection is the current saying: "A man has no need of good looks." No, a man has no need of good looks, and if he wishes to marry he need but raise his finger and as many women will respond to his sign as of old were at the disposal of Don Juan.

Such being the fruits of our economic system, it follows that the natural factors of progressive racial improvement are no longer in operation. Formerly men struggled one with another to possess women, and this struggle seemed to arise by inevitable natural law; it was dependent on the circumstance that the male, who is endowed with greater freedom and mobility because unencumbered by the work of reproduction, must court the female, who is hampered and restricted by the nature of her reproductive functions.

Only in response to such courtship would the female surrender herself to the embraces of the male. But the struggle has become a thing of the past, and it appears to be one of the proudest achievements of our progress in civilization to have abrogated this fundamental law. We have, indeed, reversed the process; so that the woman, if she is to get a husband at all, must fight for him, cheat for him, or buy him. Whilst the capacity for reproduction has become dependent upon the economic potency of the male, the act of reproduction itself has in both sexes become a mere matter of social calculation, and has entirely ceased to be a factor in natural selection.

The individual and psychological causes of the increasing prevalence of celibacy will be found chiefly in the increasing differentiation of spiritual needs, and in the consequent increasing magnitude of the demands men and women make of their sexual partners. The price of marriage is that the entire working powers of the man, and often those of the woman also, should be pledged in perpetuity; once the partnership is formed, it is ever more difficult to dissolve; its very attainment is possible only through the harmonious cooperation of hundreds of factors. Marriage practically precludes the possibility of any subsequent sexual preference, and demands as a prerequisite that there shall be harmony, not only in respect of the social position of husband and wife, but further in respect of their individual and personal inclinations, habits and opinions. If this latter demand is to-day so much more insistent than it was in former times, may we not find the explanation in the fact that the truly individual consciousness tends more and more to preponderate over the class consciousness or even the national consciousness of the individual? In earlier times the individual represented, to a much greater extent than he does to-day, the type of his country, his race, his co-linguals, his profession, his guild or his class. All such distinctions give place more and more to a cosmopolitan individualism. Within the limits of a homogeneous community, the partner in marriage could in former days be found with comparative ease, for that which was demanded was chiefly the distinctive characteristics of the members of such a community. But to-day, when a hundred individual traits of character must find in another their satisfactory complement, whilst the social conditions for marriage have to be simultaneously fulfilled, can we wonder that this union becomes increasingly difficult of attainment? Further, by a correlative manifestation, the sexual impulse tends under analysis to become progressively weaker. For the male, especially, there are innumerable ways of diverting or calming the impulse; and by recourse to prostitution, or by living in an unfettered "intimacy" he is able to gratify it to such an extent that he will not be likely to allow anyone "to make a fool of him." Perversions of every kind such as prevail in all classes of society play their part in curbing the power of the sexual impulse, of the impulse by which men and women are drawn together and led to form unions. A strong attraction towards one of the opposite sex is now apt to be regarded with mistrust from the outset; it is thought to be dangerous; it is analyzed and explained; and at length it is "happily overcome." Thus by diversion or weakening of the sexual impulse there is often effected what is regarded as a victory of reason; but we ignore the manifest purpose of nature, seeing that the true function of the sexual impulse is to secure the products of cross-fertilization.

[. . .]

The racial and biological obstacles to marriage are no more than an amplification of those that are individual in character. Why is the right man or the right woman so difficult to find? Above all, because it is at the right moment and in suitable circumstances that the right partner must be found. Somewhere in the universe this partner may exist; but in Mars, perhaps, while the other ideal sexual partner is on earth.

Sooner and oftener, however, would the desired mate be encountered did there exist a greater number of individuals whose personality is competent to satisfy and rejoice others. If one meets his or her true sexual complement, the right mate for the other has obviously also been found. Now when we say that a race undergoes degeneration, we mean no more than this: that innumerable individuals belonging to that race have deteriorated in respect of bodily and mental qualities, and that they are increasingly unable to satisfy one another's desire for happiness. It is a consequence of those conditions of our civilization whereby the working of the selective process has been falsified, that such states of mental and bodily inferiority, being transmissible by inheritance, tend increasingly to prevail.

We have traversed the entire circumference of the vicious circle, and have returned to our starting-point.

Under the conditions at present sanctioned by society, procreation must be effected within the limits of legal marriage, and for marriage to be possible a hundred different social factors must cooperate. Sexual selection is the very last thing to be considered. Children procreated as the result of a genuine sexual selection, as the fruit of a union of mutual attraction completely independent of economic or social considerations—such children must not be born. If born, they are condemned to a social environment which makes degradation inevitable. We are often assured that the terribly high death-rate among illegitimate children furnishes a proof of the unfortunate biological results of free sexual unions; but in no sense whatever can it be claimed that this death rate is a manifestation of natural law, for it is due solely to the evil social conditions artificially imposed upon the illegitimate, and far from being a proof of the necessity for the existing sexual order it furnishes an effective condemnation of that order. Among legitimate offspring, on the other hand, children are born to fathers who have exhausted their best energies in the fierce struggle for existence, and to fathers who, during the years in which they were not in a position to marry, have squandered their biological forces in the morass of prostitution; children are born to mothers who have been infected by their husbands, to mothers who have had no genuine freedom in the choice of a mate, to mothers in whom stigmata of degeneration have been ignored owing to the possession of a substantial dowry, to mothers who commonly exhibit no more than a passable average of intellectual and moral endowments—for women of exceptional capacity do not willingly surrender their freedom of choice, and therefore less often marry and reproduce their kind. Moreover, in the case of the proletariat, children are born to progenitors weakened by excessive toil, alcoholism and semi-starvation.

But the children who are not born are the children of young, beautiful, strong and healthy human beings; the children of those whose union is the outcome simply of mutual desire, of the delight each takes in the other; the children of those drawn together by the clear call of an unsophisticated sexual impulse.

In our world such children have no place.

[. . .]

To-day women are taught, in conformity with the demands of the average male, that when they give themselves they must do so unreservedly and for always; but it is precisely out of such utter self-surrender that all the tragedies of women's lives issue. The self-surrender imposes upon women a condition of slave-like dependence, and thus love lays upon them burdens which are rarely, if ever, borne by the male. If it be true that the detumescence impulse of the male is so constituted as necessarily to lead men from one woman to another, it follows that women, if they are ever to attain to a free and truly human life, must be systematically educated in such a way as to enfranchise their minds from dependence upon the male sexual impulse. If it be truly man's nature to forsake women often, women must also learn to range through several sexual experiences until they attain the one in which their spirits are at peace and their children rightly fathered:

> Till for her child a woman find
> The father fit in form and mind,
> To him unfit, and with no ruth,
> Let every woman break her troth.

As things are to-day, and in consequence of the contempt visited upon women who enter into sexual relationships outside the forms of legal marriage, a woman is intolerably dependent upon the man to whom she has once given herself. If she is as ready to leave the man as he is to leave her, she is universally stigmatized as a whore. Hence she plays a part in order to keep the man by her side, and this gives him an overwhelming advantage in their relationship, and makes him an exploiter of her mental energies.

The duplex moral code has depraved the male alike in moral character and in sexual instincts; it has made him mean-spirited; it has deprived him of the understanding how to approach love in an atmosphere of freedom. He has become the slave of a single suggestion, that of marriage. He must be kept chained up, like a watch-dog, and has forgotten how to behave himself when the chain is slipped. Although for the moment I am criticizing the sexual conduct of the average male, the reader must not suppose that I am adopting the attitude of a feminine counterpart to Strindberg, for there is nothing more remote from my mind than the spirit of the man-hater. In the existing order the sexual conduct of men and of women is equally open to criticism, and the necessary duty of criticism is equally painful in both cases.

Under the conventional code all possible sexual rights are given to the male, whereas the female has three alternatives only: marriage, celibacy, or prostitution. This last possibility involves an utter disregard of the prohibitions of our sexual morality, so relentless in other respects, and the reason for the inconsistency lies on the surface—man has need of this institution. The code is drawn up by men, and must contain provision for the satisfaction of the various demands they make in their relationships with the other sex.

Prostitution comes into existence in response to the urgency of the senses; it is a way out, and from the male point of view not altogether a bad one, since it effects for men an enfranchisement from the dominion of sensual needs, whilst leaving them entire personal freedom.

Marriage, on the other hand, viewed from the male standpoint, exists to provide a favorable social platform. The "marriage of reason" is founded upon the increase of property, and therewith of influence. It is the culmination of man's social efforts, a field for the cooperation of the sexual impulse, the reproductive impulse, and the faculties of the social climber. From this point of view, marriage, like prostitution, regarded as the work of a god dealing with the inferior creation, is not so much amiss. Between these opposite poles of the sexual life, prostitution and the marriage of reason, the male provides—for himself—a third alternative, the love-intimacy. This yields transient erotic stimulation, without furnishing social advance, but also without imposing social duties, and without the distasteful environment of prostitution. All three possibilities are at man's free disposal, whilst a woman must choose one or none, either finding satisfaction in one of the three for all her needs, or else enduring the deprivation of the most vital condition of existence.

We speak of woman's economic dependence upon man, but this is mere child's play in comparison with the sexual dependence resulting from the conditions just analyzed. A man has so much to bestow that by a woman the first comer may be hailed as a deliverer, as the giver of all good things, graciously offering marriage. "He has married her"—"Will he marry her?"—Such is the refrain that rises continually from the market of the sexes. It is not for him, but for her that everything depends upon marriage. If he does not marry, he need suffer no lack, and need incur no risk; he remains free to love, to dally, to "live." In woman's case the possibilities must be chosen singly. She must love and be married; or love and be forsaken; or, claiming the man's freedom in respect of dalliance and "living," must accept submergence in the abyss of social contempt. Can we wonder that the first of these chances, love and marriage, appears to her the most desirable, all its dangers notwithstanding?

In self-respect and genuine chastity woman has everything to gain and nothing to lose by overleaping the barriers within which her life is at present confined and by which she is now forced to grasp at marriage with any man who is willing. The complete perversion of courtship in the upper circles of society is a proof how little true sexual modesty is left to women under the dominion of the present sexual code. How small is the self-respect possible to the average woman who must snatch at any chance of attaining legalized "sexual security." The respect of the code for true chastity is trifling, since it is taken as a matter of course that the newly-wed woman shall at once and without demur surrender all to her husband, proceeding from the very outset even to the intimacy of the common bedchamber.

The women who to-day deliberately accept a life of sexual deprivation do so because they will not entertain any love relationship which may entail mental debasement, and under the existing conditions of the sexual life the danger of debasement is almost inseparable from the free intimacy. The woman throws herself away and accepts mental degradation who gives herself to a man incapable of full appreciation and understanding of her qualities, incapable of giving her a tender and whole-hearted affection. Hence the possibility for woman of genuine sexual satisfaction is dependent upon man's capacity to understand, to appreciate, and to love. But masculine capacity in these respects is at present in a declining phase, as the outcome of generations of sexual corruption and of the dominant pharisaism of the male. The inevitable consequence is that an ever larger number of free-spirited and desirable women deliberately choose a celibate life—not because they are free from the natural desires of sex, but because these desires are associated with mental requirements that cannot now obtain fulfillment.

[. . .]

Peculiarly solitary are those spoken of as new women. No light love will serve their turn, nothing but a profound experience can bring them spiritual enfranchisement; and the man of to-day with weak capacity for love and mood dehellenized is no fit mate for the new woman, for he cannot bring her such profound experience. A man the strength of whose own love builds for him a bridge upon which he can draw near to a Woman of strong individuality is a rarity and this is why women of finer clay are commonly left unmated. Their solitude is a danger, not to themselves alone, but to the race. For, as Ruth Bree has well written, "If these intellectual and fearless women die without leaving bodily offspring, if they fail to reproduce their forcible individualities, the race necessarily suffers. To the educators and teachers of the succeeding generation is then allotted the weary task of trying to enlighten the offspring of the dullards." The yearning of such women is strong, profound and lasting. So long as their spirit remains active, so long as their youth endures, so long do they believe in their star, that star under whose sign two twin souls shall be fused into an inseparable unity. But the day inevitably comes in which this yearning expires, for they have been outwearied by a fruitless pilgrimage. Maeterlinck expresses in one of his "Chansons" a woman's outpouring of such a yearning and such a resignation.

> *J'ai cherché trente ans, mes sœurs,*
>   *Òu s'est-il cache?*
> *J'ai marché trente ans, mes soeurs,*
>   *Sans m'en rapproché . . .*
>
> *J'ai marché trente ans, mes sœurs,*
>   *Et mes pieds sont las,*
> *Il était partout, mes sœurs,*
>   *Et n'existe pas . . . .*
>
> *L'heure est triste enfin, mes sœurs,*
>   *Ôtez mes sandales,*
> *Le soir meurt aussi, mes sœurs,*
>   *Et mon âme a mal . . . .*
>
> *Vous avez seize ans, mes sœurs,*
>   *Allez loin d'ici,*
> *Prenez mon bourdon, mes sœurs,*
>   *Et cherchez aussi.*

I have sought for thirty years, my sisters,
    Where hides he ever
I have sought for thirty years, my sisters,
    And found him never . . . .

I have walked for thirty years, my sisters,
    Tired are my feet and hot,
He was everywhere, my sisters,
    Existing not . . . .

The hour is sad in the end, my sisters,
    Take off my shoon,
The evening is dying, also, my sister
    My sick soul will swoon . . . .

Your years are sixteen, my sisters,
    The far plains are blue,
Take you my staff, my sisters,
        Seek also you.
        [The English translation is by Jethro Bithell. It appears in his little
            volume, *Contemporary Belgian Poetry*, Walter Scott, 1915.]

Is it conceivable that an end should ever be put to this sexual misery of women? The writer believes that it is. Even if it should be impossible for every woman to attain to a satisfactory and permanent union, in a sane sexual system every healthy woman would at least have an opportunity of being desired, and every such woman could attain to motherhood. Were not every love-intimacy shadowed by the formula, "he ought to marry her," or "he is already married," or "after all he or she is going to marry somebody else," every desirable woman who to-day remains solitary would have a hundred opportunities of being desired and loved. The possibility of being desired and loved must be thrown open freely to all women. The most essential element in this enfranchisement would be the provision of economic security for the woman whose possibilities of earning a livelihood are impaired or interrupted by motherhood. Hardly less important is the social rehabilitation of unmarried motherhood, and the demand for such rehabilitation is proudly blazoned on its flag by the "Deutsche Bund für Mutterschutz." Further, it is of importance that there should be a change in the nature of the moral preconceptions with which the partners enter upon the free love-intimacy, so that they may be liberated from the burdens upon soul and senses imposed to-day in every such intimacy. Nor could we believe complete happiness to be attainable in a unity of mother and child from which the child's father is excluded. But we regard it as beyond question that society will have to make the unity of mother and child (the question of fatherhood apart) the primary basis of its sexual order. In a word, we believe that patriarchy will prove to have been a brief social aberration, and that matriarchy will once again become the natural unit of family life. In a subsequent volume a detailed study of matriarchy will be undertaken, and proof will be offered that in human history patriarchy has, in actual fact, been no more than a transient episode, in no way founded upon nature's will. Matriarchy, on the other hand, giving expression, as the only secure family association, to the indissoluble reciprocal dependence of mother and child, reaches far back into human history to the days of the prophetesses— although even under matriarchy, if only for the reason that territorial property descended in the female line, the father of the children commonly lived with the mother in monogamic sexual union.

Even when the father is lacking to the family unit, unmarried motherhood (presupposing always that it entails neither poverty nor social contempt) is a thousand times better for a woman than that she should live out her whole life under the burden that millions of women bear to-day, that of complete renunciation of the possibilities of love and of sex. Woman's sexual enfranchisement once secured, she will no longer be condemned to remain solitary if abandoned by her first lover. Should her child lose its "natural" father, it will very probably find a better one in its mother's new companion. Man, too, when he feels himself free, in the sense in which the woman yoked by no legal ties is free, will tend to follow a natural psychical suggestion, will incline to maintain his rights in his own child, and will probably, in the free intimacy, more often remain in permanent association with the mother than he does today, when he feels "ensnared" in such a relationship. There is no ground whatever, and above all there is no eugenic ground, why a woman who has been abandoned by her lover, or one who finds her male intimate uncongenial and leaves him, should not subsequently bear children to other men with whom in the later course of her life she may form love-relationships—presupposing always that the children are healthy. Far from there existing any eugenic objection to this course, a much more rigid selective process would be at work under such conditions than obtains to-day in the unions which women contract as it were in the dark, and with one man only.

In so far as any human community needs an increase in its birth-rate, it must effect this by political and economical measures, making a direct appeal to the initiative of the mothers of the nation. Such an association between the mothers and the state will for the first time render it possible to regulate the birth-rate in accordance with a preconceived plan; whereas to-day the state is exposed to a rapid succession of crises, suffering now from overpopulation, now from under-population. There is no reason to suppose that in a reformed sexual order the actual number of births need vary very markedly from that which occurs to-day; the crucial and eminently desirable difference would be a matter of distribution and of quality. With the wide public diffusion of a knowledge of the methods of preventive sexual intercourse, and with the imposition of a social veto upon all procreative acts likely to be injurious to the race, the weakly, the diseased, and those deficient in earning power would no longer propagate to excess; neither the well-dowered daughter whose dowry is her only merit, nor the degenerate man, would perpetuate their types; comparatively unfit individuals would far more often be eliminated from the racial process, while beautiful, strong and desirable human beings would attain to procreation. There would result, not more pairing than to-day, but pairing under other forms and conditions and on the part of couples differently assorted.

Reproduction must be freed from its immurement within the barriers of marriage. Marriage will persist as the best form of sexual association, but no longer as the only recognized basis of procreation—for marriage has not proved its right to its existing monopoly in this field. We judge the tree by its fruits. In the millions of victims to celibacy and prostitution and in the stunted offspring that are born in consequence of the vitiation of the process of selection, we pay too dearly for marriage.

[. . .]

As a result of the changes here outlined, a wonderful and fully conscious play of courtship would ensue. To-day courtship, wooing, can hardly be said to occur. People marry; they buy sexual favors; they accept enforced renunciation; or they craftily "seduce" one another with the most evil intentions on both sides. True, ardently joyful, straightforward, and natural wooing of the woman by the man is rarely witnessed. Such wooing can occur only when no ill consequences can ensue to wooer or to wooed, when granting is to both an unalloyed delight. To-day, we wither in the drought which is the outcome of a false and insane code of sexual morals.

How wonderful an impulse to love would result from the social recognition of the necessity of extra-conjugal sexual intercourse and of the social rehabilitation of its practice!

PART 10

Was banning clitoridectomy humanitarian or imperialist?

Introduction

W HEN SIGMUND FREUD BEGAN investigating female sexuality for his project on infantile sexuality, he argued that by exploring the clitoris and experiencing sexual pleasure, little girls assuaged their anxiety at lacking the male phallus. However, in order to grow up, he asserted, they needed to accept their feminine status and abandon the masculine clitoris and experience orgasm in the vagina. Of course this was always difficult, since anatomically the clitoris is rich with nerves and the vagina is not. Nonetheless, slowly over the interwar period the notion that women should have vaginal, not clitoral orgasms began to spread to popular medical texts.[1]

Princess Marie Bonaparte was one of Freud's followers, trained in psychoanalysis herself. She emphasized the necessity for the vaginal orgasm and the inferiority of the clitoris even more than Freud, but she also recognized how difficult this transition was. She was frustrated because she could not experience the vaginal orgasm mandated by Freud, and underwent several operations to remedy this.[2] As Bodil Folke Frederiksen reveals, Bonaparte became very interested in the practice of clitoridectomy in Kenya, because she thought that Kenyan women might be more adjusted to their femininity as a result.

Clitoridectomy was very controversial in Kenya as part of a larger struggle between British imperialism and Kikuyu nationalism. The Kikuyu people practiced both female and male circumcision as part of an elaborate initiation rite that transformed girls and boys into adults, members of the community, ready to marry and take on community responsibilities. There is some debate about whether they practiced a minor form of just removing the tip of the clitoris, or whether they excised the entire exterior genitals of these girls.

Missionaries were horrified at this practice, and agitated for the government to control it. The British government was reluctant to interfere in what it saw as native customs, but, under pressure, in 1929 mandated that only the minor form of the operation could be carried out. The missionaries went further and denied communion to those Kikuyu who engaged in the practice. But Lynn Thomas found that in Meru, Kenya, some government officials actually encouraged the earlier performance of this rite because they thought it would deter girls from premarital sex, pregnancy, and abortions. However, this was not publicized at the time – only the effort to limit the practice.[3]

News of this controversy reached Britain, where some feminist members of parliament spoke out about it. The Duchess of Atholl's speech came as part of a larger debate in parliament over native paramountcy – the extent to which native Kenyans should be given rights to their land, and whether they should be able to vote. Atholl was a conservative member of parliament who was active in women's issues. The Duchess of Atholl compares the issue of clitorectidomy to that of suttee – in 1828, the British government in India banned the practice of burning widows on their husbands' funeral pyres. Eleanor Rathbone was a well-known feminist activist in the Labour Party, who advocated for the rights of mothers. How did Atholl and Rathbone resemble and differ from those who wanted to abolish the regulation of prostitution in the late nineteenth century?

Historian Susan Pedersen has written that it was difficult enough for them to bring up issues of women's health but nearly impossible to articulate the need for female sexual pleasure. Many doctors consulted by the British authorities assumed that the minor form of clitoridectomy, in which only the clitoris was removed, was harmless because it did not interfere with childbirth, failing to recognize its inhibiting effect on female sexual pleasure.[4]

The controversy fed into nationalist organization at this time. Britain dominated Kenya as a colony, and imported white settlers, who monopolized all the fertile land and demanded that the Kikuyu leave their own lands and work for them. In fact, the native Kenyans were prohibited from owning or renting land or growing coffee. Removed from their lands, fearing detribalization, initiation rituals were among the only ways the Kikuyu could retain their identity. But they were also organizing in modern political ways, forming the Kikuyu Central Association, to demand more rights from the British, and eventually independence. In response, the Labour Party in Britain advocated the principle of "native paramountcy." On one hand, they wanted to protect the Kikuyu against labor exploitation by white settlers. On the other, they claimed that they were not yet ready for the vote, and that the British should slowly prepare them for the modern world through education and welfare. The Kikuyu found this to be inadequate and patronizing. To resist the British, they demonstrated against the banning of clitoridectomy.

Jomo Kenyatta was one of the leaders of the KCA and himself caught in between tradition and modernity. The son of a peasant family, he went to Britain, where he eventually studied anthropology. The excerpt here is from his book, *Facing Mount Kenya*, which explained Kikuyu customs as harmonious and communitarian, rather than primitive, as portrayed by whites. Why was clitoridectomy so important to Kikuyu, according to Kenyatta? Was it written from a masculine point of view?

Notes

1   In British sexual manuals this notion first appeared in 1938; earlier manuals emphasized the clitoris. Hera Cook, *The Long Sexual Revolution: English Women, Sex, and Contraception 1800–1975* (Oxford: Oxford University Press, 2004), 209.

2   Lisa Appignanesi and John Forrester, *Freud's Women* (New York: Basic Books, 1992), 441.

3   Lynn M. Thomas, "Imperial Concerns and 'Women's Affairs': State Efforts to Regulate Clitoridectomy and Eradicate Abortion in Meru, Kenya, c.1910–1950," *Journal of African History* 39, no. 1 (1998): 121–145. For clitoridectomy more recently, see Edwins Laban Moogi Gwako, "Continuity and Change in the Practice of Clitoridectomy in Kenya: A Case-Study of the Abagusii," *Journal of Modern African Studies* 33, no. 2 (1995): 333–337.

4   Susan Pedersen, "National Bodies, Unspeakable Acts: The Sexual Politics of Colonial Policy-Making," *Journal of Modern History* 63, no. 4 (1991): 647–680.

Chapter 20

Bodil Folke Frederiksen

JOMO KENYATTA, MARIE BONAPARTE AND BRONISLAW MALINOWSKI ON CLITORIDECTOMY AND FEMALE SEXUALITY (2008)

Introduction

CONTROL OF FEMALE SEXUALITY and reproduction became highly topical in Great Britain around 1930 because of the so-called female 'circumcision' controversy. Clitoridectomy first erupted as a conflict zone in Kenya in the mid 1920s and accounts of the practice and controversy hit the press in London in 1929, shortly after the reconfirmation in Parliament by the Labour government of 'native paramountcy' in Kenya.[1] The fracas over the ownership of women's bodies took place in mission settlements, particularly in rural areas close to Nairobi, where Western education, religion and social ideals engaged and sometimes clashed with African cosmology and social organization. The controversy involved debate between international, national and local groupings, and between different versions of tradition and modernity. An emerging African nationalist modernity that incorporated elements of social organization and traditional customs, such as female 'circumcision', was, for a while, in line with the thinking and political approach of the colonial regime. A different 'scientific' and egalitarian modernity, pushed by reformist forces in the British political system and Protestant missions in Kenya, challenged the right of communities to uphold what was seen as a barbaric custom. To the leading African nationalists the perpetuation of the rites connected with female 'circumcision' and the cutting itself came to be at the heart of the anti-colonial struggle.[2]

Clitoridectomy was common among several ethnic groups in Kenya, including the Kikuyu, leaders of nationalist opposition. It involved the partial or total surgical removal of the clitoris and in many cases the labia minora and part of labia majora as an element in *irua*, an elaborate initiation into adulthood.[3] Colonial authorities were well informed of the custom and on the whole tolerated the cutting. From the mid 1920s the powerful

Protestant missions put pressure on the Kenya Government to outlaw female 'circumcision' and the whole of the *irua* ritual it was embedded in, because of its harmful effects on women's health and for reasons of the dignity and equality of women. The Church of Scotland Mission banned church members who refused to sign a declaration, the *kirore*, promising to refrain from 'circumcision' of their daughters. The leading African political organization, the Kikuyu Central Association (KCA), defended the ritual and the cutting on social and cultural grounds. In their view, 'the rite delineated right from wrong, purity from impurity, insiders from outsiders' – it constituted the deep structure of Kikuyu society.[4] The result was an upsurge of African organizations that encouraged their members to secede from missions and mission controlled education. The political crisis heightened the influence of the KCA, but also gave rise to African organizations that were in favour of a ban. The Kenya government hesitantly supported the initiatives of the Protestant missions; the metropolitan government did so more wholeheartedly, urged on by prominent feminist politicians who were appalled at what they knew of the custom and its consequences. The dissension over clitoridectomy consolidated African cultural nationalist resistance and elaborated founding ideas for the full-fledged Mau Mau liberation movement of the 1950s. It also demonstrated that visions of women's equality and liberation, as they were debated in Europe, were not at the time seen as relevant by leading African nationalists.

For a while, around 1930, African women's bodies were the battleground on which colonial officials, metropolitan politicians, Protestant missionaries and differently positioned African men and women fought.[5] Who owned women's bodies – the missionary-medical establishment, the imperial government, African men, or perhaps African women themselves? In the general clamour the voices of African women, the experts on clitoridectomy, were rarely heard. What were their experiences of the operation itself and its consequences for sexual relations and reproduction? Both in Kenya and in Britain a largely medical discourse of female reproduction and motherhood was available to the conflicting parties,[6] whereas talking in public about women's sexual desire and pleasure had to be circumspect or was not possible, although women undoubtedly did talk openly among themselves. The central argument of doctors, missionaries and politicians in favour of a ban was that clitoridectomy was harmful to each individual woman in her reproductive function and to the vitality of the population as a whole. The function of the clitoris as a site of sexual pleasure was 'unspeakable', as Susan Pedersen pointed out in her article on the debates in Great Britain: 'the simple operation on the clitoris did not affect a woman's capacity to give birth, and the medical establishment in Britain seemed unable to imagine any other arguments against the practice'.[7] The taboo on recognizing and naming female sexual pleasure contributed to the toleration of clitoridectomy.

However the silence was not complete. During this period men and women involved in the struggle for women's equality and sexual reform movements in Europe had begun to research and debate women's sexuality from the perspective of women's sexual fulfilment. It had been known for a long time that orgasm was not a precondition for conception;[8] was it also independent of men? Sigmund Freud's influential *Female Sexuality* from the early 1930s argued that a transfer of erotic sensitivity from the clitoris to the vagina occurred at adolescence and that this transfer was the basis of 'normal' sexual development for women. In Britain, Marie Stopes celebrated conjugal love with its promise of both male and female pleasure in her widely read manuals, *Married Love* and *Enduring Passion*. Others questioned the occurrence of vaginal orgasm as a 'normal' part of coition, most persistently one of Freud's prominent pupils, the French psychoanalyst Marie Bonaparte. According to her the transfer of sensitivity did not occur among large numbers of women in Europe, those that Bonaparte was familiar with, and they relied on the 'male' sexual organ, the clitoris, for their sexual satisfaction. This, she argued, caused widespread neuroses and unhappiness. As an element in her exploration of women's sexuality and in pursuit of what was 'natural', Bonaparte wanted to find out how clitoridectomy affected African women's sexual response. Her theory was that because of African free sexuality and possibly because of the prevalence of clitoridectomy, African women might be better 'vaginalized', as she expressed it, and thus more feminine than European women. In tune with earlier and contemporary discussions within and between anthropology and psychoanalysis, Bonaparte situated her research of the problematic in a framework that combined anthropological knowledge of sexuality in European and African societies with Freudian theories of the universality of the Oedipus complex. In so doing she threw herself headlong into discussions of the role of repression and sublimation of sexual drives for the development of social and intellectual capabilities of Europeans versus Africans.

Bonaparte's views on the role of 'clitoridal' sexuality, as she called it, came indirectly to influence one of the key texts of Kenyan cultural nationalism. The ethnographic monograph, *Facing Mount Kenya: the Traditional Life of the Gikuyu*, by Kenya's future president, Jomo Kenyatta, was an outcome of his Diploma dissertation, supervised by Bronislaw Malinowski at London School of Economics (LSE). Kenyatta constructed female 'circumcision', with its ritual reconfirmation of generation and gender identity, as the nucleus that held together the Kikuyu ethnic nation. Similarly Kenyatta's version of clitoridectomy, informed by his nationalist politics and Malinowski's functionalist anthropology, influenced Bonaparte's major work, *Female Sexuality*. An engagement with anthropology and psychoanalysis and a particular interest in clitoridectomy brought the three intellectuals together for a while in the mid 1930s. Their exchange of views occurred around a visit by Kenyatta to Bonaparte in Paris, arranged by Malinowski, his teacher and her friend.

The meeting and the discussions surrounding it had implications for the contemporary and our present understandings of women's sexuality in Europe and Africa. Their accounts became part of the knowledge constructions of anthropology and psychoanalysis – one discipline was central to both colonial oppression and emancipation, the other both to the consolidation of patriarchy and to movements of sexual liberation. This essay will describe the meeting in Paris and its background in the context of social-reform movements and African nationalism and will discuss the interchange between anthropology and psychoanalysis concerning women's sexual experience that surrounded it and some consequences of the knowledge generated.

The Paris meeting and its background

At the time of the meeting in Paris, early in 1935, Jomo Kenyatta was a young exile politician and student of anthropology at LSE. Marie Bonaparte (1882–1962) was a recognized writer and psychoanalyst, his senior by fifteen years. She was the great-granddaughter of Napoleon's brother, Lucien, and became the wife of Prince George of Greece and Denmark – marrying into the interrelated royal houses of Europe. Her mother died in childbirth. Marie was brought up by her father, Prince Roland, who was preoccupied with his work as a geographer and anthropologist, and his mother, Princess Pierre, a widow. As a rich child with these distinguished antecedents, Marie was protected from the world in her lonely childhood. She was sickly and imagined that she was destined to an early death, like her mother. She was subjected to a severe health regime of seclusion and a variety of medicines. Private tutors were in charge of her education – her gender and class prevented her from having a formal training, although from early on she ardently desired to learn anatomy and become a medical doctor. She coveted precise knowledge of 'the hermetic secrets of the inner structure of the human body', but lack of formal qualifications prevented her entering university.[9] Her interest in medicine and biology persisted, but from the mid 1920s, when she was in her forties, she turned to psychoanalysis in order to unearth the 'secrets' of the female human body.

Bonaparte considered herself a masculine woman, suffering from 'clitoridalism' – that is, she was unable to experience a vaginal orgasm. She attributed what she thought of as her frigidity to an 'obsessional neurosis' connected to the repression of sexuality in childhood.[10] When she was twenty-five, she married the Danish Prince George. He was thirteen years older than her and she identified him as a father substitute. Their two children, a son and a daughter, were born in 1908 and 1910. Marie was aware that her husband had homosexual tendencies, expressed in a close relationship to his ten-years-older uncle, Prince Valdemar of Denmark. She herself had had several lovers and devoted a journal to each of them.[11] In 1935, at the time of her encounter with Kenyatta, she was in her fifties, at the height of her productivity, and had just taken a new lover.

From her childhood and for the rest of her life Bonaparte was a prolific writer and thought of writing as her phallic activity.[12] She began to publish late, but had started to write as a young child. When she was between seven and ten years old, she filled five copy-books (*cahiers*) with tales, puzzles, exercises, homemade proverbs, fantastic drawings and angry, violent fragments – mostly concerned with her beloved but distant father. Her fairy tales teemed with ogres, chasms and innocent lost girls. They show that she harboured fantasies that her father and grandmother had conspired to murder her mother.

In her own account, Bonaparte had forgotten having written the notebooks until she found them after the death of her father in 1924. Over the next three years, she underwent psychoanalysis with Freud, using the *Cahiers* as the basis. She was at work on them at the time of Kenyatta's visit, and in 1939 she published the first volume out of four in French with Imago Publishers in London at her own expense – now as illustration of her early psycho-sexual development with extensive interpretative comments based on her analysis with Freud. They were later translated into English, but restricted to members of the Psychoanalytical Society. Bonaparte's first scientific essay, published in 1924, on the anatomical causes of female frigidity, foreshadowed her lifelong preoccupation with female sexuality. From the mid 1920s onwards, she wrote articles on the relationships between biology and sexuality, between psychoanalysis and anthropology and numerous psychoanalytical case stories.[13]

The background of Jomo Kenyatta (1897–1978) could not have been more different. He was born of peasants in Kenya Colony (as it was then), took part in the household economic activities of his family and was sent to the Church of Scotland Mission School at Thogoto, in Southern Kikuyuland. Here he underwent the Kikuyu circumcision rituals and was also baptized. One of his mentors was the Scots missionary and medical doctor, John W. Arthur, who was later to become his fierce opponent over the acceptability of clitoridectomy. Following his double initiation, he found work in Nairobi, married, settled in a self-built house on the outskirts of the town and in 1920 became a father. He involved himself in politics, first in the East African Association founded by a pioneer of resistance against colonialism, Harry Thuku, and later in the KCA of which he became General Secretary in 1929. For a period in the late 1920s he was the editor of *Muigwithania*, a Kikuyu newspaper – the first in any African language in Kenya.

In 1929, at the height of the crisis over clitoridectomy, the KCA sent Kenyatta to London to impress on the British government the Association's views on land alienation. He did so with the help of well-placed political friends who also encouraged him to discuss the cultural politics of clitoridectomy with the imperial government.[14] He stayed in Europe for sixteen years, interrupted only once by a return journey to Kenya. In Britain, Russia, Germany, France and Denmark Kenyatta mingled with progressive intellectuals. He had friends among Quakers, communists, pan-Africans, in the Independent Labour Party and the Labour Party. He lectured on Workers' Educational Association courses and pursued an interest in farming co-operatives as a development path that might be relevant to the post-colonial future of Kenya. After 1933 Kenyatta's political mission in so far as it was directed at the Colonial Office and establishment politicians in London had run out of steam, and not only officials but also some important friends lost interest in him. He reinvented himself as a student and an informant to linguists on Kikuyu, first at University College then at LSE, where Malinowski was instrumental in obtaining a scholarship for him.

Bonaparte and Bronislaw Malinowski (1884–1942) had met at the beginning of the 1930s, and found areas of passionate common interest, psychoanalysis being one. Malinowski was ambitious, hardworking and a victim of nervous conditions. Like Bonaparte, he was the only child of a distant, academic father. His wife, Elsie Masson, suffered from multiple sclerosis and the organization of their daily lives and that of their three children was complicated. In Marie he found an insightful friend with whom he could discuss professional as well as personal matters. How close they were is clear from a letter from 1932: 'I often return to the talks we had together, in our late quiet evenings – Shall we call them substitute psychoanalysis?'[15] Their married partners approved of the friendship, although there may have been a hint of acrimony when, later, Masson wrote to Bonaparte: 'My husband came back from Paris looking very well, and seeming also very stimulated in mind as well as in body'.[16] Her tone, when she was very ill, in a letter to her husband where she comments on his plan to visit Marie in Paris, was tolerant and humorous, but may have had an edge: 'I consign you to the care of all the out-of-work kings and princes who congregate around Marie for their dole'.[17] Elsie Masson died in 1935.

The relationship between Kenyatta, Bonaparte and Malinowski was mutually beneficial. Kenyatta was a valuable informant to both Bonaparte and Malinowski, who saw him as the prototype of the 'changing African' – a representative of modernizing educated Africans, with whom the colonial establishment would have to reckon and come to terms.[18] In the course of his seminars at the LSE Malinowski became increasingly sceptical of the superiority of white civilization. The participation in his seminars of Kenyatta and other gifted students from developing societies played a role in his disillusionment with colonial politics and strengthened his hopes of future enlightened leadership of independent African nations.[19] Kenyatta became involved in the controversial issue of Italy's invasion of Abyssinia, and increasingly in pan-African exile politics. At the beginning of the Second World War, Malinowski had left for the United States, Kenyatta was stranded in England and Bonaparte and her family lived in exile in Cape Town. She pursued her research into psychoanalysis, while Kenyatta with other African and West Indian exile politicians organized the fifth pan-African conference in Manchester in 1945 – a harbinger of the struggle for the independence of Kenya that was to preoccupy him after his return home in 1946. Around 1950 he became famous as the alleged leader of the Mau Mau revolt against British rule in Kenya and in 1953 the colonial regime imprisoned him for nine years on a conviction of 'managing Mau Mau and being a member of that society'.[20] At independence, Kenyatta was appointed president of his country and remained so until his death in 1978.

The background of the meeting between these three was the coincidence of the East African crisis over clitoridectomy with the discussion in psychoanalytical circles about the nature of female sexuality. Kenyatta was centrally involved in the former controversy, Bonaparte in the latter. During the crisis, which pitted Kikuyu nationalists against feminists, missionaries and the colonial government, Kenyatta had emerged as a spokesman for those who defended the cutting as an integral part of the social custom of initiation, on grounds of female modesty, sexual discipline and cultural nationalism.[21] Bonaparte and Kenyatta discussed their ideas on sexuality and the role of clitoridectomy with Malinowski, who was conducting influential seminars at LSE on the impact of the West in Africa: 'Culture Contact in Africa' and 'The Anthropology of Changing African Cultures'. Both Kenyatta and Bonaparte's anthropologist son, Prince Peter, were participants and they became friends. In tune with the preoccupations of Malinowski and as a scholarly rejoinder to what he regarded as 'colonial' positions on clitoridectomy, Kenyatta presented an ethnographic account of clitoridectomy and its social functions at Malinowski's seminar in November 1935. Prince Peter took notes.

At the time of the Paris meeting the friendship between Bonaparte and Malinowski was at its height. Prior to his two-month tour of Southern and Eastern Africa for the International African Institute,[22] Malinowski had scrutinized catalogues from Fortnum and Mason to find the appropriate camp equipment for a planned African safari by Bonaparte, and talked to 'one or two people in the Colonial Office' who might help her.[23] However, her plans of travelling to East Africa came to nothing. Malinowski then promised to investigate the question of clitoridectomy for her and to look for suitable informants. As a substitute for her travels in Africa, Malinowski arranged that Kenyatta should visit Bonaparte in Paris. He was eminently suited to enlighten her in view of his training as an anthropologist and since to the Kikuyu male and female circumcision was a central element of the initiation into adulthood. Malinowski informed her that Kenyatta would 'be happy to put several hours a day at your disposal in order to give you an idea of how to pronounce Kikuyu words . . . and to give you some information about the sociology of the Kikuyu'.[24] In April 1935, Kenyatta travelled to Paris at Bonaparte's expense to pay the Princess a visit. He stayed for around ten days. The meeting went well. Bonaparte took Kenyatta to Versailles, and in the shade of trees in the park they debated the physiology, psychology and politics of clitoridectomy. Shortly after the visit, Bonaparte wrote to Malinowski: 'I want to tell you that I had the greatest pleasure at receiving Kenyatta for ten days in Paris; he was really charming and we worked very well. I got a lot of information about the Kikuyu and learnt even a little of the language. It was all very interesting'.[25] Malinowski wrote back that 'Kenyatta was very grateful to you for his visit to Paris',[26] which sounds out of character. More than Kenyatta, Bonaparte was the person who had reason to be grateful: Kenyatta 'subsequently sent her a twenty-page, detailed description of the girls' initiation rites, including the excision of the clitoris'.[27]

The 'circumcision' controversy in Kenya

What were the trajectories that led Kenyatta to an interest in clitoridectomy? The struggles over emancipation of women and of peoples oppressed by colonialism were connected in the 1930s social-reform movements. In London (and later Moscow) Kenyatta was closely linked to different groupings that debated and carried out personal, political and social reform.[28] In his writings and political practice he had to deal with rapid social change in the wake of colonial modernity in East Africa. The controversy over female circumcision loomed large. The British were particularly concerned with the consequences of clitoridectomy among the Kikuyu and the related ethnic groups, Embu and Meru, who lived close to the colonial capital, Nairobi. It was well known that the cutting affected not only the clitoris but also the surrounding tissue and made sexual intercourse difficult and childbirth dangerous. In colonial attempts to regulate the custom, the difference between a 'major' and a 'minor' operation was seen as decisive and became the medical justification for not enforcing an outright ban on the custom. The tendency among medical experts and officials who took their advice was to regard the 'minor' operation as not harmful to reproductive health, their key concern. The matter was discussed at a conference of East African governors in 1926. They decided that the custom 'should not be interfered with' as it was of 'very ancient origin', but recommended that the less brutal form, the removal of the clitoris only, should be encouraged – since this operation 'would appear to be harmless'.[29] As a consequence, the Chief Native Commissioner in Kenya, G. V. Maxwell, sent a circular letter to Provincial Senior Commissioners, citing the Embu Local Native Council (LNC) as an example to be followed: they had made it 'an offence . . . to make an incision of greater extent or depth than is necessary for the removal of the clitoris during girls' circumcision'. The letter urged the officials to persuade other councils to do the same: 'It must be made clear that there is no idea of total prohibition but merely a desire, in the interests of humanity, native eugenics, and increase of population, to revert to the milder form of the operation, which is indeed more in keeping with ancient tribal usage'.[30]

The LNCs, manned by the District Commissioner and African male elders, were central institutions for carrying out British policies locally, particularly those that interfered with values upheld by the community, such as the ceremony of initiation. Here was a successful attempt to turn them into instruments of reform. However, their role was purely advisory and in spite of the adoption of the resolution by several LNCs, the decision had little effect in practice.[31] Pulled by different forces, the government positioned itself between medical enlightenment and respect for supposedly ingrained African traditions. This dual approach was in line with a policy of recognition of African customs, needed for the version of indirect rule practised in Kenya, and at the same time it showed a routine disregard of the welfare of African women, who were not a political force to reckon with.

Prominent members of the British Parliament had taken up the anti-clitoridectomy cause in 1929, and the controversy was an embarrassment for the new Labour government. The conservative Scottish politician, the Duchess of Atholl, had a long-standing interest in the social conditions of women in the colonies. At a meeting held by the Church of Scotland Mission (CSM: leading crusaders against clitoridectomy) she was alerted to the practice of clitoridectomy and the crisis in Kenya. With Eleanor Rathbone, feminist and social activist, she started the 'Committee for the Protection of Coloured Women in the

Crown Colonies'. The Committee organized an inquiry into the practice and the rites that accompanied it. Missionaries in East Africa responded and reported that 'feasting and beer drinking . . . and much immoral dancing' were part of the initiation celebrations, and 'even the old married women are painted up in . . . a heathen fashion'.[32] Armed with this and other lopsided information, Atholl made a strong speech in Parliament in the face of indifference, embarrassment and hostility from male politicians. The controversy generated divisions along gender rather than party political lines. According to Pedersen left-leaning 'radical anti-colonialists' were more preoccupied with upholding male privilege and defending white women against black men in the case of violent disturbances than with understanding the situation of African women.[33]

At the national level in Kenya, the main contenders in the conflict were the Protestant missions in Kikuyuland, particularly the Church of Scotland Mission, and the KCA. Arthur, the head of the CSM and Kenyatta's former teacher, took centre stage when he ordered that Christians who would not refrain from clitoridectomy should be refused communion. He issued a 'Memorandum on the Circumcision of Kikuyu Native Girls' where he condemned the colonial regime's conciliatory approach to the problem and related the continuation of 'the brutal ceremony' to the 'anti-European, anti-Government and anti-Mission propaganda' by the KCA on the one hand, and indifference and inactivity by the government on the other.[34]

At the local level Africans were divided and the divisions cut across generations and genders. Some African men were willing to pledge that their daughters would not be circumcised under the threat that they would otherwise be expelled from the church and miss the connected educational opportunities. Other groups of men, many of them educated at the missions, refused to give up *irua*, fearing outside influence and the erosion of control over women and land. African elders at Arthur's mission station pointed out that as a result of upholding the ban, their community would be divided in two, the educated being no longer Kikuyu but *misheni* (uncivilized people), 'since in order to get an education a young man or woman must repudiate circumcision . . . and ipso facto repudiate his elders, his clan and his tribe'.[35] Many left mission churches in protest and founded or entered independent churches and schools.[36] Women were caught in the fray. Tabitha Kanogo's account of the dilemma faced by Agnes Wairimu Hinga, a young woman at the time, torn between a traditionalist maternal uncle and a modernizing Christian brother, gives a rare insight into how women actively took part in and influenced the course of the controversy. A regional African organization, the Kikuyu Progressive Party, disagreed strongly with KCA's defence of clitoridectomy. They supported a total ban, using arguments that were parallel to those of the Europeans.[37] Modernity touched Africans in many different ways and the realities on the ground were more complex than Arthur implied. As the District Commissioner in Nyeri noted, those who resisted any modification of the custom were the 'left wing of the KCA', who also favoured 'secular education . . . beer drinking and polygamy', and they were 'the more progressive and educated members of the community'.[38] Kenyatta made the same point ten years later, when, in *Facing Mount Kenya*, he observed that 'educated, intelligent Kikuyus' still clung to the custom.[39]

This might well be a characterization of Kenyatta himself. However, in his talks on the issue in London with the parliamentary undersecretary of state at the Colonial Office, Thomas Shiels, a medical doctor, Kenyatta asserted that, 'for himself he was opposed to the practice but that the thing could only be done away with by education'.[40] At this time, he supported that medical experts should be sent to the African reserves on information campaigns. Soon after, he changed his mind. After having been back in Kenya from 1930 to 1931, Kenyatta, now General Secretary of the KCA and more than ever dependent on support from the Kikuyu, defended female circumcision as an institution 'at the very heart of Kikuyu culture'.[41] As we have seen, this was also the position of the KCA, prior to his becoming the leader.

Due to the influence of British reformers and feminists and the uncompromising stance of the Presbyterian missionaries, policies in Kenya on the practice hardened at the end of the decade: 'By the end of 1929 all LNCs except Nyeri had passed a resolution banning the severe form of clitoridectomy'.[42] The decrees were not enforced, however, and colonial policy was characterized by 'confusion and compromise'.[43] The controversy abated in the early 1930s but it had far-reaching consequences. It opened new areas of intervention by providing entry points in the management of women's sexuality that were useful to both British paternalists and African men. According to one of its first historians, John Spencer, it 'changed fundamentally relations between Africans and Europeans; between Africans and the missions and between Africans and the Government'.[44] In the view of John Lonsdale, the controversy was a 'heated exchange in a local conversation' that did not decisively alter the course of Kenyan nationalist history, or metropolitan policies.[45] According to Kanogo the conflict had enduring effects. It sharpened the tension between the Kenyan state and the cultural-nationalist Kikuyu and had far-reaching outcomes: 'the significance of the controversy in the definition of ethnicity and womanhood, lingered throughout the colonial period. It became a text in cultural nationalism and was linked to the outbreak of Mau Mau, the liberation war that rocked the colony between 1952 and 1956'. Just as importantly '[t]he clitoridectomy controversy . . . provided ample room for official privileging of Western knowledge and served to legitimate the colonial project'.[46]

Facing Mount Kenya and Female Sexuality

At the time of the meeting with Bonaparte, Kenyatta worked on *Facing Mount Kenya*. In key chapters he confronted the dominant European positions on clitoridectomy. Bonaparte was researching and writing drafts of articles that were later collected and published as *Female Sexuality*, the work that contains her most coherent arguments on the connection between clitoridectomy and female sexuality. Malinowski assisted them both. This section traces common origins of the two works. It discusses Kenyatta's treatment of the role of clitoridectomy in Kikuyu society in the light of influences from Malinowski, Bonaparte and the Kenyan settler ideologue Louis Leakey. They all made their imprint on his accounts and in his monograph they were implicit partners in the debate on the social and political implications of the management of African sexuality. The section goes on to discuss matters of women's sexuality in Bonaparte's book, relevant to the argument about clitoridectomy and women's pleasure, again in the light of the transnational conversation on women's sexuality.

Facing Mount Kenya was the outcome of Kenyatta's LSE dissertation, supervised by Malinowski. It is probably the most well-known and influential African scholarly work of its time, written according to the rules of functionalist anthropology. It represented traditional Kikuyuland, prior to colonization, as a cohesive and well-ordered society, characterized by functional interplay between humans and the environment. Kikuyu society was a mirror of European polities, demanding recognition – it was a potential nation state with customs, institutions, education, a history, norms and values.[47] It was also a society in the throes of dramatic change.

In his preface Kenyatta offers to give 'the African point of view'. He knows that some 'professional friends of Africa' will be offended when reading the book because they would prefer to remain friends of Africa for eternity, 'provided only that the African will continue to play the part of an ignorant savage so that they can monopolise the office of interpreting his mind and speaking for him'.[48] Here he refers to Leakey,[49] his fellow student, academic rival and political enemy, who had grown up in Kikuyuland as the son of the first translator of the New Testament into Kikuyu. Leakey and Kenyatta competed for funds, recognition and influence. In 1931 Leakey published a short article on female circumcision among the Kikuyu, whose ideas and actual formulations Kenyatta made use of.[50] Later, after Kenyatta's arrest in 1952 as the alleged leader of the Mau Mau uprising, Leakey helped secure his conviction.

As a counterpoint to Leakey Kenyatta questioned the legitimacy and validity of missionary and settler constructions of African sexuality and provided an anthropological background for the social regulation of sexuality:

> The large place given to sex in the initiation ceremonies is often misunderstood by Europeans, as if sexual indulgence is encouraged for its own sake; the obscenity of songs and dances and the profligacy associated with many of these ceremonies are held to prove unusual depravity. On the contrary the Africans look upon these ceremonies as a final stage, in which boys and girls must be given full knowledge in the matters relating to sex, to prepare them for future activities in their own homesteads and in the community.[51]

In the functionalist scheme of things one element, sex, could not be removed from the organic whole that constituted the initiation ceremonies. Similarly the cut itself was inseparable from the totality of interdependent elements of the rite. Kenyatta concluded that 'for the present it is impossible for a member of the tribe to imagine an initiation without clitoridectomy . . . the abolition of the surgical element in this custom means to the Gikuyu the abolition of the whole institution'.[52] He argued that the circumcision ceremony for both boys and girls had great psychological and social significance: it was a prerequisite for adulthood and full inclusion in tribe and nation, for both historical and structural reasons.

The real argument lies not in the defence of the surgical operation or its details, but in the understanding of a very important fact in the tribal psychology of the Gikuyu, namely, that this operation is still regarded as the very essence of an institution which has got enormous education, social, moral and religious implications, besides the operation.[53]

He described the young man's transformation after circumcision: 'He is a full-grown, a proper man, a full member of the tribe . . . he can think seriously of marrying and putting up his own homestead'.[54]

The chapters on 'Initiation of Boys and Girls' and 'Sex Life among Young People' give an empirical account of the cutting and the 'circumcision' ceremonies. Kenyatta's description is likely to be close to the one he presented at Malinowski's seminar in

November 1935, whose contents we know from the notes taken by Bonaparte's son, Peter, who was present, and to the account he gave Bonaparte at their meeting, six months earlier. His account was clearly written from a masculine point of view and demonstrated a strong anthropological interest in documenting tribal rituals rather than empathy with the girls who had little power to resist. The narrative drive and the abundance of details in his description of the excision and the subsequent healing process testify to his knowledge of the practice. He made light of the pain of the operation and insisted that the girls were given ample time and care to recover. He also downplayed the harmful effects in relation to birth, claiming that medical doctors only saw the cases that had gone wrong, and that the majority of Kikuyu women had easy births. When it came to the practice and consequences of clitoridectomy Kenyatta went to great lengths in order to defend his expertise. His aunt was an operator, and he claimed that his knowledge of what girls experience came from 'relatives and close friends who have gone through the initiation'.[55] He sought to position himself as an authority, in a different class from the 'well meaning anthropologists who have had experience of the difficulties of field-work in various parts of the world'.[56] As a whole *Facing Mount Kenya* is a 'masterly propaganda document', as Kenyatta's biographer notes,[57] and its author demonstrates extra care in the controversial area of female 'circumcision'.

Like Kenyatta Malinowski wanted to ferret out the social and political function and significance of female 'circumcision'. In a letter to Bonaparte he found what he called the '*idée maîtresse* of the whole thing' a puzzle. Why is it that 'the Kikuyu has taken it as a rallying point of East African nationalism?'[58] Two years later, in his address to an audience at Harvard University, he was no closer to an answer: 'That no scientific theory will be able to explain certain queer customs of kinship and domesticity may be granted . . . Why do some people practice clitoridectomy and others infibulation? Why do we find in one culture circumcision, and in another subincision? It is difficult to answer'.[59] He reported on his fieldwork among 'the Masai and the Djagga on the slopes of Mount Meru and Kilimanjaro in Tanzania' to his friend and colleague: 'I am at last among people who do practise clitoridectomy and who are very keen on it', he wrote and continued, 'I have had excellent informants in all these places, both male and female and mindful of your instructions not to miss any opportunity of studying this subject, I have worked on it pretty fully'.[60] He went on,

> the natives have a strong feeling that it is as shameful for a girl to be uncircumcised as for the boy. They regard the two operations as entirely parallel and homologous. The same word, *IRINO* (Djagga) describes both of them.

Circumcision changes young people into 'something more complete, *volkommen*, really adult and human'.[61] Malinowski and Bonaparte agreed on the 'homology' between male and female 'circumcision'. He noted the different outcomes regarding sexuality that the ceremony and operation had for young men and women:

> As regards the physiology of the matter there is a general conviction that whereas circumcision makes a boy sexually more libidinous, the girl becomes less so after the operation. So that parents are said to be keen on the operation so as to keep their daughters chaste.[62]

In the same vein Kenyatta speculated that one of the motives for what he calls 'trimming the clitoris' was the control of female sexuality – clitoridectomy would 'prevent girls from developing sexual feelings around that point'.[63] Leakey saw it differently: he thought that clitoridectomy as well as 'the custom now fallen into disuse' of 'making small cuts on the pubic area' as preparations for married life, was aimed at enhancing women's sexual pleasure.[64]

The cosmopolitan Bonaparte was not interested in cultural nationalism, but she was interested in female pleasure. To her the issue was the sources and evolution of masculinity and femininity, women's everyday experience of sexuality and the precise location of orgasm. What is the relationship between nature and culture in shaping women's reliance on either vaginal or clitoridal eroticism? Like Freud she accepted the bisexual character of humans as a fact. To her the widespread occurrence of 'clitoridalism' indicated that bisexuality persisted.

Bonaparte believed in Freud's account of female sexuality, that full sexual enjoyment for adult women implied the transfer of erotic sensations from the clitoris to the vagina – what she called 'the mysterious passage of feminine libido'.[65] Women who did not experience this transfer were exaggeratedly masculine, their Oedipal process having taken the wrong course. Why did nature play that cruel trick on women, sentencing them to an existence of unfulfilled sexual desires – 'what could cause such a frequent anomaly?'[66] In her early career Bonaparte believed that their lack of vaginal enjoyment during the sexual act might be remedied by an operation that moved the clitoris closer to the vagina entry, the 'Halban-Narjani operation'.[67] In researching the matter, she was her own primary case-material. She underwent the operation more than once.[68] In the 1930s she had dismissed the surgical approach to modelling women's sexuality as 'pre-analytical and erroneous' and argued in favour of psychoanalysis: 'Psycho-analysis . . . will be a surer and more elegant solution to such disturbances of instinct'.[69] She believed this to be true in her own case. With the help of the *Cahiers*, Freud helped her recover a crucial memory. The two-year-old Marie had been present on several occasions while her nurse and her father's groom had sexual intercourse. She thought that the retrieval of this memory helped cure her of painful psychosomatic conditions.

Bonaparte's personal interests in surgical interventions on the female sexual organs and their effects on the female libido persisted, as documented in *Female Sexuality*. This concern went along with a wish not to fundamentally question 'natural' heterosexual practices. She was convinced that a full understanding of the causes and effects of clitoridectomy might solve the puzzle of female sexuality. In order to confirm that African women were not inhibited by the 'masculinity complex' and had a more satisfactory sexual life than European women, she needed to get access to circumcised African women's sexual experience. In 'Female Mutilation among Primitive Peoples and Their Psychical Parallels in Civilization' she attempted a cross-cultural analysis of clitoridectomy. She discussed the researcher's difficulties in getting hold of reliable data that might truthfully illuminate the relation between clitoridectomy and sexual response. No 'ethnologist' had researched the question, and no black woman had, as far as Bonaparte was aware, 'surrendered . . . her secrets through psychoanalysis'.[70] Here she stated that 'in antiquity, as to-day, whole races have practised and still practise surgical operations on the external female genitals', and that these practices, 'unlike the Halban-Narjani operation, are generally not pro- but anti-clitoridal', that is they work against female pleasure.[71] As we have seen, this was the view of Kenyatta, who thought that clitoridectomy contributed to lessen and control the sexual feelings of women, thus making them feminine and receptive to men. According to Bonaparte this was also Freud's view: he thought that 'excision of the clitoris, which many tribes practise', constituted additional feminization of girls. 'Is the male, in excising that phallic vestige, the clitoris, principally concerned to achieve utmost "feminization" of the woman and . . . force her libido to take the vaginal path, now the only one left to it?' If this were the case, argued Bonaparte, it would help the transition to vaginal sexuality and African women might be 'more frequently, and better, "vaginalized" than their European sisters'.[72] On the basis of her scant evidence she concluded that if clitoridectomy, both in Europe and Africa, was aimed at diminishing the capabilities of women for orgasm, the operation was in vain.

[. . .]

The entanglement of psychoanalysis and anthropology that occurred around the meeting between Bonaparte, Kenyatta and Malinowski influenced the contemporary and also our present discourse on the universals and particulars of female sexuality. Their encounter led to the consolidation of racial and cultural stereotypes, but also to a greater freedom in talking about women's sexuality as a legitimate concern of reform movements. They all participated in the wave of social and political reform that swept over Europe in the 1930s, connecting issues of freedom for colonized peoples to emancipation of women. They were concerned with the politics of sex and gender, and the subordinate situation of women. Kenyatta did not question the subordination, Bonaparte did. However she was uneasy about accounts of sexuality that were not premised on coition as the 'natural' activity that satisfied both men and women. In her speculations on the supposedly free sexuality of Africans she indirectly confirmed notions of African intellectual inferiority, prevalent in contemporary Western anthropological and psychoanalytical literature. Bonaparte shared Malinowski's early views on the costs of evolution in terms of a loss of a natural sexuality among Westerners, and the costs of a natural sexuality among non-Western peoples in loss of civilization. Malinowski later dismissed psychoanalytic generalization and became increasingly concerned with the futility of Western paternalistic and ill-informed approaches to personality and social change.

Notes

1   See Janice Boddy, *Civilizing Women: British Crusades in Colonial Sudan*, Princeton and Oxford, 2007, p. 236.
2   There is a large literature on the crisis over clitoridectomy as it unfolded in Britain and East Africa. For an overview see John Lonsdale, 'Jomo Kenyatta, God and the Modern World', in *African Modernities: Entangled Meanings in Current Debate*, ed. Jan-George Deutsch, Peter Probst and Heike Schmidt, Oxford and Portsmouth NH, 2002, pp. 31–66, pp. 54–5. See Boddy, *Civilizing Women*, for the simultaneous and linked controversy over female circumcision in colonial Sudan.
3   The common forms of female genital cutting in colonial Kenya were the following: the removal of all or part of the clitoris; the clitoris and all or part of the labia minora; the clitoris, the labia minora and all or most of the labia majora. In the latter case the 'cut edges are stitched together so as to cover the urethra and vaginal opening, leaving only a minimal opening for the passage of urine and menstrual blood'. The two first forms are known as

clitoridectomy or excision, the third as infibulation. In Kenya the two first forms were and are by far the most common. *Female 'Circumcision' in Africa: Culture Controversy and Change*, ed. Bettina Shell-Duncan and Ylva Hernlund, Boulder and London, 2000, pp. 4, 7.

4   Tabitha Kanogo, *African Womanhood in Colonial Kenya 1900–50*, Oxford, 2005, p. 74.

5   Kanogo, *African Womanhood*, p. 74.

6   See Anna Davin, 'Imperialism and Motherhood', *History Workshop Journal* 5, 1978, pp. 9–65.

7   Susan Pedersen, 'Nationalist Bodies, Unspeakable Acts: the Sexual Politics of Colonial Policy-making', *Journal of Modern History* 63, 1991, pp. 647–80, here pp. 666–7.

8   See Thomas Laqueur, 'Orgasm, Generation, and the Politics of Reproductive Biology', in *The Making of the Modern Body: Sexuality and Society in the Nineteenth Century*, ed. Catherine Gallagher and Thomas Laqueur, Berkeley, 1987, pp. 1–2.

9   Marie Bonaparte, *À la Mémoire des disparus*, Paris, 1958, vol. 2, *L'appel des Sèves. Les souvenirs de jeunesse de Marie Bonaparte*, p. 939: 'les secrets hermétiques de la structure interne du corps humain' (my translation).

10   Celia Bertin, *Marie Bonaparte: a Life*, San Diego, New York, London, 1982, p. 146.

11   Lisa Appignanesi and John Forrester, *Freud's Women* (1992), revised edn, Harmondsworth, 2000, p. 329; Bertin, *Marie Bonaparte*, p. 94, 105.

12   Appignanesi and Forrester, *Freud's Women*, p. 330.

13   On the close links between the life of Bonaparte and her psychoanalytical work, see Nellie Thompson, 'Marie Bonaparte's Theory of Female Sexuality: Fantasy and Biology', *American Imago* 60, 2003, pp. 343–78.

14   Jeremy Murray-Brown, *Kenyatta*, London, 1972, pp. 121–6.

15   Malinowski to Bonaparte, 1 Dec. 1932, Malinowski Papers (MP). Appendix/1, Correspondence with Marie Bonaparte. The British Library of Political and Economic Science, London School of Economics.

16   14 Nov. 1934, MP, Appendix 1, Correspondence with Marie Bonaparte.

17   3 March 1935, *The Story of a Marriage: the Letters of Bronislaw Malinowski and Elsie Masson*, ed. Helena Wayne, London and New York, 1995, vol. 2, p. 219.

18   Wendy James, 'The Anthropologist as Reluctant Imperialist', in *Anthropology and the Colonial Encounter*, ed. Talal Asad, London, 1973, p. 61; George W. Stocking, *After Tylor: British Social Anthropology 1888–1951*, London, 1996, pp. 412–14.

19   Bruce Berman and John Lonsdale, 'Custom, Modernity, and the Search for Kihooto: Kenyatta, Malinowski, and the Making of *Facing Mount Kenya*', in *Anthropology, European Imperialism and the Ordering of Africa*, ed. Helen Tilley and Robert Gordon, Manchester, 2005.

20   From the court's judgement, cited by Murray-Brown, *Kenyatta*, p. 320.

21   Murray-Brown, *Kenyatta*, p. 223; Lonsdale, 'Jomo Kenyatta, God and the Modern World', pp. 54–5.

22   Stocking, *After Tylor*, p. 413.

23   Malinowski to Bonaparte, 12 Dec. 1934, MP, Appendix/1, Correspondence with Marie Bonaparte.

24   Malinowski to Bonaparte, 7 March 1935, MP, Appendix/1, Correspondence with Marie Bonaparte.

25   18 April 1935, MP, Appendix/1, Correspondence with Marie Bonaparte.

26   Malinowski to Bonaparte, 2 July 1935, MP, Appendix/1, Correspondence with Marie Bonaparte.

27   Bertin, *Marie Bonaparte*, p. 192. The whereabouts of the account is not known. However 'Notes on the visit of Jomo Kenyatta in 1935' is cited in the French edition of Berlin's biography: *Marie Bonaparte*, Paris, 1982. I thank Poul Pedersen, Århus University, for this information.

28   As can be seen in Peter Abrahams's *roman à clef*, portraying exiled Africans and local reformers in London, *A Wreath for Udomo*, London, 1956.

29   The governors' memorandum, cited by Murray-Brown, *Kenyatta*, p. 159.

30   23 Aug. 1926, Circular 28: Chief Native Commissioner to all Senior Commissioners, Public
      Record Office, CO, 533/392/1. Kanogo notes that some administrators worried that African
      women who carried out the operation would not be able to make the fine anatomical
      distinctions needed for the operation to be confined to either the *glans clitoridis*, or the
      clitoris. However, as quoted by Kanogo from a letter from a District Commissioner to
      the acting Provincial Commissioner, 7 July 1931, the 'DC from Embu confirmed that he
      had no difficulty in explaining the "glans clitoridis" to Africans. As a rule, the native appears
      to be much more familiar with the structure of the parts than does the average European'.
      Kanogo, *African Womanhood*, p. 87.
31   Lynn Thomas, *Politics of the Womb: Women, Reproduction and the State in Kenya*, Berkeley,
      2003, pp. 24, 36–7, 49.
32   'Description by Miss Brown of the Church of Scotland Mission . . . of a Circumcision of
      African Girls she Witnessed in January 1929', Liverpool University Archives, Rathbone
      Papers XIV.2.1 (7), p. 1–2, cited by Boddy, *Civilizing Women*, p. 234.
33   The metropolitan debates over the question, and the symmetry between the responses of
      British 'anti-colonialist radicals' and African nationalist spokesmen, are analysed in Pedersen,
      'Nationalist Bodies', see esp. pp. 664–5, and more fully in Boddy, *Civilizing Women*,
      chap. 9.
34   28 Aug. 1929, Memorandum on the Circumcision of Kikuyu Native Girls by John Arthur,
      M.D. Extract from Confidential File, District Commissioner's Office, Embu. Kenya National
      Archives (KNA), PC/CP/8/1/1.
35   Memorandum KNA, PC/CP/8/1/1.
36   See Derek Peterson, *Creative Writing. Translation, Bookkeeping, and the Work of Imagination in
      Colonial Kenya*, Portsmouth, 2004, pp. 110–11.
37   Kanogo, *African Womanhood*, pp. 75–80, p. 89.
38   5 Oct. 1929, Office of the District Commissioner, South Nyeri to the Senior Commissioner
      Kikuyu, KNA, PC/CP/8/1.
39   Jomo Kenyatta, *Facing Mount Kenya: the Traditional Life of the Gikuyu*, London, 1938, p. 133,
      reprint Nairobi, 1989.
40   Murray-Brown, *Kenyatta*, p. 168.
41   Murray-Brown, *Kenyatta*, p. 193. According to Lonsdale, the common view among British
      officials and settlers was that this was the first of several instances in which Kenyatta 'first
      mastered, then seemed to repudiate, an aspect of modernity', 'Kenyatta, God and the
      Modern World', p. 32.
42   Kanogo, *African Womanhood*, p. 93.
43   Thomas, *Politics of the Womb*, pp. 48–51; Kanogo, *African Womanhood*, p. 91.
44   John Spencer, *The Kenya African Union*, London, 1985, p. 71, cited in Pedersen, 'Nationalist
      Bodies', p. 651, n. 10.
45   Lonsdale, 'Jomo Kenyatta, God and the Modern World', p. 55.
46   Kanogo, *African Womanhood*, pp. 97, 89.
47   On the making of the monograph see Bruce Berman and John Lonsdale, 'Louis Leakey's
      Mau Mau: A Study in the Politics of Knowledge', *History and Anthropology* 5, 1991,
      pp. 143–204; Berman and Lonsdale, 'Custom, Modernity, and the Search for Kihooto';
      Bruce Berman, 'Ethnography as Politics, Politics as Ethnography: Kenyatta, Malinowski and
      the Making of *Facing Mount Kenya*', *Canadian Journal of African Studies* 30, 1998, pp. 313–44.
48   Kenyatta, *Facing Mount Kenya*, p. xviii.
49   As suggested by Berman and Lonsdale, 'Louis Leakey's Mau Mau', p. 162.
50   'The Kikuyu Problem of the Initiation of Girls', *The Journal of the Royal Anthropological
      Institute* LXI, 1931, pp. 277–85. For Kenyatta's use of Leakey's text, see Murray-Brown,
      Kenyatta, pp. 423–4 and Berman and Lonsdale, 'Louis Leakey's Mau Mau', p. 162 and note
      22.
51   Kenyatta, *Facing Mount Kenya*, p. 110.
52   Kenyatta, *Facing Mount Kenya*, p. 133.

53   Kenyatta, *Facing Mount Kenya*, p. 133.
54   Kenyatta, *Facing Mount Kenya*, p. 108.
55   Kenyatta, *Facing Mount Kenya*, p. 147.
56   Kenyatta, *Facing Mount Kenya*, p. 154.
57   Murray-Brown, *Kenyatta*, p. 221.
58   12 Dec. and 31 Aug. 1934, MP, Appendix/1, Correspondence with Marie Bonaparte.
59   Bronislaw Malinowski, *Sex, Culture and Myth*, New York, 1962, pp. 183–4.
60   12 Dec. and 31 Aug. 1934, MP, Appendix/1, Correspondence with Marie Bonaparte.
61   31 Aug. 1934, MP, Appendix/1, Correspondence with Marie Bonaparte.
62   31 Aug. 1934, MP, Appendix/1, Correspondence with Marie Bonaparte.
63   Kenyatta, *Facing Mount Kenya*, p. 162.
64   Leakey, 'The Kikuyu Problem', p. 279.
65   Marie Bonaparte, *Female Sexuality*, transl. John Rodker, London, 1953, reprint 1973, p. 103.
66   Bonaparte, *Female Sexuality*, p. 150.
67   This was the subject of her first scientific article, written under the pseudonym A. E. Narjani, 'Considérations sur les causes anatomiques de la frigidité chez la femme', *Bruxelles Médical* 42: 4.
68   Bertin, *Marie Bonaparte*, p. 141; Jean-Pierre Bourgeron, *Marie Bonaparte*, Paris, 1997, p. 24.
69   Bonaparte, *Female Sexuality*, pp. 150, 152.
70   Bonaparte, *Female Sexuality*, pp. 155, 156.
71   Bonaparte, *Female Sexuality*, p. 153.
72   Bonaparte, *Female Sexuality*, pp. 153, 154–5.

Chapter 21

Jomo Kenyatta

FACING MOUNT KENYA
(1953, 1978 edition)

The tribal life of the Gikuyu

Initiation of boys and girls

IT SHOULD BE POINTED OUT here that there is a strong community of educated Gikuyu opinion in defence of this custom. In the matrimonial relation, the *rite de passage* is the deciding factor. No proper Gikuyu would dream of marrying a girl who has not been circumcised, and vice versa. It is taboo for a Gikuyu man or woman to have sexual relations with someone who has not undergone this operation. If it happens, a man or a woman must go through a ceremonial purification, *korutwo thahu* or *gotahikio megiro*—namely, ritual vomiting of the evil deeds. A few detribalised Gikuyu, while they are away from home for some years, have thought fit to denounce the custom and to marry uncircumcised girls, especially from coastal tribes, thinking that they could bring them back to their fathers' homes without offending the parents. But to their surprise they found that their fathers, mothers, brothers and sisters, following the tribal custom, are not prepared to welcome as a relative-in-law anyone who has not fulfilled the ritual qualifications for matrimony. Therefore a problem has faced these semi-detribalised Gikuyu when they wanted to return to their homeland. Their parents have demanded that if their sons wished to settle down and have the blessings of the family and the clan, they must divorce the wife married outside the rigid tribal custom and then marry a girl with the approved tribal qualifications. Failing this, they have been turned out and disinherited.

In our short survey we have mentioned how the custom of clitoridectomy has been attacked on one side, and on the other how it has been defended. In view of these points the important problem is an anthropological one: it is unintelligent to discuss the emotional attitudes of either side, or to take violent sides in the question, without understanding the reasons why the educated, intelligent Gikuyu still cling to this custom.

The real argument lies not in the defence of the surgical operation or its details, but in the understanding of a very important fact in the tribal psychology of the Gikuyu—namely, that this operation is still regarded as the very essence of an institution which has enormous educational, social, moral, and religious implications, quite apart from the operation itself. For the present it is impossible for a member of the tribe to imagine an initiation without clitoridectomy. Therefore the abolition of the surgical element in this custom means to the Gikuyu the abolition of the whole institution.

The real anthropological study, therefore, is to show that clitoridectomy, like Jewish circumcision, is a mere bodily mutilation which, however, is regarded as the *conditio sine qua non* of the whole teaching of tribal law, religion, and morality.

The initiation of both sexes is the most important custom among the Gikuyu. It is looked upon as a deciding factor in giving a boy or girl the status of manhood or womanhood in the Gikuyu community. This custom is adhered to by the vast majority of African peoples and is found in almost every part of the continent. It is therefore necessary to examine the facts attached to this widespread custom in order to have some idea why the African peoples cling to this custom which, in the eyes of a good many Europeans, is nothing but a "horrible" and "painful" practice, suitable only to barbarians.

In the first place it is necessary to give the readers a clear picture of why and how this important sociobiological custom is performed.

Name of the custom

The Gikuyu name for this custom of *rite de passage* from childhood to adulthood is *irua*, i.e. circumcision, or trimming the genital organs of both sexes. The dances and songs connected with the initiation ceremony are called *mambura*, i.e. rituals or divine services. It is important to note that the moral code of the tribe is bound up with this custom and that it symbolises the unification of the whole tribal organisation. This is the principal reason why *irua* plays such an important part in the life of the Gikuyu people.

The *irua* marks the commencement of participation in various governing groups in the tribal administration, because the real age-groups begin from the day of the physical operation. The history and legends of the people are explained and remembered according to the names given to various age-groups at the time of the initiation ceremony. For example, if a devastating famine occurred at the time of the initiation, that particular *irua* group would be known as "famine" (*ng'aragu*). In the same way, the Gikuyu have been able to record the time when the European introduced a number of maladies such as syphilis into Gikuyu country, for those initiated at the time when this disease first showed itself are called *gatego*, i.e. syphilis. Historical events are recorded and remembered in the same manner. Without this custom a tribe which had no written records would not have been able to keep a record of important events and happenings in the life of the Gikuyu nation. Any Gikuyu child who is not corrupted by detribalisation is able to record in his mind the whole history and origin of the Gikuyu people through the medium of such names as Agu, Ndemi and Mathathi, etc., who were initiated hundreds of years ago.

For years there has been much criticism and agitation against *irua* of girls by certain misinformed missionary societies in East Africa, who see only the surgical side of the *irua*, and, without investigating the psychological importance attached to this custom by the Gikuyu, these missionaries draw their conclusion that the *irua* of girls is nothing but a barbarous practice and, as such, should be abolished by law.

On the other hand, the Gikuyu look upon these religious fanatics with great suspicion. The overwhelming majority of them believe that it is the secret aim of those who attack this centuries-old custom to disintegrate their social order and thereby hasten their Europeanisation. The abolition of *irua* will destroy the tribal symbol which identifies the age-groups, and prevent the Gikuyu from perpetuating that spirit of collectivism and national solidarity which they have been able to maintain from time immemorial.

[. . .]

The great ceremonial dance (matuumo)

The day before the physical operation is performed the girl is called early in the morning to have her head shaved by the sponsor. All her clothes are removed, she is given a massage, after which her naked body is decked with beads lent to her by women relatives and friends. About ten o'clock in the morning relatives and friends gather at the girl's homestead. Here a short ceremony of reunion with the ancestors of the clan is performed, and a leader is chosen to lead the procession to the homestead where the *irua* is to take place.

The girl is provided with a bell (*kegamba*) which is tied on her right leg just above the calf, or sometimes above the knee, to provide the rhythm to the procession and also for the dance. The girl is put in the middle of the procession, which moves slowly, singing ritual songs until they reach the *irua's* homestead, where the procession is joined by the other initiates who are accompanied by other processions of relatives and friends dressed in their best.

[. . .]

The *irua* candidates are lined up ready for the sacrifice which marks the end of *matuumo*. This consists of the boys running a race of about two miles to a sacred tree called *mogumo* or *motamayo*, which they have to climb and break top branches, while the girls gather round singing, and at the same time gathering the leaves and the twigs dropped by the boys.

To start the race a ceremonial horn is blown. At this point the girls, who are not allowed to participate in the race, start out walking to the tree, escorted by a group of senior warriors and women singing ritual and heroic songs. When the girls are near the tree, the ceremonial horn is again sounded, this time indicating that it is time for the boys to start the race. The boys then start running in a great excitement, as though they were going to a battle. The truth is, it is really considered a sort of fight between the spirit of childhood and that of adulthood.

The crowd which has already gathered round the tree await the arrival of the boys in order to judge the winner of the race. They shout and cheer merrily as the excited boys arrive, raising their wooden spears, ready to throw them over the sacred tree. The significance of this ceremonial racing is the fact that it determines the leader of that particular age-group. The one who reaches the tree first and throws his wooden spear over the tree is elected there and then as the leader and the spokesman of the age-group for life. It is believed that such a one is chosen by the will of the ancestral spirits in communication with Ngai, and is therefore highly respected.

The girl who arrives at the sacred tree first is also regarded in the same way. She becomes the favourite, and all try to win her affections with the hope of marrying her.

The *mogumo* ceremony occupies only a short time. As stated above, the boys climb the tree, break the top branches, while the girls collect leaves and twigs dropped on the ground. These are later tied into bunches and carried back to the homestead to keep the sacred fire burning the whole night and also to be used in other rituals, especially in making the initiates' beds. The songs rendered by the relatives and friends round the foot of the tree generally pertain to sexual knowledge. This is to give the initiates an opportunity of acquainting themselves with all necessary rules and regulations governing social relationship between men and women.

At the completion of *kuuna mogumo* (breaking of the sacred tree), the boys and girls are lined up according to the order of their adoption. Here a ceremony of taking the tribal oath (*muma wa anake*) is conducted by the elders of the ceremonial council. The initiates promise by this oath that from this day onward they will in every respect deport themselves like adults and take all responsibilities in the welfare of the community, and that they will not lag behind whenever called upon to perform any service or duty in the protection and advancement of the tribe as a whole. Furthermore, they are made to promise never to reveal the tribal secrets, even to a member of the tribe who has not yet been initiated.

[. . .]

At the end of the ceremony the boys and girls are free to go to their respective homes to rest until next morning. Care is taken to protect them from anything that might inflict wounds upon them, as the shedding of blood is regarded as an omen of ill-luck. The initiates are guarded the whole night by senior warriors against outside interference. In every home a ceremonial doctor (*mondo-mogo wa mambura*) is assigned by the traditional council (*njama ya kirera*) to protect the initiates against any possible attacks from witchcraft and also against any temptation or enticement to indulge in sexual intercourse.

How the girl is operated on

Early in the morning of the day of the physical operation the girl is called at cock-crow. She is fed with a special food (*kemere kia oomo*), eaten only on this occasion, after which she is undressed, leaving only one string of beads across her shoulder, known as *mogathe wa mwenji* (present for the barber). This is given to her sponsor as a symbol of lasting friendship and as a bond of mutual help in all matters. It also signifies that henceforth the girl is supposed to hide nothing from her sponsor nor deny her guardian anything demanded from her, even if it be the last she possesses.

After all necessary arrangements have been made, the girl is escorted to a place appointed for the meeting of all the candidates. From there they are led to a special river where they bathe. The boys are assigned to a particular place while the girls bathe at a point below them, singing in unison: "*Togwe-thamba na munja wa ecanake*," which means: "We have bathed with the cream of youth."

This is done before the sun rises, when the water is very cold. They go up to their waist in the river, dipping themselves to the breast, holding up the ceremonial leaves in their hands; then they begin shaking their wrists, dropping the leaves into the river as a sign of drowning their childhood behaviour and forgetting about it forever. The initiates spend about half an hour in the river, in order to numb their limbs and to prevent pain or loss of blood at the time of operation. The sponsors superintend to see that the initiates bathe in the correct manner, while the mothers, relatives and friends are present, painted with red and white ochre (*therega na moonyo*), singing ritual and encouraging songs. The warriors keep guard to prevent the spectators or strangers from coming too near to the bank.

[. . .]

In the meanwhile the elders select a place near the homestead where the operation is to be performed. This place is called *iteeri*.

Here a clean cowhide, tanned and polished, is spread on the ground; the ceremonial leaves called *mathakwa* are spread on the hide. The girls sit down on the hide, while their female relatives and friends form a sort of circle, several rows thick, around the girls, silently awaiting the great moment. No male is allowed to go near or even to peep through this cordon. Any man caught doing so would be severely punished.

Each of the girls sits down with her legs wide open on the hide. Her sponsor sits behind her with her legs interwoven with those of the girl, so as to keep the girl's legs in a steady, open position. The girl reclines gently against her sponsor or *motiiri*, who holds her slightly on the shoulders to prevent any bodily movement, the girl meanwhile staring skywards. After this an elderly woman, attached to the ceremonial council, comes in with very cold water, which has been preserved through the night with a steel axe in it. This water is called *mae maithanwa* (axe water). The water is thrown on the girl's sexual organ to make it numb and to arrest profuse bleeding as well as to shock the girl's nerves at the time, for she is not supposed to show any fear or make any audible sign of emotion or even to blink. To do so would be considered cowardice (*kerogi*) and make her the butt of ridicule among her companions. For this reason she is expected to keep her eyes fixed upwards until the operation is completed.

When this preparation is finished, a woman specialist, known as *moruithia*, who has studied this form of surgery from childhood, dashes out of the crowd, dressed in a very peculiar way, with her face painted with white and black ochre. This disguise tends to make her look rather terrifying, with her rhythmic movement accompanied by the rattles tied to her legs. She takes out from her pocket (*mondo*) the operating Gikuyu razor (*rwenji*), and in quick movements, and with the dexterity of a Harley Street surgeon, proceeds to operate upon the girls. With a stroke she cuts off the tip of the clitoris (*rong'otho*). As no other part of the girl's sexual organ is interfered with, this completes the girl's operation. Immediately the old woman who originally threw the water on the girls comes along with milk mixed with some herbs called *mokengeria* and *ndogamoki*, which she sprinkles on the fresh wound to reduce the pain and to check bleeding, and prevent festering or blood poisoning. In a moment each girl is covered with a new dress (cloak) by her sponsor. At this juncture the silence is broken and the crowd begins to sing joyously in these words: "*Ciana ciito ire kooma ee-ho, nea marerire-ee-ho,*" which means: "Our children are brave, ee-ho (hurrah). Did anyone cry? No one cried—hurrah!"

After this the sponsors hold the girls by the arms and slowly walk to a special hut which has been prepared for the girls. Here the girls are put to sleep on beds prepared on the ground with sweet-smelling leaves called *marerecwa*, *mataathi* and *maturanguru*. The two first mentioned are used for keeping flies away or any other insect, and also to purify the air and counteract any bad smell which may be caused by the wounds, while the last-named is purely a ceremonial herb. The leaves are changed almost daily by the sponsors who are assigned to look after the needs of the initiates (*irui*). For the first few days no visitors are allowed to see the girls, and the sponsors take great care to see that no unauthorised person approaches the hut. It is feared that if someone with evil eyes (*gethemengo*) sees the girls it will result in illness.

Healing of the wound

At the time of the surgical operation the girl hardly feels any pain for the simple reason that her limbs have been numbed, and the operation is over before she is conscious of it. It is only when she awakes after three or four hours of rest that she begins to realise that something has been done to her genital organ. The writer has learned this fact from several girls (relatives and close friends) who have gone through the initiation and who belong to the same age-group with the writer.

When the girl wakes up the nurse who is in attendance washes her with some kind of watery herb called *mahoithia* (drainers or dryers). After the washing the wound is attended with antiseptic and healing leaves called *kagutwi* or *matei* (chasers or banishers). The leaves are folded together, about two inches long, half an inch wide and quarter of an inch thick; then they are dipped in oil *maguta ma mbariki* (Gikuyu castor oil) to prevent them sticking on the wound and also to prevent the wound from shrinking. The bandage is then placed on the wound between *labia majora* to keep the two lips apart and prevent them from being drawn together while the wound heals.

The girl sits down with her legs closed together so as to keep the bandage in position. Frequently the girl is carefully examined by the nurse, and whenever she urinates, the nurse is there ready to clean the wound and put on a new bandage. The old bandage is hidden away to ensure that no man shall cross over it or put his foot on it, for such an act would bring misfortune to the man or to the girl.

For the first week after her initiation the girl is not allowed to go for a walk or even to touch with her bare hands anything in the way of food. The nurse puts the girl's food on a banana leaf, called *ngoto* or *icoya*, which serves as a plate. The leaf is lifted to the mouth without the girl actually touching its contents with her hands. The food eaten by the invalids is supplied by the parents, relatives and friends. The initiates, both boys and girls, eat collectively all food, irrespective of where it comes from, for all contributions are kept in one place in charge of the nurses and shared in common by the initiates, who refer to one another as sisters and brothers. The invalids are entertained by their sponsors, who sing them encouraging songs, in which they bring out vividly the experience they gained after they were circumcised, that in a few days their wounds will heal and soon they will be able to go out jumping and dancing. These songs have a great psychological effect on the minds of the initiates, for they strongly believe that what has happened to their predecessors will also happen to them. With this in view their thoughts rest not on the operation, but on the day when they will again appear in public as full-fledged members of the community.

On the sixth day the sponsors make a full report to the ceremonial council; if all initiates are well and can walk, a ceremony of *gotonyio* or *gociarwo* (which means to be entered or born) is arranged on the eighth day. If all are not well the ceremony is postponed until the twelfth day, for no ceremony would be arranged on the seventh, ninth or eleventh day after any event has taken place. Uneven days are considered by the Gikuyu to be unlucky for embarking on any important business.

On the day appointed the parents gather at the homestead of the *irua*, bringing with them presents in the way of beer (*njohi* or *ooke*), bananas and vegetables. The ceremony consists of killing a selected sheep, the skin of which is cut into ribbons (*ngwaro*) which are put on the wrists of the boys and girls.

[. . .]

The children have now been born again, not as the children of an individual, but of the whole tribe. The initiates address one another as "*Wanyu-Wakine,*" which means "My tribal brother or sister." When the ceremony is completed all burst into ritual song. They bid farewell to one another and then leave the homestead under the escort of their relatives. On the arrival at their respective homes a sheep or goat is killed by the parents to welcome them home again and anoint them as new members of the community (*koinokai na kohaka mwanake* or *moiretu maguta*). At this ceremony the parents are provided with brass ear-rings, as a sign of seniority. This is done when the first-born is initiated.

For a period of three or four months, according to the rules of various clans, the initiates do not participate in any work. They devote most of their time to going around the district singing the initiates' song called *waine*. In this several groups take part. The song takes place in the field and is performed only in daytime. The initiates stand in a big circle holding several sticks (*micee*) in their hands. A bunch of *micee* is held in the left hand while one stick is held in the right hand. In this manner the initiates beat the *micee* according to the rhythm of the song. The inner circle is kept clear for the favourites from various groups—namely those who were the first to reach the sacred tree. They enter the circle two by two, a boy and a girl. As they appear in the arena the sticks are beaten rhythmically by all, whilst at the same time they utter compliments. These meetings afford the initiated boys and girls opportunities of coming into contact with and knowing one another intimately.

At the end of the holiday period, a day is fixed for the initiates to return to the homestead where the *irua* took place. Here the final ceremony of cleansing or purification is performed. This is called *menjo* or *gothiga*. Up to this time the initiates have been regarded as children (*ciana*) or new-comers (*ciumeri*), and, as such, they cannot hold any responsibility in the community, for they are in their transitional period. Neither juvenile nor adult laws can be applied to them, and thus they form a sort of free community of "merry-go-round."

On the day appointed for the ceremony, people gather from far and near to join in the festival dance in which the "new-comers" are introduced into the community. The ceremony consists of shaving the heads (*kwenja*) of the boys and girls. The clothes and ornaments worn during the transitional period are discarded; their bodies are painted with red ochre mixed with oil, after which they are dressed in new clothes. The boys are provided with warriors' equipment; the girls are adorned with beads, armlets and other adornments. Then they are led to the dance, where they are introduced to the assembly as full-fledged members of the community. While the dance is going on, mothers and fathers partake of a feast of beer-drinking (*njohi*), which usually takes place during all solemn functions.

The wound normally requires a week to heal, but, of course, there are some cases which take longer, generally due to negligence on the part of the girl or the nurse in applying the healing leaves in the proper way. Such cases are few, but result in a septic condition, and the formation of much scar tissue on the area of the *labia majora*, which may make childbirth difficult. Cases of this nature sometimes find their way to hospitals and attract the attention of both the missionary and official doctors, who then and there, without careful investigation of the system of female circumcision, attack the custom of clitoridectomy in general, asserting that it is barbaric and a menace to the life of the mothers. To strengthen their attacks on this custom, these "well-wishers" have gone so far as to state that almost every first child dies as a result of this operation at the time of initiation, and that the operation is more severe to-day than it was formerly. Irresponsible statements of this kind are not to be taken too seriously, for it must not be forgotten that very few of the normal cases of childbirth ever come to the notice of European doctors. The theory that "every first child dies as a result of the operation" has no foundation at all. There are hundreds of first-born children among the Gikuyu who are still living, and the writer is one of them.

The missionaries who attack the *irua* of girls are more to be pitied than condemned, for most of their information is derived from Gikuyu converts who have been taught by these same Christians to regard the custom of female circumcision as something savage and barbaric, worthy only of heathens who live in perpetual sin under the influence of the Devil. Because of this prejudiced attitude, the missionaries are at a disadvantage in knowing the true state of affairs. Even the few scientifically minded ones are themselves so obsessed with prejudice against the custom that their objectivity is blurred in trying to unravel the mystery of the *irua*.

With such limited knowledge as they are able to acquire from their converts or from others, who invariably distort the reality of the *irua* in order to please them, these same missionaries pose as authorities on African customs. How often have we not heard such people saying: "We have lived in Africa for a number of years and we know the African mind well?" This, however, does not qualify them or entitle them to claim authority on sociological or anthropological questions. The African is in the best position properly to discuss and disclose the psychological background of tribal customs, such as *irua*, etc., and he should be given the opportunity to acquire the scientific training which will enable him to do so. This is a point which should be appreciated by well-meaning anthropologists who have had experience of the difficulties of field-work in various parts of the world.

Chapter 22

SPEECHES BY THE DUCHESS OF ATHOLL AND ELEANOR RATHBONE (1929)

Dec. 11, 1929, Hansard Parliamentary Debates, 5th series, vol. 233, cols. 599–608

Duchess of ATHOLL: I want to bring before the House some reasons why some Members of this House, who have been studying conditions amongst women and children in the Crown Colonies—women and girls particularly—feel that there is urgent need for more consideration to be given to the social well-being, health, and education of women and girls in some of our dependencies than sometimes seems to have been the case. This small group of Members of all parties who have been considering this question for some months past has met missionaries of different churches, of long standing in different Colonies, also laymen and women, among them doctors, and we are one and all deeply concerned at many of the things which we have learned bearing on the status, the health, and the welfare generally of women and girls.

In particular, we have been terribly impressed by what we have learned on a subject on which I put a question to-day to the Under-Secretary of State for the Colonies, namely, the existence of a pre-marriage rite among young girls, among many African tribes, a rite which is frequently referred to as the circumcision of girls. We have heard that this obtains in Southern Nigeria and among one tribe in Uganda, but we understand that it exists in its worst form among the Kikuyu tribe in Kenya. I am sure it will be realised that this is not an easy subject to deal with publicly. I venture to bring it before the House, because none of us can afford to forget the responsibility that has been impressed upon us from the benches opposite—the responsibility for that Colonial Empire which is directly governed from this House. We must at all times be ready to study the conditions in that Colonial Empire, particularly when we remember how little native races may be able to express themselves, and how backward they may be in respect of many of their customs.

I wish to give the House some idea of what this rite means, because I am certain it is not realised by many people in this country. I doubt very much if, even apart from

missionaries and doctors, and perhaps Government officials, there are many white people
who realise what this rite is, and what it means to the health and well-being of the girls
and women. The term applied to it is totally inadequate to give an idea of what it means.
Our Committee has been assured by medical men, and by missionaries who have attended
these women in hospital and in their homes, that the rite is nothing short of mutilation.
It consists of the actual wholesale removal of parts connected with the organs of
reproduction. The Operation is performed publicly before one or two thousand people
by an old woman of the tribe armed with an iron knife. No anæsthetic is given, and no
antiseptics are used. The old woman goes with her knife from one girl to another,
performing the operation, returning it may be once or twice to each victim. A lady
missionary steeled herself to see this operation not long ago, and has given a description
of it verified by photographs which she took. She told us that the girl has a whistle put
into her mouth so that her screams will not be heard. A medical man told us that the
operation leaves great scarring, contraction, and obstruction; natural eliminating processes
are gravely interfered with, and there is reason to believe that much blood poisoning
results. The obstruction causes terrible suffering at childbirth, and the first child is rarely
born alive. It is difficult to ascertain the extent of the mortality, because there is no
register of births or deaths, but one missionary who has attended many of these young
women in hospital in their confinement, told me recently that out of 10 cases, affecting
20 lives, only six lives survived. I have also been told of a boarding house for 60 girls of
this tribe, where a death had occurred every year lately from sometimes an apparently
trivial cause. A cut finger may turn so septic owing to the poisoning from which the girl
has suffered, that that type of injury may cause her death.

What is the policy of the Government in regard to this terrible custom? I put a question
to the Under-Secretary of State to-day on the subject and his reply was:

> The policy followed up till now by the Colonial Governments concerned has
> been to bring persuasion to bear upon the tribes which now practise the rite
> in its more brutal forms to return to the traditional and less harmful form of
> it. I am glad to say that a number of local native councils in East Africa have
> passed resolutions making illegal the severer forms of the operation.

I will ask the hon. Gentleman how he can ensure that the old women who may receive
instructions to practise the less severe form of the operation, will in fact carry out the
instructions. When the knife is in her hand, what reason is there to believe that she will
restrain herself? The committee of which I have spoken has been assured by a medical
man of standing in East Africa that, while there is this lesser form, which is not so severe
a form of mutilation as the one which I have described, it is an operation which he would
not sanction by anyone under his control. If we turn to the question of persuasion, surely
one of the best ways in which to persuade people is to give them practical demonstrations
of other and better ways; and that surely means that every opportunity should be taken
to help them to be healthy, and to help women to realise that, if they do not go through
this operation, they can become mothers with much less suffering and danger to their
children and to themselves.

When we ask what is being done in Kenya in this matter of care for women in
childbirth, we find that there are no midwives practising in the reserves; at least, that is
our information. We are told that, though there are several Government hospitals—the

hon. Gentleman who moved the Motion, I think, was misinformed on the subject of hospitals—there are only women nurses in two of them. Therefore, the majority of these hospitals are not very well equipped for attending women in their confinement. No doubt, it may be difficult to find any women to train as midwives, but Uganda shows a splendid example of what can be done in that way. We have been informed that in the Protectorate there are no less than 26 centres for maternity and child welfare, and, as a result, in the last 10 years, the infant mortality rate has dropped from 500 per thousand births—a terrible level—to not more than 130 per thousand in the kingdom of Uganda.

It seems difficult to believe that what has been possible in Uganda cannot be possible in Kenya. Kenya has its mission boarding houses and boarding schools maintained by the various missions, where African girls are taken in and given an all-round training for several years, and I have no doubt that this training is the best possible preparation for definite training as midwives. One of these boarding houses is besieged by girls wanting to come in, and a missionary who has been in charge of it has told us that she has far more applications than she can possibly satisfy—applications from girls, some of whom at least wish to escape from this mutilation. To sum up this policy of advocating the lesser rite, it seems to me that it is impossible, first of all, to guarantee that the instructions given will be carried out, and in the second place there is room for a great deal more to be done in the way of providing relief and hygienic instruction for these unhappy women. If we turn to what is said in the answer given to me as to the number of local native councils in East Africa which have passed resolutions making this severer operation illegal, I believe—

Mr. MAXTON: I do not like to interrupt the Noble Lady, but this is a Motion of a very wide nature dealing with Colonial policy with regard to coloured races, and I want to ask whether the Noble Lady is entitled to deal with what seems to be a special interest of her own and with a question which she put to the Under-Secretary at Question Time to-day.

[. . .]

Duchess of ATHOLL: If the House will allow me I will show that this is a very urgent question. In his answer to-day the Under-Secretary stated that certain native councils were trying to stop the severer form of this operation. I believe they have passed a rule instituting a punishment of one month's imprisonment and a fine of 50s. for offenders, but that, I am told, refers only to the reserves, and is easily evaded elsewhere. I have heard of a case of a Christian girl who wished to avoid being subjected to either operation, but she was seized by her relatives and obliged to submit to the severest form. Where the urgency of the question comes in is this, that an appeal was made to a native Court for damages against the operator, but the magistrate ruled that no grievous hurt had been done to the girl.

Dr. MORGAN: What is the date of that prosecution?

Duchess of ATHOLL: I believe it was in July this year. I have seen a letter of protest in regard to it in the "East African Standard" of August. The case was carried to the

Supreme Court, where the decision of the native Court was upheld, so that the woman who inflicted this terrible operation on this girl against her will has only a sentence of 30s. I am quite well aware that no Member of this House must say anything which reflects on the Courts, and so I will only say that we must presume that the Supreme Court of Kenya, in giving this decision, was carrying out the law. In that case the law must be altered, and it is for the House of Commons to show the Government of Kenya that that sort of law is not good enough. It is intolerable that a native girl who has had the courage to stand out against this custom of her tribe should be seized and forcibly operated on in this way. The letter from a well-known missionary, to which I have already alluded, referred to the fact that hundreds of young girls were anxious to escape from this operation. I must say to hon. Members that I understand the policy of British Governments of all political complexions has been to avoid interference as far as possible with native customs subject to this qualification, that they were not contrary to justice and humanity. I ask the House what could be more inhuman than the practice which I have described, and what could be more contrary to what we understand as British justice than that a girl endeavouring to escape from this terrible custom should not have the protection of a British Court.

One hon. Member just now referred to the practice of suttee. That is, I believe, the only one of the old practices of India with which we have interfered, and which we have definitely prohibited by law. I would remind the House that that definite and courageous step was taken just one hundred years ago, and I say to the House in all sincerity, and after very careful deliberation, that I regard this custom of the mutilation of girls as practised in Kenya among the Kikuyu as even more injurious to the race than suttee, terrible though suttee was. The suffering it inflicts may not be so hideous as the suffering of suttee, but certainly it is more prolonged; it may follow a girl through life, and it is more injurious to the race because it affects the health and lives of both women and children.

Some of my hon. Friends who have been serving on this committee went with me the other day to ask the Secretary of State if he would set up a Select Committee to inquire into this terrible practice, but he said he could not see his way to do so. Nevertheless, he has assured us that he is going to communicate with the Governors of the Crown Colonies on this subject, and endeavour to secure from them fuller information than he has at present. I submit that, if the information he obtains from official sources confirms the statements that have been made to the committee by several people of experience, every effort should be made to put an end to this terrible abuse. I have only to-day seen a public letter in an East African paper from the Chairman and Secretary of a committee of Kikuyu women protesting against this practice. The native elders of certainly one missionary church in Kenya have for several years taken a very strong line against it, and there are, I believe, many of the younger men among the Kikuyu who deplore it. Are we going to be more backward in our standards, lower in our standards than the Christians, or even some of the non-Christians among the Kikuyu people?

I do not wish to detain the House longer, because there is very little time left, and there are several other speakers, but I would say to the Under-Secretary how terribly concerned this committee feel about this question, and I would appeal to the hon. Gentleman to learn all he can about it, to impress upon the Governors how greatly distressed anyone is who has heard the information provided by those who have had experience of this terrible custom, to urge them to keep ever in view our trusteeship for the native races, and to allow no difficulties to stand in the way of doing everything that may be possible to end a barbarous custom which is causing untold suffering, ill-health and loss of life.

Miss RATHBONE: I beg to move, in line 10, to leave out the word "or," and, at the end of the question, to add the words "or sex."

This Amendment would make the last sentence of the Motion read as follow:

> Native self-governing institutions should be fostered; and franchise and legal rights should be based upon the principle of equality for all without regard, to race, colour, or sex.

In moving it, my motive is not to discuss the great abstract principle of sex equality, important as I believe that to be. My object is a much more immediately practical one. The Noble Lady the Member for Kinross (Duchess of Atholl) has communicated to the House some of the results of the consultations that we have been holding with those who have had intimate acquaintance with the lives of coloured women in some parts of Africa, and has dealt with the question of the effect of certain customs on the health of native women. I want very shortly to allude to another aspect of the question. We have had evidence from witnesses which has revealed to us that the position of the native women in many of these tribes—I do not say all—is one of sheer slavery, accompanied by many of the worst conditions of slavery, and carried on practically without let or hindrance from the British authorities—slavery, not to Europeans, but to men of their own race. If it be thought that the word "slavery" is an exaggeration, may I quote the definition of the word in the Slavery Convention of the League of Nations:

> Slavery is the condition or status of a person over whom any or all of the powers attaching to the right of ownership are exercised.

We have evidence that practically all the rights of ownership are, in effect, exercised over the coloured women of these races. A girl is sold by her father, often in early infancy, without choice, to the man who is destined to be her husband. Before marriage she undergoes, again without choice, at the age of 10 or 11, the cruel custom that has been described by the Noble Lady the Member for Kinross. After marriage she becomes the property of her husband, to be used by him and treated by him as he desires. If he dies, she becomes the absolute property of his next male kin, it may be his brother, his cousin, or even a little boy of her own. She may be sold by her new owner in one direction, her daughter may be sold in another direction; the sons are usually retained as the representatives of the tribe. One witness, a very cautious moderate man, evidently anxious not to exaggerate but rather impatient with the questions with which we plied him as to whether a woman had rights over real or personal property or over her children, said, "I can summarise it very shortly. So far as we can judge, a woman in these tribes has no rights at all from the moment she is born until the moment she dies." If that is not slavery, what is? To endure torture, and mutilation, to be sold in marriage to a man whom she loathes, to be obliged to endure childbirth under conditions under which childbirth is carried on, without any of the comforts of decent treatment and medical care, and separated forcibly from her children—are those things less hurtful and humiliating and degrading to humanity because the persons who perpetuate them are the blood relations of the women who endure them?

I would not have it thought that we who are responsible for this Amendment are out of sympathy with the purpose of the Motion. Most of us are in full sympathy with it. We do not wish to draw a red herring across the trail or to distract attention from the need of better relations between coloured men and white men. Two blacks do not make a white. The exploitation of coloured women by coloured men is no excuse for the exploitation of coloured men by white men. But if we are asked to accept the principle that native self-governing institutions should be fostered, and the franchise and equal rights should be based upon the principle of all without regard to sex or colour, we hope the champions of these native races will remind them that it has been an old principle that there is no slavery under the British flag. It has been a terrible shock to many of us to whom these facts are new that there is slavery under the British flag, not in small numbers, but some millions at least of women, and it is tolerated so long as you can get away under the pretence that it is a domestic custom. Many of us will never be satisfied until the full hideous truth is disclosed and made known to the women of the world and everything that can be done is done to stamp out slavery of this kind, whether by legislation, by education, or by public opinion. Let them take this message to the men of the native races. There can be no equal citizenship between coloured men and white men till there is equal citizenship between coloured men and coloured women.

PART 11

Was abortion reform motivated by eugenics, leftwing politics, or Nazi power?

Introduction

T HE INTERWAR YEARS were a time of very rapid social change and economic hardship. Public debates now featured sexuality more openly, as sex reform movements demanded greater access to birth control, and sometimes abortion. The "New Woman" appeared on the scene: she wore short skirts, worked in an office, loved the cinema, and perhaps had love affairs. But reformers also worried about the working-class mother whose husband was unemployed, who could not feed the children she had, and felt worn down and ill from repeated pregnancies. Both leftwing and rightwing movements considered eugenic ideas.[1]

Weimar Germany faced severe political turmoil and high levels of poverty and unemployment, but at the same time a modern urban culture flourished. The sex reform movement became most public in Weimar, as scores of magazines and organizations promoted not only birth control and sex education, but also eugenics, nude bathing, and gay and lesbian rights.

Abortion was commonly practiced, but the law known as section 218 punished abortion from the moment of conception. Women who had abortions, and those who provided them, could be imprisoned. In 1926, the law lessened punishments for abortion, and by 1927 "therapeutic abortion" was permitted for reasons of grave danger to health. But the authorities continued to prosecute women who had abortions, and providers. A huge movement protested against this. Searching in court records, historian Cornelie Usborne finds that many women (and men) exchanged information about how to obtain abortions through neighborhood and workplace gossip. They seemed to accept it as a necessity. She finds that older beliefs – such as claiming that women needed treatments for blocked menstruation – persisted alongside newer techniques. However, in 1933 the new Nazi regime started imposing grave penalties on abortion. Were the Nazis motivated by a concern for fetal life? Did they ban all abortions? Were Nazis successful in preventing women from having abortions?

Our primary source is an address to the World Congress on Sex Reform by Dr. Jonathan Leunbach, who was a doctor, communist, and sex reformer in Denmark in the interwar period. In Denmark at this time, young women increasingly engaged in premarital sex, especially after they were engaged, but they had to keep up the appearance of respectability – and feared pregnancy. Before 1938, birth control had become more widely available, but there were still no clinics, and it was illegal to distribute information about it. Abortion was punishable by imprisonment, but juries refused to convict most women and doctors accused of obtaining or providing abortions. This suggests that many Danes did not think abortion should be illegal, and in fact illegal abortion was widespread, if dangerous. Married working women also wanted to control their family size, facing unemployment during the difficult economy of the interwar years. As a result, many socialists joined in the sex reform movement to demand greater access to birth control, abortion, and sex education. Dr. Leunbach was one of the main campaigners on these grounds, and indeed he provided abortion in working-class areas. However, he was arrested, tried, acquitted, but then imprisoned for abortion provisions. Leunbach espoused eugenic ideas; in a 1926 book he did refer to racial conflict, but he later denied that he was racist. The mainstream medical profession, however, became concerned about the low birth rate, the danger of illegal abortions, and unhealthy pregnancies due to the lack of birth control.[2] Despite strong rightwing pressure, the Social Democrats dominated the government in the interwar years, and slowly established a welfare state. In 1938 the government passed a law legalizing birth control, providing for birth control clinics, and allowing abortion on limited grounds. A woman had to go to a Mother's Aid clinic which would provide resources for her to support a child. She could still have an abortion, with permission, if the pregnancy was the result of rape or incest, if it would damage her health, or if the fetus was damaged by a hereditary condition.

Notes

1   Ann Taylor Allen, *Feminism and Motherhood in Western Europe 1890–1970* (New York: Palgrave Macmillan, 2005), 164–169; Atina Grossmann, *Reforming Sex: The German Movement for Birth Control and Abortion Reform, 1920–1950* (New York: Oxford University Press, 1995).

2   Malcolm Potts, Peter Diggory, and John Peel, *Abortion* (Cambridge: Cambridge University Press, 1977), 121; Birgitte Søland, *Becoming Modern: Young Women and the Reconstruction of Womanhood in the 1920s* (Princeton: Princeton University Press, 2000), 86; D. V. Glass, "The Effectiveness of Abortion Legislation in Six Countries," *Modern Law Review* 2, no. 2 (1938): 121. For female sexuality in Denmark, see Bente Rosenbeck, "The Boundaries of Femininity in Denmark," *Scandinavian Journal of History* 12, no. 1 (1987): 47–62.

Chapter 23

Cornelie Usborne

CULTURES OF ABORTION IN
WEIMAR GERMANY (2007)

F OUCAULT FAMOUSLY POSTULATED that 'sexuality must not be thought of as a kind of natural given which power tries to hold in check, or as an obscure domain which knowledge tries gradually to uncover. It is the name that can be given to a historical construct.'[1] This definition revolutionized the study of sexuality which before had often been perceived as an essential and therefore unchanging biological process. Following Foucault and later constructionists, abortion should equally be conceived as a social construct, both in the way it was represented and talked about but also in the way it was defined. The meaning of abortion not only changed over time but differed also according to gender, class, location, religious denomination etc. although as we have seen, perceptions differed often less than previously thought. I do not, of course, suggest, that abortion is not anchored in a material order (abortion was a process involving objects, payment, people) or that it is not grounded in biology (for example, women's menstruation was restored); it was performed on particular occasions in certain ways with specific instruments or potions; and abortion is after all bounded by physiological phenomena such as conception and childbirth. But these physiological and material aspects are themselves open to cultural interpretation in the way they are defined and regulated, desired or feared, valued or denigrated, which renders the meaning of abortion unstable and contingent on specific contexts. It is here that this study takes issue with positivist notions of medical progress and historians of medicine who discuss scientific discoveries of reproduction as if they were part of a linear development, an upward trajectory towards the scientific truth, and as if procreation belonged to a constant biology, a 'universalized body'.

I have argued that abortion was and remains today a highly contentious issue fought over by competing groups for the right to define, organize, mediate and regulate it.[2] As Jeffrey Weeks puts it in relation to sexuality, the way it is constructed 'is a product of negotiation, struggle and human agency'.[3] In this book I have investigated the complexity of the cultures of abortion by interrogating what it meant for and how it was practised by different social actors. Instead of relying solely on authoritative accounts by law makers and policy makers which have not always responded to historical or social change, I have also drawn on the assumptions and linguistic practices of those usually marginalized in the historical analysis: aborting women, lay abortionists, pedlars of patent medicines as well as those who presented abortion in different media of popular culture. These ideological struggles are important for their own sake but they also act as a probe into the way Weimar medical cultures were organized, challenged and reconstituted. In the 1920s and early 1930s German doctors, lawyers, politicians and the Churches strove to impose their own bourgeois norms upon the meaning of conception, pregnancy and miscarriage and devised rules for reproductive behaviour. Their prescriptions were challenged more or less openly by lay practitioners, working-class women, and their accomplices. Proletarian women especially displayed alternative forms of knowledge and adhered to trusted older notions of fertility and procreation while at the same time applying modern techniques.

Gender roles and gender relations

From the findings of her oral history project about contraceptive practice in England and Wales during the first half of the twentieth century, Kate Fisher challenges the view that birth control was first and foremost a 'woman's question' or that women were responsible for the dramatic increase in the use of it. Rather than wives exerting influence on their husbands to use condoms, or 'insisting upon abstinence, turning to abortion, or adopting female methods such as caps', it was 'primarily husbands, not wives, who took responsibility for birth control strategies'. Women, Fisher claims, 'were reluctant to take an active role in the management and enforcement of birth control strategy', because they deemed this as a 'transgression of their passive and naive sexual personas'.[4] Fisher's image of women's submissiveness echoes the portrayal of working-class women's passivity in the abortion narratives of Weimar popular culture. Victimhood and vulnerability characterizes them on screen, stage and in fiction: from the proletarian mother of four in *Kreuzzug des Weibes* and Hete, the tormented and tragic heroine in *Cyankali*, or the destitute Herta in *Gilgi, eine von uns*, to the miserable protagonist of *Maria und der Paragraph*, women who found themselves pregnant against their will either took their own life or were mortally injured by botched abortions. Without much agency these women were crushed by their apparent biological fate. Contemporary reviews of the film *Cyankali* applauded such portrayal since it was thought it reflected the 'bitter truth'. One critic praised the way, 'an entire family living in poverty and destitution is hurled against the cliff of the clause [§218] and then smashed to pieces'.[5]

   In contrast, middle-class protagonists like the young teacher or the 'modern woman' in *Kreuzzug* represent the New Woman as they manage to secure a 'safe' medical termination and thus retain some control over their own body. But they achieve this at a cost and their transgression is punished. The young teacher's body is doubly expropriated, first through rape and then by having conceived a dysgenic foetus, the sole reason why she qualifies for an abortion. Likewise, the character of the 'modern woman' is condemned for the pursuit of pleasure. As von Keitz points out, she comes across as mannish in her determination to keep her figure, making her husband look effeminate as he expresses joy at his impending fatherhood in a childlike war dance.[6] Other New Woman characters like Gilgi, the heroine of Keun's eponymous novel, or Helene Baum's novel *stud.chem Helene Willfüer* survive their reproductive dilemma with feistiness and keep their ambitions intact but are burdened with single motherhood. As Krisztina Robert suggests in respect of post-First World War Britain, popular culture 'served as an arena of symbolic agitation where women's new gender roles, identities and relations were debated, constructed and contested through symbolic portrayals'.[7] This is true of Weimar Germany where aborting women portrayed in popular culture generally suffered because their desire for bodily autonomy was at odds with a still largely patriarchal society.

All the films, plays and novels I examined were remarkable in that without exception they supported abortion law reform; they all contained important ideas which questioned or subverted the dominant ideology of abortion but they were reined in by a general fear of censorship. It is instructive to be reminded of the seven-year battle with the censorship authorities waged by the director Georg Jacoby during and after the First World War to secure a licence for his abortion film *Moral und Sittlichkeit* (Sexual mores and morality), now no longer available. In 1924 it was passed and screened as *Muß die Frau Mutter warden?* (Does a woman have to become a mother?), but almost immediately banned again. It was reworked and finally released as *Frauen, hütet Eure Mutterschaft!* (Women, guard your motherhood!). As this title suggests, the censors had not only succeeded in destroying the anti-§218 message of the original script but also in 'bending it into its opposite meaning'.[8] No wonder that, as von Keitz suggests, producers and distributors tended to bow to rather than fight 'this manipulative practice by censorship authorities to ensure that films with controversial subject matter managed to get into cinemas at all'.[9] Since censors always checked the script particularly carefully, directors decided to portray transgressive behaviour on the silver screen visually rather than verbally, through a particular camera angle or through associations established by montage, while the text of the sub- or intertitles stayed within the boundaries of conventionality. In literature challenges to hegemonic discourses appear tucked away in inner monologues or asides. Abortion narratives in popular culture were thus neither at the forefront of a new ethic nor were they purely backward looking; instead they can best be described as mediating between a dominant ideology critical of lay abortionists and aborting women, on the one hand, and a popular acceptance of them, on the other.

The film *Kuhle Wampe oder Wem gehört die Welt?* is the exception to this rule. It did not feature abortion explicitly, but simply implied it as if it were completely normal. As a result it was neither pathologized nor was young Anni, the proletarian heroine, punished. In true communist style she learns to mistrust conventional rules about women's proper role and comes out fighting for a better world. She first agrees to a shot-gun engagement when she discovers she is pregnant, but then liberates herself from the shackles of petty bourgeois respectability, calls it off, and, having successfully rid herself of her pregnancy, gets on with her life in the communist youth movement and finally renews her relationship with her former boyfriend.

Anni's implied matter-of-fact approach to abortion chimes best with many of the women who had to defend themselves against the accusations of police and the courts. Rather than appearing passive, as in Fisher's interviews, or victimized, as in most popular cultural productions, they come across as active agents capable of exercising control over their fertility and their lives. Of course, my sample is self-selected in that the women examined stood accused of offences against §218 and were therefore involved in practising birth control. But German women's agency in this respect is also confirmed by surveys carried out just before or during the First World War by the Berlin dermatologist and sexologist Max Marcuse, and the Würzburg professor of gynaecology Oskar Polano.

Marcuse interviewed 100 of his proletarian female patients at his Berlin general practice. Framing his questions in such a way as to convey the assumption that contraception had been practised and pregnancies had been terminated as a matter of course, he managed to elicit extraordinarily frank answers. He found that ninety-eight women respondents thought his 'assumptions entirely natural if they related to themselves and harmless and understandable if they related to others'. Only three of Marcuse's 100 patients left contraception to their husbands and were ignorant of their precise method. All others showed that they had helped shape marital reproductive strategies either by their precise knowledge of their husbands' precautionary methods or by habitually using female contraception themselves, such as douching after intercourse or having a cap fitted. Forty women readily admitted to having had one or several abortions, apparently without 'embarrassment and inhibition', some even against their husband's wishes. Their determination to limit family size and the manner in which they inferred that birth control was their natural right is testimony to women's agency.[10]

In contrast, Marcuse's attempt to conduct the same survey on married male patients encountered great reticence even when he enquired about the relatively safe subject of contraception. Questions about abortion were warded off with replies such as, 'I don't worry about that', or 'that is my wife's business'. Only the special conditions afforded by the war, when Marcuse was in charge of a reserve army field hospital, gave him the chance of meeting more willing respondents: he selected 293 married soldiers who were well enough to be interviewed. This survey confirms that almost half of the soldiers' wives had taken on or at least shared the responsibility for family planning and, since the soldiers were not specifically asked about this, there may have been more. Typically, couples' birth control strategies ranged from husbands in charge with back-up measures by wives to wives having sole responsibility. For example, a 31-year-old postman told Marcuse that his wife applied a douche after every coitus and now had a coil inserted, too; or a 40-year-old construction worker with three children whose wife had had three miscarriages practised coitus interruptus but his wife douched immediately afterwards in case of doubt; a 27-year-old musician admitted that he did not always practise coitus interruptus but that his 26-year-old wife 'is on her guard against it'. Or a 25-year-old cashier, married for one year, no children but two miscarriages (one because the 'wife had got rid of it') admitted that only his wife used contraception. A milling cutter whose first marriage was contracted when he was aged twenty-two used no contraception at all but his wife had 'tipped' every year. This marriage ended in divorce because of adultery.[11]

Polano conducted his survey in 1914 on 500 women patients at his clinic in Würzburg; the great majority of his interviewees were married, lower-class and Catholic and it is therefore a useful counterpart to Marcuse's Berlin sample of mostly Protestant women. Polano's report omits the respondents' answers, which precludes gleaning information about husbands' and wives' gendered attitudes. But similarly to Marcuse's Berlin women, 339 of Polano's interviewees who admitted to contraception could name the precise method or appliance used by their husbands. One hundred and sixteen women said they and their husbands did not practise birth control for a variety of reasons, such as 'the desire to have children or indifference' (94), the belief that it was sinful (26), or because they were widowed or divorced (12) and husbands' refusal to cooperate with wives' express wishes (12). Only fifteen married and two single women appeared ignorant of birth control.[12]

The majority of women in my research for this book were very much part of the decision-making process about reproductive strategies, and many were in charge. What is more, their *Eigensinn* (obstinacy) in this respect showed that they resisted the dictates of medical authority both in the way they perceived abortion and in the manner of its execution. Many steadfastly clung to the notion of blocked menses, or, as it was expressed in Marcuse's survey, 'bad blood', in the face of different medical and legal definitions and in the intimidating setting of police stations or courts of law. Marcuse, out of empathy with his proletarian women patients and possibly also because he knew the limits of medical knowledge, thought this was 'not entirely without good reason'.[13] Many women refused to regard abortion as either the killing of an unborn child or a life-threatening calamity but as an everyday occurrence, even liberation from the burden of an unwanted pregnancy which was potentially disastrous in uncertain times. Women's mass violation of §218 during the Weimar Republic was in itself a sign of resistance against figures of authority, from policeman to teacher and priest. The 'scourge of abortion', much decried by the contemporary moral right but also by many liberals and men of the left, was little less than a mass rebellion against the draconian clause §218, even if judges were applying it more leniently than they were entitled to, especially in the later Weimar years. Moreover, the will to retain control over their body drove thousands of women onto the streets to demonstrate in favour of the decriminalization of abortion and it led them to petition politicians and parliament to this end.[14] Exhortations to the contrary in newspapers, travelling exhibitions, pamphlets and, as we have seen, in popular culture notwithstanding, women turned to pedlars of abortifacients, quacks and even fortune-tellers for help with unplanned pregnancies.

Yet, Kate Fisher's insistence that before the Second World War in England and Wales both husband and wife saw birth control 'as part of the male world, and a man's duty' is a useful reminder that men's role in this respect should not be overlooked. I have found plenty of evidence of men imposing their will on women, sometimes forcing them to terminate a pregnancy if this was inconvenient for the man and yet desired by the woman. There is, however, more evidence of close cooperation between husband and wife and between a young woman and her fiancé or lover, and this was true among both the working and the middle classes. According to Fisher, in England and Wales many married couples did not seem to have discussed birth control issues until well after the Second World War because it was unquestionably understood to be a man's responsibility and also because women regarded 'the act of planning . . . as cold, calculating, and an unnatural approach to family building'.[15] Furthermore, all matters sexual were a cause of acute embarrassment for British working-class couples. According to the academic and writer Richard Hoggart (b. 1918) they were very shy about certain aspects, such as talking about sex normally, or being seen naked, or even undressing before sex.[16] The sexual culture in late Imperial and Weimar Germany was markedly different: abortion featured large in many of the most popular plays, films and fiction and although censorship forced authors and scriptwriters to toe the line in some respects, the subject itself got plenty of airing. Marcuse's 1917 survey of 300 soldiers' marriages clearly shows that most men and women discussed reproduction and family limitation; even more respondents might have indicated that this was the case had they been asked about it. Well over half the answers suggest that family size and birth control was planned together either by explicitly saying so or by implying it by a precise knowledge of the wife's contraceptive method and the absence of criticism of it. Take the example of the 24-year-old postman from a small town in the Lausitz, married for three years with one child; this had arrived unplanned but now he and his wife wanted to avoid another. They had 'immediately agreed that later there was still time for the matter of having children'. In those cases where a child or more children were desired, husbands' responses show that this wish was supported by the wife.[17]

The German birth rate declined rapidly, from 31.7 per cent in the years 1906–10 to 18.4 per cent in the years 1926–30, a result of a decline in both marital and extramarital fertility. This meant a very visible decline in the average number of children per family: from 4.7 (for marriages contracted before 1905) and 3.6 (for those contracted in 1910–15) to only 2 (for marriages contracted between 1925 and 1929), much lower than the equivalent figures in England and Wales.[18] The rapidity of this demographic change was hardly possible without marital cooperation, although mentally and physically disabled veterans must have contributed to it perhaps more than was officially conceded.[19] The decline in the number of children born outside wedlock shows that single women also knew about contraception or, more likely, had access to abortion. As we have seen, however, responsibility for fertility control was also shared between the unmarried. Family planning, including abortion, may well have brought couples closer. The Hesse case study presented in Chapter 6 shows clearly the extent to which many husbands or boyfriends were involved in the planning and execution of a termination; they were often present during the operation, holding a torch to provide light for the abortionist and thus could not but witness the visceral aspects of an obstetric operation men were usually shielded from at that time; they also registered their wives' or lovers' physical and psychological reactions to it. The surviving correspondence between women who feared an unwanted pregnancy and their lovers reveals how well informed many men were about the gynaecological aspects of women's bodies but also how emotionally committed they were to help bring about a solution to their dilemma. This was to be found among all classes and in towns as well as countryside.[20] Such mutuality signified an important shift in the relationship between men and women: they talked openly about matters which their parents' generation probably found too embarrassing or distasteful to mention freely and they supported each other when the need arose. It also meant a transformation of the politics of marriage or gender relations: thanks to their growing awareness of their economic, political and social power women had become more assertive in controlling their fertility while at the same time it highlighted, as Linda Gordon suggested, 'men's diminishing social power in the family'.[21] On the other hand, women might well have resented the assumption that birth control was to be their responsibility rather than their partners', and that men should be allowed to be sexually active without such responsibilities, a point made both by Fisher and by Hera Cook in her discussion of English sex and marriage manuals after the Second World War.[22] In unmarried relationships in particular, honour played an important role. A woman's honour was damaged if her boyfriend deserted her once she was pregnant, but honour was equally important for men's strategies, which depended greatly on cultural norms of class differences between the couple and the promises given at the outset of the relationship. Much more needs to be known about men's motives and the role of masculinity in reproduction and fertility control and this would be a fertile ground for future research.

[. . .]

Of all the oppositional polarities, the differences between lower and middle classes proved of greatest importance. It was national economists like Julius Wolf or Paul Mombert who had developed the theory that wealth and the declining birth rate were causally linked. Mombert stated that fertility declined in parallel to rising wealth and social status',[23] an observation which seemed to be borne out in the statistics of the marital birth rate differentiated by class: among higher civil servants the average number of children was 3.5 for marriages contracted before 1905 but only 1.6 for those contracted between 1925 and 1929 compared to the number of children born to labourers of 4.5 and 2.1 in the same periods.[24] Class differences were also noticeable in the way abortion was practised and prosecuted. Contemporaries usually perceived abortion as a class-specific problem. One of the very first petitions to decriminalize it, sent by a group of women to the Prussian Minister of Justice, referred to 'wealthy childless women' who could afford a termination and to poor women who were criminalized.[25] Both the KPD and the SPD fought for legal reform on the grounds of class discrimination;[26] in the cultural sphere productions like *Kreuzzug, Cyankali, Madame Lu* or *Maria und der Paragraph* echoed and reinforced this notion, although others like *Gilgl* or *stud.chem. Helene Willfüer* showed that white-collar workers like Gilgi or academic women like Helene also found it impossible, or difficult, to rid themselves of an unwanted pregnancy. In 1914 Max Hirsch, another doctor and sexologist practising in Berlin, claimed that abortion among the lower classes was the main method of fertility control and that contraception was limited to the upper classes.[27] The criminal court cases examined for this book suggest that prosecutions for violation of §218 were heavily stacked against the poor. Bourgeois women certainly practised abortion, too, but they were underrepresented in crime statistics and this was for two reasons: well-to-do and educated women found it easier then lower-class women to obtain discreet help from a doctor and they had easier access to effective contraception, such as the Mensinga diaphragm, the cervical cap or the coil which usually needed fitting and regular check-ups by a doctor. This accords with Polano's findings: 81 per cent of all wives of civil servants in his randomly selected sample had used contraceptives compared to only 72 per cent of workers' wives.[28] The physical circumstances and the rhythm of daily life made it far easier for the middle classes to practise birth control more assiduously compared to the lower classes who lacked the necessary privacy, being hampered by cramped living conditions, and who often had no access to running water and heating etc. The many birth control clinics which sprang up in Weimar Germany after the end of the inflationary period catered not just for the middle classes but also for the working classes, yet those in charge found that the latter continued to prefer non-appliance methods such as coitus interruptus which cost nothing and which needed no complicated preparations.[29] A number of doctors developed their own expensive patented brands of female contraceptives, such as the Gräfenberg ring made of gold, or cervical caps in platinum which suggests that they were clearly aimed at the rich.[30] Finally, lower-class women, more than their middle-class counterparts, refused to be colonized by bourgeois ethical norms defining what constituted appropriate sexual behaviour: the biographical references to women defendants show that premarital sexual relations or the custom of 'tipping' unwanted pregnancies were frowned upon by middle-class commentators but among the poor were widely practised and accepted, often considered entirely rational, even the norm. Marcuse was astonished to find that abortion was often practised not 'as a later replacement for contraception but very often very early on as the method of choice'.[31]

Continuity and change

There is no doubt that the influence of the First World War on body history was enormous. For example, Max Hirsch, the Berlin doctor and sexologist, thought the war and the revolution had produced 'profoundly changed attitudes, life circumstances, and led to moral and economic decline'.[32] Elisabeth Domansky argued that the war had eroded the German family; the 'gendered mobilization of German society for total war' which also frequently included children and young people drafted in for public works, separated men, women and children from their families. Men's murderous experiences at the front rendered many families fatherless or undermined male authority in the home which was also challenged by 'women's and children's experience with self-sufficiency during the war'.[33] The refiguration of gender roles during the war also transformed men's and women's role in public life during the Republic, especially in the labour market and in politics. As Kathleen Canning has put it, the result of these multiple social changes was the emergence of a new female body – that of the female citizen. The body of the new *Staatsbürgerin* figures prominently during the early years of the republic, from the writing of the Weimar constitution to the campaigns of the reconstituted political parties in 1919 and 1920, to the new arenas of popular culture, consumption and mass entertainment, and to the visions of an expanded and effective welfare state.[34]

In the face of a rapidly declining birth rate and the slaughter of over two million young men in the trenches, the war had also put a new premium on women's procreative capabilities. In the interventionist Weimar welfare state young women's bodies became both a site of intervention and of power, to be disciplined by stringent regulation and to be rewarded materially and symbolically. This and their new civil rights emboldened women from all walks of life to voice their demands publicly.[35] In 1919 Adele Schreiber-Krieger, radical feminist and SPD member of the Reichstag's population select committee, called the phenomenon of the rapidly declining national fertility 'the greatest, non-violent revolution' by women, and one which 'put the key to the control of life firmly into the hands of mothers. Thus a woman in bondage becomes master and determines the fate of the family, the *Volk* and humanity'.[36] It is no coincidence that among the very first petitions sent to the Constituent Assembly was one by a group of Berlin women, without party affiliation, to 'curb coercive procreation in Germany' and to decriminalize abortion, for single women and for mothers of three children.[37] Weimar's modernity, which encouraged a 'rationalization of sexuality' – that is, a belief that the reproductive process should be controlled to suit the economic conditions and personal preferences – led to the lowest birth rate in the Western world. It also heralded a new hedonism in women's sexuality and a shift in the power of gender relations. As ever more women from the lower classes opted for abortion as their birth control method of choice, official disapproval waned, too.

Members of the medical and legal professions and the law enforcement authorities reluctantly came to tolerate, sometimes even support, abortion law reform in view of the apparent rise in abortions. The draconian penalties prescribed by the Wilhelmine criminal code were substantially modified in 1926 in favour of the aborting woman; the new law scapegoated professional abortionists instead; this was followed in 1927 by the permission of therapeutic abortion by decree. In Imperial Germany and the early Weimar years the police made many raids on suspected doctors' or quack practices but in post-inflation Weimar prosecutions generally occurred only after an abortion-related death or injury was detected or after a denunciation. This meant that the gap between theory and practice or elite attitudes to §218 and popular ideology narrowed. Even the great pillars of sexual morality, the Protestant Church, to a larger extent, and the Roman Catholic Church, to a lesser extent, and their affiliated denominational societies felt compelled to adapt to the growing popularity of family limitation in Weimar Germany in order to retain their influence in the new republic and popular support in an increasingly secular age.[38]

Individual doctors were increasingly willing to brave the storm of indignation from their invariably conservative national and local medical societies by publicly defending their own practice of terminating pregnancies on economic and social grounds, which was still illegal. Testimony of this are the highly publicized abortion trials involving doctors during the second half of the Republic, most famously the case in 1931 of the two communists Else Kienle and Friedrich Wolf, the doctor/playwright we met in Chapter 2.[39] The rural practitioner who became well known by the posthumous publication of his case material by Alfred Grotjahn was not the only one to practise terminations undetected. Another doctor from a small industrial town somewhere in Germany was able to perform abortions undisturbed by the law. In 1932 he confided to Dr Käte Frankenthal, doctor and member of the Prussian Diet for the Socialist Workers Party, that since 1922 he had performed more than 1,500 terminations. Although his patients were predominantly poor he had also helped wives and daughters of industrialists, entrepreneurs, police officers, teachers and even National Socialists.[40] In 1927 two doctors from Rheydt in the Rhineland, an area with a high number of female industrial workers, thought that agreeing to women's abortion requests was no more than a reasonable response to social hardship or, more radically, a woman's right. Although the account of this trial is found in a legal thesis of 1940, which is therefore infused with National Socialist ideology,[41] especially in its condemnation of the alleged communist propaganda resulting from the case, it is still valuable for the statistics and direct and indirect statements that it contains. In this trial the witness statements of several midwives and a medical colleague all agreed in one respect, namely that the opinion of men and women had changed fundamentally since the war. As soon as they sensed a second pregnancy women planned how to rid themselves of it out of a general distaste for the burden of children. Among working-class women and commercial abortionists alike, communist propaganda against §218 had a major effect. Women declared they would treat their body as they saw fit and nobody else had the right to determine whether the child should be carried to term.

The working-class women accused of abortion in this trial thought that to give birth to an unwanted child was sheer stupidity. 'You are mad to want another child, why don't you go to [one of the two doctors on trial] and ask him to remove it for you!'.[42]

Towards the late 1920s punitive policy softened considerably, showing to what degree 'the practice of award of punishment is influenced by cultural trends and changing world view'.[43] The German criminologist Exner conducted a study of the average penalties meted out for simple and commercial abortion within Germany as a whole during the single year of 1927. This showed that most sentences for both 'simple' and 'commercial' abortion were extraordinarily lenient. He regarded this as the result of 'a moral response to the ethics of every-day-life since the popular moral judgement of this [particular] crime is based on the principle: understanding means condoning.'[44]

Abortion in Nazi Germany

This coming together of popular practice and official policy seemed to come to a sudden halt with Hitler's assumption of power. Abortion became an important tool in the National Socialists' increasingly repressive population policy: Gabriele Czarnowski refers to it as a highly sophisticated selective programme of state-regulated reproduction according to eugenic/racist principles. It covered the entire spectrum from prosecuting and prohibiting abortion of those regarded as eugenically desirable children to permitting and enforcing it when 'undesirable' offspring were involved. Nazi population planners set out to destroy the subculture of clandestine abortion which they considered had spiralled out of control during the 'libertine' years of the Weimar Republic. The new regime introduced the necessary measures against voluntary abortion without delay. As early as May 1933 advertisements for abortion services and abortifacients were banned, an attempt to stop once and for all their widespread use of the Weimar years. At its nadir, during the Second World War the law of 1943 'To Protect Marriage, Family and Motherhood' introduced capital punishment in certain cases for hardened abortionists. This meant the killing of those who had in their turn 'killed genetically valuable' foetal life. Czarnowski certainly found a number of cases where abortionists, among them former midwives, were executed.[45] The new 1943 law also had a detrimental effect on simple abortions, that is by 'Aryan' German women who did not involve commercial operators. The normal penalty for simple abortion for a woman went up to a whole year's imprisonment and that for aiding frequently exceeded this.[46] My own research corroborates this; for example, at the beginning of June, exactly three months after the new law had come into operation, a 19-year-old domestic servant was sentenced to one year in gaol for having terminated her pregnancy, the result of a brief dalliance with a soldier on holiday in her village. Her mother, an unmarried washerwoman of forty-seven, had assisted her daughter by supplying a syringe and was sentenced even more harshly, to 15 months' imprisonment. A Dutchman who lived in the same village and had also aided in the abortion received the same penalty. The judge explained that the sentences were so harsh because the new law dictated this kind of judgement.[47]

Although the Nazi regime legalized abortion on medical grounds for the first time (as opposed to permitting it by decree of the Supreme Court, as was the case in 1927), Czarnowski argues persuasively that this apparently liberal measure was in reality repressive owing to the stringent and punitive procedure of assessment and registration. The year 1935 saw the introduction of mandatory registration and identification of every termination, miscarriage and premature birth, which made detection of criminal abortion easier. By 1936 or 1937 policing had been sharpened and Himmler had established his Headquarters to Combat Homosexuality and Abortion within the Department of Criminal Investigation. Its effectiveness is easily apparent from the increase in the number of criminal investigations into potential abortion infringements and the rising proportion of all investigations. Between Weimar and Nazi Germany the proportion of abortion cases of all criminal investigations in the *Landgericht* Mönchen-Gladbach went up from 9 per cent during the Weimar years to 11 per cent in the first six years of the Nazi regime, with an enormous increase in 1937.[48] The records of the *Landgericht* Duisburg show a similar increase.[49] And there were other legal measures to curb abortion if practised by individual women as voluntary birth control, hidden in new laws which had, on the surface, little to do with abortion (such as that against Dangerous Habitual Offenders of 1933), and the police had their own means of 'protective custody' which usually involved concentration camps.[50]

While the assessment centres put as many obstacles as possible in the way of German women of 'sound' stock seeking to terminate unwanted pregnancies, they facilitated mass abortions on Polish and Russian forced women labourers. This was the other side of the coin of Nazi abortion policy. Their programme of negative eugenics, which had the professed aim to 'cleanse the racial body' of 'inferior individuals', led to compulsory abortion for 'hereditarily diseased' women and those of 'alien races'. In July 1933, the 'Law for the Prevention of Hereditarily Diseased Progeny' paved the way for compulsory eugenic sterilization,[51] which was swiftly supplemented by the legalization of abortion on eugenic grounds. This occurred in two stages: firstly, clandestinely in a confidential memorandum sent in 1933 by the head of the Reich Medical Board to all doctors in Germany and without informing the judiciary but with the apparent backing of Hitler; secondly, by incorporating this principle into the amended Sterilization Law of 1935.[52] While the new abortion law of March 1943 introduced more severe penalties for those who performed abortions on women deemed of 'desirable' stock, it abrogated penalties if this was not the case. Polish and Czech aborting women and their accomplices, for example, were not prosecuted in German courts, nor were German abortionists who performed the operation on foreign women or those, like Jewish women, whose progeny was deemed 'undesirable'.[53]

My research has also unearthed the fact that the 1943 law caused frequent retrials when a public prosecutor pressed for a more severe sentence on aborting women and their accomplices. Thus, in October 1943, the *Landgericht* Trier increased the gaol term from four to six months for a 17-year-old female manual worker despite her employer's concern at the loss of a valuable worker and recognition of 'emotional problems caused by a pregnancy when so young and despite possessing a clean police record, her full confession and her evident remorse'. The judge ruled that 'in view of the long war and the considerable loss of valuable human life the vital strength [*Lebenskraft*] of the German *Volk* deserves increased protection and that, in contrast to opinions held before, the particular reprehensible and unacceptable nature of crimes against foetal life have come to be fully appreciated by the community'. The sentence of the young woman's accomplice, a father of three small children, was even raised from eight months' gaol to twelve months' penal servitude, on the grounds that he 'should have known that every attempt to perform an abortion on a genetically valuable woman expecting a desirable valuable child is to be regarded a crime against the vital strength of the German people'.[54]

Statistics of individual courts' records show that the determination to hand out much tougher sanctions on abortion was put into practice. In the *Landgericht* Duisburg, for example, during the last five years of the Weimar Republic only one single person was sentenced to penal servitude (under two years) but in the first years after January 1933 no less than sixteen people were thus sentenced, nine of whom to penal servitude of more than two years. At the same time the length of prison sentences also went up markedly.[55] In the *Landgericht* and *Amtsgericht* Freiburg i.Br., during the second part of the Weimar years (and the early parts of the Nazi period), two-thirds of all abortion cases were tried as misdemeanours by courts of lay assessors with a maximum penalty of three months' gaol (but in practice weeks or days or even fines were meted out), but between 1935 and 1945 as many as 12.3 per cent were tried by jury courts with much harsher penalties being meted out.[56] The same trend was noticeable in Mönchen-Gladbach.[57] In a typical case from the *Landgericht* Braunschweig from October 1942 a 27-year-old married woman had a brief affair with a lorry driver while her husband was in the army and when she suspected she was pregnant she arranged for a termination. She was sentenced to twelve months' imprisonment for this while her lover, who supplied an inappropriate instrument, went scot-free. In another case, also from 1942, an unfaithful wife received a penalty of five months' gaol simply for an attempted abortion which might well have been a natural miscarriage.[58]

Women's accomplices, their unpaid helpers, were also more severely punished, as the records of the *Landgericht* Freiburg well illustrate: prior to 1933 the vast majority received sentences of less than three months; after 1933 this gradually reversed and by 1936 the majority of accomplices were sentenced to between three and twelve months. In Mönchen-Gladbach the average length of sentence more than doubled.[59] An abortion case tried by the *Landgericht* Trier in 1938 shows how the courts inflicted increasingly harsh sentences on all involved: a 20-year-old woman, engaged to a bricklayer whom she subsequently married, had a pregnancy terminated in 1936 by a railway employee and one year later sought his help again but this time his attempts were unsuccessful and she bore a child. She received a month's prison sentence for one full and one attempted abortion, 'despite her youth and the hardship she suffered'. In the same trial a young woman living at home had been expecting an illegitimate child by a miller who said he could not marry her because he had no money. Through a friend, a local farmer, he arranged a termination by a widow. The young woman was sentenced to four months in goal. As with the other aborting woman mentioned above, the judge allowed that she had acted under duress but insisted that 'despite the mitigating circumstances the punishment should be appreciable because of the detrimental effect her actions had on the *Volk*'. The miller received a prison sentence of three months and three weeks, which was almost as harsh as that of his girlfriend, by way of punishment for his 'disgraceful behaviour' towards her, by impregnating her 'to fulfil his sexual drive', yet refusing to marry her. As for the two professional abortionists, the railwayman was sentenced to a total of three years in gaol, for one completed and one attempted abortion and for aiding with an attempted abortion on a second woman. Even though he had not acted for financial gain he had done so 'not out of compassion but to satisfy his carnal lust' (he had also forced his client to have sex with him) and had carried out his trade 'during office hours and in official railway accommodation'. His mitigating circumstances were the fact that he had no police record, his advanced age (despite being only forty) and the fact that 'he has shown himself a man in life', surely a reference to his wartime service. The harshest punishment by far was reserved for the widow: she was sentenced to a total of three years' penal servitude and a loss of all civil rights for five years for the full abortion on the young woman and two cases of attempted abortion on a domestic servant. The judge wanted her punished severely because she had 'carried out her criminal trade to the detriment of the national community even though her economic position did not force her to seek an additional income. This was aggravated by the fact that she already had a four months' gaol sentence for procuring.'[60]

Not surprisingly, the penalties for commercial abortionists went up markedly. A case from the *Schwurgericht* Trier from October 1937 shows this well: an agricultural vineyard worker also ran an abortion business with his wife. He was found guilty of three cases of commercial abortion and received the severe sentence of six years' penal servitude and loss of civil rights; his wife was sentenced to two years' penal servitude and loss of civil rights.[61] In another case, from Braunschweig, the commercial abortionist was a divorced woman of seventy-three who had a police record for offences against §218. The court considered her 'a dangerous habitual criminal', 'completely incorrigible' and a 'serious danger to the German *Volk*'. A severe sentence was demanded and duly meted out: five years' penal servitude and loss of civil rights for the same period of time.[62]

Many of the trials of the Nazi years I have investigated also show that men who had impregnated women and then aided an abortion – or, even worse, instigated the operation in the first place – were punished severely. For example, in March 1933, a 22-year-old woman from a village near Aachen was sentenced to six months' gaol for having undergone an abortion but her boyfriend was given eight months' gaol for aiding and abetting and for his 'base motives since he did not want to marry her'; even when 'she withdrew her sexual favours from him' he preferred to denounce her to the police for having an abortion rather than do the honourable thing by her.[63] In the later years of the Third Reich men were punished severely for 'avoiding [their] duty as procreator[s] of children', as proved by the case of the lover of a divorcée who received fifteen months' imprisonment for helping his girlfriend with six abortions, though she was only sentenced to ten months in gaol[64] or, similarly, when the penalty for an agricultural worker from a village near Trier for aiding with his girlfriend's attempted and unsuccessful abortion (owing to inappropriate means) was one year in gaol, while she received only nine months. The judgement was, however, revised downwards on appeal but he still received two months more in gaol than she did.[65]

No doubt as a consequence of the increased level of monitoring, doctors and other health professionals noticed a more marked tendency towards self-abortion in the Nazi era than was the case during the Weimar Republic when it was much easier to enlist the help of a professional abortionist. Some doctors commented on the surprising skill which women displayed in finding their cervix and the care they took to operate in sterile conditions.[66] Certainly, the files from the period of the Second World War in particular show the high prevalence of self-abortions.[67] Against the background of war when so many men were away at the front and a significant number of married women seemed to have started affairs with other men, or single women with married men, a number of abortion trials document the determination of women to avoid raising children born out of wedlock. But the authorities, worried about population loss and racial purity, saw it differently. Illegitimacy (as long as the progeny was thought 'eugenically desirable'), the courts now argued, was not a valid ground for abortion because, as one judge of the Cologne *Landgericht* put it, 'in today's times everything possible will be done to alleviate the situation of the unmarried mother, to bestow on her the full dignity and honour of motherhood in the eyes of the public'. Never mind that the 21-year-old woman was not only unmarried but also had lost both parents and had never had any brush with the police

before. The judge freely admitted 'emotional hardship' was outweighed by crude populationist concerns. Or, as the *Amtsgericht* Rostock declared in June 1941, in the case of a
40-year-old divorcée who had an affair with a married man, her abortion must be judged
a serious crime since this was 'an age in which prejudice against illegitimacy is no longer
important'.[68] And, in the name of preserving the existing children of 'Aryan German
parents', aborting women were given extra-long sentences if they were deemed to have
neglected their children while on wartime quests for sexual adventure,[69] a paradoxical
judgement since these children would be much more neglected when deprived of their
mothers in gaol.

Yet, despite such signs of a determined crackdown on abortion as voluntary birth
control it is perhaps surprising to find some evidence of continuity between Weimar and
Nazi abortion judicial practice, for a number of reasons. Firstly, as Czarnowski has asserted,
only a small proportion of putative criminal abortions was ever investigated under National
Socialist rule because there were never enough funds available to investigate all the
registered cases of terminations and miscarriages. Secondly, Nazi sentencing policy became
much harsher in theory but was in practice tempered by a number of amnesties benefiting
both aborting women and their accomplices, in cases when the expected prison term did
not exceed a certain duration, the exact length of which varied over time.[70] What is more,
during the early years of the Third Reich judicial practice resembled that of the Weimar
era quite closely. Contrary to official threats, some judges seem to have condoned infractions
of §218 and handed down surprisingly mild sentences for aborting women and abortionists
alike on the grounds of often spurious-sounding mitigating circumstances. These latter
seem either to have masked attitudes which were still more in tune with Weimar liberalism,
while at the same time paying lip service to Nazi ideas, or they were driven by expediency
rather than populationist concerns. Explanations proffered included one of chronology,
i.e. that the deed had taken place during the decadent Weimar years when minds were
perverted and sensibilities warped, or during the very early years of Nazi rule when the
new ideology had not yet had time to enlighten the populace. Typically, one judge
commenting on an abortion case of 1932, tried during the Nazi rule, thought the accused
was quite right to point out that her deed, or rather her submitting to it, had taken place
at a time when the community in which she lived did not regard it as unethical (1932)
and since then the state has failed to change people's minds by the appropriate public
enlightenment. Even if this incontrovertible fact cannot entirely exonerate the accused it
must, however, serve as mitigating circumstances.[71]

In a case from October 1933, where the infraction of §218 had occurred at the very
beginning of the Nazi regime, a homeopath was convicted of commercial abortion and
manslaughter. His penalty consisted merely of imprisonment for two years, six months,
presumably for the same reasons as above.[72] In another case from 1937, a husband-and-
wife team of professional abortionists were convicted on at least four counts of abortion,
performed together and the husband for a further two cases performed by himself.
Astonishingly, they were both spared penal servitude and received instead three and four
years' gaol respectively. The judge held that they should be punished severely for not
having operated with due care but that, on the other hand, they had

> carried out their criminal acts in the years 1927 to 1928, that is at a time
> when the strict National Socialist view of the totally reprehensible nature of
> abortion had not yet penetrated to the general public; when, on the contrary,

energetic propaganda on the part of certain factions for the complete decriminalization of abortion had become widespread, that means circumstances in which
the defendants' deed could have appeared in a less reprehensible light. Thus,
the deeds committed . . . could not be judged as severely as would be today.
That is why the defendants were granted mitigating circumstances and penal
servitude.

Expediency was clearly the main reason for mild sentences in a well-known case tried
in January 1935 in Frankfurt upon Oder: four doctors from Fürstenberg upon Oder, a
medical officer of health and three family doctors, were accused of having cooperated in
an abortion business; issuing false medical certificates for each other's operations; and
entering misleading data in their medical diaries. Moreover they had been found guilty
of deceiving health insurance funds by double charging them and their patients. Each was
suspected of performing illegal terminations on many women, the medical officer of health
in most, but not all, cases before 1933; his three colleagues after Hitler came to power.
The sentences of these four doctors no longer referred to the most damaging aspects of
the charge: abortion for financial gain and insurance fraud; consequently they were spared
harsh sentences and, what is more, they served only a fraction of their time in prison
either because they were pardoned or their prison term was commuted to a fine. The
official reason was either that the charge was invalidated by the statute of limitation (five
years) or, in the cases of the three medical practitioners, that it was committed in the
first few months of the Nazi regime 'at a time when the political situation was still very
fluid and the strict National Socialist attitude towards termination of pregnancy had not
yet made its way into medical circles in a sufficiently desirable manner'. The more plausible
explanation is the fact that the authorities had realized with some embarrassment that the
criminal investigation of these four doctors would deprive the local population of all medical
help. Thus, the arrest of the fourth doctor was delayed until a locum was secured. The
decision in subsequent years not to strike their names off the medical register was surely
taken for the same reason.[73]

Continuity with Imperial Germany

While I want to stress the significant liberal tendencies which developed in the sentencing
practice of the postinflation Weimar years and connect them to a greater openness to
modernity in general and reproductive self-determination in particular, there are important
continuities also between Imperial and Weimar Germany in reproductive practices. The
effect of the First World War should not be exaggerated. The continuity in working-class
patterns of fertility control from late Imperial to Weimar Germany is striking, with a
persistence of age-old trusted methods such as coitus interruptus and abortion alongside
newer methods, although infanticide was much rarer than in the nineteenth century. There
was no sharp break with women's previous strategy in that they had also taken control
of their reproductive choices before the war.

Two of Weimar's potent symbols of modernity, the New Woman and the concept
of rationalized sexuality, too, often turn out to be more ambiguous when tested against
both popular culture and the statements of hundreds of aborting women here examined.
While fictional heroines like Gilgi and Helene Willfüer celebrate the emancipated woman,

the typical image of the proletarian protagonist in literary or cinematic abortion narratives hardly resembled that of the economically independent and sexually assertive woman; nor did the lower-class victims of §218 in popular culture display the rebelliousness against husband or the state which comes across in Marcuse's and Polano's surveys or when women defended their abortion in front of the police or the judge. Popular fiction or film preferred to present women from the lower orders in their more traditional roles as suffering mothers and as victims of the vicissitudes of fertility control.

As Elizabeth Harvey has put it, 'if the "new woman" was one powerful symbol of cultural change, Berlin came to embody it in terms of geographical location. The capital of the republic became the site on which competing and conflicting visions of its modernity were – at least partially – realized'.[74] Asserting bodily autonomy was as much a characteristic of emancipated women as their role in consumerism and the new mass culture. Aborting women who sought to control their body and their sexual relationships pursued their aim in a strikingly unsentimental fashion, for example when they disposed of their foetus as if it was so much waste, or when they terminated a pregnancy against the will of their male partner. Here women were not unlike what Helmuth Lethen called the 'cold persona' of male intellectuals who hid their emotions behind a mask of detached cynicism.[75] Yet, most of these women eschewed 'scientific' contraceptives in favour of what doctors repudiated as 'primitive' and unreliable methods of postcoital douching or, more importantly, abortion, albeit practised with modern methods like the syringe. While women defendants generally seemed to be familiar with medical concepts of pregnancy and termination they also adhered to older interpretations: a delayed period could mean several things, from a physical disturbance, a sign of being unwell to a misfortune that had befallen them or their entire family. In this they echoed the eighteenth-century female patients of the physician Storch, examined by Barbara Duden; they, too, understood a lack of menstrual flow in a variety of ways: as an illness, an unborn child, or a *Mondkalb*, that is a 'mole' or a 'shadow sibling' of a real conception.[76] If late blood is perceived as a misfortune, a visit to a fortune-teller does not seem illogical. The Berlin concierge who was a popular abortionist as well as a *Kartenlegerin* and offered sympathetic magic was only one of many wise women who catered for their clients' physical and emotional needs, as in other parts of Germany. It shows that 1920s and early 1930s Berlin, the byword for modernity, continued to offer space to practices we associate with premodern times, and that women who 'rationalized' their sexuality were still attracted to enchantment and magic. If such views appear strange to some of us today, it is proof that the historian needs an imaginative sympathy with and respect for the sensibilities of the subjects under scrutiny; rationality comes in different guises, and wonder and awe are compatible with a scientific worldview.[77]

Notes

1   Michel Foucault, *History of Sexuality: Vol. 1, An Introduction* (London, 1979), 105.
2   For mediation see Willem de Blécourt and Cornelie Usborne, 'Medicine, Mediation and Meaning', in idem (eds), *Cultural Approaches to the History of Medicine. Mediating Medicine in Early Modern and Modern Europe* (Basingstoke and New York, 2004), 1–10.
3   Jeffrey Weeks, *Making Sexual History* (Cambridge, 2000), 129.
4   Kate Fisher, *Birth Control, Sex, and Marriage in Britain, 1918–1960* (Oxford: Oxford University Press, 2006), 238–39.

5   Fisher, *Birth Control, Sex and Marriage*, 238–39.

6   Max Marcuse, 'Zur Frage der Verbreitung und Methodik willkürlicher Geburten-beschränkung in Berliner Proletarierkrieisen', *Sexualprobleme* 9 (November 1913), 753, 957–73, 775.

7   Max Marcuse, *Der eheliche Präventivverkehr: seine Verbreitung, Verursachung und Methodik* (Stuttgart: Verlag Ferdinand Enke, 1917), e.g. cases 3, 6, 8, 166, 252.

8   Oskar Polano, 'Beitrag zur Frage der Geburtenbeschränkung', *Zeitschrift für Geburtshilfe und Gynäkologie* 79 (1916), 569–72.

9   Cornelie Usborne, 'Body Biological to Body Politic: Women's Demands for Reproductive Self-Determination in World War I and Early Weimar Germany', in Geoff Eley and Jan Palmowski (eds), *Citizenship and National Identity in Twentieth-Century Germany* (Palo Alto: Stanford University Press, 2008), 129–45.

10   Marcuse, 'Zur Frage der Verbreitung und Methodik', 753, 757–73, 775.

11   Marcuse, *Der eheliche Präventivverkehr*, e.g. cases 3, 6, 8, 166, 252.

12   Polano, 'Zur Frage der Geburtenbeschränkung', 569–72.

13   Marcuse, 'Zur Frage der Verbreitung', 754.

14   See Usborne, 'Body Biological to Body Politic'.

15   Fisher, *Birth Control, Sex and Marriage*, 238, 242.

16   Richard Hoggart, *The Uses of Literacy* (London, 1957), cited in Cook, *The Long Sexual Revolution*, 128.

17   Marcuse, *Der eheliche Präventivverkehr*, 18, 19, 21–29, 32–33, 37, 39–40, 47–48 etc.

18   See Usborne, *Politics of the Body*, 2, 33; Jeffrey Weeks, *Sex, Politics and Society. The Regulation of Sexuality since 1800* (London and New York, 1981), 45.

19   See Sabine Kienitz, 'Body Damage: War Disability and Constructions of Masculinity in Weimar Germany', in Karen Hagemann and Stefanie Schüler-Springorum (eds), *Home/Front: The Military, War, and Gender in Twentieth-Century Germany* (Oxford, 2002), 181–204.

20   E.g., SAM, Sta.anw. Traunstein, 15690 and 15696; ibid., AG Mü, 37153.

21   See Linda Gordon, *Woman's Body, Woman's Right*, 412.

22   Cook, *The Long Sexual Revolution*, 243; cf. idem, 'Sex and the Doctors: the Medicalization of Sexuality as a Two-war Process in Early to Mid-twentieth-century Britain', in de Blécourt and Usborne (eds), *Cultural Approaches*, 192–211.

23   Wolf, *Der Geburtenrückgang*; Paul Mombert, *Studien zur Bevölkerungsbewegung in Deutschland in den letzten jahrzehnten mit besonderer Berücksichtigung der ehelichen Fruchtbarkeit* (Karlsruhe, 1907), 162; cf. Bergmann, *Die verhütete Sexualität*, 38ff.

24   Reinhard Spree, 'Der Geburtenrückgang in Deutschland vor 1939', *Demographische Informationen*, 3 (1984), 62.

25   Geheimes Staatsarchiv Preussischer Kulturbesitz Berlin-Dahlem Rep 84a, 8231, B1 84.

26   See Usborne, *Politics of the Body*, chap. 4.

27   Max Hirsch, *Fruchtabtreibung und Präventivverkehr im Zusammenhang mit dem. Geburtenrückgang* (Würzburg, 1914), 32f.

28   Polano, 'Beitrag zur Frage der Geburtenbeschränkung', 572.

29   Marcuse, 'Der eheliche Präventivverkehr', 383f.

30   See Usborne, *Politics of the Body*, 130–31.

31   Cf. Usborne, 'Rhetoric and Resistance'; Marcuse, *Der eheliche Präventivverkehr*, 110.

32   Hirsch, *Die Fruchtabtreibung*, 41.

33   Domansky, 'Militarization and Reproduction', 445, 459.

34   Canning, *Gender History in Practice*, 182.

35   See Usborne, 'Body Biological to Body Politic'.

36   BABL, NL Schreiber, no. 60, n.d.

37   BABL, R 1501, 9347, Bl. 45.

38   See Usborne, 'The Christian Churches and the Regulation of Sexuality'; idem, *The Politics of the Body*, 71 ff.

39   See Friedrich Wolf, 'Der Stuttgarter Prozeß um den §218', in J.W. Hauer, '§218. Eine sachliche Aussprache', *Der freie Dienst*, 1 (1931), 195–99; idem, *Sturm gegen den Paragraph 218. Unser Stuttgarter Prozeß* (Berlin, 1931); Else Kienle, *Frauen. Aus dem Tagebuch einer Ärztin* (Berlin, 1932).

40   Dr Käte Frankenthal, 'Question asked in the Prussian Diet', *Korrespondenz des informationsbüros für Geburtenregelung*, 2 (1932), 4–9, 6.

41   Cf. other law theses: Jahns, *Abtreibung in Duisburg* (Düsseldorf, 1938); Krieger, 'Abtreibung in Freiburg'.

42   Inderheggen, *Abtreibung in Mönchen-Gladbach*, 19–20.

43   Inderheggen, *Abtreibung in M-Gladbach*, 131.

44   Exner cited in Inderheggen, *Abtreibung in Mönchen-Gladbach*, 131, 133–35: the study showed that 57.7 per cent of all cases which came to trial were punished with prison sentences of under three months and as many as 20.9 per cent with a fine; the most frequent (36.2 per cent) sentence for commercial abortion cases was gaol of one year and more, closely followed (31.4 per cent) by those of gaol terms between 3 and 12 months and, in third position, penal servitude (27.3 per cent), although the maximum penalty for this was penal servitude of 15 years.

45   Czarnowski, 'Women's Crimes, State Crimes', 238–39.

46   Ibid., 241.

47   LHAK, 605.2, 9965, LG Aurich, 8 June 1943.

48   Inderheggen, *Abtreibung in Mönchen-Gladbach*, 10–22: in 1937 the number of criminal investigations of suspected abortion cases went up from 97 in 1936 to 227.

49   Jahns, *Abtreibung in Duisburg*, 10.

50   Czarnowski, 'Women's Crimes, State Crimes', 247.

51   See Bock, *Zwangssterilisation*, 80ff.

52   Czarnowski, 'Women's Crimes, State Crimes', 241.

53   Ibid., 243f.

54   HSAK, 605.2, LG Trier, 13816, 22 October 1943, appeal by public prosecutor.

55   Jahns, *Abtreibung in Duisburg*, 40–42.

56   Krieger, 'Abtreibung in Freiburg i. Br.', 35–39.

57   Inderheggen, *Abtreibung in Mönchen-Gladbach*, 133, 145.

58   LHAK, 602.2, 10121; ibid., 10110, August 1942.

59   Inderheggen, *Abtreibung in Mönchen-Gladbach*, 145.

60   LHAK, 602.2, 2550, 1938.

61   LHAK, 605.2, Schwurgericht Trier, 7434, 1 October 1937.

62   Ibid., Landgericht Braunschweig, 89301, 1942.

63   Ibid., 3965, 22 March 1934.

64   Ibid., 6990, Schwurgericht Cologne, 16 March 1937.

65   Ibid., 7321, Schwurgericht Trier, 18 February 1937.

66   Czarnowski, 'Women's Crimes, State Crimes', 239, 242ff.

67   E.g., LHAK, 602.2, 9980, AG Cologne, October 1943; ibid., 10076 AG Gronau September 1942; ibid., 10110, AG Wismar, August 1942; 605.2, 10311, AG Goslar, September [??400] ibid., 10315, June 1941; 10376 AG Schwerin, September 1942; ibid., 605.2, 10495, June 1942.

68   HSAK, 605.2, 10439, LG Cologne, 11 May 1942.

69   E.g., HSAK, 605.2, 10495, 9 June 1942: a 24-year-old married woman whose husband had been drafted into the army in 1939 was said to have neglected her three young children during nightly meetings with several men.

70   Czarnowski, 'Women's Crimes, State Crimes', 247.

71   Quoted in Jahns, *Abtreibung in Duisburg*, 39.

72   LHAK, 605.2, Schwurgericht Koblenz, 4508, 31 October 1933.

73   BLHAP Pr.Br., Rep 3B, Fr.a.O., IMed, 281.

74   Harvey, 'Culture and Society in Weimar Germany', 282.
75   Helmut Lethen, *Cool Conduct: The Culture of Distance in Weimar Germany* (Berkeley, 2002); cf. Stephen Brockmann, 'Weimar Sexual Cynicism'.
76   Duden, *The Woman Beneath the Skin*.
77   Cf. Usborne, 'Rhetoric and Resistance'.

Chapter 24

Dr. J. Leunbach

ABORTION AND STERILIZATION IN DENMARK (1930)

A T LAST YEAR'S CONGRESS I had the honourable duty of reading the introductory paper at the meeting dealing with Birth Control. To-day I shall not repeat anything of what I said on that occasion, but shall content myself with a reference to the Report of the Copenhagen Congress which contains many other contributions to the subject besides my own. Birth Control furnishes so wide and important a theme that it cannot be examined exhaustively from all angles on one congress day; we have, therefore, this year also placed it on our programme as one of the main topics of discussion.

At the present moment I shall restrict myself to the question of abortion, and, in conclusion, sketch quite briefly a Danish Act recently passed with regard to sterilization.

So far as abortion is concerned, I believe that the conditions in the various Western European countries show a very large degree of resemblance, so that the conditions in Denmark can be said to be fairly typical and to depart only to a small extent from the conditions in other countries at the same cultural level.

As in all other countries with the exception of the Soviet-Union, the Criminal Code of Denmark provides severe penalties against the procuration of abortion.

The penalties apply both to the woman herself and to anyone who may assist her. The mere direction of a woman to a place where she can supposedly have an abortion produced is a punishable offence. The heaviest penalties apply to the professional abortionist, which means that a doctor risks a higher penalty than the woman herself or an unskilled non-professional helper.

In spite of the severity of the penalties the number of abortions is steadily increasing, and it is only extremely rarely that the provisions of the law are applied. The actual state of affairs is winked at so far as possible.

The hospitals treat daily many cases of intentional (so-called criminal) abortion. The doctors do know that the majority of abortions are intentional, but they are unwilling to pursue the matter further. They have no desire for certainty, for obviously it would never occur to a doctor to report a patient to the police.

The patients are discharged without receiving any instruction as to methods of contraception. Neither by the hospitals nor by the great majority of private practitioners is anything whatever done to prevent or hinder the same patients from returning time after time with repeated abortions.

Now and then it is discovered that a nurse, a midwife, or some other medically unqualified person has set up as an abortionist on a large scale. It is as a rule the fatal termination of a postabortive sepsis that leads to the discovery. A law-suit follows in which a number of women must appear either as witnesses or defendants. The end of the matter is that the professional abortionist is sent to prison for several years. Meanwhile the affair is reported in the Press and becomes a subject of gossip among the women of the community. A large number of hitherto ignorant women gather in this way the information that it is possible to get help of this kind in such cases when the occasion arises, and the luckier abortionists who have succeeded in avoiding discovery are in greater demand than ever.

The women who have terminated their pregnancies escape as a rule with a caution and a strong reprimand from the judge, and next time they must seek help elsewhere. That they are let off so easily is probably due to the fear on the part of the authorities that the carrying out of punishment that the law demands would cause too much of a sensation and would direct public attention to the precarious conditions to which the provisions give rise.

In the last generation in Denmark only two medical practitioners have been punished for production of abortion, and these cases occurred many years ago before the real abortion epidemic had begun to spread. It is only in the last ten years that abortion has assumed the form of a real social evil.

According to the letter of the law the interruption of pregnancy is strictly speaking always punishable. But nevertheless it has been the custom for the doctor to terminate a pregnancy in cases where the woman's health would otherwise be very much menaced. After all, it will therefore always be dependent on the doctor's judgment whether or no the pregnancy shall be interrupted.

Medical work in these days bears every mark of being carried on as a private capitalistic occupation. It therefore comes about that a woman who is high enough up in the social scale or is able to pay a sufficiently high fee can persuade some doctor or other to invent the medical indications necessary for the termination of an undesired pregnancy. The precise social or financial status required for the attainment of this end differ considerably in the various countries; but there is a certain tendency everywhere for the limits in these respects to become lower so that this expedient will become available to a steadily increasing number of women from the upper and middle classes.

When the doctors maintain that they will have nothing to do with the termination of pregnancy on social grounds this must be taken to mean that poverty is *not* regarded as an adequate indication while wealth, on the other hand, *is*. There is no denying that this is hardly what we could desire in the way of recognized social grounds for the induction of abortion. But society is not yet organized in the way that most of us could wish.

In Denmark it is necessary to be fairly high up the scale and to be well provided with funds in order that an abortion may be carried out easily and smoothly. I believe that the reason is partly that the Danish profession as a whole is really well circumstanced so that there are no Danish doctors who have to choose such a dangerous means of earning their daily bread. But on the other hand, if it is a question of a countess, of the wife of a wealthy business magnate, or of the daughter of a lord the risk is so small and the honour and reward so large that it requires a really well-grounded moral conviction to refuse to help such a patient. Every woman has some bodily ailment that, at all events with a little trouble, can be construed as a medical indication for the termination of her pregnancy.

It would be simply foolish to be scandalized at this state of affairs. Even the stoutest refusal on the part of the doctor will be inadequate to ensure the victory of either the moral or the criminal law. When once a woman has got into her head the idea of doing away with her unborn child, she will somehow contrive to carry her intention into practice, even if in no other way than by seeking the necessary help abroad. The result will be that the home doctor by his firmness has not merely allowed a nice little sum to slip out of his hands, but has caused the money to be sent abroad to the benefit of a rival neighbouring State. Thus, from the point of view of national economy, the doctor's conduct in such a case is seen to be absolutely reprehensible.

In such a case the individual doctor is, in fact, powerless to prevent the criminal procedure, so why should he therefore not avail himself of the goodwill, gratitude, and wealth of a patient who is most likely to combine influence with charm?

If a dog is sent by his master to the baker's for a basket of bread and on the way home is attacked by other dogs so that it is beyond his power to save the bread what can be urged against him if he yields to the temptation of sharing the dainty repast? I cannot see the right of putting the blame on the individual: the responsibility rests jointly with the existing capitalistic social order, with the prevailing class morality, and with the present criminal code.

Twenty to thirty years ago there used to happen what used to be called "a respectable accident". By this was meant a child who was brought into the world in all secrecy by a young girl from a respectable and well-to-do home, where there were sufficient means to ensure that the whole affair could be carried through with the completest discretion, so that the family honour was saved. At that time pregnancy was regarded as a condition from the natural course of which there was no way of escape.

Nowadays, on the contrary, women have realized that it is not absolutely necessary to abandon themselves to their fates, that there is a way of warding off the blow and by taking the law into their own hands, as it were, of avoiding the altogether disproportionately serious consequences of a little pardonable frivolity. The old concept of a "respectable accident", practically speaking, no longer exists. In these days a "respectable accident" will in the truest sense become an abortion and vanish before the end of the third month of pregnancy.

The protest on the part of women against giving birth to unwanted children thus achieved a decisive victory within a restricted social class. But this protest against undesired births has spread with overwhelming rapidity through the whole social scale. That it is still far from being carried through to complete victory is due neither to the lack of will on the part of the nation's women nor to moral scruples regarding the justifiability of trying to escape the consequences of sinful lust. On the contrary it is due entirely to the women's lack of power to carry through their purpose.

The law sets a heavy penalty on the procuration of abortion and therefore the doctors and the public hospitals refuse to give their support. As a consequence the women try to help themselves. If we had at our disposal some certain harmless and readily accessible method of terminating pregnancy not many unwanted children would ever see the light. But such a method we have not had up to the present.

I believe, however, that it will not be long before we have at our disposal a remedy that is so easily applicable and so absolutely harmless that every doctor can use it, and feel justified in using it, in the home of the woman so that a stay at a hospital or a clinic can be avoided.

I have for some time worked with such a remedy myself, and expect that it will be of great importance in the future. The remedy was invented by the German chemist, Heiser, who after having helped more than 11,000 women to get rid of an unwanted pregnancy was sentenced to three years' imprisonment.

The method is this: that an antiseptic paste is inserted into the uterus. The pregnancy is thereby terminated and the embryo is expelled in the course of one or two days, just as in the case of a regular abortion. In Heiser's 11,000 cases there has not been a single case of death, neither any other complications; and any after-treatment is not reported to have been necessary in any case.

In a few cases where I have applied the method and where the patients have been under observation by other doctors at a clinic, the method has turned out successful. It is the intention to have the method thoroughly tested in a greater number of cases before publication of the results. The composition of the remedy is still Heiser's trade secret and perhaps has not yet arrived at its final state. It will probably not be long before this method will be commonly known. And I believe that it will contribute to making the penalties unmaintainable.

Thus, there is not yet a ready possibility of getting an abortion produced. Therefore—and for this reason only, not on grounds of "respect for the unfolding life" or of fear of punishment—it is possible to continue to compel the women to bring children into the world against their wills.

Such at all events are the conditions in Denmark and other Scandinavian countries, and also in Germany. Presumably they are the same in England, in U.S.A. and also in France—in a word, throughout the whole domain of northern European culture.

In markedly Roman Catholic countries of Southern Europe the Church has perhaps so firm a control of morals that the protest against unwanted children may be suppressed for a number of years to come, but it is only a question of time as to how long the protest can really be held back.

Now the conditions I have just pictured are in a state of *fundamental instability*, but an instability no greater than that of so many other conditions in a society organized on private capitalistic lines. Here as in so many other spheres the workers are the sufferers, these poor and exploited masses that have beforehand to bear the hardest loads.

And it is on the weaker half of the working class, namely, the working women, that the blow of compulsory childbirth falls most heavily.

The upper class man may dismiss the problem with a pleasant smile, but then he is not affected by it in the slightest. Upper class *women* do not escape both bodily and psychic damage, but these can be got over. The working class man is oppressed by the claims of a large family and an ailing life, but *it is the working woman who has to bear the full weight of the burden.*

There is, however, a difference of the greatest significance between the problem of abortion and most other social problems. Most of the unjust and unstable conditions that arise from the capitalistic social order can be removed only by the overthrow of that social order in favour of a new and better one.

But on the contrary there exists at all events a *theoretical* possibility of a more or less satisfactory solution of the abortion problem even within the limits of a capitalistic society.

Let us go straight to the root of the matter and investigate the actual causes of the evils we wish to combat:—

The driving force is the *Women's protest against giving birth to unwanted children.*

The desire for the right of self-determination in the matter of reproduction is, as I also maintained in last year's congress, a cultural advance of first-rate importance and a necessary step in a general cultural development to which we can but give the warmest welcome. Any attempt to oppose this human development and progress may well be left to clerical, fascist, and other reactionary forces. Our problem shall be to spread the knowledge of contraceptive methods so widely that undesired pregnancies will occur only quite exceptionally. This is the most radical and thoroughgoing means of combating abortion. It is the best and most commendable way.

But we must bear clearly in mind that this will not be sufficient to meet the needs of our present actual situation. For contraceptive methods are not as yet sufficiently perfect and simple, and it must necessarily be many years before the object can be achieved in this way.

On the other hand, we can accomplish making available to all women practically as good help as is at present available to the minority in the upper classes. We are, practically speaking, at all events in the more advanced of the countries within our cultural circle, in a position to provide for any woman who wishes to procure an abortion the help necessary for the carrying out of her purpose in such a way that the danger to her health and well-being is insignificant.

This is the line that has been taken in Soviet Russia, and there it has proved possible to arrive at a tolerably satisfactory solution in this way. In Russia, however, the number of trained doctors and hospitals is too small to make it possible up to the present to stamp out the dangerous unregulated abortion completely. But in spite of this they can point to undeniably excellent results.

[. . .]

This year (1929) in Denmark a number of working women's organizations presented a petition to the Government. In sympathy with this movement we held a number of public meetings on the subject, and in these the existence of the W.L.S.R. [World League for Sexual Reform] was brought to the notice of the Danish public inasmuch as *Professor Jergenson*, as representative of the league, gave an introductory lecture. This lecture was published in *Social-Demokraten*, the organ of the present Government, and gave rise to a newspaper discussion.

In signing this petition the Danish branch of W.L.S.R. has followed the course indicated in section 3, clauses *f* and *g*, of our statutes. The text of the petition is given verbatim in *The Working Women's Information Paper* for March, 1929, from which I quote as follows:—

"On Thursday, 24th January, a delegation of working women presented the following written communication to the Ministry of Education:—

"Representations of the following organizations: The Working Women's Information Union, which represents organized women in most of the industrial occupations in Copenhagen,

"The Female Iron and Metal Workers' Trade Union, which represents 3,000 female workers, Branch 8 of the Female Workers' Trade Union, representing the organized female postal messengers, and

"The World League for Sexual Reform, with branches in twenty-two countries,

"Hereby apply to the Ministry of Education with the request that it will take steps to reform the educational programme of the elementary schools together with those of the training colleges and other institutions of education in such a way as to introduce compulsory instruction on sex questions. As the present condition is that in neither Higher Educational Institutions, Training Colleges, nor in the Schools is any instruction concerning sexual relationship given, there is also a great need for such instruction to adults who are not in attendance at any educational establishment.

"We respectfully apply to the Ministry of Education to institute such courses for adults, if possible in connection with clinics where physicians will be in attendance to give free advice to those who seek guidance in sexual matters."

On the same day the delegation was received by the Minister of Justice, and appeared before the Parliamentary Committee for the amendment of the Penal Law in order, on behalf of the same organizations, to voice the following demands:—

We request Parliament—

"1. That the new penal law shall not be allowed to include clauses that might hinder the spread of knowledge concerning, or of the use of methods of preventing, pregnancy.

"2. That the termination of a pregnancy already begun may be made permissible when it is undertaken at the request of the pregnant woman and in due order in a hospital or clinic with expert medical assistance.

"The circumstances justifying such a petition are that:—

"(a) The old penal law, in spite of its severity, has not been able to prevent numberless cases of intentional abortions. The penalties have simply meant that the law on this matter has struck at women of the poorer classes, for where sufficient means are available there will always be methods of evasion such as a trip abroad, etc. It has, on the other hand, brought death or severe life-long suffering to many less fortunately situated women by forcing them to resort to dangerous methods or to seek inexpert help. The numerous actions for infanticide must also be regarded as a consequence of this defect in the law.

"(b) The Danish State has not surrounded motherhood with such a degree of protection that working women can always contemplate with confidence and gladness the birth of a child. Such an event is often a calamity, and a working woman is therefore justified in demanding that when this is the case she is legally entitled to rid herself of an embryo whose development she does not desire.

"(c) We do not regard the termination of pregnancy as in itself desirable—on the contrary. But in our opinion to regard it as a punishable offence is a method ill calculated to combat the procuration of abortion. We regard the most wide-spread knowledge possible of contraception as the most suitable method under the present circumstances.

"(d) The Danish public is ripe for such a law. A new moral in sexual matters is on the point of developing. In support of this we can quote, among other things, more than one case in which a jury has overridden the out-of-date paragraphs of the penal code by acquitting even in cases of murder of live-born children—and fair-minded public opinion has supported these findings. Society must concede to a woman as a free human being the right of deciding how often, if at all, she shall become a mother."

Naturally this petition has not yet produced any result, but it has aroused attention both in Parliament and in the Press and among the general public. It was received with a relative degree of goodwill which even a mere five years ago would have been quite unthinkable.

In conclusion—just a few words with regard to Sterilization. In my opinion sterilization is the best and most important means available for putting into practice our ideas of eugenics. I believe that the way that gives most prospect of actually carrying out eugenics as a practical policy is by means of information distributed to the whole population through the schools and in other ways, together with the free provision of the possibility of sterilization for everyone for whom there is a fear of bringing congenitally inflicted children into the world. But on the subject of sterilization most people are either very vague or completely ignorant. The function of reproduction seems to be burdened with a powerful *taboo*—it must not be interfered with. And this applies not least to the attitude of the doctors to the question.

As an example illustrating what I have said let me just mention an Act relating to availability of sterilization, which has recently been passed in the Danish Parliament. It is the first attempt that has been made in Denmark to frame laws with an eugenic object in view. The Act bears the clearest impression of the anxious care that is taken to avoid offending against the taboo that rests on the reproductive function. Sterilization can be carried out only in institutions (for feeble-minded, epileptics, etc.), and in each individual case must the Minister of Justice give his consent.

Section 5 of the Act is a direct prohibition of sterilization that is not authorized by law and specially sanctioned by the Minister of Justice, etc., which means that if an epileptic or other hereditarily inflicted person gets a doctor to sterilize him in order that he may not bring diseased children into the world the doctor is liable to be punished.

This kind of obvious lunacy and horrible attack on personal freedom without the shadow of a reasonable justification is thus still always possible even in our enlightened age. The great majority of doctors and legislators seem to be happily at one in regarding this Act as a great advance and as charged with fairmindedness and reasonableness.

It is only the arrant out-and-out reactionaries who oppose the suggestion in the slightest, and they do so on the ground that it is in opposition to Divine law, etc.

I regard such an Act as the outcome of the previously mentioned superstition as to the power of legislative authority to arrange human affairs. As if it were not a general experience that the provisions of the law always follows, as a kind of official sanction, conditions that have already been established in the course of cultural development—in spite of, and often in direct opposition to, the existing judicial code!

In the case of eugenics I regard all legislation, both positive and negative, as mainly harmful and inhibitory of progress. The demand that in my view we must take is to remain free from interference on the part of our legislators.

PART 12

Did 1960s feminists hate sex?

Introduction

DURING THE 1960S the sexual liberation movement was influential in Denmark and Sweden, as it was all over Europe. In Denmark, university students commonly had sex before marriage, but they were usually committed to their partners and often ended up marrying them. This was not seen as a social problem. The mainstream women's rights movement was quite powerful and able to institute progress for women in jobs and equal pay, and the welfare state made it easier for women. Pornography was legalized, and sex education copiously provided. Scandinavian social democracy aimed to produce happy, healthy, respectable, productive workers and businessmen.

Yet students found this dream to be stultifying – they felt trapped within the inevitable course of going to college, marrying, getting a good career, consuming washing machines and clothes, raising families, retiring, and dying, all trapped in the capitalist machine, no matter how social democratic. By 1968, all over Scandinavia, students and other activists protested against the normative expectations of the welfare state. They started communes that challenged the norms of the bourgeois family and property ownership, and violently protested capitalism and the Vietnam War. Anchored in the universities, the movement tended to be highly theoretical. The Danes prided themselves on their bohemian heritage and sexual freedom, regarding the Swedes as rather puritanical.[1]

The sexual liberation movement, however, just expected women to be constantly available, without satisfying their own needs. First, Mette Ejlersen, in her short book *I Accuse!* pointed out that many women were diagnosed as "frigid" by husbands, boyfriends or doctors, because they could not attain the so-called vaginal orgasm. Furthermore, only 64 per cent of the university students who had sex for the first time did so voluntarily, out of desire.[2] Although sexual images were plentiful in Danish society, pornography stressed the male orgasm, ignoring the clitoris, and the most popular sex manual of the mid-twentieth century, van de Velde's *Ideal Marriage*, claimed that the female orgasm was stimulated by the male ejaculation. Ejlersen spoke to many women who felt sexually frustrated and did not know why, so she published this book to publicize the importance of the clitoris for women's sexual pleasure. Was this just an assertion of women's sexual needs, or did Ejlersen and the women she talked to have a wider feminist agenda?

The Redstockings were even more radical. A group of young feminists, they flamboyantly marched and protested to criticize the beauty ideal for women, much like the contemporaneous American women who allegedly burned bras (they actually threw bras into a trash can). As Lynn Walter writes, the Redstockings did not reject hetero-sexuality, but they wanted to engage with men in a dramatically different way. How has feminism changed since 1968?

Notes

1   Thomas Ekman Jørgensen, "The Scandinavian 1968 in a European Perspective," *Scandinavian Journal of History* 33 (2008): 326–338; Laura P. Skardhamar, "'Real Revolution' in Kana Commune," *Scandinavian Journal of History* 33 (2008): 441–463; Anette Warring, "Around 1968 – Danish Historiography," *Scandinavian Journal of History* 33 (2008): 353–365.

2   Harold T. Christensen and George R. Carpenter, "Value-Behavior Discrepancies Regarding Premarital Coitus in Three Western Cultures," *American Sociological Review* 27, no. 1 (1962): 66–74.

Lynn Walter

THE REDSTOCKING
MOVEMENT
Sex, love, and politics in 1968
(2004)

T HE 68ERS, AS A GENERATION and as a class, were the beneficiaries of
the twentieth century development of the welfare state. The post-war expansion of
higher education in particular provided opportunities, locations, and dispositions for the
formation of new social movements, most directly in the student uprising to democratize
the university. Significantly, women's increased access to higher education also put them
in a fortuitous location from which to imagine a new women's movement. Along with
reforms in educational institutions, the "post-industrial" and "post-material" generation
called upon the state, political parties, and the family to fulfill the modernist promises of
democracy, welfare, and equality.

Their confrontation with authority and the establishment shaped and was shaped by
"post-structuralist" disputations opposing the dominant socio-political paradigms and
theories, especially as represented by New Left challenges to Old Left Marxism. One
common foundation of their diverse post-structural arguments was the importance of
making theoretical space for alternative forms of agency, or collective action, in analyses
of history and social change. The significance of agency to social movement activists'
conception of their own collective action as reforming, or even revolutionizing, society
is apparent. Furthermore, the anti-hierarchical structure favored by most 68er organizations
was meant to counteract the practical implications of the post-structuralist conception
that all critical social categories are formed and maintained by power inequalities. Women's
collective action against "gender" as a hierarchical distinction is a profound example of
such thinking, and it led them to create a women's movement with an egalitarian, or
"flat", structure.

The Redstockings movement

The definitive branch of the new women's movement, the Redstockings, officially began in 1970 with a series of well-publicized actions by small groups of young women studying at higher educational institutions and quickly attracted many more young, middle-class women, the majority of whom lived in København. In contrast to established equal rights groups, the Redstockings turned their anti-authoritarian challenge toward the very same young men who were their co-activists in the student revolt and the New Left as well as in the peace, anti-EU, and anti-nuclear movements. They challenged male domination with a new political practice in the form of small, women-only, consciousness-raising "basisgruppe" that were loosely coordinated in umbrella organizations. Encapsulated in the slogan "the personal is political", their thinking was that by coming together to critically examine their own lives as women, they would become conscious of the ways in which seemingly isolated, individual problematic experiences were collective, political ones. Through this practice of "consciousness-raising," they created the political subject of a collective struggle against what was theorized as patriarchy.

Whether or not patriarchy actually existed as a *system* (as opposed to a gendered prejudice or an artifact of capitalism) was a major bone of theoretical contention between the Redstockings and the New Left. When some socialists argued that patriarchy did not exist and that, therefore, there was no foundational logic to Redstocking feminism, the implication was that their political practice was not grounded in reality or, as Birkholm (1971) argued, that it was grounded in bourgeois reality and hence, reactionary. The critique by some socialist feminists (see, e.g., Signe Arnfred & Hanne Møller 1974) that the Redstockings' practice was "anti-theory" was, at least in part, based upon this epistemological point. Nevertheless, since most Redstockings considered themselves to be socialist as well as feminist, they participated in a dialogue with the New Left on this point, despite its sometimes basic challenge to Redstocking practice (Walter 1991).

The theoretical and epistemological question of the material base of patriarchy and of feminist practice is addressed here in three concrete questions. Why did the new Danish women's movement arise; and how did it develop over time? What contributions, if any, did it make toward overcoming male domination?

The search for answers led in a direction that was not immediately apparent from the weight of the written discourse, which focused on the dialogue between socialism and feminism about theory and organizational structure. Examining texts written in the first person and about personal experience revealed that the new women's movement was collective action against the oppressive, everyday ways of thinking and interacting that perpetuate middle class femininity and masculinity as male domination. New forms of political practice developed by the Redstockings supported an uprising to oppose "the logic of love" through "the embodiment of ugliness".[1]

Judging bodies

Nine days after the first public action by a small group of Redstockings, a newspaper featured an interview with the head of an American modeling agency. She opined that:

> De fleste at de piger, der beskæftiger sig med kvindesag er grimme. Man ser sjældent en smuk kvinde stå og demonstrere for ligeret. Kvindesagskvinderne

skyder altid skylden på mændene. Det må være, fordi de enten er så grimme
eller ucharmerende, at de ikke er i stand til at gore indtryk på nogen mand.

(*Ekstra Bladet* April 17, 1970)

Most of the girls who work on women's issues are ugly. One seldom sees a
beautiful woman demonstrating for equal rights. These women always blame
men. It must be because they are either so ugly or so uncharming that they
can't impress a man.

(*Ekstra Bladet* April 17, 1970)

Accompanying this article was a picture of a young woman protester with a caption,
inviting viewers to judge for themselves, "Er der egentlig noget som helst grimt over en
rødstrømpe?" "Is there really anything ugly about a Redstocking?" Seventeen years later
came an answer in the headline in a different national newspaper: "Rødstrømperne tabte
fordi de var grimme." "The Redstockings lost because they were ugly" (*Politiken*, January
18, 1987).

Before they became Redstockings, these same young women had internalized the
cultural ways to use their own bodies to reproduce male domination in the form of a
societal beauty contest among women. The generative principle of the contest was that
women used their bodies to compete for men's attention. The judges were everyone in
society, men and women, ugly and beautiful, but the judged were the bodies of women.

The Redstockings were judged "ugly" because they confronted the embodiment of
male domination with a conscious, deliberate, and discursive break with the past
unconscious practice. For example, the very first public action by a group of Redstockings
was to walk down the avenue sporting exaggerated sexy apparel (the things they used to
make themselves more beautiful—wigs, balloons in their bras, false eyelashes) and on
reaching Rådhuspladsen to take these off and throw them in the trash. In 1972, five
Redstockings published a study of the women's magazine *eva*, which made explicit some
of the criteria for judging ideal middle class young woman's beauty (Møller *et al.* 1972).
She should be smiling, flirtatious, playful, original, soft, clean, and nonserious, as well as
wearing smart clothes and eye makeup and loved by a man. And the Redstockings? Ninon
Schloss said in her critical obituary of the movement . . .

Og da we smed kvindetøjet, smed vi jo også kvinderollen. Vi smilede aldrig,
vi var ikke venlige og opmærksomme. Vi var håndfaste, aggressive, og skabte
dårlig stemning.

(*Politiken*, Jan. 18, 1987)

And when we shed feminine clothes, we also shed women's roles. We never
smiled, we were not friendly or considerate. We were heavyhanded, aggressive,
and created a bad atmosphere.

(*Politiken* Jan. 18, 1987)

In other words, they were "ugly" in confrontation with the "beauty" as commercialized,
objectified, pacified, "pænt pige" ("good girl") and the innumerable, day-to-day practices
of female subordination. When she became a Redstocking, the beauty became the beast
and even celebrated her liberation by dancing naked at the women's summer camps.

What's love got to do with it?

In 1970 the first Redstockings' manifesto was published. Written collectively by four Redstockings—Lisbeth Dehn Holgersen, Åse Lading, Ninon Schloss and Marie-Louise Svane—and published as a newspaper editorial in the independent, left newspaper *Information*, it spoke of the "ventetid", the time before the prince comes,

> Derfor tilbringer vi ventetiden med at hækle smarte trøjer og sjaler, some vi ser labre ud i. Nød lærer nøgen kvinde. Derfor snakker vi med højskoleveninderne om, hvordan vi skal få det (os) til at lykkes, hvilken make-up, hvilken frisure, hvilken attrap. Vi stiver hinanden af med gossip om alle vores erfaringer med mænd, vi skidder og prøver sammen at beregne situationen og lægge strategien. Vi udvikler en umådelig psykologisk sans i kærlighedsanliggender—kvinder har nu mere forstand på følelser—vi spinder et psykologisk net, some vi snedigt forsøger at sænke ned over vores stakkels omkringfarende or rænkeløse helt, hovedperson og bedre halvdel. Det plejer over in købet at lykkes.
>
> (Holgersen *et al.* 1970)

> We pass the waiting time crocheting smart clothes and shawls, which we look luscious in. "Need teaches naked women . . . (to spin)." Therefore, we talk with girlfriends about how we are going to get it all to end happily. We talk about which makeup, which hairstyle, which snare. We reinforce each other with gossip about all of our experiences with men, we sit and try to figure it all out and develop a strategy . . . we spin a psychological web and cunningly try to lower it over our poor, guileless, wandering hero, main character, and better half. It usually does work, at that.
>
> (Holgersen *et al.* 1970)

Like many young women her age, a twenty-year-old hippie, interviewed for Tine Schmedes and Suzanne Giese's book *Hun*, thought "getting a man" was the key to happiness:

> Der findes ikke noget skønnere på jord end at være kvinde og ha' en dejlig mand, som ka' li én og som behandler én som "kvinde".
>
> (Schmedes and Giese 1970: 127)

> I think the women's revolt is completely ridiculous . . . There isn't anything more beautiful on this earth than to be a woman and have a wonderful man, who likes you and who treats you like a woman.
>
> (Schmedes and Giese 1970: 127)

Asked what it meant to be treated like a woman, she replied:

> Jeg elsker at være den svage, den der ska passes på—og jeg elsker at få at vide, at jeg ser dejlig ud og at han elsekr mig. Jeg ka godt li at lave mad til min fyr og pusle om ham, for det er min måde at vise ham at jeg elsker ham.
>
> (*Ibid.*: 127)

I love to be the weak one, the one who is taken care of . . . I love to know that I look beautiful and that he loves me. I like to cook for him and to do for him, because it's my way of showing him that I love him.

(*Ibid.*: 127)

And, prompted by a leading question:

Og I øvrigt tror jeg ikke at kvinder kompenserer for noget ved at gøre sig smukke. For fanden, de vil jo bare ha fat I mændene, der ka da ikke være nogen bedre grund til det. Og det er jo osse det vigtigste af alt: kærligheden. Der er ingen af os der ka leve uden kærlighed og selvfølgelig bruger man alle midler til at opnå den. Hvis jeg er grim og kedelig at se på, så er der da ingen mænd der får øje på mig, så jeg vil meget hellere være smuk så de kommer løbende alle sammen. For det synes jeg nemlig er det eneste, der virkelig er værd at arbejde på: at elske hinanden. Jeg vil godt bruge hvert sekund af mit liv på at elske dejlige mænd, for jeg synes at man kun føler man lever, når man er forelsket. Vil du ikke gi mig ret I det?

(*Ibid.*: 130)

And besides I don't think women are compensating for anything (prompted by the interviewer's leading question) by making themselves pretty. Hell, they just want to get men. There can't be any better reason than that. And it is certainly also the most important thing of all: love. There isn't anyone who can live without love and, of course, one uses every means to get it. If I were ugly and boring, then no man would look at me; I would rather be pretty, so they all come running. I think the only really worthwhile thing to work on is to love one another. I want to use every second of my life to love a wonderful man, because you feel alive when you are loved. Don't you agree?

(*Ibid.*: 130)

Her main goal in life was to be loved by men; her strategy was directed at getting and keeping love, in the form of an objectified man. However, she was critical of men as a category.

Vel er det et mandsamfund vi lever i, det er jo derfor det er sådan et lortesamfund, fordi mange mænd er så vanvittig egoistiske.

(*Ibid.*: 128)

It is a man's world we live in, and it is therefore that it is such a shitty place, because men are so insanely egotistical.

(*Ibid.*: 128)

Nevertheless,

Jeg er fuldstændig frit stillet mht alt havd jeg laver, og jeg har da valgt at leve på den her made af egen fri vilje, og jeg synes om det . . . Jeg tar det bare roligt og kræver ikke andet end at ha det så skønt som muligt hvert sekund .

(*Ibid.*: 131)

I am completely free to do what I want . . . I just take things calmly and ask
nothing more than to have it as beautiful as possible every second.

(*Ibid.*: 131)

From her perspective and that of the women's magazine *eva*, beauty and ugliness are
voluntary choices; and while there is an "objective" standard of beauty and ugly, most
women could be passably pretty, if they chose to act in ways that are beauty-making. But
who, if beauty were hers to choose, would choose ugliness? The radical nature of the
Redstockings' practice was that they chose to be "ugly", that is, to oppose the societal
beauty contest by acting "ugly".

This practical side of beauty contest with love as the imagined prize was instilled from
earliest socialization. It was objectified in structures of political economy, including the
family; and it constituted aspects of middle class feminine and masculine dispositions in
structures and institutions that support male domination. French sociologist Pierre Bourdieu
(1977) conceptualized as "habitus" the ways people unconsciously conform their everyday
behavior and motives to the intersecting hierarchical structures that constitute their position
in the world. It is meaningful from Bourdieu's analytical perspective that it was not most
men's habitus to behave as beauty contestants. A man who spent much time beautifying
himself would have been labeled "unmanly". Men, as objectified, embodied, heterosexual
love, were the prizes not the contestants. And, if a woman had the prize, then she must
have been a winner; if not, then she was a loser, no matter how "objectively" beautiful
she was.

To experience the sanctions that enforced the traditional logic of heterosexual love
could be painful, as the following stories from one of the first Redstocking books attested.
For example, Helle spoke of the shame and sadness she felt during her teenage years
because she had no breasts. She recounted an incident at a party, when one of the boys
got out the ironing board, pinned two pins on it, danced with it, and said he was dancing
with Helle. All the boys and girls laughed, and she did too. "Jeg blev nødt til at le med,
for at ikke skulle mærke min skam." "I had to laugh to cover up my shame" (Bisgaard
et al. 1971: 33). In another account, a man commented on women's liberation to a woman
with whom he had just had sex:

Jeg kender godt alle jeres ideer, og det er altsammen meget smukt, men det
er nu naturligt, at det er bedre at gå i seng med en helt ung pige end med en
ældre.

(*Ibid.*: 45)

I understand well all your ideas (about women's liberation), and they are all
very fine, but it *is* naturally better to sleep with a really young girl than with
an older one.

(*Ibid.*: 45)

Another woman related her father's lectures on the aesthetics of the human body:

Mennesket skal passe på sin krop, sagde han. En grim krop er uæstetisk. . . .
Menneskets krop er for en gangs skyld kvindens. Hans egen krop var stærkt
i forfald. Hans ben var fulde af årebetændelse og –knuder. Han var med

undtagelse af sin ølmave ret slank . . . Hans tænder var i mange år helt sorte. Han var tit syg p.gr.. sit store spiritus- og cigaretforbrug. Han blev fysisk syg, når han var sammen med kvinder, der var for fede . . . . Han havde aldrig kunnet gennemføre et samleje med en kvinde over 30 år - og han havde aldrig forelsket i en kvinde over 25 år . . . . Jeg modsagde ham aldrig, fordi jeg selv var kvinde og bange for at blive over 30 år og ubegæret.

(Ibid.: 47ff.)

My father often gives a lecture on the human body. One should take care of one's body, he says. An ugly body is unaesthetic. His legs are covered with varicose veins, he has a beer belly, his teeth are black, he's often sick from cigarettes and alcohol. He says he gets physically sick when he's with a fat woman. He could never sleep with a woman over 30 and has never loved a woman over 25. I never say anything when he says this, because I'm a woman and afraid of becoming over 30 and undesirable.

(*Ibid.*: 47ff.)

To confront such powerful sanctions demanded a political practice that challenged the "naturalness" of beauty, sexuality, and love and that constructed alternative forms, attractive and powerful enough to counter the positive reinforcements of this logic. It would require the deconstruction of the dichotomy masculinity–femininity along with the deconstruction of the dichotomy heterosexuality–homosexuality (Lützin 1990) and the construction of new collective identities and subjects.[2] Among these new identities were the Redstockings, the Lesbian Movement, and several socialist-feminist groups, such as Socialistisk Kvindegruppe, Alexandragruppe, and Gruppe 27.[3]

The establishment of the Lesbian Movement separate from the Redstockings was based upon the recognition that oppression on the basis of sexuality and gender required a separate lesbian feminist political practice. This was so for several reasons, but among these were that while becoming a lesbian feminist might be a way out of "the logic of love" for some women, it was not the way most Redstockings at that time chose to follow.

However, Redstocking practice did lead to deeper understanding of the psychology that reproduced heterosexual, feminine habitus. It was that in seeking men's love, you also seek your own domination; and, in the end, you seem to want to be dominated and cannot love him if he is not the dominant partner. This was Maria Marcus' "frygtelige sandhed" "frightful truth" (1974); Signe Arnfred, Susi Frastein and Suzanne Giese's "indre fjender" "inner enemy" (1979/80) and the basis of Suzanne Brøgger's call to "fri os fra kærlighed" "free us from love" (1974). Who would want to be "free" from love? Only "frustrated man-haters" or cold and bitter souls too "ugly" to be loved by a man (Clod 1976: 114). As the boyfriend of one of the Redstockings put it:

(Rødstrømperne) kunne sagtens spille op, være kry og provokerende og ovenpå, sålænge de var unge, og mænd stadig var interesserede i dem, seksuelt, men de skulle nok vågne op om nogle år, når de sad som sammenbidte gammeljomfruer og skrev bitre artikler, som ingen gad læse, og når ingen mænd gad have noget at gøre med dem.

(Bisgaard *et al.* 1971: 44)

(the Redstockings) are OK for now, but just wait until they get older and unattractive and sit as old, hard-bitten virgins, writing bitter articles that no one wants to read and when no man will want to have anything to do with them.

(Bisgaard *et al.* 1971: 44)

For many women heterosexual love was the cultural basis for marriage and the establishment of a nuclear family. There would have to be practical options for women to support themselves and their children before they could confront the contradiction of the logic of love.

Opportunity structures

Fortunately, in 1968, young middle-class women in Denmark did have opportunities that women in other parts of the world might well have envied. Those most frequently cited were expanded higher educational opportunities for both women and men; an economic boom, which increased the number of jobs for educated women, especially in the public and circulation sectors; the growth of social services, particularly childcare and care for the sick and elderly; and the introduction of birth control pills (Foged 1975, Richard 1978, Flensted-Jensen *et al.* 1977). All of these changes enhanced women's opportunities for economic independence from their individual male partners.

In addition to supporting social welfare services, the state played an ideological role in promoting sexual equality in the "sex-role debate" (Möberg 1962). Questions like equal pay, marital tax reform, the amelioration of women's double burden in the labor force and at home, and the expansion of care services were all being addressed before the new women's movement arose (Markussen 1980). Furthermore, Denmark had a national women's organization, The Danish Women's Society, which was active throughout the 1960s and continuing as a women's voice for sexual equality and equal rights. Thus, by 1970, when the Redstockings movement arose, there was little need for them to debate equal rights for women as a principle.

The Redstockings' class position, generation, and sexuality also contributed to opportunities for collective action. They were relatively privileged in having or studying for careers that would be fulfilling and well-paying enough to support themselves and their children without a man. They were young enough to be attractive to "their" men no matter how "ugly" they might act. And, they were in that chapter of their lives where being rescued by the prince was still possible, but they had not settled down in the castle. Moreover, lesbian members were not as tightly bound to the traditional logic and could more easily see through the "enchantment".

Of those changes in practice that preceded and supported the Redstockings' political practice, the most relevant ones are the anti-authoritarian student movement, of which many of the first Redstockings were members, and the sexual liberation that this same group of young people experienced in the late 1960s. The university and college students in Denmark were part of a general Western phenomenon of anti-authoritarian youth rebellion of the late 1960s, a rebellion that democratized the educational power structure and in Denmark led to the creation of a new political party—the Left Socialist Party. The turn of the students to the left in a critique of capitalism and the establishment included many conscious challenges to traditional lifestyles—for example, in consumption patterns, in appearance, in living arrangements, and in sexual and marriage patterns. Sexual liberation was a critique of monogamy and marriage along with a celebration of sex as a natural appetite and delight, which they thought should not be suppressed or controlled by "petit-bourgeois morality" and concepts of ownership and jealousy in relationships.

The disenchantment of the prince

A result of the new sexual practice was the uncoupling of sex and love, since you did not have to love each other to enjoy sex together. However, when sex and love were uncoupled, so, too, were couples uncoupled. If the young woman was not in love with her sexual partner, a key link chaining romantic love to marriage was broken. "Love" became even more abstract as a basis for marriage, if it did not mean sexual monogamy, at least as an ideal. Of course, love never really had meant strict sexual monogamy as a practice, as the young people pointed out in their criticism of the "hypocrisy" of their elders.

In his analysis of the impact of capitalism on Algerian peasant culture, Bourdieu examined the "disenchantment" of nature (1979) and, elsewhere, he considered the disenchantment of honor (1977). By analogy, one could say that sex was disenchanted by sexual liberation and that:

> henceforward reduced to its economic dimension only . . . the most sacred activities find themselves constituted negatively, as symbols, i.e., in a sense the word sometimes receives, as lacking concrete or material effect, in short, gratuitous, i.e. disinterested but also useless.
>
> (Bourdieu 1977: 176ff.)

The effects of the disenchantment of sex were different for young men than for young women. Young men were free to see women as sex objects. By extension, women were free to see men as sex objects (Marcus 1970) but not to imagine them as romantic love objects. A young housewife described the problems this premise created in her marriage when they both agreed that it was simply impossible not to have sex with others outside the marriage. He was good about not falling in love with the other sexual partners, but she was not so good at that (Schmedes and Giese 1970). The first Redstocking manifesto discussed the problem in terms of the increased pressures they felt to be sexually available:

> Vi er frigjorte. Endelig er vi blevet fri for at simulere ksyske og kostbare, endelig tør vi tilstå, at vi har lyst til sex. Vi tør faktisk ikke mere tilstå, at vi ind imellem rent undtagelsesvis måske ikke lige har lyst til sex. Hvis vi f.eks. har mere lyst til at snakke med ham end absolut ha noget med hans pik at gøre. Men vi hellere alt andet end misforstås og opfattes som bornerte, ufrie og (venstrefrontenens væmmeligste smædeord) frustrerede. Vi sætter alt ind på at holde positionen som venstrefrontens frigjorte damer, og paneldrengene elsker os, fordi vi vil, når de kan.
>
> (Holgersen *et al.* 1970)

We are liberated. We are finally free from feigning chastity and preciousness; finally we dare to confess that we want sex. Indeed, we dare not confess that,

on some rare occasions, we don't want sex. Say, for example, we would rather
talk with him than have anything to do with his prick. However, we would
rather do anything than be misunderstood and thought of as straitlaced, unfree,
and (the left's most contemptful label) "frustrated". We stake everything on
being the left's wonderful, liberated ladies, and the boys on the panel love us,
because we will when they can.

(Holgersen *et al.* 1970)

Sex without love, and sometimes even without desire, led to disenchantment with
the prince. He, like the emperor, was exposed and diminished.

   Together, the challenges to the logic of love that originated in sexual liberation, the
students' push to democratized authority, and the rise of a general critique of materialist
values and capitalism loosened the grip of gender, sexuality, and class habitus (Dahlerup
1998:159). In so doing they paved the way for a radical new form of feminist practice.

The Redstockings' practice

The first moments of this new practice were instances of recognition in the form of speaking
and writing, listening and reading, but not yet a well-developed discourse. Describing
the beginnings of becoming a feminist, Lisbeth Dehn Holgersen wrote that in 1969 she
attended a speech about minorities in America.

> Jeg var mægtig opflammet af den tale og lavede lynhurtigt analogier mellem
> kvindens og negerens situation: de var begge to undertrykt på grund af nogle
> fysiske ting, hudfarve og kusse, som der jo simpelthen ikke var noget at gøre
> noget ved . . . . Det stod helt klart for mig, at da jeg ikke syntes, at samfundets
> opfattelse af mig passede mig, så matte jeg ændre samfundet, således at det
> kunne acceptere sådan nogle individer som mig, og det kunne jeg kun gøre i
> fællesskab med andre kvinder, der tænkte ligesom jeg gjorde, og som følte
> sig ligeså frustrerede some jeg ved tanken om at skulle leve et liv som vore
> mødres generation af kvinder havde levet. Jeg gik i flere måneder or lurede
> med den tanke, men jeg vidste ikke rigtig, hvordan jeg skulle gribe det an.
>
> (Arnfred *et al.* 1974: 13)

> I was inflamed by that speech and made immediate analogies between women's
> and blacks' situations. They both were oppressed on the basis of some physical
> biological traits—skin color, genitals—that you could not change . . . It was
> clear to me that since society's perception of me didn't suit me, I would have
> to change society . . . and I could only do that in solidarity with other women
> who thought like me and who felt just as frustrated as I did thinking that we
> were supposed to live the lives our mothers lived. I went around thinking that
> for several months, not really knowing what to do about it.
>
> (Arnfred *et al.* 1974: 13)

Holgersen's recognition occurred before the Redstockings existed and thus, demanded
creative action. This came, prophetically, when she decided to attend a lecture by R. D.

Laing, whose book, *The Politics of Experience*, had just been translated into Danish that year. She could not get into the lecture hall because it was filled; so she and a casual acquaintance that she met there went to have a beer. As they talked they recognized that they had common problems and decided to get together a group of women who could "langsomt og sejgt ændre samfundets holdning til kvinder gennem kvinders ændrede holdning til sig selv," "slowly and steadily change society's attitudes toward women by women changing themselves" (Lisbeth in Arnfred *et al.* 1974: 14). Within a month there were twelve women in their group, and they were the ones who made the first public action on the avenue in April of 1970.

Others of the first Redstockings came from such small groups or from already existing women's or left student organizations. Once they started with a series of public actions, they drew media attention and had the chance to publicize their existence. Within a week after the first public open meeting was called, there were thirteen small groups of women who decided to call themselves after the first group, whose name came from the New York Redstockings. The media attention had contradictory effects. They became known, but through the media's lens of "good stuff", rather than through their own discourse.

To construct a discourse which could confront the disposition of lover-mother embodied in women, they would not only have to challenge unspoken, unconscious, forms of gendered domination, but also the orthodox position and the organizations which promoted it.[4] The orthodox position was that men and women are entitled to equal rights and that the institutions of the state and capitalism should support appropriate measures to insure equality. This was also the position of the Danish Women's Society, the most important longstanding feminist organization. However, as early as 1963, younger members of the Danish Women's Society raised questions about the political practice of their organization and its parliamentary path (Bryld 1963, Groes 1964). The fact that the orthodox societal position supported equality of the sexes, but not women's liberation, meant that the Redstockings had to confront existing feminist discourse and practice as well as the unconscious forms. On the other hand, it meant that their more radical discourse had cultivated soil in which to grow.

To go up against the lover-mother disposition required that they not only recognize and say that the prince had no clothes, but also, and more importantly, that the princess was naked too. This project would require a collective remaking of the engendered self.

The primary means came to be formulated as small, women-only groups with six to eight members who would meet regularly to talk to each other about their lives as women. This talk was not to be understood as therapy, even though some critics "accused" it of being so. It was to be understood as political practice with which the group's members created themselves as political agents and constructed women as historical subjects. In a non-hierarchal, supportive setting, one could come to see that one's "personal" problems had political causes, that they were common to many women in society. Over the period from 1970 to 1975, this small group form—the "basisgruppe"—increasingly defined Redstockings practice. The talk within the basisgruppe was increasingly structured, at least in theory, as the principles and procedures of basisgruppe practice became the subject of discourse by the movement as an organization (see Rødstrømpebevægelsens publications *En basisgruppe* 1975, *En dag med 120 kvinder* 1976a, and *Jordmorpjecen* 1976b). The procedures were to work against dominance by individual members, against the passivity of others, for security and support for personal challenges, against straying from the topic and slipping into familiar, "girlfriend talk" (i.e., pre-Redstocking talk). For example, the meetings were to be conducted in rounds with each person having a turn, and they were to start with a round called "siden sidst" in which the talk was about what significant conflicts or problems members experienced since the last group meeting (Agger 1977, Rødstrømpebevægelsen 1975). In its own internal practice, the group was to build each other's self-confidence, to learn to trust one another, and to develop a sense of appreciation for one's self as a woman by appreciating other women and, as a whole, to develop "sister solidarity". Thus, the group, besides being personally supportive, would also support change in practice and eventually would serve as a link in a unified feminist practice as a mass movement.

As previously mentioned, the first groups of Redstockings conducted a series of public actions as part of their political practice. These included a bus sit-in demanding that women ride for 80% fare, since their wages were 80% of men's wages, a take-over of the podium during a televised speech by a man to the Social Democratic Party on equality in the 1970s, a sit-in at the offices of the women's magazine *eva*, street theater about Third World women to oppose the World Bank Congress, demonstrations for abortion on demand, against the Common Market, for equal pay, etc. (Rødstrømpebevægelsen n.d.a: 4–12). They also wrote and published books and newspaper articles to reach a larger public. They wanted to "do something" political, in the sense of making a public political "statement", and they hoped that other basisgrupper would do likewise. That is, they hoped the basisgrupper would also conduct political actions directed outside the group itself and outside of the members' social networks.

The question of whether the movement should be more "outward" directed came to be understood as a problem with the political practice of the movement by many of its members—that is, they thought it needed to have a more centralized structure with which to make decisions on behalf of the movement as a whole. This issue first became a significant part of the Redstockings' discourse at the Tåstrup seminar in January of 1972 (Rødstrømpebevægelsen 1972) at which 200 Redstockings met to discuss the future of the movement. It ended with the Socialistisk Kvindegruppe splitting from the Redstockings, because most of the Redstockings wanted to maintain the small group, loosely-coordinated mass movement with a political practice directed at changing everyday life and conscious-ness, while those who formed the Socialistisk Kvindegruppe wanted a more coordinated, more outward-directed, more "theoretical", and more "socialist" organization.[5] Similar debates at the Helsingør Seminars in 1974 and 1976 resulted in the split-off of Alexandra-gruppe and Gruppe 27, respectively, on relatively similar grounds (Alexandragruppe 1977, Gruppe 27 1977). Since most Redstockings considered themselves to be "socialist" of one sort or another, this debate should be understood as one over practical priorities rather than a strictly socialist versus feminist one. Also, in 1974, the Lesbian Movement split from the Redstockings (Rødstrømpebevægelsen n.d.b). While this split can primarily be understood as one which reflects societal oppression on the basis of sexuality as well as gender, there was a tendency for the lesbian side of the Redstockings-Lesbian debate to parallel some of the same arguments as the Socialist-Redstocking debate with the "sides" lining up Socialist Feminist-Redstockings-Lesbian Feminist from those favoring the most centralized organization to loosest structure.

Within the Redstockings, these two debates resulted in a somewhat more centralized and formalized movement organization, but the critical significance of the basisgruppe to the definition of Redstockings' political practice was maintained. The specific outcomes were the introduction of a monthly coordination meeting to which each small group was to send a representative, an internal newsletter, an external magazine, and the refinement of procedures and principles of basisgruppe practice.[6] Thus, the Redstockings became a coordinated mass movement by 1974 (Rødstrømpebevægelsen 1976b).

The idea of a coordinated movement of small basisgrupper to work on individual practice collectively and collective practice individually was a new construction. The major purposes of the coordinated movement were to plan events and actions that would promote the formation of new basisgrupper, develop the image of the strength of the movement, and represent the movement to other political groups and to the society as a whole. As the discourse about basisgruppe practice developed, the number of groups increased. By 1976, there were approximately 110 basisgrupper in the København Redstockings (Rygård 1976b: 21) and at least that many more around the country. Also, there were groups similar to basisgrupper, but which were not officially tied to the Redstockings movement, and there were basisgrupper in the Lesbian movement.

The Redstockings never had an official analysis of the basis of women's oppression beyond the minimum foundation that:

1. Women were oppressed and exploited as women. Male domination was systematic, and the systems included both capitalism and what came to be called "patriarchy".
2. They adopted the slogan "No Women's Struggle without Class Struggle, No Class Struggle without Women's Struggle".
3. Their organizational form was non-hierarchical and based on basisgrupper.
4. The personal is political.

Despite the fact, or perhaps because of the fact, that the Redstockings had no official platform beyond this minimum, they did develop a very extensive and intensive discourse around these minimal themes, a discourse that was historically and politically new.

Bourdieu states that heretical discourses (such as the Redstockings') "derive their power from the capacity to objectify unformulated experiences, to make them public" (1977: 170). And that:

> "Private" experiences undergo nothing less than a change of state when they recognize themselves in the public objectivity of an already constituted discourse.
>
> *(Ibid.)*

And, quoting Sartre:

> Words wreak havoc when they find a name for what had up to then been lived namelessly.
>
> *(Ibid.)*

Discourse is in dialectical relation to the group which constructs it and which it constructs. Based on this conception, one could say that the Redstockings' discourse and practice constructed "women" as historical subjects of a struggle against patriarchy or male domination, that it constructed sex-for-itself. The Redstockings' practice was based upon speaking the experience of oppression and on supporting individual and collective efforts at confronting, confounding, and eventually, overcoming it. This practice was founded upon the epistemological assumption of "sex-in-itself" as an historical category.

Objectivity and subjectivity, theory and practice

What if "sex-in-itself" did not exist outside of the Redstockings' construction of it? What if their construction was a mystifying one, which served the purposes of a small segment of the population for a short period of time, but which left most women and men more confused than enlightened? What if it were a discourse constructed by a privileged segment of the middle class to promote their interests against the interests of the working class? These question, from the epistemological to the political, are ones that were part of dialogues the Redstockings had with left political parties and with socialist feminists, inside and outside of the movement. That the Redstockings confronted such basic questions in dialogue with the left at the same time that their own internal practice confronted the embodied gendered dominating practices such as accusations that they are ugly, they are not real women, they are frustrated man-haters, and that challenged the logic of love, must, in a practical sense provide evidence to support their claims to represent objective structures.

That is, the ability to collectively oppose in practice, powerful efforts to undermine or deconstruct the basis of one's understanding and practice, lends support to one's claim to confrontation with objective structures of exploitation. Also, the strength of the reaction against practical change is itself a confirmation of conflicting or contradictory structures.

However, structure reproduced in practice and "practice" as acting in ways to survive and thrive under given life conditions together do not constitute a *theory* of knowledge nor a *theory* of practice. Bourdieu places these conceptions in historical materialism as a theory of practice, but one could also tie them to theories of psychoanalysis or transformational grammar, for example. Indeed, "the logic of love" is likely to be connected to psychoanalytical object relations as well as to material life conditions of domination. The advantage of historical materialism as a model or theory of practice over other possible ones is that it is useful in explaining political practice and change. As a theory of practice, historical materialism assumes that unconscious, embodied patterns of domination represent contradictions and conflicts of interest between social categories of persons and that practice represents shifting power alignments and interests between these. Marx's critique of capitalism, as an example of historical materialism, recognizes that class conflict and interests under capitalism are objective material contradictions. Redstockings' feminism recognizes that the gender conflict and interests under patriarchy are objective material contradictions. However, both recognitions are only revealed in practice.

One of the interesting aspects of the dialogue between the left and the Redstockings was the left critique of the Redstockings' political form—its decentralized, non-hierarchical, basisgruppe, mass movement form—as being "anti-theory". The problem was that not only did "theory" (e.g., kapitallogik) not have a place for feminism, but further, it could not recognize Redstockings' practice as politics; rather, it was "navel-gazing" and "egoism", not real politics.

However, all the proposed and actual alternatives to Redstockings' practice involved more centralized organization, more "outward-directed" actions and discourse, like support for striking women workers, and in-depth analyses of the problem, clarification of the theory, and schooling in analysis and theory. Because of their emphasis on theory as opposed to Redstockings' practice, they failed to recognize that the attraction of the Redstockings movement was that it confronted embodied, unconscious, gendered habitus which daily, infinitely, and intimately reproduced male domination. This failure to understand the Redstockings' practice as politics created a situation of theory versus practice. Partly this situation was a result of the fact that Redstocking practice represented a thesis in itself and therefore, could not be advanced by a different thesis; that is, it could not be reduced to class conflict. The result was a theory gap within the Redstockings' practice, which sometimes got filled with biological reductionism or religion.[7] Redstockings' practice can be understood as an attempt to change gendered domination by changing selves collectively in a coordinated mass movement. One understanding of a mass movement is that it is made up of changes in individual practice, sometimes, to the threshold point or critical mass where structure can no longer hold. The difficulty we have in seeing an argument between spouses as politics is that, traditionally, we have drawn a distinction between the personal and the political, a distinction that made it difficult for the Redstockings to develop a theory of their practice.

The breakup of the Redstockings

By the late 1970s the Redstockings Movement began to fragment, and by 1985 the Århus Redstockings had a farewell party and closed up shop. The possible explanations run from they won to they lost (*Information* 1985, Clod 1985, Dam 1985). There is no doubt that they succeeded in changing themselves and in making changes in society and culture. The question is whether those were deep and wide enough to be sustainable without the deliberate, conscious, explicit, discursive, and coordinated challenge and reinforcement of the Redstockings as an organized movement. I am not able to answer this question, except to say that the logic of Redstockings' practice has become so much a part of women's politics that the idea of getting together with the women one works with in the factory or office, in the labor union or political party, in the schools and universities, is now commonplace. Critical aspects of the Redstockings' discourse, like patriarchy and "the personal is political", are also broadly disseminated. When I presented an earlier version of this paper to the Aalborg University women's studies faculty, some members were convinced that "the embodiment of ugliness and the logic of love" no longer held sway; that in contemporary Denmark women can beautify themselves without being part of a societal beauty contest. I hope they are correct in their assessment. The absence of a critical political practice does not necessarily mean that there is no longer any problem, and the presence of actual beauty contests must make one wonder.

In either case, it is clear that the Redstockings did not achieve all that they had hoped for. Therefore, a critical question is whether there was something about their practice and/or about the structural conditions their practice confronted that might account for the dissolution of the Redstockings movement as a movement organization.

The economic downturn, which started in the mid-1970s and culminated in the installation of a Conservative Party government in 1982, and the cutbacks in social services were threats to women's security. Such circumstances would seem to work against bold challenges to patriarchy—no time for roses, when the bread is threatened. According to Elisabeth Rygård, in her analysis from 1976:

> Krisen og arbejdløsheden har den umiddelbare virkning, at vi blir bange.
> "Mister jeg nu mit job . . . Jeg må heller la' vær at brokke mig" er sådan de
> fleste af os tænker.
>
> (Rygård 1976a: 18–19)

> The crisis and unemployment have the direct effect of making us afraid. "Will
> I lose my job? . . . I had better stop complaining", that is how most of us
> think.
>
> (Rygård 1976a: 18–19)

> I det politiske arbejde skrues bissen på: nu er der ikke tid til tant og fjas—nu
> skal der arbejdes med de virkelige problemer—og det betyder altid: de
> økonomiske alene.
>
> (Ibid. 18–19)

> In political work a tough line is taken: this is no time for all this foolishness—
> now is the time for work on *real* problems—and that always means economic
> problems.
>
> (Ibid. 18–19)

> At arbejde med kvindepolitiske spørgsmål, bliver i opgangstider anset for at
> underholdende emne, der har et skær at latterlighed over sig . . . i krisetider
> kommer den lurende foragt og undertrykkende holdning til kvindepolitik rigtig
> frem: Det bliver betragtet som luksus at beskæftige sig med kvindepolitik—
> det er det rene navlegnaskeri—får vi at vide!
>
> (Rygård 1976a: 18–19)

> In boom times the politics of the women's question is considered an entertaining
> subject . . . in crisis times the latent contempt of women's politics comes out:
> It is considered a luxury to concern yourself with women's politics—especially
> your own experience—it is pure navel-gazing, we are given to understand!
>
> (Rygård 1976a: 18–19)

Thus, one explanation for the fragmentation of the Redstockings as a coordinated movement is that patriarchy was strengthened by an economic recession.

However, since agency is central to 68ers' conception of the significance of their collective action, analyzing the reasons for the breakup of the Redstockings must go beyond structuralist answers. Their practice must also be examined. Even during the most active and expansive period in the Redstockings' history, most basisgrupper lasted no more than two years (*Internt Bladet* 1979). There was always a tendency for "old" Redstockings to drop out of the coordinated movement, taking their newly acquired feminist consciousness and experience with them to be used elsewhere. According to almost all former Redstockings, the experience they acquired as Redstockings was personally transformative, and they did not, could not, go back to their pre-Redstockings selves and to thinking and acting in their pre-Redstocking ways. That is, they did not abandon feminist practice when they dropped out of the Redstockings. They reached a point in their own lives (with time-consuming jobs and children) and in their own feminist development where the coordinated basisgruppe practice was not basic enough.

The Redstockings' practice was very time-consuming and required a great deal of personal commitment. This is evidence of the appeal and of the objective basis of the movement, but it was also its weakness, since that personal appeal had to be continually created and reinforced for it to be worth one's time and energy. The moment one "got out of it" what one personally could, it then demanded too much personal sacrifice to the general good to maintain such intense commitment. This was especially so when other facets of one's life were becoming more and more demanding, as one was no longer a childless student but rather an employed mother with a double burden of work and family.

Basisgrupper were founded on the basis of friendship, acquaintance, or by the organized movement on the basis of geography or interests. In other words, the basis of the basisgrupper was its practice and the similarities in age and personal background and history of those attracted to the movement. Unless one were lesbian and/or one's basisgruppe were also a close-knit circle of friends outside the context of group meetings and/or one lived with one's basisgruppe, the basis of the basisgruppe was feminist practice. On the other hand, it is difficult to see on what basis, other than friendship, basisgruppe practice might have been based on. Groups formed at the work place would tend to focus on work place problems and to face the complications that intimate disclosures might bring to the work environment, especially the competitive work environment of professional careers. Thus, the center collapsed as experienced Redstockings left. Their lives, changed by that experience and by life span developments, had too little use or place for the basisgruppe. Further, the split-off from the Redstockings of the Lesbian Movement took some very active members' time and energy in the direction of lesbian feminist practice.

Finally, the Redstockings found no way to use their form of politics to pressure the state and other corporate institutions directly. What demands should they make upon the state, the party, the union, the university, etc., when their practice was directed at unconscious embodied habitus? Certainly they did make demands—like abortion on demand, domestic violence shelters, women's houses, equal pay, sex quotas on party lists, opposition to the Common Market, more and better childcare, improved parental leave policy, etc. The point is that these types of demands were not based upon the Redstockings' practice but rather on more conventional forms of feminist politics like The Danish Women's Society and women's committees in political parties and unions, and in state institutions like the Equal Rights Commission. The types of demands that were basic to Redstockings' practice would require changes in individual women's and men's behavior and thinking and a politics of small, coordinated group work, work that would provide an immediate personal satisfaction as well as form the basis of a mass movement.

What happened instead was that Redstockings and other feminists became active in other political organizations; among these are the Lesbian movement, The Danish Women's Society, The Left Socialist and Socialist People's Parties, Women's Studies, and the peace and ecology movements (see Christenson 1989, Clod 1985).

Conclusion

By daring to be "ugly", the Redstockings challenged the embodied habitus of femininity at a historical moment when middle class young women and other 68ers were presented with new possibilities for collective action. They seized upon these opportunities, created a new political practice, and constructed a new feminist discourse identifying "women" as historical subjects of a struggle against patriarchy. As Bourdieu noted:

> The boundary between what goes without saying and what cannot be said for lack of an available discourse represents the dividing-line between the most radical forms of misrecognition and the awakening of political consciousness.
>
> (1977: 170)

Where is this boundary line? How do you find it? What happens when it is crossed? These are questions that I have tried to address in this look at the Redstockings movement; but it will not be 68ers, like myself, who answer them. That will be left to our granddaughters, and grandsons.

Notes

1   This is a revised version of my 1990 article, "The Embodiment of Ugliness and the Logic of Love: The Danish Redstocking Movement," *Feminist Review* (36): 103–126.

2   It would also require the deconstruction of the dichotomy heterosexuality–homosexuality since gender and sexuality are historically and politically connected. That the Lesbian movement arose within the context of the Redstocking movement is a confirmation of their political affinity. See Jackson (1987) for an excellent analysis of the relationship between women's oppression and the social construction of heterosexuality.

3   One of the key socialist-feminist critiques of Redstockings practice was that it did not attract many working class women. Their analysis was taken quite seriously by the Redstockings, as evidenced by the weight of the written discourse on tightening the structure of the movement organization in order to construct a plan of action that would take class into account and, thereby, be more useful to working class women.

4   The focus of this paper is the lover aspect of the lover-mother disposition. This is because it was initially the most important for the young women who started the Redstocking movement. The uproar against the mother disposition was just as important, but came to be a *practical* issue somewhat later in the movement as more and more Redstockings became mothers. An example of the confrontation with femininity as defined by motherhood was the often represented poster which asked "What are you going to be when you grow up, Mother?"

5   The term "socialist" is put in quotes because there were various understandings of what it meant. Most of the Redstockings considered themselves to be "socialist", in one form or another. The socialist-feminist dialogue was critical to the Redstockings' analysis of their actions.

6   Redstockings movement history in Århus followed a somewhat similar history to that of the København movement with the exception being that the Århus movement was more explicitly socialist-feminist from its beginnings. *Lands-Debat* nr. 1, 1976 contains short histories of the Redstockings in the smaller cities and towns.

7   The intellectuals of the movement in the first five years tried to find ways to analyze gender and class in the same terms. This attempt was fruitful in that it sensitized women in the movement to the importance of class and to the idea that their own demands and thinking were shaped by class. Eventually, however, the attempt to conflate gender and class into one and the same theory was not successful. A dual systems model of capitalism and patriarchy prevailed. In the meantime, the development of women's studies as a discipline with its own faculty and problem-foci has been critical to the advancement of theory during a period in which feminist practice is more fragmented.

References cited

Agger, Inger (1977) *Basisgruppe og kvindebevidsthed. En analyse af basisgruppemethoden som udviklingsproces* (København: Danmarks Pædagogisk Institut).

Alexandragruppe (1977) Position paper presented at the Socialist-Feminist Seminar, Odense (in Kvindehistoriske Samling, Statsbiblioteket, Århus).

Arnfred, Signe *et al.* (1974) *Kvinder og kvindebevægelse, 11 rødstrømpehistorier* (København: Tiderne skifter).

Arnfred, Signe and Hanne Møller (1974) "Rødstrømpebevægelsen som organisations form," in *Kvindesituation og kvindebevægelse under kapitalismen*, Signe Arnfred & Karen Syberg, eds. Copenhagen: Nordisk Sommeruniversitets skriftene no. 4.

Arnfred, Signe, Susi Frastein and Suzanne Giese (1979/80) "De indre fjender, om kvindelighedens dilemmaer" *Hug!* vol. 5, no. 24, pp.36–48.

Birkholm, Helle (1971) *VS-Bulletin* (72).

Bisgaard, Lillus *et al.* (1971) *Med søsterlig hilsen* (København: Høst & Søns Forlag and Foreningen Rødstrømperne).

Bourdieu, Pierre (1977) *Outline of a Theory of Practice*, Richard Nice, trans. (Cambridge: Cambridge Unversity Press).

—— (1979) *Algeria 1960*, Richard Nice, trans. (Cambridge: Cambridge University Press).

—— (2001) *Masculine Domination*, Richard Nice, trans. (Cambridge: Cambridge University Press).

Brøgger, Suzanne (1974) *Fri os fra kærlighed* (København: Rhodos).

Bryld, Mette (1963) "København starter ungdomskreds" *Kvinden og Samfundet* no. 11, Dec., p.169.

Christenson, Ann-Dorte (1989) *Ulydige kvinders magt—Kvindefredlejren ved Ravnstrup som politisk proces* Series om kvindeforskning (Aalborg: Aalborg Universitetsforlag).

Clod, Bente (1976) *Det autoriserede danske samleje og andre nærkampe* (København: Gyldendal).

—— (1985) "De røde strømper er grønne, gule, og blå" *Information* Aug. 21.

Dahlerup, Drude (1998) *Rødstrømperne, Den danske Rødstrømpebevægelses udvikling, nytænkning og gennemslag, 1970–1985* (København: Glydendal).

Dam, Hanne (1985) "Kvindebevægelsen har sejret sig i hjel" *Information* April 6.

Ekstra Bladet (1970) April 17.

Flensted-Jensen, Elisabeth, Susi Frastein and Annette Steen Pedersen (1977) *Mellem opgør or tilpasning, kvindebevægelse og kvindesituation i Danmark side—68* (Århus: Modtryk).

Foged, Brita (1975) *Kvindearbejde 1950–71* (Århus: Modtryk).

Groes, Lis (1964) "Nytår 1964" *Kvinden og Samfundet* no. 1, Jan., p.3.

Gruppe 27 (1977) Position paper presented at the Socialist-Feminist Seminar, Odense (in Kvindehistoriske Samling, Statsbiblioteket, Århus).

Holgersen, Lisbeth Dehn *et al.* (1970) "Something is happening, but you don't know what it is, do you, Mr. Jones" *Information* May 4 (original title in English, article in Danish).

Haavind, Hanne (1984) "Love and Power in Marriage" in *Patriarchy in a Welfare Society* Harriet Holter, ed. (Oslo: Universitetsforlaget) pp.136–167.

Information (1985) "Rødstrømpebevægelse nedlagt" Feb. 13.

Internt Bladet (1979) Debat no. 16, June (København: Rødstrømpebevægelsen) (in Kvindehistoriske Samling, Statsbiblioteket, Århus).

Jackson, Margaret (1987) "'Facts of Life' or the eroticization of women's oppression? Sexology and the social construction of sexuality" in *The Cultural Construction of Sexuality* Pat Caplan, ed. (London: Tavistock Publications) pp.52–81.

Lands-Debat (1976) no. 1 (in the papers of the Århus Rødstrømpebevægelsen, Kvindehistoriske Samling, Statsbiblioteket, Århus).

Lützin, Karin (1990) "Deconstruction of Heterosexuality" in *Feminist Approaches to Studies in the Humanities* (Copenhagen: Center for Feminist Research and Women's Studies at the University of Copenhagen) pp.121–9.

Marcus, Maria (1970) "Måske skulle du kneppe Mick Jagger" *Information* Oct. 20.

—— (1974) *Den frygtelige sandhed* (København: Tiderne skifter).

Markussen, Randi (1980) "Socialdemokratiets kvindeopfattelse og -politik fra 1960–1973" *Den jyske historiker* no. 18, pp.13–168.

Mies, Maria (1986) *Patriarchy and Accumulation on a World Scale, Women in the International Division of Labour* (London: Zed Books, Ltd.).

Möberg, Eva (1962) *Kvinnor och människor* (Stockholm: Bonniers).

Møller, Hanne *et al.* (1972) *Udsigten fra det kvindelige univers, en analyse at eva* (København: Forlaget Røde Hane).

Ortner, Sherry (1984) "Theory in Anthropology Since the Sixties" *Comparative Studies in Society and History*, vol. 26, pp.126–166.

Politiken (1987) "Rødstrømperne tabte fordi de var grimme" (An interview with Ninon Schloss) Jan. 18.

Rex, Jytte (1972) *Kvindernes bog* (København: Gyldendal).

Richard, Anne Birgitte (1978) *Kvindeoffentlighed, Om kvindelitteratur og kvindebevægelse i Danmark* (København: Gyldendal).

Rygård, Elisabeth (1976a) "Kvindekampen skal omfatte hele kvindeundertrykkelsen" *Kvinder* April, pp.18–19.

—— (1976b) "Vores praksis er vores styrke" *Kvinder* no. 8, June–July, pp.20–23.

Rødstrømpebevægelsen (n.d.a) "Rødstrømpebevægelsen i København, Forår 1970–Sommer 1974, Kort historisk gennemgang" (København: Rødstrømpebevægelsen).

—— (n.d.b) *Lesbiske, fra isolation til bevægelse* (København: Rødstrømpebevægelsen).

—— (1972) Tåstrup Seminar Rapport (in Kvindehistoriske Samling, Statsbiblioteket, Århus).

—— (1975) *En basisgruppe* (København: Rødstrømpebevægelsen).

—— (1976a) *En dag med 120 kvinder* (København: Rødstrømpebevægelsen).

—— (1976b) *Jordmorpjecen* (København: Rødstrømpebevægelsen).

Schmedes, Tine and Suzanne Giese (1970) *Hun* (København: Thaning & Appels Forlag).

Walter, Lynn (1991) "The Dialogical Identities of Danish Feminism" paper presented at the American Anthropological Association Annual Meetings, November 20–24, 1991, Chicago.

Chapter 26

Mette Ejlersen

I ACCUSE! (1969)

Thirty-three year old businesswoman, married to a sales manager:

"**I WAS MARRIED FOR SIX YEARS.** Unfortunately, I did not feel anything when I went to bed with my husband. And even though his sexual demands were not particularly heavy according to the so-called 'norm', eventually I grew to hate sex so much that I started to tremble all over, as soon as he got near me. I never told him why. I just said I wasn't in the mood. Incidentally, who first established the norm? A man or a woman? I'd very much like to know!

"In the end, we agreed to have a divorce. He couldn't have a wife who refused him admittance to her bed, and I had a permanently bad conscience because I did so. It was intolerable for both of us.

"I know that many people carry on together in similar circumstances, but I was quite able to look after myself and our two children, and I could consequently afford to divorce him. And I promised myself that there would be no more marriage for me, because I thought I just wasn't suited for the sexual side of it.

"Then I met another man. Even though I knew that I couldn't feel anything, falling in love made me just as interested in a new sexual relationship with this man, as he was interested in having one with me. And what a wonderful revelation it was to find that I *could* be satisfied."

(*Author's note:* Although you can read all this in a few moments, the conversation took us over an hour, because the truth about the clitoris and its dominating importance is still so new that most women find it almost indecent even to say the word. In exactly the same way, the previous generation trembled at using the word "intercourse", which, nowadays, is pronounced without the slightest hesitation—M.E.)

"He touched the clitoris while we were caressing each other, and this produced in me the most wonderful feelings of sensuality that I never knew existed. But, when he wanted to begin normal intercourse, I thought: 'My God! Now he'll stop, and I'll be switched off. Should I ask him to carry on? Perhaps he'll think I'm difficult or abnormal if I do.' But I didn't have to ask him anything. He did it of his own accord, while he entered me from behind. I had a climax—and I cried because I had had a climax for the first time in my life. It was so wonderful, and I was overwhelmed by an almost sublime feeling of something beautiful and clean.

"Shortly afterwards he had his climax. He noticed that I was crying, and asked me why. 'From happiness,' I said. And this was true. But I didn't tell him that it was also because it was so overwhelming. We women keep quiet about this sort of thing, even with those with whom we can talk about everything else. And, if we don't achieve this sort of happiness—well, then we don't talk about that either. At least—I believe that most women don't, neither to their partner, nor to their girl-friends, nor to their doctors. You simply don't talk about that sort of thing—silence has been in our blood for generation after generation.

"We are now married, and for myself and my husband there is nothing unusual in the fact that I can only achieve a climax through the clitoris. I sometimes carry on myself to get a climax during intercourse, while at other times I press my thighs together, and alternately press and loosen the muscles at the entrance to the vagina. This, I have discovered can bring on a climax as well.

"Now that I've told you all this, I'd like to ask a few questions in your book:

"Why is pornographic literature always babbling on about women who apparently have nothing but vaginal orgasms?

"When will we get a more truthful pornographic novel—one that mentions orgasm through the clitoris? When is it going to dawn on these literate gentlemen that their novels are based on old superstitions which have nothing to do with reality, and, in order to keep within the style of their writing, they ought to let trolls, goblins and elfs cut various sexual capers in the vagina!

"Or a literate woman who would have the courage to remove the fig leaf from the clitoris and write a book on the happiness that is hidden underneath it.

"And deliver us from those peculiar and incredible performances, where the woman 'feels her juices' spurting towards the man, as she feels him 'come' inside her. If you take too hot a douche, you don't feel it inside the vagina, but only when the water reaches the entrance to the vagina and the outer genitals. So, how can these women feel the sperm—at blood temperature? Rubbish!

"I know the truth will be unwelcome—even that women will deny it, because they don't want to betray themselves. I never thought I'd say this sort of thing either. But then, once one gets under way, it all comes out; all that has been building up for years. And I'm glad now that I've said it."

Twenty-four year old student:

"The first man with whom I really felt something, apart from the happiness of being together, and the happiness of feeling his happiness, knew all about the importance of the clitoris. He called it 'The Little King', and he was a wonderful lover, with tender hands that could give me a climax every time. But there were other sides to his character that I certainly didn't like and despite everything, I couldn't stand him any longer. So, I ended it. I still missed our sexual association terribly, but I consoled myself with thinking of what I'd heard said: 'If a woman is not interested in a man, it is not possible for her to feel anything—let alone have a climax.'

"Then by chance we met again one day, and had dinner together; afterwards we went back to his place. And, from my point of view, it was the same wonderful sexual experience, even though I still had no affection left for him. But, afterwards—my God—I almost, kicked him out of bed in sheer disgust. I know it does not sound nice when a girl says it, but don't forget that it is exactly the same with these men who buy a girl and go to bed with her on a purely 'animal basis'. Nobody condemns that kind of man.

"Vaginal orgasm? Don't know of it!"

Forty-nine year old housewife, married to a waiter:

"I was thirty-seven before it dawned on me that I wasn't frigid or 'abnormal', as one says to oneself—even though being frigid, in most doctors' opinion, is more normal in a woman than abnormal.

"I didn't tell anybody, and certainly not my husband, that I didn't feel anything when I went to bed with him. The nearest I ever got to the truth was when I asked my mother one day, who by then was quite elderly: 'Tell me quite honestly, did you ever feel anything during your intimate moments with Father?'

"Mother sat for a long time thinking carefully. Then a little hesitantly, she said: 'Ye-es. Something, I suppose. I must have done, or I wouldn't have had you two.' (My sister and myself.) But as an answer it was not very instructive, especially since I was still without children myself!

"But I didn't take it too seriously, because I knew that there was a fixed belief among women of my Mother's generation that they couldn't conceive unless they had an orgasm, a belief which must have caused them a good deal of wondering when the same women, time and time again, became pregnant without having felt the slightest thing during intercourse. But, I suppose they just thought they were the exception that proved the rule.

"It later dawned on me that certain women have indirect clitoral orgasms, which could make them believe that they are having 'vaginal' orgasms. For example, there was a girl-friend of mine who once said: 'When I got married, the sexual aspects of life were taboo between mother and daughter. Yet my mother thought she ought to have a few words with me on the subject before I entered matrimony. So she gave me the only advice she knew. She said: 'Shut your eyes and think of something else if that—you know—becomes too much of a trial for you. Then it will be all right.'

"This, of course, reveals a thing or two about that generation's complete ignorance of the subject—and their sexual submissiveness.

"I know a woman who once played a piano in a bar, and she told me the right way to go about things. I've known her since she was fourteen, when she had her first affair with a man. She's the sort who, if she hasn't got a man handy, isn't all that fussy about going with a lesbian . . ."

Since this bar-pianist struck me as being particularly interesting, I asked if I could get in contact with her. My friend went to the telephone and arranged for a meeting to take place a few days later, at her flat.

The pianist, when she arrived, turned out to be a smart girl and really lovely to look at. She arrived with an armful of beer. Her chosen form of basic diet, I was told later.

She had had great news that day. She was getting married for the second time and, since she had come straight from a tremendous all-night party, she was extremely talkative right from the start. The following are only extracts from what she said, but I ought to add that she later, when in a more sober condition, repeated her permission for me to use her comments.

She opened three bottles of beer, and offered us one each. I asked her about her new marriage.

"Well, you see there's this terribly annoying thing about me—that I love men. But it's so difficult to teach them how I want it done—and it's not because they are unwilling. All men love their little parlour games, but they're so clumsy in comparison with . . ." (she looked across at her hostess, who nodded) ". . . with girls who are 'a bit left-handed'.

"Sometimes I have the feeling that I'm the only girl in the world who tells men how we want it done. But why the hell don't more women speak up? I've known one 'experienced' man after another, and they have all been self-assured in believing that if they were to 'knock' a woman to bits the good old-fashioned way, then everything would be just rosy for both parties.

"But that's the exact opposite to what girls have told me when they've had a couple of drinks.

"I'll tell you straight out: I prefer to have it licked first—but I know that there are girls who don't like this because then the man demands the same thing. They think it's unaesthetic and abnormal and all that; understandable, I suppose, since at this point it normally becomes more difficult, because the man, as a rule, is damn clumsy when it comes to satisfying a girl with his hand, or else he can't be bothered to do it. He thinks it's stupid. He says it's difficult. He can just tolerate a little bit of caressing beforehand, but that's all—he simply can't believe that the girl wants to be satisfied all the way by this method. No, he'd sooner find a normal girl—which means a girl who denies herself, and others, tremendous pleasure, because of her play-acting.

"Perhaps there are girls who can be satisfied by the old recipe of the man thumping away. I remember one who insisted that it was the real Big Win for her, but whether she was telling the truth, I don't know. You see, her fiancé was present when she said it."

Thirty-five year old housewife, married to an accountant:

"'I took myself a lover because I finally came to the conclusion that I was frigid. He was a man with extremely wide experience in sex. He even kept a file on the women he had known, and there were several hundred. It was with him that I first learned what a climax was, because we practised moutherotics. That was how I first realised the importance of the clitoris. Even so, he still insisted that we always finish off with the really big hit— that we should have our climaxes the 'normal' way. When he cried 'I'm coming!' he expected me to 'come' too. As I was very much taken with him, I didn't mind that final bit of play-acting. Especially because he always told me beforehand when he wanted to 'come', so that I usually managed to have a clitoral climax just before. He never discovered my little subterfuge, and how could I tell him the truth? He was fully convinced that he had satisfied all those women exclusively by this last phase of intercourse. If I'd told him, he would, of course, have thought me abnormal."

Twenty-six year old secretary, married to a typesetter:

"I was amazed when, one day, one of my best friends told me that she didn't understand why there is all this discussion about sex. In her opinion there couldn't be much to discuss.

For her a climax was a foregone conclusion every time she had intercourse, and I know her well enough to know that she was telling the truth.

"I told my husband about her, and he laughed his head off. 'There you are,' he said. 'You are probably on the wrong, track after all.'

"Luckily, a couple of months later, I read a book on sex education that explained everything about indirect clitoral orgasm. I'll never forget his face when I presented the book to him on a silver tray!

"But why should it be like that? Why should the minority, who think they get vaginal orgasms, dominate the picture? It's this 'vaginal' orgasm—and men's belief in it—that the majority of women have had to face up to. I think it's about time all those that belong to this majority openly professed it. But I'm also afraid that it's going to take a long time before we dig up this whole business and bring it out into the fresh air."

Fifty year old woman, widow of a businessman:
"I had my first sexual experience when I was nineteen, and it ended with me in great wonder as to why I didn't feel anything at all.

"At that time, Van de Velde's book *Ideal Marriage* had just come out, and I studied it thoroughly—not least the descriptions of the various positions that could give me the orgasm I had heard so much of.

"I optimistically enticed my fiancé into trying several of the positions, though without telling him that I had read the book. He was, of course, delighted and thought I had the greatest natural talent of all time.

"Which was fine for him. But I still didn't know what an orgasm was. Then I read in the book that 'during normal intercourse, it is the emptying of the man's sperm that brings about the orgasm in him and the woman'. I'll never forget that sentence, because it revealed more clearly than anything else that something was wrong with me.

"The thought tortured me. I got the strangest ideas. Was I a lesbian? Was I built differently from other women?

"Another book, *The Well of Loneliness*, was being read and discussed a great deal at the time. I read it too, of course, but I never took part in any discussions. I was afraid that I might say something that would give me away and make people think that I was like the main character in the book. But, I *didn't* feel at all attracted to other girls. On the contrary, I was very much in love with my fiancé.

"One day, the pressure built up so much inside me that I cried my eyes out. My mother saw this and asked me what was the matter. But we had never discussed the subject of sex, and the best I could manage as an explanation was to blurt out: 'I'm abnormal.'

"Maybe my mother understood what I meant—maybe not. But all she said was: 'Oh, you're just as normal as everybody else.'

"In the end, I told my girl friend; we had always confided in each other, though we'd never touched on this subject before. It was too intimate. But as the boys were wild about her—she looked exactly like Ginger Rogers—and she was wild about them, I felt certain that she must be as completely normal as one should be according to Van de Velde's standards.

"'My God!' she said. 'Don't you feel anything either? I thought it was just me. We'll ask Ella.'

"Ella was her elder sister by two years and was engaged. I don't remember everything she said, but there was something about a lot of girls being what she called frigid, and there was not much anybody could do about it. And I remember that my girl friend and I talked about it privately and agreed that Ella must be frigid herself. Naturally, this didn't help us very much, but just knowing that there were many others in the same boat made the whole thing a little easier to bear.

"Then, one day, my girl friend came rushing in, very excited, and said: 'I've heard about something that ought to help us. It's an aphrodisiac, it's supposed to be very good. We'll buy some.'

"We were a bit worried about going into a chemist's and asking for it, because we thought it was on sale purely to help frigid women. But we overcame our embarrassment and brought home a paper bag full of little brown seeds. In the days that followed, we religiously ate our way through the entire contents of the bag.

"What the seeds were supposed to do, I have never discovered, but it soon became very clear to us that, as a means of awakening frigid women, they were utterly useless.

"So, we gave it up and allowed ourselves to slide down the hill, without further protest, to join the great army of frigid women.

"Luckily, we had more sense later, in fact many years later.

"I mention this little story because the problem was not only mine and my girl friend's. Little by little I learned that it was countless young women's problem in those days. A man would find it difficult to understand how terrible it is to believe oneself to be frigid, and to go through this play-acting, always with the thought: 'Am I doing it well enough to make him think I'm "normal"?'

"If a young man was convinced that he was impotent in the middle of a tremendously potent man's world, how would he feel—even though it might later dawn on him that he wasn't the only one?

"I sincerely wish that the young girls of today could be saved from what we suffered in my youth, and what followed many of us through our marriages. Because we blindly believed in the completely inaccurate information we got from books: we even had to read these books in secret because sex was a sort of silent no-man's land between parents and children.

"And how far have we really progressed? So far as I can see, all this is still taboo. That is really the reason why I agreed to talk to you."

Twenty-eight year old civil servant, formerly married to a businessman, now divorced:
"I met a married man and we fell in love with each other—wildly in love—with the inevitable result.

"Not that I didn't fight against it for a long time. I had a terribly guilty conscience because of his wife. So when it eventually happened, he was so eager and in such a state that he had a climax straight away.

"Afterwards he was in despair and asked me if I'd got something out of it too. He would always blame himself if he hadn't satisfied me especially as it was the first time we had been together.

"His happiness was my happiness—his despair my despair. So, I reassured him. I told him that all was well, 'Of course, I had been satisfied.' But, of course, this wasn't true, and I doubt whether any woman could have reached her climax during that half-minute's furious intercourse. But I thought to myself: 'My God, how I love him! It doesn't matter at all. Little by little I'll teach him what it's all about.'

"Then he said something that made me abandon this idea immediately. He said, almost with gratitude, that he thought it was a miracle that I felt that way. He had known a woman who could only be satisfied if he touched a certain spot. I knew immediately what the spot was, and I also knew that he was talking about his own wife, though he didn't say so both for her sake and mine.

"He went on to say that he sometimes had cramp in his hand because she insisted on having it that way—and that it was wonderful that I was 'normal!'

"I know my reaction will look utterly unscrupulous in black and white, but I think it was what most women would have done if it was a question of holding on to a man they couldn't live without.

"So, I expressed great surprise that any woman should want to have it that way, even though I fully sympathised with her and, only a few moments earlier, had been thinking of teaching him to do the very same thing. I actually sympathised with him: it must have been terribly strenuous, I said. How had he been able to stand it? And a lot more of the same sort of thing.

"It was disgraceful, I agree. But I felt it had been worthwhile when he said that he couldn't stand her, because I knew then that he would be able to stand her less and less the better I performed my little act.

"How many women would throw away their strongest weapon in the battle for the man they really want?

"Not many, 1 think. But, eventually, they will smart as I am now smarting. Because I got him, and now I am trapped in the sexual quagmire I created for myself. So, I can't emphasise strongly enough that we women have got to look at this business in a wider perspective; only when all men know, and all women frankly admit the truth about their sex lives are we on equal terms, both woman to woman, and sex to sex, and only then will we reach the stage where the right to have a climax will be the right of both parties.

"Regardless of how it is reached . . . ."

Thirty-three year old gymnastics teacher, married to a solicitor:

"I think we must have the reason for human sexual problems out in the open if we are to repair the old damage:

"Masses of women sacrifice satisfaction during intercourse—some because they don't know enough about it, others because they shrink from telling their partner just how they have to be acted upon—and for how long.

"Centuries of sexual suppression still weigh on them, especially on this point. Even though many now feel more free to take the part in the eroticism, as a rule they still keep quiet when it comes to the last phase; because, despite all the talk about the emancipation of women, it is still a man's world. We can regard this as being good or bad. But, if we think it's bad, then we've got to get to the root of the matter, in order to alter the situation.

"There are many manifestations of this man's world—little things that we take for granted in daily life, but which are nevertheless symptomatic.

"In many marriages, both sides want the first-born to be a boy, and the predilection for boys is continued. A mother can easily dress her baby daughter in pale blue, but if she dresses her baby boy in pink, it's always with an excuse. The girl's liking for pretty dresses and make-up is animated by the desire to make herself look feminine and attractive, and perhaps, a little weak and helpless. The boys have the desire to show self-assurance, strength, 'up-and-at-'em' virility.

"A woman takes the man's name when she marries. Exceptions are so rare that they hardly count in this connection. And nobody thinks it funny that she should do this.

"But how about the opposite?

"Impossible!

"It is a daily occurrence to see pictures in newspapers and magazines of Mrs. Director George Preben Hansen, or Mrs. Wholesaler Alfred Olsen, or Mrs. Factory-owner Sofus Sorensen and so on. But just consider for a moment the picture of a man who has been given the title of: Mr. Headmistress Gerthe Poulsen!

"Again, when a woman is admitted to a hospital, she has to fill in forms saying whether or not she is married. A man need only state his occupation.

"A man is not regarded as impotent because he grows tired of his sex life with a woman. But, if she grows tired of going to bed with him—which mainly happens because he hasn't a clue how to satisfy her—she is denounced as frigid.

"What if an attempt were made to regard men and women as equals in everything. The first outcome of this would be that the woman would become more free and consequently more truthful about sex.

"In Denmark, when referring to a woman, it is the custom to give her the title of her husband's job."

PART 13

Should prostitution be legalized or punished?

Introduction

THE SEXUAL LIBERATION MOVEMENT became mainstream in the 1970s and 1980s. In Europe, pornography became widely available. But the Redstockings' critique had yet to sink in. Simply liberating sex did not address the power relations between men and women. In Sweden, for instance, some men started to downplay the significance of rape, and claimed that penalties should be less if a woman was wearing a miniskirt. Feminists pointed out that rape was not a crime of sex, but a crime of physical violence against women. One wing of the 1980s and 1990s feminist movement also defined prostitution as the exploitation of women by men, as Yvonne Svanström writes. They resembled the women's movement of the late nineteenth century against the Contagious Diseases Acts, which demanded that the government stop sanctioning prostitution.

By the 1980s, governments also started to crack down on sexual liberation for reasons unconnected with feminism. The rapid spread of AIDS impelled governments to try to address the problem of sexually transmitted diseases. In general, Sweden has tended to be much stricter about regulating sexuality than other Scandinavian countries, especially Denmark. For instance, with AIDS Sweden made sauna clubs illegal, but Danish activists used them to reach gay men with AIDS education.[1]

The Swedish government was also concerned about prostitution for other reasons, for they feared that sexual commerce was associated with drug use and street crime. At this time, Sweden was experiencing greater immigration from Eastern European and Islamic countries, and some journalists claimed that women were being trafficked in sex rings from Russia. Furthermore, Islamic immigrants sometimes circumcised their daughters.[2] As a result of these trends, a law passed in 1999 increased penalties for rape, strengthened laws against female genital cutting (circumcision), and made soliciting prostitutes illegal.

The law was intended to punish the male customers of prostitutes, rather than the women who sold sex themselves. The idea was that this would humiliate men who went to prostitutes, rather than the women being exploited in sexual commerce. But critics debate whether the crackdown on prostitution was motivated more by concern for women exploited as prostitutes, or for fear that immigrant women from the former Soviet Union and Eastern Europe, and from the Middle East and Africa, might be contaminating Swedish boundaries, part of a general anxiety about changing boundaries?[3]

Elizabeth Bernstein engaged in an ethnographic study, interviewing women who sold sex, and their customers, as well as police officers, and perused the internet for insight into the sex trade. Streetwalking has declined in many cities, she finds, as sexual commerce has shifted to the internet. Did Bernstein find that the policing strategy was effective in deterring men from going to prostitutes? Some studies have found that the Swedish policy just drove women underground, and the internet has allowed customers to find them.[4]

Other European countries followed different policies to address prostitution. Bernstein contrasts the Swedish strategy with the Dutch strategy of tightly regulating prostitution. At first, the Dutch provided *tippelzones*, special areas outside of the city, run and constructed by the government, where men could cruise for prostitutes, and prostitutes could work, supported by social workers who provided condoms and counseling. But public opinion objected when it became clear that most of the prostitutes working there (both female-born and transsexual) were illegal or legal migrants, so the zones were shut down. However, prostitution remains legal, but brothels are tightly controlled for health and safety and working conditions. Would the Dutch or Swedish strategy be preferable?

Notes

1   Signild Vallgårda, "Problematizations and Path Dependency: HIV/AIDs Policies in Denmark and Sweden," *Medical History* 51, no. 1 (2007): 99–112.
2   Beth Maina Ahlberg *et al.*, "'It's Only a Tradition': Making Sense of Eradication Interventions and the Persistence of Female 'Circumcision' within a Swedish Context," *Critical Social Policy* 24 (2004): 50–78.
3   Don Kulick, "Sex in the New Europe: The Criminalization of Clients and Swedish Fear of Penetration," *Anthropological Theory* 3, no. 2 (2003): 205.
4   Judith Kilvington, Sophie Day, and Helen Ward, "Prostitution Policy in Europe: A Time of Change?," *Feminist Review*, 67 (2001): 78–93.

Chapter 27

Yvonne Svanström

THROUGH THE PRISM OF PROSTITUTION

Conceptions of women and sexuality in
Sweden at two fins-de-siècle (2005)

IN THE SPRING OF 2002, two separate but intertwined events made the
media in Sweden. In April a judge was sentenced to pay a fine for buying sexual services.[1]
He was caught, literally, with his pants down in the act of buying sexual services from a
woman (Domare dömd för sexbrott, *Dagens Nyheter* 2002). After the sentence, an
investigation was undertaken in order to establish whether the man was suitable to keep
his office. When interviewed about the possibilities for the sentenced judge to keep his
job, the male president of the administrative court of appeal who investigated the matter,
answered: "I have not found sufficient grounds for further action. This is a one-time
occurrence and a relatively minor crime" (Dömd domare får behålla jobbet, *Dagens Nyheter*
2002). In May the same year, an evening paper exposed a young female student at the
police academy for selling sexual services through the Internet. When asked, the male
public relations liaison for the National Swedish Police Board answered: "To be a prostitute
is not a criminal offence. However, it is highly inappropriate and unethical for somebody
who wants to become a police officer to prostitute oneself" (Gustafsson and Korsås 2002).
After discussions with the Police Academy the cadet left the school.

On 1 January 1999, a new law was passed in Sweden. The law criminalizes the purchase
of sexual services. The penalty is fines or imprisonment for no more than 6 months.[2] The
law came about after a series of discussions and lobbying in parliament, where women
members of parliament worked together across party lines. The law was presented as a
feminist law. A little more than 80 years ago, however, Sweden followed a different
tradition and regulated prostitution, as did most other countries in Europe. The regulation
of prostitution was an institutionalized way of dealing with two things: the fear of venereal
disease and the fear of "loose women's" sexuality and its effect on society. By-laws were
established which forced some women to attend medical examinations, forbade them

to walk certain streets at certain hours, and forbade them to wear certain clothes. The regulations were still in force in 1918 when they were replaced by a law which made both men and women responsible for spreading sexually transmitted diseases. Thus, Sweden has gone from regulating women in prostitution to passing a unique law which criminalizes the purchase of sexual services.

A number of feminist scholars have argued that when discussing gender relations we have to view them both in terms of stability and change. Using two analytical concepts from sociologist Eva Lundgren I want to discuss two normative systems of society: on the one hand a regulative system (laws concerning prostitution for instance) and on the other hand a constitutive system (i.e., implicit norms concerning human behaviour) (Lundgren 1993: 171–8). Social scientist Carole Pateman talks about a sexual contract, lying underneath a supposedly (gender) neutral social contract. The idea of a sexual contract shows how the view of society consisting of equal individuals is really built upon the intrinsic norm of men's access to women's bodies. The story of the sexual contract, she states, ". . . helps us to understand the mechanisms through which men claim right of sexual access to women's bodies and claim right of command over the use of women's bodies", a story about patriarchal norms which are far more difficult to change than society's legal texts (Pateman 1988: 17). On a regulative level the sexual contract is manifested in the marriage contract and the prostitution contract.

In the two cases referred to at the beginning of this article, two persons who were professionally involved in judiciary or policing activities took part in the same kind of transaction—prostitution. The judge who committed a crime buying sex was punished according to the law, but could keep his job; the police cadet who sold sexual services, which is not a criminal offence, had to leave the academy. Today Sweden has radical laws on prostitution, but patriarchal norms concerning sexuality still dominate the judicial system and public opinion. These implicit norms often rest on a long historical tradition, which makes them difficult to change. The purchase of sexual services by a man can be regarded as a one-time occurrence where he entered into a temporary contract. However, the selling of those services reflects upon a woman's character, and rather than this being a one-time occurrence it is presumed that it is part of her nature. Questions of women's rights to their own bodies have been discussed for centuries, but are still difficult to politicize, and have been seen as private questions. Thus, historian Yvonne Hirdman's description of questions of gender as "stability's changing forms" can be used to describe how attitudes to women and sexuality have changed and yet remained the same during the last hundred years (Hirdman 2001: 93–8).

In this historical exposé focus is on Sweden in the late twentieth and early twenty-first century. However, by stretching the discussion also to the late nineteenth century I will discuss the discrepancy between radical laws and traditional norms in society. I will use central legal documents to illustrate a changeable regulative system and material such as pamphlets, medical texts and feminist argumentation in journals to illustrate a historically immovable constitutive system and the fight to change it. Further, this article will show that although the Swedish state over a number of years has criminalized the purchase of sexual services—something which in practice means criminalizing a male behaviour—men's right to women's bodies still seems to be an implicit norm, and men's sexuality is still seen as women's responsibility.

The necessity of prostitution—for men's need and women's protection

In 1873 a physician, promoting brothels as a means of regulating prostitution in Sweden, stated that

> (. . .) one recognizes that the history of prostitution at all times and in all countries clearly shows that it is a necessary evil, which cannot be extinguished through any repressive action and that tolerating and monitoring the same is the only measure that can be taken to lessen this evil.
>
> (Kullberg 1873: 46)

The raison d'être for a regulation system which in Sweden singled out a certain group of women for medical and spatial control for more than sixty years, was that it was necessary. This writer referred to the long history of prostitution, a phenomenon that was said to have existed forever, which it was necessary to maintain in society but also to control. Towards the end of the nineteenth century a discussion on prostitution was part of almost every Western European nation's literary, medical and newspaper discourse, and referred to as a necessary evil. This discussion was connected with issues on morality, sexual purity, women's place in society, and conducted in public meetings, in parliaments, newspapers and journals (Manns 1997: 56–63).

The control of prostitution through regulating a number of single women was done in the name of medical, moral and public order. The fear of venereal diseases, especially syphilis, and their effect on different nations' populations was present in the discourse of several countries in nineteenth-century Europe. All the Nordic countries had arrangements where women were controlled. Denmark had officially incorporated brothels in their regulation system, while Finland, Norway and Sweden had a system of unofficial bordellos under police surveillance—in spite of brothels being prohibited in national laws (Svanström 2000: 105–08). Since 1999, prostitution is legalized in Denmark in the sense that provisions that earlier could be used against women in prostitution and sex buyers have been lifted. In Finland prostitution is not an offence, but since 1999 prostitution is prohibited in public places. A bill proposing a criminalization of the purchase of sexual services is supposed to be presented in 2005. Similar discussions have been undertaken in Norway, where prostitution is not criminalized (Skilbrei 2001: 68; Jyrkinen 2005; Smette 2003: 152–6). In the nineteenth century, arguments of moral and public order were intertwined, and physicians who in the early nineteenth century had called for regulation in the name of hygiene, later asked for measures in the name of morality. Over time, a focus on preventive measures to avoid disease turned into an administration and control of prostitution. To preserve public harmony, control had to be maintained (Svanström 2000: 235).

Although the majority of public debaters in the nineteenth century concentrated their debating efforts on explaining female sexuality and women's entry into prostitution, it was male sexuality which lay at the core. Physicians argued that prostitution was necessary because of men's sexual drive, which was more aggressive than women's: "the sexual need is incomparably less urgent for the woman than for the man. For him nature has placed the aggressive element in the sexual drive as a real instinct, comparable to other physical needs" (Bref från P.A. Levin 40). The logic of the argument was that some men, presumably unmarried, had to satisfy their sexual needs before marriage—to abstain from sexual intercourse was detrimental to men's health. Since the women they were to marry had to be respectable, i.e. virgins, these women could not be used for intercourse before marriage. Thus, men who could not (and should not, according to medical advice) control their sexuality had to visit women who prostituted themselves. Not to have a controlled prostitution would lead to unwanted consequences (such as venereal diseases)—at least for men. Then again, some debaters argued, men's sexual satisfaction was the responsibility of every woman. The later famous professor in economics, Knut Wicksell, one of the culture radicals of the 1880s promoting free sexuality and contraceptives, argued that if "respectable women" let go of their virtue and had sex with men before marriage, they would save these men and ". . . some of your sisters, whose lives he would have contributed in darkening, save them for honest men of their own class" (Wicksell 1887: 55). Thus, there was an important addendum to the rationale of a necessary prostitution for men's sake; a controlled prostitution also kept other women safe. Men who could not control their sexual urges would in the worst of cases try to satisfy their needs through assaulting respectable women. One physician argued that it was the lack of municipal brothels that forced men to assault women and led to ". . . indecent assaults and insults against the female virtue in the streets, and decency and morality is wounded in a most foul way, personal security is jeopardized and the corruption of youth is constantly lurking" (Levin 1873: 100). Thus, not only was men's sexuality the responsibility of all women, but they also had the responsibility for each other's safety. Prostituted women had to protect decent women from rape, and, through having intercourse before marriage, decent women could protect prostituted women from men—men who in theory were men they were going to marry.

Very early a connection between rape and prostitution was made in the discourse on prostitution. Seen from Carole Pateman's theoretical perspective this logic of argument is consistent with the sexual contract running as an undercurrent to the social contracts of society. Although there is a separation between the private and public sexual contract, the private wives and the public prostituted women share the responsibility for men's sexuality. Furthermore, women have the mutual responsibility for each other's safety. The private women should ease the burden of the public women by agreeing to have more sex. And public women should protect wives from sexual assault. The separation of woman as a concept into two different types of women still means that both types of women are to serve the needs of men. If they do not, women have to pay the consequences. Today this sexual contract may not be as blatantly expressed as it was in the nineteenth century, but it is still at work, both concerning prostitution and in cases of rape. In a court of law it was permitted until 1984 to ask questions on whether a woman had had sexual intercourse with a man before an alleged rape, whether she had dressed in a sexy outfit and voluntarily accompanied a man from, say, a bar. The woman could have part in the rape. After the revision of the law in 1984 it was stated that the woman's previous actions would not have any relevance for how the crime was construed. However, in practice these factors are still important for the ruling of a rape case: "What a woman expresses is interpreted by somebody else through underlying codes concerning gender and sexuality, which are based on the woman as being sexually subordinated. The boundaries for being a 'whore' have been transferred, but still serve a purpose" (Sutorius 1999: 65). The court's ruling in different rape cases depends on constitutive codes of female sexual behaviour: how much sex the woman had had before or after the crime, whether she willingly stepped into the perpetrator's car, or whether she fought violently. Jurist Anna

Kaldahl states: "The less the physical damage, the more respectable a girl needs to be to get an indictment" (Larsson 2002). In 1997 several cases of gang rape were given media attention. One of the cases has been analysed from a legal point of view. The case went all the way to the Supreme Court, and as jurist Helena Sutorius argues, it is interesting to note how all levels of the judicial system focused on the woman's behaviour: did she protest enough, could the men involved be sure that she did not want to have sex? Sutorius states: "It is interesting to note that all instances of the court focus on the woman's actions in their assessment of what the men had done, and how different conclusions are reached through the employment of different meanings and interpretations of this" (Sutorius 1999: 59). Still, underlying patriarchal views of how women should behave sexually are intertwined with how rulings are carried out in court. Expectations of women's behaviour, on a constitutive level, are still in focus, although men's behaviour is on trial. Women have themselves to blame for not staying within the boundaries of what is required of respectable women, and women should lower the risks by dressing in a way so that men do not get aroused. The undercurrent is that women whose sexuality can be questioned cannot be raped.

Whores cannot be raped—they want it, and if they indeed were raped, the injury to them would be smaller. In the late nineteenth century such opinions were almost codified. In the preparatory work for the new criminal code of 1864 one member of the committee argued for different degrees of rape depending on who was raped. The degree of inflicted harm would be less to a disrespectable woman than to a respectable woman, since ". . . the man can easily assume that the struggle put up by a lecherous woman is not genuine, and that a sleeping woman would, had she been awake, not have been disinclined for that which she at any waken moment willingly would have allowed" (Förarbeten till 1864 års lag, in: Jansson 1996: 77). For women who daily had sexual intercourse with men, a rape would not have the same detrimental consequences, especially since they, according to the argument, could not be taken by force.

Old and new feminist demands concerning prostitution

Sometime at the beginning of the twentieth century some women sent a letter to the prostitution bureau in Stockholm. In their letter the women lamented the state of society, and instead of repressing women in prostitution with regulative measures, actions should be taken against men: ". . . it is the man who should be punished and stigmatized. If the man did not pay, the woman could not have vice as a profession, thus the man is the guiltiest, and the punishment should fall upon him" (Svar på professor, undated). For these women the only possible step to take concerning prostitution was to criminalize the man who bought sexual services. At the end of the 1990s, roughly a hundred years later, similar claims from women could be heard—but this time within the democratic institutions, i.e. the Swedish parliament. In the nineteenth century, a claim to criminalize the sex buyer was a claim too radical to have any repercussions in the fight against the regulation of prostitution, which by then was fought in parliament but not abolished in Sweden until 1918.[3] However, these women's demands were formulated against a background of feminist demands that had been voiced already in the 1880s. The patriarchal ideas of women's sexual availability and the dichotomization of women into respectable and disrespectable had already been questioned in the early 1800s, but these were single protests against an unjust regulation system. In late 1878 the international organization *The British, Continental and General Federation* (the Federation) was established in Sweden, which meant that a collective of critical voices could be heard. The organization was initiated in England and worked for the abolishment of regulations of prostitution with local branches in many countries.

The radical approach of these organized protests was that sexuality was discussed without making a difference between the sexuality of "fallen" and that of respectable women. Rather, focus was on men's sexuality, and it was demanded that men change their sexual morals. Both women and men were active within the movement, but the female voices were the strongest. However, there was also self-criticism within the organization, and it was stated that middle-class women participated in laying blame on the prostituted women, and that was their unforgivable debt: "We strongly disapprove and exclude those of our own sex who have participated in the corruption of morals. But at the same time, without protest, we accept any man, although we often know for certain that he is more depraved than any of his victims" (Myhrman-Lindgren 1886: 67). Rather than criticizing women, prostitution should be a question of solidarity between women, and not a question of class: "As long as thousands and thousands of our sisters are deprived of their human rights, so long are also we humiliated, and all the respect that may be rendered to one or two of us is without significance; what is at risk here is not the individual, but all of mankind" stated one of the most radical women in 1883 (Från qvinnomötena 1883: 121). Prostitution was a question that mattered to all women.

For women to demand a change in men's sexual attitudes at a time when women did not discuss sexuality, let alone in public, was challenging. The women and men of the Federation nevertheless drew the line at free sexuality. Both men and women should be chaste until their wedding day, and sexual relations should be kept within marriage. Nevertheless, over time the radical voices within the organization were drowned by others, who, in unison with a general change in society, had the sanctity of the family and the nation as their mutual goal. This did not necessarily include the emancipation of women. Towards the turn of the century the organization working for the abolishment of the regulation of prostitution became more and more mixed up with the purity movement. Thus, the stability of the nuclear family was seen as an effective way to fight the overall lack of morality in society rather than earlier arguments that demanded women's economic independence and increased citizen's rights in society (Svanström).

Over the years the Swedish debate has at times connected prostitution to social or economic concerns, rather than seeing prostitution as exploitation of women pure and simple. The consensus among Swedish feminists, to look upon prostitution as oppression rather than as work, however, has been more or less unanimous. In 1976 a state commission was appointed to investigate the current laws on sex crimes. When the commission produced its report, it wanted to soften the rape charge and lower the penalties. Furthermore, it was suggested that the behaviour of the woman, and the way she had dressed prior to the alleged rape, should be taken into account when deciding on the severity of the crime. Again, women's sexuality and their character were in question when discussing crimes that concerned male sexual violence. However, there was unanimous agreement between the autonomous women's movement and the party organized women's federations when questioning the state commission's report on sexual violence. Thirteen different women's organizations with different political ideologies protested against the report using arguments that prostitution and rape were questions which concerned all women, and women had a right to their own bodies. This resulted in a new state commission and the demand for an additional commission to investigate prostitution (Thomsson 2000: 53).

In the 1990s, men's sexuality was in focus in the discourse of the political parties' women's federations, together with arguments that prostitution was a question which mattered to all women. In that sense, the 1990s mark a change in the Swedish parliamentary discourse on prostitution. In 1993 two state commissions had been appointed: one concerning violence against women and the other concerning prostitution. Both commissions published their reports in 1995. Political scientist Maria Wendt Höjer argues that in the report concerning violence against women, the perspective was for the first time explicitly a woman-centred perspective when it came to violence against women and rape (Wendt Höjer 2002: 155–9). However, the report on prostitution took another road. The commission suggested that both parties, the person selling sexual services and the person buying, should be criminalized. It was argued that it would be "peculiar" if only one party was seen as guilty of crime (Svanström 2004: 234). In 1998 the government bill came, and it chose to treat sexual harassment, violence against women, rape and prostitution as related problems, suggesting that the government itself saw these issues as related—prostitution was just as much a sexual offence against women as rape. Concerning prostitution, the bill proposed that only the purchase of sexual services should be criminalized (Wendt Höjer 2002: 157). The new prostitution law was established on 1 January 1999.

When voting on the government bill in 1998, all parties assured the public that they were agreeing on the different passages of the proposal concerning sexual violence against women, although not on how it should be carried out in practice (Wendt Höjer 2002: 156). When it came to criminalizing the purchase of sexual services, however, opinions differed. The discussion in parliament was formulated as a debate concerning individual rights versus a gender perspective on prostitution. Those in favour of the law argued within the gender equality framework: prostitution could not be allowed in a country which prided itself on being gender equal. Those against stated that prostitution was a social problem and not a criminal one, and the law would infringe on the rights of the individual. The bill from the Swedish government had been preceded by massive lobbying in parliament, where, for instance, the women's federations of different political parties had joined together across party lines, supporting joint party bills proposing the criminalization of the purchase of sexual services. During the period 1983–93 more than 50 party and member bills concerning prostitution were proposed, and of those about 30 proposed the criminalization of the purchase of sexual services. These came from representatives of all parties, sometimes both men and women from the same party, sometimes only women, but never groups of only men (Svanström 2004: 233). It is interesting to note, that in the ensuing parliamentary debate on whether to pass the law or not, those who were most adamant in arguing against a criminalization of the purchase of sexual services were mainly men, and those in favour were women (Svanström 2004).

To focus on men's sexuality in political terms is to try and turn a traditional discourse around, since women's sexuality has traditionally been—and to some extent still is—in focus. Questions which have been seen as private have been politicized, and men as a collective (in parliament, in the media) have been forced to debate the issue as a political question. However, these questions have been on the agenda of the women's movement for a long time and similar claims were voiced a hundred years ago. This goes to show that issues relating to sexuality have been difficult to politicize, and that there is resistance to seeing them as political questions.

Regulative and constitutive changes—stability in change

During a period of about a hundred years, the state discourse and regulations concerning prostitution has changed radically. It has gone from regulating women in prostitution to criminalizing the purchase of sexual services. The law is unique, and has in a sense turned the eye from seeing prostitution as a question of women's sexuality to a question of men and their demand for sexual services. On a regulative level there has been a radical change in how the Swedish state looks upon prostitution. However, on a constitutive level, there are still patriarchal values at work. These are at times reflected in how the law is carried out in practice.

In a report from the National Criminal Investigation Department (Rikskriminal-polisstyrelsen) problems with the implementation of the law were noted. There was a split between the political will and the priorities on behalf of the police. In some cases this could be observed in a reluctant attitude when giving resources to the work against trafficking in women for sexual exploitation. The victims were "just prostitutes" and "they want this anyway", police departments stated (Handel med kvinnor 2003: 25). The same report stated that special consideration was shown sex buyers. Public prosecutors bringing sex buyers to court while at the same time prosecuting people accused of pimping, have been criticized by certain judges holding the opinion that sex buyers should not be pilloried together with main proceedings in cases on procuring (Handel med kvinnor 2003: 26). The National Criminal Investigation Department's expert on trafficking in women stated in a newspaper interview that ". . . while used women are forced to describe what they have experienced in detail, the court seems almost uncomfortable when having to embarrass a man who has bought sexual services . . . Men seem to have a far greater understanding of why men buy sexual services, and may still not see this as a crime" (Wierup 2003).

There are, obviously, differences between how an argument such as the necessity of prostitution presented itself in the 1800s and presents itself again in the late 1900s. Women have gained a number of citizen rights in society, but women's rights to bodily integrity have been harder to attain. For more than a hundred years feminists have questioned a constitutive norm which states that men's sexuality is women's responsibility, and demanded a change in attitudes and state laws on prostitution and sexual violence. In spite of the Swedish government's political statement in these questions, and in spite of a law prohibiting the purchase of sexual services, there is still a lingering attitude that men have a right to women's bodies, and a right to sex—also within the judicial system. On a regulative level, things have changed in Sweden in the early 2000s and buying sexual services is criminalized. Constitutively, however, men's sexuality is still seen as women's responsibility. The opinion that men's sexual demands have priority over women's rights to their own bodies, is an attitude which is still at work—at times both on a regulative and a constitutive level in society.

Acknowledgements

I am indebted to my colleagues Camilla Elmhorn and Martin Gustavsson for their careful readings and suggestions on how to improve earlier versions of this article.

Notes

1   For want of a better concept and in the name of consistency I have generally used the term "sexual services" although it is gender neutral and anachronistic when discussing the nineteenth century.
2   The law is now under revision.
3   Denmark, Finland and Norway had abolished their regulation systems already in the first decade of the twentieth century, or in the late nineteenth century.

References

Bref från Dr P.A. Levin [Letter from MD P.A. Levin] (1880) *Sedlighetsvännen*, 3, pp. 37–41.
Domare dömd för sexbrott [Judge sentenced for sex crime] (2002) *Dagens Nyheter*, 12 April.
Dömd domare får behålla jobbet [Judge keeps his job] (2002) *Dagens Nyheter*, 10 May.
Från qvinnomötena [From the women's meetings] (1883) *Sedlighetsvännen*, 8, pp. 118–126.
Gustafsson, Thomas and Korsås, Erik (2002) Poliseleven är prostituerad [The police cadet is a prostitute], *Aftonbladet*, 2 May.
Handel med kvinnor, lägesrapport 5, 31 december 2002 [Trafficking in women, report of current situation 5, 31 December 2002] (2003) Rikskriminalpolisen [State Criminal Police], Kriminalunderrättelsetjänsten, Illegal invandring. www.polisen.se/inter/mediacache// 4347/4637/RKP_Rapport_2003_l. Pdf
Hirdman, Yvonne (2001) *Genus—om det stabilas föränderliga former [Gender—on the changing state of stability]* (Malmö: Liber).
Jansson, Karin (1996) Kvinnofrid ur olika perspektiv: våldtäkt, kvinnorov och andra sexuella övergrepp irca 1600–1900. (Various Perspectives on Women's Freedom), in: Görel Granström, *et al.* (Eds) *Kvinnorna och rätten: från stormaktstid till rösträttsstrid [Women and the law. From the Great Power to fighting for the right to vote]* (Uppsala: Hallgren & Fallgren).
Jyrkinen, M. (2005) The Organisation of Policy Meets the Commercialisation of Sex: Global Linkages, Policies, Technologies. *Economy and Society* 146. Helsinki: Hanken, Swedish School of Economics and Business Administration. Doctoral thesis, available at http://urn.fi/ URN:ISBN:951-555-882-4.
Kullberg, Anders (1873) Om prostitutionen och de verksammaste medlen till de veneriska sjukdomarnes hämmande, med särskildt afseende fästadt på förhållandena i Stockholm [On prostitution and the most efficient ways of fighting venereal diseases, with special concern to the situation in Stockholm], *Svenska Läkaresällskapets Nya Handlingar*, 2, V.l.
Larsson, Christina (2002) Offrets sexvanor har inte med saken att göra [The sexual habits of the victim have no relevance], *Aftonbladet*, 23 August.
Levin, Per Anders (1873) *Om prostitutionen och de verksammaste medlen till de veneriska sjukdomarnes hämmande, med särskildt afseende fästadt på förhållandena i Stockholm [On prostitution and the most efficient ways of fighting venereal diseases, with special concern to the situation in Stockholm]* (Stockholm: Norstedts).
Lundgren, Eva (1993) *Det får da være grenser for kjønn: Voldelig empiri og feministhk teori [Feminist Theory and Violent Empiricism]* (Oslo: Universitetsforlaget).
Manns, Ulla (1997) *Den sanna frigörelsen. Fredrika-Bremer-förbundet 1884–1921 [True Emancipation: Fredrika-Bremer-förbundet 1884–1921]* (Stockholm/Stehag: Brutus Östlings Bokförlag Symposion).

Millet, Kate (1969) *Sexual Politics* (London: Virago Press).

Myhrman, Lindgren, Anna (1886) Om qvinnans deltagande i Federationens arbete [On woman's participation in the Federation's work], *Sedlighetsvännen*, pp. 65–68.

Pateman, Carole (1988) *The Sexual Contract* (Cambridge: Polity Press).

Skilbrei, Liv (2001) The rise and fall of the Norwegian massage parlour: changes in the Norwegian prostitution setting in the 1990s, *Feminist Review*, 67, pp. 63–77.

Smette, Ingrid (2003) *Det seksuelle slavestand? Ein rapport om kundar i prostitusjonen [Sexual Slavery? A Report on Sex Buyers in Prostitution]* (Oslo: Pro-Sentret).

Sutorius, Helena (1999) Södertäljemålet och frågan om kvinnors sexuella självbestämmanderätt [About Women's Right to Sexual Self-Determination], in Görel Granström (Ed.), *Lika inför lagen. Rätten ur ett genusperspektiv [Equal before the Law. Justice from a Gender Perspective]* (Uppsala: Iustus).

Svanström, Yvonne (2000) *Policing Public Women: The Regulation of Prostitution in Stockholm 1812–1880* (Stockholm: Atlas Akademi).

Svanström, Yvonne (2004) Criminalising the John—a Swedish Gender Model?, in Joyce Outshoorn (Ed.), *The Politics of Prostitution. Women's Movements, Democratic States and the Globalisation of Sex Commerce* (Cambridge: Cambridge University Press).

Svanström, Yvonne (forthcoming) Offentliga kvinnor, Prostitution i Sverige 1812–1918 [Public women. Prostitution in Sweden 1812–1918].

Svar på professor Welanders bok [Answer to professor Welander's book] (Undated) Handlingar FIV, Polisdomstolens arkiv, Överståthållarämbetets arkiv, Stockholms stadsarkiv (The City Archive of Stockholm).

Thomsson, Ulrika (2000) Rätten till våra kroppar: Kvinnorörelsen och våldtäktsdebatten [The right to our bodies: The women's movement and the debate on rape], *Kvinnovetenskapligt tidskrift*, 4, pp. 51–64.

Wendt Höjer, Maria (2002) *Rädslans politik: Våld och sexualitet i den svenska demokratin [Politics of Fear. Violence and Sexuality in Swedish Democracy]* (Stockholm: Liber).

Wicksell, Knut (1887) *Om prostitutionen. Huru mildra och motverka delta samhällsonda? Två föredrag hållna vintern 1886–1887 [On Prostitution. How to Lessen and Fight this Societal Evil? Two Lectures Held in the Winter 1886–1887]* (Stockholm: Gernandts boktryckeri).

Wierup, Lars (2003) Polisen prioriterar inte sexhandeln [The police do not prioritize the trafficking in women], *Dagens Nyheter*, 14 February.

Chapter 28

Elizabeth Bernstein

TEMPORARILY YOURS

Intimacy, authenticity, and the commerce of sex (2007)

S WEDEN AND THE NETHERLANDS represent two apparently antagonistic approaches to the state regulation of commercial sex and have served as exemplars for opposing factions of feminist theorists, social activists, and policy makers around the globe. As Barbara Hobson wrote, after researching and reviewing Swedish prostitution policy in the 1980s, "differences in approach go to the heart not only of a society's organization of class and gender but also of the state's role in regulating morals and markets. The study of prostitution becomes a two-way ideological mirror."[1] Sweden has often been upheld by feminist and other social researchers as both the exemplar of the interventionist welfare state and as "the nation in which equality has proceeded further than in any other Western country."[2] Since the 1970s, many commentators have assumed that brute manifestations of sexual, gender, and class inequality such as prostitution would wither away under a Swedish-style policy regime, featuring a well-tempered market and an interventionist social welfare state.[3] In similar fashion, social libertarian strands of feminism and cultural analysis have often looked to the Netherlands for a vision of the ways in which states might endorse both sexual freedom and social welfare. For this second group of commentators, the Netherlands has stood for the utopian melding of a strong welfare state, laissez-faire moral philosophy, and harm-reduction policy agendas around "victimless crimes" involving consenting adults, such as prostitution and drugs.[4]

Some of the distinctions that social critics have sought to emphasize in the course of transnational comparisons were apparently well evidenced in 1998, when Sweden became the first country in the world to officially encode prostitution as a form of gendered violence against women by criminalizing the purchase of sex (but not its sale) in commercial sexual transactions. A mere two years later, the Netherlands took several bold steps in the opposite direction when it became one of the first Western nations to acknowledge the burgeoning sex industry as a legitimate commercial sector like any other, removing adult, consensual prostitution activity from the criminal code and instead applying occupational health, hygiene, and surety guidelines.[5]

Although feminists, sex-worker advocates, and others have often taken "criminal-ization," "decriminalization," and "legalization" to represent radically divergent approaches to the regulation of commercial sex, this chapter highlights the ways that policy approaches which appear distinct on the surface can actually serve to facilitate similar shifts on the ground. In San Francisco, Stockholm, and Amsterdam, three quite disparate versions of policy reform in the late 1990s resulted in a common series of alterations to the social geography of sexual commerce: the removal of economically disenfranchised and racially marginalized streetwalkers and their customers from gentrifying city centers; the de facto tolerance of a small tier of predominantly white and relatively privileged indoor clients and workers; and the driving of illegal migrant sex workers further underground. While the broad constellation of attitudes toward gender and sexuality as well as other components of national and local cultures, histories, and regulatory strategies are by no means irrelevant to the configuration of sexual commerce in these cities, the shared realities ushered in by larger patterns of political economy have been more definitive in shaping its predominant forms.

In the pages that follow, I examine the genesis and consequences of the criminaliza-tion of prostitution in Sweden and the legalization of prostitution in the Netherlands, noting the salience of gentrification, globalization, and the exclusion of illegal migrants in both instances. After briefly summarizing the array of strategies that the two nations have historically employed to regulate sexual commerce, I draw on my own ethnographic research and analysis of government-sponsored reports to discuss the lived impact of the two divergent regulatory strategies. In the final section of this chapter, I return to the question that has undergirded much of the scholarly and political interest in trans-national comparisons of U.S. and northern European approaches to the regulation of prostitution: whether and how contemporary state policies might be crafted toward better ends.

Overview: history and policy

Activists and scholars have noted that there are three basic strategies that states have employed in the regulation of prostitution.[6] These strategies range from formal government recognition of prostitution as a legitimate sphere of market activity (legalization), to tacit condonement (decriminalization), to official prohibition of prostitution for both buyer and seller as well as prohibition of all prostitution-related activities (criminalization). A fourth strategy might be said to combine elements from the above three approaches. In the contemporary West, the regulatory systems of Nevada, the Netherlands, and Germany are frequently cited as exemplars of the first approach, while the remaining forty-nine U.S. states have typified the third strategy since the closing of the red-light districts during the Progressive Era.[7] As we have seen, in the late 1990s the city of San Francisco shifted from a criminalized to a de facto decriminalized system within the off-street market, while applying a more intensively policed form of criminalization to outdoor, street-level transactions.

In the 1970s, both the Netherlands and Sweden shifted from a strategy of prohibition by way of public decency laws passed at the turn of the century (laws which themselves succeeded a system of regulated brothel prostitution) to a "combined strategy" involving decriminalization of the prostitute-client transaction along with harsh penalties for prostitution-related activities such as pimping and pandering,[8] The previous public decency laws, like most prohibitive policies, were designed to remove prostitutes (but not their patrons) from public streets. At the same time, both states sought to supplement their legal approaches with an array of government-funded social service programs—programs that were targeted, almost exclusively, toward female prostitutes.[9]

Through the 1980s and 1990s, the contours of the legal frameworks in the two countries and the foci of their social services began to noticeably diverge in consequential ways. As with the 1996 attempt to decriminalize prostitution in San Francisco, and the subsequent implementation of "John Schools" in diverse cities, European, municipalities, nation-states, and transnational bodies such as the European Union have found themselves scrambling to revise their prostitution policies.[10] Swedish and Dutch officials who are charged with regulating prostitution agree that the reasons for the states' revived interest in the regulation of sexual commerce are fairly straightforward: sexual commerce, regarded by some feminists as an archaic manifestation of traditional sex and gender arrangements, has not "withered away," even in what remain relatively strong welfare states such as Sweden and the Netherlands. Rather, it has taken on a wide array of new and diversified forms, which are remarkably consistent across national contexts: massage parlors, escort services, sex tourism, and cell phone and computer network contacts.[11] In addition to the extension of sexual commerce into new cultural terrains, concerns have also been stimulated by the expansion—or feared expansion—of migrant prostitution and human trafficking. The fear of trafficking has increasingly guided European prostitution policy since the early 1990s (nearly a decade before it became a pivotal domestic and foreign policy issue for the United States).[12] Significantly, neither Swedish nor Dutch feminist efforts to reform prostitution policy in the 1990s met with much success prior to the emergence of the trafficking debates. In both cases, feminist rearticulations of prostitution policy in accordance with the new framework of "trafficking" proved highly successful in gathering momentum, even if the legislation that eventually passed had some surprising consequences once put into practice. As I shall describe in the following sections, whereas in Sweden the criminalization of demand has been used to justify both the maintenance of public order and the protection of trafficked women, in the Netherlands the specter of sex trafficking has led to an explicit differentiation in social policy between "forced" and "voluntary" prostitution.[13]

The feminist state and the global sexual marketplace: criminalizing demand

> Sexuality is not something that can be bought or sold. Women are selling a totally empty body; men think they are buying something more . . . . Being a customer is like being a prostitute in that you must switch your mind off. It's like Dr. Jekyll and Mr. Hyde. That's why not all men can buy. A real, whole man who is socially functioning . . . will not be able to.
>
> ELISABETH PETTERSSON, director of the Göteborg
> Prostitution Project and member of the 1993
> Swedish Prostitution Commission[14]

> The system's commodity and market-like character . . . set limitations. It involves a bond with more or less well-masked coldness and in a certain way, a double exploitation . . .
>
> SVEN AXEL MÅNSSON, Professor of Social Welfare at the University of Göteborg and member of the 1993 Swedish Prostitution Commission[15]

In 1998, Sweden became the first country in the world to unilaterally criminalize the purchase of sex for male customers. Although clients are increasingly arrested in U.S., British, Canadian, and French cities, Sweden is the first and only country to penalize the customer—but not the prostitute—in written law. The new law was not part of the penal code but rather part of a package of laws called the Violence against Women Act, which also widened the definition of rape to include other acts in addition to sexual intercourse, increased social services for victims of domestic abuse, and stiffened penalties against genital cutting and sexual harassment.[16] Although framed in gender-neutral terms, the law understands prostitution to be a manifestation of gendered power relations, with female prostitutes serving male clients' sexual needs.[17] It thereby declares prostitution to be incompatible with the Swedish goal of gender equality.

As we have seen in our discussion of San Francisco's "John School," second-wave feminists have frequently bemoaned the sexual double standard in the treatment of prostitution by the criminal justice system (in which female sex workers are arrested, while the sexual behavior of their male clients is tacitly allowed). Apparently in response to concerns such as these, the Swedish Parliament reversed a historical trend in voting to criminalize the (presumptively male) buyer of sexual services, while leaving the (presumptively female) seller's decriminalized status intact. The text of the government bill stated plainly the Swedish Parliament's position, declaring "it is not reasonable to punish the person who sells a sexual service. In the majority of cases at least, this person is a weaker partner who is exploited by those who want only to satisfy their drives."[18] In 2002, a few years after the law's passage, the government instituted a vibrant public relations campaign that offered dramatic visual imagery promoting this view, blanketing 2,215 different public locations with color posters that informed potential customers and other citizens of sexual clients' newly criminalized (and pathologized) status.[19] One poster featuring a cluster of ordinary-looking middle-class men ominously announced that "one man in eight has bought sex." Another depicting a faceless male figure in a suit and tie declared it "time to flush the johns out of the Baltic." A third poster highlighted the gendered dimensions of the new cultural fears which were circulating around the emergence of the Internet and other new technologies: "More and more Swedish men do their shopping over the Internet . . . . It's a Crime to Buy Sex."

Though the posters and the official discourse which surrounded the law's passage both suggest that its primary objective was the extension of Sweden's celebrated "gender equality" policy to sexual as well as economic and political terrains, a closer examination of the diverse interests behind the passage of the new law reveals that gender rectitude was not the only guiding concern.[20] In origin as well as in consequence, Sweden's landmark legislation—pushed through Parliament with great fanfare by feminist Social Democratic politicians—has had as much to do with the symbolic politics surrounding questions of Swedish national identity as with questions of sex or gender per se. In fact, the Swedish Prostitution Committee's decision to implement the new law criminalizing clients emerged in tandem with heated social debates about whether or not Sweden should join the European Union. As the anthropologist Don Kulick has observed, "In the early 1990s . . . talk about prostitution had a subtext—in addition to being about the referent 'prostitution,' it was also about the EU and Sweden's relationship to it."[21] In addition to confronting the blurred boundaries between public and private and licit and illicit sex that the emergence of the Internet seemed to represent, Sweden was confronting the immediate and literal blurring of national boundaries through the specters of Europeanization and globalization. The 1998 law criminalizing the purchase of sex aimed to stabilize cultural and geopolitical boundaries simultaneously.

Though the law officially prohibits the client's behavior (a client who is uniformly depicted as white, middle-class, and computer-literate in the public relations posters), in many ways it is still the sex worker whose presence in Sweden is at issue—particularly the migrant sex worker. The national prostitution commission which ultimately recommended the new law was first established in 1993 to address a wide variety of concerns stemming from the "internationalization" of the new global order. Government officials were concerned both with an anticipated flood of migrants from the east in the wake of the recent Soviet collapse, as well as Sweden's impending and controversial entry into the European Union.[22] From its inception, one of the explicit goals of the commission was to seek a means to combat what they saw as the "free market" in sexual commerce advocated by the European "pro-prostitution lobby" and endorsed by the European Community Court. As Sven Axel Månsson, an outspoken member of the Swedish Prostitution Commission, cautioned: "A European Community member state cannot deny a foreign prostitute (from another member state) the right to work within its premises as long as prostitution is not illegal or subject to other repressive measures in that particular state. As most member states have decriminalized prostitution, [this] . . . opens the way for a free movement of 'sex workers' within Europe."[23] In language which highlighted the fear of an incursion of foreign sex workers, the Swedish Prostitution Commission declared arguments for the decriminalization of the European sex trade to be "alien to Swedish principles."[24]

Although the new Swedish policy marks an important shift from a social-service to a criminal justice system approach (the equivalent of 1.5 million U.S. dollars were given to the police, while no additional monies were given to social service agencies to enforce the new law), it has been taken by many Western feminists to represent an instance of aggressive state intervention against the incursion of global forces of inequality.[25] Government spokespersons routinely boast that the law has been an effective means of eliminating not only street prostitution but also trafficking in women.[26] Yet my own interviews with Swedish sex workers, law enforcement officials, government representatives, and activists uniformly suggest, first, that the presence of street-based and migrant sex workers in Sweden prior to the legislation was minuscule to begin with, and, second, that, if anything, the new legislation has actually served to augment, rather than delimit, the Swedish market in commercial sexual services.[27]

During our interviews, Swedish police officials routinely complained about the difficulties they faced in attempting to arrest clients, given that entrapment of any sort is illegal.[28] This is one reason, they say, that they have chosen to focus their attention on eliminating the most visible contours of commercial sex work from city streets. A second reason for the police's continued focus on street-level transactions likely has to do with what Swedish criminologists Toby Pettersson and Eva Tiby have referred to as the "problem of definition," whereby those individuals who do not conform to the stereotype of the street-based, strung-out "drug whore" (e.g., women who arrange commercial sexual contacts with their clients through Internet Web pages; male prostitutes who make contact with their clients in bars or chat rooms) may be difficult to recognize as prostitutes at all. Can "prostitution" be said to exist where there are no prostitutes? As one of Pettersson and Tiby's interviewees from the social service sector explained:

> Before [the new forms of contact came along] it was easy, black or white. Now it's become more confused somehow . . . the women who've been involved [before], it's been so obvious that they were prostitutes. ["]I'm a prostitute, kind of thing, I walk the streets.["] There's no mistaking it. But the closer you come to the other end, the more complicated it must become for the women too. It might be very good-natured and cosy, this man maybe buys dinner and yeah, then some regard it as a date. And then you get paid for it—it's a bit weird.[29]

Based on their interviews with Swedish police officials and social service workers, Pettersson and Tiby conclude that although the Swedish law explicitly sought to shift the stigma away from female prostitutes and toward male clients, "the traditional position of the bad woman as vendor and the invisible man as purchaser is preserved . . . [while] all other constellations, that may as well be considered to be prostitution, remain unproblematized."[30]

As my own police ride-alongs and various government reports reveal, urban streetwalking strolls constitute the sole focus of police attention, despite the fact that street prostitution represented a dwindling minority of the Swedish sex industry to begin with, and one in which proportionately few migrant prostitutes are employed.[31] Among the police officers, social workers, and street-based sex workers that I interviewed, there was broad consensus that the overwhelming majority of street prostitutes were Swedish citizens. While police officers admit that patrolling the streets has not accomplished much in terms of stemming the high-growth sectors of the industry—tourist-oriented strip clubs, massage parlors, and the new online services—as the following field note extract reveals, they often regard it as the most tangible way to make a difference.

> Last night I spent several hours on prostitution patrol duty with Johannes, a member of the Stockholm police squad, observing the sparse handful of female prostitutes who were still on the streets of the central business district. Johannes was intimately acquainted with each woman's face, name, and personal history ("That one, she only comes out here when she's short of money, when she's going on vacation, or when she needs money to pay the rent"). Having left the neighborhood and on our way back to my flat in the Södermalm district, Johannes gestured to what he identified as one of fourteen illegal massage parlors in the city where sexual services were readily available for purchase. As we drove past, he chuckled quietly at the hypocrisy of Swedish prostitution policy: "These it is 'too difficult' to do anything about. It takes too much time, and it requires too much evidence." Johannes's comments echoed the observations of Sonja, an exotic dancer at the "company club" that I visited yesterday.[32] To my astonishment, she remarked casually that "the police don't

care what goes on at the clubs. They're on our side [against the new law] and will wink when they ask us, 'You have a g-string on, right?'"

FIELD NOTES, JULY 2002

The Swedish sex workers that I spoke with insisted that since the law's passage, prostitution has not disappeared but rather moved underground. In cities such as Stockholm and Göteberg, with high-priced, glutted housing markets and thriving tourist industries, such enforcement strategies have conveniently served to displace streetwalkers from the very downtown areas that government and real estate officials are interested in developing.[33] As a consequence, the majority of street-walkers have switched to different forms of client networking, resorting primarily to cell phones or the Internet. As in other Western European and U.S. cities, the vast majority of prostitution activity had in any event already moved indoors, free from the supervision of social workers and the scrutiny of the police.[34] In this sense, the law has hastened a shift in the social geography of commercial sex work— one common not only to Stockholm, but also to other postindustrial cities—that was already underway.

At 8 p.m. Sven Pettersson arrives, the police officer who has been assigned to show me around the city of Göteborg's prostitution strolls. He is a small, friendly man, dressed in a tan jacket and jeans. Although his unmarked navy blue vehicle is parked in front of my hotel, we decide to go exploring on foot.

Our first destination is the city's former red-light district, which, at least at this hour, seems to consist of nothing more than an isolated, empty street and its adjacent parking lot. It is utterly unpopulated, save for a pair of rumpled women in their mid-thirties with skinny, bruised arms and blood-shot eyes. They turn to glance at us briefly before stumbling away. About fifteen minutes later, a lone, matronly Polish woman appears. Sven knows her and explains that she is now married, no longer working, and legally residing in Sweden. Like many of the police officers I have met in Sweden, Sven stresses his comfortable, quasi-familial relationship with the women, at one point even pulling out the red rose-embossed business card of a friend who has recently left the streets.

We head over to the city's main cruising area, hoping to see a few of the city's male prostitutes, but this area, too, is completely empty. We do the next segment of the tour in his car, driving over to Göteborg's three other prostitution strolls, which are pristine, orderly, and again, devoid of any discernible prostitution activity. Sven indicates the few venues in the area with checkered pasts—the mall, the video store, the parking lot where prostitutes would take their Johns. At the train station (the chief locus of street prostitution in many European cities) there has not been any activity for some time. Compared to 1995 (when a female research colleague and I walked through Göteborg's red-light district and were trailed by at least twenty or thirty cars, driven by men anxiously looking for dates), the city's street prostitution scene seems to have been radically transformed.

Before we part, I ask Sven what he thinks of Sweden's new law criminalizing the clients of prostitutes, and the 10 million crowns that was given to the police department to enforce it. I am somewhat taken aback when he issues an embarrassed laugh: "Do you want the official or the unofficial answer?" I (of course) request the latter. "The truth is that I am the whole prostitution patrol force!"

FIELD NOTES, JUNE 1999

The consequences of criminalization: Tanya's story

Prior to the new law, selling sex without an intermediary was not a crime, although "living off the earnings of a prostitute" was.[35] With the shift from the streets to the Internet, many formerly independent sex workers who were engaged in legal activity have been impelled to rely on criminal intermediaries in order to contact clients. Several women that I spoke with noted the emergence and prevalence of "Internet pimps" over the last several years, whose job it is to help women run their businesses covertly. And, at least according to some, this growth in the illegal sector of the industry has actually paved the way for the arrival of more migrant prostitutes, as well as more traffickers.

Tanya was one individual I encountered who articulated the linkages between the new Swedish prostitution law and the broader transformations occurring in the Swedish sex industry clearly and unambiguously. A former street prostitute, Tanya was currently working as a "trafficker" (her term), facilitating the passage of Estonian women into Sweden to sell sex. Although it is impossible to say that Tanya's story is in any sense typical, her professional transition encapsulated some of the broader changes in the Swedish sex market that were identified by a number of the sex workers I spoke with.

During our interview, Tanya described the way in which street clients' newly born fear of arrest eventually led her to place an ad on the Internet. Because of her transsexual background, this was a potentially dangerous arrangement for her—unlike face-to-face contacts on the street, the clients that she met online did not necessarily know what they were "getting." Often clients would show up and be disappointed that she didn't have a conventionally legible female body. "They wanted the service," she explained, "just not from me." So Tanya decided to use her Internet skills and the client contacts that she had established to help other women make the shift indoors. While her initial employees were all Scandinavian women that she knew from the streets, she eventually came to employ less expensive Estonian women instead.

In her current business, she offers what she calls "a complete service" to the women, providing everything except for visas. Once they arrive at their contact point in Sweden, Tanya secures their apartments, arranges for clients, and takes care of security. She employs only one or two women at a time and arranges for them to stay in Sweden from anywhere between one week and three months. Although she is glad that she can pay the Estonian women approximately a third less than the Swedish ones for the same work, and acknowledges that she retains custody of the women's passports while they are in her employment, she insists that the arrangement she has with them is not exploitative:[36]

> Many of the girls are still in school, so they come [to Sweden] for only a short holiday. The average number of clients per day is three or four. I know one girl who earned 120,000 kronor [~ 16,000 U.S. dollars] after seven weeks. She had that much money in her pocket when she went home!

The girls work in private apartments, normal houses. Some I can trust
and some I can't. Once, a girl disappeared with my phone and my key, and
then called to tell me that I would need to buy them back from her! So now
I'm more careful . . . . There has been plenty of talk about "slave trading" in
the business. In my case, not only do the girls want to come here to work,
but they actually pay their Estonian contact person to get in touch with me.
Most of them have done this work before . . . . It's in everybody's interest
that the girls be happy and do good work.

It's a big market, and there are many countries who are asking for them.
Sometimes, I can't even get enough girls, so I need to maintain my reputation
as a good employer. Business only goes well when everyone is happy.

Some would argue (along with Tanya herself) that the new Swedish law has backfired in
failing to curb either the demand for commercial sex or the incursion of migrant sex
workers, thereby enabling businesses like Tanya's to thrive. Together with Kulick (2003),
I would argue instead that it has served to assuage anxieties about national identity through
a series of symbolic substitutions. Anxieties about slippery national borders are deflected
onto anxieties about slippery moral borders, which affix themselves onto the bodies of
female street prostitutes. The removal of these women from public streets can thereby
pave the way for real estate developers, while bolstering Swedish national identity in the
process.

Conclusion: parallel trends

In recent decades, states and municipalities throughout North America, Australia, and
Western Europe have sought to contain a burgeoning and diversifying sex trade through
a variety of innovative measures—from stepped up enforcement against the perpetrators
of "quality of life" crimes to the legalization of brothel keeping to increased client arrests.
These efforts have arguably constituted a "third wave" of reform surrounding the state
regulation of prostitution during the last century. If the first wave occurred with the
closing of the red-light districts and the elimination of licensed brothel prostitution in the
first decades of the twentieth century, and a second wave occurred with the liberalization
of laws surrounding commercial sex in the 1970s, a new series of transformations has
occurred in tandem with the postindustrial expansion and transnationalization of sexual
commerce.

"Prosex" as well as "antiprostitution" feminists have produced diverse accounts of the
gendered meanings that comprise the commercial sex-work transaction, arguing for an
array of competing legal remedies—including decriminalization, legalization, and criminalization—and for the broader implementation of "Dutch" or "Swedish" policy models, as
we have seen. Few commentators, however, have situated their analyses within the context
of postindustrial transformations of sexuality and culture. My research demonstrates that
the failure to situate sexual commerce within a broader political-economic framework
can lead advocates to argue for opposing tactics which, once implemented, might have
surprisingly similar effects on the ground. Whether sex work is decriminalized, legalized,
or criminalized, the interests of real estate developers, municipal and national politicians,
and business owners may overshadow the concerns of feminists and sex workers.

What is arguably most remarkable about the disparate array of legal strategies that Europeans and North Americans have implemented in recent years is how singular they have been in effect: The overarching trend has been toward the elimination of prostitution from city streets, coupled with the state-facilitated (or de facto tolerated) flourishing of the indoor and online sectors of the sex trade. Despite their seeming differences, the common focus of state interventions has been on eliminating the visible manifestations of poverty and deviance (both racial and national) from urban spaces, rather than the exchange of sex for money per se.

Different policy regimes and national cultures clearly can have an impact on the scope and character of the commercial sex trade. Sweden's prohibitive attitude toward prostitution (both before and after the new law) has been manifest in a comparatively small commercial sex sector of about 2,500 prostitutes, compared with a figure of about 30,000 in the Netherlands—a country with only twice Sweden's population.[37] Conversely, the Netherlands' pragmatic recognition of the sex trade as a legitimate sphere of commerce and employment has resulted in greater social legitimacy and working conditions for at least some parties, who have the opportunity to work free from police harassment, to openly declare their occupation on their bank accounts and tax forms, and to present themselves, in the words of Yvonne (one of the brothel owners that I interviewed) as "honest, hardworking businessmen" [sic].

Given these differences, the impulse among feminists and sex-workers' rights advocates to call on the example of either country in order to advance a particular normative agenda is understandable, but it is also fraught with difficulties. One of the key problems that can emerge is a simplification of political dynamics, including a failure to consider the multiple motives of political actors, notably those which surround questions of migration, national identity, and the gentrification of cities. In the wake of European unification and other global transformations, Sweden, the Netherlands, and other countries find themselves confronting similar material and symbolic dilemmas, ones which undergird and overshadow concerns about the regulation of commercial sex.

The global restructuring of capitalist production and investment that has taken place since the 1970s has meant that legal and illegal migrants in search of many different forms of work have continued to press against Western European and U.S. borders; meanwhile, for Swedish, Dutch, and other postindustrial city dwellers, deindustrialization, unemployment, and a lack of affordable housing have become the local face of the same global processes. For Swedish and Dutch citizens, the economic hardships entailed by unification have further contributed to a fragile and wavering sense of national identity. In the face of difficult-to-remedy structural transformations such as these, both Sweden and the Netherlands have created policies which reinforce a coherent sense of national identity by more closely regulating the prostitute body. In both cases, a semblance of cleanliness and order has been created by eliminating streetwalking and—in the case of the Netherlands—concentrating sex workers in corporate-run brothels.

Both countries, furthermore, make a show of policing illegal migrants attempting to eliminate the most visible presence of migrant sex workers from public view. The national project is thereby reinforced and made to appear as "more moral" in each case—despite the fact that the policies of both countries have apparently served to strengthen the hands of the criminal networks that facilitate illegal migration. And, last, the policies of both Sweden and the Netherlands serve to better align each country with the local forces of globalization, facilitating gentrification and tourism. Despite some important surface-level contrasts, the cases of Stockholm, Amsterdam, and San Francisco demonstrate that regimes which legalize the sex trade as well as those which claim to seek its elimination share several common threads which link them to larger changes within the global economy.

Taken together, the cases also speak to a broader set of theoretical and political concerns about the state's role in achieving social reform—concerns which have long plagued feminist scholars interested in questions of prostitution, pornography, and other issues. As with the development of San Francisco's "John School," both the legalization of prostitution in the Netherlands and the criminalization of clients in Sweden were sought after and fought for by avowedly feminist constituencies. Yet as my own discussion in this chapter and the abundant literature on women's engagement with the state both reveal, feminist movements have good reason to be wary of forging alliances with nonfeminist state actors who claim to represent their best interests.[38] The question necessarily arises as to whether or not it is possible to forge a prostitution policy that simultaneously empowers sex workers and protects other women from the gendered sexualization of public space that certain feminists fear.[39] In this era of global flows of capital and culture, what are the potentials and limits of state policies that claim to speak on behalf of women?

Notes

1   Hobson (1987: 30).
2   Gelb (1989: 138), Wolfe (1989), Lenneer-Axelson (1991a). As such, it is interesting to note that it is also a country in which there has been a marked absence of any strong or tangible second-wave women's movement. The relative gender equality that Sweden is noted for has been achieved not through the civil sphere but through the early incorporation of "women's interests" into formal government institutions. According to Hobson (1999), the downsizing of the Swedish public sector in the 1990s has, however, led to a recent spate of more vocal feminist activism.
3   Hobson (1987), Jeffreys (1997), Boëthius (1999), Farley and Kelly (2000).
4   Hobson (1987), Chapkis (1997), Weitzer (2000b), Kuo (2002). "Harm reduction" refers to social-service approaches to prostitution and drug dependency that seek to reduce the associated harms without requiring the abolition of the sex industry or total abstinence by the drug user (Sorge 1991; Kilvington, Day, and Ward 2001).
5   Legalized prostitution can also be found in Austria, Germany, Australia, and New Zealand, as well as in the state of Nevada. See Outshoorn (2004), Hausbeck and Brents (2000), Perkins et al. (1994), and Jordan (2005).
6   See, e.g., Van Wesenbeeck (1995), Barry (1995), Alexander (1987), Leigh (1998), and Weitzer (2000b). Leigh (1998) articulates the differences between these models from a perspective that is akin to my own view, arguing that they merely represent "ideal types" within a field of highly complex configurations of policy.
7   The fact that the United States is often held to be a nation that relegates most of its moral issues to regulation by the market (Wolfe 1989, Esping-Andersen 1990), yet officially prohibits the exchange of sexual services for payment, might at first blush appear to present a contradiction. Although theorists writing in the utilitarian tradition have often embraced market logics to argue against state intervention in prostitution, economic logics have also been used to justify its prohibition (Satz 1995). Barbara Hobson has described a tension in the United States between a commitment to free market principles and a tradition of intervention in moral concerns, thus explaining its history of "radical swings in policy

between all-out campaigns against prostitution and sufferance of its existence" (1990: 4). On the exceptionalism of Nevada (historically rooted in a migrant mining economy and a culture of "cowboy," antifederalist libertarianism), see Hausbeck and Brents (2000).

8   Hobson (1987), Høigård and Finstad (1992), Davis (1993).

9   Less frequently, social work and reeducation programs have also attempted to target clients, as with the Swedish KAST project which began in 1997, featuring social workers doing outreach to male sexual clients and offering them counselling (Torgny Sjögren, KAST, interview, June 18, 1999). By the beginning of this decade, severe budget cuts in the Netherlands began to severely inhibit service provision of all sorts. The red-light district's Prostitution Information Center lost its government funding and the Mr. A. de Graaf Stichting, the Dutch research institute for prostitution issues, founded in 1961, closed its doors.

10   Hobson (2005), Outshoorn (2004a, 2005), Kligman (2005), Kilvington, Day, and Ward (2001).

11   Månsson (1981: 311), Jan Visser, Mr. A. de Graaf Stichting, interview, June 9, 1999.

12   Definitional struggles over what constitutes the crime and human rights violations of "trafficking" continue to abound. The most recent United Nations Protocol against Trafficking in Persons defines trafficking broadly, to encompass multiple forms of forced migration and forced labor beyond prostitution (including, most commonly, domestic work, sweatshop labor, and agricultural work). Nevertheless, many antitrafficking activists and state agents deem trafficking to be synonymous with all forms of prostitution, whether forced or voluntary (see, e.g., Saunders 2004; Saunders and Soderlund 2004).

13   On the conflation of feminism, nationalism, and antitrafficking sentiment in the passage of the 1998 Swedish law prohibiting the purchase of sex, see Kulick (2003) and Gould (2002). Joyce Outshoorn (2004b) and Marieke Van Doorninck of the Mr. A. de Graaf Stichting (interview, July 2002) have both noted the gap between Dutch feminist demands and state policies regarding the rights of illegal migrant sex workers. See also Doezema (1998) and Norwegian Ministry of Justice (2004).

14   Interview, June 18, 1999.

15   Månsson (1992: 10).

16   *Violence against Women Fact Sheet* (1999).

17   Within Sweden, variants of commercial sexual exchange that depart from the classical heterosexual exchange model of women offering services to men have been insufficiently acknowledged or understood. The crafters of a recent survey of online sexual services in Sweden were thus baffled to discover that of 2,668 entries, the majority of the sellers were men (National Board of Health and Welfare 1999).

18   *Violence against Women Fact Sheet* (1999).

19   Nordic Baltic Campaign (2002). On the relationship between the new Swedish law and the invention of a new category of "pervert" in Swedish society, see Kulick (2005).

20   Since the 1960s and 1970s, the hallmarks of Swedish gender equality policy have included state-run child care programs and generous parental leave and pension systems which have allowed Swedish women to enter the labor force in record numbers. See Florin and Nilsson (1998), Earles (2004), Hobson (1999), and Rabo (1997). Beginning in the late 1970s, feminist-identified parliamentarians sought to intervene in the sexual arena as well. Through the 1980s, antipornography legislation was made stricter through successive bans on child pornography (1980), on sexual violence in films and videos (1986), and on sexual violence in pictures and print (1989) (Bygdeman and Lindahl 1994: 72). Feminist interventions in prostitution policy date back to 1977, when the government created its first "prostitution project," sending a team of researchers and social workers to Malmö to investigate and to attempt to curb the prostitution explosion in one Swedish port city. The project gave rise to similar efforts in Göteborg, Stockholm, and Noorkjøping, and led to the government's creation of the first national prostitution commission (Månsson 1981: 311). The report that was eventually issued by the commission resulted in a new national prostitution policy which

aimed to address the problem both through legal measures and through expanded social services. In 1982, the law against vagrancy was removed from the penal code and was supplanted by several key policy revisions: profiteering (including newspaper advertising and the renting out of flats) was prohibited; pornographic "live shows" in places open to the public were banned; prostitution was criminalized for sellers under twenty years of age; and the Swedish government was required by law to fund research on methods of preventing prostitution (Swedish Prostitution Commission 1993; *Women and Men* 1995). For additional discussion of feminist interventions in Swedish sex law, see Kulick (2003, 2005).

21   Kulick (2003: 207).

22   The results of the referendum vote by which Swedish voters elected to enter the European Union were closely divided: 52.2 percent of voters were in favour, and 46.9 percent of voters were against (Kulick 2003: 214 ftnt. 15).

23   Månsson (1992: 8).

24   Swedish Prostitution Commission (1993: 3–4). The 1993 committee initially recommended the criminalization of both the buyer and the seller, arguing that bilateral criminalization would have the greatest general deterrent effect. This proposal was rejected by virtually all government parties consulted, largely on the grounds that women who were already victimized by prostitution should not be made to suffer further penalties (Norwegian Ministry of Justice 2004; interview with Anne Rygh Pedersen, Swedish Social Democratic Party, July 22, 1999).

25   See, e.g., Boëthius (1999), Farley and Kelly (2000), and Raymond (2003).

26   Winberg (2002), Ekberg (2002), Swedish Ministry of Foreign Affairs (2003), Orback (2005).

27   Before the passage of the new law, there were never more than 1,000 street prostitutes in all of Sweden, even according to the most liberal estimates (Kulick 2003: 200), with street prostitution consisting of no more than a third of the overall market (Norwegian Ministry of Justice 2004). Data collected through the 1990s reveal that approximately one quarter of Swedish prostitutes were migrants, compared to upward of 50 percent and as much as 80 percent in countries such as the Netherlands and Germany (Randers-Pehrson and Jessen 2000: I; TAMPEP 2002: 243ff).

28   Unlike in the United States, even the use of police decoys is considered entrapment. As of 2001, the police had made eighty-six arrests and twenty convictions (Anders Gripelov, head of the Prostitution Patrol Force, interview, July 8, 2002).

29   Pettersson and Tiby (2003: 163). Another definitional difficulty is entailed by the Swedish law's equation of the crime of prostitution with the purchase of a "temporary sexual relationship." ("Anyone who for remuneration procures a temporary sexual relationship will be guilty—if their action is not punishable by some other offense according to the penal code—of purchasing sexual services, and will be sentenced to fines or prison for not more than six months.") As Kulick rightfully inquires: "What does 'temporary' mean exactly? Should it cover regular clients, who maintain long term relationships with individual sex workers, or are they exempt from prosecution? And . . . what exactly constitutes 'a sexual relationship'? . . . what exactly has to be done to whom for a given interaction to be considered 'sexual'?" (2003: 202).

30   Pettersson and Tiby (2003: 154).

31   The Swedish police have been involved in only one case which involved sex purchased indoors. In a 2003 case associated with trafficking, a list of clients was found by the police while going through the computer records of a Stockholm brothel. Due to strict laws against entrapment, the police conduct no undercover operations in brothels—whether or not trafficking is suspected (Norwegian Ministry of Justice 2004: 10).

32   Swedish "company clubs" are the approximate equivalent of "gentleman's clubs" in the United States.

33   On the law's exclusion of Swedish sex workers from city streets, see also Östergren (2004); on the spatialization of social hierarchy in Sweden, see Pred (2000).

34   Roane (1998), Israely (2000), Davies and Wonke (2000).

35   The penal code provides that a person "promoting or improperly deriving economic advantage from another person having casual sexual relations in return for payment can be convicted of procuring and imprisoned for up to four years . . . Procuring can include, not only the more traditional activities of the pimp or the panderer, but also other forms of promotion such as sex advertisements in newspapers, travel arrangements and so on. Special penal liability—the same as for procuring—is incurred . . . by a property owner when a tenanted apartment is used for prostitution" (Swedish Prostitution Commission 1993: 3).

36   As Tanya explained to me, "For a Swedish girl working by herself, it's usually 1,500 [kronor] for an hour of services. Sometimes, on the street, the client would be able to bargain her down to 1,000 kr. Now that it's only drug addicts left on the street, the price has gone way down. A blow job was usually 500 kr. So when I started to employ Swedish girls, I would charge 1,500 to 3,000 (for a half hour or one hour), and take half. Now if I want to make the same profit with the Estonian girls, I pay 500 kronor per girl, which leaves 750 for me for a half hour date. The meeting costs the client 1,250. So it's slightly cheaper for him, and he gets a higher quality girl. For a one-hour date, the price is 1,600 to 2,500. The girl gets 500 for half an hour, and 800 for one hour. But actually, I have found that the girls are happy with even less, anywhere from 300 to 500, so I have started paying that." At the time the interview was conducted, the exchange rate was approximately 9 kronor to the dollar. Thus, each woman would earn approximately $30 to $50 for a half-hour date, while Tanya would earn $80. For an hour date, the women whom Tanya employed would earn approximately $90, and Tanya would earn $180.

37   Randers-Pehrson and Jessen (2000: I), TAMPEP (2002: 242). Providing precise statistical counts of sex-industry workers is notoriously difficult, as numbers are generally gleaned from police or social workers; using official counts of identifiable prostitutes as measures of the size of the sex industry in general presents even greater difficulties. Nonetheless, the numbers can serve as a rough portrait of differences in the scope and character of sexual commerce in diverse contexts.

38   See, e.g., Walkowitz (1980), Beisel (1997), Luker (1998), and Brown (1995).

39   The sexualization of public culture has also inspired antiprostitution activism on the part of women's organizations that do not consider themselves feminist. Evangelical Christian women have historically played an active role in shaping prostitution policy not only in the United States but also in countries such as Norway, Britain, and the Netherlands (Hobson 1987).

References

Alexander, Priscilla. 1987, "Prostitution: A Difficult Issue for Feminists", in Fréderique Delacoste and Priscilla Alexander, eds. *Sex work: writings by women in the sex industry*. London: Virago Press.

Barry, Kathleen. 1995. *The prostitution of sexuality*. New York: New York University Press.

Boethius, Maria-Pia. 1999. "Current Sweden: The End of Prostitution in Sweden?" Svenska Instituetet, http://www.si.ed.infoSweden/604.cs?hit1_Prostitution@hit2 (last accessed Feb. 26, 2001.)

Brown, Wendy. 1995. *States of injury: power and freedom in late modernity*. Princeton, N.J.: Princeton University Press.

Bygdeman, Marc, and Katarina Lindahl. 1994. *Sex education and reproductive health in Sweden in the twentieth century*. Report for the International Conference on Population and Development in Cairo.

Chapkis, W. 1997. *Live sex acts: women performing erotic labor*. New York: Routledge.

Davis, Fania. 1995. Letter to James A. Quadra, San Francisco Deputy City Attorney, RE: *Dotson v. Yee, San Francisco Task Force on Prostitution Final Report*, app. D.

Davis, Guy and Anthony Wonke. 2000. "Media: We Want Porn: Virtual Brothels in Amsterdam." *Guardian* (London), Nov. 13, p. 8.

Doezema, Jo. 1998. "Forced to Choose: Beyond the Voluntary v. Forced Feminism Dichotomy." In *Global sex workers: rights, resistance, and redefinition*. Edited by K. Kempadoo and J. Doezema. New York: Routledge.

Earles, Kimberley. 2004. "Women and the Assault on Welfare in Sweden." *Socialism and Democracy* 18 (1): 107–35.

Ekberg, Gunilla. 2002. "The International Debate about Prostitution and Trafficking in Women: Refuting the Arguments." *Seminar on the Effects of Legalization of Prostitution Activities—A Critical Analysis*. Stockholm, Regeringskansliet.

Esping-Anderson, Gosta. 1990. *The Three Worlds of Welfare Capitalism*. Princeton: Princeton University Press.

Farley, Melissa, and Vanessa Kelly. 2000. "Prostitution: A Critical Review of the Medical and Social Sciences Literature." *Women and Criminal Justice* 11 (4): 29–64.

Florin, C. and B. Nilsson. 1998. "Something in the Nature of a Bloodless Revolution," in *State policy and gender system in the two German states and Sweden 1945–1989*. Edited by R. Torstendahl. Uppsala: Distribution, Dept. of History, [Uppsala universitet].

Gelb, Joyce. 1989. *Feminism and politics: a comparative perspective*. Berkeley: University of California Press.

Gould, Arthur. 2002. "Sweden's Law on Prostitution." *Transnational prostitution: changing patterns in a global context*. Edited by S. Thorbek and B. Pattanaik. London: Zed Books.

Hausbeck, Kathryn and Barbara Brents. 2000. "Inside Nevada's Brothel Industry." In *Sex for sale: prostitution, pornography, and the sex industry*. Edited by R. J. Weitzer. New York: Routledge.

Hobson, Barbara. 1999. "Women's Collective Agency." *Extending citizenship, reconfiguring states*. Edited by M. P. Hanagan and C. Tilly. Lanham, Md.: Rowman & Littlefield Publishers.

Hobson, Barbara Meil. 1987. *Uneasy virtue: the politics of prostitution and the American Reform tradition*. New York: Basic Books.

Hoigard, Cecilie, and Liv Finstad. 2002. *Backstreets: Prostitution, Money and Love*, trans. Katherine Hanson, Nancy Snipe and Barbara Wilson. University Park: Pennsylvania University Press.

Israely, Jeff. 2000. "Old Trade, New Tack: Italy Considers Legalizing Prostitution in Order to Control It." *San Francisco Chronicle*, Sept. 25, p.A12.

Jeffreys, Sheila. 1997. *The Idea of Prostitution*. North Melbourne: Spiniflex.

Jordan, Jan. 2005. *The Sex Industry in New Zealand: A Literature Review*. Wellington: New Zealand Ministry of Justice. http://www.courts.govt.nz/pubs/reports/2005/sex-industry-in-nz-literature-review/index.html (last accessed June 15, 2005).

Kilvington, Judith, Sophie Day, and Helen Ward. 2001. "Prostitution Policy in Europe: A Time of Change?" *Feminist Review* 67: 78–93.

Kligman, Gail, and Stephanie Limoncelli. 2005. "Trafficking Women after Socialism: To, through, and from Eastern Europe." *Social Politics* 12 (1): 118–140.

Kulick, Don. 2003. "Sex in the New Europe: The Criminalization of Clients and Swedish Fear of Penetration." *Anthropological Theory* 3 (2): 199–218.

Kulick, Don. 1998. *Travesti: sex, gender, and culture among Brazilian transgendered prostitutes*. Chicago, IL: University of Chicago Press.

Kuo, Lenore. 2002. *Prostitution policy revolutionizing practice through a gendered perspective*. New York: New York University Press.

Leigh, Carol. 2004. "A Brief History of Prostitution in San Francisco." *San Francisco Task Force on Prostitution Final Report* app. D: Testimony, History, Index.

Leneer-Axelson, Barbro. 1991a. "Swedish Men and Equality." Paper presented at the Department of Social Work, University of Göteborg.

Luker, Kristin. 1998. "Sex, Social Hygiene, and the State: The Double-Edged Sword of Social Reform." *Theory and Society* 27 (5): 601–634.

Mansson, Sven-Axel. 1992. "Brothel Europe: International Prostitution and Traffic in Women." Unpublished Manuscript.

Mansson, Sven-Axel. 1981. *Konshandelns Framjare Och Profitorer*. Lund: Doxa.

National Board of Health and Welfare. 1999. Kännedom om prostitution. March 7, 2001. http://www.sos.se/sos/publ/refereng/0003005e.htm.

Nordic Baltic Campaign against Trafficking in Women. 2002. *Final Report*. Nordic Council of Ministers, http://www.nordicbalticcampaign.org.

Norwegian Ministry of Justice and Police Affairs 2004. *Purchasing Sexual Services in Sweden and the Netherlands*. Ed. Ulf Stridbeck (G-0637).

Orback, Jens. 2005. "Legal and Other Normative Means to Combat Trafficking in Women and Girls. Speech by the Swedish Minister for Gender Equality at the Forty-Ninth Session of the United Nations Commission on the Status of Women, March. 1.

Ostergren, Petra. 2004. "Sexworkers' Critique of Swedish Prostitution Policy." Article available at http://www.petrostergren.com.

Outshoorn, Joyce. 2005, "The Political Debates on Prostitution and Trafficking of Women." *Social Politics* 12 (1) (spring 2005): 141–155.

Perkins, Roberta, Garreet Prestage, Rachel Sharp and Frances Lovejoy, eds. 1994. *Sex work and sex workers in Australia*. Sydney: University of South Wales Press.

Pettersson, Toby and Eva Tiby. 2003. "The Production and Reproduction of Prostitution." *Journal of Scandinavian Studies I Criminology and Crime Prevention*. 3: 154–72.

Pred, Allan. 2000. *Even in Sweden: racisms, racialized spaces, and the popular geographical imagination*. Berkeley: University of California Press.

Rabo, Annika. 1997. "Gender Equality in Post-Welfare Sweden." In *Anthropology of policy: critical perspectives on governance and power*. Edited by C. Shore and S. Wright. New York: Routledge.

Randers-Pehrson, Arne, and Liv Jessen. 2000. European Network for HIV-STD Prevention in Prostitution. *Northern Regional Report, 2000*. Available at http://www.europap.net/ (accessed March 2001).

Raymond, Janice. 2003. "Ten Reasons for Not Legalizing Prostitution." *Journal of Trauma and Practice* 2: 315–32.

Roane, Kit. 1998. "Prostitutes on Wane in New York Streets but Take to Internet." *New York Times* Feb. 23, pp. Al and B4.

Satz, Debra. 1995. "Markets in Women's Sexual Labor," *Ethics* 106 (1): 63–85.

Saunders, Penelope. "Prohibiting Sex Work Projects, Restricting Women's Rights: The International Impact of the 2003 U.S. Global AIDS Act." *Health and Human Rights* 7 (2): 179–93.

Saunders, Penelope and Gretchen Soderlund. 2004. "Threat or Opportunity? Sexuality, Gender, and the Ebb and Flow of Traffic as Discourse," *Canadian Journal of Women's Studies* 22 (3,4): 16–24.

Sorge, Rod. "Harm Reduction: A New Approach to Drug Services." *Health/PAC Bulletin* (winter): 70–99.

Swedish Ministry of Foreign Affairs. 2003. *Poverty and trafficking in human beings*. Stockholm: Regeringskanliet.

Swedish Prostitution Commission. 1995. Betänkande av 1993 ars Prostitution-sutreding. SOU:15. English Summary.

TAMPEP (Transnational AIDS/STD Prevention Among Migrant Prostitutes I Europe Project). 2002. *Final Report*, Vol. 1.

Van Wesenbeeck, Ine. 1995. *Prostitutes' well being and risk*. Amsterdam: VU University Press.

Violence against Women Fact Sheet 1999. News and Information from the Swedish Government Offices on Issues Related to Violence Against Women. July 6. http://www.kvinnifrid.gov.se/regeringen/faktaeng.htm.

Walkowitz, Judith R. 1980. *Prostitution and Victorian society: women, class, and the state*. New York: Cambridge University Press.

Weitzer, Ron. 2000. "The Politics of Prostitution in America." In *Sex for sale: prostitution, pornography, and the sex industry*. Edited by R. J. Weitzer. New York: Routledge.

Winberg, Margareta. 2002. "Speech by the Deputy Prime Minister." *Seminar on the effects of legalization of prostitution activities: a critical analysis*. Stockholm: Regeringskanliet.

Wolfe, Alan. *Whose keeper? Social science and moral obligation*. Berkeley: University of California Press.

Women and men in Sweden. Facts and figures. Stockholm: SCB.

Index

aboriginal 167
abortion 4, 8–9, 38; in Denmark 288–94, 313; in Germany 267–84
abstinence 116
Acton, William 162
adultery 7, 56, 60, 90, 92, 145, 149, 158
Aeschines 7, 14, 19, 20–35
Africans 236, 238, 326; *see also* Kenya
AIDS 325
Alcibiades 20
alcoholism 226
American *see also* United States; 2, 10, 141, 147, 162, 296, 299
amrad 71, 75
Amsterdam 338, 347
anal intercourse 24–5, 59, 63–4, 184
Anderson, Benedict 168
Anderson, Wilda 104
anthropology 5, 145–6, 165, 194, 234, 239, 253
anus 25, 65
Ariori 95–6
aristocracy 27, 191, 289
Aristogeiton 14, 26, 27, 33
Aristophanes 26
Aristotle 19, 21, 24, 25
Aristotle's Masterpiece 1, 116, 130
army 162, 168
ascetism 40, 42, 47, 89

Atholl, Duchess of 234, 242, 260–4
Austin, Sarah 122
Australia 165–6, 171, 345
Austria 4, 195
autobiography 186, 187, 189, 205

Baudelaire, Charles 194
Baümer, Gertrude 217
Belgium 161, 178, 188
Berlin 179, 207, 210, 272, 275–6, 284
Bernstein, Elizabeth 5, 326, 337
BfM *see* League for the Protection of Motherhood
birth control 4, 9, 115, 220; in Denmark 288–94; in Weimar Germany 267–8, 270–3, 277
birth control pill 304
birth rate 116, 127, 231, 268, 274, 276
bisexuality 184, 199, 218, 220, 247
Blagden, Isa 147, 151
Bloch, Iwan 216
Bodichon, Barbara Leigh Smith 119, 120
Bonaparte, Marie 5, 233, 238, 244, 247, 248
Bougainville, Louis de 95–6, 100–1, 107
Bourdieu, Pierre 302, 305, 309–10
Bowman, Annie 167
boys, as erotic objects: in ancient Greece: 14; in early Islamic cultures 33, 68–77
Bree, Ruth 228

Britain: birth control in 270, 273; government of 233, 236; Victorian 7, 10, 115, 118–27; 144–52
Browning, Elizabeth and Robert 150–1
Burma 170
Butler, Josephine 9, 119, 162
Butler, Judith 5, 145

Caine, Nathaniel 166
Canning, Kathleen 276
capitalism 220, 289, 290, 292, 295, 304, 306, 307, 309, 346
Carlyle, Thomas 123
celibacy 38, 42, 49, 225, 227–8, 231
census 165–7, 173
chastity: and venereal disease, 137–8; critique of 305; in ancient Greece 26, 33, 38; in early Christianity 42, 46–9; in Islam 64, 88; in imperial Germany 210, 228; in Victorian England 123
childbirth 9, 234, 242, 261, 264, 291
children 104, 112; eugenics and 223, 226; sexual development of 198, 199; sexual initiation of 258–9
Chinese 166–8, 179
Christianity 7; and abortion 270, 272, 277, 291; as opposed to Islam 60; early 37–57; in Britain 120–1; in imperial Germany 212; Krafft-Ebing and 196; morality and 95–6, 105, 108; see also missionaries
cinaedus 6, 13, 18, 19, 24–5
circumcision see also clitoridectomy; 233, 236–46, 252–9, 325
citizenship 2, 19, 191, 265, 276
class consciousness 225, 309; see also middle class, working class
clitoridectomy 233–4, 236, 241–6, 252–9, 261–5, 340
clitoris 1, 5; and Freud 233, 237–8, 242, 247–8; in 1960s 296, 317–24; in nineteenth century 116, 131, 135, 137; see also orgasm, clitoridectomy
Cobbe, Frances Power 151
Cohn, Bernard 165
coitus interruptus 272, 275, 283
communism 268, 271, 277
conception 132–4, 270
condoms 270
consciousness raising 298, 307–9
Contagious Diseases Acts 4, 8–9, 120–1, 161–8, 325
Cook, Hera 2–3, 115

Coontz, Stephanie 144
Copenhagen 288, 292, 298
Crocker, Leslie G. 104
cross-dressing 102, 149, 204
Crow, Emma 148
Cushman, Charlotte 142, 147–51
Czarnowski, Gabriele 278, 282

Danish Women's Society 307, 313
Darwinism 3, 192
Das, Veena 165
Davidson, James 14
Demosthenes 17, 32
Denmark 9, 10, 268, 288–314, 325
desire, sexual 2, 7, 13, 16, 35, 115; and clitoris 247; in Imperial Germany 215–16, 219; in Krafft-Ebing 184, 191, 198
Dickens, Charles 120
Dickinson, Edward Ross 4, 209, 211
Diderot, Denis 5, 96–106
discourse 3–5, 10, 119, 298, 307
divorce 38, 42, 56, 120, 145, 220, 317
Dohm, Hedwig 211
Dover, Kenneth 13
Duc, Aimée 195

Edmondson, Joseph 162, 175
effeminacy 68
Ejlersen, Mette 1, 9, 295, 317
Elberskirchen, Johanna 216, 219
Ellis, Havelock 4
El-Rouayheb, Khaled 7, 59
Enlightenment 95, 99, 100, 105
eros 16, 2–7
Essenes 37, 44
Estonia 344–5
eugenics 3–4; in imperial Germany 220, 231, 242, 267–8, 278–9, 281; in Nazi Germany 279; in Weimar Germany 267; in Denmark 294; Krafft-Ebing and 209–10
eunuchs 37–55, 199
evolution 216, 220, 223; see also Darwinism

Faderman, Lilian 152
feminism 9; in Britain 234, 236; in Denmark 296–314, 324; in Germany 210, 211 216, 224; in Sweden 325, 328, 331–5, 339, 341, 345
fertility: cults 46; in Britain 116, 121–2, 126; in Germany 270, 272, 274–6, 283; in Tahiti 96, 104

fetishism 189, 191–5
film 270
Finland 329
Fisher, Kate 270–1, 273
Flaubert, Gustave 194
Flesch, Max 214
Florence 6
Foucault, Michel 2–5, 7, 9, 13, 38, 59, 115, 118, 184, 269
France: abortion in 191; culture of 103; prostitution in 161, 179
fraternal patriarchy 102–3
Fredericksen, Bodil Folke 233
Freud, Sigmund 6, 233, 237–9, 247–8
friendship 7, 85, 141, 150, 152, 184
Frost, Ginger 125

galli 38, 46, 49
gay rights 279
Germany: imperial 211–20, 231, 242, 267–8; Weimar 8, 10, 195, 267–71, 278–9, 281, 283, 291
Gikuyu see Kikuyu
gonorrhea 138
Goodman, Dena 99
Gray, Effie 122
Greece, ancient 6, 7, 13–35, 37, 44–5, 59
Greg, William 166

Haeckel, Ernest 210
Halban-Narjani operation 247
Halperin, David 14
Hammerton, James 120
Harmodius 14, 26–7, 33
Harvey, Elizabeth 284
Hausen, Karen 212
Hays, Matilda 147
hermaphrodite 137, 200
hetairai 13, 17
heteronormativity 3, 5
heterosexuality 198–9, 209, 211, 212, 303, 304
Hipparchus 14
Hirschman, Charles 168
Hitler, Adolf 278, 279, 283
Hobson, Barbara 333, 337
Hoggart, Richard 273
Homer 16
homosexuality (same-sex eroticism) 2–7, 9; and sexology 183–207; German rights movement 212, 220; in ancient Greece 13–35, 37, 38, 145–6, 149; in Denmark 303; in Islamic world 63–5, 91, 93; in Nazi Germany 279
Hong Kong 165, 168, 172, 179–80
honor 29, 33, 35, 45, 61, 63, 70–3, 305
Hosmer, Harriet 150, 151
husbands, female 150

Ibn Hazm 7, 59
illegitimacy 124–6, 226, 281–2
immigration 325, 326, 339, 342, 346
imperialism 5, 95, 101, 162–81, 253, 260
incest 103, 146, 147, 148
India 161–3, 171, 177, 179, 180, 263
infanticide 283, 293
internet 326, 339–42, 344
irua 242, 253–9
Islam 6–7, 45, 59–93, 325

Jerome 48–9
Jesus 37–57, 130
Josephus 43–4
Judaism and Jews 37, 43, 44, 279

Kahn, Dr. Joseph 2, 116, 135
Kanigo, Tabitha 243–4
Kenya 5, 233–4, 236, 237–48, 252–63
Kenyatta, Jomo 5, 6, 234, 238, 239–48
Kertbeny, Karl Maria 184
Key, Ellen 216
Kikuyu 233–4, 236, 240, 243–5, 252–9, 263
Kikuyu Central Association 237
kinaidos see also cinaedus; 13
Kingsley, Fanny 122
Kisch, Heinrich 213
kleptomania 194
Koran 59
Krafft-Ebing, Richard 4, 5, 183, 186–98, 214
Kuefler, Mathew 38
Kulick, Don 341, 345

Labour Party 234, 240
Ladies' National Association 162
Lange, Helene 216
League for the Protection of Motherhood 210, 213, 230
Leakey, Louis 244–5
lesbianism (female-female eroticism) 8, 60, 142, 148–59; and Krafft-Ebing 184, 195, 204–6; in Denmark 303, 308, 313, 320, 321; in Weimar Germany 267
Leunbach, Dr. Jonathan 9, 268, 288

Levine, Philippa 161, 164
Lévi-Strauss, Claude 146–7
libertine 65, 76, 104, 111, 194, 278
Lister, Anne 8, 142, 156–9
liwāṭ 63, 76, 77
Lochrie, Karma 3, 7
Lombroso, Cesare 196, 214
London 187
love 26–7, 60; biologization of 220; crisis in
    212–15; critique of 304; nature of 82–5;
    intimacy and 228; romantic 305–6
lūṭī 63–6
Lutyens, Edwin and Emily 123

ma'būn 63–6, 77
Maeterlinck, Maurice 229
Malay Straits 165, 168, 172
Malinowski, Bronislav 238, 246, 248
Månsson, Sven Axel 340–1
Maori 224
Marcus, Sharon 8, 142
Marcuse, Max 214, 271, 273–4, 284
marriage 6–8; crisis in 210, 212, 215, 220;
    critique of 223–31; female 141, 145–52,
    148; gay 144; in ancient Greece 41;
    Britain, 120–5, 141, 244, 130, 144; in
    Islam 74; in Kenya 252, 264; in Tahiti
    111; romantic love and 305
Marxism 297
masculinity 2, 40–55, 77
masochism 183, 189, 192, 193–4
Mason, Michael 120
masturbation 2, 116, 123, 198, 200–6
matriarchy 230
Mau Mau movement 237, 241, 244
Mayreder, Rosa 216
Mediterranean 61, 69
Meisel-Hess, Grete 4, 9, 210, 223
menstruation 8, 193, 205, 268–9, 273,
    284
Merrill, Lisa 147
Michel, Robert 209
Middle Ages 2, 6, 59
middle class 4, 213, 289, 304, 332
midwives 261–2, 277–8, 289
Mill, John Stuart 123
missionaries 5, 233, 236–7, 242, 243–4,
    253, 258, 260, 262–3
Moll, Albert 189, 207, 213
monogamy 102, 148–9, 217, 305
Montesquieu 99
Moscovici, Claudia 96

motherhood: in Denmark 293; in imperial
    Germany 214, 210, 216–17, 219, 230; in
    Kenya 237; in Weimar Germany 271,
    278; single 104, 219, 230, 281
Moxnes, Halvor 7, 37–8

National League of German Women's
    Associations 216
nationalism 5–6, 233, 238, 241, 244, 246–7
native paramountcy 234
nature, concepts of: in ancient Greece 24–6,
    33, 35; in Britain 130, 152, 158; in Islam
    89, 96, 99, 102, 108; in Krafft-Ebing 188,
    206; women's 212, 215, 224–5
Nazis 10, 268, 277, 278, 281, 282
Netherlands 326, 337, 345, 346
New Left 297–8
Nigeria 260
norm 3, 317; see also heteronormative
North, Lydia 122

Obscene Publications Act of 1857 116
Oedipus complex 238
Oosterhuis, Harry 5, 186
orgasm 5, 116; vaginal or clitoral 233, 237,
    238, 247, 295, 317–24
orientalism 166
Origen 48–9
Ottoman empire 59, 63

Paget, James 122
paragraph 175 184
Paris 187; prostitution in 176, 178
Pateman, Carol 328, 330
patriarchy 102–3, 220, 230, 238, 298,
    309–12, 314, 334; see also fraternal
    patriarchy
Paul, the apostle 38
pederasty in Islamic world 61, 63–7, 72–7;
    Krafft-Ebing and 200, 202
Pedersen, Susan 234, 237
pedophilia 193
penetration 8, 13, 25, 61–4, 69, 70
penis 1–2, 14, 24–6, 62, 65, 67, 71–2, 131,
    137–9, 202
Pericles 19–20
Persia 60
Peterson, M.J. 122
phallus 233
Philo 43–4
philosophy 95, 99
Plato 17, 19, 24–6, 85, 184

Poland 279
Polano, Oskar 271, 284
police: in Australia 171; in Germany 179, 271, 273, 277, 279–81, 284, 288; in India 168, in Netherlands 346; in Paris 161, 176; in Sweden 326, 327–9, 338, 334, 341–3
polygamy 145, 147–9, 215, 216, 243
Pompeii 17
population 231, 276, 278, 281–3, 294
pornography 1, 149, 295, 318, 325, 347
Potter, Georgina 123
pregnancy 1, 115, 119, 134, 234, 267, 270–5, 277–84, 289–91, 293; fear of 200, 218, 268; prenuptial 124
premarital sex 268, 330
privacy 19, 20, 145, 275
procreation 1, 198, 214, 216, 226, 270
prostitution 4, 6: male 14, 17, 19, 23–4, 29, 31, 33, 38, 65, 74; in Britain 120, 126, 161; in colonies 162–81; feminists and 210, 220, 223, 224; as sexual service 225, 227, 328; in modern era 325–39; in Sweden 328–35, 337–9; in Netherlands 337–9; in Germany 191, 203, 338; in United States 338
psychiatry 186, 194; French 194–5; German 211
psychoanalysis 145, 239, 247

queerness 5–6, 37, 51

race 137, 161, 165, 168; and eugenics 223, 225–6, 268, 279; and gender 306; and prostitution 338; theories of 215
rape: of males 6, 61, 64, 69, 192; of women 102, 114, 209, 268, 270, 325, 330–3, 340
Rathbone, Eleanor 234, 242, 260, 263
Redstockings 9, 296–314
religion 89–92, 102, 104–5, 107–8, 110, 213, 216, 253; see also Christianity, Islam, Judaism
repression 2–3, 115, 119, 238
reproduction 2, 37; and abortion 269, 274, 292; and sexual crisis 210, 216, 223–5; in Britain 183; in Kenya 231, 236–7; in Tahiti 102–4, 121; see also procreation
Robert, Krisztina 271
Rome 2, 5–6, 17, 37, 44, 46
Rousseau, Jean-Jacques 99, 142
Rubin, Gayle 145–6

Ruskin, John 122–3
Russia 279, 325; see also Soviet Union

Sachse, Christoph 212
Sade, Marquis de 194
sadism 183, 194
Said, Edward 166
Sand, George 150
Schreiber, Adele 216
Schreiber-Krieger, Adele 276
self 3, 6, 43, 62, 119, 145, 188, 198, 307–8
self-control 38, 41, 45, 124, 126, 194
Sen, Sudipta 168
sex change 187
sex education 122, 293, 325
sex manuals 1
sex reform: in imperial Germany 212, 216, 219–20, 236; in Weimar Germany 267
sexology 3–5, 145, 183, 209; in imperial Germany 212–18, 220; in Weimar Germany 272, 275–6
sexual identity 3, 6, 65, 198, 220
sexual liberation movement 295, 304, 325
sexual morality 103, 107
sexuality, definition of 3
Showalter, Elaine 121
Singapore 169
Sissa, Giulia 14
slavery 13, 30, 33, 45, 59, 86
Smith-Rosenberg, Carroll 141–2, 152
Social Democrats 268, 276, 292, 295, 308, 340
socialism 268, 304, 313
socialist feminists 298, 308
sodomy 2, 6–7, 62–3, 65–6, 68–9
Soviet Union 288, 292, 326, 341
Spain 59, 87
Spivak, Gayatri 167
Stebbin, Emma 147–9
sterilization 288, 294
Stockholm 331, 388, 342–3, 347
Stoler, Ann 167
Stopes, Marie 237
Strindberg, August 209, 227
Sufism 59
suicide 190
suttee (sati) 234, 263
Svanström, Yvonne 325, 327
Sweden 9, 10, 295, 325, 328–35, 337–46
symposium 17, 26–7
syphilis 105, 121, 138–9, 168, 223, 253, 329

Tahiti 5, 95–106
Therapeutae 44
Thomas, Lynn 233
Timarchus 7, 14, 19–35
transsexual 326
twilight moments 7

Uganda 260–2
Ulrichs, Karl Heinrichs 5, 184
United States 291, 338, 345
universality of morals 98
uranism 184, 195
urnings 186, 188, 190, 191, 192, 204
Usborne, Cornelie 8, 267, 269

vagina 1–2, 63, 72, 131, 135, 137, 233,
    237, 318
Van de Velde, Theodore 296
venereal disease 4, 105, 121, 138, 161–2,
    168, 177, 200; and prostitution 329;
    see also syphilis
Vicinus, Martha 7
virginity 38, 131, 135, 137, 205, 329
Viswanathan, Gauri 165
vocabulary, sexual 1–2, 7–10, 118

Walker, Sarah 122
Walter, Lynn 296, 297
war 124: World War I 219, 220, 271–2,
    276, 283, 289–91; World War II 273,
    278; Vietnam 295
Wardlaw, Ralph 166
Weeks, Jeffrey 269
welfare state 276, 295, 297, 337
Well of Loneliness 321
Westermarck, Edvard 224
Winkler, John 14
W.L.S.R. (World League for Sexual Reform)
    292–3
women 17, 26, 44, 91: African 237; as
    alternative sexual objects 68, 71, 74, 76;
    and sexology 193, 194; and suffrage 121;
    attacking marriage 223; in Victorian Britain
    118–25; Kenyan 263; nature of 212–13; new
    228, 267, 270, 283; sexual drive of 122,
    131, 215–19; movement of, see feminism
working class 4, 9, 121, 124, 125–6, 191: in
    Denmark 29; in Weimar Germany
    267–70, 277, 283–4
Working Women's Information Union 292
World Congress on Sex Reform 268, 288

Desire

A History of European Sexuality

Anna Clark

'Provides a valuable overview of the history of sexuality in Europe since classical antiquity, synthesising as it does a mass of studies of specific regions and periods which have appeared during the last two decades.'

Lesley Hall, *Wellcome Library, UK*

Desire: A History of European Sexuality is a survey of sexuality in Europe from the Greeks to the present. The book traces two concepts of sexual desire that have competed throughout European history: desire as dangerous, polluting, and disorderly, and desire as creative, transcendent, even revolutionary. Following these changing attitudes through the major turning points of European history, Anna Clark concludes by demonstrating that western European sexual culture is quite distinct from many other cultures, and asks whether the vision of sexual desire as revolutionary, even transcendent, has faded in the modern secular era.

While *Desire* builds on the work of dozens of historians, it also takes a fresh approach. Explaining how authorities tried to manage sexual desire and sometimes failed, the book introduces the concept of 'twilight moments' to describe activities seen as shameful or dishonourable, but which were tolerated when concealed by shadows. Other topics addressed include:

- Sex in Greece and Rome
- Divine desire in Judaism and early Christianity
- New attitudes toward sexuality in the seventeenth and eighteenth centuries
- Victorian twilights.

Written in a lively and engaging style, this new survey contains many fascinating anecdotes, and draws on a rich array of sources including poetry, novels, pornography and film as well as court records, autobiographies and personal letters. *Desire* integrates the history of heterosexuality with same-sex desire, focuses on the emotions of love as well as the passions of lust, and explores the politics of sex as well as personal experiences.

ISBN: 978–0–415–77517–5 (hbk)
ISBN: 978–0–415–77518–2 (pbk)

Available at all good bookshops

For ordering and further information please visit:
www.routledge.com

RELATED TITLES FROM ROUTLEDGE

Her Husband was a Woman!

Women's Gender-Crossing in Modern British Popular Culture

Alison Oram

'Astonishing' reports of women masquerading as men frequently appear in the mass media from the turn of the twentieth century to the 1960s.

Alison Oram's pioneering study of women's gender-crossing explores the popular press to analyse how women's cross-gender behaviour and same-sex desires were presented to ordinary working-class and lower middle-class people. It breaks new ground in focusing on the representation of female sexualities within the broad sweep of popular culture rather than in fiction and professional literature.

Her Husband was a Woman! surveys these engaging stories of cross-dressing in mass-circulation newspapers and places them in the wider context of variety theatre, fairgrounds and other popular entertainment. Oram catalogues the changing perception of female cross-dressing and its relationship to contemporary ways of writing about gender and desire in the popular press. In the early twentieth century cross-dressing women were not condemned by the press for being socially transgressive, but celebrated for their trickster joking and success in performing masculinity. While there may have been earlier 'knowingness', it was not until after the Second World War that cross-dressing was explicitly linked to lesbianism or transsexuality in popular culture.

Illustrated with newspaper cuttings and postcards, *Her Husband was a Woman!* is an essential resource for students and researchers, revising assumptions about the history of modern gender and sexual identities, especially lesbianism and transgender.

ISBN: 978–0–415–40006–0 (hbk)
ISBN: 978–0–415–40007–7 (pbk)

Available at all good bookshops

For ordering and further information please visit:
www.routledge.com

Images of Ancient Greek Pederasty

Boys Were Their Gods

Andrew Lear

Greek pederasty, or paiderastia – the social custom of erotic relations between adult men and adolescent boys – was a central characteristic of Greek culture. Both Greeks and non-Greeks saw it, along with the gymnasium with its intimate connection to pederasty, as markers of Greek identity. It is an important theme in Greek literature, from poetry to comedy to philosophy – and in Greek art as well. In Athenian vase-painting, in particular – the painted scenes that decorate clay drinking vessels produced in Athens between the 6th and the 4th centuries BC – pederasty is a major theme: indeed, pederastic courtship is one of the mortal activities most commonly depicted.

This lavishly illustrated book brings together, for the first time, all of the different ways in which vase-painting portrays or refers to pederasty, from scenes of courtship, foreplay, and sex, to scenes of Zeus with his boy-love Ganymede, to painted inscriptions praising the beauty of boys. The book shows how painters used the language of vase-painting – what we call 'iconography' – to cast pederasty in an idealizing light, portraying it as part of a world in which beautiful elite males display praiseworthy attitudes, such as moderation, and engage in approved activities, such as hunting, athletics, and the symposium. The book also incorporates a comprehensive catalogue of relevant vase-paintings, compiled by noted archaeologist Keith DeVries. It is the most comprehensive treatment available of an institution that has few modern parallels.

ISBN: 978–0–415–22367–6 (hbk)
ISBN: 978–0–415–22368–3 (pbk)

Gender in World History

Second edition

Peter N. Stearns

Covering societies from classical times to the twenty-first century, *Gender in World History* is a fascinating exploration of what happens to established ideas about men and women, and their roles, when different cultural systems come into contact. This book breaks new ground to facilitate a consistent approach to gender in a world history context.

This second edition is completely updated, including:

- expanded introductions to each chronological section
- extensive discussion of the contemporary era bringing it right up to date
- new chapters on international influences in the first half of the twentieth century and globalization in the latter part of the twentieth century
- engagement with the recent work done on gender history and theory.

Coming right up to the present day, *Gender in World History* is essential reading for students of world history.

ISBN: 978–0–415–39588–5 (hbk)
ISBN: 978–0–415–39589–2 (pbk)

Available at all good bookshops

For ordering and further information please visit:
www.routledge.com

Women's History, Britain 1700–1850

Hannah Barker and Elaine Chalus

Here for the first time is a comprehensive history of the women of Britain during a period of dramatic change. Placing women's experiences in the context of these major social, economic and cultural shifts that accompanied the industrial and commercial transformations, Hannah Barker and Elaine Chalus paint a fascinating picture of the change, revolution, and continuity that were encountered by women of this time.

A thorough and well-balanced selection of individual chapters by leading field experts and dynamic new scholars, combine original research with a discussion of current secondary literature, and the contributors examine areas as diverse as enlightenment, politics, religion, education, sexuality, family, work, poverty, and consumption.

Providing a captivating overview of women and their lives, this book is an essential purchase for the study of women's history, and, providing delightful little gems of knowledge and insight, it will also appeal to any reader with an interest in this fascinating topic.

ISBN: 978–0–415–29176–7 (hbk)
ISBN: 978–0–415–29177–4 (pbk)

Available at all good bookshops

For ordering and further information please visit:
www.routledge.com

RELATED TITLES FROM ROUTLEDGE

Women's History, Britain 1850–1945

An Introduction

Edited by June Purvis

This edited collection includes chapters, written by experts in their field, on the suffrage movement, race and empire, industrialisation, the impact of war and women's literature, health, the family, education, sexuality, work and politics. Each contribution provides an overview of the main issues and debates within each area and offers suggestions for further reading. This book not only provides an invaluable introduction to every aspect of women's participation in the political, social and economic history of Britain, but also brings the reader up to date with current historical thinking on the study of women's history itself. This is an invaluable and concise overview of an essential area of historical and contemporary study.

ISBN: 978–1–85728–319–8 (hbk)
ISBN: 978–0–415–23889–2 (pbk)

Available at all good bookshops

For ordering and further information please visit:
www.routledge.com

Women, Gender and Religious Cultures in Britain, 1800–1940

Edited by Sue Morgan, Jacqueline de Vries

This volume is the first comprehensive overview of women, gender and religious change in modern Britain spanning from the evangelical revival of the early 1800s to interwar debates over women's roles and ministry.

This collection of pieces by key scholars combines cross-disciplinary insights from history, gender studies, theology, literature, religious studies, sexuality and postcolonial studies. The book takes a thematic approach, providing students and scholars with a clear and comparative examination of ten significant areas of cultural activity that both shaped, and were shaped by women's religious beliefs and practices: family life, literary and theological discourses, philanthropic networks, sisterhoods and deaconess institutions, revivals and preaching ministry, missionary organisations, national and transnational political reform networks, sexual ideas and practices, feminist communities, and alternative spiritual traditions. Together, the volume challenges widely-held truisms about the increasingly private and domesticated nature of faith, the feminisation of religion and the relationship between secularisation and modern life.

Including case studies, further reading lists, and a survey of the existing scholarship, and with a British rather than Anglo-centric approach, this is an ideal book for anyone interested in women's religious experiences across the nineteenth and twentieth centuries.

ISBN: 978–0–415–23115–2 (hbk)
ISBN: 978–0–415–23213–5 (pbk)

Available at all good bookshops

For ordering and further information please visit:
www.routledge.com

Routledge
Taylor & Francis Group

The Sixties

A Journal of History, Politics and Culture
New to Routledge for 2008!

EDITORS:
Jeremy Varon, *Drew University, USA*
Michael S. Foley, *CUNY Graduate Center, USA*
John McMillian, *Harvard University, USA*

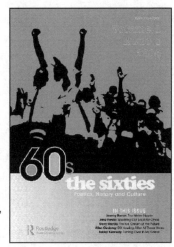

No recent decade has been so powerfully transformative in the United States and much of the world as the 1960s. The era's social movements - from civil rights, to feminism, student and youth protest, environmentalism, and nascent conservativism - dramatically changed the political culture of the developed west. Meanwhile, the decade's decolonization struggles altered the nature and balance of global power. In Communist Europe, incipient democracy movements set the stage for the revolutions that ended the Cold War. Collectively, these movements gave the 1960s their signal identity, and dominate understandings of their historical legacy.

Whether in the United States, or across the globe, no recent decade has had such an enduring grip on politics, culture, and consciousness as the 1960s.

The Sixties: A Journal of History, Politics and Culture, will feature cross-disciplinary, accessible and cutting-edge scholarship from academics and public intellectuals. In addition to research essays and book reviews, *The Sixties* will include conversations, interviews, graphics, and analyses of the ways the 1960s continue to be constructed in contemporary popular culture.

SUBSCRIPTION RATES
Volume 1, 2008, 2 issues per year
Print ISSN 1754-1328
Online ISSN 1754-1336
Institutional rate (print and online): US$257; £132; €206
Institutional rate (online access only): US$244; £125; €195
Personal rate (print only): US$49; £25; €39

informaworld™

A world of specialist information for the academic, professional and business communities. To find out more go to: **www.informaworld.com**

eupdates
Taylor & Francis Group

Register your email address at **www.informaworld.com/eupdates** to receive information on books, journals and other news within your areas of interest.

For further information, please contact Customer Services at either of the following:
T&F Informa UK Ltd, Sheepen Place, Colchester, Essex, CO3 3LP, UK
Tel: +44 (0) 20 7017 5544 Fax: 44 (0) 20 7017 5198
Email: tf.enquiries@informa.com
Taylor & Francis Inc, 325 Chestnut Street, Philadelphia, PA 19106, USA
Tel: +1 800 354 1420 (toll-free calls from within the US)
or +1 215 625 8900 (calls from overseas) Fax: +1 215 625 2940
Email: customerservice@taylorandfrancis.com

View an online sample issue at:
www.informaworld.com/thesixties

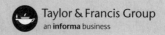

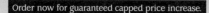
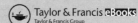